# World Religions

## Eastern Traditions

# World Religions
## Eastern Traditions

**Third Edition**

Edited by

**Willard G. Oxtoby**

**Roy C. Amore**

OXFORD

UNIVERSITY PRESS

# OXFORD
UNIVERSITY PRESS

8 Sampson Mews, Suite 204, Don Mills, Ontario M3C 0H5
www.oupcanada.com

Oxford University Press is a department of the University of Oxford.
It furthers the University's objective of excellence in research, scholarship,
and education by publishing worldwide in

Oxford   New York

Auckland   Cape Town   Dar es Salaam   Hong Kong   Karachi
Kuala Lumpur   Madrid   Melbourne   Mexico City   Nairobi
New Delhi   Shanghai   Taipei   Toronto

With offices in

Argentina   Austria   Brazil   Chile   Czech Republic   France   Greece
Guatemala   Hungary   Italy   Japan   Poland   Portugal   Singapore
South Korea   Switzerland   Thailand   Turkey   Ukraine   Vietnam

Oxford is a trade mark of Oxford University Press
in the UK and in certain other countries

Published in Canada by Oxford University Press

**Library and Archives Canada Cataloguing in Publication**

World religions : eastern traditions / edited by Willard G. Oxtoby & Roy C. Amore. — 3rd ed.

Includes bibliographical references and index.

ISBN 978-0-19-542676-2

1. Religions.  I. Oxtoby, Willard G. (Willard

Gurdon), 1933–2003  II. Amore, Roy C., 1942–

BL80.3.W66 2009      200      C2009-905223-7

Cover Credit: Annie Griffiths Belt

Oxford University Press is committed to our environment. This book is printed on Forest Stewardship
Council certified paper, harvested from a responsibly managed forest.

Printed and bound in the United States of America.

2  3  4  –  13  12  11

# Contents

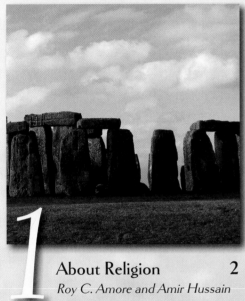

## 1 About Religion    2
*Roy C. Amore and Amir Hussain*

## 2 Hindu Traditions    28
*Vasudha Narayanan*

## 3 Sikh Traditions    106
*Pashaura Singh*

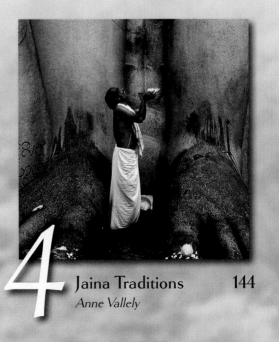

## 4 Jaina Traditions    144
*Anne Vallely*

# Contributors

**ROY C. AMORE** has extensive research experience in Asia. His books include *Two Masters, One Message*, comparing the lives and teachings of Christ and Buddha, and *Lustful Maidens and Ascetic Kings: Buddhist and Hindu Stories of Life*. He is professor in the Department of Political Science and associate dean, administration, Faculty of Arts and Social Sciences, at the University of Windsor and is currently writing a book on religion and politics.

**AMIR HUSSAIN** is professor in the Department of Theological Studies at Loyola Marymount University in Los Angeles, where he teaches courses on Islam and world religions. A Canadian of Pakistani origin, he is the author of *Oil and Water: Two Faiths, One God,* an introduction to Islam for North Americans.

**VASUDHA NARAYANAN** is distinguished professor in the Department of Religion and director of the Center for the Study of Hindu Traditions at the University of Florida. A past president of the American Academy of Religion, she is the author or editor of seven books and has written more than a hundred articles and chapters in books. Her current research focuses on Hindu traditions in Cambodia.

**JOHN K. NELSON** is associate professor in the Department of Theology and Religious Studies at the University of San Francisco. Trained as a cultural anthropologist, he is the author of two books on Shinto as well as a documentary film on Yasukuni Shrine, and is actively researching contemporary Buddhism in Japan and North America.

**The late WILLARD G. OXTOBY**, the original editor of this work, was professor emeritus at the University of Toronto, where he launched the graduate program in the study of religion. His books include *Experiencing India: European Descriptions and Impressions* and *The Meaning of Other Faiths*.

**ALAN F. SEGAL** is professor of religion and Ingeborg Rennert professor of Jewish studies at Barnard College, Columbia University. He has written extensively in the fields of comparative religion, Judaism, and early Christianity. His books include *Rebecca's Children, Paul the Convert,* and *Life after Death: A History of the Afterlife in Western Religion.*

**PASHAURA SINGH** is professor and Dr Jasbir Singh Saini endowed chair in Sikh and Punjabi studies at the University of California, Riverside. He has authored three Oxford monographs, co-edited three conference volumes, and contributed articles to academic journals, books, and encyclopedias. His recent book, *Life and Work of Guru Arjan: History, Memory, and Biography in the Sikh Tradition* (OUP, 2006) was a bestseller in India.

**ANNE VALLELY** is associate professor in the Department of Classics and Religious Studies at the University of Ottawa, where she teaches courses on South Asian traditions (especially Jainism and Hinduism), as well as nature and religion. Her book *Guardians of the Transcendent: An Ethnography of a Jain Ascetic Community* (2002) is an anthropological study of Jain female ascetics. Her co-edited volume *Animal Others and the Human Imagination* will be published in 2010.

**TERRY TAK-LING WOO** teaches at York University and the University of Toronto, Scarborough. She is involved with courses that introduce the study of religion and East Asian religions. Her research interests include women in Chinese religions and Chinese religions in diaspora.

# Important Features of This Edition

This third edition of *World Religions: Eastern Traditions* incorporates several features introduced in the single-volume *Concise Introduction to World Religions* (2007). Perhaps the most significant improvement over earlier versions of the full two-volume set is the fact that all the major traditions are now presented in the same way, following an organizational pattern that moves from Origins through Crystallization, Differentiation, Practice, and Cultural Expressions to Interaction and Adaptation. Other highlights include:

- New introductory and concluding chapters by Roy Amore and Amir Hussain (editor of the companion Western Traditions book), common to both volumes;

- New chapters on Sikhism, Jainism, Japanese traditions, and the religions of China and Korea;

- New pedagogy, including 'Traditions at a Glance' boxes, 'Sites' boxes, recommended websites, and bolded key terms (defined in end-of-chapter glossaries);

- Boxed excerpts from scripture and other essential texts; and

- A striking new four-colour design.

To better reflect the richness and diversity of each religious tradition and its adherents, the text has been completely redesigned in a vibrant four-colour palette, with a thoroughly revamped art program that features an expanded range of beautiful, meticulously chosen photographs, now in full colour.

Chapter 3

Sikh
Traditions

~ Pashaura Singh ~

**Traditions at a Glance boxes** give readers a summary of the basics at the start of each chapter.

## Traditions at a Glance

**Numbers**
Confucians: Estimates range from 6 to 8 million.
Daoists: Estimates range from 2.5 to 3.5 million.
Chinese Universalist or Popular Religion: Estimates range from 385 to 405 million.
Korean Shamanism and Popular Religion: Estimates range from 1 to 7 million.

**Distribution**
Confucians and Daoists live in East Asia, Australia, New Zealand, Southeast Asia, North and West Europe, North America, and a few other places. Korean and Chinese popular religions are found primarily in East Asia, with small pockets in diasporic communities in North America and Europe.

**Founders and Teachers**
Mythological founders and heroes include Yao, Shun, and Yu in China, and Tangun in Korea. Famous first teachers—some mythical, some historic—include the Yellow Emperor, Confucius, and Laozi in China, and Ch'oe Ch'ung in Korea.

**Deities**
For Confucians the place of a deity is filled either by Heaven or by Heaven and Earth together. For some Daoists, the Way functions as a deity; others look to what is in effect a bureaucracy of deities. Popular religions, both Korean and Chinese, include deities from various traditions.

**Authoritative Texts**
For Confucians, the Classics from the Zhou and Han are the foundational texts. For Daoists, Laozi is fundamental, with variations from sect to sect. The popular and shamanistic religions tend not to be textually oriented.

**Noteworthy Teachings**
None of the East Asian teachings are radically exclusive. Daoism and Confucianism share cultural and social space with each other and popular religions even if they differ doctrinally. The two elite religions hold a common utopian view of a peaceful and harmonious society in which people are devoted to self-cultivation and discipline, try to be good, live frugally, and serve the community.

heart-mind (**xin**) so as to restore its natural unity, emptiness, and tranquillity. It is in the recovery of this original heavenly emotional state that the self is transformed and brought into harmony with Heaven and Earth. This is a cosmic harmony, a harmony for all: humans, ghosts and spirits, deities, Heaven and Earth alike.

This commitment to harmony is above all a commitment to individual cultivation according to the Way. The cultivation of moral and spiritual nobility, of sagehood, requires both internal and external ritual practices: for example, both the stilling of the 'heart-mind' and the performance of sacrifices. The collective, apparently secular

## Sites

**CHINA**

**Beijing** The Imperial Palace complex, also known as the Forbidden City, includes the Tiantan (Altar or Temple of Heaven), where the Ming and Qing emperors performed the grandest sacrifices. The city is also home to the Taimiao, the ancestral temple of both dynasties; a Confucian temple dedicated to scholar-officials; various Daoist and Buddhist temples; and the tombs of the later Ming emperors.

**Qufu** The complex of monuments in the birth place of Confucius, in Shandong, includes a temple, a cemetery, and a family mansion. The cemetery contains Confucius' tomb and the remains of more than 100,000 of his descendants.

**Nanjing** The first capital city of the Ming, whose emperor, Hongwu, is buried here in the Xiaoling Tomb. Scholar-officials were trained in this thriving ancient metropolis, at the Confucian Academy. The Jinghai Temple is dedicated to the goddess of the sea, in honour of China's great Muslim seafaring admiral, Zhenghe.

**Wudangshan** Mount Wudang in Hubei is known for its many Daoist monasteries. It is also home to an organized complex of palaces and temples, built mostly during the Ming, and contains Daoist buildings from as early as the seventh century. The buildings include some of the finest examples in Chinese art and architecture.

**Xi'an** The capital for numerous dynasties, the city and its environs are home to the famous terracotta warrior guardians; numerous Daoist and Buddhist temples; and Huashan, one of the five sacred mountains of Daoism.

**KOREA**

**Seoul** The Changdeogung Palace (Palace of Prospering Virtue) complex was established by T'aejong, the first king of the Choson dynasty. It includes Jongmyo, the oldest and most authentic of preserved Confucian royal shrines, which are dedicated to the ancestors of Choson. It houses tablets bearing teachings of the royal family.

**Sites boxes** draw attention to locations of special significance to each tradition.

**Timelines** help to place religious developments in historical context.

---

## Timeline

| | |
|---|---|
| c. 2700 BCE | Evidence of Indus Valley civilization |
| c. 1750?–1500 | Earliest Vedic compositions |
| c. 600 | Production of *Upanishads* |
| c. 500 | Production of Hindu epics begins |
| 326 | Greek armies in India under Alexander |
| c. 272 | Accession of King Ashoka |
| c. 200 | First contacts with Southeast Asia |
| c. 200 BCE–200 CE | Composition of *Bhagavad Gita* |
| c. 200 CE | Compilation of *Laws of Manu* and *Natya Sastra* completed |
| c. 500 | Beginnings of tantric tradition |
| c. 700–900 | Alvars and Nayanmars, Tamil *bhakti* poets |
| c. 700–800 | Shankara's Advaita Vedanta |
| 1017 | Traditional birth date of Ramanuja, Vaishnava philosopher (d. 1137) |
| 1100–1150 | Angkor Wat built in Cambodia |
| 1398 | Traditional birth date of Kabir, North Indian *bhakti* poet (d. 1518) |
| c. 1400 | Major endowments at Tirumala–Tirupati temple |
| 1486 | Birth of Chaitanya, Bengali Vaishnava *bhakti* leader (d. 1583) |
| c. 1543 | Birth of Tulsidas, North Indian *bhakti* poet (d. 1623) |
| 1757 | British rule established in Calcutta |
| 1828 | Ram Mohan Roy founds Brahmo Samaj |
| 1836 | Birth of Ramakrishna Paramahamsa (d. 1886) |
| 1875 | Dayananda Sarasvati founds Arya Samaj |
| 1893 | Vivekananda attends World's Parliament of Religions in Chicago |
| 1905–6 | Vedanta Temple built in San Francisco |
| 1926 | Birth of Sathya Sai Baba |
| 1959 | Maharishi Mahesh Yogi brings transcendental meditation to America and Europe |
| 1965 | A.C. Bhaktivedanta Swami Prabhupada, founder of ISKCON, sails to America |
| 1977 | Hindu temples consecrated in New York and Pittsburgh |

Hindus may consider many things—from astronomy and astrology to music and dance, from phonetics to plants—essential in the practice of their religion. It would be impossible to do justice to all the subjects that fall under the rubric of the sacred for Hindus. Therefore the following discussion will include a number of features not usually covered by the term 'religion' in the Western world.

### ORIGINS

The origins of Hinduism have been much debated. The standard view in the early twentieth century was that it had grown from a fusion of the indigenous religions of the Indus Valley with the faith of the Aryans, an Indo-European people

---

to thirty thousand. In this way the civil service came to be filled with men trained in the official Confucian curriculum, which included the Five Classics and the 'six arts'. As these men learned in Confucianism, gradually replaced the feudal aristocracy of the Zhou in government, Confucius' vision of the noble person as one defined by character and merit rather than birth moved closer to reality.

Some scholars have suggested that Emperor Wu chose Confucianism as the state orthodoxy because the Confucian idea of the Mandate of Heaven served to legitimate his authority. In fact, however, the Confucian literature expected the emperor's authority to be circumscribed by ministers who would counsel restraint and discourage extravagance. According to the tradition, it was both the right and the duty of ministers to restrain

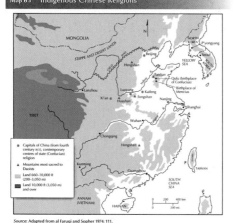

**Map 6.1    Indigenous Chinese Religions**

*Source: Adapted from al Faruqi and Sopher 1974: 111.*

---

**Informative maps** provide useful reference points.

## Document Boxes

Document boxes provide a generous selection of excerpts from scripture and other important writings.

## Focus Boxes

Focus boxes offer additional information on selected subjects.

**End-of-chapter glossaries** enhance understanding of key concepts; **further readings** and **recommended websites** provide an excellent starting point for further research and study.

 **Extensive ancillary package.**

**For Instructors:** an Instructor's Manual, a Test Generator, and PowerPoint slides.

**For Students:** a Student Study Guide.

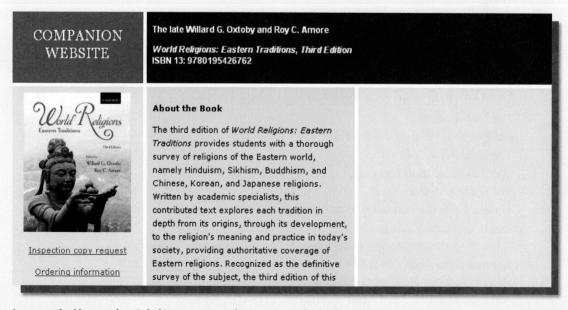

**COMPANION WEBSITE**

The late Willard G. Oxtoby and Roy C. Amore
*World Religions: Eastern Traditions, Third Edition*
ISBN 13: 9780195426762

**About the Book**

The third edition of *World Religions: Eastern Traditions* provides students with a thorough survey of religions of the Eastern world, namely Hinduism, Sikhism, Buddhism, and Chinese, Korean, and Japanese religions. Written by academic specialists, this contributed text explores each tradition in depth from its origins, through its development, to the religion's meaning and practice in today's society, providing authoritative coverage of Eastern religions. Recognized as the definitive survey of the subject, the third edition of this

Inspection copy request

Ordering information

*Instructors should contact their Oxford University Press sales representative for details on these supplements and for login and password information.*

# Foreword

Will Oxtoby seemed to know everything there was to know about the world's religions. Having majored in philosophy, he completed his Ph.D. in Near Eastern Studies at Princeton and, after learning Hebrew and Arabic, began his career as a Bible professor at McGill. Before long, however, he was enticed into the Persian gardens of Zoroastrianism. Exploring the relationships between Zoroastrianism and early Second Temple period Judaism required him to learn Avestan, the classical Persian language, which in turn required a working knowledge of Sanskrit. By the time he began teaching the history of religion at Yale, he already had half the world's traditions within his purview. He had also developed strong views on the teaching of religion.

He put those views into practice as the founding director of the University of Toronto's Centre for the Study of Religions. Will himself had begun his exploration of other faiths from a Presbyterian perspective, and he wanted to emphasize that anyone with strong roots in a particular religious tradition cannot help bringing certain assumptions to the study of other traditions. In this respect, the believer and the non-believer start from a similar place: both may find it difficult to appreciate an unfamiliar tradition from the insider's point of view.

Will also wanted his students to understand that the truths of religion do not reveal themselves to the casual eye. Close observation is required even when the observer is an insider to the faith. And a capacity for critical analysis is no less essential for those exploring their own traditions than a sympathetic openness to difference is for outsiders seeking to understand religious experiences that they do not share.

In a sense, Will's entire career reflected his conviction that religion plays a central role in the lives of most people around the world, and that we cannot understand others without understanding their faiths. He also believed that it is only by making the effort to understand other religions that we can truly begin to understand our own.

Will was among the first to identify Iran's Islamic revolution as an event of worldwide religious significance—an early expression of a much broader revitalization of religion that was likely to bring with it dangers as well as rewards. A decade later, he recognized the collapse of the Soviet Union as another event of enormous religious importance, and not just because it opened the way for a religious revival in Eastern Europe. It was significant, Will suggested, because the demise of an explicitly atheistic, Marxist-inspired state could be attributed—at least in part—to a contradiction within Marxism. Marx himself had justly criticized religion as an instrument of oppression, serving the authoritarian state. Yet some of the fundamental principles on which Marx based his critique would be quite at home in any number of religions, and in many ways Marxism itself could be seen as a religion (especially one of the Western Abrahamic variety). The communist system had gained power by promising to end tyranny and alleviate human misery. Having done the very opposite, it was justly condemned by its own principles.

In the course of his career, Will came to believe ever more deeply in the plurality of truth. With that belief came the conviction that human efforts to understand truth must be plural as well. In Will's view, truth was not the possession of any single religion or school of thought: it was something that emerged in the process of comparison and dialogue. Thus every religion must be recognized as having its own purchase on truth, and every individual—believer, unbeliever, and everyone in between—as having a potentially valid perspective; then all those perspectives have to become part of a wide-open, ongoing dialogue. The spirit behind such dialogue Will called pluralism, and it was in that spirit that these textbooks were conceived.

*Alan F. Segal*
*Barnard College*
*Columbia University*

# Preface

I t is an honour for me to have been asked to edit this third edition of the late Will Oxtoby's *World Religions: Eastern Traditions*. Many years ago, at a conference where I had made some remarks on Buddhism, Will asked if I had time to go for a coffee. He told me about a project he was planning with Oxford University Press: a two-volume world religions text that would, among other things, pay close attention to the history of each major tradition. Although he would write the chapter on Christianity himself, for the other traditions he wanted to find specialists who would be willing to adopt the overall approach he had in mind, balancing sympathy with critical analysis. As the coffee break continued, we agreed that the ideal contributor would be a scholar who was either an insider to the tradition in question or who identified with it strongly enough to bridge the insider–outsider gap (see Chapter 1 of this book). I was asked to share the writing of the Buddhism chapter with Professor Julia Ching.

Will believed that only those who loved classroom teaching could write a good textbook. He chose his contributors accordingly, and when the first edition of *World Religions* was published, in 1996, both volumes were warmly received by professors and students alike. It wasn't long before Will was planning a second edition and urging us to make notes for revisions.

By the time the second edition appeared, in 2002, Will was already planning a single-volume version. Sadly, neither he nor his wife Julia lived to see it take shape. Nevertheless, *A Concise Introduction to World Religions* (2007) was organized according to a new, more formal chapter structure he had designed for it. This third edition of the two-volume set reflects the revised chapter structure and the rich colour format introduced in the *Concise* volume. In addition, new contributors have brought fresh perspectives to several traditions. Yet together, Amir Hussain, the editor of the new Western volume, and I have tried to stay true to Will Oxtoby's vision.

Will wrote in his original foreword that before 1979, many people used to ask him why he was wasting his time on something as unimportant as religion, but that those questions stopped after Iran's Islamic Revolution. I have a similar story. Before I moved over to political science, I taught in a religious studies department. Sometimes political science students would ask me why anyone interested in politics would bother with religion. Since the attacks of September 2001, not a single student has raised that question. On the contrary, understanding the world's major religious traditions seems more important now than ever before.

## Acknowledgements

First I wish to express my appreciation to all the teachers/scholars who have contributed to this volume. Four new authors were recruited for this edition, all of whom chose to write brand-new chapters. Together with the returning authors, they have produced a sound and engaging text, and several of them also contributed photographs for their chapters. I enjoyed working with Amir Hussain on the chapters that open and close this book. I also deeply appreciate the support and advice on content I have received from my wife, Michelle Morrison, and from many of my students at the University of Windsor.

At Oxford University Press I would like to thank Katherine Skene for her encouragement, Jennifer Mueller for her developmental guidance, and Sally Livingston for her hands-on editorial work. With Amir, I am also grateful to the following reviewers, whose comments on the second edition helped to shape this one:

Martin Adam, University of Victoria
Edward Chung, University of Prince Edward Island
Husain Khimjee, Wilfrid Laurier University
Edward Smith, University of Guelph
Marie Taylor, Lakehead University
Ayse Tuzlak, University of Calgary

Finally, on behalf of all the authors, I wish to thank the many practitioners of Eastern religious traditions who, over the years, have answered our questions, posed for our cameras, and allowed us to observe them at worship, sometimes even inviting us to take tea with them or share their food. It is, after all, their spiritual lives that this book is all about.

*Roy C. Amore*
*September 2009*
*University of Windsor*

*World Religions*

Eastern Traditions

# Chapter 1

# *About Religion*

Roy C. Amore ✎ Amir Hussain

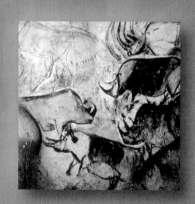

# 🌿 Looking Both Ways from Stonehenge: Basic Human Religion

Standing on the west side of **Stonehenge**, we watch the sun rise through the circle of massive standing stones. Within the outer circle is a grouping of paired stones capped by lintels and arranged in a horseshoe pattern, opening towards the rising sun. At the centre of the horseshoe lies a flat stone that was once thought to have served as an altar for sacrifices. Today, however, it is believed that the centre stone originally stood upright, marking the spot where an observer would stand to watch the movements of the sun and stars.

The Stonehenge we know today is what remains of a structure erected between 3,500 and 4,000 years ago. But the site had already been used as a burial ground for centuries before that time: researchers believe that the remains of as many as 240 people, probably from a single ruling family, were interred there between roughly 3000 and 2500 CE.[1] The structure itself is generally believed to have been used for ceremonial purposes, and its orientation—towards the point where the sun rises at the summer solstice—is what has led many to think it might have been designed to serve as a kind of astronomical observatory.

Ignoring the crowd of tourists, we position ourselves behind the central stone to note the position of the rising sun in relation to the 'heel stone' on the horizon more than 60 metres away. Today, on the morning of the summer solstice, the sun rises in the northeast, just to the left of the heel stone. It's easy to imagine that this day—the longest of the year and the only one on which the sun rises to the north side of the heel stone—would have been the occasion for some kind of ceremony in ancient times; that the entire community would have gathered at dawn to watch as someone with special authority—perhaps a priest, perhaps the local chief or ruler—confirmed the position of the rising sun. It's also easy to imagine the sense of order in the universe that would have come from knowing exactly when and where the sun would change course.

Tomorrow the sun will rise behind the heel stone, and it will continue its (apparent) journey towards the south for the next six months. Then in late December, at the winter solstice, the sun will appear to reverse course and begin travelling northwards again. Many centuries after people first gathered at Stonehenge, the Romans would celebrate this day as marking the annual 'rebirth' of the sun—the high point of the festival they called Saturnalia. And in the fourth century CE, the Christians in Rome would choose this same time of the year to celebrate the birth of their risen lord. Christmas was to combine the unrestrained revelry of the Roman midwinter festival, marked by feasting, gift-giving, and general merriment, with the celebration of the coming to earth of a deity incarnate.

## Looking Back from Stonehenge

There are a few concepts, shared by virtually all human cultures, that seem fundamental to what we call religion: powerful gods, sacred places, a life of some kind after death, the presence in the physical world of spirits that interact with humans in various ways. These concepts are so old and so widespread that no one can say where or when they first emerged.

### Three Worlds

Historically, it seems that humans around the globe have imagined the world to consist of three levels—sky, earth, and underworld. The uppermost level, the sky, has typically been considered the home of the greatest deities. Exactly how this concept developed is impossible to know, but we can guess that the awesome power of storms was one contributing factor. Another was very likely

◄ Stonehenge (© Nick Hawkes/Alamy).

The 'high place' at Petra, Jordan (Roy C. Amore).

the apparent movement of the sun, the stars, and the planets across the sky. Observing the varying patterns could well have led early humans to believe that the heavenly bodies were living entities animated by their own individual spirits—in effect, gods and goddesses.

The very highest level, in the heavens above the clouds and stars, was thought to be the home of the highest deity, typically referred to by names such as Sky Father, Creator, or King of Heaven. This deity—invariably male—was the forerunner of the god of the monotheistic religions. Under the earth lived the spirits of serpents (surviving as the cobras, or **nagas**, in the religions of India) or reptilian monsters (surviving in dragon lore); perhaps because they were associated with dark and hidden places, they were usually imagined as evil. Finally, between the sky and the underworld lay the earth: the intermediate level where humans lived.

## Sacred Places

Around the world, there are certain types of places where humans tend to feel they are in the presence of some unusual energy or power. Such places are regarded as set apart from the everyday world and are treated with special respect. Among these sacred places (the word 'sacred' means 'set aside') are mountains and hilltops—the places closest to the sky-dwelling deities. In the ancient Middle East, for instance, worship was often conducted at ritual centres known simply as '**high places**'. People gathered at these sites to win the favour of the deities by offering them food, drink, praise, and prayer. One widely known example is the altar area on the cliff above the ancient city of Petra in Jordan (familiar to many people from the Indiana Jones films).

Great rivers and waterfalls are often regarded as sacred as well. And in Japan virtually every feature of the natural landscape—from great mountains and waterfalls to trees and stones—was traditionally believed to be animated by its own god or spirit (*kami*).

## Animal Spirits

Another common and longstanding human tendency has been to attribute spirits to animals, either individually or as members of a family with a kind of collective guardian spirit. For this reason, traditional hunting societies have typically sought to ensure that the animals they kill for food are treated with the proper respect, lest other members of those species be frightened away or refuse to let themselves be caught.

In addition, body parts from the most impressive animals—bulls, bears, lions, eagles—have often been used as 'power objects', to help make contact with the spirits of these animals. In many cultures, people have attributed magical properties to objects such as bear claws or eagle feathers, wearing them as amulets or hanging them in the doorways of their homes for protection from evil spirits.

## Death and Burial

From ancient times, humans have taken great care with the burial of their dead. The body might be positioned with the head facing east, the 'first direction', where the sun rises, or placed in the fetal position, suggesting a hope for rebirth into a different realm. These burial positions in themselves would not be enough to prove a belief in an afterlife; however, most such graves have also contained, along with the remains of the dead, 'grave goods' of various kinds. Some of these provisions for the afterlife likely belonged to the person in life; some appear to be specially made replicas; and some are rare, presumably costly items such

A reconstruction of an Egyptian burial from the fourth century BCE at the British Museum in London; the naturally preserved body of a man is surrounded by a variety of grave goods (Alex Segre/Alamy).

as precious stones. Apparently the living were willing to sacrifice important resources to help the dead in the afterlife.

The belief that deceased ancestors can play a role in guiding the living members of their families appears to be especially widespread. Traditions such as the Japanese **Obon**, the Mexican **Day of the Dead**, and the Christian **All-Saints Day** and **Hallowe'en** all reflect the belief that the souls of the dead return to earth once a year to share a ritual meal with the living.

### Why Are Humans Religious?

The reasons why humans tend to be religious are far too numerous and complex to be reduced to a single answer. All we can say with any certainty is that religion seems to grow out of human experiences: from the fear of death to the hope for a good afterlife, from the uncertainty surrounding natural events to the sense of control over nature provided by a priest who could predict the change of seasons and the movement of the planets. Religion emerges through the experience of good or bad powers that are sensed in dreams, in sacred spaces, and in certain humans and animals.

Religion has many emotional dimensions, including fear, awe, love, and hate. But it also has intellectual dimensions, including curiosity about what causes things to happen, a sense of order in the universe that suggests the presence of a creator, and the drive to make sense out of human experience.

The nature of religious belief and practice has changed through the centuries, so we must guard against taking the religion of any particular time and place as the norm. What we can safely say is that religion is such an ancient aspect of human experience that it has become part of human nature. For this reason some scholars have given our species, *Homo sapiens*, a second name: *Homo religiosus*.

## ❧ TEN WAVES OF RELIGION

Most of the chapters in this book focus on individual religions, but it may be useful to begin with a broader perspective. What follows is a brief overview of some of the major developments in the history of what the late Canadian scholar Wilfred Cantwell Smith called 'religion in the singular', meaning the history of human religiosity in the broadest sense.

Looking forward from ancient Stonehenge, we can see a number of patterns emerge in different parts of the world, some of them almost simultaneously. Around 500 BCE, for example, several new religious traditions began to form under the

leadership of a great prophet or sage. And by the first century of the Common Era, the concept of a god born in human form was taking root in many parts of the world.

The history of religion is complex, and any attempt to explain broad patterns and trends runs the risk of oversimplification. Even so, if we want to understand how apparently similar ideas might have taken root in cultures that are otherwise very different, it may be useful to think of the way, over time, an island is shaped by the waves that break on its shores. At the most fundamental level, every wave adds some sand and takes some away, so that the contours of the shoreline are constantly changing. In addition, however, great storms occasionally carry the seeds of new vegetation from one island to another, modifying the environment of the second island and creating new conditions that will support other new species, some of which may be very similar to those already living on the first island.

In the same way, some religious ideas may actually have been carried from their places of origin to other cultures, while others may have developed more or less independently, in response to changing environmental—or social, or economic—conditions.

Just as a great storm will bring new plants to the shore, some of which will take root and eventually choke out earlier arrivals, so from time to time major 'waves' have introduced new religious concepts and practices to different human cultures. Where the soil and climate were suitable, the new elements were able to take root, and in time some of them may have replaced older ones.

Countless small waves have undoubtedly caused additional changes of local importance, but we will focus on the big waves, the ones that have brought similar changes to several traditions around the world. Although the following discussion identifies ten such waves, they are by no means the only ones: other scholars would likely propose somewhat different lists.

## Wave 1: Shamanism

One very early wave appears to have carried the ritual specialist—in essence, a kind of priest—that we know today as a **shaman**. (Other terms include 'medicine man', 'soul doctor', and 'witchdoctor'.) The word 'shaman' comes from a specific central Asian culture, but it has become the generic term for a person who acts as an intermediary between humans and the spirit world.

### Hunting Rituals

Many ancient cave drawings depict hunting scenes in which a human figure seems to be performing a dance of some kind. Based on what we know of later hunting societies, we can guess that the figure is a shaman performing a ritual either to ensure a successful hunt or to appease the spirits of the hunted species.

It's not hard to imagine why such societies would have sought ways to influence the outcome of the hunt. Indeed, it seems that the more dangerous the endeavour, the more likely humans were to surround it with rituals. As the anthropologist Bronislaw Malinowski pointed out in his book *Magic, Science and Religion*, the Trobriand Islanders he studied did not perform any special ceremonies before fishing in the lagoon, but they never failed to perform rituals before setting out to fish in the open ocean. This suggests that religious behaviour is, at least in part, a way of coping with dangerous situations.

In addition, though, as we have seen, early humans believed that the spirits of the animals they hunted had to be appeased. Thus a special ritual might be performed to mark the first goose kill of the season, in the hope that other geese would not be frightened away from the hunting grounds.

Such rituals reflect humans' concern over the future food supply, but they also reveal something about the nature of human belief in spirits. From very ancient times, it seems, humans have believed that the spirit—whether of an animal killed

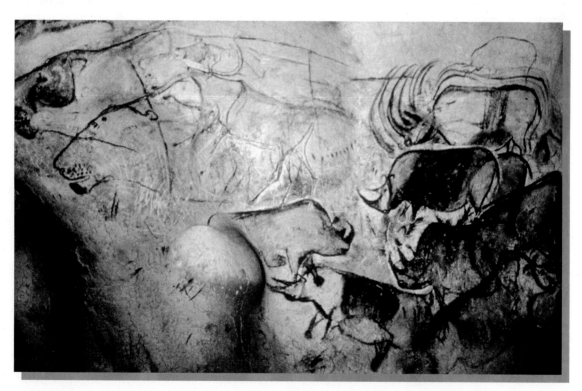

Animal images from the Chauvet cave in southern France, dated c. 30,000 BCE (AP photo/Jean Clottes).

for food or of a human being—survives death and can communicate with others of its kind.

### Coping with Unfriendly Spirits

The spirits associated with natural phenomena—from animals to storms or mountains and rivers—have typically been believed to behave towards humans just as humans behave towards one another. Strategies for dealing with unfriendly spirits, therefore, are usually based on what works with humans.

Many cultures have believed wild, uninhabited areas to be guarded by resident spirits. In some cases these spirits have taken the form of monsters or mythical beasts; in others, of 'little people' such as trolls (common in the folklore of Scandinavia, for example).

Unfriendly spirits were of particular concern to those who ventured into the forest as hunters or gatherers, but they were not confined to the wilderness. Pain and disease of all kinds—from toothache to appendicitis to mental illness—were also attributed to possession by malevolent spirits or demons. In Sri Lanka, those suffering from certain illnesses were advised to have a shaman sacrifice a chicken as an offering to the 'graveyard demon', effectively bribing him to go away; in such cases a second chicken, still alive, would be given to the shaman who performed the ritual. Another approach was to frighten the demon away, either by threatening to invoke another, stronger spiritual power, such as the spirit guide of the shaman, to drive him off, or by making threatening gestures or loud noises. The firecrackers still used in some East Asian rituals are examples of the latter approach.

### The Shaman

The most important resource of all, however, has been the shaman. Shamans are still active in a number of cultures today. The way they operate varies, but certain patterns seem to be almost universal, which in itself suggests that the way of the shaman is very ancient. Sometimes the child of a shaman will follow in the parent's footsteps, but more often a shaman will be 'called' to the role by his or her psychic abilities, as manifested in some extraordinary vision or revelation, or perhaps a near-death experience.

Candidates for the role of shaman face a long and rigorous apprenticeship that often includes a vision quest, in the course of which they are likely to confront terrifying apparitions. Typically the questor will acquire a guiding spirit, sometimes the spirit of a particular animal (perhaps a bear or an eagle, whose claws or feathers the shaman may wear to draw strength from its special powers) and sometimes a more human-like spirit (a god or goddess). This spirit then continues to serve as a guide and protector throughout the shaman's life.

To communicate with the spirit world, the shaman enters a trance state (often induced by rhythmic chanting or drumming). According to Mircea Eliade in his classic *Shamanism: Archaic Techniques of Ecstasy*, contact is then made in one of two ways. In the first, the shaman's soul leaves his body (which may appear lifeless) and travels to the realm where the spirits live; this way is described as 'ecstatic' (from a Greek root meaning to 'stand outside'). In the second, the shaman calls the spirit into her own body and is possessed by it; in such cases the shaman may take on the voice and personality of the spirit, or mimic its way of moving.

In either case, after regaining normal consciousness the shaman announces what he has learned about the problem at hand and what should be done about it. Typically, the problem is traced to the anger of a particular spirit; the shaman then explains the reason for that anger and what must be done to appease the spirit: in most cases the appropriate response is to perform a ritual sacrifice of some kind.

## Wave 2: Connecting to the Cosmos

Our second wave is the one that inspired the building of structures like Stonehenge. People of the Neolithic ('new rock') era went to extraordinary lengths to create sacred areas by assembling huge stones in complex patterns. In some cases the motivation may have been political: perhaps a leader wanted to demonstrate his power over the people under his command. In others, however, the main reason undoubtedly had something to do with religion—for instance, the need for a public space where the rituals essential to the society—weddings, puberty rites, funerals—could be performed.

## Discerning the Cosmic Cycles

Ritual centres such as Stonehenge may also have served purposes that we might think of as scientific or technical, but that their builders would have associated with religion. One very important function of priests was to track the seasons and determine the best time for seasonal activities such as

Stonehenge (David MacDonald).

planting. In addition to tracking the north–south movements of the sun, the people of the Neolithic era paid careful attention to the phases of the moon and the rising positions of certain constellations. The horizon was divided into segments named after the planet or constellation associated with that section. What we now call astrology developed as a way of understanding the cycle of the seasons and how humans fitted into it, collectively and individually. In ancient times no important decision would have been made without consulting an expert in the movements of the sun, moon, planets, and constellations. Even in modern times, many people, including political leaders, consult an astrologer before making major decisions.

## Hilltop Tombs

We suggested earlier that two powerful reasons behind human religion are the fear of death and the idea of an afterlife. Ancient cultures around the world appear to have favoured high places as burial sites. Where there were no hills, artificial ones were sometimes built, at least for the most important members of the society. The pyramids of Egypt and the stupas of Asia are both examples of this practice. In the pyramids, shafts extending from the burial chambers towards important stars connected the deceased with the cosmos. Similarly in Buddhist stupas, a wooden pole— later, a vertical stone structure—extended above the burial mound to connect the earth with the heavens. Scholars refer to this kind of symbolic link between earth and sky as an *axis mundi* ('world axis').

## Animals and Gods

Another common feature of Neolithic religion was a tendency to associate certain animals with specific deities. One very early example comes from the ancient (c. 7000–5000 BCE) city of Catalhoyuk ('forked mound'), near Konya in modern Turkey, where a small sculpture was found of a woman flanked by two large felines. James Mellaart, the archaeologist who first excavated the site in the 1960s, believed she represented a mother goddess seated on a throne. Although this interpretation has been disputed,[2] we know that the ancient Egyptians had a cat goddess named Bast who was revered as a symbol of both motherliness and hunting prowess. And the fierce Hindu goddess Durga is usually depicted riding either a lion or tiger. (One Christmas card from modern India shows the Virgin Mary riding a tiger in the same fashion.)

A statue of the Hindu bull god Nandi at Lepakshi, Andrha Pradesh (© Hornbil Images / Alamy).

### The Bull God

A similar pattern of association links the most powerful male deities with the strength and virility of the bull. In Greek mythology, the great god Zeus took the form of a white bull when he abducted the Phoenician princess Europa. A creature known as the minotaur—half man, half bull—was said to have been kept in a labyrinth beneath the ancient palace of Knossos, on the island of Crete, where frescos show people leaping over the horns of a bull. Greek temples often displayed bull horns near their altars. And in India a bull named Nandi is the sacred mount of the great god Shiva.

The association of the bull with the creator god can even be seen in Judaism, which strictly forbade the use of any image to represent its invisible God. When Moses returns from the mountain and finds that his brother Aaron, the first high priest, has allowed the people to worship an image of a golden calf or bullock, he denounces this practice as idolatry. Centuries later, one of Solomon's sons is severely chastised for installing bull images in the temples he has built.

## Wave 3: Temple Religion

A third wave brought larger temples, more elaborate sacrificial rituals, and, with the latter, the development of a priestly class endowed with unusual power, prestige, and wealth. This wave played an enormous role in shaping many traditions, including Judaism, Chinese religion, and Hinduism, beginning roughly three thousand years ago.

### Indo-European Priests

'Indo-European' is a modern term referring to a language family and cultural system that eventually stretched from India all the way through Europe; it does not designate any particular ethnic group. The Indo-European (IE) cultural system has been one of the most important in human history. It may have originated in the region around the Black Sea, but that is only one of many theories that scholars have proposed.

From the vocabulary of 'proto-IE', as reconstructed by linguists, it is clear that the IE people hunted, practised metallurgy, rode horses, drove chariots, and waged war, among other things. Farming, however, appears not to have been part

## The Sacrifice

When they divided the Man [*Purusha*, the primal Person sacrificed by the gods to create the world], into how many parts did they disperse him? What became of his mouth, what of his arms, what were his two thighs and his two feet called? His mouth was the brahmin, his arms were made into the nobles, his two thighs were the populace, and from his feet the servants were born (Doniger O'Flaherty 1975: 26).

Three times a year all your males shall appear before the Lord your God at the place which he will choose: at the feast of unleavened bread, at the feast of weeks, and at the feast of booths. They shall not appear before the Lord empty-handed: All shall give as they are able, according to the blessing of the Lord your God that he has given you (from Moses' instructions to the people of Israel; Deuteronomy 16:16–17).

of their culture: the fact that the IE vocabulary related to agriculture differs from one place to another suggests that in farming the Indo-Europeans simply adopted existing local practices.

Everywhere the IE warriors conquered, they set up a social system with four basic divisions, the top three of which consisted of priests, warriors, and middle-class commoners. In India these groups are known respectively as the brahmins, kshatriyas, and vaishyas. In ancient times each of these groups had a special clothing colour; thus today in India *varna* ('colour') is still the standard term for 'class'. The priests performed rituals, kept the calendar, taught the young, and advised the kings; within the warrior class, the top clans were the rulers; while the middle-class 'commoners' earned their living as merchants or farmers. Finally, all local people, no matter how wealthy or accomplished, were relegated to the servant (shudra) class.

The four-level social system was given mythic status in the *Rig Veda*, according to which the world came into being through the sacrifice of a 'cosmic person' (*Purusha*). Out of his mouth came the brahmin priests, whose job was to chant the

sacred hymns and syllables. The warriors came from his arms, the middle class from his thighs, and the servants from his feet. Even today, this ancient hymn continues to buttress the social class structure of India.

Over a period of about a thousand years, beginning around 2500 BCE, the Indo-Europeans took control of the territories that are now Afghanistan, northwest India, Pakistan, Turkey, Greece, Rome, central Europe, and, for a while, even Egypt. Their religious culture was similar to most of its counterparts four to five thousand years ago, with many deities, including a 'sky father' (a name that survives in Greek Zeus Pater, Latin Jupiter, and Sanskrit Dyaus Pitar) and a storm god (Indra in India, Thor in Scandinavia); they sang hymns to female deities, such as the goddess of dawn; and they had a hereditary priesthood to offer sacrifices to the gods.

Although the IE people did not necessarily invent the system of hereditary priesthood, they certainly contributed to its spread. In addition to Hindu brahmins, examples include the ancient Roman priests and Celtic Druids. These priests enjoyed great power and prestige, and sometimes were resented by non-priests. (One ancient Indian text includes a parody in which dogs, acting like priests, dance around a fire chanting '*Om* let us eat, *om* let us drink'.[3])

### Priests and Temples Elsewhere

We actually know when the first Jewish temple was built. After David had been chosen as king of both the northern kingdom of Israel and the southern kingdom of Judah, he captured the Jebusite city now known as Jerusalem. He transformed the city into a proper capital, complete with a grand palace for himself and an organized priesthood. His son Solomon took the next step, building the first temple in the mid-tenth century BCE. The priests attached to the temple soon made it the only site where sacrificial rituals could be performed.

The Jewish priesthood was hereditary. All those who served in the temple as assistants to the priests were required to be Levites (from the tribe of Levi), and priests themselves had to be not only Levites but direct descendants of Aaron, the brother of Moses who was the original high priest.

Priests became a powerful social class in many other parts of the world as well, including Africa, Asia, and the Americas. In some cultures they were a hereditary class, and in others they were recruited. Typically, the role of priest was reserved for males, females being considered impure because of the menstrual cycle; the Vestal Virgins of ancient Rome, who tended the sacred fires and performed rituals, were among the very few exceptions to the general rule.

## Wave 4: Prophetic Religion

The word 'prophet' derives from Greek and has two related meanings, one referring to a person who speaks on behalf of a deity and one referring to a person who foresees or predicts the future. The terms are often conflated because prophets delivering messages from the deity often warned of disasters to come if God's will was not obeyed. The site of the temple at Delphi, Greece, where a virgin priestess under the inspiration of Apollo delivered prophecies, had been considered sacred for centuries, maybe millennia, before the glory days of classical Greece. It must have seemed a natural spot for making contact with the divine and receiving sacred knowledge: high up a mountainside, close to the gods, with a natural cave that resembled the entrance to a womb (*delphys* in Greek, representing the mysterious female energy) and a standing stone or *omphalos* (navel of the earth), representing the male energy and the connection between heaven and earth.

This sacred site dates back at least three thousand years, to a time before the rise of classical

The ruins of the temple at Delphi (Steven Vidler/Eurasia Press/Corbis).

Greece, when the oracle was believed to be inspired not by Apollo but by the earth goddess Gaia. Eventually males took control of the sacred site, but even in classical times the virgin priestesses would prepare themselves to receive Apollo's message by bathing in an artesian spring and breathing intoxicating fumes from a fissure in the earth—both water and fumes issuing from Gaia, the earth.

Those wishing to consult the oracle had to climb the mountain, make known their request, pay a fee, and sacrifice a black goat before their question would be put to the oracle. The priestess would take her place over the fissure and, in an ecstatic trance, deliver Apollo's message, which was typically unintelligible and had to be translated into ordinary language by a male priest. Interpreting the real-world significance of a prophecy was not so simple, however. In one famous case, a Greek leader who asked what would happen if he went to war with another state was told that a great country would fall; accordingly, he went to war—but the country that fell was his own. Similarly in the Oedipus myth, the oracle's prophecy that the infant would grow up to kill his father and marry his mother was fulfilled in spite of the measures taken to avoid that fate.

### Abrahamic Prophetic Traditions

In 586 BCE the people of Israel were forcibly removed from their homeland and exiled to Babylon. The centuries that followed the 'Babylonian captivity' were the defining period for the concept of prophecy as it developed in the three monotheistic traditions that trace their origins to the prophet Abraham. Often, the Jewish prophets' messages were directed towards the people of Israel as a whole, warning of the disasters that loomed if they did not follow God's demands.

Christianity saw Jesus and certain events surrounding his life as the fulfillment of Hebrew prophecies. And Islam in turn recognized the Hebrew prophets, beginning with Abraham and including Jesus, as the forerunners of the Prophet Muhammad, the last and greatest of all, the messenger (*rasul*) who received God's final revelations. Muslims understand Muhammad to have been the 'seal of the prophets': no other prophet will follow him, since he has delivered the message of God in its entirety. As with earlier prophetic traditions, the Day of Judgment (or Day of Doom) and the concepts of heaven and hell are central to Islam.

### Zarathustra, Prophet of the Wise Lord

Zarathustra (or Zoroaster) was a prophet figure who lived more than 2,500 years ago, probably in the region of eastern Iran or Afghanistan. Although we know little about his life, he left behind a collection of poems devoted to a 'wise lord' called Ahura Mazda. The religion that developed around his teachings, which came to be known as Zoroastrianism, played an important part in the development of monotheism.

The concepts of heaven and hell also owe a lot to the Zoroastrians, who believed that evil-doers were condemned to hell at their death, but that eventually a great day of judgment would come when the souls of all the dead would be made to pass through a fiery wall. Those who had been virtuous in life would pass through the fire without pain, while the rest would be cleansed of their remaining sin and permitted to enter paradise (a term believed to derive from a Persian word meaning garden).

The threat of hell and the promise of heaven were powerful tools for any prophet seeking to persuade people to behave as they believed the deity demanded.

## Wave 5: The Energy God

Yet another important wave of change arrived around 2,500 years ago. Among the ideas it carried was one that, although it has never been the focus of a major tradition, continues to inspire important minorities in cultures around the world. That

## Divine Energy

The Dao that can be told of
Is not the Absolute Dao;
The Names that can be given
Are not Absolute Names.
The Nameless is the origin of Heaven and Earth;
The Named is the Mother of All Things
    (from Laozi in the *Daodejing*; Lin Yutang 1948: 41).

This finest essence, the whole universe has it as its Self: That is the Real: That is the Self: That *you* are, Svetaketu! (from the *Chandogya Upanishad* 6.9; Zaehner 1966: 110).

idea concerns the nature of the divine and where it is to be found. Specifically, it suggests that the divine is neither a 'sky-father' nor an 'earth-mother', but a force, an energy, that is found by looking within. This is not a god that issues commandments, answers prayers, or in any way interacts with humans as a human. It does not create in the usual fashion of gods, or direct the course of history, or dictate the fate of individuals. In fact, some have suggested that it may have more in common with the principles of modern physics than with the traditional gods of most religions. This divinity simply exists—or rather, 'underlies' everything that exists.

Among the traditions that developed in the wake of this wave were the Daoism of China, the Upanishadic wisdom of India, and the pre-Socratic philosophy of the early Greek world.

### Finding the Dao Within

The sage who became known as Laozi ('Master Lao') lived in northern China around 600 BCE. According to legend, he worked for the government as an archivist. At night students would visit his home to hear his words of wisdom about life, especially how to live in harmony with one's inner nature. But Lao had what we might call a mid-life crisis. Dissatisfied with his job and the social and political life of his time, he is said to have left home and set out to the west, riding on a water buffalo (an event that became a favourite subject for artists). Apparently he had not even said goodbye to his students, but one of them happened to be working as a guard at the border. Shocked to learn that his master was leaving China, he begged Lao to record his teachings before leaving.

So Lao paused at the border long enough to write down the fundamentals of his thought in a series of beautiful, if cryptic, verses that were eventually collected in a small volume called **Daodejing** (or *Tao De Ching*), meaning the book (*jing*) about the *Dao* and its power (*de*). It became and remains one of the world's most influential books.

What did Laozi write that has spoken to so many through the millennia? He begins with what became one of the most famous opening lines in history: 'The *Dao* that can be described is not the eternal *Dao*. The name that can be named is not the eternal name.' In general usage the word *Dao* means 'the way', but here it refers to the mysterious energy that underlies all things. Laozi is warning readers that words cannot adequately describe the *Dao*. Ogden Nash, a twentieth-century poet noted

Laozi and the water buffalo; a sculpture from the Song dynasty (960–1279) (Burnstein Collection/Corbis).

the water over time. The water in the ox hoofprint will evaporate and return to the sky, to fall again when the time is right.

### 'That Is You': Sitting near the Sages of Old India

A worldview similar to that of Daoism took shape in northern India around the same time. The texts it produced, known as the **Upanishads** (a Sanskrit term meaning literally 'sitting-up-near' the master), were reserved for the most advanced students when they were composed, between roughly 1500 and 600 BCE.

What the Daoist sages called the *Dao* the Upanishadic masters called *sat* (usually translated in English as 'being', 'truth', or 'the real'). In one Upanishad there is the story of a young man named Svetaketu who has just completed his studies with the brahmin priests. Back at home, his father, who is a king and therefore a member of the warrior class, asks Svetaketu what his priestly teachers taught him about the original source of all things. When Svetaketu admits that he was not taught about that subject, his father undertakes to instruct him in the secret wisdom.

for combining insight and humour, captured the same idea this way: 'Whatever the mind comes at, God is not that.'

In traditional cultures, people talk about the characteristics of various deities—their loving nature, or anger, or jealousy, or desire for a particular kind of behaviour. But the absolute, the eternal *Dao*, has no such attributes. Thus Laozi uses poetic imagery to give us some insights into its nature. Unlike Athena, Zeus, Yahweh, or Indra, the *Dao* does not have a 'personality', and there is no reason for humans to fear, love, or appease it.

Rather, Laozi says, the *Dao* is like water: it will take on the shape of whatever container we pour it into. Falling from the sky, it may seem content to lie in the hollow made by the footprint of an ox in the muddy road. Raining on the rocky mountaintop, it tumbles all the way down. Water seems malleable, passive and without a will of its own. Yet a mountain will be worn down by

The first lesson has to do with the need for sleep and food; then the real teaching begins. The father has Svetaketu bring a bowl of water and taste it. Then he has him put a lump of sea salt into the water. The next morning Svetaketu sees that the lump of salt is no longer visible; he tastes the water and finds it salty. We can imagine his impatience at being instructed in something he already knows. But his father has a bigger point in mind. He tells Svetaketu that just as the salt is invisible yet present in the water, so also there is a hidden essence present throughout the world. That hidden essence, the force that energizes everything, is the highest reality, the father says, and that reality is you (*tat tvam asi*; 'that you are'). The Upanishadic master is initiating his son into a new religious worldview that understands 'god' as an energy hidden within and sustaining everything. And that great energy, that ultimate reality, '*tat tvam asi*'—that is you.

### The First Principle: Greek Philosophy before Socrates

The same wave influenced Greek thought around 2,500 years ago as well. The Greek-speaking philosophers of Ionia (now southwestern Turkey) began to ask the same questions as Svetaketu's father: What is the first principle, the first cause, the source from which all else comes? Starting from the science of the day, which held there to be four primal elements—earth, air, fire, and water—they wanted to determine which of those four came first. Although their methods were those of philosophy rather than scientific experimentation, their attempt to understand the causal principle underlying all things—without bringing in a god as the final cause—marked a major advance towards the development of the scientific worldview.

### Later Theistic Mysticism

European religious thought eventually reflected the influence of this wave as well. German Christian mystics such as Jacob Böhme (1575–1624) would use terms such as *Ungrund* ('ungrounded') or *Urgrund* ('original ground') to refer to the divine as primal cause. Christian, Jewish, and Muslim mystics alike believed in a god beyond the reaches of human understanding.

## Wave 6: Purity and Monasticism

At almost the same time that the 'energy god' worldview was establishing itself in China, India, and Greek culture, another spiritual development of great importance was forming in India. The earliest historical records come from the region of what is now northern India around 2,500 years ago, but the tradition itself claims to have much older roots. Its followers typically sought spiritual enlightenment through asceticism—intense bodily discipline. Their ethic was one of non-violence towards all creatures, and their goal was to perfect the human potential for purity of mind.

### Ganges Spirituality

English has no specific term for the new type of religion that came into bloom in the region of the Ganges river around 500 BCE. By that time the Indo-European cultural system, including the religion of the brahmin priests, was firmly established in what is now northern India. We can never know for certain what earlier traditions that religion displaced, since the written sources we rely on were the products of the brahmins themselves. However, linguistic and archaeological data lend support to the theory that two of the world's great living religions—Jainism and Buddhism—were rooted in the pre-brahminic traditions of the Ganges region.

Along the banks of the river were many camps where spiritual masters of various persuasions operated what were in effect open-air seminaries. Though some of the teachers were brahmins, others were committed to the idea that it was wrong to harm any living creature. Their followers rejected the killing of animals for food, and some even objected to farming, because hoeing and plowing would harm organisms living in the soil. While the brahmin masters continued to perform their animal sacrifices, the masters committed to the principle of non-harm (*ahimsa*) denounced that tradition. Some of the latter—among them the Jaina master Mahavira—went so far as to require their disciples to cover their mouths and noses and strain their drinking water, in order to avoid causing harm to microscopic insects.

Leaving the world of day-to-day life to follow the path of spiritual enlightenment through rigorous ascetic discipline, the students who gathered around these masters took vows of poverty and celibacy, and considered themselves to have 'departed the world'. The Buddhist and Jaina monastic traditions trace their roots to these ascetics, and it is possible that Indian monasticism played a role in the development of Western monasticism as well.

One more difference between the Indo-European and 'Gangetic' cultural systems is worth mentioning here. In the IE system, priests were recruited only from the brahmin social class. In the Ganges tradition, by contrast, the notion of a hereditary priesthood is rejected entirely: anyone, however humble, can choose to lead the life of a holy person. As the Buddha would teach his followers, the status of the 'true brahmin' is not a birthright, but must be earned through meritorious conduct.

## Wave 7: Mystery Religion

'Mystery religion' refers to a wave of Greek and Roman traditions in which the core teachings and rituals were kept secret from outsiders and revealed only to those prepared to undergo initiation in the hope of securing blessings during this life and a heavenly paradise in the afterlife. Such religions became so popular during the Roman period that they presented a threat to the power and influence of the official Roman priesthood (not to be confused with the Roman Catholic priesthood).

The Eleusinian mystery tradition may be the oldest. Named for an ancient Greek town called Eleusis, it grew out of the myth of the young Persephone or Kore ('girl') who is abducted by the god of the dead (Hades) and taken down into the underworld. With the disappearance of this young girl—a potent symbol of growth and fertility—everything on earth begins to die. This imperils not only humans but the gods themselves, who depend on humans to feed them through sacrifices. The girl's mother, Demeter, is therefore allowed to descend into the underworld and bring her back.

Scholars understand the Persephone myth to be based on the seasonal cycles of stagnation during the winter and renewal in the spring. Members of her cult believed that by identifying themselves with the dying and rising goddess through the celebration of seasonal rituals, they too would triumph over death.

Initiates into the mysteries associated with the god Dionysus were also following a very ancient tradition. Through rituals that included the drinking of wine, ecstatic dancing, and, perhaps, the eating of mind-altering plants, participants were able to enter into ecstatic states of consciousness in which they believed that their god would ensure a pleasant afterlife. Another popular mystery cult, dedicated to the goddess Isis, had Egyptian origins.

Many scholars have suggested that mystery cults such as these may have influenced the development of Christianity. The early Christians were initiated into the new cult by undergoing baptism. They then joined an inner circle of people whose faith centred on the death and resurrection of Jesus and who hoped that by following Christ they would secure blessings during this life and a place in heaven after death. Although Christianity developed out of Judaism, its theological structure does seem to have been influenced, however indirectly, by the mystery wave of religion.

## Wave 8: God on Earth

### The Avatar

Long before the word 'avatar' came into use in computer games, *avatara* was a Sanskrit theological term for the 'coming down' of a god to earth. In the earlier stages of religion there were many stories of gods and goddesses who came down to earth, but there are two major differences in the avatar stories.

First, the avatar is a god in a truly human form—as a later Christian creed put it, 'fully God and fully man'—whereas the ancient gods

## Avatar Gods

For the protection of the good,
For the destruction of evildoers,
For the setting up of righteousness,
I come into being, age after age.
    (Krishna to Arjuna in the *Bhagavad Gita*; Zaehner 1966: 267).

Have this mind among yourselves, which you have in Christ Jesus, who, though he was in the form of God, did not count equality with God a thing to be grasped, but emptied himself, taking the form of a servant, being born in the likeness of men. And being found in human form he humbled himself. . . . (St Paul to the Christians of Philippi; Philippians 2:6–7).

came down to earth as gods. For example, in the ancient Indian story of Princess Dhamayanti, the father of a beautiful princess holds a party to which he invites all the marriageable princes from various kingdoms. Four gods also attend the party, however, all disguised as the handsome prince Nala, whom the princess already plans to choose. She is disturbed to see five look-alikes, but is finally able to distinguish the four imposters from the real Prince Nala because the gods do not sweat and are floating slightly above the ground. She marries the human prince, and they live happily ever after.

Unlike the gods at Dhamayanti's party, the avatar gods walk on the ground, perspire, get hungry, sleep, and are in every way human. They are incarnated in a human womb, are born, grow up, teach, save the world from evil, and eventually die. As a Christian layman once told me, 'You have to understand that we Christians worship a god in diapers.' His choice of words was unusual, but his theology was solid, and it leads us to the second major change brought by the avatar wave.

This second innovation is the fact that the avatar god is a saviour figure in at least two ways. Not only does he save the world from some evil power, such as Satan or a demonic king, but he saves those who put their faith in him from hell and ensures that they have a place in heaven. In the religions of the avatar wave, the ritual of sacrifice is replaced by the ritual of placing faith in the saviour god.

The biography of the saviour gods follows a well-known pattern. Typically, the avatar god has a special, non-sexual conception. His mother is chosen to bear him because she is exceptionally pure, and an angel or prophet announces to her that the child she is carrying has a special destiny. The saviour's birth, usually in a rustic setting, is surrounded by miracles, which often include a fortuitous star or constellation pattern in the night sky. Wise persons foresee the child's greatness. An evil king tries to kill the baby, but kills another baby, or babies, instead. The child has special powers, and as an adult is able to work miracles. He typically marries and has a child before embarking on his religious mission. His death represents a triumph over evil and the cosmos responds with earthquakes and other natural signs. Upon dying, he returns to the heavens to preside over a paradise in which his followers hope to join him after they die.

The avatar wave hit Asia and the Middle East approximately two thousand years ago. Among Hindus its impact was reflected in the worship of Krishna; among Buddhists in the veneration of Amitabha Buddha (the figure who would become Amida in Japan), and among Jews in the rise of Christianity.

### Krishna, Avatara of Vishnu

In some Hindu stories Vishnu is the ultimate deity, the god who lies at the origin of everything there is, including the creator god Brahman. Vishnu lies on his cosmic serpent, sometimes identified with the Milky Way, and out of his navel grows a lotus plant. From the lotus Brahman is born as the first of all creations; then the universe and all its material and spiritual energies follow. This is not exactly a mythic version of the big bang theory, but it comes close. Life evolves, over an unimaginable number of years, out of the divine energy at the centre of the universe. After the universe has run its allotted course, the process reverses from evolution to involution. Over an equally long period of time, eventually all things return into Vishnu, as if crossing the event horizon into a black hole. There all energy lies dormant as Vishnu sleeps, before the whole process begins again.

Another storyline about Vishnu sees him as the protector of the world. When earth gets into trouble, he comes down to save us. The first five *avataras* of Vishnu took the form of animals, and they protected the world from natural disasters in its formative millennia. The next four avatars are humans, the most important of whom is Krishna. His exploits are narrated in several different Hindu sources. The most famous is the *Bhagavad Gita*—the 'Song of the Lord', a small section of the epic *Mahabharata*. The latter tells of a great war between two houses of the royal family. Krishna is a relative of both houses and is recruited by both armies, but chooses to fight for neither. Instead, he agrees to drive the chariot of Arjuna, one of the five princes who lead one army.

At the beginning of the Gita, just before the battle, Arjuna asks Krishna to drive the chariot into the neutral zone between the two great armies, so that he can get a better look at the enemy. But when he sees his adversaries more closely, he loses his will to fight, telling Krishna that he recognizes among them his cousins, his old teachers, and others he remembers from childhood.

Krishna counsels him to take up his bow and fight, for that is his duty as a warrior. Arjuna has misgivings, however, and they begin a long conversation about morality or duty (dharma) and the eternal soul that cannot die even though the body may be killed in battle. Krishna teaches with such great authority that soon Arjuna asks how he knows so much. Krishna replies that he is a god of gods, that he is the energy behind all the categories of spirits and gods. When Arjuna asks for proof, Krishna grants him the eye of a god, with which he sees the splendors and mysteries of the universe as a god would.

In the end, Arjuna accepts the divinity of his chariot-driving cousin, acts on his advice, fights alongside his brothers, and wins the war. More important, however, is what Arjuna learns from Krishna about the many ways to lead a good religious life. These include the *yoga* (way) of good works (*karma yoga*), the way of deep spiritual wisdom (*jnana yoga*), and the way of faithful devotion to Krishna (*bhakti yoga*). Of these, the path of faithful devotion is the most highly recommended because it is the easiest and the most certain. The real saving power comes not from the wisdom or discipline of the individual, but from the saving power of the god. Krishna promises that those who practise devotion to him will go to his heaven when they die.

Another source offers stories about other parts of Krishna's life. We learn from it that Krishna was born under the rule of an evil king who was secretly part of a demonic plot to take over the world. One day King Kamsa is driving the wedding chariot of a female relative when an old man—a prophet figure—yells out to the king and tells him he is assisting in the marriage of a woman whose eighth child will grow up to kill him. The king is about to call off the wedding, but the bride pleads with him to reconsider, even promising that when she has children, Kamsa can do with them as he wishes. Kamsa agrees, the marriage takes place, and he proceeds to kill her children as they are born. On the night of the fateful eighth birth, the father is told in a dream to take the baby to safety with relatives across the river. This he does, replacing his child with a baby girl born the same evening.

When the king's guards hear the baby crying, they awaken the king, who smashes the infant's head on the ground. As the baby's soul rises towards heaven, it tells Kamsa that the baby who will grow up to kill him is still alive. That child is Krishna, and when he grows up he fulfills his destiny, saving the world from the evil represented by Kamsa and his demons.

### Amitabha, the Buddha of Saving Grace

The avatar wave gave Buddhism the story of Amitabha Buddha, in which a prince intent on achieving buddhahood makes forty-eight vows, a number of which focus on helping others towards the same goal. Among them is a promise to establish a paradise free of all suffering, disease, and ill will, in which those who put their trust in Amitabha Buddha will be reborn after their death. His followers hope that if they sincerely profess their faith in his saving power, they will be rewarded with rebirth in that 'Pure Land'.

### Jesus the Christ: God Come Down

The Christian doctrine of the trinity affirms that the one God exists in three persons: those of the father, the son, and the holy spirit. In formulating this doctrine, the Christians departed radically from the theology proclaimed by Abraham and Moses. There is no room in Jewish thought for an avatar god, but that was the direction in which Christian

thought developed. The prologue to the Gospel of John identifies Jesus with the divine Logos—the word of God that was present before creation. The New Testament says that Jesus 'emptied himself of divinity' and came down for the salvation of the world. His conception is through the spirit of god rather than by normal sexual intercourse. An angel announces the significance of the pregnancy to his mother. The birth is associated with a special star. Shepherds overhear the angels rejoicing and come to revere the infant, according to Luke's gospel. In Matthew's gospel, magi from the East follow a special star and bring gifts to the child.

For Christians, Jesus became the ultimate god who had died on the cross on behalf of his followers and rose on the third day. By participating in the sacred rituals—the sacraments of baptism and the eucharist—and placing their trust in Jesus as Lord, Christians could expect to go to heaven after their death.

So Christianity starts with the Hebrew scriptures and the monotheism of Moses and incorporates into them the avatar pattern, as well as elements of the mystery traditions, to form a new religion. Many Jews resisted these changes, but some accepted them in the belief that God had in fact offered the world a new dispensation.

## Wave 9: Scriptural Religion

The ninth wave is hard to date. The earliest scriptures we have are the Zoroastrian Avesta of Persia, the Hindu Vedas, and the Torah of Judaism, all of which took shape approximately three thousand years ago. This wave came much later, however, when different groups began to insist that their particular scriptures were the literal words of God, and to make adherence to those scriptures the focus of their religious life.

The scripturalism wave manifested itself in Rabbinic Judaism in the centuries following the destruction of the Jerusalem temple in 70 CE. It emerged in full force with the rise of Islam, destined

## The Word of God

We have sent it down as an Arabic Qur'an, in order that you may learn wisdom (from the Qur'an, 12:2).

In the beginning was the Word, and the Word was with God, and the Word was God. The same was in the beginning with God. All things were made by him, and without him was not any thing made that was made (John 1:1–3, KJV).

And the Word was made flesh and dwelt among us (John 1:14, KJV).

to become one of the two most influential religions of all time. It also played a large role in Protestant Christianity, in which the authority of scripture replaced that of tradition and the papacy.

### Living by Torah

During the Jews' exile in Babylon the priests were not able to perform the traditional temple rituals, and so the Jews turned to the rabbis—scholars of the Torah with special expertise in Jewish law and ritual. In this way scripture began to play a more important role in Jewish life, a role that became even more important after the destruction of the second temple in 70 CE. Since that time, Jewish religious life has centred on interpretation of the scripture.

### The Word of God

Two or three generations passed after the death of Jesus before the gospels were written, and the Christian canon did not take shape until well into the third century CE. But once the books of the canon were fixed, the Church came to emphasize scripture as a divinely inspired source of faith and practice. The Bible became as central to Christianity as the Torah was to Judaism. Christians commonly refer to the scripture as the word of God,

and some believe that the Bible was literally dictated by God to its human authors.

### God's Final Prophet

The scriptural wave reached its greatest height in Islam. The surahs that make up the Qur'an are believed to be the sacred words of God as revealed to the Prophet Muhammad by an angel, recorded by scribes, and compiled as a collection after his death. In its essence, therefore, the Qur'an is considered to be an oral text, meant to be recited—always in the original Arabic—rather than read. Nevertheless, the written Qur'an is treated with great respect. No other book is to be placed on top of the Qur'an, and before opening the book, the reader is expected to be in the same state of ritual purity required to perform the daily prayers.

### The Lotus Sutra

The teachings of the Buddha were transmitted orally for centuries before they were first written down, some two thousand years ago. Although Buddhists revered these texts, their practice did not centre on them. Later, the Mahayana and Vajrayana schools added many more texts to their respective canons, but Buddhists in general did not attribute any special properties to the scriptures themselves. That changed in the 1200s, when a Japanese monk named Nichiren instructed his followers to place their faith in the power of his favourite scripture, the *Lotus Sutra*, and chant their homage to it, just as followers of the Pure Land school chanted homage to Amitabha/Amida Buddha.

### Creation through the Word of God

A number of scriptural traditions have maintained that their scriptures were in existence before the creation of the world. The medieval book of Jewish mysticism known as the *Zohar*, for example, teaches that the Torah played a role in the creation of the world. The prologue to the Gospel of John in the New Testament talks about creation through the Word (*logos* in Greek). And Islam understands the Qur'an to have existed in the mind of God before creation.

This idea has ancient roots. In old Israel, Egypt, India, and elsewhere, it was assumed that the deities would not have performed the physical work of creation themselves, like ordinary humans: rather, like kings, they would have commanded that the work be done: 'Let there be light.' Thus the divine word took on a special role in later theologies. In traditional Hindu thought the goddess of speech, Vac, played this role. How could the scriptures—the actual words of the Torah, Bible, or Qur'an—be present in the mind of God at the time of creation, thousands of years before the historical events they describe? The answer for believers is that God knows the future. Outsiders might argue that this calls into question the concept of free will: If the deity knows everything in advance, how can humans be free to choose? What use is it to try to persuade people to do the right thing if the deity has already determined what each of them will do? Such questions have led to lively theological debates in many religious traditions.

## Wave 10: Fundamentalism

Our final wave began to take shape in the mid-twentieth century and is still unfolding today. In time it may prove to have been merely a sub-wave of scripturalism. Nevertheless, for those of us living in the aftermath of 9/11, it often seems as if the current wave of violent religious fundamentalism represents something new in the human experience.

The term 'fundamentalism' was first used in the early twentieth century to refer to a variety of American Protestantism characterized by a fervent belief in the absolute, literal truth of the Bible. Adherents of this type of Protestantism reject all forms of secularism that they perceive as inconsistent with biblical tradition. Thus many send their children to religious schools because the public system teaches 'secular' values; some even refuse to vote because the democratic system is a human creation not mentioned in scripture. Not surprisingly, Protestant fundamentalists reject the authority of science and strongly object to the concept of evolution and the idea that the universe is billions of years old. In addition, many scholars have noted that fundamentalist groups tend to be male-dominated and to understand male–female relations and roles from a hierarchical, patriarchal perspective.

Similar movements exist within most religious traditions. Yet however convinced these groups are that their god is the only true one, and that their way of believing and worshipping is the only true way, the majority of their adherents have no desire to force their convictions on others. At the same time, within all these groups there are militant minorities who are prepared to use violence, whether to convert others, to defend the true believers, or to take revenge on perceived enemies. To understand how this wave has taken shape and is developing today, we will look at both regular religious fundamentalism and the more militant varieties in our concluding chapter.

A re-enactment of the crucifixion at a Christian rally in Washington, DC (Erik Freeland/Corbis).

# 🌿 WHY STUDY RELIGION?

The first and most obvious reason to study religion is that it exists. Not all humans would lay claim to religious beliefs, but humans in general have been religious from time immemorial.

A closely related reason is that religion has played such an important role in human affairs. People go to war over religious identities, make great art to serve religious communities or express their spirituality. People spend significant amounts of their time, money, and energy on religious activities and institutions. People seek to change social norms, or to prevent change, out of religious conviction. In short, religion so pervades the human world that it demands our attention regardless of whether it plays a direct role in our own personal life.

It is also common to study religion for more personal reasons. You may want to know more about the tradition you, or someone close to you, grew up in. You may want to study other religions in order to understand other people's beliefs, or to look at your own beliefs from a different perspective. You may also want to arm yourself with knowledge in order to bring others around to your way of thinking, or to defend your beliefs against the arguments of those who might try to convert you to theirs.

## Insider versus Outsider

Most people learn about their own religion from their parents, their teachers at religious schools, or other members of the same religious community.

Naturally, people tend to accept the teachings of their religion as true and assume that the teachings of other religions are false, or at least less true. As 'insiders' we may find it disturbing when 'outsiders' challenge our beliefs or suggest that the history of 'our religion' may not be exactly as we have been taught.

One of the advantages of a book such as this is that it helps us appreciate our own traditions from both insider and outsider points of view. When approaching an unfamiliar religious tradition, outsiders need to be sensitive to the ways in which it serves the needs of its followers. For their part, insiders need to understand how their own tradition looks from the outside.

The insider–outsider matter is more complex than we might imagine, for there are many kinds of insiders. Is your Muslim friend a Sunni or a Shi'i? If a Shi'i, does she belong to the Twelver branch or one of the Sevener branches? Which variety of Buddhism does your classmate practise—Theravada, Mahayana, or Vajrayana? If Mahayana, which school? Is your Christian neighbour Protestant, Catholic, or Orthodox? A Protestant may well be an 'outsider' to Catholic Christianity. A Zen Buddhist could have trouble seeing any connection between his practice and an elaborate Vajrayana ritual. Because each religion has many subdivisions, in these volumes we will speak of traditions in the plural. We hope our readers will keep in mind the diversity behind the monolithic labels.

## Some Practical Matters

The East–West division of our two volumes is quite conventional, but it is problematic for several reasons. For one thing, the so-called 'Western' religions arose in what we now term the Middle East: they are Western only in the sense that they were widely adopted in the West. A related problem is that there is no clear dividing line between East and West. As the late Will Oxtoby pointed out in an earlier edition of this text, 'the East was everything to the east of Europe' until well into the twentieth century:

> The Orient began where the Orient Express ran: Istanbul. For some purposes, it even included North Africa and began with Morocco. . . . A century ago, Islam was thought to be an Eastern religion, and Westerners who studied it were called orientalists.

For those of us living in the twenty-first century, though, the biggest problem with the East–West division is that all the religions discussed in these volumes are now found throughout the world. Thus our Eastern volume focuses on traditions that developed in the East and are still centred there, while its Western counterpart focuses mainly on those that developed in the Middle East and now predominate in the Middle East, Europe, Africa, and the Americas.

For dates we use BCE ('Before the Common Era') rather than BC ('Before Christ'), and CE ('Common Era') rather than AD ('Anno Domini', Latin for 'in the year of our lord'). For dates that are obviously in the Common Era, the 'CE' will be implied.

Finally, it is difficult to decide whether a book like this should use diacritical marks on foreign words. Scholars of religion writing for other scholars typically use diacritics for precision in transliterating foreign terms into English. Since this is an introductory text, we have chosen not to use diacritics because students often find them more confusing than helpful. Anyone who wishes to do more research on a religious tradition will soon encounter them, however.

Whether or not you are religious yourself, we invite you to delve into the study of several religious traditions that have played central roles both in the lives of individual humans and in the civilizations they have built around the world.

# Glossary

**All Saints Day**  A Christian festival honouring all the departed saints; held in the West on 1 November.

**Daodejing**  The Daoist 'Classic of the Way and Power', compiled roughly 2,500 years ago and traditionally attributed to Laozi.

**Day of the Dead**  A Mexican festival honouring the dead.

**Hallowe'en**  Now a popular secular holiday, held on 31 October; originally celebrated as the 'Eve' of All Saints Day.

**high places**  Sacred areas located on hill- or mountain-tops; such places existed throughout the ancient Near East.

**naga**  A mythical cobra living in the underworld, often associated with water and fertility in Indian religions.

**Obon**  A Japanese festival honouring ancestors.

**shaman**  A type of priest, widespread among hunter-gatherer societies, who communicates with the spirit world on behalf of the people.

**Stonehenge**  One of several ancient rock structures thought to have been constructed for ritual purposes.

**Upanishads**  Hindu religious texts thought to have been composed between 1500 and 600 BCE.

# References

Ballter, Michael. 2005. *The Goddess and the Bull: Catalhoyuk: An Archaeological Journey to the Dawn of Civilization*. New York: Free Press.

Doniger O'Flaherty, Wendy. 1975. *Hindu Myths: A Sourcebook Translated from the Sanskrit*. Harmondsworth: Penguin Classics.

Eliade, Mircea. [1951] 1964. *Shamanism: Archaic Techniques of Ecstasy*. Translated by Willard R. Trask. Princeton: Princeton University Press.

Lin, Yutang, 1948. *The Wisdom of Laotse*. New York: The Modern Library.

Malinowski, Bronislaw. 1948. *Magic, Science and Religion*. Boston: Beacon Press.

# Notes

1. Marc Kaufman, 'Researchers Say Stonehenge Was a Family Burial Ground', *Washington Post*, 30 May 2008: A1.

2. Michael Ballter, *The Goddess and the Bull: Catalhoyuk: An Archaeological Journey to the Dawn of Civilization* (New York: Free Press, 2005).

3. Chandogya Upanishad I, xii, in R.C. Zaehner, ed. *Hindu Scriptures* (London: Everyman's Library, 1966), 84.

# Chapter 2

# Hindu Traditions

ॐ Vasudha Narayanan ॐ

The earliest compositions in the Hindu tradition are said to have been 'revealed' to *rishis* (visionaries or seers) through both sight and sound; thus the sacred words are called *shruti* ('that which is heard'). This dual emphasis on seeing and hearing the sacred is characteristic of the Hindu tradition.

When Hindus go on a pilgrimage or visit a temple, they seek an experience known as a **darshana**: to see and be seen by a particular deity or **guru** (holy teacher). But Hindus also believe in the importance of uttering prayers aloud. Reciting Sanskrit texts in the temple or recounting in a vernacular language the stories of the gods, chanting a prayer or singing a devotional song or meditating on a holy **mantra**—these are just some of the ways in which Hindus actively live their tradition through its sacred words In short, Hindus experience the divine through both sight and sound.

It is hard to identify common denominators in Hinduism. While some texts and some deities are widely accepted, there is no single text, deity, or teacher that all Hindus would consider supremely authoritative. There is a corpus of holy works, but many non-literate Hindus may not even have heard of them. Similarly, there are many local deities with local names who may or may not be identified with pan-Indian gods. The Hindu tradition is in fact many traditions encompassing hundreds of communities and sectarian movements, each of which has its own hallowed canon, its own sacred place, and its own concept of the supreme deity.

## 'Hinduism'

The word 'Hinduism', like the word 'India' itself, is derived from 'Sind': the name of the region—now in Pakistan—of the river Sindhu (Indus). The term was given currency by the British colonizers of India in the eighteenth and nineteenth centuries. To them, 'Hinduism' essentially meant the religion of those Indians—the majority of the population—who were not Muslims, although a few smaller groups, including Jainas, Parsis, Christians, Jews, and sometimes Sikhs, were also recognized. As a term for religious identity, 'Hinduism' did not catch on until the nineteenth century. Thus anyone who tries to look for the term in books printed earlier is unlikely to find it.

There are approximately 900 million Hindus in the world today. When they are asked about their religious identity, however, they generally refer not to Hinduism but rather to their particular caste or community. An alternative term designating a comprehensive tradition is *sanatana dharma* ('eternal faith'), but it is common in only a few parts of India and in some classes of society. The term is seldom used to refer to local manifestations of the faith.

Under Indian law the term 'Hindu' applies not only to members of a Hindu 'denomination' such as Vira Shaiva or Brahmo Samaj, but also to 'any other person domiciled in the territories to which [the Hindu Family Act] extends who is *not a Muslim, Christian, Parsi, or Jew* by religion' (italics added). In effect, India's legal system uses 'Hindu' to refer to anyone who does not profess one of the specified religions, all of which originated outside India.

In the same way we must recognize that what we call 'Hinduism' encompasses an amazing plurality of traditions, and that no single holy book, dogma, or religious leader is authoritative for all of them. We can make some generalizations and trace some important lines of historical continuity, but only as long as we keep in mind their limitations.

The very concept of religion in the Western, post-Enlightenment sense is only loosely applicable to the Hindu tradition. Some Hindus consider the Sanskrit word **dharma** to come close to 'religion', but they recognize that this is true in a limited way. 'Dharma' for Hindus means righteousness, justice, faith, duty, a religious and social obligation, but it does not cover all that is sacred for the Hindu.

◀ The Gangaur festival, honouring the goddess Parvati, is celebrated throughout Rajasthan every spring (© Craig Lovell/Corbis).

# Timeline

| | |
|---|---|
| c. 2700 BCE | Evidence of Indus Valley civilization |
| c. 1750?–1500 | Earliest Vedic compositions |
| c. 600 | Production of *Upanishads* |
| c. 500 | Production of Hindu epics begins |
| 326 | Greek armies in India under Alexander |
| c. 272 | Accession of King Ashoka |
| c. 200 | First contacts with Southeast Asia |
| c. 200 BCE–200 CE | Composition of *Bhagavad Gita* |
| c. 200 CE | Compilation of *Laws of Manu* and *Natya Sastra* completed |
| c. 500 | Beginnings of tantric tradition |
| c. 700–900 | Alvars and Nayanmars, Tamil *bhakti* poets |
| c. 700–800 | Shankara's Advaita Vedanta |
| 1017 | Traditional birth date of Ramanuja, Vaishnava philosopher (d. 1137) |
| 1100–1150 | Angkor Wat built in Cambodia |
| 1398 | Traditional birth date of Kabir, North Indian *bhakti* poet (d. 1518) |
| c. 1400 | Major endowments at Tirumala–Tirupati temple |
| 1486 | Birth of Chaitanya, Bengali Vaishnava *bhakti* leader (d. 1583) |
| c. 1543 | Birth of Tulsidas, North Indian *bhakti* poet (d. 1623) |
| 1757 | British rule established in Calcutta |
| 1828 | Ram Mohan Roy founds Brahmo Samaj |
| 1836 | Birth of Ramakrishna Paramahamsa (d. 1886) |
| 1875 | Dayananda Sarasvati founds Arya Samaj |
| 1893 | Vivekananda attends World's Parliament of Religions in Chicago |
| 1905–6 | Vedanta Temple built in San Francisco |
| 1926 | Birth of Sathya Sai Baba |
| 1959 | Maharishi Mahesh Yogi brings transcendental meditation to America and Europe |
| 1965 | A.C. Bhaktivedenta Swami Prabhupada, founder of ISKCON, sails to America |
| 1977 | Hindu temples consecrated in New York and Pittsburgh |

Hindus may consider many things—from astronomy and astrology to music and dance, from phonetics to plants—essential in the practice of their religion. It would be impossible to do justice to all the subjects that fall under the rubric of the sacred for Hindus. Therefore the following discussion will include a number of features not usually covered by the term 'religion' in the Western world.

# ORIGINS

The origins of Hinduism have been much debated. The standard view in the early twentieth century was that it had grown from a fusion of the indigenous religions of the Indus Valley with the faith of the Aryans, an Indo-European people

## Traditions at a Glance

### Numbers
Approximately 900 million to one billion around the world.

### Distribution
Primarily India; large numbers in the United States, Canada, and Western Europe, as well as many parts of South and Southeast Asia.

### Principal Historical Periods

| | |
|---|---|
| c. 2500–600 BCE | Indus Valley civilization; composition of the Vedas |
| c. 500 BCE–1000 CE | Composition of epics and *Puranas* |
| 600–1600 | Devotional poetry in local languages |
| 13th–18th centuries | Northern India under Muslim rule |
| mid-1700s–1947 | British colonial period |

### Founders and Leaders
Important early figures include Shankara, Ramanuja, Madhva, Vallabha, Ramananda, Chaitanya, Swami Narayanan, Ramakrishna, and Vivekananda. Among the hundreds of teachers who have attracted followings in the last century alone are Aurobindo, Ramana Maharishi, Maharishi Mahesh Yogi, Sathya Sai Baba, Anandamayi Ma, and Ma Amritananda Mayi.

### Deities
Hindu philosophy recognizes one supreme being (the ineffable Brahman) who is not limited by gender and may take countless forms; classical rhetoric typically refers to 330 million. Some sectarian traditions identify the supreme deity as Vishnu, some as Shiva, and some as a form of the Goddess. The supreme being may be understood as male, female, androgynous, or beyond gender.

### Authoritative Texts
The Vedas are technically considered the most authoritative texts, though the epics (the *Ramayana* and the *Mahabharata*, including the *Bhagavad Gita*), the *Puranas*, and several works in regional languages have also been very important.

### Noteworthy Teachings
In general, most Hindus recognize a supreme being, variously conceived—personal for some, impersonal for others. Most think of the human soul as immortal and believe that when it reaches liberation it will be freed from the shackles of karma and rebirth. Specific teachings vary depending on sectarian tradition, region, and community.

usually thought to have migrated there sometime between 1750 and 1500 BCE. More recently, however, several different theories have been proposed. Some scholars maintain that the Indo-Europeans migrated into India from other parts of Asia; others insist there is demonstrable evidence that the Indian subcontinent itself was their original homeland.

## The Harappa Culture

In 1926 excavations revealed the remains of several large towns on the banks of the Indus River in what is now Pakistan. Two of these towns, known today as Mohenjo Daro ('Mound of the Dead') and Harappa, were more than 480 kilometres (300 miles) apart. Yet archaeological evidence suggested a certain uniformity in the culture across the entire northwestern part of the subcontinent. Similar objects found in towns hundreds of kilometres apart suggest continuous travel and communication between them, and although the culture is still widely identified with the Indus Valley, some scholars prefer to call it the Harappa culture because it extends well beyond the Indus basin itself.

It is generally believed that the towns were in existence by about 2750 BCE, though some historians push the date back several centuries. Inscriptions on carved seals show that this culture had a written language, though no one has yet been able to decipher the script with any assurance. What we do know is that the people of the Harappa civilization were impressive builders who lived in what appear to have been planned cities. In the citadel mound at Mohenjo Daro there is a huge swimming-pool-like structure (archaeologists call it 'the Great Bath'), surrounded by porticos and flights of stairs. The care with which the complex was built has led scholars to believe that it was designed for religious rituals of some sort. Some of the houses also appear to have included a room with a fire altar, suggesting a domestic fire ritual. Stone sculptures and terracotta statuettes of what looks like a mother goddess may have been used as icons in worship.

From the buildings tentatively identified as worship halls archaeologists have unearthed some stone sculptures and large numbers of terracotta figurines. Scholars surmise that some were used as icons in worship. These include statuettes of what seems to be a mother goddess—a female figure wearing a short skirt, abundant jewellery, and a fan-shaped head-dress with two little cups on either side. Smoke stains in these cups suggest that they were used for offerings of fire or incense. Because these images were common in this civilization and are similar to figures found in other excavations, it is thought that they may represent an early form of the deity who came to be known as the Goddess. Some Western scholars believe that goddess worship is indicative of a society in which women enjoyed high status, but we have no hard evidence to support this thesis in the case of the Harappan civilization. And though goddesses have certainly been worshipped in the later Hindu tradition, women were not necessarily held in high esteem in all strata of society.

In addition, excavations around the Indus River have yielded approximately two thousand flat seals and many amulets. A few of the seals represent a man seated on a low throne in what looks like a **yoga** posture. The man's headdress and the animals around him suggest that this figure may be a prototype of the deity who came to be known as Shiva.

Another recurrent theme on the seals is that of a spirit emerging from a *pipal* tree and worshippers standing in front of it. The *pipal* tree has been a part of the Hindu tradition for about 2,500 years. If it indeed had religious significance during the Indus Valley period, this has been one of the more enduring features of the religious tradition. On some seals a horned person is emerging from the *pipal* tree and a row of seven figures with long braids is standing in front of it; the notion of seven beings is important in later Hindu mythology. These figures have been identified both as seven holy men (*rishis*) and as seven goddesses of later Hindu myths.

Scholars are not yet sure how the people who lived in these cities disposed of their dead. Since the manner of disposal frequently reveals religious convictions, this is an important gap in our knowledge. No large burial sites have been found, though it is possible that some land used for this purpose was later flooded and now lies under water. The small number of graves that have been discovered are oriented on a north–south axis. In a few of them objects were buried with the bodies, perhaps to serve the dead in an afterlife.

Graves containing more than one body are more difficult to interpret. The additional remains may be those of attendants. But it is also possible that wives were interred with their husbands, reflecting an early version of **sati**—the culturally expected suicide of a widow, who throws herself onto her husband's funeral pyre. In that connection, the fragmentary evidence of multiple burials in the Indus Valley gives rise to a new set of speculations. It is supposed that most bodies were cremated around the river bank. However, some pots hold collections of bones, and it is possible that both cremation and burial were practised. There is no agreement about what might have brought the Indus Valley civilization to an end. Some scholars think it was destroyed by Indo-European invaders from Central Asia around 1750 BCE. Other theories centre on flooding or epidemics that might have driven the population farther east.

In any event, some elements of their religious traditions survived the early centuries of Indo-European cultural domination. From the fragmentary evidence and clues found in the Indus Valley, as well as in other regions of India, we can tentatively say that some features of the Hindu religion as practised today go back before 1750 BCE to Mohenjo Daro and Harappa.

We know even less of the early history in other parts of the subcontinent than we do of the Indus Valley civilization. Nevertheless, scholars have observed a curious fact in some sites of archaeological importance. They have noticed an intriguing correspondence between places frequented by people about four thousand years ago and sites that are of religious significance today. For example, some places that were inhabited and popular four thousand years ago, like the Gudiyam caves near Madras, are today seen as abodes of the divine. While there is some debate over whether there has been a

continuous belief in the sacredness of a particular place such as Gudiyam for the last four thousand years, this pattern is repeated in so many sites that it is considered significant. It seems likely that at least some of these elements have been part of the religious culture of the subcontinent for the last four to five thousand years.

## The Indo-Europeans

Who were the Indo-Europeans? This question is still debated. Scholars use the term 'Indo-European' (or 'Indo-Aryan') to refer to the family of languages of which Sanskrit is one. Western scholars in the nineteenth century noted the similarities between some Indian and European languages. For example, the Sanskrit word **jnana** is a cognate of the English word 'knowledge'; 'lack of knowledge' is ajnana in Sanskrit and 'ignorance' in English. There are hundreds of similar cognates, including the words for 'father' and 'mother'. The Indo-European languages also have many grammatical structures in common. Based on linguistic evidence, nineteenth-century scholars posited a theory of migration that would account for the resemblances. According to this theory, people from Central Asia began migrating to widely distant regions at some time between 2000 BCE and 1500 BCE. Some moved west and north into what is now Europe, from Ireland to Scandinavia. Others headed south or east and settled in the region of Iran, where they called themselves Aryans—a name that eventually acquired a class connotation, coming to mean 'noble ones'.

Many scholars believe that the Indo-Europeans originated in Central Asia and that the migration began around 2000 BCE. Others think the migrants originated in the general region of modern Turkey and began spreading out as much as four thousand years earlier. The latter suggest that it was a peaceful migration undertaken by a growing agricultural population in need of additional land.

Yet another school of thought holds that the original home of the Indo-Europeans was actually

## Map 2.1    Hinduism

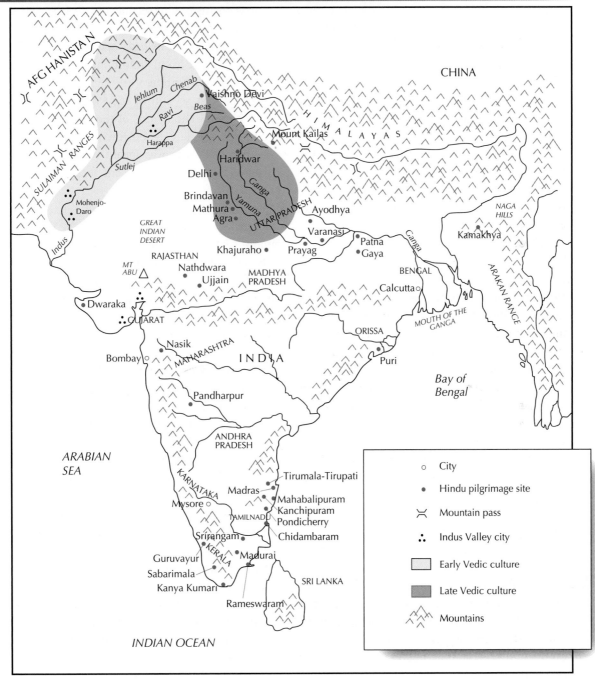

the Indian subcontinent. Proponents of this theory base their arguments on astronomical data and contradictory evidence concerning a great river that was said to have flowed from the mountains to the sea in the region of the Harappan civilization. They identify this river as the legendary Sarasvati, which according to an ancient Hindu text (the *Rig Veda*) had five Aryan tribes living on its banks, yet has been shown by geologists to have run dry by the time that the Aryans were supposed to have entered India (i.e., around 1750 BCE). If the Aryans were there before the Sarasvati dried up, the theory goes, their dates must be pushed back to the time of the Harappan civilization or even earlier.

None of the evidence is conclusive, and some of these theories are clearly motivated by political, racial, religious, and nationalist agendas. Evidence from many areas of study has been drawn into the debate: Vedic philology, comparative philology, linguistic paleontology, linguistics, archeology, astronomy, geography, and geology, as well as religious traditions.

What we know is that the Indo-Europeans composed many poems and, eventually, manuals on rituals and philosophy. They committed these traditions to memory using various mnemonic devices to ensure correct pronunciation, rhythm, and intonation, and passed them from generation to generation by word of mouth.

## The Vedas

The earliest surviving Indo-European compositions are the **Vedas** (from the Sanskrit for 'knowledge'); these are the works collectively known as *shruti* ('that which was heard'). The Vedic *rishis* 'saw' the mantras and transmitted them to their disciples, starting an oral tradition that has continued to the present.

Traditionally regarded as revealed scripture, the Vedas are now generally thought to have been composed between roughly 1500 BCE (some scholars put the earliest date closer to 1750 BCE)

and 600 BCE. There are four Vedic collections: *Rig, Sama, Yajur,* and *Atharva*. Each of these collections in turn consists of four sections: hymns (*Samhitas;* the earliest parts), directions for the performance of sacred rituals (*Brahmanas*), compositions for the forest' (*Aranyakas*), and philosophical works called the **Upanishads** ('sitting near [the teacher]').

The earliest section of the *Rig Veda* contains 1,028 hymns. The hymns of the *Sama Veda* and *Yajur Veda* are largely borrowed from the *Rig,* and the *Sama Veda* was meant to be sung. The *Upanishads* are the most recent sections of each collection.

Each *Veda* has its own *Upanishads*—philosophical works composed around 600 BCE. Thus the famous *Chandogya Upanishad* belongs to the *Sama Veda*, the *Brihadaranyaka* and *Taittiriya Upanishads* are affixed to the *Yajur Veda*, and the *Aitreya Upanishad* belongs to the *Rig Veda*.

The *Atharva Veda* differs from the other three Vedas in that it includes material that scholars consider non-Aryan, such as incantations and remedies to ward off illness and evil spirits. Unlike the hymns of the other Vedas, these chants were used for purposes other than sacrificial rituals. Some call for harm to befall one's enemies, such as 5.29: 'pierce his eyes, pierce his heart, break his tongue'. One verse (7.38) refers to the use of herbs to make a lover return, and another (7.50) requests luck in gambling.

In the Hindu tradition the term **Vedas** denotes the whole corpus, starting with the hymns, continuing through the ritual treatises, and concluding with the texts of a more philosophical character. Many Orientalists and Western Indologists, however, have used *Veda* only for the hymns, the *samhita* portion of each collection. This narrower use of the term is generally not accepted by Hindus.

### The Status of the Vedas

Almost all educated Hindus would describe the Vedas as their most sacred texts; yet most would be hard pressed to identify their contents. Although considered to be extremely important by all orthodox philosophers and theological treatises, the Vedas are not books that people keep in their homes. Rather, they are ritual texts that Hindus understand as representing eternal sound, eternal words passed on through the generations without change. A few hymns from them are recited regularly at home as well as in temple liturgies, and the philosophical sections have often been translated and commented upon, but the rest of the Vedas are known only to a handful of ritual specialists and to Sanskrit scholars familiar with the early Vedic form of the language.

The Vedas are particularly significant to the **brahmins**, the class that has historically considered itself the 'highest' in Hindu society. For many centuries, acceptance as an orthodox member of the society we call Hindu depended on acceptance of the Vedas as authoritative. As custodians of the Vedas, the brahmins reserved for themselves the authority to study and teach these holy words. Though members of two other classes were technically 'allowed' to study the Vedas, in time this privilege was lost and, in some cases, abandoned.

Historically, the Vedas were treated as 'revealed' scripture, though the source of the revelation was not necessarily a deity. In medieval times brahmin commentators considered the Vedas to represent 'eternal truth' and 'eternal sound', coeval with God. All schools of medieval thought agreed that the Vedas have a transcendental aspect and an authoritative nature. They differed, however, on the significance of their status as divine (*apauruseya*, literally 'superhuman'; not composed by man).

Followers of the Nyaya ('logic') school of philosophy believed that God was the author of the Vedas and that, since God is perfect, the Vedas are infallible. Many other Hindu schools took different views. Two that continue to be influential, the Mimamsa and Vedanta schools, say that the Vedas are eternal and of non-human origin. The Vedic seers (*rishis*) 'saw' the mantras and transmitted them; they did not invent or compose them. The words have a fixed order that must be

maintained by a tradition of recitation. The Vedic seers transmitted the words to their disciples, establishing an oral tradition that has come down to the present.

Not being composed by human beings, the Vedas are considered faultless, the perfect and supreme source of knowledge. From them we can learn about the Supreme Being, and their authority grants credibility to particular doctrines. But the Mimamsakas do not assume that any being, divine or otherwise, played a role in their composition. Except for the Nyaya school, orthodox Hindus have not necessarily attributed the perfection of the Vedas to a divine composer.

The Vedic collections have served as manuals of ritual for all the many strands of the Hindu tradition. Some sections have been recited and acted on without major changes for at least two thousand years. Interpretations, however, have not been static. In every generation, specialists in Vedic hermeneutics have worked to make the texts' messages relevant to the particular time and place.

Several works have been more popular among Hindus generally, but the theoretical, ritual, and epistemological significance of the Vedas has been unquestioned. Thus the highest honour that could be given to any Hindu religious text was to describe it as the 'fifth Veda'.

Among the works that have been accorded this title are the **Mahabharata**, one of two great Hindu epics; Bharata's *Natya Sastra*, an important treatise on dance and performance composed around the beginning of the Common Era; and a number of vernacular compositions from South India, especially the *Tiruvaymoli* ('sacred utterance') of Nammalvar (ninth century) and the *Periya Puranam* (twelfth century), a collection of the life stories of saints who were devotees of Shiva.

These texts made no attempt either to imitate the *Vedas* or to comment on them. Their status as 'fifth Vedas' derived solely from the fact that Hindus thought they reflected the wisdom embodied in the four original Vedas, making their eternal truth relevant to a new place and time.

## The Vedic Hymns

The figures that were to become the principal Hindu deities—goddesses like Sri (Lakshmi) and gods like Narayana (Vishnu)—are rarely mentioned in the *samhitas*; only the later Vedic hymns address them directly. Rather, the earliest hymns of the Vedas speak of many deities who in time would be superseded, and many of the stories they allude to would not be familiar to most Hindus today.

Indra, for instance, is a warrior god who battles other cosmic powers. Agni is the god of fire who was believed to serve as a messenger, carrying to the deities the offerings that humans placed in the sacrificial fire. Soma is the name of a god identified with the moon, but also of a plant-based elixir, used for ritual purposes, that some modern scholars believe was derived from a hallucinogenic mushroom.

Sarasvati, as we have seen, was the name given to a great river. But Sarasvati was also a goddess described in the *Rig Veda* as beautiful and fortunate, the inspirer of noble thoughts, giving rise to truthful words. By the time the ritualistic sections called the **Brahmanas** were composed, Sarasvati had taken over the attributes formerly associated with the goddess Vac ('speech'), who appeared in the early verses of the *Rig Veda* as the consort of the creator Prajapati. Now Sarasvati is speech incarnate, the power of the word, and the mother of the *Veda*s.

In addition, some texts refer to Sarasvati as Gayatri ('singer') and Savitri ('sun'), and in this guise she is associated with learning. To this day, young boys recite the *Gayatri* mantra, dedicated to the sun, as part of the ceremony that marks their initiation into the life of a student.

The early hymns typically offer praise to the gods; thus the river Indus is praised for giving cattle, children, horses, and food. But many of them also include petitions—not for salvation or eternal bliss (in fact, the idea of an afterlife is rarely mentioned) but rather for a good and happy life on this earth. Thus Agni is asked to protect those who praise him, and Indra is asked to crush the worshipper's enemies. A *rishi* named Sobhari simply requests 'all good things', but a woman poet named Ghosa specifically asks to be cured of her white-tinted skin, so that she may marry and live happily with her husband. Another woman poet, Apala, asks Indra for lush hair to grow on her head as well as her father's, and for crops to grow in her father's barren fields.

One of the dominant features of Vedic religious life was the ritual sacrifice (*yajna*), typically performed using fire. From simple domestic affairs to elaborate community events, these sacrifices were conducted by ritual specialists and priests who supervised the making of altars, the sacrifice of animals, and the recitation of the hymns. Many rituals also involved the making, offering, and drinking of the *soma* elixir.

A delicate connection was understood to exist between the rituals and the maintenance of cosmic and earthly order, or *rta*. *Rta* is truth and justice, the rightness of things that makes harmony and peace possible on earth and in the heavens. Although it is an impersonal cosmic principle, it was upheld by Vedic gods like Varuna.

A number of hymns composed around 1000 BCE speculate on the origins of the universe. One, entitled 'The Creation Hymn', expresses wonder at the creation of the universe from nothing and ends with the suggestion that perhaps no one knows how it all came to be.

Another account, however, describes how the universe itself was created through the cosmic sacrifice of the primeval man (*Purusha*). This account, entitled the 'Hymn to the Supreme Person' (*Purusha Sukta*), is important even today in both domestic and temple rituals, and has figured continuously in the tradition for some three thousand years. Straining to capture infinity in words, the composer uses the notion of a 'thousand' to evoke what cannot be measured or perhaps even imagined:

> (1) The cosmic person has a thousand
> heads
> a thousand eyes and feet

## The Creation Hymn, *Rig Veda* 10.129

There was neither non-existence nor existence then; there was neither the realm of space nor the sky which is beyond. What stirred? Where? In whose protection? Was there water, bottomlessly deep?

There was neither death nor immortality then. There was no distinguishing sign of night nor of day. That one breathed, windless, by its own impulse. Other than that there was nothing beyond.

Darkness was hidden by darkness in the beginning; with no distinguishing sign, all this was water. The life force that was covered with emptiness, that one arose through the power of heat.

Desire came upon that one in the beginning; that was the first seed of mind. Poets seeking in their heart with wisdom found the bond of existence in non-existence.

Their cord was extended across. Was there below? Was there above? There were seed-placers; there were powers. There was impulse beneath; there was giving-forth above.

Who really knows? Who will here proclaim it? Whence was it produced? Whence is this creation? The gods came afterwards, with the creation of this universe. Who then knows whence it has arisen?

Whence this creation has arisen—perhaps it formed itself, or perhaps it did not—the one who looks down on it, in the highest heaven, only he knows—or perhaps he does not know (Doniger O'Flaherty 1981: 25–6).

It covers the earth on all sides
and extends ten finger-lengths beyond

(2) The cosmic person is everything
all that has been and will be. . . .

Various elements of the universe are said to have arisen from this sacrifice:

(13) From his mind came the moon
from his eye, the sun
Indra and Agni from his mouth
the wind came from his breath.

(14) From his navel came space
from his head, the sky
from his feet, earth;
from his ears, the four directions
thus the worlds were created.

In this context an idea is introduced that will change forever the religious and social countenance of the Hindu tradition:

(12) From his mouth came the priestly class
from his arms, the rulers.
The producers came from his legs;    *humans*
from his feet came the servant class.

Thus the origins of the four classes (*varnas*) of Hindu society are traced to the initial cosmic sacrifice. Though this verse is the first explicit reference to what came to be called the caste system, it is likely that the stratification of society had already taken place long before the *Rig Veda* was composed.

### *The* Upanishads

By the time of the *Aranyakas* and *Upanishads*, in the seventh and sixth centuries BCE, the early Vedic emphasis on placating the gods through ritual sacrifice had given way to critical philosophical inquiry. This period—a little before and perhaps during the lives of Gautama Buddha and the Jaina teacher Mahavira—was a time of intellectual ferment, of questioning—and rejecting—authoritarian structures.

Yet the *Upanishads* do not totally reject the early hymns and sacrificial rituals. Instead, they rethink and reformulate them. Thus some rituals are interpreted allegorically, and the symbolic structures of the sacrifices are analyzed in some detail.

Most of the *Upanishads* take the form of conversations—between a teacher and a student, between a husband and wife, or between fellow philosophers. In the beginning of one study session a teacher exclaims: 'May we work with vigour; may our study illumine us both. May there be no discord between us. *Om*. Let there be peace, peace, peace' (*Taittiriya Upanishad* 11.1.1). After years of Vedic instruction, a departing student receives moving advice from his guru (teacher):

> Speak the truth. Practice virtue. Do not neglect to study every day. Do not neglect truth, virtue, studying or teaching. . . . Be one to whom your mother is a god, your father is a god, your teacher is a god, a guest is like a god. . . . Give with faith . . . give liberally, give with modesty . . . give with sympathy. . . . This is the command. This is the teaching. This is the secret of the *Veda*. . . . (*Taittiriya Upanishad* 1.11.1–6).

### Karma and Samsara

It is in the *Upanishads* that we find the earliest discussions of several concepts central to the later Hindu tradition, among them the concept of **karma**. The literal meaning of 'karma' is 'action', especially ritual action, but in these books the word eventually comes to refer to a system of rewards and punishments attached to various actions. This system of cause and effect may require several lifetimes to work out. Thus the concept of karma implies a continuing cycle of death and rebirth or reincarnation called **samsara**. To achieve

liberation (*moksha*) from this cycle, according to the *Upanishads*, requires a transforming experiential wisdom. Those who attain that wisdom become immortal (*a-mrta*, 'without death').

A frequent theme of the *Upanishads* is the quest for a unifying truth. This 'higher' knowledge is clearly distinguished from the 'lower' knowledge that can be conceptualized and expressed in words. Its nature cannot be explained or taught: it can only be evoked, as in this question posed by the seeker in the *Mundaka Upanishad*: 'What is it that, being known, all else becomes known?' (1.1.3). The *Brihadaranyaka Upanishad* of the *Yajur Veda* reflects the quest for enlightenment in these lines:

> Lead me from the unreal to reality
> Lead me from darkness to light
> Lead me from death to immortality
> *Om*, let there be peace, peace, peace.

Significantly, in later centuries the 'higher wisdom' is not connected with any Vedic or book learning or conceptual knowledge. It is only through the experience of enlightenment that one is freed from the birth-and-death cycle.

### Atman and Brahman

At the heart of this wisdom is experiential knowledge of the relationship between the human soul (**Atman**) and the Supreme Being (**Brahman**). Brahman pervades and yet transcends not only human thought but the universe itself. Ultimately, Brahman cannot be described any more than infinity can be contained.

To know Brahman is to enter a new state of consciousness. The *Taittiriya Upanishad* associates Brahman with existence or truth (*satya*), knowledge (*jnana*), infinity (*ananta*), consciousness (*chit*), and bliss (*ananda*); elsewhere Brahman is described as the hidden, inner controller of the human soul and the frame over which the universe is woven.

Many passages of the *Upanishads* discuss the relationship between Atman and Brahman, but invariably they suggest rather than specify the connection between the two. In one famous conversation in the *Chandogya Upanishad*, a father asks his son to dissolve salt in water and says that Brahman and Atman are united in a similar manner. The father ends his teaching with a famous dictum—*tat tvam asi* ('you are that')—in which 'that' refers to Brahman and 'you' to Atman. More than a thousand years later, philosophers still differed in their interpretations of this passage. For Shankara in the eighth century, 'you are that' indicated that Brahman and Atman were identical. On the other hand, for Ramanuja in the eleventh century it meant that the two were inseparably united but not identical.

We learn more of the relationship between Brahman and Atman elsewhere in the *Upanishads*. In some passages, the sage Yajnavalkya refers to Brahman as the hidden, inner controller of the human soul (Atman); in others, as the frame and the substance of the universe. In the latter analogy the reference is to a weaving loom: the universe is said to be woven over Brahman.

The *Upanishads* represent the beginnings of Hindu philosophical thought; in the opinion of some, they also represent the best. The quest for a unifying knowledge or higher wisdom is a recurring theme in various systems of Hindu philosophical reasoning, and continues to preoccupy thinkers today.

### Women in the Vedas

We have already mentioned Ghosa and Apala as two women poets named in the early *Samhitas*; a third was Lopamudra, a philosopher and poet. The *Upanishads* also identify a number of women who participated in the quest for ultimate truth and sought salvific knowledge in both domestic and public forums. In the *Brihadaranyaka Upanishad*, for instance, Maitreyi, the wife of the sage Yajnavalkya, questions him in depth about the nature of reality, and a woman philosopher named

## How Many Gods Are There?

Vidagdha Shakalyah asked: 'Yajnavalkya, how many gods are there?'

He answered . . . in line with the ritual prayer, '. . . three hundred and three, and three and three thousand.'

'Yes, but Yajnavalkya, how many gods are there, really?'

'Thirty-three.'

'Yes, but really, how many gods are there, Yajnavalkya?'

'Six.'

'Yes, but really, how many gods are there, Yajnavalkya?'

'Three.' . . .

'Yes, but really, how many gods are there, Yajnavalkya?'

'One and a half.'

'Yes, but really, how many gods are there, Yajnavalkya?'

'One.'

'Yes, but who are those three hundred and three and three thousand and three?'

'They are but the powers of the gods; there are only thirty-three gods' (*Brihadaranyaka Upanishad* 3.9.1–2; trans. Vasudha Narayanan).

## Gargi Vachaknavi Questions Yajnavalkya

Then Vachaknavi said, 'Venerable Brahmanas, I shall ask him two questions. If he answers me these, none of you can defeat him in arguments about Brahman.' 'Ask, Gargi' [said he].

She said, 'As a warrior son of the Kasis or the Videhas might rise up against you, having strung his unstrung bow and having taken in his hand two pointed foe-piercing arrows, even so, O Yajnavalkya, do I face you with two questions. Answer me these.' 'Ask, Gargi.'

She said, 'That, O Yajnavalkya, of which they say, it is above the heaven, it is beneath the earth, that which is between these two, the heaven and the earth, that which the people call the past, the present and the future, across what is that woven, like warp and woof?'

He said, 'That which is above the heaven, that which is beneath the earth, that which is between these two, heaven and earth, that which the people call the past, the present, and the future, across space is that woven, like warp and woof.'

She said, 'Adoration to you, Yajnavalkya, who have answered this question for me. Prepare yourself for the other.' 'Ask, Gargi.'

She said, 'That, O Yajnavalkya, of which they say, it is above the heaven, it is beneath the earth, that which is between these two, the heaven and the earth, that which the people call the past, the present, and the future, across what is that woven like warp and woof?'

He said, 'That which is above the sky, that which is beneath the earth, that which is between these two, sky and earth, that which the people call the past, the present, and the future, across space is that woven like warp and woof. Across what is space woven like warp and woof?'

He said, 'That, O Gargi, the knowers of Brahman call the Imperishable. It is neither gross nor fine, neither short nor long, neither glowing red (like fire) nor adhesive (like water). (It is) neither shadow nor darkness, neither air nor space, unattached, without taste, without smell, without eyes, without ears, without voice, without mind, without radiance, without breath, without a mouth, without measure, having no within and no without. It eats nothing and no one eats it.'

'Verily, at the command of that Imperishable, O Gargi, the sun and the moon stand in their respective positions. At the command of that Imperishable, O Gargi, heaven and earth stand in their respective positions. At the command of the Imperishable, O Gargi, what are called moments, hours, days and nights, half-months, months, seasons, years stand in their respective positions. At the command of that Imperishable, O Gargi, some rivers flow to the east from the white (snowy) mountains, others to the west in whatever direction each flows. By the command of that Imperishable, O Gargi, men praise those who give, the gods (are desirous of) the sacrificer and the fathers are desirous of the darvi offering.'

'Whosoever, O Gargi, in this world, without knowing this Imperishable performs sacrifices, worships, performs austerities for a thousand years, his work will have an end; whosoever, O Gargi, without knowing this Imperishable departs from this world, is pitiable. But, O Gargi, he who knowing the Imperishable departs from this world is a Brahmana (a knower of Brahman).

'Verily, that Imperishable, O Gargi, is unseen but is the seer, is unheard but is the hearer, unthought but is the thinker, unknown but is the knower. There is no other seer but this, there is no other hearer but this, there is no other thinker but this, there is no other knower but this. By this Imperishable, O Gargi, is space woven like warp and woof.'

She said, 'Venerable Brahmana, you may think it a great thing if you get off from him though bowing to him. Not one of you will defeat him in arguments about Brahman.' Thereupon [Gargi] Vachaknavi kept silent (*Brihadaranyaka Upanishad* 3.8; Radhakrishnan 1953: 230–4).

Gargi Vachaknavi challenges him in a public debate. When he does not answer to her satisfaction, Gargi presses the question, and eventually she pronounces a judgment about him to her fellow philosophers, saying that he is indeed wise. Apparently Gargi and Maitreyi were honoured and respected for their wisdom, as were dozens of other women whose names appear in the *Upanishads* and elsewhere in the *Vedas*.

These women were among the teachers through whom the sacred knowledge was transmitted. Whereas in the *Upanishads'* lists of teachers the father's name is frequently mentioned, in others the teachers are identified as the sons of particular women. In the *Brihadaranyaka Upanishad* (VI.5.1) roughly forty-five teachers are listed with their mothers' names instead of their fathers'. So, while it is clear that a male spiritual lineage is generally accepted (after all, it is the male teachers who are being named), it is possible that some teachers received spiritual instruction from their mothers.

# ❧ CRYSTALLIZATION

## Classical Hinduism

The literature that was composed after the Vedas, starting around 500 BCE, was recognized to be of human origin and was loosely called **smrti** ('that which is remembered'). Though theoretically of lesser authority than the 'revealed' *shruti*, this material was nonetheless considered inspired, and it has played a far more important role in the lives of Hindus for the last 2,500 years. There are three types of *smrti*: epics (*itihasas*), ancient stories (**Puranas**), and codes of law and ethics (*dharmashastras*). (The term *smrti* can also refer to the codes alone.)

For many Hindus the phrase 'sacred books' refers specifically to two epics, the **Ramayana** ('Story of Rama') and the *Mahabharata* ('Great [Epic of] India' or 'Great [Sons of] Bharata'). The best-known works in the Hindu tradition, these stories are told to children by their parents and invariably constitute their first and most lasting encounter with Hindu scripture.

## *The* Ramayana

The *Ramayana* has been memorized, recited, sung, danced, enjoyed, and experienced emotionally, intellectually, and spiritually for 2,500 years. It has been a source of inspiration for generations of devotees in India and elsewhere. The epic is performed as theatre and as dance in places of Hindu (and Buddhist) cultural influence throughout Southeast Asia, and its characters are well known as far away as Cambodia, Thailand, and Indonesia.

The hero of the *Ramayana* is the young prince Rama, whose father, Dasaratha, has decided to abdicate in favour of his son. On the eve of the coronation, however, a heartbroken Dasaratha is forced to exile Rama because of an earlier promise made to one of his wives. Rama accepts cheerfully and leaves for the forest, accompanied by his beautiful wife, Sita, and his half-brother Lakshmana, who both refuse to be separated from him. Bharata, the brother who has now been named king, returns from a trip to discover that Rama has gone into exile and his father has died of grief. He finds Rama and begs him to return, but Rama refuses because he feels he must respect his father's decision to banish him. He asks Bharata to rule as his regent.

While in the forest, Sita is captured by Ravana, the demon king of Lanka. Rama, full of sorrow at being separated from his wife, sets out to search for her with the aid of his brother and a group of monkeys led by Hanuman, a monkey with divine ancestry. It is Hanuman who finds Sita and reports her whereabouts to Rama, who, with the monkeys' help, goes to war with Ravana. After a long battle, Rama kills Ravana and is reunited with Sita. They eventually return to the capital and are crowned. Rama is considered such a just king that *Ram rajya* ('kingdom or rule of Rama') is the Hindu political ideal.

Rama is also the ideal son and husband, at least in most of the story, and Sita as well has been idealized both for her own qualities and for her relationship with her husband. In a sequel to the *Ramayana*, however, Rama's subjects become suspicious about Sita's virtue following her captivity in Ravana's grove. Because there is no way of proving her innocence, and he does not want to create a legal precedent for excusing a wife who has slept outside her husband's home, Rama banishes his own wife, who by now is pregnant.

The exiled Sita gives birth to twins. Some years later, the twins prepare to meet Rama in battle, and it is then that Sita tells them he is their father. There is a brief reunion. Rama asks Sita to prove her innocence in public by undergoing some ordeal, but Sita refuses and asks Mother Earth to take her back. She is then swallowed by the ground.

Many Hindus have seen Sita as the ideal wife because she follows her husband to the forest. Others see her as a model of strength and virtue in her own right. She complies with her husband as he does with her; their love is one worthy of emulation. Yet she is also a woman who stands her ground when asked by her husband to prove her virtue. On one occasion, in Lanka, she acquiesces, but the second time she gently but firmly refuses and so rules out any possibility of a reunion. There have been other versions of this tale called *Sitayana*, which tell the story from Sita's viewpoint. Even conservative commentators agree with the time-honoured saying 'sitayas charitam mahat' ('the deeds of Sita are indeed great').

Rama is a paragon of human virtue, and in later centuries he came to be seen as an incarnation of Vishnu. Temples dedicated to Rama and Sita are found in many parts of the world.

## The Mahabharata *and the* Bhagavad Gita

With approximately 100,000 verses, the *Mahabharata* is said to be the longest poem in the world. It is not found in many homes, but many people own copies of an extract from it called the **Bhagavad Gita**.

The *Mahabharata* is the story of the great (*maha*) struggle among the descendants of a king named Bharata. The main part of the story concerns a war between the Pandavas and the Kauravas. Though they are cousins, the Kauravas try to cheat the Pandavas out of their share of the kingdom and will not accept peace. A battle ensues in which all the major kingdoms are forced to take sides. Krishna, by this time considered to be the ninth incarnation of the god Vishnu, is on the side of the Pandavas. Though he refuses to take up arms, he nevertheless agrees to serve as charioteer for the warrior Arjuna, who in later centuries would come to be seen as symbolizing the human soul in quest of salvation.

Just as the war is about to begin, Arjuna, who has hitherto been portrayed as a hero emerging victorious from several battles, becomes distressed at the thought of fighting his relatives. Putting down his bow, he asks Krishna whether it is correct to fight a war in which many lives will be lost, especially one against one's own kin. Krishna replies that it is correct to fight for what is right; one must try peaceful means, but if they fail one must fight for righteousness ('dharma'). The conversation between Arjuna and Krishna, which unfolds across eighteen chapters, constitutes the *Bhagavad Gita*.

One of the holiest books in the Hindu tradition, the *Gita* teaches loving devotion to Krishna and the importance of selfless action as Krishna instructs Arjuna on the nature of God and the human soul, and how to reach liberation. It was probably written sometime between 200 BCE and 200 CE, and for centuries people learned it by heart. In verses that are still recited at Hindu funerals, Krishna describes the soul as existing beyond the reach of the mind and the senses, unaffected by physical nature. Just as human beings exchange old clothes for new ones, so the human soul discards one body and puts on another through the ages, until it acquires the knowledge that will free it forever from the cycle of birth and death.

Thus Arjuna is told not to grieve at what is about to take place; however, he is also warned that if he does not fight for righteousness, he will be guilty of moral cowardice and will have to face the consequences of quitting at a time when it was

## From the *Bhagavad Gita*

*On the immortality of the soul:*
Our bodies are known to end, but the embodied self is enduring, indestructible, and immeasurable; therefore, Arjuna, fight the battle!

He who thinks this self a killer and he who thinks it killed, both fail to understand it does not kill, nor is it killed.

It is not born, it does not die; having been, it will never not be; unborn, enduring, constant, and primordial, it is not killed when the body is killed. . . .

As a man discards worn-out clothes to put on new and different ones, so the embodied self discards its worn-out bodies to take on other new ones.

Weapons do not cut it, fire does not burn it, waters do not wet it, wind does not wither it. It cannot be cut or burned; it cannot be wet or withered; it is enduring, all-pervasive, fixed, immovable, and timeless. . . .

*On the way of action:*
Be intent on action, not on the fruits of action; avoid attraction to the fruits and attachment to inaction!

Perform actions, firm in discipline, relinquishing attachment; be impartial to failure and success— this equanimity is called discipline. . . .

Wise men disciplined by understanding relinquish the fruit born of action; freed from these bonds of rebirth, they reach a place beyond decay. . . .

When suffering does not disturb his mind, when his craving for pleasures has vanished, when attraction, fear, and anger are gone, he is called a sage whose thought is sure.

When he shows no preference in fortune or misfortune and neither exults nor hates, his insight is sure. . . .

*On the mystery and purpose of incarnation:*
Though myself unborn, undying, the lord of creatures, I fashion nature, which is mine, and I come into being through my own magic.

Whenever sacred duty decays and chaos prevails, then, I create myself, Arjuna.

To protect men of virtue and destroy men who do evil to set the standard of sacred duty, I appear in age after age. . . .

*On the nature of God and the way of devotion:*
Always glorifying me, striving, firm in their vows, paying me homage with devotion, they worship me, always disciplined. . . .

I am the universal father, mother, granter of all, grandfather, object of knowledge, purifier, holy syllable OM, threefold sacred love.

*Continued*

I am the way, sustainer, lord, witness, shelter, refuge, friend, source, dissolution, stability, treasure, and unchanging seed.

I am heat that withholds and sends down the rains; I am immortality and death; both being and nonbeing am I. . . .

Men who worship me, thinking solely of me, always disciplined, win the reward I secure.

When devoted men sacrifice to other deities with faith, they sacrifice to me, Arjuna, however aberrant the rites.

I am the enjoyer and the lord of all sacrifices; they do not know me in reality, and so they fail. . . .

The leaf or flower or fruit or water that he offers with devotion, I take from the man of self-restraint in response to his devotion.

Whatever you do—what you take, what you offer, what you give, what penances you perform—do as an offering to me, Arjuna!

You will be freed from the bonds of action, from the fruit of fortune and misfortune; armed with the discipline of renunciation, your self liberated, you will join me. . . .

If he is devoted solely to me, even a violent criminal must be deemed a man of virtue, for his resolve is right. . . .

Keep me in your mind and devotion, sacrifice to me, bow to me, discipline your self toward me, and you will reach me!

(Miller 1986: 32–87)

his duty (dharma) to wage a just war and protect the people.

Krishna also makes several statements about himself that mark an important shift in Hindu theology. In the *Upanishads* the sages were reluctant to describe Brahman; but in the *Bhagavad Gita* Krishna reveals himself as the ultimate deity, a personal god, filled with love for human beings, who incarnates himself periodically to protect them. Whereas the Supreme Being of the *Upanishads* was beyond human conceptualization, the deity of the *Bhagavad Gita* is loving and gracious. Krishna describes himself as the goal, supporter, lord, witness, refuge, sanctuary, and friend of the human being, as well as the origin, dissolution, and maintenance of the universe. Many of the traditions within Hinduism have retained this overtly theistic flavour. When Arjuna is unsure about Krishna's claim to be God incarnate, Krishna reveals his cosmic form. Arjuna quakes at this vision and is filled with love and awe. Trembling, he seeks forgiveness of Krishna and implores him to resume his normal form.

## The Three Ways to Liberation

In the course of the *Gita* Krishna describes three ways to liberation—or, as some Hindus believe, three aspects of one way to liberation—from the cycle of birth and death: (1) the way of action, (2) the way of knowledge, and (3) the way of devotion. Each way (*marga*) is also a discipline (*yoga*).

The way of action (*karma yoga*) is the path of unselfish duty performed neither in fear of punishment nor in hope of reward. Acting with the expectation of future reward leads to bondage and unhappiness. If our hopes are disappointed we may respond with anger or grief, and even if we do receive the expected reward we will not be satisfied for long. Soon that goal will be replaced with another, leading to further action—and further accumulation of karma, which only leads to further rebirth.

Other books of the time pointed out that even the 'good' karma acquired by performing good deeds is ultimately bad, because to enjoy the good karma we must be reborn. A thirteenth-century Hindu philosopher, Pillai Lokacharya, described good karma as 'golden handcuffs'. Therefore Krishna urges Arjuna to act without attachment to the consequences. Evil will not touch the person who acts according to his dharma, just as water does not cling to a lotus leaf. All actions are to be offered to Krishna. By discarding the fruits of our action, we attain abiding peace.

Krishna also explains the way of knowledge (*jnana yoga*): through scriptural knowledge, one may achieve a transforming wisdom that also destroys one's past karma. True knowledge is an insight into the real nature of the universe, divine power, and the human soul. Later philosophers say that when we hear scripture, ask questions, clarify doubts, and eventually meditate on this knowledge, we achieve liberation.

The third way—the one emphasized most throughout the *Gita*—is the way of devotion (*bhakti yoga*). If there is a general amnesty offered to those who sin, it is through devotion. Ultimately, Krishna makes his promise to Arjuna: if we surrender to him, he will forgive all our sins (*Gita* 18:66).

## The Deities of Classical Hinduism

The period of the Gupta empire (c. 320–540) was one of great cultural and scholarly activity. In mathematics the concept of zero was introduced along with the decimal system. Around 499 Aryabhatta established both the value of pi (3.14) and the length of the solar year (365.3586 days); he also proposed that the earth is spherical and rotates on its axis. As commercial activity increased, so did contact with Greek and Roman trade missions from the Mediterranean, and coastal towns flourished, particularly in southern India.

The Gupta period also saw a surge in religious and literary activity. Temple building was encouraged, pilgrimages were undertaken, and playwrights used religious themes in their dramas. Hindus, Jainas, and Buddhists all composed poems and plays that reveal a great deal about religious trends of the time. Temple architecture, literature, astronomy, and astrology received royal patronage.

Hinduism had by no means been dormant during the previous seven centuries; the *Bhagavad Gita*, to take only one example, comes from that era. Nevertheless, what we know in retrospect as Hindu traditions had been overshadowed to some degree by the spread of Buddhist teachings and institutions. Now, under the Guptas, Buddhist influences receded and Hinduism came to dominate India. Eventually, some Hindu texts would even assimilate Siddhartha Gautama, the Buddha, as one of the incarnations of Vishnu.

It would be impossible to identify the precise time when the transition occurred, but from the Gupta era onward three deities become increasingly prominent: Vishnu, Shiva, and Shiva's consort, variously known as Parvati, Devi, or simply 'the Goddess'. Devotees who give primacy to Vishnu are termed Vaishnavas; those who focus on Shiva are termed Shaivas; and followers of the Goddess are called Shaktas, in reference to her role as the *shakti* ('power') of her divine consort.

Starting around 300 BCE and continuing until a little after 1000 CE, numerous texts known as *Puranas* (from the Sanskrit for 'old') were composed that retold the 'old tales' or ancient lore of the Hindu tradition, shifting the emphasis away from the major Vedic gods and goddesses in favour of other deities. In the Hindu tradition nothing is ever really discarded. Older deities or concepts may be ignored for centuries, but eventually they are discovered afresh. As we have seen, a prototype for Shiva may have existed as long ago as the ancient Harappa culture, and Vishnu was mentioned as a minor figure in the early Vedic hymns. These gods moved to the forefront in the first millennium of the Common Era. In the process, the Hindu tradition as we know it today crystallized.

### Vishnu

Vishnu ('the all-pervasive one') is portrayed as coming to Earth in various forms, animal and human, to rid the world of evil and establish dharma or righteousness. In the first of these incarnations (**avataras**) he appears as a fish who saves Manu, the primeval man. This story was originally part of the Vedic literature, but is expanded in the *Puranas*.

While bathing in a lake, Manu finds a small fish in his hand. The fish speaks to him and asks him to take it home and put it in a jar. The next day it has expanded to fill the jar. Now Manu is asked to put the fish in a lake, which it outgrows overnight, then into a river, and finally the ocean. The fish, who is really Vishnu, then tells Manu that a great flood is coming, and that he must build a boat and put his family in it, along with the seven sages or *rishis*, and 'the seeds of all the animals'. Manu does as he is told. When the flood sweeps the earth, those on the ship survive. This story is sharply reminiscent of flood myths in other religious traditions.

Eventually, Vishnu will have ten incarnations in the present cycle of creation. Nine are said to have already happened, and the tenth is expected at the end of this age. Vishnu's incarnations appear in some of the earliest carvings in India and in Southeast Asia. Some of the earliest carvings of the Gupta period, dated c. 400 CE, depict Vishnu's second and third incarnations, as a tortoise and as a boar who saves the goddess earth. These magnificent carvings are in Udayagiri caves, in the modern state of Madhya Pradesh. The story of the tortoise incarnation is relatively unimportant in India, but it became very popular in Cambodia. In this powerful narrative, the celestial beings (*devas*) and demons (*asuras*) churn an ocean of milk to make the nectar of immortality, using a (good) snake, Vasuki, as the churning rope. In 2004, when a memorial was built in Siem Reap, Cambodia, for those killed by the Khmer Rouge regime, the entire park was circled by *devas* and *asuras* holding a rope, in the act of churning for *amrita*, the nectar of immortality.

Vishnu's seventh incarnation was Rama, the hero of the epic, and according to some narratives the ninth was the Buddha, who may have diverted attention away from Hindu teachings but is praised by some interpreters for the emphasis he gave to non-violence.

In other texts Vishnu's ninth incarnation is Krishna, whom we have already met in the *Bhagavad Gita*. The *Puranas* tell other stories from the life of Krishna: the delightful infant, the mischievous toddler who steals the butter he loves, the youth who steals the hearts of the cowherd girls and dances away the moonlit nights in their company. Some of the later *Puranas* celebrate the love of Krishna and his beloved Radha.

In many other incarnations Vishnu is accompanied by his consort Sri (Lakshmi), the goddess of good fortune, who bestows grace in this world and the next, blessing her worshippers not only with wealth but eventually with liberation. All stores display pictures of her, and so do most homes.

### Shiva

Like Vishnu, Shiva emerged as a great god in the post-Upanishadic era. Unlike Vishnu, however,

Vishnu and Lakshmi in the interval between the destruction of one universe and the beginning of the next, when Brahma will emerge from the lotus flower to carry out the work of creation. A painting from the Punjab hills, c. 1870 (Victoria and Albert Museum; http://collections.vam.ac.uk/objectid/O68861).

he did not reveal himself sequentially, through a series of incarnations. Instead, Shiva expresses the manifold aspects of his power by appearing simultaneously in paradoxical roles: as creator and destroyer, exuberant dancer and austere yogi. The wedding portrait of Shiva and his divine consort, Parvati, is an important part of his tradition, and his creative energy is often represented in the symbolic form of a **linga** (a conical or cylindrical stone column). Popular throughout India, stories of Shiva and his local manifestations—for instance, as Sundaresvara in the city of Madurai—are beloved by Hindus.

### The Goddess

The great Goddess also appears in multiple forms, though the lines between them are not always clearly defined (Western scholars tend to emphasize the distinctions, while Hindus generally blur them). Her cult seems to have been a somewhat later development. Though many goddesses appear in the *Vedas*, none of them were all-powerful. Likewise, the epics and the early *Puranas* honour many consort goddesses, but no supreme female deity. It is only in the later *Puranas* that we begin to see explicit references to worship of a goddess not just as an appendage to a male deity but as the ultimate power, the creator of the universe, and the redeemer of human beings. She was sometimes considered to be the *shakti* or power of Shiva, but frequently her independence from the male deity was stressed.

The most familiar manifestation of the Goddess, or Devi, is Parvati, the wife of Shiva, though in this benevolent aspect she may also be called Amba or Ambika ('little mother'). Durga is her warrior aspect, represented iconographically with a smiling countenance and a handful of weapons. As Kali the Goddess is fierce and wild, a dark, dishevelled figure who wears a garland of skulls; yet even in this manifestation, her devotees call her 'mother'. In addition there are countless local goddesses with distinctive names and histories who are all manifestations of the same Goddess.

Festivals like the autumn celebration of **Navaratri** ('nine nights') are dedicated to the Goddess, and millions of Hindus offer her fervent devotions every day. The continuing importance of the Goddess is a distinctive characteristic of the Hindu tradition.

### Sarasvati

In the *Puranas* the Vedic goddess Sarasvati becomes the goddess of learning. Although she is the consort of a creator god named **Brahma** (a minor deity, not to be confused with Brahman), their relationship is not celebrated iconographically, as the unions of Vishnu and Lakshmi or Shiva and Parvati are.

Rather, Sarasvati seems to enjoy a certain autonomy: portraits usually depict her alone, without Brahma or any other male god. She is a beautiful young woman with a white sari and a golden crown over flowing hair, radiant with wisdom, sitting gracefully on a rock beside a river. She has four hands; two of them hold a stringed musical instrument called a *vina*, another holds a string of beads, and the last holds a manuscript. The *vina* symbolizes music and the manuscript learning, while the beads signify the counting and recitation of holy names, which leads to transformative knowledge or wisdom.

It seems that writing was associated with pollution until well into the Common Era. Yet Sarasvati's manuscript came to symbolize her mastery of writing and books, and by the thirteenth century a library was called *Sarasvati bhandaram*, or 'the storehouse of Sarasvati'. Some texts also portray Sarasvati as the source of the **devanagari** script used for writing the Sanskrit language. All these themes coalesce in later Hindu tradition, yielding the composite picture of Sarasvati as the patron goddess of arts and education, music and letters.

### Other Deities

Three other gods are also very popular. Ganesha, the elephant-headed son of Shiva and Parvati, is probably the most beloved god in all of Hinduism. He is seen as a remover of all obstacles and hindrances, and no new project or venture begins without a propitiatory offering for him, or at least a prayer. Murugan, another son of Shiva, is popular in the Tamil region of South India. And the monkey god Hanuman (also known as Maruti), a model devotee of Rama and Sita, is everyone's protector.

In South India Vishnu, Shiva, and Devi are frequently known by local names and temples devoted to them are seldom referred to as Vishnu or Shiva temples. Thus Vishnu is known in the Tirupati hills and Srirangam as Venkateshwara ('lord of the Venkata hill') or Ranganatha ('lord of the stage' or *ranga*). Each manifestation has not only a unique personality, but a mythical history that links it with a particular place. These myths are recorded in books called *Sthala Puranas* ('*Puranas* about the place'). Local manifestation is extremely important in Hinduism. Every village has its own deity, and it can take considerable effort to connect those deities with pan-Indian gods and goddesses.

Gods and goddesses in the Hindu pantheon intervene on behalf of human beings, as we see in the story of the gracious Parvati, who comes down as Meenakshi, a princess, and begins a new dynasty (the Pandyans, who ruled a kingdom of the same name in South India in the first millennium CE), thus nurturing her subjects. This faith can be seen when a person prays to Ganesha for help in finding lost keys or getting out of a difficult situation.

Sri or Lakshmi is called the mother of all creation, who bestows wisdom and salvation and is grace incarnate. Many teachers have composed hymns celebrating her compassion and wisdom. Vedanta Desika (1268–1369) describes her thus:

> She fulfils all [our] desires. She is noble, she gives prosperity,
> she is filled with good thoughts; she gives righteousness, pleasure, attainment and liberation (*dharma kamartha moksha da*).
> She gives the highest state (*parinirvana*) . . . she helps one cross the ocean of life and death. . . .

Sri is said to serve as a mediator between human beings and God in the matter of salvation, but at least one community—the Sri Vaishnava—is divided regarding her status in relation to God (Vishnu). Followers of Vedanta Desika believe Sri to be equal to and coeval with Vishnu, capable of saving human beings on her own instead of just interceding on behalf of human beings. On the other hand, followers of Pillai Lokacharya (1264–1369) believe that, although she is an elevated soul, she is not equal with Vishnu, and is therefore incapable of granting salvation on her own.

## The Hindu 'Trinity'

The notion of the *trimurti* ('three forms') seems to have been part of the Hindu tradition since at least the fourth century.

In the symbolism of *trimurti*, the gods Brahma, Vishnu, and Shiva either coalesce into one form with three faces, or are represented as equal. This has sometimes been interpreted as implying a polytheistic belief in three gods: Brahma the creator, Vishnu the preserver, and Shiva the destroyer. This interpretation contains a grain of truth, for the *trimurti* concept does effectively bring together the three great functions of a supreme god and distribute them among three distinct deities. But it is more misleading than informative in two ways.

First, it suggests that Hindus give equal importance to all three gods. In practice, however, most sectarian Hindu worshippers focus their devotions on only one deity, whether Shiva, Vishnu, the Goddess in one of her multiple forms, or a local deity who may be unknown in other parts of India. Such devotees consider the other deities important but secondary to their own faith and practice. Furthermore, although Vishnu and Shiva are certainly popular, Brahma has not been worshipped as a supreme deity for more than two millennia (and perhaps never was). Though portrayed in mythology as the creator god, he himself is only the agent of the supreme deity who created him; that deity, at whose pleasure Brahma creates the universe, may be Vishnu, Shiva, or the Goddess, depending on the worshipper's sect.

Second, the 'polytheistic' interpretation of *trimurti* suggests that creation, preservation, and destruction are functions that can be performed separately. But in fact followers of Vishnu or Shiva commonly understand creation, preservation, and destruction to be three parts of an integrated process for which their own particular supreme god is responsible. In this context, destruction is not unplanned, nor is it final: it is simply one phase in the ongoing evolution and devolution of the universe. All of creation temporarily enters or becomes one with Vishnu or Shiva until a new cycle of creation begins again. The cycle of creation will continue as long as there are souls caught up in the wheel of life and death. It is in this sense that devotees of Shiva, Vishnu, or the Goddess see their own chosen deity as the creator, the maintainer, and the destroyer of the universe.

## Ages of Time

The *Puranas* refer to those cosmic cycles of creation and destruction as the days and nights of Brahma. Each day of Brahma contains approximately 4,320 million earthly years, and the nights of Brahma are equally long. A year of Brahma is made up of 360 such days, and Brahma lives for 100 years. Each cycle therefore amounts to 311,040,000 million earthly years, at the end of which the entire cosmos is drawn into the body of Vishnu or Shiva (depending on which *Purana* one is reading), where it remains until another Brahma is evolved.

*Cycles*

Each day of Brahma contains fourteen secondary cycles of creation and destruction called *manavantaras*, each of which lasts 306,720,000 years. During the long intervals between *manavantaras*, the world is recreated and a new Manu or primeval man appears and once again begins the human race.

Each *manavantara* in turn contains seventy-one great eons (*maha yugas*), each of which is divided into four eons (*yugas*). A single one of these eons is the basic cycle. The golden age (*krta yuga*) lasts 1,728,000 earthly years. During this time dharma or righteousness is envisioned as a bull standing firmly on all four legs. The Treta age is shorter, 1,296,000 earthly years; dharma is then on three legs. The Dvapara age lasts half as long as the golden age; thus for 864,000 earthly years dharma hops on two legs. Finally, during the *kali yuga*, the worst of all possible ages, dharma is reduced to one leg. This age lasts for 432,000 earthly years, during which the world becomes progressively worse. It is in this degenerate *kali yuga*—which, according to traditional Hindu reckoning, began around 3102 BCE—that we live today.

There is a steady decline through the *yugas* in morality, righteousness, life span, and human satisfaction. At the end of the *kali yuga*—obviously still a long time off—there will be no righteousness, no virtue, no trace of justice. When the world ends, seven scorching suns will dry up the oceans, there will be wondrously shaped clouds, torrential rains will fall, and eventually the cosmos will be absorbed into Vishnu. The *Puranas* deal with astronomical units of time; the age of the earth and of the human being is infinitesimally small in relation to the eons of time the universe goes through. Although, according to many Hindu systems of thought, it is entirely possible for human beings

to end their own cycle of birth and death through transforming wisdom and/or devotion, the cycles of creation and destruction of the universe are independent of the human being's attaining *moksha* or liberation.

Temples represent the spatial and temporal cosmos. Thus their architecture sometimes reflects the Puranic cycles of time. At the great Vishnu temple of Angkor Wat in Cambodia, for instance, the causeways and passages were designed so that their measurements (when calculated in the units used in the building of the temple) would represent the numbers of years in various cycles of time.

## Caste and the *Laws of Manu*

'Caste' is used as a shorthand term to refer to the thousands of social and occupational divisions that have developed from the simple fourfold structure laid out in the 'Hymn to the Supreme Person': priests, rulers, merchants, and servants. There are more than one thousand *jatis* ('birth groups') in India, and people routinely identify themselves by their *jati*. Underlying this hierarchical system is the idea that people are born with different spiritual propensities. Ritual practices, dietary rules, and sometimes dialects differ between castes, and inter-caste marriage is still relatively rare. Although the modern word 'caste' signifies both the four broad *varnas* and the minutely divided *jatis*, Western scholars sometimes translate *varna* as 'class' and *jati* as 'caste'.

By the first centuries of the Common Era, many treatises had been written regarding the nature of righteousness, moral duty, and law. Called the *dharmashastras*, these are the foundations of later Hindu laws. The most famous is the *Manava Dharmashastra* ('Laws of Manu'), attributed to the primordial man that Vishnu saved from the flood. These were probably codified around the first century, for they reflect the social norms of that time: the caste system is firmly in place, and women have slipped to an inferior position from

## Becoming a Brahmin

Nahusha asked Yudhishthira:
'Who can be said to be a brahmin, O King?'
Yudhishthira replied:
'O lord of Serpents! The one who is truthful,
is generous, is patient, is virtuous, has empathy,
is tranquil, and has compassion—such a person is a brahmin'
  (*Mahabharata Vana Parva*, 177.15, trans. Vasudha Narayanan).

the relatively high status they enjoyed in the period of the Vedas.

When reading this text we have to understand that in many parts of India the rules it laid down were not followed strictly. We also have to take its pronouncements on women with a grain of salt. The upper classes were generally called 'twice born', in reference to the initiatory rite by which the males of these social groups were spiritually reborn as sons of their religious teachers. This rite, the **upanayana**, marked a boy's initiation into studenthood—the first of four stages in life. The *dharmashastras* set out the roles and duties of the four principal castes that make up Hindu society: brahmins (priests), **kshatriyas** (rulers, warriors), **vaishyas** (merchants), and **shudras** (servants). The brahmins were (and are still) the priestly class, the only group in Hindu society authorized to teach the Vedas. Although not all members of the brahmin community were priests, all enjoyed the power and prestige associated with spiritual learning.

The dharma of the kshatriya class (who were permitted to study but not to teach the Vedas) was to protect the people and the country. In the Hindu tradition, past and present, lines of descent are all-important. Thus many kings sought to confirm their legitimacy by tracing their ancestry to the primeval progenitors of humanity—either the sun (*surya vamsa*) or the moon (*chandra vamsa*)—and even usurpers of thrones invoked divine

antecedents. Later Hindu rituals explicitly emphasized kshatriya families' divine connections. The *Laws of Manu* describe in detail the duties of a king. He is to strive to conquer his senses, for only those who have conquered their own senses can lead or control others. He must shun not only the vices of pleasure—hunting, gambling, drinking, women—but also the vices that arise from wrath, such as violence, envy, and slander.

Members of the mercantile class (vaishyas) were responsible for most commercial transactions, as well as agricultural work, including the raising of cattle. The power of wealth and economic decisions lay with this class, whose members were permitted to study the Vedas but not to teach them.

The last class mentioned formally in the *dharmashastras* is the shudras. The *dharmashastras* say that it is the duty of shudras to serve the other classes; they would not be permitted to accumulate wealth even if they had the opportunity to do so. There was no kind of power that shudras could acquire, and the only shudras to be treated with any respect were the elderly. As the *Laws of Manu* put it, 'The seniority of brahmins comes from sacred knowledge, that of kshatriyas from valour, vaishyas from wealth, and shudras, only from old age.'

In practice, however, the caste system is far more complex and flexible than the *dharmashastras* suggest. For example, the Vellalas of South India wielded considerable economic and political power, even though the brahmins considered them a shudra caste. They were wealthy landowners, and the *dharmashastra* prohibitions do not seem to have had any effect on their fortunes.

The *Laws of Manu*, as well the *Bhagavad Gita*, tell us that it is better to do one's own dharma imperfectly than to do another person's well. However, the law books acknowledge that in times of adversity one may do other tasks, and they list these in order of preference for each class. While these codes of law emphasize the importance of marrying within one's own class, they recognize that mixed marriages take place quite often, and so they go on to list the kind of subcastes that emerge from various permutations. A marriage is generally acceptable if the male partner is of a higher caste. If the woman is higher, however, their offspring are considered of a lower caste than either parent.

Also part of India's social fabric are various 'outcastes': groups officially excluded from the caste system either because they originated in mixed marriages in the distant past or, more often, because they are associated with occupations deemed polluting, such as dealing with corpses or working with animal hides (the English word 'pariah' comes from the Tamil for 'drummer'—an outcaste occupation because drums were made of animal hides stretched taut over a frame). Until the nineteenth century, caste was only one factor among the many considered in the judicial process and in society itself. Legal cases were decided with reference to the immediate circumstances, and local customs were no less important than written texts—sometimes more so. It was India's British colonial rulers who, assuming that the caste laws were binding, attributed a new authority to them.

The caste system is such a strong social force in India that even non-Hindu communities such as the Christians, Jainas, and Sikhs have been influenced by it. Nadar Christians from the south, for instance, will marry only people of the same caste, and similar restrictions are observed all over India. In Southeast Asia, on the other hand, the caste system bears little resemblance to the Indian model. Inscriptions after the eighth century show that Manu was known, as were the *varna* and *jati* systems, and brahmins were honoured and several held high positions. However, the rest of society seems to be organized in different ways, and the king, in some cases, actually awarded specific caste status to various groups. The caste system still functions to a limited extent in some diasporas but has been significantly diluted among Hindu groups in North America.

## The Stages and Goals of Life

The dharma texts of the classical period recognized four stages of life (**ashramas**) for males from the three higher classes in society. First, a young boy was initiated into studenthood, during which he was to remain celibate and concentrate on learning. Education was to be provided for all those who desired it, and families were to support students. Although the early epics suggest that girls could also become students, it is likely that this right had been withdrawn by the first century, when the *Laws of Manu* were codified.

In the next stage the young man was to repay his debts to society and his forefathers, and his spiritual debt to the gods, by marrying and earning a living to support his family and other students. It was the householder's dharma to be employed and lead a conjugal life with his partner in dharma (*saha-dharmacarini*). Most men never went beyond these two stages, and for many the student phase was probably not particularly important.

Even so, the *Laws of Manu* describes two more stages. When a man's children have grown and become householders themselves, he and his wife may retire to the forest and live a simple life devoted to recitation of the Vedas. Finally, in the last stage, an elderly man would renounce the material world altogether and take up the ascetic life of the **samnyasin**. His old personality was now dead; he owned nothing, relied on food given as alms, and spent the rest of his days seeking enlightenment and cultivating detachment from life. This kind of formal renunciation became rare with the increasing popularity of the *Bhagavad Gita*, which stresses controlled engagement with the world.

The literature of the period just before the beginning of the Common Era also recognized a number of aims that human beings strive for. These are neither good nor bad in themselves, but may become immoral if they are pursued at an inappropriate time of life or with inappropriate intensity. The aims are dharma, the discharging of one's duties; *artha*, wealth and power in all forms; *kama*, sensual pleasure of many types, including sexual pleasure and the appreciation of beauty; and finally, *moksha*, or liberation from the cycle of birth and death. The last was sometimes seen as belonging to a different category, but texts like the *Gita* made it clear that we may strive for liberation even in daily work as long as we act without attachment.

# ❧ DIFFERENTIATION

## Vedanta

Six schools of philosophy are recognized within the Hindu tradition—Samkhya, Nyaya, Vaisheshika, Mimamsa, Yoga, and Vedanta—and elements of all six can be seen in modern Hinduism. Yoga has attracted a wide popular following in recent years, but as a philosophical school Vedanta is by far the most important. Vedanta ('end of the Vedas') has engaged Hindu thinkers for more than a thousand years. Although the term 'Vedanta' traditionally denoted the *Upanishads*, in popular usage it more often refers to systems of thought based on a coherent interpretation of the *Upanishads* together with the *Bhagavad Gita* and the *Brahma Sutras* (a collection of roughly five hundred aphorisms summarizing the teachings of those texts).

An important early interpreter of Vedanta was Shankara (fl. c. 800). For him, reality is non-dual (*advaita*): the only reality is Brahman, and this reality is indescribable, without attributes. Brahman and Atman (the human soul) are identical; Shankara interprets the Upanishadic phrase 'you are that' in a literal way and upholds the unity of what most people perceive as two distinct entities. Under the influence of *maya* we delude ourselves into believing that we are different from Brahman, but when the illusion is dispelled, the soul is liberated by the realization of its true nature. Liberation, therefore, is the removal of ignorance and the dispelling of illusion through the power of transforming knowledge. That goal can be reached in this life; human beings can achieve liberation while still embodied (*jivanmukti*). Final release, however, will come only after the death of the body. Those liberated in this life act without binding desire and help others to achieve liberation.

Shankara also posits three levels of reality. He recognizes that human beings believe life is real, but points out that when we are asleep we also believe that what happens in our dreams is real. Only when we wake up do we discover that what we dreamt was not real. So too in this cycle of life and death, we believe that all we experience is real. And it is—until we are liberated and wake up to the truth about our identity. One might argue that there is a difference: that the dream seems true only to the individual dreamer, whereas the phenomenal world seems real to millions who seem to share the same reality. But the school of Shankara would say that our limited reality is the result of ignorance and illusion. With the transformative knowledge spoken of in the *Upanishads*, we recognize that we are in reality Brahman and are liberated from the cycle of life and death. But that cycle goes on for the other souls still caught in the snares of *maya*.

Shankara's philosophy was criticized by later philosophers like Ramanuja and Madhva. One of their principal objections is connected with the status of *maya*: if *maya* is real, then there are *two* realities: Brahman and *maya*. If *maya* were unreal, Shankara's critics argue, surely it could not be the cause of the cosmic delusion attributed to it. Shankara tries to circumvent this objection by saying that *maya* is indescribable, neither real nor unreal, and his followers would say that in the ultimate state of liberation, which is totally ineffable, such criticisms are not valid in any case.

Ramanuja (traditionally 1017–1137) was the most significant interpreter of theistic Vedanta for the Sri Vaishnava community—the devotees of Vishnu and his consorts Sri (Lakshmi) and Bhu (the goddess Earth)—in South India. In his commentaries on the *Brahma Sutras* and the *Gita*, as well as his independent treatises, Ramanuja proclaims the supremacy of Vishnu–Narayana and emphasizes that devotion to Vishnu will lead to ultimate liberation. He challenges Shankara's interpretation of scripture, especially regarding *maya*, and his belief that the supreme reality (Brahman) is without attributes. For Ramanuja, Vishnu (whose name literally means 'all-pervasive') is immanent throughout the universe, pervading all souls and material substances, but also transcending them. Thus from one viewpoint there is a single reality, Brahman; but from another viewpoint Brahman is qualified by souls and matter. Since the human soul is the body and the servant of the Supreme Being, liberation is portrayed not as the realization that the two are the same, but rather as the intuitive, joyful, and total realization of the soul's relationship with the lord. (*moksha*)

The Sri Vaishnava community differs from other Hindu traditions in that it reveres as sacred not only Sanskrit texts like the Vedas, the *Bhagavad Gita*, the epics, and the *Puranas* but also the Tamil compositions of the **Alvars**: twelve South Indian poet-saints who lived between the eighth and tenth centuries CE. Specifically, the Sri Vaishnavas hold the *Tiruvaymoli* of Nammalvar to be the *Tamil* (or *Dravida*) *Veda* and refer to their scriptural heritage as *ubhaya vedanta* or dual Vedic theology.

The community also considers the 108 temples that the Alvars glorified in their poems to be heaven on earth. Worship in these Vishnu temples includes selections from Sanskrit and Tamil scripture. In the Sanskrit devotional hymns of the Sri Vaishnava community, following the Puranic literature, Vishnu is portrayed as reigning over *vaikuntha* or heaven. The liberated human soul, after cleansing itself in the waters of the river Viraja, which encircles heaven, approaches Vishnu and his consort Sri, renders loving service, and is never separated from them. The Sri Vaishnava tradition reveres Ramanuja as a saviour of the community, and his image is found in many temples.

The philosopher Madhva (c. 1199–1278) is unique in the Hindu tradition in classifying some souls as eternally bound. For him there are different grades of enjoyment and bliss even in liberation. He is also one of the explicitly dualistic Vedanta philosophers, holding that the human soul and Brahman are ultimately separate and not identical in any way.

## Yoga

Yoga is the physical and mental discipline through which practitioners 'yoke' their spirit to the divine. Many Hindu texts have held it in high regard and the word has had many meanings in the history of the Hindu tradition. Its origins are obscure, though some scholars have pointed out that seals from the Harappan culture portray a man sitting in what looks like a yogic position.

For many Hindus the classic yoga text is a collection of short, aphoristic fragments called the *Yoga Sutras*, finalized sometime in the early centuries of the Common Era and attributed to Patanjali. We do not know who Patanjali was, but he is said to have lived in the second century BCE. It is likely that yoga had been an important feature of religious life in India for centuries before the text was written.

Patanjali's yoga is a system of moral, mental, and physical discipline and meditation with a particular object, either physical or mental, as the 'single point' of focus. It is described as having eight 'limbs' or disciplines. The first of these, *yama*, consists of restraints: avoidance of violence, falsehood, stealing, sexual activity, and avarice. (Interestingly, the same prohibitions are part of the 'right conduct' taught by the Jaina tradition.) The second, *niyama*, consists of positive practices such as cleanliness (internal and external purity), equanimity, asceticism (what Patanjali calls 'heat', a kind of energetic concentration), the theoretical study of yoga, and the effort to make God the focus of one's activities. In addition Patanjali recommends a number of bodily postures and breathing techniques.

A crucial aspect of yoga practice is learning to detach the mind from the domination of external sensory stimuli. Perfection in concentration (*dharana*) and meditation (*dhyana*) lead to *samadhi*: absorption into and union with the divine. There are various stages of *samadhi*, but the ultimate stage is complete emancipation from the cycle of life and death. This state is variously described as a coming together, uniting, and transcending of polarities; empty and full, neither life nor death, and yet both. In short, this final liberation cannot be adequately described in human language.

Although Patanjali's yoga is widely considered the classical form, there are numerous variations. 'Yoga' is often used in a general way to designate any form of meditation or practice with ascetic tendencies, and in the broadest terms it may refer to any path that leads to final emancipation. Thus in the *Bhagavad Gita* the way of action is called *karma yoga* and the way of devotion as *bhakti yoga*. In some interpretations of these forms, the eight 'limbs' of classical yoga are not present; *bhakti yoga* simply comes to mean *bhakti marga*, the way of devotion. In this context yoga becomes a way of self-abnegation, in which the worshipper seeks union with the Supreme Being through passionate devotion. Some philosophers, including Ramanuja, have said that *bhakti yoga* includes elements of Patanjali's yoga, but many Hindus use the term

Students at the Shiv Yoga Mandir School in Badami, Karnataka (Frederic Soltan/Sygma/Corbis).

'yoga' much more loosely. Although its theoretical aspects have had considerable importance in particular times and traditions, Patanjali's yoga has not enjoyed mass popularity over the years, and few religious teachers have regarded it as a separate path to liberation. Recent decades have seen increasing interest in the physical aspects of yoga, especially in the West, but that interest does not always extend to the psychological and theoretical foundations of the practice.

## Tantra

The tantric component of the Hindu tradition is hard to define, partly because advocates and detractors portray it in very different lights. Essentially **tantra** consists of a body of ritual practices—occasionally sexual—and the texts interpreting them, which appear to be independent of the Vedic tradition.

'Tantra' may be derived come from a root word meaning 'to stretch' or 'expand'. It began to gain importance in the Hindu and Buddhist traditions in about the fifth century. Some scholars believe it originated in the indigenous culture of the subcontinent and re-emerged more than a millennium after the Aryan conquest. Others see it as a later development external (though not in opposition) to the Vedic tradition. A number of other movements within Hinduism, including Shaivism and Vaishnavism, incorporated elements of tantra in their own practice. For example, when images of deities are installed in temples, large geometric drawings (*mandalas*) representing gods or goddesses and the cosmos are drawn on the floor and used as objects of meditation and ritual.

Tantrism developed its own form of yoga, known as _kundalini_, centred on the *shakti* or power of the Goddess, which is said to lie coiled like a serpent at the base of the spine. When awakened, this power rises through six chakras or 'wheels' within the body to reach the final chakra under the skull known as the thousand-petalled lotus.

The ultimate aim of this form of yoga is to awaken the power of the *kundalini* and allow it to unite with the divine being, who is in the thousand-petalled lotus. When this union is achieved, the practitioner is granted visions and psychic powers that eventually lead to emancipation (*moksha*).

There are many variants of tantrism, but the main division is between the 'left-handed' and 'right-handed' schools. As the left hand was considered inauspicious, the term 'left-handed' was applied to movements that did not meet with the approval of the larger or more established schools. 'Left-handed' practices centred on the ritual performance of activities forbidden in everyday life, such as drinking liquor, eating fish and meat, and having sexual intercourse with a partner other than one's spouse. These activities were disapproved of in many other Hindu circles, so that to a large extent left-handed tantrism remained esoteric. The 'right-handed' school was more conservative.

One may also see divisions in tantra along sectarian lines: the Shaiva, Shakta, and Vaishnava communities all have their own canons of texts called *tantras*.

## Ayurvedic Medicine

Medicine made great progress in the Hindu world in the first millennium. One of the most important systems was called **Ayurveda**: the *veda* (knowledge) of enhancing life. The physician or *vaidya* ('one who is learned') promotes both longevity and quality of life. The prototype is a deity called Dhanavantari, sometimes identified as an incarnation of Vishnu. The South Indian parallel to Ayurveda is the Tamil system called Siddha.

At some time during the last three centuries BCE, the surgeon Sushruta and the physician Charaka presented theories that they claimed had been transmitted to them by the gods. These teachings reflected an understanding of illness as a lack of balance among three elements: air, phlegm, and bile. This analytic approach recalls Greek and

Chinese medical theories of roughly the same period. The *Sushruta Samhita* begins by declaring that the physician's aim is 'to cure the diseases of the sick, to protect the healthy, to prolong life', while the *Charaka Samhita* includes a detailed statement of the ethics required of a physician. In these respects, the ancient roots of Ayurvedic medicine seem strikingly modern. With the growth of tantra after about 500, however, the Ayurvedic literature devoted increasing attention to ritual as a complement to treatment with medicines.

Today in India, Ayurveda serves as a bridge between modern international medicine and traditional Indian religio-philosophical theories. Ayurvedic clinical practice relies on specific remedies and therapies, just as modern medicine does, while Ayurvedic theory draws on elements of tantra and yoga. It shares their outlook on life and the world, but puts greater emphasis on health than on spiritual attainment.

## Hinduism in Southeast Asia

Hindu culture today is associated almost exclusively with the Indian peninsula, but its influence can still be found across Southeast Asia. Archeological evidence suggests that extensive trade links were established by the second century CE, and both Hindu and Buddhist texts in India refer to Southeast Asia as the land of gold (*suvarna bhumi*) and gems. Chinese texts from about the third century CE refer to kings of Funan (a kingdom in ancient Cambodia) with Indian names. Sanskrit inscriptions are seen in the Khmer empire beginning about the late fifth century CE. Until the fourteenth century, Hindu narratives and temple-building traditions were popular across much of Southeast Asia, especially in Cambodia.

Cultural connections between India and Southeast Asia were also widespread. Many Sanskrit inscriptions and thousands of icons and sculptures portraying Hindu deities indicate that Hindu influences were pervasive in Cambodia, Thailand, Laos, Vietnam, Java, Indonesia, and Bali. Most of the popular Hindu deities are seen in temple iconography all over Southeast Asia. While the features and clothing are distinctively local in texture, the attributes, weapons, and other iconographic signifiers clearly identify them as the Hindu deities. One of the largest Hindu temples in the world is Angkor Wat, built by King Suryavarman II in the twelfth century CE and dedicated to Vishnu. And kings and queens of Cambodia had names reminiscent of Indian–Hindu royalty—names such as Jayavarman, Indravarman, Mahendravarman, and Indira-Lakshmi.

Even so, Hindu traditions in Southeast Asia, as elsewhere, took on distinctive local characteristics. The Khmer people of Cambodia, for instance, emphasized some stories that were not so important in India, and temples in Cambodia, Laos, and Indonesia are often strikingly similar to their counterparts on the subcontinent in their basic design, yet strikingly different in effect.

Shiva, Vishnu, and Lakshmi were all popular in Southeast Asia, but so was an amalgam of Vishnu and Shiva—a god named Hari-Hara, particularly in Cambodia. Portrayed in reliefs in the Badami caves (c. sixth century CE, Northern Karnataka) but otherwise little known in India, Hari-Hara appears in many Cambodian inscriptions after the seventh century; we also see him represented in many icons. In addition, icons of Brahma, Vishnu, Shiva, Ganesha, Murugan, Nandi (a bull sacred to Shiva), Garuda (the 'eagle mount' of Vishnu), the nine planets worshipped by Hindus, and other deities have been found all over Southeast Asia. A few inscriptions also refer to amalgamated deities like Ardha-narisvara (a combination of Shiva and the goddess Parvati).

One of the most widely worshipped deities across Southeast Asia was Shiva, particularly as represented by the creative symbol of the *linga*. In Cambodia, Shiva is usually depicted with two wives, Uma and Ganga. In the *Puranas*, the river Ganga is said to reside in the hair of Shiva, but

A statuette of Ganesha from Malaysia (Corbis).

other narratives refer to the river itself as a deity, a consort of Shiva. Local rivers in Cambodia came to be considered holy, among them the rivers flowing from a hill called Phnom Kulen (near Siem Reap, Cambodia), to irrigate Angkor. The sacred nature of these rivers was proclaimed in carvings made on rocks on their banks, which emphasized their identification with the Ganga.

Carvings of Vishnu, in various incarnations, can also be found in temples across South and Southeast Asia. Starting with the endowments of Queen Kulaprabhavati in the late fifth century, we find many endowments to Vishnu temples in Cambodia. Knowledge of Indian Vaishnava texts, including the two epics, was widespread, at least among the elite, and even though Shaivism and other forms of Hinduism were largely displaced by Buddhism by the fifteenth century, the *Ramayana* continues to thrive through the performing arts.

The Prambanan temple near Yogyakarta, Indonesia, is just one of many in the region whose walls are carved with scenes from the *Ramayana* and the *Puranas*.

The Prambanan temple also has shrines for Brahma and Vishnu, although the main shrine is dedicated to Shiva. In fact, most of the temples in Southeast Asia were home to more than one deity: Shiva, Vishnu, and Devi—the great goddess—were frequently worshipped in the same building. Sectarian affiliation and devotion to either Shiva or Vishnu seems to have been flexible within families as well.

Many inscriptions, especially in Cambodia, trace matrilineal as well as patrilineal descent. We can also note the importance given to biological ancestry, the pride taken in brahmin ancestors who were learned in the Vedas. The title *vrahmana* (Sanskrit *brahmana*, a brahmin) is also attached to some names in Khmer. However, despite the great respect shown to the brahmins in Cambodian (as well as Thai) culture, the caste system as we know it in India did not exist in that region. Studies show that new castes were created by the king, who seems to have had the power to bestow caste identities on his subjects. It may be that the caste system in Cambodia was largely ceremonial, or of relevance only to brahmins and royalty.

There seems to have been a strong matrilineal tendency in Cambodia, and it is not possible to say whether it is a local phenomenon or one that was imported from parts of South India. The famous inscription called the Sdok Kak Thom (c. 1052), one of the most important sources of information about Cambodian culture, speaks of many generations of kings and priests, many through a matrilineal descent. Many women seem to have held royal offices, and they certainly executed many pious and charitable works. We also hear of many queens—Indra-lakshmi, Kambuja-raja-lakshmi, and Jayaraja-devi—through inscriptions, and they seem to have wielded considerable power. Claims to the throne seem to have been made by royal women as well as men.

Although Hinduism is not practised in Southeast Asia today, except by immigrants, cultural traditions associated with it still linger. Dances with Indian themes, particularly stories connected with the *Ramayana* and Tamil works such as the *Manimekalai* (c. second to fifth centuries CE) are part of almost every cultural event, and names of Indian origins are still common among people in Indonesia, Thailand, and Cambodia.

## South Indian Devotion (*Bhakti*)

The standard portrait of Vedic and classical Hinduism is based on the culture of the northern part of the Indian subcontinent. But South India—that is, the region south of the Vindhya mountains—had a flourishing cultural life of its own by 400 BCE and possibly earlier. It was here that an entirely new type of Hindu devotion (**bhakti**) emerged and spread throughout India.

A sophisticated body of literature in the Tamil language existed two thousand years ago. Its earliest components are a number of poems on secular themes that are thought to have been composed at the time of three great Tamil academies. Known as the *Sangam* (Academy) poems, they fall into two groups: one dealing with the outer (*puram*) world of warfare, the valour of kings, chivalry, and honour, the other with the inner (*akam*) world of love and romance, of secret meetings, anguished separation, and the overwhelming joy of union.

The Tamil language has a long history of sophisticated poetry, drama, and grammatical analysis. The earliest extant Tamil composition shows some undeniable similarities to Sanskrit literature, and the early poems of love and war include many words borrowed from Sanskrit. Tamil literature on the whole, however, is neither imitative of nor derived from early Sanskrit material.

The oldest collections of Tamil poems, known as the *Ettutokai* (Eight Anthologies) and the *Pattupattu* (Ten Songs) were probably composed between the first and the third centuries. Lost for more than a thousand years, they were rediscovered in the nineteenth century. Five basic situations or moods are associated with five distinct landscape settings (*tinai*). Thus in the *akam* poems the seashore represents separation between lovers, and a jasmine flower symbolizes a woman patiently waiting for her beloved. The underlying meaning of each poem would have been instantly clear to the audiences that heard it recited.

Religious literature apparently began to flourish after the fifth century. The *Paripatal* is a work included in an anthology of early classical poetry but is probably later than most other poems in that collection. Several poems in the *Paripatal* are addressed to Vishnu, and other hymns are written in praise of Murugan (the son of Shiva and Parvati)—still a popular god in the south.

The *bhakti* movement represented a major shift in Hindu culture. It arose sometime around the sixth century, when poet-devotees of Vishnu and Shiva began travelling from temple to temple singing the praises of their chosen deity not in formal Sanskrit but in Tamil—the mother tongue of the people, the language of intimacy and powerful emotion. By the twelfth century, seventy-five of these devotees had been recognized as saints: sixty-three devotees of Shiva known as the Nayanmars ('masters') and twelve devotees of Vishnu known as the Alvars ('those "immersed deep" in the love of Vishnu').

Composed between the seventh and ninth centuries, the vernacular songs of the Alvars were introduced into the temple liturgy as early as the tenth century, challenging orthodox claims that Sanskrit was the exclusive vehicle for revelation and theological communication. Moreover, brahmin theologians honoured their authors as ideal devotees. This response was extraordinarily significant, for some of the Alvars came from lower-caste (perhaps even outcaste) backgrounds and one of them—Andal (see the box on page 62)—was a woman. Selections from their works, collected in the eleventh century as the *Nalayira Divya Prabandham*, or *Sacred Collect of Four Thousand Verses*, are recited daily in temples and in homes by the

## From the Songs of Andal

*Andal ('she who rules') was an eighth-century Alvar who is worshipped in many South Indian temples dedicated to Vishnu. Her passionate poetry is not only recited and sung by the Vaishnava community today, but is broadcast over every radio station in Tamilnadu and Karnataka in the month of December. Tradition says that she refused to marry and longed for union with Vishnu—a wish that her biographers claim was fulfilled. Thus in her life as well as her work Andal represents a radical alternative to Manu's view of women and their role. Icons of Andal are found in major South Indian Hindu temples in Toronto, Chicago, New York, Atlanta, Orlando, Livermore, and in many other parts of the world.*

A thousand elephants circle,
as Narana, Lord of virtues,
walks in front of me.
Golden jars brim with water;
Festive flags and pennants fly through this town,
eager to welcome him—
I saw this in a dream, my friend!
Drums beat happy sounds; conches were blown.
Under the canopy strung heavy with pearls,
Madhusuda, my love, filled with virtue,
came and clasped the palm of my hand
I saw this in a dream, my friend!
Those with eloquent mouths recited the good Vedas,
With mantras they placed
the green leaves and the grass in a circle.
The lord, strong as a raging elephant,
softly held my hand as we circled the fire.
I saw this in a dream, my friend!
    (*Nachchiyar Tirumoli* 1.1 and 1.6–7; trans. Vasudha Narayanan)

Sri Vaishnava community, which considers them the Tamil equivalents of the Sanskrit Vedas.

The poems of the Alvars follow the literary conventions of earlier Tamil poetry, incorporating the symbols of the *akam* and *puram* poems. Vishnu is seen as a lover and a king, both accessible and remote, gracious and grand. In their songs of devotion, the Alvars seek from Vishnu both the embrace of the beloved and the protection of the king.

Many incidents from the *Ramayana*, *Mahabharata*, and *Puranas* make their way into the Alvars' songs, along with some stories not found in

any of these sources. Above all, the poets focus on the supremacy of Vishnu-Narayana, emphasizing that his incarnations as Rama or Krishna and his presence in the temple point to both his ability and desire to save all beings. In the eighth century, Kulacekara Alvar expressed his longing to see Rama in the temple at Tillai (the modern city of Chidambaram):

In the beautiful city of Ayodhya, encircled by
    towers,
a flame that lit up all the worlds
appeared in the Solar race

and gave life to all the heavens.
This warrior, with dazzling eyes,
Rama, dark as a cloud,
the First One, My Lord,
is in Chitrakuta, city of Tillai.
When is the day
when my eyes can behold him
and rejoice?
     (*Perumal Tirumoli* 10.1)

Sometimes the Alvars identify themselves with characters from the epics or the *Puranas*, expressing their longing for Vishnu by speaking in the voice of one who is separated from Rama or Krishna. A royal devotee of Rama, Kulacekara Alvar imagines the grief felt by Dasaratha, the father of Rama, after banishing his son to the forest:

Without hearing him call me 'Father' with
     pride and with love,
Without clasping his chest adorned with gems
     to mine,
Without embracing him, without smoothing
     his forehead,

Without seeing his graceful gait, majestic like
     the elephant,
Without seeing his face [glowing] like the
     lotus,
          I wretched one,
          having lost my son, my lord,
          Still live.
     (*Perumal Tirumoli* 9.6)

In other instances a poet will speak in the voice of a character from the old secular Tamil poems of romance and chivalry.

Many of the Tamil saints, both Vaishnava and Shaiva, travelled all over South India and parts of the north, visiting temples in which their chosen deity was enshrined. In this way pilgrimage became an important feature of the Hindu tradition, and as the character of Vishnu or Shiva varied from one region to another, individual places were glorified along with the lord himself. Eventually, 108 sites came to be known as sacred places in which Vishnu abides, and the number was even higher for the Shaiva tradition. The Vira Shaiva movement gained popularity in what is now the state of Karnataka, in the twelfth century. The *vachanas*, or

## 'Heaven on Earth', from the *Perumal Tirumoli*

The poet of the Perumal Tirumoli, Kulacekara Alvar, is said to have been the king of the Chera kingdom (Kerala). Expressing his devotion to Vishnu, he sometimes assumes the identity of a character in the epics or the Puranas, and often identifies manifestations of the deity in local temples with various incarnations of Vishnu.

This is the temple of him who became
the divine fish, tortoise, boar, lion and dwarf.
He became Rama in three forms, he became Kanna,
and as Kalki he will end [these worlds].
This is Srirangam, where the swan and its mate
swing on the lotus blossoms, embrace on flowery beds,
and revel in the red pollen strewn around the river
     (*Perumal Tirumoli* 4.9.9, trans. Vasudha Narayanan).

sayings, of their poet-saints—who also included a woman, Akka Mahadevi—made explicit their contempt for the caste system. Rejecting temple worship, the Vira Shaivas preferred to express their devotion to Shiva symbolically, by carrying a small *linga*.

## From the *Tiruvaymoli*

*Although philosophical texts say that the soul is beyond gender, devotional poets have often used the language of human love to express their feelings for the divine. In the following extracts from the* Tiruvaymoli—*the ninth-century masterpiece that is considered to be one of the 'fifth Vedas'—the poet Nammalvar speaks in the voice of a young girl who longs for Vishnu as she would for a human lover (the indented lines refer to various incarnations of Vishnu).*

Where do I go from here?
I can't stand the soft bells, the gentle breeze,
the dark water-lily, darkness that conquers day,
dulcet notes, jasmines, the refreshing air.
The Lord, my beguiling one,
    who creates, bores through,
    swallows and spews this earth,
    who measures here and beyond,
does not come.
Why should I live?
    (*Tiruvaymoli* 9.9.2; trans. by Vasudha Narayanan)

*In another section Nammalvar speaks in the voice of a cowherd girl longing for Krishna (addressed here as 'Kanna'):*

My fragrant shoulders, slender as bamboo shoots,
have become weak, alas!
Blind to my pining,
not heeding of my loneliness,
The cuckoo birds coo, alas!
Peacocks mate and dance, alas!
When you go to graze the cattle,
a day seems like a thousand ages, alas!
Your lotus eyes pierce me;
Kanna, you're unfair, you're unfair.

You're unfair, Kanna, you're unfair!
When you make love and embrace my full breasts,
a tidal wave of pleasure, unchecked by our union,

*Continued*

rises to the firmament, and soars beyond,
making my wits drown in the flood.
And then it all recedes like a dream.
My passion permeates my inner life
and throbs in every cell of my body.
My soul cannot bear the burden
when I am separated from you.
Every time you go to graze the cows,
        I die.

I shall die if you go to graze the cows,
for my soul is ablaze with the fire of my breath,
I have no companion.
I shall not live to see your dark body dance.
When you leave me, the day never ends;
my twin eyes, shaped like *kayal* fish,
swim in tears that never end.
Born as cowherd girls in a herder clan,
a humble state,
Our loneliness is death.

You were gone the whole day,
grazing cows Kanna!
Your soothing words burn my soul.
evening tramples like a rogue elephant
and the fragrance of jasmine buds,
loosening my bonds, blows upon me.
Embrace my beautiful breasts
with the fragrance of the wild jasmine
upon your radiant chest.
Give me the nectar of your mouth,
and adorn my lowly head
with your jeweled lotus hands.
        (*Tiruvaymoli* 10.3.1, 2, 3, and 5; trans. by Vasudha Narayanan)

### Classical Carnatic Music

Music has been part of Hindu worship ever since the time of the *Veda*s. The mystical syllable **om** was considered the beginning of sound in the universe and a manifestation of the Supreme Being. Knowledge of the nature of sound and its proper expression was therefore considered to be religious knowledge. The *Veda*s specify the different kinds of pitch and tone by which the verses were to be recited. The exalted status of the *Sama Veda* was in part a reflection of the melodious way in which it was to be sung.

Classical music was for the most part religious in nature. Treatises on music refer to a divine line of teachers, frequently beginning with the deities Shiva and Parvati, and honour Sarasvati as the patron goddess of the fine arts. Bharata's *Natya Sastra*, a classical text on dance and mime composed around the beginning of the Common Era, speaks of the performing arts as a spiritual path to liberation. Some later *Puranas*, such as the *Brhad-dharma*, say that Vishnu and Sri are manifested as Nada Brahman or the Supreme Being in the form of sound.

Properly controlled and articulated, sound itself could lead to mystical experience. Thus the sound of a hymn was considered no less important than the words. *Nadopasana*, meditation through sound, became a popular religious practice. The Alvars composed their poems to be sung and danced. Many devotional poet-composers addressed their songs to the deities.

What we know today as carnatic music—the classical music of South India—began to take its distinctive present form in the fifteenth century, when the musicians Purandaradasa and Anna-macharya introduced a number of new *ragas* (musical modes based on specific scales) accompanied by particular rhythmic beats. As devotees of Vishnu in particular sacred places (Pandharpur in Maharashtra and Tirupati in Andhra Pradesh), they developed these new *ragas* to sing his praises.

This form of music was raised to new heights in the eighteenth century by three musicians who apparently never met one another, although they were all born in the same village in Tamilnadu at about the same time. Diksitar wrote in praise of Parvati, while Shyama Shastri composed some three hundred songs devoted mainly to the Goddess. The third, Tyagaraja (1767–1847), composed intensely moving songs in praise of Rama, became the most renowned poet-musician of South India, and is considered one of the world's greatest composers.

His father, Rama Brahma, who was well versed in the Vedas, had been given a sacred mantra that bore the name of Rama, and was well known for his discourses on the *Ramayana*, which must have influenced his son. According to legend, Tyagaraja wrote some 24,000 *krtis* or songs. Slightly more than seven hundred survive today, of which roughly two dozen are in Sanskrit; the rest are in the Telugu language. He also wrote two story-poems. After meditating on the Rama mantra, he reportedly had visions of the lord Rama and his devotion increased. Tyagaraja envisions Rama as his protector and companion:

> Show pity and shower your mercy on me
> Rama, son of King Dasaratha. . . .
> At the mere thought of you my skin
> just tingles all over, Rama . . . .
> When I long for you with love,
> the whole world becomes a straw.
> When you are near me—
> what, me worry? . . .
> Did you take the avatar
> of Rama just for my sake?
> Did you walk this earth
> to save poor servants like me?
> . . . You are Tyagaraja's
> sole companion Rama
> show pity and shower your mercy on me,
> Rama, son of King Dasaratha.
> (Jackson 1991: 188–9)

Tyagaraja became an ascetic towards the end of his life. In his songs, *bhakti* is the means by which the devotee seeks to approach Rama. Finally, though, the joy of the song and the experience of devotion become ends in themselves:

> Devotion steeped in the nectar
> of melodious tones and modes
> Is the celestial bliss,
> O my heart and soul
> (Jackson 1991: 334).

Tyagaraja's music is still sung at wedding concerts, songfests, on radio and television broadcasts, and in many homes today; internet sites also carry a wide selection of his compositions. Every spring, South Indian Hindus in America hold music festivals in his honour.

## North Indian Bhakti

Having begun in South India, the *bhakti* tradition gradually spread to the north. Under the Islamic sultanate established in Delhi in the twelfth century, relations between Muslims and Hindus were sometimes hostile, and several Hindu temples were looted and razed to the ground. On the other hand, the synergy made possible by the coming together of cultural influences from the Middle East and India gave rise to extraordinary innovations in all the arts, from music and dance to poetry and architecture.

North Indian *bhakti* resembled its southern counterpart both in its use of vernacular languages and in the fact that it was open to people of every caste, from high to low. The two differed, however, in the focus of their devotion. South Indian *bhakti* was generally addressed to a particular deity—either Vishnu or Shiva—but in the north the object of devotion was often Rama or Krishna, or sometimes the divine being without a form. The sometimes synergistic relationship that developed between Hindus and Muslims in northern India was reflected in the delightful, sometimes poignant works composed in the vernacular by poet-singers of the Sant ('holy person' or 'truth') tradition. Emphasizing the *nirguna* ('without attributes') Brahman of the *Upanishads*, the Sants held the divinity to be without form. Hence their worship had nothing to do with physical images, and—unlike the Tamil poet-saints, who travelled from temple to temple precisely in order to express their devotion to local manifestations of their chosen deity—they expressed their devotion either in poetry or in silent meditation. At the same time they rejected distinctions between religious communities. Among the most important Sant poets was Kabir, a Hindu weaver from Varanasi whose life is said to have spanned more than a hundred years (1398–1518). In his insistence that God is beyond the particularities of any religious community, Kabir had much in common with a Punjabi religious leader named Nanak (1469–1539) and a Sufi Muslim teacher named Dadu (1544–1603). All three men attracted followers. In time, the disciples of Kabir and Dadu were reabsorbed into the general populations of Hindus and Muslims respectively, but Nanak's ultimately formed a separate community—the Sikhs. Kabir was one of several Sant poets whose works became part of the Sikh scripture.

Two other important poets in North India were Surdas and Tulsidas. Surdas (c. 1483–1563), who settled just south of Delhi near Agra, was a blind singer and poet whose compositions are in a dialect of Hindi. In his *Sursagar*, the youthful Krishna is celebrated in poetry valued by many Hindus. Krishna is the mischievous butter thief, but also the irresistible flute player, and the verses celebrate Radha's affection for him as a model of *bhakti*. Tulsidas (1543?–1623) is perhaps best-known for his *Lake of the Deeds of Rama*, a retelling or translation of the ever-popular *Ramayana* in verses that have their own beauty and have inspired hundreds of traditional storytellers and millions of Rama devotees in Hindi-speaking areas. Large sections of this work are learned by heart: sidewalk vendors, shopkeepers, housewives, and learned people can all quote from it even today.

An early exponent of Krishna devotion was the twelfth-century poet Jayadeva, who is thought to have lived in the eastern city of Puri on the Bay of Bengal. His Sanskrit work *Gita Govinda* ('Song of the Cowherd') extols the love of Radha and Krishna; it also contains a reference to the Buddha as an incarnation of Krishna–Vishnu, filled with compassion.

Finally, a Bengali contemporary of Surdas was Chaitanya (1486–1583). At the age of thirty-four he took the religious name Krishna-Chaitanya, 'he whose consciousness is Krishna'. Chaitanya's views have an overtone of the faith-versus-works dialectic that Christians find in Saint Paul and Martin Luther

## From Kabir

Go naked if you want,
Put on animal skins.
What does it matter till you see the inward Ram?
If the union yogis seek
Came from roaming about in the buff,
Every deer in the forest would be saved. . . .
Pundit, how can you be so dumb?
You're going to drown, along with all your kin
Unless you start speaking of Ram.
Vedas, Puranas—why read them?
It's like loading an ass with sandalwood!
Unless you catch on and learn how Ram's name goes,
How will you reach the end of the road?
You slaughter living beings and call it religion:
Hey brother, what would irreligion be?
'Great Saint'—that's how you love to greet each other:
Who then would you call a murderer?
Your mind is blind. You've no knowledge of yourselves.
Tell me, brother, how can you teach anyone else?
Wisdom is a thing you sell for worldly gain,
So there goes your human birth—in vain.
    (Hawley and Juergensmeyer 1988: 50–1)

and that Buddhists find in the Japanese Pure Land teachings of Shinran—that in the *kali yuga*, our present degenerate age, humans lack the capacity to fulfil all the requirements of religious action and duty; the only way to liberation is through trusting devotion to a loving and gracious deity.

For Chaitanya, however, the ultimate goal was not liberation from attachment in the traditional sense but rather the active enjoyment of his intense spiritual love of Krishna—a passionate love like the one that the cowherd girls felt for him. Chaitanya is said to have led people through the streets, singing about his lord and urging others to join him in chanting Krishna's names. Eventually, many of his followers came to believe that Krishna and Radha were present in Chaitanya himself.

Chaitanya's movement had waned somewhat by the late nineteenth century, but it was revived through the efforts of a government official named Kedarnath Datta (1838–1914) who took the name Bhaktivinode Thakur, and his son Bimalprasad Datta (1874–1937; religious name Bhaktisiddanta Sarasvati). A pupil of the younger Datta, Abhaycaran De (1896–1977), who took the name A.C. Bhaktivedanta, then carried this lineage abroad, launching the International Society for Krishna Consciousness—better known as the Hare Krishna movement—in New York in 1966. Both its theology, locating divine grace in Krishna, and its practice, centred on devotional chanting, can be traced directly to Chaitanya.

What has been the legacy of the *bhakti* movement? With its spread, the message of the Sanskrit

## From Mirabai

*Mirabai (1450?–1547) was a Rajput princess in Gujarat. Left a widow when she was still a young woman, she became a devotee of Krishna and wrote passionate poetry about her love for him.*

Sister, I had a dream that I wed
the Lord of those who live in need:
Five hundred sixty thousand people came
and the Lord of Braj was the groom.
In dream they set up a wedding arch;
in dream he grasped my hand;
in dream he led me around the wedding fire
and I became unshakably his bride.
Mira's been granted her mountain-lifting Lord:
from living past lives, a prize.
  (Caturvedi, no. 27; Hawley and Juergensmeyer 1988: 137)

scriptures was reinforced by powerful devotional works, many of which have come to function as scripture themselves. Composed in vernacular languages, these poems and songs offer the faithful far more guidance, inspiration, consolation, hope, and wisdom than the Vedas have ever done. This is not to say that the vernacular literature is at variance with the Vedas. Rather, the poet-saints made what they perceived to be the message of the Vedas accessible to everyone, inspiring devotion and preparing devotees to receive the shower of divine grace.

## Reform and Revival

It was the Portuguese explorer Vasco da Gama (1469–1524) who fulfilled Columbus's ambition of finding a sea route to India from Europe. When he landed in Calicut, on the western coast of India in 1498, he opened the way to the Indian subcontinent for a long line of traders, missionaries, and eventually rulers. Before long, the Dutch, English, and French were also travelling to India, where they soon established settlements. Early European scholarship in Indian languages, especially Sanskrit, led to the historical reconstruction of the movements of the Indo-European people from Central Asia. Studies in comparative philology pioneered the theory of a common Indo-European ancestry. This was the first glimpse that Hindus received of their pre-Vedic historical antecedents.

In time the foreign powers became involved in local politics, and possession of territory became one of their goals. As the Mughal empire disintegrated in the early eighteenth century, many chieftains attempted to acquire parcels of land and to enlist English or French help in their efforts. Eventually large parts of the Indian subcontinent were loosely united under British control. In the past, most Hindu and Muslim rulers had accepted a large degree of local autonomy, but the British felt a moral and political obligation to govern and impose sweeping changes without regard to local tradition or practice At the same time, foreign missionaries were severely critical not only of what they saw as Hindu 'idolatry', but of the caste system and practices such as *sati*. The foreigners were not the only ones to call for change, however. Some Hindu intellectuals were equally convinced of the need for reform. Among them was Ram Mohan Roy.

### The Brahmo Samaj

Ram Mohan Roy (1772–1833) was born into an orthodox brahmin family in western Bengal. The details of his education are unclear, but he is said to have studied the Qur'an as well as the Vedas, and may also have explored Buddhism. Eventually joining the East India Company, he became familiar with Western social life and the Christian scriptures and formed close ties with members of the Unitarian movement. He rejected the Christian belief in Jesus as the son of God, but admired him as a compassionate human being, and in 1820 he published a book called *The Precepts of Jesus: The Guide to Peace and Happiness*, in which he emphasized the compatibility of Jesus' moral teachings with the Hindu tradition.

Roy believed that if Hindus could read their own scriptures they would recognize that practices such as *sati* were not part of classical Hinduism and had no place in Hindu society. Therefore he translated extracts from Sanskrit texts into Bengali and English and distributed his works for free. In 1828 he established a society to hold regular discussions on the nature of Brahman as it appears in the *Upanishads*. This organization, which came to be called the Brahmo Samaj ('congregation of Brahman'), emphasized monotheism, rationalism, humanism, and social reform. Although Roy rejected most of the stories from the epics and the *Puranas* as myths that stood in the way of reason and social reform, he drew on the Vedas, particularly the *Upanishads*, to defend Hinduism against missionary attacks. At the same time, together with the Unitarians, he accused the missionaries, who believed in the Christian Trinity, of straying away from monotheism. A pioneer in the area of women's rights, including the right to education, he fought to abolish *sati*, founded new periodicals, and established educational institutions.

The Brahmo Samaj has never become a mainstream movement. Nevertheless, it revitalized Hinduism at a critical time in its history by calling attention both to inhumane practices and to the need for education and reform, and in so doing played a major part in the modernization of Indian society.

### The Arya Samaj

The Arya Samaj was established in 1875 by Dayananda Sarasvati (1824–83). Born into a brahmin family in Gujurat, he left home at the age of twenty-one to avoid an arranged marriage and take up the life of an ascetic. After fifteen years as a wandering yogi, he studied Sanskrit under a charismatic guru named Virajananda, who taught that the only true Hindu scriptures were the early Vedas and rejected as false all later additions to Hindu tradition, including the worship of images. On leaving his teacher, Dayananda promised that he would work to reform Hinduism in accordance with the true teachings of the Vedas.

Dayananda believed that the Vedas were literally revealed by God, and that the vision of Hinduism they presented could be revived by stripping away later human accretions such as votive rituals and social customs such as *sati*, and teaching young people about their true Vedic heritage. To that end, he founded many educational institutions.

Dayananda also believed that the Vedic teachings were not at variance with science or reason. He rejected the notion of a personal saviour god; in fact, he rejected any anthropomorphic vision of the divine. He believed that the human soul is in some way coeval with the deity. A radical feature of Dayananda's teaching is the idea that total elimination of *karma* is almost impossible, and that therefore it is not possible to attain eternal liberation. In his view, the ideal was not renunciation but rather a full, active life of service to other human beings: working to uplift humanity in itself would promote the welfare of both the body and the soul.

### The Ramakrishna Movement

Ramakrishna Paramahamsa (1836–86; born Gadadhar Chatterjee) was a Bengali raised in the Vaishnava *bhakti* tradition, cultivating ecstatic trance experiences. In his early twenties he was employed as a priest by a wealthy widow who was building a temple to the goddess Kali; by his account, he experienced the Divine Mother as an ocean of love. From the age of twenty-five he took instruction in tantra as well as Vedanta. He concluded that all religions lead in the same direction and that all are equally true.

Following his death, his disciples in Calcutta formed the Ramakrishna Mission to spread his eclectic ideas. Among them was Swami Vivekananda (Narendranath Datta, 1862–1902), a former member of the Brahmo Samaj who believed that Western science could help India make material progress, while Indian spirituality could help the West along the path to enlightenment. As a Hindu participant in the 1893 World's Parliament of Religions in Chicago, and subsequently as a lecturer in America and Europe, he presented an interpretation of Shankara's non-dualist (*advaita*) Vedanta in which Brahman is the only reality. As a consequence of the attention he attracted, it was this philosophy that the West generally came to consider the definitive form of Hinduism.

Under Vivekananda's leadership, the movement established a monastic order and a philanthropic mission, both dedicated to humanitarian service. In keeping with Ramakrishna's ecumenical vision, it encouraged non-sectarian worship. It also ignored caste distinctions, opening hundreds of educational and medical institutions for the welfare of all. The Ramakrishna movement's introduction of a Hindu presence into this field of activity was particularly significant because until then most of India's new medical and educational institutions had been run by Christian missionaries.

The monastic wing of the movement maintains that renunciation promotes spiritual growth. Unlike other monastic orders, however, it insists that its members should not be isolated ascetics, but should live in and for the world, giving humanitarian service to others.

### The Aurobindo Ashram

Nationalism and yoga come together in the philosophy of Aurobindo Ghose (1872–1950), who was sent from Calcutta to England for schooling at the age of seven and did not return to India until he was twenty.

The maturing of Ghose's views over the years can be seen in his writings. At an early age he devoted his energies to the Indian nationalist campaign for independence from Britain. Understanding nationalism as a kind of religion, he saw human beings as instruments of God—whom he did not define—and nationalism as the work of God in India.

As a Bengali, Aurobindo admired Ramakrishna, who came from the same region. Perhaps influenced by Ramakrishna's devotion to the goddess Kali, he identified the goddess Bhawani—the mother of the universe and the *shakti* of the supreme Brahman—the infinite energy coming from what is eternal in the world and in human beings.

But Aurobindo went further than most religious thinkers, identifying this personified *shakti* as India. He believed that the Absolute itself was the force behind the Indian independence movement, and that India was to be the teacher of all nations. True patriotism, he said, identifies the motherland with both divine and maternal power, and sees the fight for independence as the way to spiritual liberation. In espousing these ideas, Aurobindo had more in common with some of the early Bengali freedom fighters than with Vedanta philosophers.

In 1908, however, Aurobindo was imprisoned on suspicion of sedition, and while in prison he underwent several mystical experiences. (In one of them, he felt the presence of Vivekananda.) These experiences convinced him that the quest for Indian independence was of lesser value than the spread of Vedanta philosophy. Following this spiritual awakening, he said that *sanatana dharma* ('the eternal faith') goes beyond nationalism, and is not circumscribed by geographic boundaries. Rather, the Hindu religion is the eternal religion because it is universal and embraces all others.

In 1910 Aurobindo felt an inner call to go to the French territory of Pondicherry in southeastern

India. There he devoted himself to yoga, writing, and reinterpretation of the Vedas in the light of what he had learned from his mystic experience. Though inspired by Vivekananda's leadership, Aurobindo disagreed with his view of the universe as illusory, a manifestation of *maya*. Rather, he believed that the universe was ultimately real.

Aurobindo's philosophy, based on his own experiences and his understanding of the *Upanishads*, describes the path of salvation as a two-way street. While human beings strive through yoga to ascend upwards, enlightenment descends from above. The meeting of these two energies—the human energy, striving for wisdom, and the supreme energy coming down from above—creates a new 'gnostic' individual. This enlightenment experience makes final liberation possible, and eventually everyone will be liberated.

In 1914 Aurobindo found a collaborator in a Frenchwoman named Mira Richard (b. Alfassa, 1878–1973). Together they established a model spiritual centre in Pondicherry that attracted hundreds of followers. After Aurobindo's death, 'the Mother', as Mira Richard was known, led the Aurobindo *ashram* ('retreat centre') until her death at the age of ninety-five.

### The Theosophical Society

Founded in New York City in 1875, the Theosophical Society took its name from a mystic 'divine wisdom' tradition in Western philosophy that can be traced back as far as ancient Greece. The founders of the Society, however, associated their beliefs specifically with Hindu Vedanta.

Helena P. Blavatsky (1831–91) had left her Russian aristocrat husband shortly after their marriage and claimed to have travelled the world in search of enlightenment—even spending seven years in Tibet under the guidance of Hindu spiritual teachers. She was already promoting theosophical ideas as early as 1858, and in 1875 she organized the Theosophical Society in collaboration with two Americans, a lawyer-journalist named Henry S. Olcott and a lawyer named William Q. Judge (1851–96).

Blavatsky's books *Isis Unveiled* (1877) and *The Secret Doctrine* (1888) presented her views as a blend of Vedanta with Egyptian snake worship (which she attributes to Tibet), medieval European alchemy, and cosmological theories of nineteenth-century science. Written in English, these works circulated in spiritualist circles in the West and among some educated Indians.

In 1878 Blavatsky and Olcott moved to India and established the world headquarters of the Theosophical Society in a suburb of Madras. This strengthened two false impressions: that their eclectic international movement was an authentically Hindu phenomenon, and that Vedanta was the definitive expression of Hinduism. It also helped to perpetuate the misleading idea, still current in certain circles both in India and abroad, that the Indian people possess some special spiritual insight. One need only consider the religio-communal violence that characterized India in the twentieth century to know that the Theosophists' image of India is debatable at best.

## ❧ PRACTICE

## The Sacred Syllable *Om*

The word *om* is recited at the beginning and end of all Hindu and Jaina prayers and recitations of scripture; it is used by Buddhists as well, particularly in Tibetan Vajrayana. The word is understood to have three sounds, *a–u–m*, with the diphthong *au* producing an *o* sound. The sound of *om*, which begins deep in the body and ends at the lips, is considered auspicious. Its history in the Hindu tradition is ancient; the *Mandukya Upanishad* discusses its meaning and power. Hindu philosophers and sectarian communities all agree that *om* is the most sacred sound.

At the same time, almost every Hindu community has speculated about the meaning of *om*, and the speculations vary widely. Some say it represents the supreme reality or Brahman. Many Hindu philosophers have believed that *om* was present at the beginning of the manifest universe and that it contains the essence of true knowledge. Some say that its three sounds represent the three worlds: earth, atmosphere, and heaven. Others say that they represent the essence of the three *Vedas*: *Rig*, *Yajur*, and *Sama*. Some derive the word from the Sanskrit verbal root *av-*, meaning 'that which protects'.

According to followers of the philosopher Shankara, that is, non-dualist interpreters of Vedanta, the three sounds *a*, *u*, and *m* have the following experiential meanings:

- *A* stands for the world that we see when we are awake, the person who is experiencing it, and the waking experience.
- *U* stands for the dream world, the dreamer, and the dream experience.
- *M* represents the sleep world, the sleeper, and the sleep experience.
- These three states we experience on this earth, while a fourth, unspoken syllable represents the state of liberation.

Some Vaishnava devotees, on the other hand, say that *a* represents Vishnu, *u* denotes the human being, and the meaning of *m* is the relationship between the two. Other Vaishnavas say that the sounds represent Vishnu, Sri, and the devotee.

Thus Hindus agree that *om* is the most sacred sound but disagree regarding its meaning. In a sense, then, the sound of *om* is a whole greater than the sum of its parts, exceeding in significance the many meanings attributed to it.

## Temple Worship

The Vedic literature does not indicate any trace of temple worship. In the Harappa culture, however, it seems that some buildings may have been set apart for worship, and some figures seem to have an iconic status. When exactly temples began to figure in Hindu worship is uncertain. South India has some temples that have survived from the seventh or eighth century CE, but those in the north tend to be more recent, since many were destroyed either by Muslim rulers or by various invaders. However, caves with carvings depicting incarnations of Vishnu as well as icons of Shiva, found near Bhopal, Madhya Pradesh, suggest that worship at public shrines was established by the early fifth century. Magnificent cave carvings can also be seen at the fifth-century site of Udayagiri (near Bhopal in the modern state of Madhya Pradesh) and the sixth-century site of Badami, the capital of the Chalukya empire. Temples are a common part of the Indian landscape now, but there are many regional variations in architecture and patterns of worship.

Deities in Hindu temples are treated like kings and queens. (The Tamil word for temple is *koil*, 'house of the king'.) The **murtis**—variously translated as 'idols', 'icons', 'forms', or 'objects to be worshipped'—are given a ritual bath, adorned, carried in procession, and honoured with all the marks of hospitality offered to royal guests, including canopies to shelter them, fans to keep them cool, and music and dance to entertain them. Wedding rituals between the God and Goddess are celebrated, as are various other festivals. In the Srirangam temple, there are special festivities for 250 days a year. All this is done because, in most cases, the enshrined image is regarded as God. Devotees believe that the presence of God in the temple does not detract from his or her presence in heaven, immanence in the world, or presence in a human soul. The deity is always complete and whole, no matter how many forms he or she may be manifest in at any given time. Generally, in Hinduism, there is no tradition of congregational prayer in the style of Christian or Muslim worship. Rather, the priest prays on behalf of devotees, presents offerings of fruit, flowers, or coconut to the deity, and then gives back some of the blessed objects to the devotees. The food thus presented is considered ennobled because it is now **prasada** (literally 'clarity', but meaning 'divine favour'), a gift from the deity. Traditionally, Hindu priests have been primarily ritual specialists rather than counsellors, though they may be taking on a more pastoral role today in the Americas.

Because there are so many philosophical and sectarian traditions within Hinduism, understandings of the *murti* vary widely. Many Hindus believe that, once consecrated, the image in the temple becomes not a symbol of God but God himself, fully present in image form in order to make himself accessible. The image in the temple, then, is a direct analogue to the incarnation (*avatara*) of Vishnu as Rama or as Krishna in times past. Others, however, believe that the image in a temple is only a symbol of a higher reality, and some—including members of the Brahmo Samaj and Vira Shaiva movements—have rejected images altogether. Adherents of Shankara's non-dual Vedanta, for their part, believe that the supreme reality is not personified. Theoretically, Brahman is identical to the human soul, Atman, and it is transforming wisdom, not *bhakti*, that leads to liberation. Therefore Vedantins have no reason to worship in a temple. In practice, however, even they throng to shrines to express their devotion.

Temple festivals celebrate events portrayed in the local myths as well as more generic observances. At Madurai in Tamilnadu, for instance, the Meenakshi-Sundaresvara temple complex honours Meenakshi, a manifestation of Parvati who is also portrayed as a princess of the local Pandyan dynasty. After a military career in which she is said to have conquered many chiefs, she marries Sundaresvara, who is seen to be Shiva himself. The wedding of the god and goddess is celebrated with much pomp and joy every year at a festival attended by pilgrims in the hundreds of thousands.

Vishnu temples in South India also have large shrines for the goddess Sri or Lakshmi. Similarly, temples dedicated to a manifestation of Shiva or Parvati usually include a shrine for that deity's consort. The processional image of Vishnu in the inner shrine always shows him with his consorts Sri and Bhu, the goddess of the earth. In Sri's own shrine, however, she is represented alone and is only occasionally accompanied by an image of Vishnu. In other words, while Vishnu is worshipped only in conjunction with Sri, Sri may evidently be worshipped alone, and several festivals are celebrated for her exclusively.

Temples to Murugan, a son of Shiva and Parvati, are popular in the Tamil region of South India, though they are uncommon in the north. Hanuman, who figures in the story of Rama and Sita, is venerated both at temples and at home shrines. Many temples also contain representations of the nine planets, which may cause harm if they are not propitiated. Especially dreaded is Shani or Saturn, who is said to wreak havoc unless he is appeased by proper prayers or rites.

Temples to the creator god Brahma or his consort Sarasvati, the goddess of learning, are rare. The reason is usually associated with a Shaiva story in which Brahma is said to have told a lie, for which he is cursed and told that he will not be worshipped in any temple; the curse seems to include Sarasvati. Nevertheless, there are a few temples dedicated to them. Karambanur or Uttamar koil, near Srirangam in Tamilnadu, for instance, is an early syncretic temple with separate shrines to Shiva, Parvati, Vishnu, Lakshmi, Brahma, and Sarasvati. Students frequent the shrine of Sarasvati, especially on the eve of an examination. She is also worshipped at a famous temple at Sringeri, Karnataka, where she is known as Sharada. Devotion to Sarasvati is most evident in domestic worship, however. Children recite prayers to her daily, and students carry little pictures of her to school.

Although most of the temples in northern India today date from after the end of the Mughal period, architectural guides from as early as the fifth century suggest that at least some elements of temple design and construction have remained constant.

A temple has a correlation to the universe itself and to the body of divine beings, and is therefore planned with care. In the Sri Vaishnava community, the temple is said to be heaven on earth. An ideal temple has seven enclosures (*prakaras*) and is located near a body of water of some kind— whether the sea, a river, a pond, a spring, or an artificial pool (called a 'tank' in India)—which automatically becomes holy. Devotees making a formal pilgrimage from a faraway place sometimes bathe in the water before entering the temple. In South Indian temples, the enclosures have gateways over which stand large towers (*gopuras*); the tallest one in the Srirangam temple is approximately 83 metres (270 feet) high. The towers are an essential part of the religious landscape, and in popular religion even a vision of the temple tower is said to be enough to destroy one's sins.

Devotees frequently walk around the temple inside one of the enclosures; this 'circumambulation' of the deity is an essential part of the temple visit. They may perform an *archana* ('formal worship') in which the priest praises the deity by reciting his or her names. Devotees also bow down before the deity. Sometimes they will go to the temple kitchen for *prasada*. In some temples devotees must buy the *prasada*; in others it is provided at no charge from endowments made by patrons in the past. Such patrons frequently earmark their donations for particular charitable deeds or functions in the temple, and their donations are inscribed on stone plaques on the temple walls.

Women, especially those from royal families, were liberal benefactors of temples and other institutions. In the year 966, in Tiru Venkatam (Tirupati), a woman called Samavai donated money for the temple to celebrate some festivals and consecrate a silver processional image of Vishnu (known here as Venkateshwara). A record of her endowment, inscribed in stone, concludes with the phrase *Sri vaishnava rakshai* ('by the protection of the Sri Vaishnavas'). Within a short time

Samavai also donated two parcels of land, totalling roughly 10 hectares (23 acres) and ordered that the revenues derived from them be used for major festivals. She also gave a large number of jewels to the temple for the adornment of the image of the lord. Today this temple has the largest endowments and revenues of any in India.

Studies by epigraphers and art historians show that Samavai was not an isolated example. We know, for instance, that queens of the South Indian Chola dynasty (c. 846–1279) were enthusiastic patrons of Shiva temples and religious causes around the tenth century. At that time, a South Indian queen called Sembiyan Mahadevi gave major endowments to many Shiva temples.

The inscriptions recording endowments represent a tangible honour for the many patrons over the centuries who have generously donated funds. In addition, the large amounts of money received point to the temples' power as economic institutions. Inscriptions are an important source of information about a temple and the social life of the times. For example, the fact that women like Samavai were able to make such donations suggests a certain independence both of lifestyle and of income.

Hindu temples may have been built in Vietnam as early as the fourth or fifth century, and some of the largest temples to Shiva and Vishnu are found in the region of the Khmer empire, which stretched from modern Cambodia to parts of Thailand and Laos. Although there are striking similarities to temples and iconographic styles in different parts of India, including the states along the eastern coast, the Southeast Asian buildings have their own architectural idiom. Shiva temples are shaped like mountains; the large mountain-temples at Bakheng and Bakong in the Siem Reap area of Cambodia, for instance, look more like Borubodur, the Buddhist temple in Indonesia, than those in India. The large Vishnu temple of Angkor Wat in Cambodia, like many temples in India (and Central America as well), is situated and built according to astronomical calculations:

The great temple of Angkor Wat, where the sun rises directly over the central tower at the time of the equinox in spring and fall (Vasudha Narayanan).

the sun rises directly behind the central tower at the time of the spring and autumn equinoxes. The Udayagiri cave complex may also reflect astronomical knowledge, since it is situated close to the latitude where the Tropic of Cancer—the northernmost point where the sun appears to stand directly overhead at noon on the summer solstice—would have been around 400 CE.

Some temples in India have minimal funds, but others are very well endowed. An example is the Vishnu temple at Tiru Venkatam (the Tirupati hills in Andhra Pradesh). Vishnu here is known as Venkateshwara, or 'lord of the Venkata hills'. (A branch of this temple in the United States is discussed at the end of this chapter.) The temple at Tiru Venkatam is referred to in Tamil texts from the fifth century, and the Alvars frequently sang about it. Although it enjoyed royal patronage in the past, it is only in the last century that it began attracting large numbers of pilgrims and substantial revenues. The popularity of the temple is said to have increased dramatically after a major reconsecration in 1958.

The wealth of this temple is frequently commented upon by the media. Cars and diamonds are collected, along with an average of 20 kilograms (640 troy ounces) of gold every month, from various pieces of jewellery deposited in the collection box. Until 1965, when the government took them over, it owned more than six hundred villages. The enormous revenues of the temple are used for charitable purposes, universities, educational institutions, and hospitals. Today, some believe the Tirumala-Tirupati temple complex to be one of the wealthiest religious institutions in the world, second only to the Vatican.

## Sculptural and Pictorial Symbolism

### The Naga

One of the earliest symbols in the Hindu tradition may be the *naga* (serpent). In many villages (as well as quiet spots in large cities) there are sacred trees surrounded with small stone images of intertwined snakes, which are venerated with spots of red powder (the same kumkum powder that is used to adorn women's foreheads). Women come to these open-air shrines to worship at particular times of the year, or when they want to make a wish regarding a matter such as childbirth. *Nagas*

The dancing Shiva, carved in the sandstone of the Badami caves in northern Karnataka (Vasudha Narayanan).

are also important in the iconography of Shiva and Vishnu.

In Cambodia balustrades in the form of large *nagas* are an integral part of the Hindu and Buddhist temple landscapes. Cambodian narratives trace the descent of the kingdom from a Hindu prince from India and a *naga* princess.

### The Dance of Shiva

Iconographically, Shiva is often portrayed as a cosmic dancer known as Nataraja, the king of the dance. In this form Shiva is the archetype of both the dancer and the ascetic, symbolizing mastery over universal energy on the one hand and absolute inner tranquillity on the other.

In the classic Nataraja representation, Shiva has four hands. One of the right hands holds an hourglass-shaped drum, symbolizing sound—both speech and the divine truth heard through revelation. The other right hand is making a gesture that grants fearlessness to the devotee. One of the left hands holds a flame, symbolizing the destruction of the world at the end of time. The feet grant salvation and are worshipped to obtain union with Shiva. The left foot, representing the refuge of the devotee, is raised, signifying liberation. The other left hand points to this foot.

Dancing through the creation and destruction of the cosmos, Shiva–Nataraja is the master of both *tandava*, the fierce, violent dance that gives rise to energy, and *lasya*, the gentle, lyric dance representing tenderness and grace. The entire universe shakes when he dances; Krishna sings for him, the snake around his neck sways, and drops of the Ganga River, which he holds in his hair, fall to the earth.

### The Linga

In temples Shiva is usually represented by a *linga*: an upright shaft, typically made of stone, placed in a receptacle called a *yoni*, which symbolizes the womb. Although *linga* is generally translated into English as 'phallus', and in Sanskrit *linga* means 'distinguishing symbol', Hindus do not normally think of it as a physical object. Rather, it serves as a reference point to the spiritual potential in all of creation, and specifically to the positive energies of Shiva. The union of the *yoni* and *linga* is a reminder that male and female forces are united in generating the universe. Although Shiva is stereotyped as the 'destroyer' in some literature, it is his creative role that is represented in the temple.

### Erotic Sculpture

People from other cultures have often been shocked by temple sculptures celebrating *kama*, sensual love. Probably the most famous examples of such art are found at Khajuraho (c. 1000 CE), in the state of Madhya Pradesh, southeast of Delhi, and Konarak (c. 1250), in the eastern coastal state of Orissa. Although many other temples also contain erotic sculpture, it is frequently kept in inconspicuous niches or corners.

Some art historians have speculated that the sculptures may have been intended to serve an educational purpose for young men who as students were isolated from society, in order to prepare them for adult life in a world where *kama*—sensual enjoyment—of all kinds was considered a legitimate goal and spouses were expected to be partners in *kama* as well as dharma. Other scholars have suggested that such scenes illustrate passages from various myths and literary works such as the *Puranas*.

### Forehead Marks

Perhaps the most common visual sign of Hindu culture is the forehead mark or **tilaka** ('small, like a *tila* or sesame seed'), especially the red dot (*bindi*) traditionally worn by married women. In many parts of India, however, men—ascetics and temple priests—also wear various forehead marks in the context of religious rituals. Like many elements in the Hindu traditions, a forehead mark may be interpreted in various ways, depending on the gender and marital status of the person wearing

it, the occasion for which it is worn, the sectarian community from which the wearer comes, and, occasionally, his or her caste.

At the simplest level the forehead mark is decorative. In this spirit, unmarried and Christian as well as married Hindu women today wear *bindis*, and the traditional dot of kumkum powder has been largely replaced by stickers in a wide variety of shapes and colours. Thus many people today do not think of forehead marks as having anything to do with religion. Yet their value is more than cosmetic. Married women see the *bindi* as a symbol of the role that they play in society. Other marks indicate the wearer's sectarian affiliation. When worn correctly in ritual situations, the shape and colour indicate not only which god or goddess the person worships, but also the socio-religious community to which he or she belongs.

The materials used to create the mark depend on the wearer's sectarian affiliation and the purpose

A married woman wearing a *bindi* (© Steve Evans).

for which the mark is worn. Marks denoting affiliation to a particular deity may be made with white clay, sandalwood paste, smoke-collyrium, flower petals, or ash. In general, followers of Vishnu, Krishna, and Lakshmi wear vertical marks; worshippers of Shiva and Parvati wear horizontal or slightly curved crescent marks made of ash or other substances with a red dot in the middle; and a combination of dots and crescents usually indicates a preference for the Goddess (Devi) in one of her many manifestations. Other variations are instantly identifiable to those familiar with India's many philosophical traditions.

## Domestic Worship

One of the most significant ways in which Hindus express their devotion to a deity or a spiritual teacher is through rituals performed in the home; such worship is usually called **puja**. Many Hindu households set aside some space—if only a cabinet shelf—for a shrine to hold pictures or small images of the revered figure, whether god or guru.

The rituals performed in the home are simplified versions of temple rituals, led by family members rather than priests. In the home as in the temple, the deity is treated with all the hospitality accorded to an honoured guest. Daily puja typically consists of simple acts in which all family members can take part, such as lighting oil lamps and incense sticks, reciting prayers, or offering food to the deity. More elaborate rituals, however—such as the puja offered to Satyanarayana (a particular manifestation of Vishnu) on full-moon days—may involve a priest or other specialist.

Significantly, a number of domestic rituals are specific to the women of the household. In many parts of India, women gather on certain days of the year to celebrate the goddess by fasting and feasting, and then perform what are called 'auspiciousness' rituals for the happiness of the entire family. Other women's rituals are found only in certain geographic regions. In the south, for example,

women often gather before a major family celebration (such as a wedding) to ask for the blessing of a particular group of female ancestors: those who have had the good fortune to die before their husbands and therefore have preserved their status as *sumangalis* or 'auspicious women'. Such women are believed to have immense power to influence the success of any ritual. In northern India, during some domestic festivals such as Navaratri (see below) young virgin girls are venerated by other women who believe that they are temporary manifestations of the Goddess.

In the home as in the temple, worshippers participate in the myths associated with the various deities. At the same time, in speaking a prayer or singing a hymn, they take part in the passion of the composer. Thus in Sri Vaishnava worship, devotees who recite a verse of Andal's are to some extent participating in Andal's own devotion, and through this identification they link themselves with the devotional community extending through time.

## The Significance of Food

The Hindu tradition is preoccupied with food: not just what kind of food we eat, where and when we do so, and how it is prepared, but who prepares it, who has the right to be offered it first, and who may be given the leftovers. Certain dates and lunar phases require either fasting or feasting. Furthermore, there are technical distinctions among fasts: some demand abstention from all food, others only from grain or rice. According to some texts, one can win liberation from the cycle of life and death simply by observing the right kinds of fast.

Contrary to a common Western stereotype, most Hindus are not vegetarians. Nor does vegetarianism for Hindus mean abstaining from dairy products. Generally speaking, vegetarianism is a matter of community and caste. The strictest Hindu vegetarians are generally the Vaishnavas, who are found all over India. In addition, most brahmins are vegetarian—except in Bengal, Orissa, and Kashmir. In the West, members of the International Society for Krishna Consciousness (the Hare Krishna movement) not only abstain from meat, fish, and fowl, but also avoid certain vegetables that are thought to have negative properties, such as onions and garlic.

These dietary prohibitions and habits are based on the idea that food reflects the general qualities of nature: purity, energy, and inertia. The properties of food include both those that are intrinsic to it and those that are circumstantial. Pure foods such as dairy products and many vegetables are thought to foster spiritual inclinations. By contrast, meat, poultry, and onions are believed to give rise to passion and action, while stale food and liquor are seen as encouraging sloth. Thus a strict vegetarian diet is prescribed for people who are expected to cultivate spiritual tranquillity and avoid passion, such as brahmins, Vaishnavas, and widows.

In addition, the nature of a given food is thought to be influenced by the inherent qualities of the person who cooks it. For this reason it was common even in the mid-twentieth century for strictly observant brahmins to eat only food prepared by people of their own caste.

Food is also auspicious and inauspicious. Weddings, funerals, ancestral rites, and birthdays require the use of auspicious lentils, spices, and vegetables. What one feeds the forefathers is different from what one feeds the gods and human beings; rituals associated with death involve different kinds of food from life-promoting rituals. Turmeric powder, for example, is auspicious, while sesame seed is inauspicious. Similarly, food prepared for ritual use in temple and death ceremonies is restricted to traditional ingredients; innovations such as potatoes and red peppers (both hot and sweet), introduced to India by Europeans in the last few centuries, are to be avoided.

A central element in temple rituals is the offering of food to the deity, after which the 'leftovers' are served to devotees as *prasada*. Inscriptions on the walls of medieval temples show that most endowments were intended for food offerings, and in the case of the temple at Tirupati they include detailed instructions for the preparation of offerings. The latter is one of a number of pilgrimage centres that eventually became famous for particular kinds of *prasada*. The cooking and distribution of *prasada* is now a multi-million-dollar industry at such temples.

Beyond the practicalities of use or avoidance, food appears in Hindu thought as an important symbol of spiritual experience. In a well-known story about the eighth-century Tamil poet-saint Nammalvar, the Supreme Being appears as the spiritual and physical nourisher of all human beings. Nammalvar has spent the first sixteen years of his life in a yogic trance, and has never eaten or spoken. Then an elderly brahmin is guided to him by a vision of light. To test Nammalvar, this man asks him a question: 'If a little thing is born out of the stomach of a dead thing, what will it eat and where will it lie?' When Nammalvar, speaking for the first time in his life, replies, 'It eats that, and lies there,' the old man is convinced of his wisdom and becomes his disciple. This exchange is usually paraphrased as follows: If a human soul takes on a body (since flesh in itself is considered to be a 'dead' or inanimate substance), what will nourish it, and what is its support? Nammalvar answers that the sustenance and support of the human soul is the Supreme Being, in this case Vishnu. The idea of a mystical union between food and the person who eats it is suggested in the *Taittiriya Upanishad* (part of the *Yajur Veda*):

> Oh, wonderful! Oh, wonderful! Oh,
>   Wonderful!
> I am food! I am food! I am food!
> I am a food-eater! I am a food-eater! I am a
>   food-eater!
>       (*Taittiriya Upanishad* III.10.5)

Theologians through the centuries have debated the significance of this passage, but most have interpreted it as referring to the experience of the Vedic sacrificer, who identifies himself with Brahman both as food and as eater. This verse is recited as part of the weekly temple liturgy in Vishnu temples all over the world.

Food also plays an important role both in Ayurvedic medicine and in various regional traditions that rely on different foods to rectify imbalances of 'cold' and 'heat' accumulated in the body.

## The Annual Festival Cycle

In the Hindu tradition there is a festival of some kind almost every month of the year. The most popular are the birthdays of Rama, Krishna, and Ganesha; the precise dates for these celebrations vary from year to year with the lunar calendar, but they always fall within the same periods.

Some festivals are specific to certain regions. **Holi**, for instance, is a North Indian festival celebrated in March or April with bonfires to enact the destruction of evil, and exuberant throwing of coloured powder to symbolize the vibrant colours of spring. It commemorates the fourth incarnation of Vishnu, when he took the form of a man-lion in order to save the life of his devotee Prahlada. Vishnu's fifth incarnation, as a dwarf-brahmin, is celebrated in the state of Kerala in a late-summer festival called Onam. Other festivals, like Navaratri and **Deepavali** (known colloquially as Divali in some areas) are more or less pan-Hindu. A detailed discussion of Navaratri will give us an idea of the complexity of the variations in observance across the many Hindu communities.

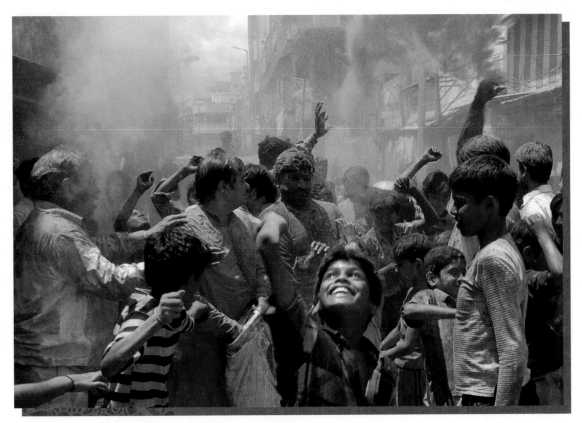

Celebrating Holi in Hyderabad (AP Photo/Mahesh Kumar A.).

## Navaratri

The festival of Navaratri ('nine nights') begins on the new moon that appears between 15 September and 14 October and is celebrated all over India, but in different ways and for different reasons.

In Tamilnadu, for instance, Navaratri is largely a festival for women. Exquisite dolls representing the goddesses Sarasvati, Lakshmi, and Durga are arranged in elaborate tableaux depicting scenes from the epics and *Puranas*. Every evening, women and children dressed in bright silks visit one another, admire the dolls, play musical instruments, and sing songs from the classical repertoire in praise of one or another of the goddesses. It is a joyous time of music and beauty, and a glorious celebration of womanhood. On the last two days—a special countrywide holiday—large pictures of Lakshmi and Sarasvati, draped with garlands of fresh flowers, are placed in front of the display of dolls and worshipped.

In the state of West Bengal, by contrast, the same nine or ten days are dedicated to a festival called Durga Puja, commemorating the goddess Durga's killing of the buffalo-demon Mahisa. Devotees make sumptuous statues of Durga for her spirit to inhabit; then, after nine nights, they immerse the statues in water to symbolize her return to the formless state.

In the state of Gujarat, Navaratri is celebrated with two special dances. In the circular dance called *garbha*, a sacred lamp is kept in the centre of the circle as a manifestation of the goddess. The second dance, called *dandiya*, is performed with sticks and recalls the dance that Krishna is said to have performed with the cowherd girls.

In many parts of northern India women will invite seven pre-pubescent girls to a home during Navaratri for veneration as representatives of the goddess Durga.

According to some traditions, it was during the same nine nights and ten days that Rama battled Ravana. In Ramnagar, a city near Varanasi (Banaras) on the river Ganga, people act out the story of the *Ramayana* in a play called *Ramlila* and on the tenth day celebrate Rama's victory. Little boys play the parts of Rama and his brothers in what is considered to be India's largest outdoor theatre, spanning several hectares.

Some Hindus believe that it was on the ninth day of Navaratri that Arjuna found the weapons he had hidden a year before and paid respects to them before entering battle. Because of this story, the last two days, dedicated to Lakshmi and Sarasvati, are called *Ayudha Puja* ('veneration of weapons and machines'): cars and buses are draped with garlands, while computers and typewriters are blessed with sacred powders and given the day off work. The ninth day of the festival honours Sarasvati, the patron of learning and music. All the musical instruments in the house, any writing device, and selected textbooks are kept in front of her image, to be blessed by her for the rest of the year.

In many parts of India, the last day of the festival is dedicated to Lakshmi. This is a time for fresh starts: to begin new ventures and new account books, to learn new prayers and music, to acquire new knowledge, and to honour traditional teachers. On the last days of the Navaratri festival, the fortune of learning, the wealth of wisdom, and the joy of music are said to be given by the grace of the goddesses.

## Deepavali

*Deepa* means 'lamp' and *vali* means 'necklace' or 'row'. Thus Deepavali (or Divali) means 'necklace of lights'. It is celebrated at the time of the new moon between 15 October and 14 November. Hindus all over the world decorate their houses with lights, set off firecrackers, and wear new clothes. In some parts of India, Deepavali marks the beginning of a new year, but that is only one of several reasons for the festival. As in the case of Navaratri, the significance of Deepavali varies from region to region.

In South India, for instance, Deepavali celebrates the dawn when Krishna is said to have killed Narakasura, a demon from the nether world, thus ensuring the victory of light over darkness. In

North India, however, Deepavali marks the return of Rama to Ayodhya and his coronation. And in Gujarat it is the beginning of the new year, when businesses open new account books and new clothes are worn. Presents are exchanged in some communities, and it is generally a time of feasting. In Tamilnadu, it is said that the river Ganga itself is present in all the waters on Deepavali day. People get up at three or four in the morning for a special purifying bath, and members of some communities greet one another by asking 'Have you had a bath in the river Ganga?'

## Life-Cycle Rites

Every culture has its rites of passage: rituals that mark the transitions from one stage of life to another. In some of the *dharmashastra* texts the discussion of the life-cycle sacraments begins with the birth of a child. In others the first sacrament is marriage, for it is in this context, properly speaking, that each new life will begin.

Two factors are important to note in discussing life-cycle rites. First, not all are pan-Hindu, and even those that are do not necessarily have the same importance in all communities. Second, many important rites, especially those involving girls or women, are not discussed in the classical texts—possibly because those texts were written by men. Women were considered merely as partners to males, who were the main focus of the books. It may also be that some of these rites developed after the texts were written. We shall discuss first the normative *dharmashastra* sacraments, and then look at a few rites of passage that have more localized regional importance.

The English word 'auspiciousness' has become the standard translation for a category of concepts for which Sanskrit uses four different terms: *kalyana, mangala, shubha,* and *sri*. Certain kinds of people, animals, rituals, smells, sounds, and foods are considered auspicious: that is, they are thought to have the power to bring about good fortune and a good quality of existence (*su asti*). Marriage is called 'the auspicious ceremony' in Tamil, and in some North Indian usage the word *shubha* ('auspicious') precedes the word *vivaha* ('marriage'). Auspicious times are chosen for the performance of all sacraments; these times depend on the horoscope of the person concerned, which is cast at birth.

The right hand is associated with auspicious activities, such as gift-giving, eating, and wedding rituals. The left hand is associated with the inauspicious and the impure: insults, bodily hygiene, and funerary rituals, which include those honouring ancestors.

### Birth Rituals

The cycle of sacraments (*samskaras*; literally, 'perfecting') begins before birth. The time at which a child is conceived, the rituals administered to a pregnant woman, and her behaviour during pregnancy are all thought to condition the personality of the child. Thus, in traditional usage, there was a ritual for proper conception of a child, and mantras were to be uttered before the man and woman came together. The *Upanishads* describe specific rituals to be followed if one wanted a learned daughter or a heroic son; in later times, however, daughters were rarely desired. Although the conception sacrament has been largely discarded, it survives in some communities as one of the rituals observed on the wedding night. Some *dharmashastras* suggest that it is a husband's duty to approach his wife for intercourse at particular times of the month, and a few even go so far as to say that a man who does not do so is guilty of abortion. Abortion has generally been considered sinful, but the texts apparently have little influence on modern Hindu life: abortion is legal in India and rarely a subject of debate in Hindu religious discourse.

Many communities in India also follow two other prenatal rites called *pumsavana* ('seeking a male offspring') and *simanta* ('hair parting'). Although formerly performed in the fifth month of pregnancy, today they are performed much later to ensure the safe birth of a son.

At the moment of birth, care must be taken to note the exact time, to ensure an accurate horoscope. The first ceremony performed after the birth, called *jatakarma* ('birth action'), was supposed to precede the cutting of the umbilical cord, but it is now done much later. The *jatakarma* rites include *medhjanana* ('birth of intelligence'), in which the father prays for the intellectual well-being of the child, and *ayushya*, in which he prays for longevity for himself and for the child, saying, 'May we see a hundred autumns, may we hear a hundred autumns.' The ceremony ends with a request for the infant's physical well-being and strength.

## Initiation Rituals

The ritual that initiates a young brahmin boy into the study of the Vedas is called *upanayana* or *brahma upadesha*. The word *upanayana* can mean either 'acquiring the extra eye of knowledge' or 'coming close to a teacher' to get knowledge; *brahma upadesha* refers to receipt of the sacred teaching (*upadesha*) concerning the Supreme Being (Brahman).

The *upanayana* ritual is traditionally performed around the age of eight and initiates the boy into the first stage of life, called *brahmacharya*—literally 'travelling on the path that will disclose the Supreme Being' (that is, studenthood). At this stage the student was supposed to concentrate on acquiring knowledge, not wealth. Therefore he did not work for a living; rather, it was the society's duty to support and feed him. In the past, the student would often live in his teacher's house, begging his food from other households and taking it home for his teacher's wife to prepare for him. It has been suggested that girls may have undergone a similar initiation in the early Vedic era, but if that was the case, the practice had been discontinued by the time the *Upanishads* were composed (c. 600 BCE).

The *upanayana* ceremony takes two days to complete. On the first day, the boy is bathed in water into which the essence of all the sacred and life-giving waters has been invoked through the recitation of sacred verses from the *Vedas*. This

ritual is called *udaga shanti* ('peace brought on the waters'), and in a larger sense it seeks peace on all the waters and lands of the earth. The verses end with repeated requests for *shanti* (peace): peace for the individual, for the soul, the body, the divine beings, the family, the community, and the entire earth. In order for the initiation sacrament to be valid, the boy must have undergone all the sacraments prescribed for earlier stages in the life cycle (naming, the first feeding of solid food, hair cutting, and so on). On the second day, therefore, before the actual rituals begin, the family priest quickly repeats all these rituals, just in case they have not been performed properly. During the ritual the boy is given a sacred 'thread' or cord to wear over his left shoulder. The meaning of this cord is unclear. Some think it represents an upper garment that the student would wear when he was fit to perform a sacrifice. Others think it symbolizes a spiritual umbilical cord representing the boy's connection to his teacher—the spiritual parent through whom he will be reborn. The boy is now taught how to eat properly, thanking earth for his food and asking divine beings to bless it. He may then be given garlands brought from various temples as a sign of divine blessing.

Then comes the central part of the ritual: the actual *brahma upadesha*, or imparting of the sacred teaching. As the boy sits with his father and the priest sits under a silk cloth (thought by some scholars to symbolize the spiritual womb) a sacred mantra is given to him that he will be expected to chant 108 times in succession, three times each day. Known as the *Gayatri* or sun mantra, it is very short—'I meditate on the brilliance of the sun; may it illumine my mind'—but it is considered the most important of all mantras. The boy is then taken outside and shown the sun, the source of light, knowledge, and immortality. He has to twine his fingers in a particular way to ward off the harmful rays while looking directly at the heart of the sun.

Finally, the boy must beg his food for the day, though nowadays this begging is only symbolic.

Since it is considered meritorious for women to feed brahmin boys, all the women attending the ceremony (starting with the boy's mother) line up to give him three scoops of raw rice. The boy says, 'O generous lady, give me food' three times, and three times the rice is placed on his plate.

Today, of course, the initiate no longer goes to live with his teacher, and most boys do not undertake any Vedic studies. The initiation ceremony was traditionally part of the life cycle for male members of all three of the higher castes, but it is now rarely performed outside the brahmin community. Efforts are underway to introduce similar initiation ceremonies for young girls.

### Weddings

According to the *dharmashastra* codes of law and ethics, a man is born with debts to the sages, the gods, and the ancestors. A wife helps him repay these debts. The debt to the gods is discharged through the correct performance of domestic and social rituals with—and only with—his wife; the debt to the ancestors, by having children. A wife is a man's partner in fulfilling dharma, and without her a man cannot fully perform his religious obligations.

Hindu scriptures suggest that there is no higher ideal for a woman than to be a faithful wife. In the myth of Savitri, for example, the princess Savitri chooses to marry Satyavan even though it has been predicted that he has just one more year to live. She repeats a prayer taught to her by a divine minstrel for the longevity of her husband. A year later, Yama, the god of death, comes to claim Satyavan, but Savitri follows them to the end of the earth. Touched by her devotion, Yama grants her three wishes—anything except the life of her husband. Savitri's third wish is for a hundred sons, and since at that time no Hindu wife could properly have sons out of wedlock, Yama is forced to relinquish his grip on Satyavan's life. In this way Savitri became the symbol of the faithful wife. In South India her triumph over death is celebrated in a domestic ritual in which married women request happiness with their husbands, and unmarried girls request a happy married life.

Wedding ceremonies in India vary widely from region to region. In some communities in Kerala, the rite may take less than a half hour; in other areas it may last five days.

Before a wedding can be arranged, the parents of the prospective bride must find a suitable bridegroom; for this they often rely on the help of friends and extended family. Ideally, he will come from the same geographic region, speak the same language, and belong to the same community and subcommunity, though he must belong to a different *gotra* or clan. He should be compatible with the bride in education, looks, age, and outlook, and the two families should be of similar socio-economic status.

When a possible husband is finally found, the family will compare his horoscope with that of the bride. The purpose of this reading is not only to assess compatibility and character but also to balance the ups and downs in the partners' future lives. Thus calculations are made to determine which years are likely to be difficult ones for each: to avoid acute adversity, those years that are expected to be bad for the husband will be better ones for the wife, and vice versa. Family astrologers are employed to analyze the horoscopes, and their predictions are eagerly awaited.

To select a mate, parents sometimes obtain several horoscopes and have them analyzed in order to eliminate unsuitable candidates from the start. In the past the search for prospective partners was conducted largely through informal networks, but today much of this work is done by formal marriage bureaus and non-profit organizations. The Sunday newspapers devote three or four pages to matrimonial advertisements listing all the qualifications required of a prospective mate, from caste and community background to language and dietary preferences. Today computers are often used to cast children's horoscopes as soon as they are born. When the horoscopes match, the young people and their families meet to decide whether they like each other—a decision that sometimes takes little more than a brief look at one another. At this point both parties have the right either to opt out or to request more time to get acquainted.

Obviously, arranged marriages are less common today than they were when young women were largely sheltered from the world outside the home. Now that men and women increasingly study and work together, a couple may meet and decide to get married with or without the families' approval. Such marriages often cross boundaries of caste and community—even language and geography.

When an arranged meeting does lead to a betrothal, arrangements are often made for the bride's parents to give the groom's family a 'gift' (sometimes referred to as a 'dowry') in the form either of cash or of goods. There is no religious sanction for this practice; in fact, scriptural prescriptions refer to the transaction as moving in the other direction, from the groom's parents to the bride. Although the practice is now illegal, it remains quite common.

The marriage ceremony itself must include several basic features if it is to be considered legal. These include the *kanya dana* (the gift of the virgin by the father), *pani grahana* (the clasping of hands), *sapta padi* (taking seven steps together around fire, which is the eternal witness), and *mangalya dharana* (the giving of 'auspiciousness' to the bride). In addition, the bride and bridegroom usually exchange garlands.

Some weddings include lavish exchanges of presents with friends and extended family members, processions on horseback or in antique cars, feasting, entertainment, and fireworks. The festive atmosphere often recalls a fairground, with vibrant splashes of colour and plenty of noise. Everyone has a good time, and relatively little attention is paid to the bride and groom.

The ceremony itself lasts several hours and for the bride may involve several changes of elaborate clothing and jewels. Often the couple sit on a platform near a fire, to which offerings are made. The bride's parents have an active role to play, as do the groom's sister and the bride's brother and maternal uncle at particular moments in the ritual, but the hundreds of guests are free to come and go as they please. During the *kanya dana* or 'giving of the virgin', the father of the bride quotes from the *Ramayana*, reciting the words spoken by Janaka, the father of Sita, as he gives her in marriage to Rama: 'This is Sita, my daughter; she will be your partner in dharma.' *language of the epics*

The groom's family then presents the bride with the 'gift of auspiciousness': a gold necklace, a string of black beads, or a simple yellow thread carrying the insignia of the god the family worships (a conch and discus symbolizing Vishnu, for instance, or a *linga* symbolizing Shiva).

In South India the groom fastens this string or the necklace around the bride's neck as her symbol of marriage (corresponding to a wedding ring in the West). She will wear it for the duration of her marriage. There is no equivalent symbol for the groom, although men who have put on the sacred thread will wear a double set of threads after they marry.

In the central rite of the wedding, when the bride and the bridegroom take seven steps around the fire together, the groom says:

Take the first step; Vishnu will follow you. You will not want for food for the rest of your life. Take the second step; Vishnu will guard your health. Take the third step; Vishnu will follow you and see that you may observe all religious rituals. Take the fourth step; Vishnu, following you, will grant you happiness. Take the fifth step; Vishnu will follow and grant you cattle and kine. Take the sixth step; let Vishnu follow you and let us enjoy the pleasures of the season. Take the seventh step; Vishnu will follow you. We shall worship together.

Then, clasping the bride's hand (*pani grahana*), the groom says:

You have taken seven steps with me; be my friend. We who have taken seven steps together have become companions. I have attained your friendship; I shall not forsake that friendship. Do not discard our relationship.

Let us live together; let us think together. We have come to a right and fitting stage of our lives; let us be happy and prosperous, thinking good thoughts.

Let there be no difference in our hopes and efforts; let us attain our desires. And so we join ourselves (our lives). Let us be of one mind, let us act together and enjoy through all our senses, without any difference.

You are the song (*Sama*), I am the lyric (*Rig*), I am *Sama*, you are *Rig*. I am the sky, you are the earth. I am the seed; you shall bear my seed. I am thought; you are speech. I am the song, you are the lyric. Be conformable to me; O lady of sweet unsullied words, O gem of a woman, come with me; let us have children and attain prosperity together.

Many of these verses come from sections of the Vedas that prescribe ritual. The officiating priest recites the mantras, which the bride and groom repeat after him. It is worth noting that these passages from the Vedas refer to the wife not as her husband's possession or servant, but rather as his partner in dharma and his companion and friend in love. For most communities, the central rituals must be conducted near a sacred fire. The importance of fire (*agni*) can be traced as far back as the coming of the Indo-European people to India around 1500 BCE. Fire was considered the master of the house, the eternal witness to all the rituals marking the milestones in a human life. Oblations are made to the fire as part of the prenatal rites, when the child is one year old, when a man reaches sixty, and yet again if he reaches eighty. Finally, when life is over, the body is committed to fire. Without a fire as witness, therefore, the

wedding will not be valid. In another ritual, the groom bends down and places the bride's foot on a firm, heavy stone. The fact that he touches her feet is significant in itself, for this is an unequivocal gesture of respect in Hindu culture. He then places rings on her toes, saying, 'Stand on this stone, be firm and steady as this stone. Stand conquering those who oppose you; be victorious over your enemies.' Like the passages from the Vedas cited above, this rousing speech suggests a view of a wife's role that has nothing to do with servitude.

Later in the evening the new husband and wife are taken outside for a ritual called *Arundhati darshana* ('the sighting of Arundhati'). In Indian astrology, the seven brightest stars of the Great Bear constellation (the Big Dipper) represent the seven sages, one of whom (Vasistha) is accompanied by a companion star identified as his wife, Arundhati—a symbol of fidelity throughout India. Just as the stars Vasistha and Arundhati remain close through the years, so the newlyweds are urged to stay together forever.

### Funeral Rites

We have noted elsewhere that nothing in the Hindu tradition is ever really discarded. Funeral rites reflect different combinations of elements from the Vedas and the *Bhagavad Gita* with elements specific to individual regions and communities (Shaiva, Vaishnava, etc.). Except for infants and ascetics (who may be buried), cremation by fire is the final sacrament in most communities. No fire is to be lit or tended in the house where the death occurred until the cremation fire has been lit, and the family of the deceased is considered to live in a state of pollution for a period of time that varies from twelve days to almost a year after the death. Each religious community has its own list of scriptures to recite from. Although the funeral rituals for most Hindu communities would include portions of the *Vedas* and the *Bhagavad Gita*, many would also include recitations from texts sacred only to that specific community. The Sri Vaishnava community, for example, recites Nammalvar's

*Tiruvaymoli*, in which the poet-saint expresses his longing to be united with Vishnu.

The funeral rituals are usually performed by the eldest son of the deceased. For the first few days the spirit of the deceased is a *preta* (ghost). To quench the thirst resulting from the body's fiery cremation, the spirit is offered water and balls of rice. Some of these rituals go back to the earliest Vedic times, when the dead were thought to live on the far side of the moon and thus to need food for their journey.

After a designated period of time, the length of which varies depending on caste, the injunctions relating to pollution are lifted in an 'adoption of auspiciousness' ceremony. On every new-moon day the departed soul is offered food in the form of libations with sesame seeds and water. After a year, the anniversary of the death is marked with further ceremonies, and the family is then freed from all constraints.

## Women's Rituals

Most women's rituals are domestic, undertaken for the welfare of the family and earthly happiness, but a few are intended solely for personal salvation or liberation. Many practices, such as worship at home shrines or temples, pilgrimages, and the singing of devotional songs, are similar to those undertaken by men, but some are unique to married women whose husbands are alive. Underlying many of the rites is the notion that women are powerful and that the rites they perform have potency. Though many women's rituals share certain features, the differences among the many communities, castes, and regions are so great that generalizations should be avoided.

### Early History

We have already noted that upper-caste girls may have been permitted to study the Vedas in the ancient past. The epics tell of women lighting and tending the sacrificial fire to make ritual offerings to the gods. They also refer to women ascetics, who would presumably have undergone renunciatory rites similar to those required of men. These privileges appear to have been withdrawn by the beginning of the Common Era, however.

### Calendrical Rituals Today

Many traditional women's rituals are no longer practised today, but a number of votive rituals (*vrata*) are still observed on particular days during specific lunar months. These rituals involve the welfare of others—whether the husband, the extended family, or the community—and only unmarried women or married women whose husbands are alive may participate in them; widows are excluded. Although Sanskrit manuals say that performing these rites will enable a woman to attain final liberation from the cycle of birth and death, most participants ask only for more worldly rewards, such as marriage or for a long life for their husbands.

After prayers to the family deity, the women may eat a meal together and distribute emblems of auspiciousness such as betel leaves, bananas, coconuts, turmeric, and kumkum powder. The rituals may take anywhere between a few minutes and five days to complete, with periods of fasting alternating with communal eating.

In South India many women's rituals are performed during the month of Adi (15 July–14 August). Married women were traditionally enjoined to stay celibate during this month. Many women pray to the goddess Lakshmi for domestic happiness. There are a variety of rituals connected with various castes. Women of some castes carry special pots of water and other ritual items to the temples of local goddesses and perform rites in their honour for the benefit of the entire family. Others cook rice and milk dishes in the temples of the local goddesses and distribute the food. In the temple of Draupadi Amman, women and men alike enter a trance state and walk over hot coals in a ceremony called 'walking on flowers'.

In North India many women's rites focus on the welfare of male relatives. In late summer, for example, girls tie a protective cord around the wrists of their brothers. And in October–November, women undertake two fasts (*karva chauth* and *ahoi ashtami*) for the well-being of their husbands, as well as one for the health of their sons. These daytime fasts are broken only after the stars come out in the evening.

### Women's Life-Cycle Rituals

In the upper castes the standard life-cycle rituals associated with childhood, marriage, and death are much the same for both sexes. There are many other sacraments associated with women, however, that have not received scriptural ratification. Some of these rites are local in nature, specific to certain regions and communities.

In the past, for instance, many communities would celebrate a young girl's first menstrual period, since this 'blossoming' meant that she was ready for marriage. Today urban communities tend to consider this tradition old-fashioned, but it is still practised in rural areas. The girl is showered with gifts of money or clothing by her family, and the ritual celebration often resembles a mini-wedding.

Special rituals may also attend pregnancy, especially the first. In a popular South Indian ritual called 'bracelets and amulets' the pregnant woman is dressed in a heavy silk sari, and women of all ages slip bangles and bracelets onto her arm. In earlier days a bangle-seller was invited and the woman's parents gave all the guests glass bracelets that were supposed to safeguard them from evil spirits.

In another rite the expectant mother's hair is adorned with flowers, to enhance the natural radiance that is often said to accompany pregnancy. In the Hindu tradition married women often wear flowers in their hair, but normally only a bride's hair is completely woven with flowers. Rituals such as these acknowledge the importance of a woman's body and celebrate its life-bearing potential.

### Attitudes towards Women

On the whole, the view of women expressed in the Hindu scriptures has been contradictory. Woman is portrayed—often by the same author—as servant and goddess, strumpet and saint, the protected daughter and the powerful matriarch, the shunned widow and the worshipped wife.

The *Laws of Manu* (c. 200 CE) make women's inferior status in Hindu society at that time only too clear. Male commentators through the centuries have approvingly quoted statements like this: 'Though destitute of virtue, or seeking pleasure elsewhere, or devoid of good qualities, a husband must be constantly worshipped as a god by a faithful wife' (*Manu* 5.154).

Manu goes on to say that a wife is the goddess of fortune and auspiciousness (*Manu* 9.26) and that only if women are honoured will the gods be pleased and the religious rituals prove beneficial (*Manu* 3.56). On balance, however, the negative statements outweigh the positive ones. Perhaps the most famous of his pronouncements on women is the following:

> By a girl, by a young woman or even by an aged one, nothing must be done independently, even in her own house. In childhood a female must be subject to her father, in youth to her husband, when her lord is dead, to her sons; a woman must never be independent (*Manu* 5.147–8).

Statements like this one, and the weight given to them by later commentators, did much to influence Western notions of Hindu women. As influential as Manu has been in some communities and at certain times, however, his views cannot be considered prescriptive or normative. Women in the Vedic age composed hymns and took part in philosophical debates. In fact, Manu's dictates were not necessarily followed. Medieval women were more than dutiful wives. As we have seen, women composed poetry, endowed temples, gave religious advice and wrote scholarly works, including commentary on scripture. Far from being ostracized or condemned, those women were respected, honoured, and in some cases even venerated. Despite Manu and his successors, many women of the upper socio-economic groups enjoyed both religious and financial independence and made substantial contributions to literature and the fine arts.

Some of the contradictions in Hindu thinking about women can be traced to the concept of auspiciousness. Auspiciousness refers primarily to prosperity in this life—prosperity being associated above all with wealth and progeny. Thus cattle, elephants, kings, and married women with the potential to bear children are all said to be auspicious, as are birth and marriage rituals, because they are associated with the promotion of three human goals recognized by classical scriptures: dharma (duty), *artha* (prosperity), and *kama* (sensual pleasure). There is also a second level of auspiciousness, however, that is related to the fourth and ultimate human goal: *moksha* (liberation). The two levels of auspiciousness have been implicit in Hindu religious literature and rituals. In many contexts, women have auspiciousness in different degrees, which determine the levels of their acceptance.

In the classical literature of the *dharmashastras* and in practice, it is auspicious to be married because it is only in marriage that one can fulfil one's dharmic obligations. The ideal is the *sumangali*, the married woman who is a full partner in dharma, *artha*, and *kama*, through whom children are born, and through whom wealth and religious merit are accumulated. Only a married woman may be called *Srimat* (the one with *sri* or auspiciousness) or *griha-Lakshmi* (the goddess of the house). She is the most honoured woman in Hindu society, especially if she bears children, and after death, her body is adorned for the funeral rites. Traditionally, a Hindu wife's dharma included not only total obedience and loyalty to her husband in life but fidelity to his memory after his death. Some of these notions are still adhered to in Hindu life. A wife may occasionally be abandoned, but social pressures make it difficult if not impossible for a woman to leave her husband.

These traditional attitudes were reflected in literature and the media as late as the 1970s. For example, when *A Doll's House*, by the Norwegian playwright Henrik Ibsen (1828–1906), was adapted in the western Indian regional language of Marathi, the ending was altered. In the original version, the heroine Nora becomes convinced that her husband is not worthy of her love and leaves him to build an independent life. But the Marathi adaptation allows the Indian version of Nora no opportunity for unchaste behaviour: after leaving her husband, she goes to live with his parents and serve them dutifully.

In the *Puranas*, which reflect codes of conduct dating back two thousand years, the dharma of a faithful wife was to worship and serve her husband as god. The ideal wife, according to a line from the *Padma Purana* (probably written after the eleventh century), would combine the qualities of a slave in service to her husband, a harlot in love, a mother in offering him nourishment, and a counsellor in times of need.

It is paradoxical but consistent with the Hindu value system that the truly faithful wife, having surrendered all power over her own life to her husband, was said to gain virtually limitless power—power so great as to burn up the world and stop the motion of the sun and the moon. The *Puranas* and the oral tradition contain many stories about the power of such women to save lives and even perform miracles. In the first century, Manu himself seems to recognize the necessity of treating women with due respect:

Where women are honoured, there the gods are pleased; but where they are not honoured, no sacred rite yields rewards. Where the female relations live in grief, the family soon perishes; but that family where they are not unhappy ever prospers. The houses on which female relations, not being duly honoured, pronounce a curse, perish completely, as if destroyed by magic (*Manu* 3.56–8).

The virtuous dead are also believed to have significant power. As we have seen, married women regularly perform rituals in honour of the family's dead *sumangalis*. A *sumangali* ancestor retains the power to influence the well-being of the family. When propitiated, she radiates auspiciousness; when offended, she has the power to curse. In this context she is held to be almost more powerful, morally, than the man; she is as worthy of worship as her husband.

In traditional Hindu society, courtesans usually came from certain castes and families. In some communities, women were ritually dedicated to a temple and married to its deity. Such a woman became a *devadasi* ('servant of the god'). Since the deity is immortal, she could never be widowed. Rather, she was continually 'wedded' through her sexual liaisons and therefore was said to be continually, eternally auspicious (*nitya sumangali*). In principle her presence anywhere, at any time, was auspicious. In practice, however, such women have generally been treated as prostitutes and ostracized from mainstream society.

'Public' prostitutes were distinguished, at least in theory, from temple prostitutes. As a profession, prostitution was certainly established by the fourth century BCE. In a chapter called 'The Superintendent of Prostitutes', Chankaya (c. fourth century BCE?) in his famous book *Arthasastra,* clearly outlined the duties of, and taxation procedures for, prostitutes. In the beginning of the Common Era, the *Kama Sutra* described in detail the complex art of the woman about town. Even the *Mahabharata* includes references to prostitution.

All these texts refer to the woman's duties to a king, his guests, and his retinue. If a prostitute receives the money and then defaults, the fine is eight times the amount paid by her client. Her taxes are two days' wages per month. A prostitute who kills her lover is to be thrown to the dogs. A king must pay a monthly maintenance stipend not only to retired courtesans themselves but also to their instructors in the many arts of the refined prostitute. A total of sixty-four arts are listed, including art,

arithmetic, carpentry, logic, magic, mimicry, music, poetry, and swordplay. In addition, kings are advised that prostitutes can render useful service by spying and extracting information from other spies.

With a definite place and role in society, prostitutes had their own dharma. In prostitution as in every area of Hindu life, one who performed her dharma scrupulously was thought to acquire great powers. In one story, the celebrated king Ashoka (c. third century BCE) asks whether anyone can make the river Ganga flow upstream. When a courtesan accepts the challenge and succeeds, the king asks her how she was able to accomplish this miracle. The prostitute answers that she treats all her clients equally, regardless of caste. To serve them is her act of truth or dharma, and fulfilling it gives her extraordinary power. Other stories, however, depict prostitutes in an unfavourable light, and women from the so-called higher classes were instructed never to go near them.

### Adulteresses

Before the time of Manu female infidelity was considered regrettable but was not absolutely condemned. Once an adulteress had performed the prescribed penances and purification rituals, she was allowed to resume a reasonably normal life; her menstrual cycle erased her lapses.

From roughly the first century onward, however, an unfaithful wife was considered worse than a prostitute. According to Manu, a wife who is disloyal to her husband 'is censured among men, and (in her next life) is reborn in the womb of a jackal and tormented by diseases, the punishment of her sin'. In literature, there have been stories as in the popular short-story collection called *Vetalapanchavimshati* (c. eighth century CE) about unfaithful wives, but they have been forgotten, and the adulteress has never become a cultural archetype. The only possible exception to this rule is Radha, who—according to some sacred texts—was married but left her husband for Krishna. In Radha's case, renunciation of the marriage vow is interpreted as symbolizing the depth of her love

Krishna (known locally as Shyamasundara, 'the dark handsome one') and Radha are the presiding deities of the New Raman Reti temple in Alachua, Florida (Vasudha Narayanan).

The common blessing for a woman, 'May your husband live long' is self explanatory. Although the strict code of conduct prescribed for widows is no longer operative in its most restrictive and oppressive aspects, there are certain disabilities associated with widowhood. She is debarred from active participation in auspicious occasions. Besides the items of decoration associated with the married state, she is expected to discard colourful clothes, glass bangles, wearing of flowers, and attractive jewellery. Plain white colour is associated with widowhood, and by implication is forbidden traditionally for Sumangali, i.e., one whose husband is alive. The widows of Bengal, who abstain from fish, the Kammas and Reddy widows of Andhra Pradesh who give up meat are not yet extinct. Among the Brahmin and also among such non-Brahmin communities who do not have the custom of widow remarriage, there are a number of ways for restricting the life of a widow so that she gets little pleasure out of life and her natural desires are suppressed.

for Krishna, and she is seen as representing an ideal human soul, one who is ready to renounce everything to be with the lord. In short, Radha's action is interpreted in a spiritual rather than a social context.

## Widows

Widows have traditionally been considered inauspicious, bad omens for anyone who encounters them. In some Indian languages, the word for 'widow' is a term of abuse, and even in educated, reform-oriented circles, vestiges of this attitude remain. Even today, widows may be visually differentiated from other women in society. In many communities, they remove the ornamental mark or *tilaka* that unmarried girls and married women wear on their foreheads, and until the mid-twentieth century, brahmin widows in South India underwent tonsure (shaving of the head).

The position of widows in the twentieth century is summed up in *Toward Equality: Report of the Committee on the Status of Women in India*, an official publication of the government's Ministry of Education and Social Welfare (1974):

Significantly, the report concludes the above passage by stating, 'A distinct contrast between the status of a widow and a Sumangali (an ideally auspicious woman) is characteristic of India as a whole.'

The status of widows, like that of adulteresses, was not nearly so low before the beginning of the Common Era. In some cases, a widow was allowed to remarry; or if she was childless, a brother-in-law was appointed by the family to have relations with her until she gave birth to a son. The fourth-century BCE *Arthasastra* outlines a number of courses a widow could take, and recommends special financial bonuses if she remained true to her husband's memory. Over time, however, the status of widows deteriorated. Eventually, in-heritance rights were denied to sons fathered by brothers-in-law, and by the time of Manu absolute chastity was recommended for widows.

*Sati* (often spelled 'suttee' in the West) was for some centuries a way for a widow to retain her honoured status as a *sumangali*. The practice was outlawed as homicide by the British in 1829, but it has continued to resurface from time to time. In 1987, for instance, a woman named Roop Kanwar committed *sati* in front of hundreds of witnesses.

The so-called higher castes were considered the trend-setters regarding suicide and attitudes to widows in general. Brahmin women did not gen-erally practise *sati*, but after the fourteenth century (especially in northern India), widows of the ksha-triya caste made it a point of honour to die with their husbands. Though there were no injunctions for women in other castes to commit *sati* or dis-figure themselves in any way, they adopted those practices to imitate the 'higher' classes. Thus even though women of the 'lower' castes have tradition-ally been seen as enjoying somewhat more free-dom than their upper-caste counterparts, this was not always the case in practice.

Mothers, especially those with sons, were an important exception to the ill-treatment meted out to widows. We see this attitude reflected in scriptural texts such as the *Skanda Purana*: 'except-ing one's widowed mother, all widows are void of auspiciousness' (*Skanda Purana* III, ch. 7, 50–1). A mother, whatever her faults, should never be abandoned by her son. Even Manu says that the mother is 'a thousand times' more important than the father (*Manu* II.145).

Efforts to improve the lot of widows have been ongoing since the 1829 proscription of *sati* and the 1856 legalization of remarriage by widows. One notable activist was Pandita Ramabai (1858–1922),

a brahmin who converted to Christianity after her husband's death and became an important social reformer. Another was Mrs Subbalakshmi (1886–1969; known as 'Sister Subbalakshmi' in Tamilnadu). Married at the age of eleven, she was widowed shortly thereafter but had the good for-tune to come from a progressive family: her par-ents allowed her to continue her education, and in the first half of the twentieth century she worked hard for the education of widows.

### Women and Pollution

With a few exceptions (among them the Vira Shaiva), most Hindu communities have tradition-ally regarded menstruation as physically polluting. Menstruating women were excluded from every-day life, and even though strict segregation is no longer widespread, vestiges of the old attitudes remain. Frequently, menstruating women are prohibited from cooking and most communities still do not permit menstruating women to attend a place of worship or participate in any religious ritual, and even Vira Shaiva households may pro-hibit menstruating women from cooking. Virtually all Hindu women take a purifying ritual bath on the fourth day.

The same concept of pollution extends to child-birth. Even though the birth of a child is a happy and auspicious occasion, it is thought to render the entire family ritually impure. For several days after the birth, the family cannot go to a temple or celebrate an auspicious event, and the mother, who may bleed for up to six weeks after giving birth, is treated as if she were menstruating.

# 🌿 INTERACTION AND ADAPTATION

## Religious Leaders

For more than 20,000 years Hindus have vener-ated holy men and women. The *Taittiriya Upani-shad* exhorts a departing student to consider his *acharya* (religious instructor) as a god, and there have been countless other gurus, ascetics, mediums, storytellers, and **sadhus** ('holy men') who have commanded anything from obedience to veneration. It would not be an exaggeration to say that for many Hindus, the primary religious experience is mediated by someone they believe to be in some way divine.

This is no less true of modern times than of the ancient past. Followers of Sri Sathya Sai Baba (Sathya Narayan Raju, b. 1926), a charismatic teacher from Andhra Pradesh in the south, believe him to be an *avatara*. The heads of three monasteries established by the philosopher Shankara in the eighth century continue to exercise considerable influence among educated urban people, as do a number of intellectual Vedantic commentators. In their interpretation of the ancient scriptures and their mediation of traditional values, we see the dynamic and adaptable nature of the Hindu tradition.

All *acharyas* are gurus, but not all gurus are *acharyas*. Most *acharyas* belong to specific lineage and teach a particular sectarian tradition. Gurus, by contrast, are not necessarily connected to any particular tradition, and they tend to emphasize more 'universal' and humanist messages, stressing the divinity in all human beings and encouraging their followers to transcend caste and community distinctions. Another difference is that *acharyas* are almost invariably male, while many women have been gurus. An example is Ma Amritananda Mayi ('Ammachi'), the leader of a movement that sponsors an international network of charitable, humanitarian, educational, and medical institutions. Known as the 'hugging guru', she is one of the most popular religious leaders in the world today.

Many charismatic teachers are called *swami* ('master') by their followers. Others take their titles from the ancient Vedic 'seers' known as *rishis*. An example is the founder of the Transcendental Meditation movement, popularly known in the west as TM. Maharishi ('great seer') Mahesh Yogi

(1911?–2008) is probably one of the most influential teachers in the Western world.

Mohandas Karamchand Gandhi (1869–1948) is best known for his successful use of non-violent protest in the campaign to gain India's independence from British colonial rule. The title 'Mahatma' ('great soul') was given to him by Rabindranath Tagore, India's famed poet and Nobel laureate.

Born in coastal Gujarat and trained as a barrister in England, Gandhi practised law in South Africa from 1893 to 1915. It was there, in response to the racial discrimination faced by the Indian minority, that he began experimenting with civil disobedience and passive resistance as vehicles for protest. After his return to India, where he became the leader of the Indian National Congress in 1921, he combined the techniques he had developed in South Africa with practices drawn from India's Hindu and Jaina religious traditions and applied them to the campaign for India's freedom.

In particular, Gandhi emphasized the principle of non-violence (*ahimsa*) and developed a strategy of non-violent resistance called *satyagraha* ('truth-force'). Also borrowed from religious observances was his practice of fasting, which he used both as a means of 'self-purification' and as a psychological weapon. Gandhi's fasts drew attention to social injustices and the atrocities perpetuated by the British authorities. Faced with brutality, he refused to retaliate, saying that 'An eye for an eye makes the world blind.' Another major influence was the *Bhagavad Gita*, which he first became acquainted with as a student in England and understood as an allegory of the conflict between good and evil within human beings. It remained his guide throughout his life.

In addition to his political work, Gandhi promoted social reform, especially with respect to the notion of 'untouchability'. He gave the generic name 'Harijan' ('children of God') to the outcaste communities. Although the latter today reject the name as patronizing, it drew attention to discriminatory practices within Hindu society.

Less successful were Gandhi's efforts to promote peace between Muslims and Hindus in the context of the achievement of independence in August 1947. For Gandhi, the violence that accompanied the partitioning of the subcontinent represented a major failure. Within a few months, on 30 January 1948, he was assassinated by a Hindu incensed by what he perceived to be Gandhi's championing of Muslim causes. Since then, Gandhi's influence has made itself felt in many parts of the world, but perhaps most notably in the US movement for civil rights under the leadership of Martin Luther King, Jr.

## Hinduism and the Environment

The history of environmental activism in India is sometimes traced as far back as the late fifteenth century, when a guru named Jambho-ji—inspired by the pastoral life of Krishna the cowherd—taught his followers to minimize harm to the natural world. The community he established took the name Bishnoi, after the twenty-nine ('bish-noi') most important of his teachings, which included everything from vegetarianism to water conservation and the protection of trees. Based in Rajasthan, the Bishnoi have continued to follow those teachings for more than five hundred years.

Environmental responsibility is by no means confined to the Bishnoi, however. Today, growing numbers of Hindu leaders and institutions are drawing on the classic texts to encourage eco-activism. Visitors to the Venkateshwara temple in Tirumala-Tirupati, for instance, are greeted by billboards proclaiming *vriksho rakshati: rakshatah* ('Trees, when protected, protect us'), and the temple authorities have emphasized a line from the *Matsya Purana* in which the goddess Parvati declares that 'One tree is equal to ten sons.' In a culture where sons are so highly prized, the force of this statement is striking.

The Tirumala-Tirupati temple has also established a large nursery on the surrounding hills. In addition to plants of many varieties, the temple grows tree saplings, which pilgrims are given as

*prasada* and are encouraged to plant at home. Apart from this consciousness-raising venture, the temple invites pilgrims to offer donations for the purchase and planting of trees and plants. Donors are honoured with a special *darshana* (viewing of the deity) in the inner shrine, and their names are displayed on the trees they pay for.

Religious teachers and institutions retrieve and re-envision the meaning of the Vedas by emphasizing the sections that speak of peace and harmony. The *Song of Peace* (*shanti path*), for example, composed more than three millennia ago, has become a source of inspiration for environmental activists:

> May there be peace in the skies, peace in the atmosphere, peace on earth, peace in the waters. May the healing plants and trees bring peace; may there be peace [on and from] the world, the deity. May there be peace in the world, peace on peace. May that peace come to me! (*Yajur Veda* 36.17).

## Modern Reproductive Technology

Of all the technological innovations developed in recent years, those associated with reproduction tend to be among the most controversial. Yet Hindus appear on the whole to be quite accepting of intervention in this area. In the case of assisted reproduction, this acceptance is probably not surprising: the traditional teachings on dharma have always emphasized that reproduction is a primary duty. Thus many Hindus today accept artificial insemination, for example, although the husband is generally the only acceptable donor. In particular, members of the 'higher' castes, which set great store by their lineage, are more likely to seek technological help than to adopt a child of unknown background.

In fact, many stories about supernatural or 'unnatural' means of conception and childbirth can be found in the classic literature. In the *Mahabharata*, a queen named Gandhari grows one hundred sons in brass jars. In other texts, an embryo is transplanted from one woman to another, Krishna's brother Balarama is transplanted into another womb, and deities are invoked to 'fertilize' women whose husbands cannot procreate.

The ethical considerations become more complex where issues such as contraception and gender selection are concerned. For thousands of years, male children were more welcome than females, largely because of the traditional duty to the ancestors: in a patriarchal, patrilineal society, sons would continue the family line and could be counted on to look after their parents in old age, whereas daughters would be of benefit only to their husbands' families. Indeed, the cost of providing a dowry for a daughter represented a significant financial burden for many families.

Today sonograms and amniocentesis are often used for the express purpose of ascertaining the sex of the fetus early in pregnancy, so that female fetuses can be aborted. As a result, the numbers of female births have dropped dramatically in recent years.

The *dharmashastra* texts maintain that the unborn fetus has life; according to popular belief and stories from the *Puranas*, it is even capable of hearing and learning from the conversations that take place around it. Nevertheless, abortions are legal in India and are accepted without any strong dissent from religious leaders or prolonged editorial, legislative, or judicial debate.

Thus it appears that the dharma texts do not have the compelling authority for Hindus today that their counterparts in some other religious traditions do for their adherents.

## The Hindu Diaspora

When the first brahmins crossed the seas to Cambodia and Indonesia, early in the first millennium CE, it was not long before they began building temples. The process of emigration has continued. Since the 1970s Hindu immigrants have been transforming their new homes in North America into sacred places.

Places of worship were established as early as 1906 in the San Francisco area, but the first really ambitious attempt to reproduce the traditional architecture and atmosphere of a Vaishnava sacred place was the Sri Venkateshwara temple in Penn Hills, a suburb of Pittsburgh, Pennsylvania, built in 1976. The Penn Hills temple enshrines a manifestation of Vishnu as Venkateshwara, lord of the hill known as Venkata ('that which can burn sins') in the South Indian state of Andra Pradesh. (Other Venkateshwara temples have been established in California, Illinois, and Georgia.) The Penn Hills temple was built with the help, backing, and blessing of one of the oldest, richest, and most popular temples in India, the Venkateshwara temple at Tiru Venkatam.

Despite devotees' desire to maintain sacred traditions and remain faithful to the architectural forms common in India, some compromises and innovations have been necessary. As far as possible, for example, the ritual calendar has been adapted to fit the American secular calendar, since many festival organizers live far from the temple and long weekends are often the only time they can travel. Nevertheless, the land on which the temple is located is considered no less sacred than the land in India where Tiru Venkatam stands. The devotees celebrate the significance of having Venkateshwara dwelling on American soil with his consort Sri (known locally as 'the lady of the lotus' or Padmavati). In a popular song that was recorded and sold to temple visitors in the 1980s, the following verse is sung in Sanskrit:

> Victory to Govinda [Krishna], who lives in
>   America,
> Victory to Govinda, who is united with
>   Radha who lives on Penn Hills,
> Victory to the Teacher, Victory to Krishna.

The idea that the Penn Hills temple is located on sacred land is not merely abstract. Devotees see the entire Pittsburgh area as geographically similar to the sacred land of India. Drawing on Puranic lore, the Penn Hills devotees see their temple's physical location—at the confluence of three rivers, one of them subterranean—as recalling the sacred place in India where the rivers Ganga and Yamuna meet the underground Sarasvati. As they described it in 1986:

> Pittsburgh, endowed with hills and a multitude of trees as well as the confluence of the three rivers, namely, the Allegheny, the Monongehela, and the subterranean river (brought up via the 60 foot high fountain at downtown) to form the Ohio river is indeed a perfect choice for building the first and most authentic temple to house Lord Venkateshwara. The evergrowing crowds that have been coming to *the city with the thriveni Sangama* [confluence of three rivers] to worship at the Temple with the *three vimanas* reassure our belief that the venerable Gods chose this place and the emerald green hillock to reside in.

The concept of sacred land is not unique to the Penn Hills devotees. Republicans from the Hindu community in the Dallas–Fort Worth area understand the notion of *karmabhumi*—the land where actions bear fruit, where actions produce merit or demerit—in a far broader sense than the authors of the *dharmashastras* intended. An 'Asian Indian Caucus Booklet' circulated by a small group of Hindus at the Republican party convention in Dallas in 1984 underlines the importance of sacred land to many Hindus. Reporting on the convention, the writer V.S. Naipaul quoted from the booklet:

> Indians immigrated to the USA to pursue their 'DREAM' to achieve fully their potentials in this land of 'Opportunities'. They came in pursuit of their dreams, visions, happiness and to achieve excellence. . . . During the last few years most of the people have changed from 'Green card holder' status to that of 'US CITIZENS', thus enabling

themselves to be full participants in socio-economic and political processes. They have chosen, by their free will, the USA as the 'KARMABHUMI'—the land of karma or action.

That a place outside India could be the *karmabhumi* is a new idea in Hinduism. According to the lawmakers, the land of the Aryas where the black antelope roams was the only land that could be called *karmabhumi*. Apparently some Hindus in America have extended the concept to the big-sky rangeland where the deer and the antelope play.

### Miracles and Temple-Building

Statues of Venkateshwara and his consorts were carved in India, then brought to the United States, and consecration rituals were performed at Penn Hills. Although the establishment of the temple was almost a miracle in itself, given the bureaucratic red tape involved, the temple does not have an origin myth. Other temples in America do, however. An origin myth involves a dream or vision, or the 'discovery' of the form of the deity in natural formations such as mountains or caves.

Generally these origin myths are associated with Shaiva temples, especially if there is a strong connection with American devotees. Thus the Light of Truth Universal Shrine temple at Yogaville, Virginia, was established in response to a vision experienced by Swami Satchidananda (b. 1919) of the Divine Life Mission. Overlooking the temple is a mountain called Kailas, after the traditional abode of Shiva. The Iraivan/Kadavul temple on Kauai, Hawaii, was built in 1970 by Swami Shivaya Subramuniyaswami (1927–2001), who was born in the United States and initiated in Sri Lanka. In 1975 he had three visions of Shiva walking in the meadows near the Wailua River. Twelve years later, a rare Shiva *linga*, a six-sided quartz crystal, was discovered and taken to Kauai from Arkansas. A new Iraivan temple is now being built of stone carved in Bangalore and shipped to Hawaii. It is expected to last for a thousand and one years.

Perhaps the most unusual temple with mythic origins is the one at Wahiawa (Oahu), Hawaii, now run entirely by Hindus from India. This temple is dedicated to Visvanatha (translated as 'lord of the universe'), and the organization in charge of it is called the Lord of the Universe Society. The Shiva *linga* at the Wahiawa temple, said to be a healing stone, is believed to be the embodiment of the Hawaiian god Lono, a priest-healer of ancient times whom the Hindus believe to be a manifestation of Shiva. According to another myth, this stone represents two sisters from Kauai who are turned into rocks. Classic hierophany (manifestation of the divine) is seen in this statement issued by the society:

> The Sacred Healing Stone has been discovered and rediscovered. Several people have experienced healings, visions, dreams and profound feeling of peace and well-being after coming into contact with the Healing Stone and its powers. . . . [In] March 1988, some Indians were taken to the Healing Stone by their friends and they were awe-stricken by the resemblance of the Sacred Healing Stone to Lord Shiva in the form of a Shiva Lingam. . . . In April 1988 a special Pooja was organized. It became apparent to those who attended the Pooja that this place was indeed special, sacred and holy (Sengupta n.d.).

When overseas Hindu communities build a temple, they gain a local place of worship with formally consecrated icons, where sacraments can be conducted and offerings of devotion made. They also establish an institution that will educate the younger American-born generation through weekly language and religion classes, frequent lectures, sponsorship of classical music and dance (which have a broad religious base in India), summer camps, and an outreach bulletin.

New temples are springing up all over the North American landscape. In many cases the community hall is built even before the shrine. This emphasis on community life is understandable at a time when Hindus are trying to assert their identity in a society where they feel culturally and linguistically marginalized. The community hall is a place where different groups can meet for classes in language, music, and dance.

Significantly, disputes arise within the North American community over which deity is to be enshrined and what mode of worship is to be adopted. Devotees of Vishnu, Shiva, the Goddess, or Ganesha, or those who worship Vishnu as Rama or Krishna, want the temple to be primarily dedicated to that deity. In this way a temple intended to unite the Hindu community in the diaspora frequently gives rise to division. The reason is clear: as we noted at the outset, Hinduism is not a unitary tradition. It is not a single identity, and it lacks a united community and central authority. Because of its diversity, reaching consensus is almost impossible. Lines are drawn along sectarian, caste, and regional lines, and debates continue as they have throughout history.

# CONCLUSION: THE FUTURE OF HINDUISM

As the communities in the diaspora face the challenges of raising a new generation in the faith, Hindus in many parts of the world are actively working to define Hinduism. Many of the statements made in the context of self-definition are questionable and may not be historically true. Examples include statements such as 'Hinduism is not a religion, it is a way of life,' or 'Hinduism is a tolerant religion.' The difficulty of proving or disproving such claims only underscores the complexities of a religious tradition that has evolved through more than three thousand years of recorded history—five thousand if the Harappa culture is included.

The dynamism of the many Hindu traditions is unmistakable. Vedanta is continually being interpreted. People continue to experience possession by deities, to situate their homes in auspicious directions, and to choose religiously correct times for happy events. Temples continue to be built, consecrated, and preserved. The sacred words of the Vedas and the *smrti* literature are still broadcast widely. Manuscripts are being restored, edited, and published, and new technologies are making the literature more widely accessible; the tradition confining the sacred word to particular castes is gone forever. The airwaves are flooded with religious programs, horoscopes are cast and matched by computer, surgeries are scheduled for auspicious times. In short, Hinduism continues to adapt to changing times and different lands.

## Sites

Almost every village has a locally important temple, and countless hills, mountains, rivers, and groves are considered sacred. The following list is only a very small sample.

**Badrinath, Uttaranchal** An important pilgrimage site, high in the mountains, with a temple of Vishnu in the form of the sages Nara and Narayana; one of 108 sacred places for the Sri Vaishnava community.

**Chidambaram, Tamilnadu** The abode of Nataraja, the Dancing Shiva, a large temple complex with shrines to both Shiva and Vishnu.

**Guruvayur, Kerala** This temple dedicated to the youthful Krishna draws millions of pilgrims every year.

**Haridwar, Uttaranchal** One of seven holy sites identified in the *Puranas*. Located on the banks of the river Ganga, it is one of the cities where a great festival called Kumbha Mela is held.

**Kamakhya, Assam** One of the most important Shakti *peethas* (sites where the power of the Goddess is said to be palpably felt). The temple is dedicated to the goddess Kamakhya, a form of Shakti/Parvati/Durga.

**Kanchipuram, Tamilnadu** A temple town important for at least two millennia, home to dozens of temples dedicated to Vishnu and Shiva.

**Kanya Kumari, Tamilnadu** A small temple town at the southernmost tip of the Indian peninsula, famous for its temple dedicated to Parvati.

**Madurai, Tamilnadu** A large city, important for more than two thousand years and home to dozens of temples including a famous complex dedicated to the goddess Meenakshi (a form of Parvati) and the god Sundaresvara (Shiva).

**Mathura and Brindavan, Uttar Pradesh** A city and a complex of pastoral and urban pilgrimage sites nearby, all associated with incidents in the early life of Krishna.

*Continued*

**Mount Kailas** An important peak in the Himalayan range, said to be the abode of Lord Shiva.

**Nathdwara, Rajasthan** Home of a celebrated temple to Krishna in the form of Srinathji, in which legend says he lifted up the mountain Govardhana. Located near Udaipur.

**Pandharpur, Maharashtra** Home of a temple to Vithoba or Vitthala (a form of Vishnu) and Rukmini (Lakshmi).

**Prayag, Uttar Pradesh** The holy site where the Ganga and Yamuna rivers are said to come together with a legendary subterranean river called Saraswati.

**Puri, Orissa** Site of a temple dedicated to Jagannath (a form of Vishnu), his brother Balabhadra, and their sister, Subhadra. Also the site of a famous festival (Ratha Yatra) in which Lord Jagannath (the origin of the English word 'juggernaut') is taken through the streets on a huge chariot.

**Sabarimala, Kerala** A temple to Ayyappan, set in the hills of Kerala and site of an important pilgrimage where millions of pilgrims, almost all male, congregate every January. Women are ordinarily forbidden to make the pilgrimage.

**Srirangam, Tamilnadu** An island temple-town in the Kaveri river, where Vishnu, here called Ranganatha ('Lord of the stage'), reclines on the serpent Ananta ('infinity'); one of the most important pilgrimage sites for the followers of Vishnu, celebrated in the poems of the Alvars.

**Tirumala-Tirupati** (also known as **Tiruvenkatam**), **Andhra Pradesh** Probably one of the most important pilgrimage sites in India. The temple, located on seven hills, is dedicated to Venkateshwara (Vishnu) and is said to be the richest religious institution in the world next to the Vatican.

**Vaishno Devi, Jammu and Kashmir** Located at an elevation of more than 1,580 metres, this temple is dedicated to the Goddess Vaishno Devi, who is sometimes perceived as a form of Durga and sometimes as an amalgamation of all the major goddesses.

**Varanasi, Uttar Pradesh** Also known as Kasi or Banaras; one of the holiest cities in India, located on the banks of the river Ganga. After cremation, many Hindus' ashes are brought here to be ritually submerged in the waters.

# Glossary

**acharya**  The leading teacher of a sect or the head of a monastery.

**advaita**  Shankara's school of philosophy, which holds that there is only one ultimate reality, the indescribable Brahman, with which the Atman or self is identical.

**Alvars**  Twelve devotional poets in South India whose works are central to the *bhakti* tradition.

**artha**  Wealth and power; one of the three classical aims in life.

**ashramas**  Four stages in the life of an upper-class male: student, householder, forest-dweller, and ascetic.

**Atman**  The individual self, held by Upanishadic and Vedantic thought to be identical with Brahman, the world-soul.

**avatara**  A 'descent' or incarnation of a deity in earthly form.

**Ayurveda**  A system of traditional medicine, understood as a teaching transmitted from the sages.

**Bhagavad Gita**  A section of the *Mahabharata* epic recounting a conversation between Krishna and the warrior Arjuna, in which Krishna explains the nature of God and the human soul.

**bhakti**  Loving devotion to a deity seen as a gracious being who enters the world for the benefit of humans.

**Brahma**  A creator god; not to be confused with Brahman.

**Brahman**  The world-soul, sometimes understood in impersonal terms.

**Brahmanas**  Texts regarding ritual.

**brahmin**  A member of the priestly class.

**darshana**  Seeing and being seen by the deity in the temple or by a holy teacher; the experience of beholding with faith.

**Deepavali**  (Divali) Festival of light in October–November, when lamps are lit.

**devanagari**  The alphabet used to write Sanskrit and northern Indian vernacular languages such as Hindi and Bengali.

**dharma**  Religious and social duty, including both righteousness and faith.

**guru**  A spiritual teacher.

**Holi**  Spring festival celebrated by throwing brightly coloured water or powder.

**jnana**  Knowledge; along with action and devotion, one of the three avenues to liberation explained in the *Bhagavad Gita*.

**kama**  Sensual (not merely sexual) pleasure; one of the three classical aims of life.

**karma**  Action, good and bad, as it is believed to determine the quality of rebirth in future lives.

**kshatriya**  A member of the warrior class in ancient Hindu society.

**linga**  A conical or cylindrical stone column, sometimes considered phallic, symbolic of the god Shiva.

**Mahabharata**  A very long epic poem, one section of which is the *Bhagavad Gita*.

**mantra**  An expression of one or more syllables, chanted repeatedly as a focus of concentration in devotion.

**moksha**  Liberation from the cycle of birth and death; one of the three classical aims in life.

**murti**  A form or personification in which divinity is manifested.

**Navaratri**  'Nine nights'; an autumn festival honouring the Goddess.

**om**  A syllable chanted in meditation, interpreted as representing ultimate reality, or the universe, or the relationship of the devotee to the deity.

**prasada**  A gift from the deity, especially food that has been presented to the god's temple image, blessed, and returned to the devotee.

**puja**  Ritual household worship of the deity, commonly involving oil lamps, incense, prayers, and food offerings.

**Puranas**  'Old tales', stories about deities that became important after the Vedic period.

**Ramayana**  An epic recounting the life of Lord Rama, an incarnation of the god Vishnu.

**rishi**  A seer; the composers of the ancient Vedic hymns are viewed as *rishis*.

**sadhu**  A holy man.

**samnyasin**  A religious ascetic; one who has reached the fourth of the classical stages of life for Hindu males after student, householder, and forest-dweller.

**samsara**  The continuing cycle of rebirths.

**sati**  The self-sacrifice of a widow who throws herself onto her deceased husband's funeral pyre.

**shruti**  'What is heard'; the sacred literature of the Vedic and Upanishadic periods, recited orally by the brahmin priests for many centuries before being written down.

**shudra**  A member of the lowest of the four major classes, usually translated as 'servant', though some groups within the *shudra* class could be quite prosperous.

**smrti**  'What is remembered', a body of ancient Hindu literature, including the epics, *Puranas*, and law codes, formed after the *shruti* and passed down in written tradition.

**tantra**    An esoteric school outside the Vedic and brahminical tradition, which emerged around the fifth century and centred on a number of controversial ritual practices, some of them sexual.

*tilaka*    A dot or mark on the forehead made with coloured powder.

*upanayana*    The initiation of a young brahmin boy into ritual responsibility, in which he is given a cord to wear over his left shoulder and a mantra to recite and is sent to beg for food for the day.

*Upanishads*    Philosophical texts in the form of reported conversations on the theory of the Vedic ritual and the nature of knowledge, composed around the sixth century BCE.

**vaishya**    A member of the third or mercantile class in the ancient fourfold class structure.

**Vedas**    The four collections of hymns and ritual texts that constitute the oldest and most highly respected Hindu sacred literature.

**yoga**    A practice and discipline that may involve a philosophical system and mental concentration as well as physical postures and exercises.

# Further Reading

Baird, Robert D. 1993. *Religions and Law in Independent India*. New Delhi: Manohar. Takes up some problems of the status of various groups.

_____, ed. 1995. *Religion in Modern India*. 3rd ed. New Delhi: Manohar. Good individual chapters on nineteenth- and twentieth-century sectarian movements.

Basham, Arthur Llewellyn. 1954. *The Wonder That Was India*. London: Sidgwick & Jackson. Arguably still the definitive introduction to the pre-Muslim culture of the subcontinent.

Beny, Roloff, and Aubrey Menen. 1969. *India*. London: Thames and Hudson. Menen's text interspersed with Beny's photographs in this coffee-table book provides a lively 60-page introduction to the culture—opinionated and provocative.

Bhattacharji, Sukumari. 1970. *The Indian Theogony: A Comparative Study of Indian Mythology from the Vedas to the* Puranas. Cambridge: Cambridge University Press. Good for tracing the shift from Vedic to other deities as the focus of devotion.

Blurton, T. Richard. 1992. *Hindu Art*. London: British Museum Press; Cambridge: Harvard University Press. A good introductory survey.

Brown, C. Mackenzie. 1990. *The Triumph of the Goddess: The Canonical Models and Theological Visions of the* Devi-Bhagavata Purana. Albany: State University of New York Press. Study of a text important for feminine manifestations of deity.

Bumiller, Elisabeth. 1990. *May You Be the Mother of a Hundred Sons. A Journey among the Women of India*. New York: Random House. Useful insights into Indian society.

Chapple, Christopher, and Mary Evelyn Tucker, eds. 2000. *Hinduism and Ecology: The Intersection of Earth, Sky, and Water*. Cambridge, MA: Center for the Study of World Religions, Harvard Divinity School. Part of an important series in which various traditions address current environmental issues.

Chatfield, Charles, ed. 1976. *The Americanization of Gandhi: Images of the Mahatma*. New York: Garland. Includes American applications of Gandhi's ideas concerning the struggle for racial justice.

de Bary, William Theodore, ed. 1958 *Sources of Indian Tradition*. New York: Columbia University Press. The classic sourcebook: well selected, well introduced.

Dimock, Edward C., Jr., and Denise Levertov, trans. 1967. *In Praise of Krishna: Songs from the Bengali*. Garden City, NY: Doubleday. Lyrical expressions of devotion in eastern India.

Doniger O'Flaherty, Wendy, ed. and trans. 1988. *Textual Sources for the Study of Hinduism*. Manchester: Manchester University Press. A good sourcebook in a rather compressed format, covering the main phases of the Hindu tradition.

Eck, Diana L. 1981. *Darcan: Seeing the Divine Image in India*. Chambersburg, Penn.: Anima Books. Brief but authoritative, on the significance of coming into the presence of the deity.

Embree, Ainslie T., ed. *Sources of Indian Tradition*. 2nd ed. 2 vols. New York: Columbia University Press. 1988. Expands on the de Bary first edition but drops a few items in the process.

Erndl, Kathleen M. 1993. *Victory to the Mother: The Hindu Goddess of Northwest India in Myth, Ritual, and Symbol*. New York: Oxford University Press. Well focused on one region.

Felton, Monica G. 1967. *A Child Widow's Story*. New York: Harcourt, Brace & World. Brings concreteness to description of social situations.

Findly, Ellison B. 1985. 'Gargi at the King's Court: Women and Philosophic Innovation in Ancient India'. In Yvonne Y. Haddad and Ellison B. Findly, eds. *Women, Religion and Social Change*, 37–58. Albany: State University of New York Press. Shows that intellectual activity was not totally limited to males.

Harlan, Lindsey, and Paul B. Courtright, eds. 1995. *From the Margins of Hindu Marriage: Essays on Gender, Religion, and Culture*. New York: Oxford University Press. A useful collection.

Hawley, John S., and Donna M. Wulff. 1982. *The Divine Consort: Radha and the Goddesses of India*. Berkeley: Berkeley Religious Studies Series. Another useful work on feminine aspects of the Hindu tradition.

_____. 1996. *Devi: Goddesses of India*. Berkeley: University of California Press. Expands on the theme of the previous work.

Hiriyanna, Mysore. 1985. *The Essentials of Indian Philosophy*. London: Allen and Unwin. A frequently consulted, accessible introduction.

Jones, Kenneth W. 1976. *Arya Dharm: Hindu Consciousness in 19th-century Punjab*. Berkeley: University of California Press. Describes Dayananda Sarasvati's Arya Samaj and its legacy in modern India.

Kinsley, David. 1986. *Hindu Goddesses: Visions of the Divine Feminine in the Hindu Religious Tradition*. Berkeley: University of California Press. Separate chapters on individual figures.

_____. 1997. *Tantric Visions of the Divine Feminine: The Ten Mahavidyas*. Berkeley: University of California Press. Responsible approach to a controversial topic.

Leslie, Julia, ed. 1991. *Roles and Rituals for Hindu Women*. London: Pinter; Rutherford, NJ: Fairleigh Dickinson University Press. A coherent set of essays on the subject.

Lopez, Donald S., Jr., ed. 1995. *Religions of India in Practice*. Princeton: Princeton University Press. A sourcebook containing a fine range of material; strong on ritual.

Marglin, Frédérique, and John B. Carman, eds. 1985. *Purity and Auspiciousness in Indian Society*. Leiden: E.J. Brill. A useful collection, in an anthropological series.

Michell, George. 1989. *The Penguin Guide to the Monuments of India*. Vol. 1. London: Penguin. Local maps, plans, and descriptions of pre-Mughal Indian temples and other sites.

Miller, Barbara Stoler, trans. 1977. *Love Song of the Dark Lord: Jayadeva's Gitagovinda*. New York: Columbia University Press. An important *bhakti* text.

Narayan, R.K. 1972. *Ramayana: A Shortened Modern Prose Version of the Indian Epic*. New York: Viking. A useful point of access to this classic.

Narayanan, Vasudha. 1994. *The Vernacular Veda: Revelation, Recitation, and Ritual Practice*. Columbia: University of South Carolina Press. The ritual use of the *Tiruvaymoli* among India's scheduled castes as well as brahmins.

_____. 1996. '"One Tree Is Equal to Ten Sons": Hindu Responses to the Problems of Ecology, Population, and Consumption'. *Journal of the American Academy of Religion* 65: 291–332. Discusses some classic resources for addressing concerns of today.

Olivelle, Patrick, trans. 1996. *Upanisads*. New York: Oxford University Press.

———, trans. 1997. *The Pancatantra: The Book of India's Folk Wisdom*. New York: Oxford University Press.

———, trans. 1999. *Dharmasutras: The Law Codes of Atastamba, Gautama, Baudhyayana, and Vasistha*. New York: Oxford University Press. This and the two foregoing items are lucid translations of influential texts.

Orr, Leslie C. 2000. *Donors, Devotees, and Daughters of God: Temple Women in Medieval Tamilnadu*. New York: Oxford University Press. Provides a useful corrective to prescriptive male writings in Sanskrit on Hindu women.

Radhakrishnan, Sarvepalli, and Charles A. Moore, eds. 1957. *A Source Book in Indian Philosophy*. Princeton: Princeton University Press. Still the best anthology for philosophical texts.

Rajagopalachari, Chakravarti. 1953. *Mahabharata*. Bombay: Bharatiya Vidya Bhavan. A sampling from this vast epic.

Ramanujan, A.K., trans. 1981. *Hymns for the Drowning: Poems for Vishnu by Nammawvar*. Princeton: Princeton University Press. An excellent source for Tamil *bhakti*.

Rangacharya, Adya, trans. 1986. *The Natyasastra: English Translation with Critical Notes*. Bangalore: IBH Prakashana. A text frequently considered India's fifth *Veda*, important for the role of the performing arts in modern Hindu tradition.

Renou, Louis. 1964. *Indian Literature*. New York: Walker. One of the best concise introductory surveys.

Richman, Paula, ed. 1991. *Many Ramayanas: The Diversity of a Narrative Tradition in South Asia*. Berkeley: University of California Press. Reflects the importance of the *Ramayana* in vernacular South Asian tradition.

———, ed. 2000. *Questioning Ramayanas: A South Asian Tradition*. Delhi: Oxford University Press.

Roy, Kumkum, ed. 1999. *Women in Early Indian Society*. Delhi: Manohar. A useful collection of articles on both Hindu and Buddhist women.

von Stietencron, Heinrich. 1989. 'Hinduism: On the Proper Use of a Deceptive Term'. In Günther D. Sontheimer and Hermann Kulke, eds. *Hinduism Reconsidered*, 11–27. New Delhi: Manohar. One of the best discussions of the problem of viewing Hinduism as a single 'religion'.

Waghorne, Joanne P., Norman Cutler, and Vasudha Narayanan, eds. 1985. *Gods of Flesh, Gods of Stone: The Embodiment of Divinity in India*. New York: Columbia University Press. Explores a range of forms in which Hindus see deity manifested.

Williams, Raymond Brady, ed. 1992. *A Sacred Thread: Modern Transmission of Hindu Traditions in India and Abroad*. Chambersburg, PA: Anima. A good description of the diaspora in the 1970s and 1980s.

Wujastyk, Dominik, intro. and trans. 1998. *The Roots of Ayurveda: Selections from Sanskrit Medical Writings*. Delhi: Penguin. Useful for the relationship between traditional Indian medicine and religion.

Zimmer, Heinrich. 1946. *Myths and Symbols in Indian Art and Civilization*. New York: Pantheon. A classic study, still often cited.

# Recommended Websites

http://www.sacred-texts.com/hin/index.htm
  Free online translations (mostly late-nineteenth to early-twentieth century) of the Vedas, epics, *Puranas, Yoga Sutras, smrti* literature, etc.

http://www.sscnet.ucla.edu/southasia/
  Very good links for South Asian culture, religions, and history.

http://www.wabashcenter.wabash.edu/resources/result_browse.aspx?topic=569&pid=361
A meta-site with links to many useful resources, including course syllabi.

http://www.columbia.edu/itc/mealac/pritchett/00generallinks/index.html
A good site with links to many resources on South Asia.

http://virtualvillage.wesleyan.edu/
An on-the-ground look at a 'virtual village' in North India.

http://www.veda.harekrsna.cz/encyclopedia/index.htm
Links to articles on various topics in Hinduism from an ISKCON perspective.

http://www.sathyasai.org/
The official site of Sri Sathya Sai Baba, maintained by his devotees.

http://prapatti.com/
Texts and MP3 audios of several Tamil and Sanskrit Vaishnava prayers.

http://www.hindupedia.com/en/Main_Page
An online encyclopedia offering 'a traditional perspective' on the Hindu religion and way of life.

http://www.hinduismtoday.com/
A popular magazine based in Hawaii, rooted in the classical Shaiva tradition, but offering articles of interest to Hindus all over the world.

# References

Carman, John B., and Vasudha Narayanan, trans. 1989. *The Tamil Veda: Pillan's Interpretation of the Tiruvaymoli*. Chicago: University of Chicago Press.

Doniger, Wendy, and Brian K. Smith, trans. 1981. *The Laws of Manu*. London: Penguin.

Doniger O'Flaherty, Wendy, ed. and trans. 1981. *The Rig Veda: An Anthology, One Hundred and Eight Hymns*. Harmondsworth: Penguin.

Hawley, John S., and Mark Juergensmeyer, trans. 1988. *Songs of the Saints of India*. New York: Oxford University Press.

India. Ministry of Education and Social Welfare. 1984. *Toward Equality: Report of the Status of Women in India*. New Delhi: Ministry of Education and Social Welfare.

Jackson, William J., trans. 1991. *Tyagaraja: Life and Lyrics*. Delhi: Oxford University Press.

Kennedy, Melville T. 1925. *The Chaitanya Movement: A Study of the Vaishnavism of Bengal*. Calcutta: Association Press.

Lipski, Alexander. 1977. *Life and Teachings of Sri Anandamayi Ma*. Delhi: Motilal Banarsidass.

Miller, Barbara Stoler, trans. 1986. *The Bhagavad-Gita: Krishna's Counsel in Time of War*. New York: Columbia University Press.

Naipaul, V[idhiadar] S. 1984. 'Among the Republicans'. *New York Review of Books* 31, 16: 5–17.

Nielsen, N.C., et al., eds. 1993. *Religions of the World*. 3rd ed. New York: St Martin's Press.

Radhakrishnan, Sarvepalli, trans. 1953. *The Principal Upanisads*. London: Allen and Unwin.

Sengupta, D. n.d. 'The Historic Healing Stone—L.O.T.U.S.'. Kauai: Lord of the Universe Society.

Tagore, Rabindranath, trans. 1915. *One Hundred Poems of Kabir*. London: Macmillan.

Venkateshwara Temple. 1986. 'Kavachas for the Deities'. Pittsburgh: Venkateshwara Temple.

Chapter **3**

# Sikh
# Traditions

≫ Pashaura Singh ≪

The Punjabi word *Sikh* means 'disciple'. People who identify themselves as Sikhs are disciples of **Akal Purakh** ('Timeless Being', God), the ten Sikh **Gurus**, and the sacred scripture called the **Adi Granth** ('Original Book'). The youngest of India's indigenous religions, Sikhism emerged in the Punjab approximately five centuries ago and quickly distinguished itself from the region's other religious traditions in its doctrines, practices, and orientation—away from ascetic renunciation and towards active engagement with the world.

Today the global Sikh population numbers approximately 25 million, of whom more than 20 million live in India, mainly in the state of Punjab. Sikhs make up only about 2 per cent of the country's one billion people, but their contributions to its political and economic life are significant. The rest of the world's Sikhs are part of a global diaspora that includes substantial communities in Southeast Asia, Australia, New Zealand, East Africa, Britain, and North America, established through successive waves of emigration.

##  ORIGINS

The religious environment of the fifteenth-century Punjab was suffused with the thought of the North Indian **Sants**. The founder of the Sikh tradition, Guru Nanak (1469–1539), shared both the mystic and the iconoclastic tendencies of 'poet-saints' such as Kabir, Ravidas, and Namdev. Nevertheless, Nanak declared his independence from the prevailing thought forms of his day and sought to kindle the fire of independence in his disciples.

The foundation of the tradition he created was his own belief in the possibility of achieving spiritual liberation in a single lifetime through meditation on the divine Name (***nam***) and the living of an ethical life in the world. The interaction of this ideology with two environmental factors—the rural base of Punjabi society and the historical circumstances of the period during which Nanak's successors elaborated on the foundations he laid—determined the historical development of Sikhism.

The name Punjab (literally, 'five waters') refers to the five rivers (Jehlum, Chenab, Ravi, Beas, and Sutlej) that define the region, all of which are tributaries of the Indus. The central Punjab has a rich layer of fertile soil resulting from the changing course of rivers and heavy rainfall. Historically, this region has served as a geographical crossroads where the cultures of the Middle East, Central Asia, and India have interacted in

### The Nath Tradition

The various Nath sects all claimed descent from a semi-legendary yogi named Gorakhnath and all promulgated hatha yoga—a formidably difficult system of physical postures and breath-control—as the means of spiritual liberation. Nath doctrine affirmed that the rigorous practice of hatha-yoga induced a psycho-physical process whereby the spirit could ascend to mystical bliss (*sahaj*). Stressing the irrelevance of caste to spiritual liberation, the folly of sacred languages and scriptures, and the futility of temple worship and pilgrimage, while emphasizing interior devotion, the Nath yogis had a strong influence on the Sant tradition of North India. During the period of Guru Nanak, the Nath yogis were an important force in the religious milieu of the Punjab, and the use of Nath terminology in Guru Nanak's hymns suggests that he engaged in a number of debates with them.

◀ The Golden Temple, illuminated in celebration of Guru Granth Sahib's anniversary (Munish Sharma/Reuters/Landov).

# Timeline

| | |
|---|---|
| **1469** | Birth of Guru Nanak, the founder of the Sikh tradition |
| **1499** | Guru Nanak's mystical experience |
| **1519** | Establishment of the first Sikh community at Kartarpur |
| **1539** | Guru Nanak is succeeded by Guru Angad |
| **1577** | Guru Ram Das establishes the town of Ramdaspur (Amritsar) |
| **1604** | The Adi Granth is compiled under Guru Arjan's supervision |
| **1606** | Guru Arjan's martyrdom by the orders of Emperor Jahangir |
| **1675** | Guru Tegh Bahadur's martyrdom by the orders of Emperor Aurangzeb |
| **1699** | Guru Gobind Singh organizes the Khalsa |
| **1708** | Succession of personal Gurus ends with the death of Guru Gobind Singh; from now on the scripture is the Guru, attaining the title of Guru Granth Sahib |
| **1765** | Sikhs capture Lahore |
| **1799** | Punjab united under Maharaja Ranjit Singh |
| **1849** | Annexation of the Punjab by the British |
| **1865** | Publication of the first printed edition of the Guru Granth Sahib |
| **1873** | Singh Sabha movement is established |
| **1892** | Singh Sabha establishes Khalsa College in Amritsar |
| **1920** | Shiromani Gurdwara Prabandhak Committee (SGPC) is established |
| **1925** | Sikh Gurdwara Act gives the SGPC legal authority over all gurdwaras |
| **1947** | Punjab partitioned between India and Pakistan |
| **1973** | Anandpur Sahib Resolution is passed by the Akali Dal |
| **1984** | Indian army attacks the Golden Temple and other gurdwaras in the Punjab |
| **1999** | Sikhs celebrate the tri-centenary of the Khalsa |
| **2004** | Manmohan Singh is elected the first Sikh prime minister of India |
| **2008** | Tri-centenary celebration of the installation as Guru of the Guru Granth Sahib |

various ways, and through which a series of Muslim invaders—Afghans, Arabs, Iranians, Turks—had made forays into the region since at least the eighth century CE.

Sufi Islam had already become established in the Punjab by the eleventh century, and with the establishment of the Delhi Sultanate, in the thirteenth century, three Sufi orders from Iraq and Persia moved into northern India. By the fifteenth century the Buddhists had disappeared from the Punjab, although a few Jaina ascetics had survived. There were also three distinct Hindu communities devoted to Shiva, Vishnu, and Devi (the Goddess), respectively, along with a cluster of tantra-influenced yogic sects known collectively as the Nath tradition. It is only in the context of this diverse religious universe that the development of the Sikh tradition can be understood, for

# Traditions at a Glance

**Numbers**
25 million around the world.

**Distribution**
Primarily northern India, especially Punjab, Haryana, and Delhi, with minorities in other provinces of India and many other countries, including Canada, the United States (especially California), and Britain.

**Founders and Leaders**
Founded by Guru Nanak c. 1500 CE, and developed over the following two centuries by a succession of nine other inspired teachers, the last of whom, Guru Gobind Singh, died in 1708.

**Deity**
The Supreme Being is considered to be One and without form. Guru Nanak refers to the deity as Akal Purakh ('Timeless Person'), Kartar ('Creator'), and Nirankar ('Formless'), among many other names.

**Authoritative Texts**
The Adi Granth (also known as Guru Granth Sahib) is a compilation of divinely inspired hymns by six Gurus, fifteen poet-saints, and fifteen Sikh bards; the Dasam Granth, a collection of hymns made in the time of the tenth Guru, is also revered as a secondary scripture.

**Noteworthy Teachings**
There is One Supreme Reality, never incarnated. In addition to reverence for the Gurus and the sacred scriptures, Sikhs emphasize egalitarianism, tolerance, service to others, and righteous life in this world as the way to ultimate liberation from the cycle of rebirth.

it required the Sikhs to define themselves in an ongoing process of interaction and lively debate.

## Guru Nanak

Guru Nanak was born in 1469 to an upper-caste professional khatri ('merchant') family in the village of Talwandi (Nankana Sahib), not far from what is now Lahore, Pakistan. At the time of his birth much of northern India, including the Punjab, had been under Muslim control for more than two centuries. In his lifetime, Guru Nanak witnessed the dominance of the Lodhi Sultanate,

and its final extinction by Mughal Emperor Babur (1483–1530) in 1526. By the time Babur came to power, Guru Nanak had already established a community of his followers in the village of Kartarpur ('The Creator's Abode'). For the next two centuries the Sikh tradition evolved in the historical context of the Mughal rule in India.

### Guru Nanak's Mystical Experience

Much of the material concerning Guru Nanak's life comes from hagiographical *janam-sakhis* ('birth narratives') that were first written down roughly seven decades after his death but had

## Map 3.1 The Punjab

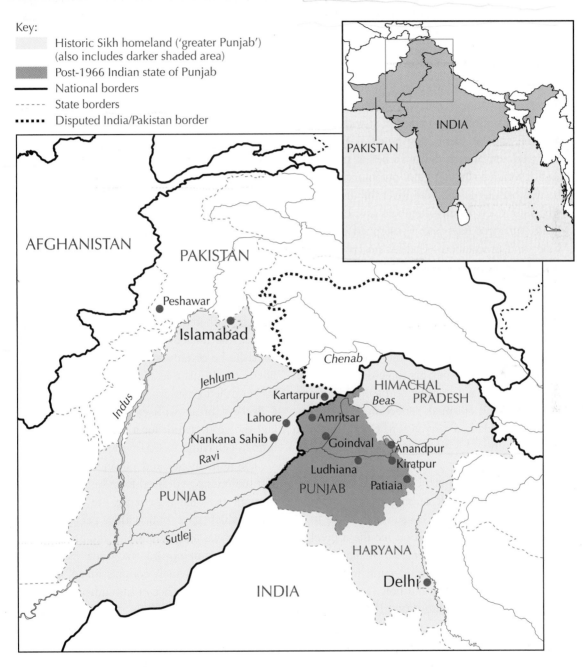

Key:

Historic Sikh homeland ('greater Punjab')
(also includes darker shaded area)

Post-1966 Indian state of Punjab

National borders

State borders

Disputed India/Pakistan border

*Source*: Adapted from Nesbitt 2005: 9.

begun circulating orally during his lifetime. His life may be divided into three distinct phases: an early contemplative period; a mystic enlightenment followed by years of pilgrimage and debate; and a conclusion in which he and his growing community of disciples established the first Sikh community.

Employed as a steward by a local Muslim nobleman, the young Nanak worked diligently at his job. But his mind was preoccupied with spiritual matters, and he spent long hours at the beginning and end of each day absorbed in meditation and devotional singing. Early one morning, while he was bathing in the Vein River, he disappeared without a trace. Family members gave him up for dead, but three days later he stepped out of the water and proclaimed: 'There is no Hindu, there is no Muslim.'

The significance of this statement becomes clear in the context of a religious culture divided between the conflicting truth claims of the Islamic and Hindu traditions. Nanak pointed the way towards the common humanity underlying the external divisions. After his three-day immersion in the waters—a metaphor of dissolution, transformation, and spiritual perfection—Nanak was ready to proclaim a new vision. One of his own hymns describes his experience:

> I was a minstrel out of work; the Lord assigned me the task of singing the Divine Word day and night. He summoned me to his Court and bestowed on me the robe of honour for singing his praises. On me he bestowed the Divine Nectar (*amrit*) in a cup, the nectar of his true and holy Name. (M1, *Var Majh* 27, Adi Granth / AG 150)[1]

This hymn is intensely autobiographical, explicitly pointing out Guru Nanak's own understanding of his divine mission and marking the beginning of his ministry to preach the message of the divine Name. He was then thirty years of age, had been married for more than a decade, and was the father of two young sons, Sri Chand and Lakhmi Das. Yet he left his family behind to set out on a series of journeys to both Hindu and Muslim places of pilgrimage in India and abroad. In the course of his travels he encountered the leaders of different religious persuasions and tested the veracity of his own ideas through dialogue with them.

### Foundation of the Sikh Panth

At the end of his spiritual travels Guru Nanak purchased a parcel of land on the right bank of the Ravi River in central Punjab, where he founded the village of Kartarpur in 1519. There he lived for the rest of his life as the 'spiritual guide' of a new religious community. His charismatic personality and teaching won him many disciples, who received the message of liberation through religious hymns of unique genius and notable beauty. They began to use these hymns in devotional singing (**kirtan**) as part of congregational worship. The first Sikh families who gathered around Guru Nanak at Kartarpur formed the nucleus of the Nanak-**Panth** (Path of Nanak), the community who followed his path to liberation. In his role as what the sociologist Max Weber called an 'ethical prophet', Nanak called for a decisive break with existing formulations and laid the groundwork for a new, rational model of human behaviour based on divine authority.

The authenticity and power of Guru Nanak's spiritual message derived from his direct access—through personal experience—to Divine Reality itself, which gave him with a perspective from which he was able to interpret and assess the various elements of existing traditions. He conceived of his work as divinely commissioned, and he demanded the obedience of his audience as an ethical duty.

The 974 hymns of Guru Nanak that are preserved in the Adi Granth offer the most authoritative account of his teachings. Thoroughly familiar with the texts, beliefs, and practices of the existing traditions, Guru Nanak made a very clear distinction between their teachings and practices and his own. He frequently refers to contemporary Hindus,

Vaishnavas, Jainas, Nath yogis, Sufis, and Muslim scholars (the *ulama* or 'theologians'). In his *Siddh Gosti* ('Discourse with the Siddhas', AG 939–46), for instance, he critiques Nath beliefs and contrasts his own path of spirituality with theirs. In another composition he offers a critique of a ritual dance of Vaishnavas (AG 465). Defining his own path against the Hindu and Muslim conventions of the day, including ritual and pilgrimage, temple and mosque, brahmin and mullah, Vedas and Qur'an, at the same time he defined the 'true Hindu' and 'true Muslim' as opposed to the false believer who continued to follow the conventional forms. In so doing he invited true devotees of both religions to follow his own path of inner spirituality based on ethical values.

## Guru Nanak's Message to Different Audiences

*Guru Nanak addressed his Muslim audience as follows:*

Make mercy your mosque and devotion your prayer mat,
    Righteousness your Qur'an;
Meekness your circumcising, goodness your fasting;
    For thus the true Muslim expresses his faith.
Make good works your Ka`bah, take truth your Pir
    Compassion your creed and your prayer.
Let service to God be the beads which you tell
    And God will exalt you to glory.
        (M1, *Var Majh*, AG 140–1)

*To the 'twice-born' Hindus, he said:*

Make compassion the cotton, contentment the thread,
    Continence the knot, and truth the twist.
This is the sacred thread of the soul,
    If you possess it, O Brahmin, then place it on me.
It does not break or become soiled with filth.
    This can neither be burnt, nor lost.
Blessed are the mortals, O Nanak,
    Who wear such a thread round their neck.
        (M1, *Var Asa*, AG 471)

*Guru Nanak encountered the Nath yogis in their own terms:*

Make contentment your earrings, modesty your begging-bowl and wallet,
    And meditation on the Lord your ashes.
Let the fear of death be your patched garment;
    Be chaste like a virgin; make faith in God, your staff.
Your great Yogic sect (*ai panthi*) should be universal brotherhood,
    And self-control the conquest of the world.
        (M1, *Japu 28*, AG 6)

Guru Nanak rightly understood that his listeners would comprehend his message more clearly if it was expressed in the language of their own religious heritage. Thus he reached out to his Muslim audience by using Islamic concepts and used Nath terminology with the yogis. The message in each case, however, reflected Guru Nanak's own understanding of the divine truth.

Guru Nanak, as founder, was the central authority for the Kartarpur community. He prescribed the daily routine, in which communal devotions—Nanak's *Japji* ('Honoured Recitation') was recited in the early hours of the morning, and *So Dar* ('That Door') and *Arti* ('Adoration') were sung in the evening—were balanced with agricultural work for sustenance. He defined the ideal person as a *Gurmukh* ('one oriented towards the Guru') who practised the threefold discipline of *nam dan ishnan*, 'the divine Name, charity and purity' (AG 942). Corresponding to the cognitive, the communal, and the personal aspects of the evolving Sikh identity, these three features—*nam* (relation to the Divine), *dan* (relation to the society), and *ishnan* (relation to self)—established a balance between the development of the individual and the society. For Guru Nanak, the true spiritual

## Guru Nanak on Women

*Guru Nanak's campaign for egalitarian reform was not limited to the caste system. He spoke out clearly against the inferior position assigned to women in Punjabi society, as the following verse from his celebrated Asa Ki Var ('Ballad in the Asa mode') shows:*

From women born, shaped in the womb,
To woman betrothed and wed;
We are bound to women by ties of affection,
On women man's future depends.
If one woman dies he seeks another;
With a woman he orders his life.
Why then should one speak evil of women,
They who give birth to kings?
Women also are born from women;
    None takes birth except from a woman.
Only the True One [Akal Purakh/God], Nanak [Guru Nanak often addresses himself],
    needs no help from a woman.
Blessed are they, both men and women,
    Who endlessly praise their Lord.
Blessed are they in the True One's court,
    There shall their faces shine.
        (M1, *Var Asa*, AG 473; McLeod 1997: 241–2)

*Nanak's egalitarian ideas about women set him far apart from the medieval poet-saints of North India, particularly Kabir, who described woman as 'a black cobra', 'the pit of hell', and 'the refuse of the world' (Kabir Granthavali: 30.2, 30.16, and 30.20).*

life required that 'one should live on what one has earned through hard work and share with others the fruit of one's exertion' (AG 1245). Service, self-respect, truthful living, humility, sweetness of the tongue, and taking only one's rightful share were among the virtues most highly prized in the pursuit of liberation.

Guru Nanak's spiritual message found expression at Kartarpur through three key institutions: the *sangat* ('holy fellowship') where all felt that they belonged to one large spiritual fraternity; the *dharamsala*, the original form of the Sikh place of worship; and the **langar**: the communal meal, prepared as a community service by members of the *sangat*, that is served to everyone attending the **gurdwara** (the Sikh place of worship) and that requires people of all castes and conditions to sit side-by-side in status-free rows—female next to male, socially high next to socially low, ritually pure next to ritually impure—and share the same food. This was the first practical expression of Guru Nanak's spiritual mission to reform society. The institution of the *langar* promoted egalitarianism, community service, unity, and belonging while striking down a major aspect of the caste system. In so doing it

marked a major step in the process of defining a distinctive Sikh identity.

### Lineage of Gurus

Finally, Guru Nanak created the institution of the Guru, who became the central authority in community life. Before his death in 1539, he designated his disciple Lehna as his successor by renaming him Angad, meaning my 'own limb'. Thus a lineage was established that would continue from the appointment of Guru Angad (1504–52) to the death of Guru Gobind Singh (1666–1708), the tenth and the last human Guru of the Sikhs.

## The Ten Gurus

Guru Nanak's decision regarding the succession was the most significant step in the development of the early Sikh Panth, for he not only promoted Angad to the status of 'Guru' within his own lifetime, but bowed before his own successor, becoming a disciple himself. In this act of humility, Guru Nanak clearly asserted both the primacy of the message over the messenger and the objective independence of the power behind divine revelation. In this way he gave the office of Guru charismatic authority and established that the Guru is 'one', whatever form the occupant of the office may take.

Guru Angad consolidated the nascent Sikh Panth in the face of a challenge mounted by Guru Nanak's eldest son, Sri Chand, the founder of the ascetic Udasi sect. The sixty-two *shaloks* ('couplets' or 'stanzas') composed by Guru Angad throw light on the historical situation of the Panth during his period and mark the doctrinal boundaries of the Sikh faith in strict

Sikh women worshipping at Jalandhar (Reuters/Munish Sharma/Landov).

conformity with Guru Nanak's message. He established a new Sikh centre at Khadur, where his wife Khivi ran the community kitchen (also called the *langar*) and added a dessert of rice boiled in milk to the standard vegetarian meal. This addition was a sign of the Sikhs' ability to attract contributions substantial enough to offer generous meals to one and all.

Guru Angad refined the **Gurmukhi** ('from the Guru's mouth') script in which the Guru's hymns were recorded. The original Gurmukhi script was a systematization of the business shorthand that Guru Nanak used to write the Punjabi language as a young man. Apparently the early Gurus had no objection to the idea of an overlap between everyday life and the life of the spirit. Thus the use of the Gurmukhi script signals the early Sikhs' emphatic rejection of the hegemonic authority attributed to Sanskrit, Arabic, and Persian in the scholarly circles of the time. At the same time, the use of Gurmukhi reinforced the distinct identity of the Sikhs. In fact, language has been the single most important factor in the preservation of the Sikh cultural heritage. For Punjabis, the idea that spiritual truth could be inscribed in their own native language created a sense of empowerment that had been conspicuously absent.

The third Guru, Amar Das (1479–1574), introduced a variety of institutional innovations that helped to reinforce the cohesion and unity of the ever-growing Sikh Panth. In addition to founding the town of Goindval (southeast of Amritsar on the river Beas), he established two annual festivals (Divali and Baisakhi) that provided regular opportunities for the growing community to get together and meet the Guru; introduced a system of twenty-two *manjis* ('cots' or seats of authority) as bases for missionaries seeking to attract new converts, and oversaw the preparation of the Goindval *pothis* ('volumes'): the initial collection of the compositions of the first three Gurus and some of the medieval poet-saints.

These early steps towards the establishment of a more comprehensive administrative system speak of the rapidity with which Guru Nanak's message was gaining ground, and also of the practical wisdom of those charged with sustaining the movement. The second- and third-generation disciples had to find ways to convey that message without the benefit of direct emotional experience. In every religious tradition, translation into a standard written form and objectification in rituals and ceremonies become imperative as time removes new converts further and further from the lives of the founder and the original disciples.

As the geographical base of the Panth expanded, missionaries needed copies of the *bani* ('divine Word') that they could carry with them, and growing numbers of Sikhs needed a common frame of reference for communal worship. Thus Guru Amar Das had scribes make copies of the hymns for distribution

As important as these innovations were, the reforms that Guru Amar Das instituted regarding women were perhaps even more significant. He abolished not only the wearing of the veil but the practice of *sati*, and permitted widows to remarry. He also appointed women as missionaries (roughly half of the original twenty-two *manjis* were held by women) and gave all Sikh women equal rights with men to conduct prayers and other ceremonies in the congregational setting.

The fourth Guru, Ram Das (1534–81), established a town called Ramdaspur in 1577 and ordered the construction of a large bathing pool there. (After the pool was completed, the town was renamed Amritsar, 'nectar of immortality'.) The new building projects required considerable financial and logistical mobilization for which the appointment of 'deputies' (*masands*) became necessary to deal with increasingly complex administrative demands. The fact that the Panth was equal to such an endeavour is an indication of the support that Guru Nanak's message had attracted in just a few decades.

In addition, Guru Ram Das contributed 679 new hymns to the collection that made up the Sikh scripture, and expanded the number of melodies (*ragas*) specified for their singing from 19 to 30. Together, the musicality and the emotional appeal of his hymns had a tremendous impact on his audience. The liturgical requirement not only to recite but to sing the sacred Word became part of the very definition of Sikhism, and contributed significantly to Sikhs' self-image as a distinct and cohesive community. Indeed, the process of distinguishing between 'us' and 'them' was effectively completed during the period of Guru Ram Das, who proclaimed the 'loyal Sikhs of the Gurus (*gursikhs*)' to be spiritually greater than the 'Bhagats, Sants, and Sadhs' (AG 649).

The fifth Guru, Arjan (1563–1606), inherited a vibrant religious community. His twenty-five years as Guru were marked by several far-reaching institutional developments. First, he built the Darbar Sahib ('Divine Court', also known as Harimandir Sahib and, later, as the 'Golden Temple') in the sacred pool of Amritsar, a shining monument that remains the central symbol of the Sikh faith to this day. Its foundation was laid in January 1589 and the construction was completed in a decade. Second, he took it on himself to organize the scriptural corpus he had inherited into the Adi Granth, the definitive statement of Sikhism's unique spiritual stance. Third, by the end of the sixteenth century the Sikh Panth had developed a strong sense of independent identity: as Guru Arjan asserted, 'We are neither Hindu nor Musalman' (AG 1136).

By the mid-seventeenth century, the author of a Persian study of different religious systems (*Dabistan-i-Mazahib*) was able to comment that 'there were not many cities in the inhabited countries where some Sikhs were not to be found'. In fact, the growth of Sikhism was so significant that it attracted the unfavourable attention of the Mughal authorities.

Bathing in the Pool of Nectar (Raghu Rai/Magnum).

### Rise of Sikh–Mughal Conflict

To a large extent, the peaceful growth of the Sikh Panth through the sixteenth century can be attributed to the liberal policy of Emperor Akbar (r. 1556–1605). Within eight months of Akbar's death, however, Guru Arjan himself was dead, executed at Lahore by order of the new emperor, Jahangir (r. 1605–28). This 'first martyrdom' was a turning point in Sikh history, pushing the community in the direction of self-consciousness, separatism, and militancy. In short, Guru Arjan's martyrdom became the decisive factor in the crystallization of the Sikh Panth.

The sixth Guru, Hargobind (1595–1644), signalled this new direction when, at his investiture, he donned two swords, one symbolizing spiritual (*piri*) and the other temporal (*miri*) authority. One symbol of this new temporal authority was Hargobind's construction, in 1609, of the Akal Takhat ('Throne of the Timeless Being') facing the Darbar Sahib, to resolve internal disputes within the community. Under his direct leadership the Sikh Panth took up arms to defend itself against Mughal hostility. The new emphasis on worldly affairs did not mean that the Sikhs had abandoned their spiritual base. Rather, as a Sikh theologian of the period, Bhai Gurdas, explained, in adopting a martial orientation the Guru was simply 'hedging the orchard of the Sikh faith with the hardy and thorny *kikar* tree'. After four skirmishes with Mughal troops, Guru Hargobind withdrew from Amritsar to the Shivalik hills—beyond the jurisdiction of the Mughal state—and Kiratpur became the new centre of the mainline Sikh tradition.

Relations with the Mughal authorities eased under the seventh and eighth Gurus, Har Rai (1630–61) and Harkrishan (1655–64), although the Gurus held court to adjudicate on temporal issues within the Panth and kept a regular force of Sikh horsemen. But the increasing strength of the Sikh movement during the period of the ninth Guru, Tegh Bahadur (1621–75) once again attracted Mughal attention in the 1670s. Guru Tegh Bahadur encouraged his followers to be fearless in their pursuit of a just society: 'He who holds none in fear, nor is afraid of anyone, is acknowledged as a man of true wisdom' (AG 1427). In so doing, he posed a direct challenge to Emperor Aurangzeb (r. 1658–1707), who had imposed Islamic laws and taxes, and ordered the replacement of Hindu temples with mosques. Guru Tegh Bahadur was summoned to Delhi, and when he refused to embrace Islam he was publicly executed on 11 November 1675. If the martyrdom of Guru Arjan had helped to bring the Sikh Panth together, this second martyrdom helped to make human rights and freedom of conscience central to its identity.

### The Khalsa

Tradition holds that the Sikhs who were present at Guru Tegh Bahadur's execution concealed their identity for fear of meeting a similar fate. For this reason the tenth Guru, Gobind Singh, resolved to impose on his followers an outward form that would make them instantly recognizable. He restructured the Panth and created the **Khalsa** ('pure'), an order of loyal Sikhs bound by a common identity and discipline (*rahit*). On **Baisakhi Day** 1699 at Anandpur, Guru Gobind Singh called for volunteers and initiated as the nucleus of the new order the 'Cherished Five' (*Panj Piare*) who were the first to respond. To this day, the Khalsa initiation ceremony follows the pattern established in 1699: initiates drink a sweet 'nectar' (**amrit sanskar**) that has been stirred with a two-edged sword and sanctified by the recitation of five liturgical prayers.

The launch of the Khalsa was the culmination of the formative period in the development of Sikhism. But it was only one in a series of major reforms instituted by Guru Gobind Singh. After adding a collection of the works of his father, Guru Tegh Bahadur, to the Adi Granth, he closed the Sikh canon. And before he passed away in 1708, he brought to an end the succession of human Gurus. Thereafter, the authority of the Guru would be invested not in an individual but in the scripture (Guru-Granth) and the corporate community

(Guru-Panth). Together, Guru-Granth and Guru-Panth would continue the process of consolidating the Sikh tradition through the eighteenth century.

# CRYSTALLIZATION

The term 'crystallization' comes from Wilfred Cantwell Smith, who identified a number of standard stages in the development of a religious tradition. The process begins with the vision of a mystic whose preaching attracts followers and continues with the organization of a community, the positing of an intellectual ideal of that community, and the development of its institutions. Smith maintains that in the case of Sikhism the last two stages were reached under the fifth Guru, Arjan, and the tenth, Gobind Singh. In his view, the concept 'Sikhism' must be understood as the 'total complex of Sikh religious practices and rites, scriptures and doctrines, history and institutions' as they developed over a period of two centuries. Of course crystallization is an ongoing process, one that continues as the community is obliged to respond to changing conditions.

The sword is one of the most important symbols of the Sikh identity (Reuters/Landov).

## The Sacred Scriptures

The Adi Granth is the primary scripture of the Sikhs. It includes the works of the first five Gurus and the ninth, plus material by four bards (Satta, Balvand, Sundar, and Mardana), eleven Bhatts ('court poets' who composed and recited panegyrics in praise of the Gurus), and fifteen Bhagats ('devotees' of the Sant, Sufi, and Bhakti traditions, including the medieval poets Kabir, Namdev, Ravidas, and Shaikh Farid)—a total of thirty-six contributors stretching historically from the twelfth century to the seventeenth. The standard version of this collection contains a total of 1,430 pages, *standard* and every copy is identical in terms of the material printed on individual pages.

The text of the Adi Granth is divided into three major sections. The introductory section includes three liturgical prayers. The middle section, which contains the bulk of the material, is divided into thirty-one major *ragas*, or musical patterns. The final section includes an epilogue consisting of miscellaneous works.

The second sacred collection, the Dasam Granth, is attributed to the tenth Guru, Gobind Singh, but it must have extended beyond his time to include the writings of others as well. Mani Singh compiled the collection early in the eighteenth century. Its 1,428 pages offer four major types of compositions: devotional texts, autobiographical works, miscellaneous writings, and a collection of mythical narratives and popular anecdotes.

The third category of sacred literature consists of works by Bhai ('Brother') Gurdas (c. 1558–1637) and Bhai Nand Lal Goya (1633–1715). Along with the sacred

## From the Sacred Writings of the Sikhs

*Guru Nanak exalts the divine Name:*

If in this life I should live to eternity, nourished by nothing save air;
If I should dwell in the darkest of dungeons, sense never resting in sleep;
Yet must your glory transcend all my striving; no words can encompass the Name.
    (*Refrain*) He who is truly the Spirit Eternal, immanent, blissful serene;
    Only by grace can we learn of our Master, only by grace can we tell.
If I were slain and my body dismembered, pressed in a hand-mill and ground;
If I were burnt in a fire all-consuming, mingled with ashes and dust;
Yet must your glory transcend all my striving, no words can encompass the Name.
If as a bird I could soar to the heavens, a hundred such realms in my reach;
If I could change so that none might perceive me and live without food, without drink;
Yet must your glory transcend all my striving; no words can encompass the Name.
If I could read with the eye of intelligence paper of infinite weight;
If I could with the winds everlasting, pens dipped in oceans of ink;
Yet must your glory transcend all my striving, no words can encompass the Name.
    (M1, *Siri Ragu* 2, AG 14–15; McLeod 1984: 41)

*The third Guru, Amar Das, addresses the Brahmins' pride in the traditional learning that they had monopolized:*

He who is truly a dutiful Brahmin will cast off his burden of human desire,
Each day performing his God-given duty, each day repeating God's Name.
To such as submit God imparts divine learning, and those who obey him live virtuous lives.
He who is truly a dutiful Brahmin wins honour when summoned to God.
    (M3, *Malar* 10, AG 1261; McLeod 1984: 47)

*The tenth Guru, Gobind Singh, praises the sword. This passage, often repeated at Sikh functions, has now come to serve as the national anthem of the Khalsa:*

Reverently I salute the Sword with affection and devotion.
Grant, I pray, your divine assistance that this book may be brought to completion.
Thee I invoke, All-conquering Sword, Destroyer of evil, Ornament of the brave.
Powerful your arm and radiant your glory, your splendour as dazzling as the brightness of the sun.
Joy of the devout and Scourge of the wicked, Vanquisher of sin, I seek your protection.
Hail to the world's Creator and Sustainer, my invincible Protector of the Sword!
    (*Bachitar Natak*, Dasam Granth, 39; McLeod 1984: 58)

compositions of the Gurus, their works are approved in the official manual of the *Sikh Rahit Maryada* ('Sikh Code of Conduct') for singing in the gurdwara.

The last category of Sikh literature is made up of three distinct genres. The *janam-sakhis* ('birth narratives') are hagiographical accounts of Guru Nanak's life dating from the seventeenth century but based on earlier oral traditions. The *rahit-namas* ('manuals of code of conduct') provide rare insight into the evolution of the Khalsa code in the course of the eighteenth and nineteenth centuries. And the *gur-bilas* ('splendour of the Guru') literature of the eighteenth and nineteenth centuries praises the mighty deeds of the two great warrior Gurus, Hargobind and Gobind Singh, in particular.

Finally, it is important to emphasize that the Adi Granth is set apart from other Sikh texts not only by the richness and semantic density of its content, but because it is inextricably embedded in daily life. For Sikhs, the scripture is not merely to be read, or even to be understood, but to be appropriated and interiorized, to be practised and lived.

## The Khalsa

Three aspects of the institution created by Guru Gobind Singh on Baisakhi Day 1699 are particularly significant. First, it was understood that, in undergoing the *amrit* ceremony, the Khalsa initiates were 'reborn' in the house of the Guru. From that day forward, Guru Gobind Singh would be their spiritual father and his wife, Sahib Kaur, their spiritual mother. As part of their new identity, male members of the Khalsa were given the new surname *Singh* ('lion') and female initiates were given the surname *Kaur* ('princess'). Their birthplace became Kesgarh Sahib (the gurdwara that commemorates the founding of the Khalsa) and their home Anandpur Sahib (the town where Kesgarh Sahib is situated). The new collective identity conferred on the Khalsa initiates gave them a powerful sense of belonging.

Second, the Guru himself received the nectar of the double-edged sword from the hands of the Cherished Five, becoming part of the Khalsa Panth, subject to its collective will. In so doing, he symbolically transferred his spiritual authority to the Five and paved the way for the termination of personal Guruship. Finally, it was at the inauguration of the Khalsa that Guru Gobind Singh delivered the nucleus of what would become the *Rahit*

('Code of Conduct') of the order. To ensure that Khalsa members would never seek to conceal their identity as Sikhs, he made five physical symbols mandatory:

1. *Kes*, unshorn hair, symbolizing spirituality and saintliness;
2. *Kangha*, a wooden comb, signifying order and discipline in life;
3. *Kirpan*, a miniature sword, symbolizing divine grace, dignity, and courage;
4. *Kara*, a steel 'wrist-ring', signifying responsibility and allegiance to the Guru; and
5. *Kachh*, a pair of short breeches, symbolizing moral restraint.

Known (from their Punjabi names) as the **Five Ks** (*panj kakke*), these outward symbols of the divine Word imply a direct correlation between *bani* ('divine utterance') and *bana* ('Khalsa dress'). Every morning, in putting on the various items of dress (including the turban in the case of male Sikhs) while reciting prayers, Khalsa Sikhs dress themselves in the word of God; their minds are purified and inspired, and their bodies are girded to do battle with the day's temptations.

In addition to cutting the hair, three other sins are specifically prohibited: using tobacco (this injunction was later expanded to include all intoxicants); committing adultery; and eating meat that has not come from an animal killed with a single blow.

## Sikh Doctrine

The primary source of Sikh doctrine is the Adi Granth. Its first words are Guru Nanak's invocation of One God (*1-Oankar*) in the **Mul Mantar** ('Seed Formula'). This succinct expression of the nature of the Ultimate Reality is the fundamental statement of Sikh belief:

There is One ('1') Supreme Being, the Eternal Reality, the Creator, without fear and devoid of enmity, immortal, never incarnated, self-existent, known by grace through the Guru. The Eternal One, from the beginning, through all time, present now, the Everlasting Reality. (AG 1)

By beginning with 'One' (the original Punjabi text uses the numeral rather than the word), Guru Nanak emphasizes the singularity of the divine; as he put it in a later hymn, the Supreme Being has 'no relatives, no mother, no father, no wife, no son, no rival who may become a potential contender' (AG 597). At the same time he draws attention to the unity of Akal Purakh, the Eternal One, the source as well as the goal of all that exists. The Mul Mantar illuminates the way Sikh doctrine understands a Divine Reality that is at once transcendent and immanent, a personal God of grace for his humblest devotee. The vital expression of the One is through the many, through the infinite plurality of creation. This understanding of the One distinguishes the Sikh interpretation of 'monotheism' from its interpretation in the Abrahamic traditions.

The Sikh Gurus were fiercely opposed to any anthropomorphic conception of the divine. The creator and sustainer of the universe watches over it as lovingly as any parent. Like a father he runs the world with justice, and destroys evil and supports good, and like a mother she is the source of love and grace, and responds to the devotion of her humblest followers. Simultaneously 'Father, Mother, Friend, and Brother' (AG 268), God is without gender.

In general, then, Sikh tradition worships a transcendent (*nirguna*, 'without attributes'), non-incarnate, universal God. Yet this God is also described as immanent (*saguna*, 'with attributes'), and is partly embodied in the divine Name (*nam*) as well as the collective Words (*bani*) and persons of the Gurus. Only through personal experience can he be truly known.

## Creation

According to Guru Nanak's cosmology hymn, the universe was brought into being by the divine order, will, or command (**hukam**). This *hukam* is an all-embracing principle, the sum total of all divinely instituted laws; and it is a revelation of the nature of God:

> For endless eons, there was only darkness.
> Nothing except the divine order existed.
> No day or night, no moon or sun.
> The Creator alone was absorbed in a primal
>     state of contemplation . . .
> When the Creator so willed, creation came
>     into being . . .
> The Un-manifest One revealed itself in the
>     Creation.
>     (AG 1035–6)

Elsewhere Guru Nanak describes how 'From the True One came air and from air came water; from water he created the three worlds [sky, earth, and netherworld] and infused in every heart his own light' (AG 19). As the creation of Akal Purakh, the physical universe is real but subject to constant change. In Sikh cosmology, the world is divinely inspired, the place that provides human beings with the opportunity to perform their duty and achieve union with Akal Purakh. Since 'all of us carry the fruits of our deeds', the actions we take during our earthly existence are important (AG 4).

## Value of Human Life

A human being is a microcosm (*pind*) of the macrocosm (*brahmand*) in the Sikh worldview. For Guru Nanak, human life is worth a 'diamond', but its value drops to a 'farthing' if we do not realize our true spiritual nature (AG 156). In his *Suhi* hymn, he proclaims:

> One is blessed with the rarest opportunity
> of the human birth through the grace of the
> Guru. One's mind and body become dyed

deep red (with the love of the divine Name) if one is able to win the approval of the True Guru. (AG 751)

For Guru Arjan, human life is the most delightful experience possible (AG 966), and the human being is the epitome of Creation: 'All other creation is subject to you, O man/woman! You reign supreme on this earth' (AG 374). Like Guru Nanak, he emphasizes the opportunity that human life provides to remember the divine Name and ultimately to join with Akal Purakh: 'Precious this life you receive as a human, with it the chance to find the Lord' (AG 15). But those who seek the divine beloved while participating in the delights of the world are rare.

### Karam, Sansar, and Divine Grace

The notions of *karam* (/karma, 'actions', the principle of moral cause and effect) and *sansar* (/samsara, 'reincarnation') are fundamental to all religious traditions originating in India. In other Indian religions, karma is popularly understood as an inexorable, impersonal law. In Sikh doctrine, however, karam is not inexorable, not absolute. Rather, it is subject to the 'divine order' (*hukam*), a higher, all-embracing principle that is the sum total of all the divinely instituted laws in the cosmos. For Sikhs, karam is not an impersonal law, but a principle that can be overridden in the name of justice by Akal Purakh's omnipotent grace. In fact, divine grace always takes precedence over the law of karam in the Sikh teachings, and can even break the chain of adverse karam.

### Divine Revelation    *mystical union*

Guru Nanak used three key terms to describe the nature of divine revelation in its totality: *nam* ('divine Name'), *shabad* ('divine Word'), and *guru* ('divine Preceptor'). *Nam* refers to the divine presence that is manifest everywhere around and within us, though most people fail to perceive it because of the self-centred desire for personal gratification.

This self-centredness (*haumai*, meaning 'I, I' or 'me, mine') separates us from Akal Purakh, and thus we continue to suffer within the cycle of rebirth (*sansar*). Akal Purakh, however, looks graciously on human suffering. Thus he reveals himself through the Guru by uttering the *shabad* ('divine Word') that will communicate a sufficient understanding of the *nam* ('divine Name') to those who are able to 'hear' it. The *shabad* is the utterance that, once heard, awakens the hearer to the reality of the divine Name, immanent in all that lies around and within.

### Remembering the Divine Name

Traditionally, *haumai* is the source of five evil impulses: lust, anger, covetousness, attachment to worldly things, and pride. Under its influence humans become 'self-willed' (*manmukh*), so attached to worldly pleasures that they forget the divine Name and waste their entire lives in evil and suffering. To achieve spiritual liberation within one's lifetime it is necessary to transcend the influence of *haumai* by adopting the strictly interior discipline of **nam-simaran** or 'remembering the divine Name'.

There are three levels to this discipline, ranging from the repetition of a sacred word, usually *Vahiguru* ('Praise to the Eternal Guru'), through the devotional singing of hymns with the congregation, to sophisticated meditation on the nature of Akal Purakh. The first and the third levels are undertaken in private, while the second involves public, communal activity. The main purpose of *nam-simaran* is to bring practitioners into harmony with the divine order (*hukam*). Ever-growing wonder in spiritual life ultimately leads to a condition of blissful 'equanimity' (*sahaj*), when the spirit ascends to the 'realm of Truth': the fifth and the last stage, in which the soul finds mystical union with Akal Purakh.

The primacy of divine grace over personal effort is fundamental to Guru Nanak's theology. Yet there is neither fatalism nor passive acceptance in this view of life. Rather, personal effort in the form of good actions is seen as an integral part of spiritual discipline: 'With your own hands carve out your own destiny' (AG 474). By teaching his followers to see their own 'free' will as part of Akal Purakh's will, Guru Nanak encouraged them to create their own destinies. The necessity of balance between meditative worship and righteous life in the world is summed up in the following triple commandment: earn your living through honest labour, adore the divine Name, and share the fruits of your labour with others.

## Four Notions of Guruship

In Indic traditions the guru is a human teacher who communicates divine knowledge and guides disciples along the path to liberation. In Sikhism, however, the term 'guru' has evolved over time to encompass four types of spiritual authority: the eternal Guru, the personal Guru, Guru-Granth, and Guru-Panth.

### God as Guru

Guru Nanak uses the term Guru in three basic senses: to refer to Akal Purakh himself, to the voice of Akal Purakh, and to the Word, the Truth of Akal Purakh. To experience the eternal Guru is to experience divine guidance. Guru Nanak himself acknowledges Akal Purakh as his Guru: 'He who is the infinite, supreme God is the Guru whom Nanak has met' (AG 599). In Sikh usage, therefore, the Guru is the voice of Akal Purakh, mystically uttered within the human heart, mind, and soul (*man*).

Akal Purakh is often characterized as *Nirankar*, 'the One without Form'. Guru Arjan states explicitly that 'The True Guru is *Niranjan* [the One who is wholly apart from all that is darkness and untruth—hence the 'One who is himself Truth', God]. Do not believe that he is in the form of a human being' (AG 895).

Sikhs evoke the absolute knowledge and power of the divine Name by chanting '*Vahiguru! Vahiguru!*' ('Hail the Guru'). The sound vibrations of this phrase are believed to be supremely powerful.

In addition, the Sikh scripture often uses Hindu and Muslim names for God. Hindu (particularly Vaishnava) names such as Ram, Hari, Govind, Mukand, Madhav, Murari, Sarangpani, Parmeshvar, and Jagdish, and Muslim names such as Allah, Khuda, Rahim, Karim, and Sahib, express different aspects of Akal Purakh, as Guru Nanak recognized (AG 1168). And Guru Arjan provided a comprehensive list of the names from various contemporary religious traditions associated with different attributes of God (AG 1083). These names acquire meaning and significance in the Sikh context, however, only when they are refracted through the lens of the Mul Mantar. Most important, the 'truth of the Name' (*satinamu*) is a reality that lies beyond any name.

### The Teacher as Guru

The personal Guru functions as the channel through which the voice of Akal Purakh becomes audible. Nanak became the embodiment of the eternal Guru only when he received the divine Word and conveyed it to his disciples. The same spirit manifested itself in his successors. In fact, Guru Nanak bypassed the claims of his own son, Sri Chand, who was disqualified by his ascetic ideals, in favour of a more worthy disciple. Guru Angad followed the example of his Master when he chose his elderly disciple Amar Das over his own sons. The third Guru, however, designated as his successor his son-in-law, Ram Das. The latter's youngest son, Arjan, was the direct ancestor of all the later Gurus. Nevertheless, in each case the succession went to the most suitable candidate, not automatically from father to eldest son.

In Sikh doctrine, a theory of spiritual succession known as 'the unity of the office of the Guru' meant that there was no difference between the founder and the successors: all represented one and the same light, just as a single flame ignites a series of torches. The same principle can be seen in the Adi Granth, where all the Gurus sign their compositions 'Nanak' and each is identified by the codeword *Mahala* ('King') with an appropriate number. Thus the compositions labelled 'Mahala 1' (M 1) are by Guru Nanak, while those labelled M 2, 3, 4, 5, and 9 are by Guru Angad, Guru Amar Das, Guru Ram Das, Guru Arjan, and Guru Tegh Bahadur, respectively (the sixth, seventh, and eighth Gurus did not contribute any hymns to the corpus).

### The Scripture as Guru

Sikhs normally refer to the Adi Granth as the Guru Granth Sahib ('Honourable Scripture Guru'). In so doing, they acknowledge their faith in the scripture as the successor to Guru Gobind Singh, with the same status, authority, and functions, in terms both of personal piety and of collective identity, as any of the ten personal Gurus. The Adi Granth has become the perennial source of divine guidance for Sikhs, and it is treated with the most profound respect.

The Adi Granth is more authoritative than the secondary Sikh scripture, the Dasam Granth, which contains the works attributed to the tenth (*dasam*) Guru, Gobind Singh. It is also the authoritative

basis of the most important Sikh doctrines, rituals, and social and ethical positions. Simply to be in the presence of the Guru Granth Sahib, or to hear a sentence read aloud from it, makes Sikhs feel that they are on sacred ground.

### The Community as Guru

The phrase 'Guru-Panth' is employed in two senses: one, 'the Panth *of* the Guru', refers to the Sikh community; the other, 'the Panth *as* the Guru', refers to the Guru-Panth doctrine, which developed from the earlier idea that the Guru is mystically present in the congregation. At the inauguration of the Khalsa in 1699, Guru Gobind Singh symbolically transferred his authority to the 'Cherished Five' when he received initiation from their hands. Sainapati, the near-contemporary author of *Gur Sobha* (1711 CE), recorded that Guru Gobind Singh designated the Khalsa as the collective embodiment of his divine mandate:

> Upon the Khalsa which I have created I shall bestow the succession. The Khalsa is my

The *Panj Piare* (Cherished Five) leading a Khalsa Day parade in Surrey, BC (THE CANADIAN PRESS/Darryl Dyck).

physical form and I am one with the Khalsa. To all eternity I am manifest in the Khalsa. Those whose hearts are purged of falsehood will be known as the true Khalsa; and the Khalsa, freed from error and illusion, will be my true Guru.

As the elite group within the Panth, the Khalsa has always claimed to speak authoritatively on behalf of the whole, although at times non-Khalsa Sikhs have interpreted the doctrine of Guru-Panth as conferring authority on the broader community. In practice, consensus is achieved by following democratic traditions.

## Sikh Ethics

The Adi Granth opens with a composition of Guru Nanak's known as the *Japji*, in which a fundamental question is raised: 'How is Truth to be attained, how the veil of falsehood torn aside?' The Guru answers his own question: 'Nanak, thus it is written: Submit to the divine Order (*hukam*), walk in its way' (AG 1). In other words, Truth is obtained not by intellectual effort or cunning, but by personal commitment alone. To know Truth one must live it. The seeker of the divine Truth must live an ethical life. In this context Guru Nanak explicitly says: 'Truth is the highest virtue, but higher still is truthful living' (AG 62). Indeed, truthful conduct is at the heart of Guru Nanak's message. Cultivating virtues such as wisdom, contentment, justice, humility, truthfulness, temperance, love, forgiveness, charity, purity, and fear of Akal Purakh not only enriches personal life but also promotes socially responsible living, hard work, and sharing. In contrast to the Hindu tradition, in which holy men live by begging alms, Sikhism rejects both begging and withdrawal from social participation.

### Service

The key to a righteous life is to render service (*seva*) to others. Such service must be voluntary and undertaken without any desire for self-glorification. Nor should the one who gives aid sit in judgment on those who receive it. The Sikh Prayer (*Ardas*) emphasizes the importance of 'seeing but not judging', urging the faithful to reflect on the merit of those 'who magnanimously pardoned the faults of others'. The ideals are social equality and human brotherhood. Therefore any kind of discrimination based on caste or gender is expressly rejected. The Gurus also emphasized the importance of optimism in the face of adversity, and preferred moderate living and disciplined worldliness to asceticism and self-mortification.

### Justice

Guru Nanak held justice to be the primary duty of the ruler and the administrator. Thus he severely condemned the contemporary Muslim jurists (*qazi*) who were believed to take bribes and have no concern for truth. 'To deprive others of their rights must be avoided as scrupulously as Muslims avoid the pork and the Hindus consider beef as a taboo' (AG 141). In short, Guru Nanak regarded the violation of human rights as a serious moral offence.

The Sikh view of justice is based on two principles: first, respect for the rights of others; second, the non-exploitation of others. To treat everyone's right as sacred is a necessary constituent of justice. Those who are truly just will not exploit others even if they have the means and opportunity for doing so.

Guru Gobind Singh taught that, in the pursuit of justice, peaceful means of negotiation must be tried. Only when all such efforts have failed does it become legitimate to draw the sword in defence of righteousness. A famous verse from the *Zafarnama* ('Letter of Victory')—a long poem addressed to Emperor Aurangzeb after the latter, instead of negotiating, had sent his forces against the Sikhs—makes this point explicitly: 'When all other methods have been explored and all other means have been tried, then may the sword be drawn from the scabbard, then may the sword be used' (verse 22). The use of force is allowed in Sikh doctrine, but only in defence of justice and then only as a last resort. Moreover, in the face of tyranny no sacrifice is too great, 'It does not matter if my four sons have been killed; the Khalsa is still there at my back' (verse 78). For the Sikhs of the Khalsa, the quest for justice is the primary ethical duty.

### Oneness of Humankind and Religion

Sikhism is dedicated to the defence of human rights and resistance against injustice. It strives to eliminate poverty and to offer voluntary help to the less privileged. It is committed to the ideal of universal brotherhood, with an altruistic concern for humanity as a whole. In a celebrated passage from the *Akal Ustat* ('Praise of the Immortal One'), Guru Gobind Singh declares that 'humankind is one, and all people belong to a single humanity' (verse 85). Here it is important to underline the Guru's role as a conciliator who tried to persuade the Mughals to walk the ways of peace. Even though he had to spend the greater part of his life fighting battles forced on him by Hindu hill rajas and Mughal authorities, a longing for peace and fellowship may be seen in a passage from the *Akal Ustat*:

> The temple and the mosque are the same, so are the Hindu worship (*puja*) and Muslim prayer (*namaz*). All people are one; it is through error that they appear different. . . . Allah and Abhekh are the same, the Purana and the Qur'an are the same. They are all alike, all the creation of the One (verse 86).

The above verses emphasize the belief that the differences dividing people are in reality meaningless. In fact, all people are fundamentally the same because they all are the creations of the same Supreme Being. To this day, Sikhs conclude their morning and evening prayers with the words 'in

thy will, O Lord, may peace and prosperity come to one and all.'

##  PRACTICE

### Prayer

Devout Sikhs rise during the 'ambrosial hours' (*amritvela*, the last watch of the night, between 3 a.m. and 6 a.m.) and begin their daily routine with approximately an hour of devotions, beginning with meditation on the divine Name and continuing with recitation of five liturgical prayers, including Guru Nanak's *Japji* ('Honoured Recitation') and Guru Gobind Singh's *Jap Sahib* ('Master Recitation'). Evening prayers are selected from a collection of hymns entitled *Sodar Rahiras* ('Supplication at That Door'), and the *Kirtan Sohila* ('Song of Praise') is recited before retiring for the night. These prayers are learnt by heart in childhood and recited from memory every day. Thus they are always available to provide guidance. In fact, knowing the *gurbani* ('Guru's Utterances') by

---

**Daily Routine of Liturgical Prayers**

The Early Morning Order (3–6 a.m.)

1. *Japji* ('Honoured Recitation')

2. *Jap Sahib* ('Master Recitation')

3. The Ten *Savayyas* ('Ten Panegyrics')

4. *Benati Chaupai* ('Verses of Petition')

5. *Anand Sahib* ('Song of Bliss')

The Evening Prayer

*Sodar Rahiras* ('Supplication at That Door')

The Bedtime Prayer

*Kirtan Sohila* ('Song of Praise')

heart is often compared with having a supply of cash on hand and ready for use whenever it may be needed.

## Congregational Worship

In every gurdwara a large copy of the Guru Granth Sahib is reverently wrapped in expensive cloth and installed ceremoniously every morning on a cushioned, canopied stand called the *palki* ('palanquin'). There is a broad aisle leading from the main entrance to the Guru Granth Sahib at the opposite end of the hall. All who enter the gurdwara are expected to cover their heads, remove their shoes, and bow before the sacred volume by touching the floor with their foreheads. Worshippers sit on the floor, and it is the Punjabi custom for men to sit on the right side of the hall and women on the left, but this is not mandatory.

Sikhism has no ordained priesthood. Instead, every gurdwara has a *granthi* ('reader') who, in

The *granthi* reads from the Guru Granth Sahib inside the Golden Temple of Amritsar (Willard G. Oxtoby).

addition to reading from the Guru Granth Sahib, takes care of the book and serves as custodian of the gurdwara. The office is open to men and women alike, though in practice most *granthis* are men.

Worship consists mainly of *kirtan*—the congregational singing of devotional hymns, led and accompanied by musicians (*ragis*) playing harmoniums and the small drums called *tabla*. Through *kirtan* the devotees attune themselves to the divine Word and vibrate in harmony with it. Many today believe that this traditional practice helps them cope with the additional obstacles that a modern technological society puts in the way of their spiritual life.

At some time during the service, either the *granthi* or a traditional Sikh scholar (*giani*) may deliver a homily (*katha*) based on a particular hymn or scriptural passage appropriate to the occasion. Then all present will join in reciting the *Ardas* ('Petition', the Sikh Prayer), which invokes divine grace and recalls the rich heritage of the community.

The Sikh understanding of the Adi Granth as living Guru is most evident in the practice known as 'taking the Guru's Word' (*vak laina*) or 'seeking a divine command' (*hukam laina*). As a mark of respect, a ceremonial fan (*chauri*) is waved over the Guru Granth Sahib. Then the book is opened at random and the first hymn on the left-hand page is read aloud in its entirety (beginning on the previous page if necessary). In this way the congregation hears the Guru's **Vak** ('Saying') for that particular moment or occasion. Taken in the morning, the Vak is the divine lesson that will serve as the inspiration for personal meditation throughout the day; taken in the evening, it brings the day to a close with a new perspective on its particular joys and sorrows. The whole *sangat* (congregation) receives the Vak at the conclusion of different ceremonies.

The reading of the Vak is followed by the distribution of **karah prashad**—a sweet, rich paste of flour, sugar, and butter that has been 'sanctified' first by the recitation of prayers during its preparation and then by resting next to the scripture during the service. Symbolically, it represents

*Langar* at a Toronto gurdwara (Stephen Epstein/Ponkawonka.com).

the bestowal of divine blessings on all who receive *karah prashad*. At the end of congregational worship everyone shares in the *langar* prepared and served by volunteers as part of the community service expected of all Sikhs. All present, Sikhs and non-Sikhs alike, sit together to share a traditional vegetarian meal—usually flat bread, bean stew, and curry. This custom is a powerful reminder of the egalitarian spirit that is so central to Sikhism.

## The Annual Festival Cycle

The most important festival day in the Sikh calendar is Baisakhi (Vaisakhi) Day, which usually falls on 13 April. Celebrated throughout India as New Year's Day, it has been considered the birthday of the Sikh community ever since Guru Gobind Singh inaugurated the Khalsa on Baisakhi Day in 1699. Sikhs also celebrate the autumn festival of lights, Divali, as the day when Guru Hargobind was released from imprisonment under the Mughal emperor Jahangir. Harimandir Sahib (the Golden Temple) in Amritsar is illuminated for the occasion. These two seasonal festivals were introduced by the third Guru, Amar Das, and Guru Gobind Singh added a third: Hola Mahalla, the day after the Hindu festival of Holi (March/April), is celebrated with military exercises and various athletic and literary contests.

The anniversaries of the births and deaths of the Gurus are marked by the 'unbroken reading' (*akhand path*) of the entire Sikh scripture by a team of readers over a period of roughly forty-eight hours. Such occasions are called *Gurpurbs* ('holidays associated with the Gurus'). The birthdays of Guru Nanak (usually in November) and Guru Gobind Singh (December/January) and the martyrdom days of Guru Arjan (May/June) and Guru Tegh Bahadur (November/December) in particular are celebrated around the world.

## Life-Cycle Rituals

At the centre of every important life-cycle ritual is the Guru Granth Sahib.

### Naming a Child

When a child is to be named, family members take the baby to the gurdwara and present the *karah prashad* that will be distributed after the actual ceremony to the Guru Granth Sahib. After various prayers of thanks and a recitation of *Ardas*, the Guru Granth Sahib is opened at random and the first letter of the first composition on the left-hand page is noted; then a name beginning with the same letter is chosen. In this way the child takes his or her identity from the Guru's word and begins life as a Sikh. Then a boy is given the second name *Singh* ('Lion') and a girl the second name *Kaur* ('Princess'). *Amrit* is applied to the eyes and head; the infant is given a sip of the sweetened water to drink; and the first five stanzas of Guru Nanak's *Japji* are recited.

### Marriage

'They are not said to be husband and wife, who merely sit together. Rather, they alone are called husband and wife who have one soul in two bodies' (AG 788). This proclamation of the third Guru, Amar Das, has become the basis of the Sikh view of marriage, which emphasizes the necessity of spiritual compatibility between the spouses. In a traditional society where the family is more important than the individual, the fact that Sikh marriages have traditionally been arranged is not inconsistent with that principle.

To be legal, a Sikh wedding must take place in the presence of the Guru Granth Sahib. The bride and groom circumambulate the sacred scripture four times, once for each of their four vows:

1. to lead an action-oriented life based on righteousness and never to shun obligations of family and society;
2. to maintain bonds of reverence and dignity between one another;
3. to keep enthusiasm for life alive in the face of adverse circumstances and to remain detached from worldly attachments; and
4. to cultivate a balanced approach in life, avoiding all extremes.

The circular movement around the scripture symbolizes the primordial cycle of life in which there is no beginning and no end, while the four marital vows reflect the ideals that the Sikh tradition considers the keys to a blissful life.

### Khalsa Initiation

The Khalsa initiation ceremony (*amrit sanskar*) must also take place in the presence of the Guru Granth Sahib. There is no fixed age for initiation: all that is required is that the candidate be willing and able to accept the Khalsa discipline. Five Khalsa Sikhs, representing the original Cherished Five (*Panj Piare*), conduct the ceremony. Each recites from memory one of the five liturgical prayers while stirring the sweetened water (*amrit*) with a double-edged sword.

The novices then drink the *amrit* five times so that their bodies are purified of five vices (lust, anger, greed, attachment, and pride), and five times the *amrit* is sprinkled on their eyes to transform their outlook towards life. Finally, the *amrit* is poured on their heads five times, sanctifying their hair so that they will preserve its natural form and listen to the voice of conscience. At each stage of the ceremony, the initiates repeat the words *Vahiguru Ji Ka Khalsa! Vahiguru Ji Ki Fateh!* ('Khalsa belongs to the Wonderful Lord! Victory belongs to the Wonderful Lord!'). Thus a person becomes a Khalsa Sikh through the transforming power of the sacred word and the sacred nectar (*amrit*). At the conclusion of the ceremony, a Vak is read aloud and *karah prashad* is distributed.

### Death

For a dedicated Sikh (*Gurmukh*), death is a joy to be welcomed when it comes, for it means the perfecting of his or her union with Akal Purakh

## From Sikh Hymns and Prayers

*Despite his militancy, Guru Gobind Singh shares with Guru Nanak a sense that religious boundaries are irrelevant to God:*

There is no difference between a temple and a mosque, nor between the prayers of a Hindu and a Muslim. Though differences seem to mark and distinguish, all men/women are in reality the same.

Gods and demons, celestial beings, men called Muslims and others called Hindus—such differences are trivial, inconsequential, the outward results of locality and dress.

With eyes the same, the ears and body, all possessing a common form—all are in fact a single creation, the elements of nature in a uniform blend.

Allah is the same as the God of the Hindus, Puran and Qur'an are the same. All are the same, none is separate; a single form, a single creation (*Akal Ustat, Dasam Granth*, 19–20; McLeod 1984: 57).

*Bhai Gurdas likewise declares the irrelevance of external religious observances:*

If bathing at *tiraths* ['pilgrimage centres'] procures liberation, frogs, for sure, must be saved;
And likewise the banyan, with dangling tresses, if growing hair long sets one free.
If the need can be served by roaming unclad the deer of the forest must surely be pious;
So too the ass which rolls in the dust if limbs smeared with ashes can purchase salvation.
Saved are the cattle, mute in the fields, if silence produces deliverance.
Only the Guru can bring us salvation; only the Guru can set a man free (*Varan Bhai Gurdas*, 36:14; McLeod 1984: 67).

*The Sikh Prayer called the Ardas, standardized by the 1930s, contains a roll call of the ten Gurus. Sri Hari Krishan, included in it, is the child who became the eighth Guru, and should not be confused with the Hare Krishna movement arising from Hindu Vaishnavism in Bengal:*

Having first remembered God, turn your thoughts to Guru Nanak; Angad Guru, Amar Das, each
    with Ram Das grant us aid.
Arjan and Hargobind, think of them and Har Rai.
Dwell on Sri Hari Krishan, he whose sight dispels all pain.
Think of Guru Tegh Bahadur; thus shall every treasure come.
May they grant their gracious guidance, help and strength in every place.
May the tenth Master, the revered Guru Gobind Singh, also grant us 'help and strength in every place.
The light which shone from each of the ten Masters shines now from the sacred pages of the Guru
    Granth Sahib.
Turn your thoughts to its message and call on God, saying, *Vahiguru!* (*Chandi di Var, Dasam Granth*,
119; McLeod 1984: 104).

*Martyrdom is a frequent theme in Sikh history, motivating Sikhs to persevere in struggles today:*

These loyal members of the Khalsa who gave their heads for their faith; who were hacked limb from limb, scalped, broken on the wheel, or sawn asunder, who sacrificed their lives for the protection of hallowed gurdwaras never forsaking their faith; and who were steadfast in their loyalty to the uncut hair of the true Sikh: reflect on their merits, O Khalsa, and call on God, saying, *Vahiguru!* (*Ardas*; McLeod 1984: 104).

and a final release from the cycle of rebirth. For a self-willed person (*Manmukh*), by contrast, death means the culmination of his or her separation from the Divine and perpetuation of the process of reincarnation.

Hymns from the Guru Granth Sahib are sung both in the period preceding the cremation and in the post-cremation rites. In India, the body of the deceased is bathed, dressed in new clothes, and placed on a pyre for cremation. The ashes are then disposed of in a nearby stream or river. In the diaspora, however, the rituals associated with death have had to undergo significant changes. Family and friends gather around the body at a funeral home with the necessary facilities for cremation. The body is placed in a casket where people may scatter flower petals as a tribute. Following devotional singing and eulogy, *Ardas* is offered by the *granthi*. Then the casket is pushed on a trolley to the cremation furnace, usually accompanied by family and friends. While the casket is burning, the congregation recites the late-evening prayer, *Kirtan Sohila*.

In addition, a reading of the entire scripture takes place either at home or in a gurdwara—a process that may take up to ten days to complete. At the conclusion of the reading a 'completion' ceremony is held when the final prayers are offered in the memory of the deceased.

# 🏵 DIFFERENTIATION

## Encounter with Modernity

The Khalsa spent most of its first century fighting the armies of Mughals and Afghan invaders. Finally, in 1799, Ranjit Singh (1780–1839) succeeded in unifying the Punjab, taking control of Lahore and declaring himself Maharaja. For the next four decades the Sikh community enjoyed more settled political conditions, and with territorial expansion as far as Peshawar in the west, people of different cultural and religious backgrounds were attracted into the fold of Sikhism. The appearance of the Golden Temple today owes a great deal to the generous patronage of the Maharaja, who also employed scribes to make beautiful copies of the Sikh scripture that were sent as gifts to the Sikh *Takhats* ('Thrones', the traditional seats of authority at Amritsar, Anandpur, Patna, and Nander) and other major historical gurdwaras.

Although Maharaja Ranjit Singh himself was a Khalsa Sikh, his rule was marked by religious diversity within the Sikh Panth. Khalsa members, in their drive to carve out an empire for themselves, realized that for their project to succeed they required allies both inside and outside the Sikh Panth. Therefore they forged an internal alliance with the **Sehaj-dharis**: Sikhs who lived as members of the Nanak Panth but did not accept the Khalsa code of conduct. The Khalsa conceded the religious culture of the *Sehaj-dharis* to be legitimate even though, in keeping with the inclusive approach of their sovereign, the latter revered Hindu scriptures as well as the Guru Granth Sahib and the Dasam Granth, and in some cases even worshipped Hindu images.

### Sikh Reform Movements

After the death of Maharaja Ranjit Singh in 1839, his successors could not withstand the pressure exerted by the advancing British forces. After two Anglo–Sikh wars, in 1846 and 1849, the Sikh kingdom was annexed to the British empire. With the loss of the Punjab's independence the Sikhs were no longer the masters of their own kingdom. It was in this context that three reform movements emerged in the second half of the nineteenth century, each attempting to restore the sense of a distinct spiritual identity to a people whose religious tradition was now just one among a vast array of traditions now encompassed within colonial India.

## The Nirankaris

Baba Dayal Das (1783–1853) was the founder of a renewal movement devoted to purging Sikhism of

Hindu influences (especially image worship) and recalling Sikhs to the worship of the 'formless and invisible God' (*Nirankar*). Dayal Das's followers revered his *Hukam-nama* ('Book of Ordinances') alongside the Guru Granth Sahib and recognized a line of personal Gurus descending from him. Although they did not equate this line with the succession of ten Gurus ending with Guru Gobind Singh, and did not reject the orthodox doctrine according to which the Guru is eternally present in the sacred scripture, they believed that Baba Dayal was dispatched by God to recall the Panth to obedience and renew the Sikh tradition.

The Nirankari movement survives today, although its numbers do not exceed a few thousand and they have remained on the periphery of the Panth. They claim that it was Baba Dayal Das who instituted the distinctively Sikh marriage ceremony, in which the Sikh scripture replaced the fire at the centre of the older Hindu rite.

## The Namdharis

The Namdharis took their name from their emphasis on the divine Name. Their leader, Baba Ram Singh (1816–84), was the first reformer to stress the importance of the Khalsa under colonial rule. He reinstituted the order of Sant ('Devout') Khalsa in 1862, creating his own initiation ritual and an austere rule of conduct stressing, in addition to chanting the divine *nam*, a vegetarian diet and all-white dress.

As the number of his followers grew, Baba Ram Singh took on an increasingly active role in the public sphere, promoting boycotts of various kinds as a form of non-violent resistance to the British occupation of the Punjab. After the British gave permission for the slaughter of cows—banned under Maharaja Ranjit Singh—to resume, a number of Muslim butchers in Amritsar and Ludhiana were killed by Namdhari extremists. In the background of the mutiny of 1857 the British crushed the Namdhari movement, sending Baba Ram Singh into exile, and executing more than sixty Namdharis without trial in a particularly horrifying way—tying them over the mouths of canons and blasting their bodies to pieces. The Namdharis came to be seen as political martyrs and forerunners of the Gandhian movement for the independence of India.

After Ram Singh's death, the Namdharis developed a doctrine of religious authority similar to the Shi'i Muslim doctrine of the hidden Imam, maintaining that Guru Gobind Singh did not die in 1708 but went into hiding, that Baba Ram Singh succeeded him as the twelfth Guru; and that although Ram Singh in turn went into hiding as well, some day he will return.

## The Singh Sabha Movement

Among the most important contributions to the modernization of the Sikh tradition were the educational initiatives of the **Singh Sabha** ('Society of the Singhs'). Established in 1873 by four prominent Sikh reformers, the Singh Sabha sought to reaffirm Sikh identity in the face of two threats: the casual reversion to Hindu practices during the period of Punjabi independence under Maharaja Ranjit Singh and the active proselytizing efforts not only of the Hindu Arya Samaj, but of Christian missionaries.

By the end of the nineteenth century the Tat ('Pure' or 'True') Khalsa, the dominant wing of the Singh Sabha, had eradicated the last traces of religious diversity within the Sikh Panth and established clear norms of belief and practice. In effect, they made the Khalsa tradition the standard of orthodoxy for all Sikhs.

In the twentieth century the Tat Khalsa reformers also contributed to two important legal changes. First, in 1909, they obtained legal recognition of the distinctive Sikh wedding ritual in the Anand Marriage Act (1909). Then in the 1920s they helped to re-establish direct Khalsa control of the major historical gurdwaras, many of which had fallen into the hands of corrupt *mahants* ('custodians') supported by the British. Inspired by the Tat Khalsa ideal, the Akali movement of the 1920s eventually secured British assent to the Sikh Gurdwara Act (1925), under which control of all gurdwaras passed to the Shiromani Gurdwara Prabandhak Committee (SGPC; 'Chief Management Committee of Sikh Shrines'). The Akalis were the forerunners of the modern political party known as the Akali Dal ('army of the immortal').

### SGPC Rahit Manual

Control of the gurdwaras gave the SGPC enormous political and economic influence. By 1950 it had established itself as the central authority on all questions of religious discipline, and in that year it published a manual entitled *Sikh Rahit Maryada*, which has ever since been regarded as the authoritative guide to orthodox Sikh doctrine and behaviour.

Based on the teachings of the Guru Granth Sahib, supplemented with teachings from revered Sikh leaders, the *Sikh Rahit Maryada* enjoins Sikhs to cultivate a pure and pious inner spirituality (*bani*), to adopt the Five Ks as external signs of virtuous conduct (*bana*), and to abstain from the four cardinal sins (hair-cutting, adultery, intoxicants, and meat obtained through the slow bleeding or religious sacrifice that has not been killed with a single blow).

The manual encourages the worship of God and meditation on his name, undergoing Khalsa initiation, and attending divine services. It also calls on Sikhs to earn a living honestly and truthfully, to share selflessly with the needy and less fortunate in order to further the well-being of all, to nurture virtues such as compassion, honesty, generosity, patience, perseverance, and humility, and to avoid superstitions, idols, and images.

Not punitive in intent or effect, the *Sikh Rahit Maryada* encourages devotees to attune their daily lives to the will of God. It calls for tolerance of those who stray as well as those who, though they follow the teachings of Guru Granth Sahib, have not yet accepted the full discipline of the Khalsa; instead of condemning these *Sehaj-dharis*

('gradualists'), it assumes that in time they will progress to the point where they will join the Khalsa. The only code of conduct sanctioned by the Akal Takhat—the highest seat of religious and temporal authority among Sikhs—the *Sikh Rahit Maryada* is distributed free of charge by the SGPC, and is now available in Hindi and English as well as Punjabi, in acknowledgement of the needs of Sikhs living outside their historical homeland.

### Variations in Modern Sikhism

Although the *Sikh Rahit Maryada* tends to represent Sikhism as a single coherent orthodoxy, at the popular level the Sikh Panth today encompasses a number of variations. For instance, the Khalsa itself includes a distinctive order called the Nihangs, who are rigorous in the observance of the Khalsa *Rahit* and, having renounced all fear of death, are ready to die for their faith at any time. Their garments are always blue, with some saffron and white, and on their heads they wear a high turban surmounted by a piece of cloth called a *pharhara* ('standard' or 'flag'). In North America some Sikhs occasionally wear Nihang dress on special occasions such as Baisakhi Day.

Another group within the Khalsa calls itself the Akhand Kirtani Jatha ('continuous singing of the Sikh scriptures') and follows its own special discipline that includes an entirely vegetarian diet and requires that female members wear a small turban.

In fact, the Sikh Panth has never been monolithic or homogeneous, and in recent years the Internet has allowed many groups to claim that they represent the 'true' Panth. Of the 25 million Sikhs in the world today, only about 20 per cent are orthodox **Amrit-dharis** ('initiated'). But many other Sikhs follow most of the Khalsa code even though they have not been initiated. (Those who 'retain their hair' are known as **Kes-dharis**.)

Less conspicuous are the many Sikhs (especially in North America and the United Kingdom) who do cut their hair but do not consider themselves to be 'lesser Sikhs' in any way. Many of these people use the Khalsa names 'Singh' and 'Kaur' without inhibition. In fact, they are the majority in the diaspora, and they play active roles both in the community's ritual life and in the management of the gurdwaras.

These semi-observant Sikhs are often confused with the *Sehaj-dharis* who have never accepted the Khalsa discipline. Although the *Sehaj-dharis* practise *nam-simaran* and follow the teachings of the Adi Granth, they do not observe the *Khalsa Rahit*. The number of *Sehaj-dharis* has declined in the last few decades, but they certainly have not disappeared completely.

Finally, there are Khalsa Sikhs—especially in the diaspora—who have committed one or more of the four sins after initiation. These lapsed *Amrit-dharis* are known as 'Patit Sikhs' ('Apostates'). It should be emphasized that none of these categories are necessarily permanent. Individuals go through different stages in life, and their status within the Panth changes accordingly. In short, there is no single way of being a Sikh.

# 🌿 CULTURAL EXPRESSIONS

## Cultural Norms of Family and Society

Guru Nanak believed that the key to liberation lay not in ascetic renunciation but in the life of the householder. His successors shared that belief, upholding the ideal of family life in their own lives as well as in their teachings. The third Guru, Amar Das, proclaimed, 'Family life is superior to ascetic life in sectarian garb because it is from householders that ascetics meet their needs by begging' (AG 586). To understand family relationships, one must address issues of caste and gender from the Sikh perspective.

Doctrinally, caste has never been one of the defining criteria of Sikh identity. In fact, rejection of caste-based discrimination was a fundamental feature of Sikhism from the beginning. Moreover, the *Sikh Rahit Maryada* explicitly states that 'No account should be taken of caste' in the selection of a marriage partner. This is the ideal, however. In practice, most Sikhs still marry within their own caste group, though inter-caste marriages are becoming more common among urban professionals, in India and elsewhere.

In Punjabi society, marriage creates a connection not just between two individuals but, more important, between two groups of kin. It is in this context that the concept of honour (*iz-zat*) continues to play a significant role in family relationships.

The Sikh Gurus approached issues of gender within the parameters of a traditional patriarchal society. Thus despite their egalitarian principles and efforts to foster respect for womanhood, their ideas about women were inseparable from their ideas about family: in their view, the ideal woman was defined by her conduct in the context of family life, as a good daughter, a good sister, a good wife and mother. They condemned men as well as women who did not observe the cultural norms of modesty and honour in their lives. There was no tolerance for any kind of premarital or extramarital sexual activity, and rape was regarded as a particularly serious violation, for the dishonour it brought to the family meant the loss of social standing in the community. Furthermore, the rules governing the Khalsa are clearly egalitarian in principle. Those who seek initiation cannot be accepted without their spouses; hence the proportions of male and female initiates are roughly equal. And Khalsa women wear all of the Five Ks.

In practice, however, males still dominate most Sikh institutions, and many Sikh women continue to live in a society based on patriarchal cultural assumptions. In this respect they differ little from their counterparts in any of India's major religious communities. Even so, Sikh women have been asserting themselves with growing success in recent years. In the area of reproductive rights, for instance, they successfully argued the case for abortion under certain circumstances. As a result, although Sikhism does not condone abortion for the purpose of sex selection, or as a form of birth control, it does permit medical abortion when the mother's life is in danger, or in cases of incest or rape.

## Music, Art, and Literature

Sikhism is the only world religion in which song has been the primary medium for the founder's message. Sacred music has been at the heart of the Sikh devotional experience from the beginning. In specifying the *ragas* (melodies) to which the hymns were to be sung, Guru Nanak and his successors sought to promote harmony and balance in the minds of listeners and performers. Any *raga* likely to arouse passion was therefore either excluded altogether or adapted to produce a gentler effect.

### Art

The earliest examples of Sikh graphic art are illuminated scriptures dating from the late sixteenth and early seventeenth centuries. Sikh scribes followed the Qur'anic tradition of decorating the margins and the opening pages of the text with abstract designs and floral motifs. The earliest extant paintings of Guru Nanak appear in a *janam-sakhi* (birth-narrative) from the mid-1600s.

Both fine and applied arts flourished under the patronage of Maharaja Ranjit Singh. In addition to painting, sculpture, armour, brassware, jewellery, and textiles, a distinctive

Sikh architecture developed at the Sikh court in the first half of the nineteenth century. Murals and frescoes depicting major events from Sikh history can still be seen at historic gurdwaras including the Darbar Sahib in Amritsar.

Two great Sikh artists emerged in the twentieth century. Sobha Singh (1901–86) was skilled in the Western classical technique of oil painting, but he drew his themes from the romantic lore of the Punjab, the Indian epics, and the Sikh tradition; he is particularly well known for his portraits of the Gurus. Kirpal Singh (1923–90) specialized in realistic capturing on canvas episodes from Sikh history, including awe-inspiring scenes of martyrs and the realistic portrayal of battle scenes. Some of his works are displayed in the Central Sikh Museum in the Darbar Sahib complex.

*Nineteen Eighty-Four,* by The Singh Twins, 1998 (© The Singh Twins: www.singhtwins.co.uk).

A number of Sikh women have also made names for themselves as artists. Amrita Shergill (1911–41), for instance, has been described as the Frida Kahlo of India. Raised largely in Europe, she studied art in Paris but returned to India in 1934 and explored village life in a series of paintings that have been declared National Art Treasures. Arpana Caur (b. 1954) is a bold modern painter who addresses current issues and events directly. The Singh Twins (b. 1966), born in England, apply styles and techniques of the classic Indian miniature tradition to contemporary themes. Their painting *Nineteen Eighty-Four*, inspired by the storming of the Golden Temple, is a powerful reflection not only on the event itself but on the responses it evoked in the Sikh diaspora.[2]

### Literature

A rich literary tradition began with the introduction of the Gurmukhi script used to record the hymns of the Gurus. The influence of the Adi Granth is clear in the works of early poets such as Bhai Gurdas. The first Punjabi prose form was the *janam-sakhi*, which remained the dominant literary genre before the emergence of the twentieth-century novel. It is easy to see the impact of Sikh devotional literature on the writings of celebrated early modern authors such as Kahn Singh Nabha (1861–1938), the poet Bhai Vir Singh (1872–1957), and Mohan Singh Vaid (1881–1936), who wrote stories, novels, and plays as well as many works of non-fiction. All these writers emphasized optimism, resolute determination, faith, and love towards fellow human beings. Max Arthur Macauliffe (1837–1913) was an administrator in the British colonial government who became interested in Sikhism in the 1860s and devoted his life to the translation of the Sikh scriptures. Writers such as these played a leadership role in the Singh Sabha reform movement of the late nineteenth and early twentieth centuries. Although much contemporary Punjabi literature reflects Western influences, Sikh devotional literature is still a source of inspiration for the passionate lyricism of the new generation of writers such as Harinder Singh Mehboob.

# 🌿 INTERACTION AND ADAPTATION

## Twentieth-Century India

### Doctrinal Authority

By 1950, as we have seen, the Shiromani Gurdwara Prabandhak Committee (SGPC) had become the principal voice of authority in both religious and political affairs for the worldwide Sikh community. Although it has often been challenged by Sikhs living outside the Punjab, the SGPC is a democratic institution that claims to speak on behalf of the majority of Sikhs, and hence to represent the authority of the Guru-Panth.

The ultimate authority, however, is the Akal Takhat in Amritsar. The most important of the five *Takhats*, the Akal Takhat may issue edicts (*hukam-namas*) that provide guidance or clarification on any aspect of Sikh doctrine or practice. It may punish any Sikh charged with a violation of religious discipline or with activity 'prejudicial' to Sikh interests and unity; it may also recognize individuals who have performed outstanding service or made sacrifices for the sake of the Sikh cause.

### The Partition of India

In 1947 the British withdrew from India and the subcontinent was partitioned to create two independent republics of India and Pakistan. Partition was especially hard for the Sikhs because it split the Punjab into two. Most of the 2.5 million Sikhs living on the Pakistani side fled as refugees; though many settled in the new Indian state of Punjab, some moved on to major cities elsewhere in India.

Since 1976 the Constitution of India has defined the republic as a secular state, and Article 25 guarantees the right to freedom of religion.

However, a sub-clause of the same Article states that 'persons professing the Sikh, Jaina, or Buddhist religion' will be considered to fall within the general category of Hinduism. When the original Constitution was drafted, the Sikh members of the Constituent Assembly refused to sign the document because it did not recognize the Sikhs as a group with an independent identity. Since that time, Sikh and Hindu politicians alike have deliberately stirred up popular resentment on both sides for political purposes.

In 2002 the National Commission to Review the Constitution recommended that the wording of Article 25 be amended to refer specifically to the three religious groups—Sikhs, Jainas, and Buddhists—that are currently covered under the default term 'Hindu'. To date, however, this amendment has not been enacted.

### 'Operation Blue Star'

In 1973 the main political party of the Sikhs, Akali Dal, passed the Anandpur Sahib Resolution, demanding increased autonomy for all the states of India. Over the following years, relations with the Indian government became increasingly strained as a result. In an apparent attempt to sow dissension in the Akali ranks, the Congress government encouraged the rise of a charismatic young militant named Jarnail Singh Bhindranvale (1947–84). But this strategy backfired in the spring of 1984, when a group of armed radicals led by Bhindranvale decided to provoke a confrontation with the government by occupying the Akal Takhat building inside the Golden Temple complex. The government responded by sending in the army. The assault that followed—code-named 'Operation Blue Star'—resulted in the deaths of many Sikhs, including Bhindranvale, as well as the destruction of the Akal Takhat and severe damage to the Golden Temple itself.

A few months later, on 31 October 1984, Prime Minister Indira Gandhi was assassinated by her own Sikh bodyguards. For several days unchecked Hindu mobs in Delhi and elsewhere killed thousands of Sikhs. As a consequence of these events, 1984 became a turning point in the history of the Sikhs, precipitating an identity crisis within the Panth and dividing Sikhs around the world into two camps, liberal and fundamentalist.

## The Sikh Diaspora

Over the last century more than one million Sikhs have left India for foreign lands. Wherever they have settled—in Singapore, Malaysia, Thailand, Hong Kong, Australia, New Zealand, East Africa, and the United Kingdom, as well as Canada and the United States—they have carried their sacred scripture with them and established their own places of worship. Today there are more than five hundred gurdwaras in North America and the United Kingdom alone.

New cultural environments have required some adaptation. In diaspora gurdwaras, for instance, congregational services are usually held on Sunday, not because it is the holy day—in India there is no specific day for worship—but because it is the only day when most Sikhs are free to attend services.

Western societies have also presented Sikh spirituality with serious challenges. Turban-wearing Sikhs have frequently faced discrimination by prospective employers, and Khalsa Sikhs have had to negotiate with various institutions for permission to wear the *kirpan* as a religious symbol. At the same time, a gradual loss of fluency in the Punjabi language means that younger Sikhs are at growing risk of theological illiteracy. Diaspora Sikhs, fully aware that assimilation is making steady progress among the second and third generations, have responded with concerted efforts to revive interest in Sikh traditions and identity.

To meet the challenges of life in Western societies, many gurdwaras now hold 'Sunday school' classes for children, and many Sikh families now worship at home—in both Punjabi and English— as well as at the gurdwara. Another innovative response has been to organize Sikh Youth Camps offering continuous exposure to Sikh spirituality, values, and traditions.

## Punjabi Sikhs and White Sikhs

Around 1970 a number of yoga students in Toronto and Los Angeles were inspired by their teacher, a Sikh named Harbhajan Singh Puri (Yogi Bhajan), to convert to the Sikh faith and join his Healthy, Happy, Holy Organization ('3HO'). Eventually renamed Sikh Dharma, the organization has since established chapters or *ashrams* in various North American cities.

All members of this organization—male and female—wear the same costume of white turbans, tunics, and tight trousers, and for this reason they have come to be known as 'White Sikhs'. They live and raise families in communal houses, spending long hours in meditation and chanting as well as yoga practice.

Punjabi Sikhs in general praise the strict Khalsa-style discipline of the White Sikhs. In other respects, however, the White Sikh culture is seen as quite alien. In the Punjab, for instance—as in India as a whole—white clothing is normally a sign of mourning; only the Namdharis dress entirely in white. And the only Sikh women who wear turbans are members of the Akhand Kirtani Jatha. Finally, the concept of *izzat* ('prestige' or 'honour'), which plays such an important part in Punjabi culture and society, is irrelevant to the White Sikhs. Even in North America, therefore, Punjabi Sikhs have tended to distance themselves from the White Sikhs.

## ❧ RECENT DEVELOPMENTS

In the last few decades Sikhs in North America have received a great deal of media attention. Unfortunately, much of this attention has been negative, based on stereotypes rather than knowledge

of Sikh traditions. In the United States, the first victim of the racial backlash that followed the terrorist attacks of September 2001 was—perhaps not surprisingly—a Sikh, Balbir Singh Sodhi of Arizona, who was shot dead by a self-described 'patriot' who mistook him for a Muslim. People simply do not know who Sikhs are.

Among the issues that have attracted particular attention have been the right to wear turbans in the workplace and *kirpans* in public schools, the Indian army's assault on the Golden Temple, the Air India bombing of 1985 (in which 329 people—most of them Canadian citizens—died), and, most recently, the acquittal of the two Vancouver men who were suspected of having played major roles in the bombing conspiracy. In response to the largely negative public attention attracted by issues such as these, various efforts have been undertaken to encourage discussion and correct public misunderstanding.

The first North American conference on Sikh studies was held in 1976 at the University of California, Berkeley. Participants at that conference generally felt that Sikhism was indeed 'the forgotten tradition' among scholarly circles in North America. This is no longer the case. In the last two decades the scholarly literature on Sikhism has grown steadily, and the mistaken notion that Sikhism offers a synthesis of Hindu and Muslim ideals has been almost entirely abandoned. Today there are eight endowed chairs in Sikh studies in North America, and Sikhism is increasingly recognized in undergraduate academic programs.

The Sikh community has been involved in a process of 'renewal and redefinition' throughout its history, and that process has only intensified in recent years. Today, the question 'Who is a Sikh?' is the subject of often acrimonious debate in online discussions among the various Sikh networks. Each generation of Sikhs has to respond to this question in the light of new historical circumstances while addressing the larger issues of orthodoxy and orthopraxy. Not surprisingly, diaspora Sikhs approach these issues from different perspectives, depending on the cultural and political contexts they come from. In many cases they rediscover their identity through their interaction with other religious and ethnic communities. New challenges demand new responses, especially in a postmodern world where notions of self, gender, and authority are subject to constant questioning. Thus the process of Sikh identity-formation is a dynamic and ongoing phenomenon.

## Sites

**Amritsar, Punjab** The holiest of all places for Sikhs, Amritsar is the site of the Darbar Sahib (the Golden Temple) and was named for the 'pool of nectar' that surrounds the shrine. Facing the Golden Temple and connected to it by a causeway is the Akal Takhat ('Eternal Throne'), the most important of five seats of authority within the Sikh world.

**Anandpur, Punjab** The birthplace of the Khalsa; the Takhat Sri Kesgarh Sahib stands on the spot where Guru Gobind Singh is said to have created the 'Cherished Five' (*Panj Piare*) in 1699.

**Talwandi Sabo, Punjab** Guru Gobind Singh stayed here for several months c. 1705; site of the Takhat Sri Damdama Sahib.

**Patna, Bihar** The birthplace of Guru Gobind Singh and the site of the Takhat Sri Patna Sahib.

**Nanded, Maharashtra** The place where Guru Gobind Singh died and the site of the Takhat Sri Hazur Sahib.

# Glossary

**Adi Granth**   Literally, 'original book'; first compiled by Guru Arjan in 1604 and invested with supreme authority as the Guru Granth Sahib after the death of Guru Gobind Singh.

**Akal Purakh**   'The One Beyond Time', God.

**Amrit-dhari**   'Nectar-bearer'; an initiated member of the Khalsa.

**Baisakhi**   An Indian new year's holiday in mid-April, when Sikhs celebrate the birthday of the Khalsa.

**Five Ks**   The five marks of Khalsa identity: *kes* (uncut hair), *kangha* (wooden comb), *kirpan* (sword), *kara* (wrist ring), and *kachh* (short breeches).

**gurdwara**   Literally, 'Guru's door'; the Sikh place of worship.

**Guru**   'Teacher'; either a spiritual person or the divine inner voice.

**hukam**   'Divine order, will, or command'; an all-embracing principle, the sum total of all divinely instituted laws; a revelation of the nature of God.

**janam-sakhis**   'Birth testimonies'; traditional accounts of the life of Guru Nanak.

**karah prashad**   A sweet pudding or paste of flour, sugar, and butter that is prepared in an iron (*karah*) bowl with prayers, placed in the presence of the Sikh scripture during worship, and then distributed in the congregation.

**Kes-dhari**   Literally, 'hair-bearer'; a Sikh who affirms his identity by wearing unshorn hair.

**Khalsa**   Literally, 'pure' or 'crown estate'; hence an order of Sikhs bound by common identity and discipline.

**kirtan**   The singing of hymns from the scriptures in worship.

**langar**   The term for both the community kitchen and the meal that is prepared there and served to all present in the congregation.

**miri-piri**   The doctrine that the Guru possesses temporal (*miri*) as well as spiritual (*piri*) authority.

**Mul Mantar**   Literally, 'Basic Formula'; the opening creedal statement of the Adi Granth, declaring the eternity and transcendence of God, the creator.

**nam**   'The divine Name'.

**nam-simaran**   'Remembrance of the divine Name', especially the devotional practice of meditating on the divine Name.

**Panth**   Literally, 'path'; hence the Sikh community.

**Rahit**   The code of conduct for the Khalsa.

**Sants**   Ascetic poets who believed divinity to exist beyond all forms or description.

**Sehaj-dhari**   Literally, a 'gradualist'; a Sikh who follows the teachings of the Gurus but has not accepted the Khalsa discipline.

**Singh Sabha**   Literally, 'Society of Singhs'; a revival movement established in 1873 that redefined the norms of Sikh doctrine and practice.

**Vak**   'Saying'; a passage from the Guru Granth Sahib chosen at random and read aloud to the congregation as the lesson of the day.

# Further Reading

Dusenbery, Verne A. 2008. *Sikhs at Large: Religion, Culture, and Politics*. New Delhi: Oxford University Press. A collection of essays bringing together different perspectives on the cultural and political dimensions of the Sikh diaspora and of Sikhism as a global religion.

Fenech, Louis E. 2008. *The Darbar of the Sikh Gurus: The Court of God in the World of Men*. New Delhi: Oxford University Press. Traces the evolving nature of the court of the Sikh Gurus in the broader historical context of Indo-Persian courtly tradition.

Grewal, J.S. 1991. *The New Cambridge History of India: The Sikhs of the Punjab*. Cambridge: Cambridge University Press. A classic chronological study of Sikh history from the beginnings to the present day.

Jakobsh, Doris R. 2003. *Relocating Gender in Sikh History: Transformation, Meaning and Identity*. New Delhi:

Oxford University Press. A recent study examining the development of gender ideals under the Sikh Gurus, and their adaptation and in some cases transformation by the new intellectual elite of the Singh Sabha during the colonial period.

McLeod, W.H. 1984. *Textual Sources for the Study of Sikhism*. Manchester: Manchester University Press. An anthology of selections covering all aspects of Sikh belief, worship, and practice.

———. 1999. *Sikhs and Sikhism*. New Delhi: Oxford University Press. An omnibus edition of four classic studies on the history and evolution of Sikhs and Sikhism by one of the world's leading scholars in the field.

———. 2002. *The Sikhs of the Khalsa*. New Delhi: Oxford University Press. A study of how the *Rahit* or 'the code of belief and conduct' came into being, how it developed in response to historical circumstances, and why it still retains an unchallenged hold over all who consider themselves Khalsa Sikhs.

Nesbitt, Eleanor. 2005. *Sikhism: A Very Short Introduction*. Oxford: Oxford University Press. An ethnographic introduction to Sikhism, its teachings, practices, rituals, and festivals.

Oberoi, Harjot. 1994. *Construction of Religious Boundaries*. New Delhi: Oxford University Press. A major reinterpretation of Sikh religion and society during the colonial period.

Singh, Harbans, ed. 1992–8. *The Encyclopaedia of Sikhism*, 4 vols. Patiala: Punjabi University. A four-volume reference work covering Sikh life and letters, history and philosophy, customs and rituals, social and religious movements, art and architecture, and locales and shrines.

Singh, Nikky-Guninder Kaur. 2005. *The Birth of the Khalsa: A Feminist Re-Memory of Sikh Identity*. Albany: State University of New York Press. Explores the institution of the Khalsa from a feminist perspective, questioning the ways in which Sikh tradition has constructed a hyper-masculine Sikh identity.

Singh, Pashaura. 2006. *Life and Work of Guru Arjan: History, Memory and Biography in the Sikh Tradition*. New Delhi: Oxford University Press. A reconstruction of the life and work of the fifth Sikh Guru, based on history, collective memory, tradition, and mythic representation.

# Recommended Websites

http://www.columbia.edu/itc/mealac/pritchett/00generallinks/index.html
  A good site with links to many resources on South Asia.

www.sikhs.org
  The Sikhism Home Page, Brampton, Ontario, Canada.

www.sikhnet.com
  SikhNet, Espanola, New Mexico, USA.

www.sgpc.net
  Shiromani Gurdwara Parbandhak Committee, Amritsar, Punjab, India.

www.sikhchic.com
  Online magazine: journey through the Sikh universe.

# References

McLeod, W.H. 1984. *Textual Sources for the Study of Sikhism*. Manchester: Manchester University Press.

————. 1989. *Who Is a Sikh? Problem of Sikh Identity*. Oxford: Clarendon Press.

————. 1997. *Sikhism*. London: Penguin Books.

Singh, Pashaura. 2006. *Life and Work of Guru Arjan: History, Memory and Biography in the Sikh Tradition*. New Delhi: Oxford University Press.

# Notes

This chapter is dedicated to the memory of my teacher, Professor Willard G. Oxtoby.

1. This reference means that the passage quoted comes from the 27th stanza of the ballad (*Var*) in the musical measure *Majh*, by Guru Nanak (M1), on page 150 of the Adi Granth (AG).

2. For a discussion of this work by the artists themselves, see <http://www.sikhchic.com/article-detail.php?cat=21&id=747>. *Nineteen Eighty-Four and the Via Dolorosa Project* (2009) is a semi-autobiographical documentary film in which the artists draw parallels with the Christian faith.

# Chapter 4

# Jaina Traditions

≈ Anne Vallely ≈

A frail monk sits cross-legged on a bed, leaning against the wall for support as his followers enter the room. Everyone knows this is the last time they will gather for *darshana*—to pay homage to their guru and receive his blessing—for he has taken the vow of *sallekhana* and the process is nearing its end. *Sallekhana* is the ritual death achieved at the end of a long fast. No Jaina is required to undertake such a fast; in fact, Jainas are expressly forbidden to cause harm to any living being, whether in thought, speech, or action. But the Jaina path is one of renunciation—of departure from life during life—and *sallekhana* is merely its logical end. Voluntary death is the most radical statement possible of detachment from the body and the world. A dispassionate death is a triumph for the eternal soul on its journey towards perfection.

## OVERVIEW

Jainism confronts us with a simple yet extraordinary message: the path to happiness, truth, and self-realization is the path of restraint. Happiness is the product not of doing but of not-doing; not of embracing the world but of disengaging from it.

It is this emphasis on restraint that gives Jainism its distinctive ascetic character. To study the Jaina tradition, however, is to realize that it cannot be contained within such narrow bounds. For one thing, the Jaina community is equally well known for its business acumen, worldly success, and strong social identity—in other words, for its effective, dynamic engagement with the world.

Outsiders often perceive a paradoxical disjunction between the Jaina community's this-worldly achievements and its other-worldly ethos. But this seeming paradox reflects the spirit of the tradition: the path of renunciation is a path of transformative power. The power of renunciation lies not in opposing worldly power, but rather in transcending and subsuming it. Some of the most interesting dimensions of Jainism can be traced to this interplay between the worldly and the other-worldly, both in scripture and in lived practice. Ultimately, following the Jaina path means withdrawing from the world—not just from its sorrows but also from its ephemeral joys, from family and community, from desires and pride, even from one's own body.

Conquering our attachment to the world is the most difficult of all battles, but for Jainas it is the only battle worth engaging. Such is the message of the **Jinas** ('victors' or 'conquerors'), the twenty-four ascetic–prophets—the most recent of whom was **Mahavira** (c. 599–527 BCE)—who taught the path to eternal happiness.

Jainism is a tradition that expresses itself ritually through the veneration and emulation of the Jinas (also known as '**Tirthankaras**'—builders of bridges across the ocean of birth and death, or *samsara*). The Jina is the highest expression of the Jaina ideal, and the focus of the Jaina devotional apparatus. A commanding figure who could just as easily have been a worldly *chakravartin*—the ideal benevolent ruler—endowed with all the powers and possessions the world has to offer, the Jina 'conquers' the world by turning his back on it. Indeed, the Jina is venerated in both his potentialities—as the regal *chakravartin*, magnificently bejewelled and crowned, and as the unadorned **Arhat**, deep in meditation, entirely detached from worldly concerns. World renouncer and world conqueror, though antithetical in their orientations, both trace their beginnings to the auspicious karma accrued from a life of non-violence. Restraint, self-discipline, and commitment not to harm are the starting points for the Jina and the *chakravartin* alike.

To grasp the vigorous, even forceful character of Jainism, we need to keep in mind that the Jaina

◀ Pilgrims pray at the feet of the colossal statue of Bahubali (Raghu Rai/Magnum).

# Timeline

| | |
|---|---|
| c. 850 BCE | Parsavanath, the 23rd Tirthankara |
| 599–527 | Traditional dates of Mahavira |
| 4th century | Possible beginning of split within Jaina community with southward migration of one group |
| 2nd century CE | Umasvati, Digambara author of the *Tatthvartha Sutra* |
| 5th century | First Jaina temples |
| 9th century | Jinasena, Svetambara philosopher |
| 10th century | Colossal statue of Bahubali erected in Shravanabelagola, Karnataka |
| 11th century | Dilwara temple complex in Rajasthan |
| 12th century | Hemachandra, Svetambara philosopher |
| 15th century | Lonkashaha initiates reform in the Svetambara tradition |
| 16th century | Banarsidass initiates reform in the Digambara tradition |
| 17th century | Beginning of Svetambara Sthanakvasi subsect |
| 18th century | Beginning of Svetambara Terapanthi subsect |
| 20th century | Revitalization of the Bhattaraka tradition within the Digambara sect |

path of renunciation is one not of retreat from the harshness of the world, but of triumph over it. The world surrenders its bounty spontaneously to those who conquer it through detachment—though of course the true renouncer is indifferent to such rewards.

For Jainas the highest possible value is non-violence. So central is this value that Jainas commonly express the essence of their tradition in three words: 'ahimsa paramo dharma' ('non-violence is the supreme path'). This is not to say that Jainas seek to eradicate the violence of the world. In a universe where every life exists only at the expense of others, such a commitment would be futile; furthermore, any engagement with the world only causes us to sink deeper into its depths, generating ever more karma to fasten to our souls. Rather, the Jaina commitment to

non-violence is a commitment to radical non-interference.

Jainas equate non-violence with renunciation because it is only through the total cessation of activity—of mind, speech, and body—that one can truly avoid harming others and, consequently, oneself.

We are surrounded by countless life forms, many of which are invisible to the eye. All possess an eternal soul (*jiva*), and none desires to be harmed. Yet their omnipresence means that we cannot perform any action without causing them harm. And in causing them harm, we harm ourselves, for every act of violence we perpetrate increases the negative karma attached to our souls, impeding our ability to know our true selves. Lack of intention to commit harm is an important mitigating factor. But even unintended acts of harm still result in some degree of karmic

imp.

No.23

# Traditions at a Glance

## Numbers
Estimates range from five to eight million worldwide.

## Distribution
Primarily India; smaller numbers in East Africa, England, and North America.

## Principal Historical Periods

| | |
|---|---|
| 599–527 BCE | Traditional dates of Mahavira |
| c. 310 BCE | Beginning of the split within the Jaina community |
| 2nd century BCE | Possible composition of *Kalpa Sutra* |
| 6th century CE | Crystallization of Svetambara sect |
| 17th century | Emergence of the Svetambara Sthanakvasi subsect |
| 18th century | Emergence of the Svetambara Terapanthi subsect |

## Founders and Leaders
The 24 Jinas or Tirthankaras: [*bridge*] a series of 'ford-builders' who achieved perfect enlightenment and serve as guides for other human beings. The most important Tirthankaras are the two most recent, Parsavanath and Mahavira.

## Deities
None in philosophy; a few minor deities in popular practice; some Jainas also worship Hindu deities such as Lakshmi. Although the Tirthankaras are not gods, their images are revered by many Jainas.

## Authoritative Texts
All Jainas agree that the earliest texts were lost long ago. The Svetambara sect reveres a collection called the *Agama*, consisting of various later treatises known as the *Angas*, as well as the *Kalpa Sutra*, which contains the life stories of the Tirthankaras. The Digambara sect believes that the original *Angas* were lost as well and focus instead on a set of texts called *Prakaranas* (treatises).

## Noteworthy Teachings
The soul is caught in karmic bondage as a result of violence, both intended and unintended, done to other beings. Non-violence is the most important principle, in thought, word, and deed. Freed from karma, the soul attains crystal purity.

bondage—though that karma is less heavy, dark, and damaging than the kind created when the harm is intentional.

Jainism tells us that attachment to the world, our bodies, and the cultivation of our personalities comes at the expense of knowing our true Self.

The Self has nothing to do with this world—not with its sounds, its colours, or its rhythms, nor with our own talents, aptitudes, or experiences, nor even with the relationships we forge with others. The worldly, social selves constructed with such care from the time of our birth are no more than elaborate sand castles, washed away with each wave of the ocean of *samsara*.

The Self is fundamentally other. Its deep, silent tranquillity is indifferent to the cacophony of the world. And precisely because the soul does not lobby for the attention of our consciousness, its presence is easy to ignore amidst the endless distractions created by the demands of the body. Nevertheless, the soul is luminous, radiating peace, and on very rare occasions our conscious minds may catch a glimpse of its magnificence. Jainas call this momentary awakening **samyak darshan** ('right faith' or 'correct intuition' into the workings of the world), and it is the starting point of Jainism

In the absence of *samyak darshan* Jainism makes little sense. The restraint and self-discipline it calls for are challenges to be undertaken only by those with an awareness of both the uniqueness of human birth—the only incarnation from which liberation can be attained—and the perils of worldly attachment.

According to Jainas, there is only one path to emancipation: the path of self-discipline and non-harm. Yet this singular path leads to a remarkable range of Jaina communities, and the lived traditions of Jainism vary widely in both interpretation and practice. In fact, diversity is one of the distinguishing characteristics of Jainism.

The most fundamental distinction is the one between the two Jaina sects: **Digambara** (naked or 'sky-clad') and **Svetambara** (white-clad). This sectarian split occurred some two hundred years after the death of Mahavira, and was the product of enduring differences in views regarding ascetic practice, women's spiritual capacity, and the nature of the Jina, among other things.

Other issues that divide Jainas include the worship of images or idols, the use of 'living beings' such as flowers, water, and fire in worship, and the need for a guru to guide one's spiritual development. Despite the diversity of their interpretations, however, all Jainas share the commitment to renunciation and non-violence that is the heart of the tradition. The message of restraint is unambiguously conveyed by the 'sky-clad' ascetics who literally embody the principle of renunciation, but it is also present in the beliefs and practices of lay Jainas, including those who live in a context of plenty. Out of the clamorous diversity of Jaina expression emerges the unbroken and unvarying message that non-violence is the only path to liberation.

# ORIGINS

Jainism appeared on the historical scene sometime between the ninth and sixth centuries BCE as part of the same *shramana* ('world-renouncing') movement that gave rise to Buddhism. The imprecise dating reflects the meagre data that historians have at their disposal. The later date is the more commonly accepted because the historicity of Mahavira (born Vardhamana Jnatrpura) has been widely established. The earlier date is associated with the life of the twenty-third Tirthankara, Parsavanath, for which the evidence is limited to the occasional scriptural reference (for instance, Mahavira's parents were said to be devotees of the lineage of Parsavanath).

The followers of Mahavira, like other *shramana* groups (most notably the followers of the Buddha), rejected the brahminical orthodoxy of the day. As their name implies, the 'world renouncers' considered the brahmins' preoccupation with cosmic and social order to be fundamentally flawed. All the elements that went into maintaining that order—the hierarchical caste system, the elaborate liturgy, the rituals, and above all the cult of sacrifice—were anathema to the renouncers.

United in their condemnation of the status quo, the *shramanas* also held similar views regarding the need for salvation from a meaningless cosmos. All regarded the cosmic order not as the creation of a transcendent, cosmic god—the existence of which they denied—but rather as a purposeless place of

*[handwritten margin note: early Vedas, Brahminism]*

Digambara Jainas greet the saint Acharya Vidyasagar Maharaj with a procession (Ian Berry/Magnum).

suffering that must be transcended. Finally, each *shramana* group claimed a unique insight into the workings of the cosmos, as well as the means to escape its confines and attain *moksha*/nirvana. Despite their similarities, therefore, the various *shramana* groups developed as distinct traditions and even rivals.

Mahavira is said to have been born to a ruling family in the region of Nepal–northeastern India. Our knowledge of his life is derived from very limited scriptural sources (Jaina texts and parts of the Buddhist Pali canon). Almost all that can be said with any authority is that he was a historical personage whose teachings on restraint attracted a considerable number of disciples and lay followers.

Nevertheless, the Jaina tradition has many tales of the teacher they call Mahavira, or 'Great Hero', beginning with the miraculous transfer of his embryo from the womb of a brahmin woman

named Devananda to that of Queen Trisala (which unequivocally established the supremacy of the kshatriya caste over the brahmins). Indeed, Jainas are familiar not only with Mahavira's biography, but with many of those from his previous births. Accounts of his life are retold and re-enacted throughout the year, but especially during the festival known to Svetambara Jainas as Paryushana and to Digambara Jainas as Daslakshana.

Discussion of origins in any religion is often fraught with ambiguities, as historicity and mythology are interwoven in such complex ways that they become hard to separate. The ambiguities are multiplied in the case of Jainism, because the Jainas have both a strong sense of historical continuity and an equally strong sense of being embedded in a system of eternally recurring time, cycles of generation and degeneration so vast that mythohistorical particularities, though 'real' (never illusory), are ultimately meaningless.

Svetambara nuns devoted to Lord Bahubali on the road to Sravanabelgola (Frédéric Soltan/Sygma/Corbis).

Jainas believe that the cycles of generation (*ut-sarpini*) and degeneration (*avasarpini*) produce predictable patterns in social, moral, and physical life. Thus within each cycle of generation and degeneration alike there are periods that favour the emergence of Jinas who teach the path of liberation. For Jainas, therefore, Mahavira—far from being the founder of Jainism—is merely the final Jina of the current degenerate time period. In the next cycle, which will be one of generation, another twenty-four Jinas will appear, preaching the same wisdom. And during the cycle of decline that will inevitably follow, yet another twenty-four will appear, and so on, in an unending cycle of decay and growth.

In this context linear time carries very little weight. Jainas can be said to be both diachronically and synchronically oriented, moving nimbly between the two perspectives. Most crucially, however, Jainas assert that Jainism—like the cosmos itself—has no point of origin. Just as the cosmos has existed from 'beginningless time', so too has the struggle for liberation from it—as well as the truth about how to attain salvation. 'Jainism' is simply the name we give to this path. By declaring the cosmos to be eternal, Jainism directs our attention away from the fruitless question of origins to the more pressing existential issue of our bondage in *samsara* (the cycle of birth and death).

Jainism is overwhelmingly concerned with conveying its message of restraint. This task is urgent because, even though the message is eternal, it is accessible only to certain incarnations (human beings alone), residing in specific regions of the cosmos (the *karmabhumi*, or realms of action) and, as noted above, within limited time periods. If these conditions are not present, the message is out of reach. Thus we who are living in this world, at this moment, are among the privileged, and we must not squander our chance to escape.

## The Life of Mahavira in the *Kalpa Sutra*

### Mahavira's Birth

[When] the Venerable Ascetic Mahavira was born, . . . [there] rained down on the palace of King Siddhartha one great shower of silver, gold, diamonds, clothes, ornaments, leaves, flowers, . . . sandal powder, and riches.

. . . [His parents] prepared plenty of food, drink, spices, and sweetmeats, invited their friends, relations, kinsmen. . . . His three names have thus been recorded: by his parents he was called Vard- hamana; because he is devoid of love and hate, he is called sramana (i.e., Ascetic); because he stands fast in the midst of dangers and fears, patiently bears hardships and calamities, adheres to the chosen rules of penance, is wise, indifferent to pleasure and pain, rich in control . . . the name Venerable Ascetic Mahavira has been given him by the gods (Jacobi 1884: 251–6).

### Enlightenment

When the Venerable Ascetic Mahavira had become a Jina and Arhat, he was a Kevalin [liberated one], omniscient and comprehending all objects; he knew and saw all conditions of the world, of gods, men, and demons: whence they came, whither they go, whether they are born as men or ani- mals or become gods or hell beings, the ideas, the thoughts of their minds, the food, doings, desires, the open and secret deeds of all the living beings in the whole world; he the Arhat for whom there is no secret, knew and saw all conditions of living beings in the world, what they thought, spoke, or did at any moment (Jacobi 1884: 263–4).

### Mahavira's Physical Death

In the fourth month of that rainy season . . . in the town of Papa . . . the Venerable Ascetic Mahavira died, went off, quitted the world, cut asunder the ties of birth, old age, and death; became a Siddha, a Buddha, a Mukta, a maker of the end (to all misery), finally liberated, freed from all pains ... [that night, the kings who had gathered there said]: 'since the light of intelligence is gone, let us make an illumination of material matter' (Jacobi 1884: 264–6).

## CRYSTALLIZATION

Mahavira established Jainism as a four-fold com- munity (**caturvidhyasangha**) made up of monks, nuns, laymen, and laywomen. His open accep- tance of women in his sangha is noteworthy, particularly since the *shramana* groups generally regarded women as 'objects of desire', to be avoid- ed lest they distract male ascetics from their path. (The Buddha's initial reluctance to permit women to join his order is well known.)

It is true that many Jaina scriptures suggest a mistrust of women, and that until recently nuns have never held positions of authority within the order. Even so, they have always been pres- ent in large numbers, and they have played an integral part in the sangha's operations. Mahavi- ra's sanctioning of the involvement of women as well as men was crucial to the success of the developing community, as was his recognition of the interdependence between householders and mendicants.

For its first thirty years the sangha was held together by the charismatic example of the living Jina. It is said that Mahavira's sangha grew to include 36,000 nuns and 14,000 monks, as well as 318,000 laywomen and 159,000 laymen (Jaini 1979: 37). The preponderance of nuns over monks—highly unusual for a religious order in India—has remained a distinguishing feature of Jainism throughout its history.

At the age of seventy-two Mahavira 'left his body' and attained *moksha*. For Jainas, *moksha* is a state of complete detachment from the world, a state from which communication with those still in the cycle of *samsara* is impossible. Thus Mahavira's followers were deprived of the sort of post-mortem cult typical of some other religious traditions, in which followers have sought to maintain contact with their central figures through prayer. Instead, the Jainas faced the enormous challenge of sustaining their tradition without any hope of spiritual guidance from the Jina.

Mahavira's disciples assumed leadership of the community, but the process of institutionalization soon gave rise to dissension. Within two centuries of Mahavira's death, the once cohesive Jaina community had begun to split into two discrete traditions, with two distinctive collections of scriptures that were at variance with one another. The precise causes of the split remain unknown, but many sources suggest that the turning point came in the fourth century BCE, when one group moved south (possibly in response to a severe famine in the north). Thereafter the two groups developed in isolation. Differences inevitably arose, and in time each group came to see the other as deviating from the vision of Mahavira, and therefore as inauthentic.

That the northern group had abandoned Mahavira's principle of nudity and begun wearing a white robe was a particular abomination to the southerners, for whom nudity was among the most elemental expressions of non-attachment and non-violence. The northerners argued that a simple garment had no bearing on spiritual progress. Nevertheless, the matter of clothing was such a central and visible difference that it became the basis for the two groups' self-identification. Eventually, in the early centuries of the Common Era, the northerners came to be known as the Svetambara (white-clad) and the southerners as the Digambara (sky-clad, or naked). The lay followers of both groups (including the fully clothed lay followers of the naked monks) likewise took on these appellations as markers of their religious identity.

This was not the only point of division, however. Another important disagreement involved women's eligibility for initiation into the order. The Digambaras' insistence on nudity meant that women were, *a priori*, disqualified from taking the vows of renunciation. The Svetambaras, by

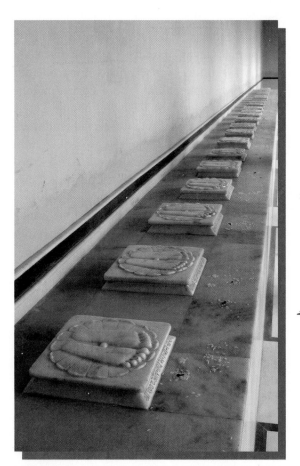

Marble footprints symbolize the departed Tirthankaras (Gabriel Jones).

contrast, imposed no such condition and therefore did permit women to join them.

Both groups regard women's bodies as inferior to men's in that they are weaker by nature. Therefore the ascetic path is more difficult for them. For the Svetambaras, however, the female body is not an insurmountable obstacle; they permit women full initiation, and even maintain that the nineteenth Jina (Mallinath) was female. Digambaras vehemently disagree, arguing that asceticism requires a powerful, 'adamantine' body, which women lack (Jaini 1979: 39). They believe that rebirth in a male body is a prerequisite for full renunciation, but in the interim they permit women to become *aryikas* (noble women) and lead a life of semi-renunciation.

Finally, the nature of the Jina's omniscience when embodied (that is, while in life) came to be a point of contention between the two groups. According to the Digambaras, one who is omniscient must already have transcended bodily appetites and functions. Thus the Jina has no need of normal bodily activities such as sleep or the consumption and elimination of food, and does not preach but rather communicates by a divine, supernatural sound. The Svetambara, by contrast, believe that all embodied beings are subject to bodily demands; therefore the omniscient Jina eats, sleeps, and communicates in the regular way through the spoken word.

## Sacred Literature

Scholars of religion today acknowledge that the boundaries separating one religion from another have never been as watertight as the scriptures of those religions suggest they are. The creation of a sacred literature or canon might seem to require the existence of a well-defined community. But in practice the development of such a community may depend (at least in part) on the creation of such a canon. While a socially recognized community of some kind must have existed in order for a canon to develop, it would always have been,

and continues to be, more porous than scriptures suggest.

The sacred literature of the Jainas is said to have been transmitted by the Jina Mahavira to his followers, but it is not believed to have originated with him. In our time cycle, the eternal teachings were first propounded by the Jina **Rsabha**, and then promulgated anew by each succeeding prophet. Mahavira's teachings were committed to memory by his closest disciples, the *ganadharas*, who then transmitted them orally to other disciples, who in turn passed them along down the generations. Thus the Jaina canon (*Agama*) for many years existed as a purely oral tradition. The entire *Agama* consists of three main branches: the *Purva* ('the ancient'), concerned with Jaina metaphysics, cosmology, and philosophy; the *Anga* ('the limbs'), which includes discussion of mendicant conduct, doctrine, karma, and religious narratives; and the *Angabahya* ('ancillary limbs'), a subsidiary collection of commentaries on the above topics, along with dialogues on topics such as astrology and the cycles of time.

The canon was faithfully preserved and transmitted orally from generation to generation within the ascetic orders for more than two hundred years. In the early fourth century BCE, however, northern India was struck by a devastating famine that is said to have continued for twelve years. The Jaina canon was nearly lost altogether as both the ascetics and the householders, whom they depended on for sustenance, struggled to survive.

From this point on, what actually happened to the *Agama* becomes sketchy and contentious. The *Purvas*—the most ancient section, believed to date back to the time of Parsavanath, in the ninth century BCE—disappeared, although it is thought that much of the content was contained in the final section of the *Anga*, called the *Drstivada*. Unfortunately, according to the Svetambaras, the *Drstivada* was also lost to memory, but its essence was preserved through mnemonic allusions in a text contained within the *Angabahya*.

## From the *Bhaktamara Stotra*

*The Bhaktamara Stotra is one of the most beloved Jaina texts. It is addressed to Adinatha—another name for Rsabha, the first Tirthankara.*

In the fullness of faith
I bow
to the feet of the Jina,
shining as they reflect the gems in the crowns
of the gods
who bow down in devotion,
illuminating the darkness
of oppressive sin,
a refuge in the beginning of time
for all souls
lost in the ocean of birth (1)

. . .

Praising you
instantly destroys
the sinful karma that binds
embodied souls
to endless rebirth
just as the sun's rays
instantly shatter
the all-embracing
bee-black
endless dark night (7)

. . .

Gods like Hari and Hara
don't have your shining knowledge.
Light is glorious
in a glittering jewel
but not in a piece
of even the best glass.

I think it is good
that after seeing
Hari, Hara, and the rest of the gods
my heart is pleased

only with you.
I have gained so much in this world
by seeing you
o lord.
None other can steal my mind,
not even in my next life (20–1)

. . .

Praise to you,
o lord,
remover of the pain
of the three worlds.
Praise to you,
stainless ornament
of the earth's surface.
Praise to you,
supreme lord
of the triple world.
Praise to you,
o Jina,
you dry up
the ocean of rebirth (26)

. . .

O Jina King
Laksmi comes quickly to Manatunga,
who forever wears around his neck
your garland of praise,
woven from the qualities
of my bhakti
and adorned by the multihued flowers
of radiant color (44)

(*Bhaktamara Stotra, Manatunga*, 1, 7, 20–1, 26, 44; Cort 2005: 95–8).

The Digambaras, however, claim that they managed to retain much of the *Drstivada*, and they eventually put it in writing around the second century CE. This work, called the *Satkhandagama*, was the first Jaina scripture to be preserved in written form, and it is one of only two canonical works that the Digambaras recognize as authoritative. The other is the *Kasayaprabhrta*, a second text

No. 28

based on the *Drstivada* and written down during the same period. They reject the scriptures retained by the Svetambaras as inauthentic deviations from the original canon.

In addition to the *Agamas*, vast collections of post-canonical writing were produced by the learned *acharyas* (mendicant scholars) of both the Svetambara and Digambara sects, including Jinasena, Hemachandra, Kundakunda, Haribhadra, and Umasvati. Known collectively as *Anuyogas* ('branches of scripture'), their writings achieved canonical status within their respective traditions and are today among the most celebrated works of ancient and medieval Indian philosophy.

The seemingly intractable dispute over the Svetambara and Digambara canons aside, the gulf between the two groups is not as wide as it may appear. Many fundamental ideas—on the nature of the soul, karma, non-violence, the cosmos—are common to both groups, as are many practices. It would be patently wrong to suggest that differences do not exist within Jainism on these fundamentals, but there is enough consensus across sectarian lines to permit us to consider them 'tenets' of the tradition.

The **Tatthvartha Sutra** of Umasvati (second century CE) merits special note here. It is an extraordinarily comprehensive treatment of the fundamentals of the tradition, and remains a cherished manuscript among both Svetambara and Digambara communities. The recent text *Saman Suttam* (1974)[1] is the first cross-sectarian effort to produce a concise summary of Jaina thought. Following are the fundamentals of Jaina cosmology on which the two sects agree.

## Cosmology

Jainas believe that the entire cosmos (*loka*) is made up of six eternal substances, called *dravya*, and that knowledge of these *dravya* is an important step towards self-perfection. These substances are classified in two broad categories—*jiva* (soul) and *ajiva* (non-soul). *Jiva* is an eternal substance with consciousness. Souls caught in the cycle of rebirth (*samsara*) are often referred to as *samsari jiva*, whereas those that are liberated are referred to as *muktatma*. *Ajiva* is a substance without consciousness and consists of five types: *pudgala* (pure matter), *kala* (time), *dharma* (principle of motion), *adharma* (principle of rest), and *akash* (space). The latter four—all variants of *pudgala*—are 'supportive' forms, without which existence would not be possible.

*Pudgala* is a concrete substance with the attributes of touch, taste, smell, and colour. Although it has no special function, in its most subtle form it is the basis of all matter and energy. All activities of the mind and body, including thought and speech, are considered to be *pudgala*. All worldly knowledge is acquired by means of *pudgala*—including the knowledge of how to free ourselves from it! Indeed, it is only through perception, which is also a form of *pudgala*, that we can know the cosmos and its contents.

Thus *pudgala* is not antithetical to *jiva*. It is neutral in this regard, although its natural tendency is to become attached both to other forms of matter and to *jiva*. This is an important point, because the renouncers typically speak of matter in highly negative terms (for example, referring to the world as vomit, or the body as a trap). Those terms are chosen largely for rhetorical impact, however, for *pudgala* is *jiva*'s friend as well as its foe. The effective omnipresence of *pudgala* makes this unavoidable. The worldly soul that seeks release from it is nevertheless utterly dependent on it.

The most fundamental existential problem, shared by all beings in the cosmos, is the fact that *jiva* and *ajiva* are thoroughly enmeshed. This is what prevents the soul from achieving a state of bliss, for bliss can be experienced only in a state of purity and separation from all that is not-soul. Jainas do not posit an original state of separation from which there was a 'fall'. Instead they assert that this state of entanglement is eternal, 'without beginning', and we are constantly exacerbating it, since every activity of the mind as well as the body causes vibrations that create ever more particles of sticky, binding karma. These karmic particles come in two types—auspicious ('good karma', called **punya)** and inauspicious ('bad karma', called **paap)**—but ultimately all forms of karma must be purged. The forces behind those karma-creating activities, and hence the root causes of our bondage, are the passions.

This is the quandary from which the Jaina path of self-restraint offers a coherent way out. Through self-restraint, Jainas believe, we can discipline the passions and eventually quell them. By limiting—eventually, eliminating—the inflow of karma and cleansing the soul of all the karmic particles that have become encrusted on it through eternity, we can eliminate the cause of the soul's suffering. The process of purging is called *nirjara*, and it is the purpose behind most Jaina practices. Normally, karma dissolves when (after giving its pain or pleasure) it comes to fruition. But karma can be made to 'ripen' and vanish prematurely through the practice of certain austerities, and this is the aim of ascetic discipline. Among the austerities, or *tapas*, that cause karma to dissociate from the soul are fasting, the study of the *Agamas*, and meditation.

The Jaina view of the soul's lonely, blundering voyage through endless time within a violent and purposeless cosmos is a harsh one, from which the only sensible response is escape. The tradition crystallized around ideas that explain our predicament, and practices that offer a way out.

# ✤ DIFFERENTIATION

As a tiny, heterodox minority within the vast Indian mosaic, Jainas have always been vulnerable to assimilation. How they have managed to differentiate themselves, expand, and thrive when other world-renouncing traditions have not remains a curiosity. Paradoxically, the success of 'other-worldly' Jainism likely owes much to its 'this-worldly' know-how. The skills required to forge alliances with ruling elites and make inroads into established economic structures were key to its survival in the medieval period (fifth through seventeenth centuries). The Jaina tradition developed those skills early on, in the first two centuries of its existence, when it enjoyed the patronage of the kshatriya rulers.

In the final centuries before the beginning of the Common Era, the fate of all the *shramana* groups, including the Buddhists as well as the Jainas, depended on their ability to secure royal patronage. The socio-political 'alliance' between the kshatriyas and the various *shramanas* was rooted in a shared ideological opposition to brahminic orthodoxy. The fact that Mahavira came from a kshatriya clan was a sign of the kshatriyas' ascent. The alliance was mutually beneficial: the *shramanas* prospered with the economic support of the kshatriyas, while the latter gained in a myriad of ways through the extension of their popular support.

In the fourth century BCE, however, Emperor Ashoka converted to Buddhism and the balance of power shifted. The Jainas slowly retreated from their original centres of power in eastern India (Magadha), towards the more peripheral (at that time) northwestern regions of Rajasthan, Gujarat, and Punjab, as well as into the southern areas of what are now Maharashtra and Karnataka. Nevertheless, the wealth and—more important—the political skills that Jainas had acquired from serving (in legal positions, as advisers, etc.) at the various kshatriya courts gave them a worldly acumen that would serve them well long after their royal support had disappeared.

By the third century BCE, the once unified Jaina *caturvidhyasangha* had begun to separate into the two groups that, centuries later, would become the Svetambaras and Digambaras. The split was reinforced by the geographical repositioning of the Svetambaras in the northwest and the Digambaras in the south. Yet Jainas of both sects managed to prosper and gain positions of importance in their new environments. Although their influence with local elites was always limited, their skills, especially in trade, enabled them to establish secure communities.

Jaina philosophy flourished over the following centuries. Among the *acharyas* who produced important treatises were the Digambaras Umasvati (the second-century author of the *Tatthvartha Sutra*), his contemporary Kundakunda, and Haribhadra in the seventh century, and the Svetambaras Jinasena in the ninth century and Hemachandra in the twelfth. Together, the philosophical works of the *acharyas* constitute an enormous and celebrated body of sacred literature.

The social organization of the Jaina community retained its 'fourfold' character throughout the medieval period, preserving the interdependence between householders and renouncers. Instead of establishing large monasteries, as the Buddhists did, the Jaina ascetics continued to rely directly on householders for sustenance. Rules of ascetic practice placed severe restrictions on personal possessions and comforts. Householders were keenly aware of these rules, and because of their direct involvement in the lives of renouncers, they acted as unofficial enforcers of proper conduct. These were likely factors in the absence of the development of large Jaina monasteries. It has been suggested that the Jainas resisted the wave of Hindu devotionalism, and the arrival of Islam, in the twelfth century far more successfully than the Buddhists did, precisely because of their social organization. The Buddhist monasteries also relied on the support of their lay followers, but never to the extent that the Jaina ascetics relied on Jaina householders, who provided mendicants with sustenance as often as three times a day. The latter played a central role in the perpetuation of Jaina tradition, and for that reason they may have been less vulnerable than their Buddhist counterparts to the rise of the Hindu *bhakti* movement. Furthermore, whereas the concentration of the Buddhist monks and scriptures in large, wealthy monasteries made them easy targets for marauding armies, the Jainas were dispersed throughout the society and had no property to plunder. Thus

the decentralized nature of Jaina groups may have inadvertently contributed to their survival.

# Reform

Idol (*murti*) veneration became an established feature of Jainism very early its history (third century BCE), but the first Jaina temples did not appear until the early medieval period (c. fifth century CE)—an era of widespread temple construction. With time and growing affluence, the temples became the anchors of Jaina religious life, sites not only of devotion but of interaction between householders and the mendicants who gathered there.

Temple building and maintenance, as well as idol-veneration, continue to be central religious activities for most Jainas, as well as important factors in the transmission of the tradition. Today, however, the care and management of temples is almost exclusively the responsibility of the laity. (The only exception to the rule of enforced itinerancy developed in the last century, with the revitalization of the Bhattaraka tradition within the Digambara sect; *bhattarakas* are semi-ascetics who control the religious community's assets and are involved in the administration of temples.) The general absence of settled, temple-based communities of mendicants today can be traced to a number of powerful reform movements that arose between the fifteenth and seventeenth centuries and effectively reinvigorated the tradition of ascetic discipline among both Svetambara and Digambara Jainas.

The reformers saw a direct correlation between the proliferation of temples and what they considered to be a growing laxity on the part of many Jaina ascetics, who gradually abandoned their itinerant way of life for the relative comfort of a settled life in and around the temples. Although murmurs of protest against the laxity and considerable wealth of these *caityavasis* (temple-dwellers) could be heard as early as the eleventh century, it was not until the 1400s that the practice of dwelling in temples was forcefully condemned.

One of the five Dilwara temples at Mount Abu in Rajasthan, built between the eleventh and thirteenth centuries (Willard G. Oxtoby).

A lay reformer named Lonkashaha was the first in the Svetambara tradition to question the wealth and power of the *caityavasis*. He also challenged their deviation from the principle of *samyama* (restraint), and criticized idol-worship and temple-building as contrary not only to the ethos of renunciation but also to the vow of non-violence, given that the construction of idols and temples involved unnecessary violence to living beings. Lonkashaha's uncompromising critique effectively put an end to the institution of the *caityavasis*.

Temples and idols were at the heart of the lay community's devotional practices, and ordinary Jainas were not easily persuaded by Lonkashaha's arguments. In time, though, he succeeded in establishing an ascetic 'lineage' (*gaccha*) called the Lonkagaccha. Today it has all but died out, but it gave rise to two groups that are highly influential among Svetambara Jainas: Sthanakvasis (a sect opposed to temple-based Jainism whose renouncers reside in halls known as *sthanaks* on their peripatetic travels), and Terapanthis (a reform movement within the Sthanakvasis that opposed the use of *sthanaks* as well as temples).

Major changes took place in the Digambara tradition as well, initiated by the lay poet Banarsidass in the sixteenth century. Like Lonkashaha, Banarsidass criticized what he considered to be the excessive ritualism and unnecessary violence (the use of flowers, for instance) associated with temple worship. At the same time he denounced a group of quasi-ascetic clerics called the *bhattarakas*. Analogous to the Svetambara *caityavasis* but with greater political clout, the *bhattarakas* served both as guardians of the temples and as intermediaries between the naked ascetics and the ruling elites—a role that, in addition to gaining them power and wealth, made them vulnerable to corruption.

The Digambaras responded to these critiques with sweeping reforms that led to the decline (though not the disappearance) of the *bhattarakas*. The revitalization sparked by the reformers' critiques put both the Svetambara and Digambara orders in positions of significant strength as they entered the modern period.

# ❧ PRACTICE

The importance that Jainism attaches to practice is one of the tradition's defining features. Correct practice (*samyak caritra*) constitutes one of the 'Three Jewels' of the tradition, along with correct intuition (*samyak darshan*) and correct knowledge (*samyak jnana*). Although all three are equally fundamental, correct practice tends to overshadow

The Great Head Bathing Ceremony of Lord Bahubali (Frédéric Soltan/Sygma/Corbis).

the others because it is so conspicuous. Jainas are everywhere known by their practices—from their strict avoidance of certain very common foods to the Digambara ascetics' insistence on nudity. Before we look at specific practices, however, it is important to grasp the special significance that the concept of practice has in Jainism, and how it is grounded in Jaina metaphysics.

The Jaina emphasis on practice reflects an understanding of the world and human suffering as *real*—not illusory—and in need of active human intervention. This understanding stands in sharp contrast to that of Vedanta-Hinduism and Buddhism, which essentially see the world and human suffering as products of thought and perception, and therefore focus on changing consciousness as the way to freedom. While Jainas recognize that lack of consciousness plays a key role in the problems of earthly existence, they also believe that those problems are constituted from physical realities that must be dealt with physically through practices such as penance and fasting.

We have already described the Jaina view of the eternal soul (*jiva*) and matter (*ajiva*) as enmeshed in a labyrinthine web that will never be untangled without concrete action. Because our entrapment is real in a physical sense—not just an illusory state that can be dispelled through clearer thinking—our enlightenment hinges as much on our practice as it does on our worldview. Good intentions, for Jainas, can never be enough; action must always be the foremost consideration. It is for this reason that renouncers follow an ascetic discipline designed to heighten their awareness of how they move their bodies in and through space—how they walk, sit, lie down, speak, hold items, collect alms, sleep, go to the toilet, etc. It is no exaggeration to say that the focus on practice is a defining feature of the Jaina path.

The elaborate edifice of Jaina practice aims to purify the soul of the *pudgala* that clings to it. By shedding obstructive karma, the soul becomes free to manifest its true, radiant and powerful nature. Practices are of two types: defensive and offensive.

*No. 29*

Defensive strategies, such as inculcating detachment and mindfulness, work to impede the accumulation of new karma (a process called *samvara*), while practices such as fasting, meditation, and various forms of physical discipline work to 'burn off' old karma. Jainas call this process *nirjara*.

The hallmarks of Jaina practice—ascetic discipline, dietary restrictions, fasting, **samayika** (state of equanimity), **pratikramana** (prayer of forgiveness), *sallekhana* (fast to death), even Jina puja (worship of the Jinas)—are undertaken, by both renouncers and householders, with the aim of purification, and the dual processes of *samvara* and *nirjara*. The main difference between the paths of the renouncer and the householder lies in the degree of purification they permit; the renouncer's life is structured by a series of vows (**mahavratas**) that make it nearly impossible for new karma to develop.

Because renouncers are largely shielded from the risk of accumulating new karma, they can devote their time to whittling away the karmic load they carry. Householders, immersed as they are in worldly activities—working, raising families, preparing food—are awash in karmic influences. Nevertheless, they can limit the influx of negative karma (*paap*) through lay practices (**anuvratas**) such as fasting or limiting possessions, travel, cosmetics, and so on; many women in particular undertake these moderate exercises in restraint. What marks such activities as characteristically Jaina is that they all involve disengagement from the world. Even devotional activities (Jina puja, for example) that outwardly resemble Hindu forms of worship are interpreted by Jainas as practices that foster worldly detachment.

Ideally, the lives of Jainas, whether renouncers or householders, are governed by a series of vows (*mahavratas* or *anuvratas*) that limit worldly engagement, discipline the body, and help the soul develop the tools it will need for its eventual liberation. Thus Jainism is unequivocally a *shramana* or renouncer tradition even though the vast majority of Jainas at any given time have always been householders enthusiastically, and successfully, involved in worldly pursuits.

Jainism is nevertheless a *shramana* tradition because its defining framework is thoroughly ascetic in character. It creates and moulds religious identity by asking the faithful to accept increasingly restrictive boundaries. The main difference between the *mahavratas* of the mendicants and the *anuvratas* of the householders is the degree to which the vows restrict worldly engagement.

## Ascetic Practice

The *mahavratas* are five 'great vows' accepted by everyone who takes up the life of a Jaina ascetic (*muni* or *sadhvi*): Ahimsa (non-harm), *satya* (truthfulness), *asteya* (non-stealing), *brahmacharya* (celibacy), and *aparigraha* (non-possession/non-attachment). It is said that Mahavira established celibacy as a separate vow, independent of the fourth vow of non-attachment under which it had been incorporated, during the time of Parsavanath.

Although the discourse of renunciation refers often to the poetic image of the solitary wanderer, initiation into the renouncer path is very much a collective endeavour. Aspiring ascetics must first seek and receive permission from their families (or spouses), as well as from the leader of a mendicant order.

In addition, the ascetic orders impose certain restrictions themselves. Neither sect accepts individuals who are physically, emotionally, or mentally fragile. The renouncer path was not designed as a refuge for those on the margins of conventional society; it is an arduous path suitable only for the courageous, committed, and stalwart. It is for this reason that the Digambara sect continues to claim that women's physical and emotional natures make them unsuitable for the ascetic life. The female body's 'femaleness'—determined as it is by karma—is seen as too great an impediment, making the already challenging life of mendicancy impossible. In other words, the renouncer path is to be undertaken only by those who have both the

*Monks and nuns*

spiritual desire and the physical fortitude for a life of denial.

By drawing the Self back from worldly concerns, the vows create the conditions in which its true vitality and force can be unveiled. The first vow (*ahimsa*) is the weightiest of the five; Jainas commonly say that it effectively encompasses all the others. In effect, *ahimsa* forbids all involvement with the world and ensures that no action is undertaken spontaneously, without restraint. Because the vow of *ahimsa* is total and unconditional in its application, renouncers must be concerned to cause no harm—through speech, action, or thought—even to 'one-sensed' beings (invisible air-bodied beings, water, fire, earth) as well as plants, insects, animals, and fellow human beings. Avoiding harm to human beings and animals is easy compared to avoiding harm to water and air and other minute forms of life (all of which

*radical understanding of non-violence*

are equally endowed with an eternal soul); this is a monumental challenge and is the main reason behind the Jaina insistence on correct practice.

*Munis* and *sadhvis* are not permitted to prepare their own food, since even harvesting plants or boiling water inevitably causes harm to living beings. Thus the ascetics depend entirely on the generosity of householders, and even so they must be vigilant to maintain their vow of *ahimsa*. They are permitted only a small portion of the householder's 'leftovers'; they cannot accept food that has been prepared expressly for them, as this would implicate them in whatever violence that preparation entailed; and the food and water they receive in their alms bowls must already have been cooked, boiled, or peeled (in the case of fruits) to ensure that it is *ajiv* (without life).

It is critical to understand the rationale underpinning these practices. The path of renunciation

## From the *Acaranga Sutra* on Good Conduct

He who injures these (earth bodies) does not comprehend and renounce the sinful acts; he who does not injure these, comprehends and renounces the sinful acts. Knowing them, a wise man should not act sinfully towards the earth, nor cause others to act so, nor allow others to act so. He who knows these causes of sin relating to earth, is called a reward-knowing sage. Thus I say (Jacobi 1884: 10–11).

. . . the sage who walks the beaten track (to liberation), regards the world in a different way. 'Knowing thus (the nature of) acts in all regards, he does not kill,' he controls himself, he is not overbearing.

Comprehending that pleasure (and pain) are individual, advising kindness, he will not engage in any work in the whole world: keeping before him the one (great aim, liberation), and not turning aside, 'living humbly, unattached to any creature.' The rich in (control) who with a mind endowed with all penetration (recognises) that a bad deed should not be done, will not go after it. What you acknowledge as righteousness, that you acknowledge as sagedom . . .; what you acknowledge as sagedom, that you acknowledge as righteousness. It is inconsistent with weak, sinning, sensual, ill-conducted house-inhabiting men. 'A sage, acquiring sagedom, should subdue his body.' 'The heroes who look at everything with indifference, use mean and rough (food, &c.)'. Such a man is said to have crossed the flood (of life), to be a sage, to have passed over (the samsara) to be liberated, to have ceased (from acts). Thus I say (Jacobi 1884: 46–7).

is open to all, irrespective of caste, gender, or social position. But it is extremely demanding, and Jainas know that very few will ever be able to take it. The overwhelming majority who remain householders therefore accept, implicitly or explicitly, that a certain amount of violence will be a regular part of their lives. For these people, support for the renouncers is both a duty and an honour—with the additional benefit of earning them merit or good karma (*punya*). More important, it sustains a system in which the ideal of living without doing harm remains a genuine possibility for anyone with the requisite strength of character.

The *mahavrata* of *ahimsa* prohibits outright many aspects of the renouncers' former householder lives, and no aspect of embodied existence escapes the framework of restraint: eating, talking, sleeping, walking, defecating, urinating, thinking, even dreaming—all must be disciplined in nonharm. Renouncers must not walk on grass or in the rain, for to do so would cause them harm; wherever they step they must look carefully to be sure they do not harm anything on the ground; they are forbidden from using electricity and flush toilets (which cause harm to fire-bodied and water-bodied beings respectively); and their minds are subject to continuous self-censure as they try to eliminate anger, jealousy, greed, and desire. Negative or aggressive thoughts are believed to accrue bad karma (*paap*) in much the same way that stepping on an insect would. The restrictions on

speech, body, and thought contained within the principle vow of *ahimsa* are potentially limitless.

The subsidiary vows of non-attachment, truthfulness, non-stealing, and celibacy reinforce and enlarge the vow of *ahimsa*. The vows of truthfulness and non-stealing forbid false speech and the use of anything that has not been freely given. *Brahmacharya* is more than a vow of celibacy: it is a vow to renounce all desire. Even dreams of a 'carnal' nature have the power to attract karma, and therefore require penance. The vow of *aparigraha* entails the renunciation not only of all possessions (home, clothing, money, etc.) but of all attachments, whether to places, people, things—or even dogmatic ideas.

In addition to the *mahavratas*, which specify actions to be avoided, there are six 'obligatory actions' that renouncers are required to perform, some of which will be discussed in detail below. In brief, they are equanimity (*samayika*), praise to the Jinas (Jina puja), homage to teacher (*vandana*), repentance (*pratikramana*), body-abandonment (*kayotsarga*), and, finally, the more general pledge to renounce all transgressions (*pratyakhyana*).

Taken together, the *mahavratas* and obligatory actions can appear overwhelming. But it is important to bear in mind that the constraints they impose are not seen as barriers to freedom. Rather, they are understood as catalysts to self-realization, the means to the sublime state of unconditional freedom, permanent bliss, and omniscience. Furthermore, each step along the way to self-realization is believed to bring benefits for the community as well as the individual. For Jainas, the renouncers embody a spiritual power that can work miracles—though of course they are not supposed to use their powers for 'worldly' purposes.

The path to the very highest levels of self-realization has fourteen stages (**gunasthanas**). Householders rarely rise above the fifth step, and must fully renounce worldly life if they wish to go beyond it. Nevertheless, the householder path offers considerable opportunities for spiritual progress as well.

## The Mahavratas

1. Non-violence (*ahimsa*)

2. Truth (*satya*)

3. Non-stealing (*asteya*)

4. Chastity (*brahmacharya*)

5. Non-possession/non-attachment (*aparigraha*)

## Householder Practice

The *anuvratas* are the 'small (or lesser) vows' that govern lay life and are normally taken without any formal ceremony. Modelled on the mendicant's *mahavratas*, they reflect the same aspiration to limit worldly engagement. They are identical in name and number to the *mahavratas*, but are interpreted and applied more leniently.

For instance, the *ahimsa anuvrata* is partial, not total. It prohibits the consumption of certain foods (see pp. 164–5), as well as eating after dark (when injury to insects is more likely). But it does not concern itself with one-sensed beings, accepting that harm to them is unavoidable for householders. The subsidiary vows work in a similar manner: truthfulness and non-stealing are emphasized in much the same way as in the *mahavratas*, but celibacy is redefined to mean chastity in marriage.

Similarly, the *anuvrata* of *aparigraha* does not require householders to live without possessions. Instead, it demands that they scrutinize their psychological attachment to their possessions.

The *anuvratas* are seen as establishing a compromise between worldly existence and spiritual progress. They do not interfere with the householder's ability to lead a 'normal' existence. Quite the contrary: Jainas have long been among the wealthiest, most literate, and most accomplished communities in India. And from the Jaina perspective, there is a direct connection between their socio-economic success and their religious vows.

### Reflection–Meditation

Whereas the *mahavratas* and *anuvratas* seek to discipline embodied activities, the practice of *samayika* seeks to halt them altogether. *Samayika* is a daily period of 48 minutes reserved for meditation or reflection, during which the practitioner seeks to leave the concerns of body behind and 'dwell in the soul'. Through the practice of *samayika*, the Jaina seeks a state of equanimity by striving to remain indifferent to attachments and aversions, sufferings and pleasures. In the absence of such ultimately meaningless distractions, the Self can experience and enjoy itself. Jainas believe that the practice of *samayika* offers a foretaste of the joyous state that final release will bring.

### Fasting and Dietary Practices

Closely connected in intent with *samayika* is fasting, a practice so widespread among Jainas that it can be considered emblematic of the tradition. The word Jainas use for 'fast' is **upvas** (literally, 'to be near the soul'); this term underscores their belief that in order to get close to the soul we must get away from the worldly demands of the body and ego. Like the daily practice of *samayika*, fasting facilitates withdrawal from worldly activities so as to focus on the soul. At the same time fasting is considered a highly effective means of eliminating karma.

Jainas are renowned for their fasts, which are legendarily long, frequent, and arduous. Lay women, in particular, are celebrated for their heroic fasting, which is believed to benefit their families as well as themselves. The entire household gains social prestige from the pious acts that the women perform, and the auspicious karma created by fasting can bring karmic rewards for the family.

The (primarily) male equivalent of the female practice of fasting is the practice of making public donations (*dana*) for worthy causes such as religious celebrations or temple construction. Such practices likewise have the dual benefit of being socially prestigious and accruing religious merit. It is worth repeating that Jainas do not consider prosperity and spirituality to be incompatible. Worldly advantages such as wealth, beauty, health, and intelligence are regarded, at least in part, as the products of auspicious karma acquired through a life of detachment and restraint.

Fasting rituals (including the fast that leads to death) can be seen as logical extensions of a dietary ethos that is an integral part of the Jaina spiritual path. In fact, Jaina dietary rules are for many outsiders the best-known aspect of the tradition. Jainas are meticulous in eating no meat, fish, or eggs (though most do consume dairy products). They also prohibit the consumption of fruits with many seeds (because each seed is a potential life) and root vegetables such as potatoes, carrots, onions, and garlic (because of the violence involved in digging them out of the ground). Alcohol is also rejected.

Jainas recognize that eating is as much about death as it is about life: in order to sustain life, life must be destroyed. Thus fruits with a single stone may be eaten, along with legumes, grains, and leafy vegetables of all kinds, 'provided they were harvested and prepared with kindness and care' (Jaini 1990: 6).

Jaina dietary restrictions are the culinary expression of a philosophy of non-attachment that is most forcefully expressed in the practice of *sallekhana*, the ritual fast that brings life to an end.

## The Fast to Death   *salle khang*

Jainas boast that whereas other traditions celebrate birth, they celebrate death. This statement is a powerful reminder that they trace their origins to the *shramana* tradition in which the highest goal was to escape embodied existence. A death that is 'celebrated' is one that has been accepted voluntarily and with equanimity, indicating total detachment from the body and the world. We recall that the root of 'Jainism' is the Sanskrit word *Jina*—the 'one who has conquered' his ego, greed, and attachment to the world, even his body.

For Jainas the ideal death is voluntary, achieved through the ritual fast called *sallekhana*. Although *sallekhana* is not the universal practice, it is not uncommon even among householders. It is seen as a fitting and highly auspicious conclusion to a life dedicated to self-discipline and detachment. To be able to 'discard the body' without pain or fear, and greet death with calmness and equanimity, is to reap the ultimate reward of a life lived in accordance with Jaina principles.

In addition, *sallekhana* is believed to be highly advantageous for the soul as it journeys forward.

A Jaina ascetic who has taken the vow of *sallekhana* prays (Frédéric Soltan/Sygma/Corbis).

A dispassionate death results in a powerful expulsion of *paap* (bad karma) while attracting the *punya* (good karma) required to ensure a good rebirth either in a heavenly realm or in a spiritually advanced human state. Jainas believe that at the moment of physical death, the karma-saturated soul will be instantaneously propelled into a new incarnation, determined by its karma. (A soul free of all karma, instead of being reborn, would ascend to the realm of liberation, **siddha loka**; but that is not possible in the current time cycle.)

*hope for better rebirth*

If the Jaina ideal is detachment, a progressive withdrawal from life during life, then *sallekhana* becomes its logical conclusion. The title of an essay on the subject by James Laidlaw captures this idea beautifully: 'A Life Worth Leaving' (2005). For Jainas, therefore, *sallekhana* is the natural culmination of a life dedicated to the discipline of detachment from the world; it is the ultimate embodiment of Jaina values, paradoxically achieved through a kind of dis-embodiment. Whether or not they choose *sallekhana*, Jainas endeavour to accept the inevitability of death with self-control and serene detachment.

## Jaina Astrology

Jaina astrology has received relatively little scholarly attention, but it is a subject of great interest in the community itself. The complex and unique ways in which Jainas use astrological charts is beyond the scope of this chapter. Nevertheless, it is worth noting that the practice points to an aspect of Jainism that is easily overlooked, namely its recognition of the role that external forces play in the process of self-realization. We have seen that Jainas eschew any notion of a creator god, and—with no hope of divine assistance—emphasize self-reliance along the path to liberation. Under these circumstances it is essential to make use of all possible means. Astrology, as it turns out, is one means, especially useful for the insight it offers into the manipulation of karma for both spiritual and worldly benefit.

The Jaina interest in astrology is noteworthy for at least two reasons. First, it sheds light on the Jaina understanding of karma/*pudgala* as something with positive as well as negative aspects. Second, to the extent that astrology is a proactive art that seeks to pre-empt misfortune and take advantage of opportunity, it reminds us that Jaina renunciation is not a matter of flight from the world but rather of a resolute fight to overcome it.

## Jina Worship    (venerating the jinas)

The objects of Jaina worship are the twenty-four perfected beings known as the Jinas. Temples are constructed to house icons of them, pilgrimages are made to places associated with them, and they are worshipped daily in prayer. Although four of

the Jinas are especially revered (Mahavira, Parsavanath, Neminath, Rsabha), all receive regular devotions.

The main festivals celebrate events in the lives of the Jinas, especially Mahavira, as do the exquisite Jaina miniature paintings, while Jaina sculpture is devoted almost exclusively to portraits of the Jinas in meditation. Even among the Sthanakvasis and Terapanthis, who reject image worship, the Jinas are ubiquitous in narrative and prayer. Clearly, then, to be a Jaina is to be a worshipper of the Jinas.

And yet the Jinas are profoundly absent. Having perfected themselves, they are indifferent to their worshippers, whose transient worldly concerns are literally 'beneath them'. The existence of a lively, emotional cult of devotion within a tradition centred on dispassionate renunciation of all attachments may seem paradoxical, but Jainas insist that the real purpose of devotion is self-transformation through surrender to the ideal that the Jina embodies.

What most Jainas mean by 'self-transformation' through Jina puja, however, is not terribly different from what we find in theistic traditions. Proper devotional practice leads to proper mental activity, which in turn leads to the elimination of negative karma and the attraction of good karma. In this way devotional practice produces karmic 'blessings' even if the Jina who is the ostensible object of that practice is indifferent to it. Again, one of the most fundamental tenets of the Jaina tradition is its rejection of the concept of a creator God who intervenes in human affairs. Here we see how the proper manipulation of karma makes such a figure superfluous.

The central prayer in Jainism, called the **Namokar Mantra**, suggests how the devotional cult operates. The first part begins by proclaiming homage to the Jinas ('Namo Arihantanum'), then to all liberated beings ('Namo Siddhanum'), to *acharyas*, ('Namo Ayariyanam'), to religious leaders ('Namo Uwajayahanum'), and finally to all renouncers everywhere ('Namo loe savva sahu-nam'). The second part consists of the statement 'This five-fold mantra destroys all sins and is the most powerful of all auspicious mantras.'

Terapanthis and Sthanakvasis are uncomfortable with the quasi-miraculous language of the latter section and therefore omit it. But most Jainas consider it an integral part of the prayer. As such, it provides insight into the way Jaina devotionalism parallels the devotionalism of theistic cults even though devotees expect nothing from the objects of their devotion. What is important is the power of the mantra itself to produce good karma.

Puja assists the devotee in two ways, helping him or her along the path of self-realization and at the same time bringing 'worldly' benefits. The beneficent power of good karma (*punya*), earned through devotional practice, makes a reciprocal relationship with a god unnecessary (see Cort 2001). It is important to add here that even though the Jaina devotional cult operates within its own non-theistic framework, Jainas also venerate gods and goddesses who are believed to reside in heavenly realms. These divinities (e.g., Padmavati, the female guardian deity of Parsavanath, or the Hindu god Ganesh) *are* capable of interceding on behalf of their followers. Jainas worship and

## The *Sakra Stava* (Hymn of Indra)

*'Sakra' is an alternative name for the god Indra. This hymn, in which the god praises the Jinas, is recited by observant Jainas.*

[Indra, the god of the celestial one, spoke thus]:

'My obeisance to my Lords, the Arhats, the prime ones, the Tirthankaras, the enlightened ones, the best of men, the lions among men, the exalted elephants among men, lotus among men.
Transcending the world they rule the world, think of the well-being of the world.
Illuminating all, they dispel fear, bestow vision, show the path, give shelter, life, enlightenment.
Obeisance to the bestowers of *dharma*, the teachers of *dharma*, the leaders of *dharma*, the charioteers of *dharma*, the monarchs of the four regions of *dharma*,
To them, who have uncovered the veil and have found unerring knowledge and vision, the islands in the ocean, the shelter, the goal, the support.
Obeisance to the Jinas—the victors—who have reached the goal and who help others reach it.
The enlightened ones, the free ones, who bestow freedom, the Jinas victorious over fear, who have known all and can reveal all, who have reached that supreme state which is unimpeded, eternal, cosmic and beatific, which is beyond disease and destruction, where the cycle of birth ceases; the goal, the fulfillment,
My obeisance to the *Sramana Bhagvan Mahavira*
The initiator, the ultimate Tirthankara, who has come to fulfill the promise of earlier Tirthankaras.
I bow to him who is there—in Devananda's womb from here—my place in heaven.
May he take cognizance of me.'

With these words, Indra paid his homage to *Sramana Bhagvan Mahavira* and, facing east, resumed his seat on the throne (*Kalpa Sutra* 2; Lath 1984: 29–33).

pray to them for assistance in worldly matters, but not for assistance along the path of liberation.

# CULTURAL EXPRESSIONS

The Jaina community is rich in cultural expressions, with celebrated temples, festivals, art, and literature, as well as active philanthropy. That Jainas are culturally strong and conspicuous throughout India raises an interesting question: how can a tradition that attributes the highest values to renunciation sustain itself culturally in so robust a manner? Before considering the most significant examples of Jaina cultural expression, it is important to understand how, despite their ethos of withdrawal from mundane temporal concerns, Jainas have such a solid presence in the world.

Although the Jaina message is that the path to freedom is one of restraint and withdrawal, this is not a forcefully normative statement: from the Jaina perspective it simply reflects a sober assessment of the way the world works. To be a 'good' Jaina does not require adoption of a mendicant's life, though this is unequivocally the ideal. The tradition accommodates varying degrees of renunciation, and overtly recognizes human shortcomings in this regard.

Each living being is a bundle of karmic proclivities that compel us to engage with the external world. Only human beings are capable of taming these proclivities; yet very few of us even recognize their presence, let alone seek to eradicate them. Jainas use the epithet 'Maharaja' ('Great King' or 'Great Ruler') for those who try (the renouncers). The best that most of us can aim for is to control our inclinations by living our lives in a framework of samyak darshan ('correct faith'). To lead the life of a disciplined householder is perfectly respectable, as long as it is done in the context of samyak darshan.

What ignites the spark of spiritual awareness depends on the individual. For some it may be a powerful artistic experience; for others it may be a philosophical tract, or participation in a public festival. Therefore all cultural expressions that inculcate samyak darshan are valued. Building a temple, creating a work of art, celebrating a festival—all help to bring a community together in celebration of shared Jaina values. The tenth-century Digambara acharya Nemicandra praised 'the great monks and acharyas who have established the celebration of festivals . . . due to which even the downtrodden and condemned people become religious' (cited in Jain 2008).

Music, art, temple architecture, festivals, and rituals are all vehicles for celebration of the tradition. Their ultimate purpose, writes Shugan C. Jain, is to 'take followers away from worldly pleasures and bring them back to the path of spiritual purification' (2008).

## Festivals

The Jaina ritual calendar revolves around three major festivals, with many minor ones in between. The three are Divali, which coincides with the start of the New Year in November–December; **Mahavira Jayanti** in spring; and, most important, Paryushana/Daslakshana, in August–September.

Although it is common to think of Divali as a Hindu or even pan-Indian festival of light, many Jainas believe it began as a Jaina commemoration of the moksha of Mahavira and over time was co-opted by other traditions. For Jainas, the 'light' that Divali celebrates is the light of omniscience. While Hindus celebrate the defeat of the evil King Ravana and the establishment of social and cosmic order with the return of Lord Rama, Jainas commemorate their Lord's transcendence of society and the cosmos altogether.

Even so, Jaina celebrations of Divali do not differ markedly from those of their Hindu neighbours. For example, because Divali coincides with the new year, the Hindu goddess of wealth, Sri Lakshmi, is enthusiastically worshipped by all. And because the festival marks the start of a new financial year, members of the business community (of which Jainas constitute an important segment) are especially fervent in showing their appreciation of the goddess. Of course, the ascetics are never far away to remind the Jainas that the greatest wealth is *moksha* itself. Once again it is important to remember that financial success, in itself, is not considered antithetical to the Jaina ideal: as long as one does not become covetous, the possession of wealth is regarded as an indicator of an auspicious life.

No. 34 Mahavira Jayanti is a joyous festival held in the month of *caitra* (March–April). Celebrating the birth of Lord Mahavira, it is an occasion for great pageantry, with shops, streets, and temples

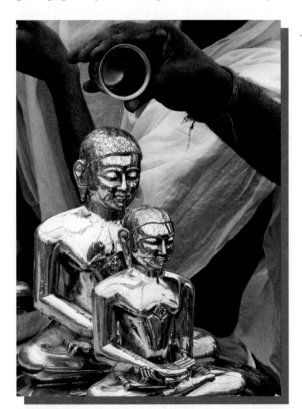

A worshipper pours water on statues of Lord Mahavira as part of the Mahavira Jayanti celebration (Raj Patidar/ Reuters/Landov).

all sumptuously decorated. Jainas enthusiastically undertake pilgrimages, listen to sermons, sing devotional hymns, and take part in pujas as well as ritual re-enactments of the wondrous events associated with Mahavira's birth. Ritual actors in heavenly costume play the roles of the adoring gods and goddesses, who descend from the heavens to pay the baby homage and carry him to the mythical Mount Meru, where he is ceremoniously given his first bath and his name. To perform the role of Indra, the king of the gods, or his queen Indrani is especially meritorious, and the right to do so is usually won at auctions that generate huge sums of money for various philanthropic and social service organizations.

The most important of all Jaina festivals, however, is Paryushana/Daslakshana (the Svetambara and Digambara names for the festival, respectively). This festival is celebrated at the end of the summer rainy season—a four-month period of such lush fecundity that renouncers are forbidden to travel during it, lest they cause unnecessary violence to the innumerable sentient beings that the rains bring to life.

The literal meaning of Paryushana is 'abiding together'—a reference to the sustained interaction that takes place between householders and renouncers during the summer. Obliged to stay in one place, the renouncers must seek alms from the same local householders for several months, and the latter take advantage of this daily contact to seek the renouncers' advice on all sorts of spiritual and worldly issues. Paryushana comes at a time of transition in the annual calendar, marking the end of the rains and the resumption of the renouncers' peripatetic rounds. It is the climax of a period of heightened religiosity.

Although Paryushana is a festival of restraint, it is celebrated with characteristic Jaina enthusiasm. The end of the eight-day festival, called Samvatsari Pratikraman, is a day of introspection, confession of sins, and fasting. The penultimate day is celebrated as the Day of Forgiveness (Kshamavani),

*Not on study guide* [handwritten marginal note]

when Jainas seek to wipe the slate clean with one another and with the world itself by asking and offering forgiveness for all harms.

Forgiveness is fundamental to social interaction and amity. For Jainas, however, it is equally important in the context of erasing the obligations that tie us to the world. Forgiveness—or, more accurately, 'detached forgiveness'—is essential to self-control and renunciation. To 'clean the slate' with all beings in the world, Jainas recite the universal prayer, *Micchami Dukkadam*:

> We forgive all living beings
> We seek pardon from all living beings
> We are friendly towards all living beings,
> And we seek enmity with none.

*No. 35* An interesting 'minor' festival is Astanika, celebrated three times a year, in spring, summer, and fall. It reveals the importance that Jaina cosmology attributes to human birth, for it is only during Astanika periods that the minor gods have the opportunity to worship the Jinas —an opportunity that humans enjoy throughout their lives. In Jaina cosmology, those minor gods are reaping the fruits of good karma earned in a previous human life. When that karma is exhausted, however, their sojourn in the heavens will end. Then they will have to return to the earth and resume the human work of eliminating bad karma. During their time in the heavenly realms, they have no opportunity to purify their souls except during the Astanika intervals when they can travel to the legendary Nandishwara Island and worship the Jinas. Nandishwara Island is a unique plane within Jaina cosmography, home to fifty-two naturally formed Jaina temples and more than five thousand Jaina idols of liberated beings (*siddhas*). Humans have no access to Nandishwara Island, but celebrate Astanika by building replicas of the island and its temples, and performing puja before them. Jainas claim that this practice earns good karma and wins them worldly favours from the gods.

Almost all Jaina cultural expressions (art, ritual, iconography) are tied in one way or another to the Five Auspicious Events (*Panch Kalyanaka*) in the lives of the Jinas: conception, birth, renunciation, omniscience, and *moksha*. These five paradigmatic events are universally celebrated and powerfully inform the Jaina religious imagination. They are vividly represented in sculptures and miniature paintings, re-enacted in theatre and ritual, and devotedly described in narrative—most famously in the ancient *Kalpa Sutra* text. They are also closely associated with pilgrimages, since every *tirtha* (site of devotion) is linked with one or more of them.

The centrality of the Jinas in the cultural expressions of Jainism—in its rituals and iconography, and as an ethical archetype—is overwhelming. Ultimately, however, Jainism insists that the Jinas are irrelevant: self-realization is not dependent on them, and since the Jinas have by definition passed out of this world into a state of liberation, any connection they might have had with life in this world is radically absent. Clearly, the Jina is not central to Jaina metaphysics in the way that God is central in theistic traditions. Nevertheless, the Jina is the bedrock on which the Jaina imagination has developed and around which Jaina devotional life revolves.

# INTERACTION AND ADAPTATION

An important factor in the success of Jainism has been Jainas' ability to maintain good relations with their religious neighbours, particularly Hindus. Because Jainas have never made up more than a small proportion of the communities they live in, a capacity for effective interaction with non-Jainas has been essential.

Jainas themselves credit their adaptive success to their commitment to *ahimsa*: non-violence in thought, speech, and deed makes for easy friendship. Another factor encouraging broadmindedness and compromise is the doctrine of *anekantavada*: literally meaning 'not one-sided', it teaches that all human truth claims are partial and context-bound, and that intolerance is the product of confusing partiality with truth.

Of course Jainism is not a relativist epistemology. It unequivocally affirms the existence of Truth, as well as its ultimate attainability, and it has strategically used this doctrine to dismiss the rival philosophies of Buddhism and Hindu Vedanta as *ekanta* (one-sided). At the same time it maintains that, among those who have not reached enlightenment, no one can claim more than partial understanding. This perspective may very well foster—as Jainas claim it does—a general attitude of tolerance towards difference.

We have seen how Jainism's ethical principles—the restrictions it places on dietary practices, livelihoods, and so on—serve as 'fences' to keep the violence of worldly life at bay. Socially, however, Jainism has never erected fences to ensure religious purity. To insist on exclusion would likely have doomed a community so small and vulnerable. Instead, Jainas seek the closest possible integration with their neighbours, adopting local languages and customs while safeguarding their fundamental practices and beliefs.

According to Padmanabh Jaini, a prominent scholar of Jainism and Buddhism, the Jaina *acharyas* were prescient when they recommended 'cautious integration' with neighbouring peoples and practices. Well aware of the risk of assimilation into Hindu culture, they also recognized the necessity of forging close social and economic ties with non-Jainas. The *acharya* Jinasena (ninth century CE) went the furthest in prescribing selective integration, and his ideas have been enormously influential.

Jinasena did this in two ways. First, he defined some Hindu practices as falling outside the sphere of religion and taught that Jainas should feel free to adopt any local custom that did not conflict with their basic tenets. Second, he 'Jaina-ized' other Hindu practices, re-interpreting them in terms of Jaina doctrine so that they could be adopted without fear of assimilation. So, for example, he developed a Jaina version of the age-old Hindu *samskaras* (life-cycle rituals), creating an interpretive overlay for Hindu rituals that had already been widely adopted by Jaina householders.

In addition, Jinasena redefined the caste system—an institution that Mahavira had soundly denounced—so as to rationalize it and ease social intercourse for Jainas living in a caste-bound society. Thus he argued that the caste system was not—as the brahmins claimed—divinely ordained, but simply a product of economic and political expediency. He also argued that 'brahmin' should be an honorific title reserved for those who lead righteous lives, not a status ascribed at birth. In this way Jinasena was able to argue that Jainas, because of their superior ethical conduct, were the true brahmins.

Perhaps because of its individualist ontology, emphasizing the solitary nature of the soul, Jainism is not inclined to question the 'authenticity' of its followers. So, for instance, Jainas rarely debate who is and who is not a 'true' Jaina. This is not necessarily the case with the question of 'true' Jaina practices, however. The absorption of Hindu influences into Jainism (e.g., theistic elements, ritual practices) has gone on for a long time, and for most Jainas it has not been a cause for anxiety. This situation may be changing somewhat today. In the current climate of religious revival, as the symbolic boundaries between traditions are hardening, these issues appear to be taking on increasing significance.

# ❧ RECENT DEVELOPMENTS

For the last half century Jainism—like many other traditions—has been undergoing a profound revitalization. One factor has been its geographic spread beyond south Asia to the far reaches of the globe. Sizeable Jaina communities now exist in England, the United States, and Canada, and this diaspora is contributing to some significant new developments.

Outside India, for example, the renunciatory ethos becomes harder to sustain, and seemingly less important for Jaina religious identity. Although Jainas everywhere retain their philosophical commitment to the *ahimsa* principle, in diaspora communities it is often expressed in the 'worldly' terms of animal rights, ecological health, and societal improvement; aspirations to self-purification and world transcendence seem to be less common. A similar shift is occurring with respect to dietary practices, which are no longer inextricably tied to the ideology of renunciation; the connection with the *ahimsa* principle remains close, however. What we seem to be witnessing is a redefinition of *ahimsa* and a de-coupling of the previously inseparable relationship between *ahimsa* and renunciation.

Many examples attest to the resurgence of Jaina religious identity within India. For instance, efforts to have Jainism legally recognized as a distinct tradition, independent of Hinduism, have been under way for more than a century, but in the last few years they have gained enough popular momentum to reach the level of Supreme Court arbitration. In addition, census data show that increasing numbers of Jainas are now identifying Jainism as their 'religion' rather than their 'caste' or 'sect'. Meanwhile, the number of Jaina schools and institutions are growing, and after decades of dormancy the Digambaras are reviving the practice of naked mendicancy.

Modernizing Jaina reformers present their tradition as progressive, environmentally responsible, egalitarian, and scientifically avant-garde. For example, there is a strong tendency to argue that Jaina theories of the cosmos not only resonate with science but actually anticipate them, and that modern science in due course will confirm Mahavira's vision of the cosmos (see Gelra 2007).

The influential Svetambara Terapanthi sect has vigorously marketed 'Insight Meditation' (*Preksha Dhyann*) as a scientifically informed therapeutic practice. In the last fifteen years, Terapanthis have set up a number of sophisticated meditation centres in India, England, and the US that attract Indians and foreigners alike. This effort to reach out beyond the Jaina community is interesting both because it is a new development and because it reflects a desire to position Jainism within the global community.

If recognition as a 'world religion' depended solely on scope and influence, Jainism would always have merited inclusion in the club. The impact of the *shramana* tradition on Indian culture and religious expression has been immeasurable, and Jainism has been its principal flag-bearer for more than 2,600 years.

To qualify as a 'world religion', however, a tradition must also possess both a universal aspect and a certain singular or exclusive quality—something that distinguishes it from all other traditions. Over the past two centuries, Jainas have actively asserted both their difference from rival traditions (especially Hinduism) and the universal significance of their principles, especially *ahimsa*.

For Jainism, as for all religious traditions today, remaining relevant is an enormous challenge. Jainas have enthusiastically taken up the task of reframing their ancient tradition to fit the contemporary context, and its revival speaks to their success. With its doctrines of non-violence and non-attachment, and its repudiation of intellectual dogmatism, Jainism has a great deal to offer the modern world.

# Sites

**Dilwara Temples** An exquisite complex of white marble temples on Mount Abu, Rajasthan, dating from the eleventh century.

**Ranakpur Temples** Another beautiful complex, also in Rajasthan, dating from the fifteenth century.

**Palitana, Gujarat** A major pilgrimage site with an extensive temple complex dating from the eleventh century.

**Gwalior Fort, Madhya Pradesh** Site of enormous rock-cut sculptures of Jinas.

**Sammet Shikarji, Bihar** An important pilgrimage site where it is claimed that twenty-three of the twenty-four Jinas achieved omniscience.

**Shravanabelagola, Karnataka** Home of the colossal (18-metre) statue of the renouncer Bahubali (also known as Gomateshwara), and the site of an enormous pilgrimage once every twelve years.

**Jaina Centre, Leicester, England** The first Jaina temple outside India, consecrated in 1980.

**Jaina Center of Greater Boston** The first such centre in North America.

# Glossary

*ajiva* Non-soul, non-consciousness; *ajiva* is also referred to as 'matter' or 'karma'.

*anuvratas* Five vows modelled on the great vows of the renouncers but modified to make them applicable to lay life: non-violence, truthfulness, non-stealing, non-attachment, and chastity.

*caturvidhyasangha* Literally, 'four-fold community'; the community consisting of monks, nuns, laymen, and laywomen.

**Digambaras** Early sectarian node within Jainism with its own sacred scriptures; identified by the male mendicant practice of nudity.

*gunasthanas* Stages or steps of spiritual progress, numbering fourteen in total.

**Jina** Literally, 'conqueror'; an epithet for the 24 ascetic–prophets who conquered the world of desire and suffering, and taught the path to eternal happiness; alternatively called Tirthankara.

*jiva* Eternal soul/consciousness; all living beings are endowed with *jiva*.

**Mahavira** Literally, 'Great Hero'; epithet of the 24th and final Jina of our time cycle, born Vardhamana Jnatrpura in the sixth century BCE.

**Mahavira Jayanti** A joyous spring festival celebrating the birth of Mahavira.

*mahavratas* The five 'great vows' adopted by renouncers: absolute non-violence, truthfulness, non-stealing, non-attachment, and celibacy.

**Namokar Mantra** The central prayer in Jainism.

*paap* Karmic particles of an inauspicious nature ('bad karma').

**pratikramana** Ritual practice of repentance.

**punya** Karmic particles of an auspicious nature ('good karma').

**Rsabha** The first Tirthankara of our current time cycle; also called Adinath.

**sallekhana** A ritual fast to death undertaken voluntarily, usually in old age or illness.

**samayika** A desired state of equanimity; ritual practice of meditation.

**samyak darshan** Right vision, faith, or intuition into the basic truth of the cosmos; spiritual growth is dependent upon the attainment of *samyak darshan*.

**siddha loka** Final abode of the liberated *jiva*.

**Svetambara** One of the two early sectarian nodes within Jainism; mendicants wear simple white robes.

**Tatthvartha Sutra** An important philosophical text accepted by all Jaina sects, composed by Umasvati in the second century CE.

**Tirthankara** Literally, 'ford-maker'; epithet for the 24 Jinas who, through their teachings, created a ford across the ocean of *samsara*.

**upvas** Literally, 'to be near the soul'; term used to denote ritual fasting.

# Further Reading

Babb, Lawrence A. 1996. *Absent Lord: Ascetics and Kings in a Jain Ritual Culture*. Berkeley: University of California Press.

Banks, Marcus. 1992. *Organizing Jainism in India and England*. Oxford: Clarendon.

Carrithers, Michael, and Caroline Humphrey, eds. 1991. *The Assembly of Listeners: Jains in Society*. Cambridge: Cambridge University Press.

Cort, John E. 2001. *Jains in the World: Religious Values and Ideology in India*. New York and Delhi: Oxford University Press.

Dundas, Paul. 2002. *The Jains*. 2nd ed. London: Routledge. A comprehensive overview of Jainism and an excellent introduction to the subject.

Jaini, Padmanabh S. 1979. *The Jaina Path of Purification*. Berkeley: University of California Press. The standard general study of Jainism.

Laidlaw, James. 1995. *Riches and Renunciation: Religion, Economy, and Society among the Jains*. Oxford: Oxford University Press.

# Recommended Websites

http://www.jaindharmonline.com
A portal dedicated to Jainism and Jaina dharma; it contains information and links to news articles.

http://www.jainstudies.org
The International Summer School for Jain Studies.

http://www.jainworld.com
Jainism Global Resource Center, USA.

http://pluralism.org/wrgb/traditions/jainism
Resources from Harvard University's Pluralism Project.

# References

Cort, John E. 2001. *Jains in the World: Religious Values and Ideology in India*. New York and Delhi: Oxford University Press.

———. 2005. 'Devotional Culture in Jainism: Manatunga and His *Bhaktamara Stotra*'. In James Blumenthal, ed. *Incompatible Visions: South Asian Religions in History and Culture*. Madison, WI: Center for South Asia, University of Wisconsin-Madison.

Gelra, M.R. 2007. *Science in Jainism*. Ladnun, Rajasthan: Jain Vishva Bharati Institute.

Jacobi, Hermann, trans. 1884. *Jaina Sutras*, Part I. In F. Max Müller, ed., *Sacred Books of the East*, 22. Oxford: Clarendon Press.

Jain, S.C. 2008. 'Jain Festivals'. Unpublished manuscript prepared for the International Summer School of Jain Studies.

Jaini, Padmanabh S. 1979. *The Jaina Path of Purification*. Berkeley: University of California Press.

———. 1990. 'Ahimsa'. Inaugural Roop Lal Jain Lecture, Centre for South Asian Studies, University of Toronto.

Laidlaw, James. 2005. 'A Life Worth Leaving: Fasting to Death as Telos of a Jain Religious Life'. *Economy and Society* 34, 2: 178–99.

Lath, M., trans. 1984. *Kalpa Sutra*. V. Sagar, ed. Jaipur: Prakrit Bharati.

# Note

1. This text was compiled by Jinendra Varni and published by Sarva Seva Sangh Prakashan, India. It was translated into English in 1993 by T.K. Tukol and K.K. Dixit.

Chapter

# 5

# Buddhist Traditions

❧ Roy C. Amore ❧

At the heart of Buddhism are three elements known as the 'Three Jewels' or the 'Triple Gem': the Buddha, the Dharma (teachings), and the Sangha (congregation). Buddhists express their faith in these elements by saying they 'take refuge' in them. Recitation of the 'Three Refuges' mantra has been a regular part of virtually every Buddhist ceremony for approximately 2,500 years.

## OVERVIEW

With his last words to his disciples—'Everything that arises also passes away, so strive for what has not arisen—the Buddha passed into **nirvana** some 2,500 years ago. After a deep enlightenment experience at the age of thirty-five, he had spent the remaining forty-five years of his life teaching that all worldly phenomena are transient, caught up in a cycle of arising and passing away. He set the wheel of **dharma** (teaching) in motion, established a community (**sangha**) of disciples, and charged his followers to carry the dharma to all regions of the world. The missionary effort succeeded. Today there are Buddhists in nearly every country in the world, and Buddhism is the dominant religion in many parts of East, South, and Southeast Asia.

Buddhism has three main traditions or 'vehicles', all of which originated in India. The earliest is **Theravada** (also known as **Hinayana**), which spread to Southeast Asia; the second is **Mahayana**, which became the principal school in East Asia; and the third is **Vajrayana**, which developed out of Mahayana and became closely associated with

### Buddhist Vehicles and Schools

1. Theravada (sometimes called Hinayana, the 'Little Vehicle'), now dominant in Sri Lanka and Southeast Asia: the only survivor of the eighteen sects that existed in the third century BCE
2. Mahayana (the 'Great Vehicle'), now dominant in East Asia and Vietnam:
   - Madhyamika in India, Sanlun in China
   - Yogacara in India, Faxiang in China
   - Tiantai in China, Tendai in Japan
   - Huayan in China, Kegon in Japan
   - Zhenyan in China, Shingon in Japan
   - Pure Land, Jingtu in China, Jodo in Japan
   - Chan in China, Son in Korea, Zen in Japan
     — Linji in China, Rinzai in Japan
     — Caodong in China, Soto in Japan
   - Nichiren in Japan
3. Vajrayana (the 'Diamond Vehicle'), now dominant in Tibet and the Himalayas:
   - Gelugpa ('Yellow Hats')
   - Kargyu ('Red Hats')
   - Karma-pa ('Black Hats')
   - Nyingma ('Ancient' school)

◀ Theravada monks and novices at the Phu That stupa in Udomxai, Laos (Amanda Ahn/© dbimages/Alamy).

# Timeline

| | |
|---|---|
| **c. 531 (or 589 or 413)** BCE | Shakyamuni's enlightenment |
| **c. 496 (or 544 or 368)** | Shakyamuni's *parinirvana* or passing |
| **c. 395** | First Buddhist council |
| **c. 273** | Accession of King Ashoka |
| **c. 225** | Mahendra takes Theravada Buddhism to Sri Lanka |
| **c. 67** CE | Buddhism takes root in China |
| **c. 100** | Emergence of Indian Mahayana |
| **c. 200** | Nagarjuna, Madhyamika philosopher |
| **c. 350** | Asanga and Vasubandhu, Yogacara philosophers |
| **372** | Buddhism introduced to Korea from China |
| **c. 500** | Emergence of tantra in India |
| **604** | 'Prince' Shotoku, Japanese regent and patron of Buddhism, issues Seventeen-Article Constitution |
| **c. 750** | Padmasambhava takes Vajrayana Buddhism to Tibet |
| **806** | Shingon (tantric) Buddhism introduced to Japan |
| **845** | Persecution of Buddhism in China |
| **1173** | Birth of Shinran, Japanese Pure Land thinker (d. 1262) |
| **1222** | Birth of Nichiren, founder of the Japanese sect devoted to the *Lotus Sutra* (d. 1282) |
| **1603** | Tokugawa regime takes power in Japan; Buddhism is put under strict state control |
| **c. 1617** | Dalai Lamas become rulers of Tibet |
| **c. 1900** | Beginnings of Buddhist missionary activity in the West |
| **1956** | B.R. Ambedkar (1891–1956) converts to Buddhism, leading to the conversion of 380,000 other dalits and re-establishing Buddhism in India |
| **1959** | China takes over Tibet; the Dalai Lama and many other Tibetans flee to India |
| **1963** | Thich Quang Duc immolates himself in protest against the persecution of Buddhists in South Vietnam |
| **2001** | Taliban forces destroy colossal Buddhist statues along ancient trade route in Afghanistan |

the Himalayan region. All three traditions also have followers in Europe and North America.

# ✤ ORIGINS

## Religious Life in Ancient India

The tradition identified in Chapter 1 as 'Ganges Spirituality' developed at a time when northern India was one of the most active centres of civilization in the world. Its location, halfway between the Bay of Bengal to the east and the Arabian Sea to the west, gave it easy access to a trading route that stretched across the Indian subcontinent. By 500 BCE trade was thriving, enriching the merchant (vaishya) class, and giving rise to a new money-based economy, while agriculture flourished on the large estates owned by the kshatriyas and brahmins and worked by commoners and slaves.

Hidden beneath the peace and prosperity, however, were social and ideological tensions that went beyond the usual tensions between the upper and lower classes. The new money economy had created a large urban merchant class with wealth and financial power but without either the land or the social status of the traditional landowning classes. The brahmins and kshatriyas who considered themselves to represent the mouth and arms of the cosmic Person looked down on the new urban rich.

Perhaps the most important cultural tension, however, was between the religion of the brahmins and the traditional religious beliefs and practices of the region. We noted in Chapter 1 that while the brahmins considered animal sacrifice central to their sacred tradition, the ascetic masters—among them the Jaina master Mahavira and **Shakyamuni** Buddha—took the ethic of *ahimsa* so seriously that they denounced even that ritual practice.

Another major difference between the brahmin and ascetic traditions had to do with the role of deities. In the former, the deities required regular praise and ritual offerings, and in return they would respond to devotees' requests for assistance.

Some of the major deities were recognized by the other traditions as well—especially the creator god Brahma and the storm god Indra. For the most part, though, deities played quite a small role in the non-brahminic traditions. Minor gods might provide practical help from time to time, but there was no question of asking the gods for assistance along the spiritual path. The liberation that the ascetics sought could be achieved only through their own efforts. As an East Asian Zen Buddhist master put it much later, 'If there is anything to take hold of, you must take hold of it for yourself.' The spiritual masters led the way, but the disciples had to walk the path themselves, without any supernatural assistance. A verse of the *Dhammapada*, a collection that is a favourite of Buddhists everywhere, puts it this way: 'You must strive for yourselves. The Tathagatas [buddhas] are only your guides. Meditative persons who follow their path will overcome the bonds of Mara [death]' (*Dhammapada* no. 276).

It was in this environment that Buddhism originated. Some aspects of Buddhist thought were major innovations: the concept of the impermanence of the human self or soul, for instance, and the idea of social egalitarianism. But others—including the notions of **karma** and successive reincarnations, the ideal of ascetic withdrawal from the world, and the belief that numerous gods, demons, and spirits play active roles in human life—were common to all the traditions of the Ganges region.

Among the students along the ancient Ganges was a prince from the small kingdom of the Shakya people in what is now southern Nepal. Named Siddhartha Gautama, he was to become known first as Shakyamuni, the 'Shakyan sage', and eventually as the Buddha of the current age.

## The First Gem: The Buddha

### *The Bodhisattva Vow and Previous Lives*
Buddhism, like Hinduism and Jainism, understands the cosmos in terms of an endless succession of universes arising and passing away.

## Traditions at a Glance

### Numbers
Most estimates range between 200 and 300 million.

### Distribution
South, Southeast, and East Asia, plus minorities in Europe and North America.

### Founder
Shakyamuni Buddha, who taught in northern India 2,500 years ago; believed to be the most recent in a long line of major buddhas.

### Principal Historical Periods

| | |
|---|---|
| 5th to 1st century BCE | Early Indian Buddhism; the roots of the Theravada tradition, which eventually spread to Sri Lanka and Southeast Asia |
| 1st century CE | Mahayana emerges and later spreads to Southeast, Central, and East Asia |
| 5th century CE | Vajrayana emerges and begins spreading to the Himalayan region |

### Deities
The Buddha is not worshipped as a god; rather, he is venerated as a fully enlightened human being. Regional variants of Buddhism have often incorporated local gods and spirits. Mahayana developed a theory of three bodies of the Buddha, linking the historic buddhas to a cosmic force.

### Authoritative Texts
Theravada has the *Tripitaka* ('Three Baskets'): *vinaya* (monastic rules), *sutras* (discourses), and *abhidharma* (systematic treatises). Mahayana has a great number of texts in various languages, including Chinese, Japanese, and Tibetan. Vajrayana has the Kanjur (tantric texts) and Tanjur (commentaries).

### Noteworthy Teachings
The Three Characteristics of Existence are suffering, impermanence, and no-self. The Four Noble Truths are suffering, origin of suffering, cessation of suffering, and the Eightfold Path. Other notable teachings include karma, rebirth, and nirvana. In addition, the Mahayana and Vajrayana schools stress the emptiness (non-absoluteness) of all things. All schools emphasize non-violence and compassion for all living beings.

---

Our current universe, having evolved millions of earthly years before the present, was already in the declining phase of its life cycle when Shakyamuni, the Buddha of the present age, was born. In every era, when the inevitable decline in morality and truth—that is, dharma—becomes severe, a highly developed being is born to become the buddha for that era. (In the same way, Hindu tradition maintains that the lord Krishna comes to save the earth when dharma has declined.)

Although many Buddhists believe in gods and spirits, no almighty god is needed to mastermind the arrival of a new buddha: such a highly developed being is aware of the state of the world and knows when the time has come. Buddhists tell the story of Gautama Buddha, or Shakyamuni, as the Buddha for our era, with the understanding that there have been buddhas in previous eras and there will be buddhas in subsequent ones. Each era is considered to have only one fully enlightened, teaching buddha, but there are numerous other beings in every age who are thought to have achieved some degree of enlightenment. Among them are *pratyeka buddhas* (hermits who live in isolation from the world and do not teach), **Arhats** ('worthy ones', frequently translated as 'saints'), and **bodhisattvas** (those who have dedicated themselves to achieving buddhahood). All the Buddhist traditions agree that Shakyamuni lived to the age of eighty, but scholars are not certain when he lived. Some Indian and Western Buddhologists who have correlated the Buddhist chronicles with Greek evidence believe he was born in 566 BCE; others argue for 563. In Sri Lanka and Southeast Asia, however, the standard birth date is several decades earlier (624 BCE), while Japanese scholars, relying on Chinese and Tibetan texts, have adopted a later date of 448 BCE.

Significantly, Shakyamuni achieves enlightenment through his own reflective and meditative efforts. He has, however, nearly perfected his 'mind of enlightenment' through hundreds of previous lives. Unlike the Hindu *avatara* or Christian god incarnate, the Buddha, Shakyamuni, is not a god on earth but simply a human being who has perfected the spiritual potential of all living creatures.

What is special about the Buddha is the spiritual and intellectual power of his insight. That manifestation of power, the ability to free people from entrapment in suffering, is what Buddhists have in mind when they say that they take refuge in the Buddha.

Before we relate the narrative of Shakyamuni, we must clarify an item of terminology. Usage distinguishes between a buddha as an already enlightened being and a bodhisattva as one who has vowed to seek enlightenment but has not yet attained it. Thus for the period of his younger years in quest of enlightenment, Siddhartha is termed a bodhisattva, but in his mature teaching following his enlightenment, he is referred to as the Buddha. This chapter will refer to Shakyamuni as 'the Buddha' (with a capital 'B'), but to any other enlightened being, in the generic sense, as 'a buddha' (lower-case).

The story of the Buddha, as Buddhists tell it, has its beginning in earlier ages. During the lifetime of one previous buddha, a young man comes upon a crowd of people filling mud holes in the road in anticipation of the arrival of the buddha of that era. But the buddha comes before one mud hole is filled, and so the young man puts himself into the hole to serve as a stepping-stone. Instead of stepping on him, however, the buddha announces that the young man will become a buddha himself in the distant future.

The young man takes the startling prophecy to heart and vows to work towards full enlightenment. The act of solemnly promising to work towards buddhahood is called taking a 'bodhisattva' vow. The term *bodhi* in the first part of the compound means 'enlightenment', and *sattva* means 'being', as in the phrase 'human being'. After the young man in our story dies, his karma complex—the matrix of all his past actions—gives rise to a new being. In short, he is reborn, as are all living beings. Over many lives he makes progress towards purifying his inner nature. Stories of more than five-hundred of his lives are preserved in a collection called *Jataka* ('birth stories').

The best known and most beloved of the *Jataka* tales is the final one, which tells the story of the bodhisattva's last incarnation before he becomes the Buddha. Here the bodhisattva is reborn as a prince named Vessantara, who as a young boy bodhisattva takes a vow of perfect generosity: whenever he is asked for something, he will give it. The consequences of this promise are not terribly serious as long as he is a child, but eventually his father, following an old royal custom of India, retires and passes the throne to him.

No one complains much when Vessantara gives food and clothing from the public treasury to the poor, for his generosity is credited with bringing rains and prosperity to the kingdom. But when he gives the kingdom's lucky white elephant to citizens of a rival kingdom, the people demand that his father resume the throne and banish Vessantara. Yet even in exile he continues to give away everything he is asked for, up to and including his wife and children. Finally his father intervenes, Vessantara is reunited with his family, and we learn that the gods have been guiding events in order to give him the opportunity to test his resolve. Vessantara's strict adherence to his vow serves as a model for Buddhist self-discipline.

### Siddhartha's Birth and Childhood

After Vessantara dies, he is not reborn immediately. Rather, the new being generated by his karma complex waits in heaven until the time comes when the dharma of the previous buddha has been lost and a new 'wheel turner' is needed to set the wheel of dharma (the *dharmachakra*) in motion once again. Finally, when the world needs him, he chooses to be born into the ruling family of a small kingdom in what is now southern Nepal.

The story of the Buddha's birth and childhood varies to some extent among the Buddhist traditions. What follows is a very brief version, based on the early Pali-language account preserved in the Theravada tradition. (Later versions tend to be longer and to include many more miracles.) According to this early account, then, the queen of the Shakya people, Mahamaya, is keeping a vow of sexual abstinence in observance of a festival. One afternoon she takes a nap and dreams she is carried by the four 'world protectors' to a pleasant grove of trees. (The world protectors are minor gods who look after the earth, one for each cardinal direction. Although Buddhists do not believe that enlightenment requires any kind of divine intervention, they do imagine minor gods to play an active role in the unfolding of events.)

In the grove, a spiritual being in the form of a sacred white elephant—albino elephants were associated with good fortune—descends from the heavens and miraculously enters through her side, where it becomes the embryo of the Buddha-to-be. After a pregnancy marked by supernatural signs—Mahamaya can see the child in her womb—she sets out for her home city, intending to give birth there. While she stops to rest at a roadside park known as Lumbini, the baby is born through her right side as she holds onto a tree branch for support. In later Buddhist accounts, the tree miraculously lowers its branch to assist her, flowers appear out of season, and streams of hot and cold water rain down from the sky to wash the baby. In the Theravada tradition, the birth takes place on the full-moon day of the month called **Vaishakha** ('rains'), which usually falls in April or May of the Western calendar (East Asian Buddhists follow a different tradition). A bright light illuminates the world that night, to mark the holy event. In the ancient world, the birth of an extraordinary person was often thought to be marked by unusual astral events, such as a bright light or an auspicious alignment of the planets.

It is interesting to compare the birth stories of Buddha and Jesus. Both are conceived without normal sexual intercourse. Buddha's mother is married but under a vow of celibacy, and Mary is an unwed virgin. Both infants are born outside the house, Jesus in a stable and Buddha in a grove. A bright light announces both births, and sages forecast their future greatness. Angels appear in the sky to announce the births, to shepherds in one case and a meditating sage in the other.

The infant bodhisattva is presented to the father, King Shuddhodana, who holds a naming festival. The name chosen for him, Siddhartha, can be translated as 'he who achieves success'. But Buddhists rarely use it, preferring the titles that refer to his spiritual role, such as Shakyamuni or (Lord) Buddha.

During the naming ceremony, various brahmins offer predictions based on their reading of his physical features. Later Buddhist texts report that they find thirty-two major bodily signs and more than eighty minor ones. The most significant features can be seen in the Buddha statues that became popular approximately five centuries after his death. His unusually long ear lobes are a sign of great spiritual wisdom; his golden complexion shows his inner tranquillity, and the wheel patterns on the soles of his feet point to his role as wheel-turner. On the basis of these signs, the brahmins predict an extraordinary destiny for the young prince. If he stays 'in the world', he will become a great emperor, ruling far more than the little Shakya kingdom. But if he 'departs the world', he will achieve the highest possible goal for a monk, becoming a fully enlightened buddha.

His father, the king, wants Siddhartha to become a great emperor, so he orders that no evidence of sickness, old age, or death be allowed near the boy, lest knowledge of life's inevitable suffering lead him to renounce the world and become a monk. Evidently the early Buddhists who told this story shared the view of those modern scholars who see religion as a response to the adversities of life and suggest that, in the absence of adversity, humans would have little reason to pursue the spiritual path. As the Buddha explained to his followers, his early life was that of a pampered prince:

> I was delicate, most delicate, supremely delicate. Lily pools were made for me at my father's house solely for my benefit. Blue lilies flowered in one, white lilies in another, red lilies in a third. I had three palaces; one for the Winter, one for the Summer and one for the Rains (*Anguttara Nikaya* iii.38; Nanamoli 1972: 8).

There are only a few stories of the bodhisattva's childhood. In one of them he amazes his first teacher when he shows that he already knows the various alphabets. In another he wins a martial arts tournament even though he has shown little interest in war. In the most significant of these stories, the boy is sitting in the shade of a rose-apple tree watching his father perform a spring ground-breaking ritual when he enters a meditational trance, during which the shadow of the tree miraculously stands still even though the sun moves. The memory of this wakeful meditation state will play a role in his eventual achievement of enlightenment.

### The Four Sights and the Great Departure

Despite all King Shuddhodana's precautions, Siddhartha learns the bitter truth of life's sorrows around the time of his thirtieth birthday. By then he is happily married (the earliest sources do not refer to his wife by name, but later texts call her Yasodhara) and the father of a son named Rahula. Going for a chariot ride through the royal park, the prince happens to see four sights that will alter the course of his life. The first three—a sick man, a suffering old man, and a dead man—awaken him to life's problems. When he asks what is wrong with these men, his chariot driver answers honestly, revealing to him for the first time the harsh realities of life. The Buddha would later explain to his disciples what he learned from seeing the reality of sickness:

> When an untaught ordinary man, who is subject to sickness, not safe from sickness, sees another who is sick, he is shocked, humiliated and disgusted; for he forgets that he himself is no exception. But I too am subject to sickness, not safe from sickness, and so it cannot befit me to be shocked, humiliated and disgusted on seeing another who is sick. When I considered this, the vanity of health entirely left me (*Anguttara Nikaya* iii. 38; Nanamoli 1972: 8).

The fourth and final sight is a monk, whose aura of tranquil detachment from the world suggests that there is a way to overcome the suffering

## From the *Dhammapada*

*Many of the Buddhist* sutras *include one or more verses that sum up the teaching. These memory verses were eventually collected as a separate work called the* Dhammapada, *'fundamentals of Dharma'. The verses from Chapter One concern the pure mind.*

1. The mind is the source of all mental actions [dharmas],
   mind is the chief of the mental actions, and they are made by the mind.
   If, by an impure mind, one speaks or acts,
   then suffering follows the mind as a cartwheel follows the footprint of the ox.
2. The mind is the source of all mental states,
   mind is their leader, and they are made by the mind.
   If, by a pure mind, one speaks or acts, then happiness follows the mind like a shadow.
3. 'I was abused.' 'I was beaten.' 'I was hurt.' 'I was robbed.'
   Those who dwell excessively on such thoughts never get out of their hating state of mind.
4. 'I was abused.' 'I was beaten.' 'I was hurt.' 'I was robbed.'
   Those who leave such thoughts behind get out of their hating state of mind.
5. In this world hatreds are never ended by more hating.
   Hatreds are only ended by loving kindness.
   This is an eternal truth [dharma].
6. Some people do not know that we must restrain ourselves.
   But others know this and settle their quarrels.
7. One who dwells on personal gratifications, overindulges the senses, overeats, is
   indolent and lazy,
   that person is overthrown by Mara [Death] like an old, weak tree in a windstorm.
8. One who dwells in meditation on the bodily impurities, keeps the senses under
   control, eats moderately, has faith and disciplined energy,
   that person stands against Mara like a rocky mountain.
9. Whoever puts on the ochre robe but lacks purity, self-control, and truthfulness,
   that person is not worthy of the robe.
10. Whoever puts on the ochre robe and is pure, self-controlled, and truthful,
    that person is truly worthy of the robe.
11. Mistaking the unessential for the important,
    and mistaking the essential for the unimportant,
    some persons, dwelling in wrong-mindedness,
    never realize that which is really essential.
12. Knowing the essential to be important,
    and knowing the unessential to be unimportant,
    other persons, dwelling in rightmindedness,
    reach that which is really essential.

of life after all. To this day, Buddhist monks often say that what first attracted them to join the sangha (the monastic order) was seeing, as children, the calmness and serenity of the older monks and nuns as they passed through the streets on their daily alms-seeking rounds.

On returning home the bodhisattva ponders the four sights. That night, with the help of the four world protectors, he flees the palace, along with his horse and servant. Many Buddhist temples have murals depicting this event, known as the Great Departure.

Having departed the worldly life, the bodhisattva dismisses his servant and horse, exchanges his princely clothes for those of a poor hunter, obtains an alms bowl, and begins a new life as one of the wandering students seeking spiritual truth along the banks of the Ganges. Determined to learn all eight levels of classical yoga, he soon masters the six levels known to his first guru. He then finds one who is able to teach him the seventh level as well, but even the deep tranquillity of the seventh level is not enough to satisfy the bodhisattva.

Therefore, with five other students, he embarks on an independent program of rigorous ascetic discipline. After six years he is subsisting on nothing more than one palmful of water and one of food per day. He becomes so emaciated that he loses consciousness, but the four world protectors preserve him.

### Enlightenment

Now convinced that even the most extreme asceticism cannot bring about the enlightenment he seeks, the bodhisattva leaves the cave where he has been living and goes to a pleasant town now called Bodh Gaya ('bodh' being short for 'enlightenment). There he resumes eating and drinking, but he still needs a method. Then he remembers the wakeful meditational trance he experienced spontaneously as a child:

> I thought of a time when my Sakyan father was working and I was sitting in the cool shade of a rose-apple tree: quite secluded from sensual desires, secluded from unprofitable things I had entered upon and abided in the first meditation, which is accompanied by thinking and exploring with

happiness and pleasure born of seclusion. I thought: Might that be the way to enlightenment? Then, following up that memory there came the recognition that this was the way to enlightenment (*Majjhima Nikaya*; Nanamoli 1972: 21).

Choosing a pleasant spot beside a cool river, under a *pipal* tree (a large fig tree considered sacred in India at least as far back as the Harappa civilization, known thereafter to Buddhists as the Bodhi tree), he sits to meditate and vows that he will not get up until he has achieved nirvana.

According to some versions of the story, it is at this point, just before dusk on the evening of the full-moon day in the month of Vaishakha, that Mara, the lord of death, arrives. Mara plays a role in Buddhism similar in some ways to that of Satan in Christianity. His main function is to come for people at death and oversee their rebirth in an appropriate place. But he wants to exercise power over events in this world as well. Determined to thwart the bodhisattva's attempt to achieve enlightenment, Mara summons his daughters—whose names suggest greed, boredom, and desire—to tempt him. When that fails, Mara offers him any worldly wish, if only he will return home and live a life of good karma (merit) as a householder. The bodhisattva refuses.

Now Mara becomes violent. He sends in his sons—whose names suggest fear and anger—to assault the bodhisattva. But the bodhisattva's spiritual power is so great that it surrounds and protects him from attack like a force field.

Having failed in his efforts to tempt and threaten the bodhisattva, Mara challenges him to a debate. Mara himself claims to be the one worthy to sit on the Bodhi Seat—the place of enlightenment—on this auspicious night and accuses the bodhisattva of being unworthy. With his sons and daughters cheering him on, Mara thinks he has the upper hand. But the bodhisattva has the truth on his side. He responds that he has the merit of the generosity, courage, and wisdom perfected through

Bodh Gaya, the place of the Buddha's enlightenment and a major pilgrimage site. The Bodhi tree is visible behind the small stupa in the foreground. Beyond that is a large modern temple (Roy C. Amore).

countless previous lives, and calls upon the Earth herself to stand witness on his behalf. The resulting earthquake drives Mara away. Buddhists today understand this story as symbolizing the surfacing of the last remnants of the mind's deep impurities, which the bodhisattva must overcome before he can attain liberation.

With Mara defeated, the bodhisattva begins to meditate in his own way—the reverse of the way taught by the yoga masters. A yogi seeks to move ever deeper into unconsciousness, drawing in the conscious mind as a turtle draws in its head and limbs, in effect shutting out the world. The bodhisattva, by contrast, meditates to become more conscious, more aware, more mindful.

In ancient India soldiers divided the night into three watches. The same concept can be seen in Buddhism. During the first watch, the bodhisattva remembers his own past lives; the ability to do this is considered one of the psychic powers that come with spiritual advancement, but it should not be a goal in itself. During the second watch, he acquires deeper insight into the working of karma, understanding how the past lives of various

people have been reflected in later incarnations. During the third watch of the night, he turns his awareness to the question of how to put an end to suffering and in due course arrives at what will become known as the Four Noble Truths.

Finally, just before dawn, the bodhisattva enters the state of complete awareness, of total insight into the nature of reality. After hundreds of lives, he has fulfilled his bodhisattva vow. He is no longer a being (*sattva*) striving for enlightenment (*bodhi*); he is now a buddha, a 'fully enlightened one': 'I had direct knowledge. Birth is exhausted, the Holy Life has been lived out, what was to be done is done, there is no more of this to come' (*Majjhima Nikaya*; Nanamoli 1972: 25).

Having completed his journey to full enlightenment, he has earned the title Tathagata ('thus-gone one'). It is this title that the Buddha will most often use to refer to himself. For example: 'Whatever a Tathagata utters, speaks, and proclaims between the day of his enlightenment and the day he dies, all that is factual, not otherwise, and that is why he is called "Tathagata"' (*Anguttara Nikaya* ii.22; Dhammika 1989: 50).

Another term for the state of enlightenment or *bodhi* that the Buddha has reached is 'nirvana' ('*nibbana*' in Pali). This state has two aspects, negative and positive. In its negative aspect nirvana has the sense of 'putting out the fires' of greed, hatred, and delusion. In its positive aspect nirvana is the experience of transcendent happiness. A poem by Patacara—one of the first ordained Buddhist women—expresses the way the positive and negative meanings of nirvana come together in the perfect happiness that arrives when evil desires have been extinguished. In the first verse she expresses her longing for nirvana and her frustration at not attaining it despite all her efforts; in the second verse she recalls how the breakthrough finally came as she was turning down the wick on her oil lamp:

> With ploughshares ploughing up the fields, with seed
> Sown in the breast of earth, men win their crops,
> Enjoy their gains and nourish wife and child.
> Why cannot I, whose life is pure, who seek
> To do the Master's will, no sluggard am,
> Nor puffed up, win Nibbana's bliss?
>
> One day, bathing my feet, I sit and watch
> The water as it trickles down the slope.
> Thereby I set my heart in steadfastness,
> As one doth train a horse of noble breed.
> Then going to my cell, I take my lamp,
> And seated on my couch I watch the flame.
> Grasping the pin, I pull the wick right down
> Into the oil . . .
> Lo! the Nibbana of the little lamp!
> Emancipation dawns! My heart is free!
> (*Songs of Sisters*, Rhys Davids 1964: 73)

Reflecting on his experience, the new Buddha wonders whether the way to enlightenment can be taught. He decides that it can, and so begins a teaching career motivated by compassion for all living beings.

### Setting the Wheel in Motion

The new Buddha's first impulse is to seek out and teach his two former yoga teachers, but his psychic powers tell him that both have died. Thus he decides to begin by teaching the five *shramanas* who were his companions during his years of ascetic discipline. Perceiving (again using his psychic powers) that they can be found at a deer park known as Sarnath near Varanasi (Banaras), he sets out and on the way encounters two merchants, sometimes said to be Burmese, who show their respect by offering him food.

In a sense, this act marks the beginning of institutional Buddhism, which depends on the material support (food, medicine, robes, financial donations) given by laypeople in return for the spiritual gifts offered by ordained Buddhists (dharma teaching, chanting, guidance). This pattern of reciprocal giving has remained central to all forms of Buddhism to the present day.

On arriving at the deer park, the Buddha is at first shunned by his five friends because he has abandoned the rigorous discipline they so value, but when they see his aura they recognize that he has attained nirvana, and ask to know how he did it. He responds with his first **sutra**, often referred to as the 'Wheel Turning' sermon or discourse because it marks the moment when the wheel of true dharma is once again set in motion.

Another name for this first discourse is the 'Instruction on the Middle Path', for in it the Buddha encourages his former companions to follow a path of moderation between indulgence and asceticism. As long as he lived the life of a pampered prince he did not advance spiritually. Yet the years of ascetic discipline left him too weak to make any real progress. Only after he began to eat, drink, and sleep in moderation was he able to reach enlightenment.

In time, this principle of moderation would be developed into a general ethic of the Middle Way. Some interpreters consider this principle so central to the tradition that they refer to Buddhism itself as 'the Middle Way'.

Having counselled the five to abandon their ascetic practices, the Buddha begins to explain the insight into suffering that he gained while meditating under the Bodhi tree. After a few days of instruction in the Four Noble Truths and the Eightfold Path for overcoming suffering, the Buddha ordains the five as his first disciples and sends them forth to teach the dharma to others.

Shakyamuni and his five fellow ascetics in the deer park at Sarnath, the site of his first sermon (Roy C. Amore).

### *Entering* Parinirvana

For the next forty-five years the Buddha travels throughout the Middle Region, ordaining disciples and teaching thousands of lay followers, including various local kings. He also ordains several members of his own family, one of whom—his cousin Devadatta—eventually leads a group of dissident disciples in revolt, and makes more than one attempt on his life.

His body is becoming weak as he nears eighty, but he continues to travel. Finally, one day he and his disciples are dining with the leader of a local tribal group when an odd-smelling dish is brought to the table. He asks his host to serve it only to him, not to his disciples. On eating the dish, he falls ill. When it becomes apparent that he is dying, the Compassionate One tells his disciples not to blame the host, who meant well. They ask whom they should follow if he dies, and he tells them to follow the dharma. Thus in Buddhism no individual has absolute authority, although there are senior authorities in particular traditions (the Dalai **Lama** in the Gelugpa sect of Vajrayana, for example).

On his deathbed—in a grove of trees at Kushinagar—the Buddha meditates up through the eight yoga stages, back down through them, and finally back up through the first four. Then, at the moment of death, he experiences ***parinirvana***: the final end of the cycle of rebirth, the total cessation of suffering, the perfection of happiness. Until that moment he has been in the state known as nirvana 'with remainder'—the highest level of nirvana possible for one still living.

## A Woman's Compassionate Wisdom

*Compassion is a major value in Buddhism, as may be seen in this Buddhist story of a woman whose compassion for her sick husband not only comforts him but brings him back to health.*

Once, while the Lord was staying among the Bhaggis on the Crocodile Hill . . . , the good man Nakulapita lay sick, ailing and grievously ill. And his wife Nakulamata said to him: 'I beg you, good man, do not die worried, for the Lord has said that the fate of the worried is not good. Maybe you think: "Alas, when I am gone, my wife will be unable to support the children or keep the household together." But do not think like that, for I am skilled in spinning cotton and carding wool, and I will manage to support the children and keep the household together after you are gone.

'Or maybe you think: "My wife will take another husband after I am gone." But do not think that, for you and I know that for sixteen years we have lived as householders in the holy life [that is, as celibates, practising strict sexual abstinence].

'Or maybe you think: "My wife, after I am gone, will have no desire to see the Lord or to see the monks." But do not think like that, for my desire to see them shall be even greater.

'Or maybe you think: "After I am gone, my wife will not have a calm mind." But do not think like that, for as long as the Lord has female disciples dressed in white, living at home, who gain that state, I shall be one. And if any doubt it, let them ask the Lord.

'Or maybe you think: "My wife will not win a firm foundation, a firm foothold in this Dhamma and discipline. She will not win comfort, dissolve doubt, be free from uncertainty, become confident, self-reliant, and live by the Teacher's words." But do not think like that, either. For as long as the Lord has female disciples dressed in white . . . I shall be one.'

Now, while Nakulapita was being counselled thus by his wife, even as he lay there his sickness subsided and he recovered. And not long after, he got up, and leaning on a stick, Nakulapita went to visit the Lord and told him what had happened. And the Lord said: 'It has been a gain; you have greatly gained from having Nakulamata as your counsellor and teacher, full of compassion for you, and desiring your welfare' (adapted from Dhammika 1989: 111–13).

Buddhism does not elaborate on the nature of *parinirvana*—'nirvana without remainder': such a state is by definition beyond human understanding. What is important, and fundamental to Buddhism, is the reality of that state and the potential of all living beings to attain it.

## CRYSTALLIZATION

The crystallization of the Buddhist tradition began with the transformation of the Buddha's discourses into a set of doctrinal teachings, the dharma, and the movement towards an institutionalized monastic system. We will begin with the Dharma, the Second Gem, and then turn to the Third Gem, the Sangha.

## The Second Gem: The Dharma

Avoid doing all evil deeds,
cultivate doing good deeds,
and purify the mind—
this is the teaching of all buddhas.
(*Dhammapada* 183)

## From the *Itivuttaka*

*The* Itivuttaka *('So I heard') is a collection of the Buddha's teachings said to have been made by Khujjuttara, a lay woman of the servant class who used it to teach other women. Each section begins with the expression 'So I heard' ('Itivuttaka').*

Even if one should seize the hem of my robe and walk step by step behind me, if he is covetous in his desires, fierce in his longings, malevolent of heart, with corrupt mind, careless and unrestrained, noisy and distracted and with sense uncontrolled, he is far from me. And why? He does not see the Dhamma, and not seeing the Dhamma, he does not see me. Even if one lives a hundred miles away, if he is not covetous in his desires, not fierce in his longings, with a kind heart and pure mind, mindful, composed, calmed, one-pointed and with senses restrained, then indeed, he is near to me and I am near to him. And why? He sees the Dhamma, and seeing the Dhamma, sees me (Dhammika 1989: 49–50).

To 'take refuge in the dharma' is to have confidence in the eternal truth of the Buddha's teachings. 'Dharma' (in Pali, *dhamma*) is a central concept in Buddhist thought, and the range of its meanings and associations extends well beyond the meaning of 'dharma' in the Hindu context.

In classical Indian culture generally, the Sanskrit word 'dharma' carries the sense of social and moral obligation. The *Bhagavad Gita*, for instance, assumes that each individual's dharma is the duty appropriate to the caste and the life situation into which he or she born. (Thus the law codes governing Hindu society came to be called the *dharmashastra*s.)

It is no surprise, then, that the 'dharma' referred to in Buddhist texts is sometimes translated as 'law'. Buddhist usage, however, reflects the root meaning of 'dharma': 'that which holds'. In fact, the Sanskrit 'dharma' is related to the Latin word *firma*; thus in English we could understand 'dharma' to mean 'teachings that are firm'—that is, eternal truths. For Buddhists, these eternal truths include the laws of nature, the reality of spiritual forces such as karma, and the rules of moral conduct or duty. Believing the Buddha's understanding of those realities to be definitive, generations of thinkers studied and

systematized his insights, creating a program of instruction that anyone seeking enlightenment could follow.

### The Four Noble Truths

At the core of the Buddha's first sermon in the deer park were the Four Noble Truths about suffering and the Eightfold Path to overcoming it:

1. Noble Truth of Suffering: No living being can escape suffering (**duhkha**). Birth, sickness, senility, and death are all occasions of suffering, whether physical or psychological.
2. Noble Truth of Origin: Suffering arises from craving (*trishna*), from excessive desire.
3. Noble Truth of Cessation: Suffering will cease when desire ceases.
4. Noble Truth of the Eightfold Path: It is possible to put an end to desire, and hence to suffering, by following eight principles of self-improvement.

### The Eightfold Path

The eight principles that make up the Eightfold Path are not sequential, like the steps on a ladder. All are equally important, and each depends on all the rest. Thus none of them can be properly observed in isolation. They must work in concord, like the petals of a flower unfolding together. They are right understanding (specifically of the Four Noble Truths), right thought (free of sensuous desire, ill-will, and cruelty), right speech, right conduct, right livelihood, right effort, right mindfulness, and right meditation.

## The Three Characteristics of Existence

Existence has three characteristics, according to the Buddhist dharma: suffering, impermanence, and no-self. 'Suffering', as a characteristic of existence, refers to all the varieties of pain and deprivation, physical and psychological, that humans are subject to. 'Impermanence' is the passing nature of all things. Remember the last words of the Buddha: 'Everything that arises also passes away.' With the exceptions of empty space and nirvana, nothing in life is static: everything is in process. Some philosophies, both in India and in the West, treat change as a problem to be overcome and attribute permanence to what they value most highly; by contrast, Buddhist thought regards change as a fact.

Finally, the concept of no-self draws attention to the psychological implications of that existential impermanence. The Sanskrit term **anatman** means 'without Atman': but what is Atman? The Hindu understanding at the time of Shakyamuni is reflected in the *Upanishads*, where Atman represents the eternal self or soul in humans and is related to Brahman, the underlying energy of the universe. For many Hindus, the innermost self is the most stable and abidingly real feature of the individual, because it participates in the reality of the universe.

The Buddha proposed that no such eternal, unchanging self exists. And in denying the existence of a self, he made the concept of ownership radically unsustainable for his followers: if there is no 'I', there can be no 'mine'. The *anatman* concept does not mean that there is 'no person' or 'no personality' in the ordinary English sense of those terms. In fact, Buddhist teachings about the self

address the components of personality, the *skandhas*, in some detail, suggesting that personality is the product of shifting, arbitrary circumstance. In that respect, Buddhist notions of personality have more in common with modern psychological theory than they do with either Hindu or Western religious notions of an eternal soul. What Buddhist personality theory implies is that wise people, recognizing the impermanence of all things—including themselves—will not become emotionally attached either to material goods or to fixed images of themselves.

## The Three Instructions

There is a story about a young Buddhist monk named Buddhaghosa, who goes to the main monastery in ancient Sri Lanka, requesting permission to use its library for his research and writing on the dharma. To test him, the abbot assigns him the task of commenting on a verse to the effect that once one has become established in morality (*sila*) one should go on to perfect one's concentration (**samadhi**) and wisdom (**prajna**). In response, Buddhaghosa writes what was to become a very famous commentary called *The Path of Purity* in which he expands on the meaning of the three instructions.

Morality, *sila*, is the essential foundation. Perfecting concentration means developing a mental state in which one is focused, tranquil, and alert. This *samadhi* state of mind is helpful in every aspect of life, but it is especially important if one is to move to the third level, the state of higher wisdom, without which one cannot attain nirvana. One of the central insights gained at that third level is the nature of causality.

The principle of causality is a thread that runs throughout the Buddha's dharma. To appreciate its function, think of a pool table. To observe this world of changing circumstances is like observing a pool table where the balls are colliding with one another and the cushions, repeatedly causing one another to change directions: each time you blink, you see a new configuration of pool balls, caused by the previous configuration. With this image in mind, we can now turn to one of the more difficult expressions of Buddhist higher wisdom.

### The Twelve Stages of Dependent Origination

The standard term for this understanding of causality—in which everything that arises does so in response to other factors, and will in turn cause changes in other things—is *pratitya-samutpada*, usually translated as 'dependent origination' or 'conditioned coproduction'. Because early Buddhist teachers delivered the dharma teachings orally, they tended to use visual images and numbered lists to help fix them in listeners' minds. Thus Buddhist dharma uses the image of a wheel with twelve spokes (not to be confused with the eight-spoked wheel that symbolizes the Eightfold Path) to express the view of life as a cycle of interdependent stages or dimensions.

The twelve links of the chain of dependent origination may be further divided into three stages, reflecting the movement from a past life through the present one and on to the future:

| | | |
|---|---|---|
| Past | 1. | Ignorance, leading to |
| | 2. | karma formations, leading to |
| Present | 3. | a new individual 'consciousness', leading to |
| | 4. | a new body-mind complex, leading to |
| | 5. | the bases of sensing, leading to |
| | 6. | sense impressions, leading to |
| | 7. | conscious feelings, leading to |
| | 8. | craving, leading to |
| | 9. | clinging to (grasping for) things, leading to |
| | 10. | 'becoming' (the drive to be reborn), leading to |
| Future | 11. | rebirth, leading to |
| | 12. | old age and death |

The process does not stop with the twelfth link, of course, since old age and death lead to yet another birth, and so the wheel of rebirth turns on and on. Buddhists have analyzed this wheel from many viewpoints and with many similes, but the heart of the matter is always the same: all living beings are in process and will be reborn over and over again until they realize nirvana.

## *Tripitaka*: The Three Baskets of Sacred Texts

Shakyamuni did not write down any of his teachings, nor did he assign anyone the task of recording his words. This was entirely in keeping with the Hindu tradition, in which writing was associated with commerce. The sacred teachings of the Hindus were the exclusive preserve of the priests who committed them to memory and transmitted them by sound alone. In fact, the Hindu ritual formulas were understood to have an acoustic effectiveness that would be lost if they were not spoken and heard. Thus for its first four hundred years or so, the Buddhist sangha was content to recite the teachings from memory.

To manage the work of passing along the teachings, various **bhikshus** were assigned the task of memorizing selected portions. At the early conferences of all sangha members, one of the most important tasks was to recite the teachings in their entirety.

At the first council, held long after Shakyamuni's death, *Bhikshu* Ananda, who had been his travelling companion, is said to have recited the discourses (*sutras*) on dharma ascribed to Shakyamuni. *Bhikshu* Upali is credited with reciting the section on monastic rules (**vinaya**). The systematic treatises (*abhidharma*) composed after Shakyamuni's *parinirvana* were recited at a later meeting. The oral teachings were finally put into writing by the Theravada monks of Sri Lanka in the first century CE, after a famine had reduced the monks' numbers so drastically as to threaten the survival of the oral tradition. The fact that Theravada Buddhists refer to their scriptures as the **Tripitaka** ('three baskets') suggests that the manuscript copies of the three types of texts—written on palm leaves strung together and bundled like Venetian blinds—may have been stored in three baskets. The collection survives in the Pali language, a vernacular derived in part from Sanskrit, and is therefore referred to as the Pali canon.

The *Sutra Pitaka*, or 'discourse basket,' contains the talks on dharma attributed to Shakyamuni or his early disciples. The discourse is often presented as a response to a question from a disciple. The beginning of the *sutra* gives the setting in a stylized manner. The following opening of the 'Discourse on the Lesser Analysis of Deeds' is typical:

> Thus have I heard: At one time the Lord was staying near Savatthi in the Jeta Grove in Anathapindika's monastery. Then the brahmin youth Subha, Todeyya's son, approached the Lord; having approached, he exchanged greetings with the Lord; having conversed in a friendly and courteous way, he sat down at a respectful distance. As he was sitting down at a respectful distance the brahmin youth Subha, Todeyya's son, spoke thus to the Lord: 'Now, good Gotama, what is the cause, what the reason that lowness and excellence are to be seen among human beings while they are in human form?' (Horner 1967, 3: 248–9)

Subha has asked the timeless question of why bad things happen to apparently good people. Shakyamuni, referred to here by the title *bhagavan* ('Lord'), then explains to Subha how the karma accumulated through actions in past lives causes some people to suffer short, unhappy lives and others to enjoy long, blessed lives.

There are five sections (*nikayas*) of the *Sutra Pitaka*, the first 'basket'. In the ancient world, texts were usually organized not chronologically or alphabetically, but by length, from longest to shortest. (The same principle was followed by the early Muslims in organizing the sequence of the *surahs*

that make up the Qur'an.) There are a few exceptions, however. The *sutras* in the 'Kindred Sayings' section are organized around topics, while the 'Gradual Sayings' are arranged in numerical lists (four truths, four kinds of humans, and so on).

The second basket, the *Vinaya* ('discipline') *Pitaka*, contains both the rules of monastic discipline and stories about how Shakyamuni came to institute each rule.

Finally, the *Abhidharma* (Further Discourses) *Pitaka* contains seven books by unnamed early Buddhists who systematically analyzed every conceivable aspect of reality in the light of various Buddhist principles. For example, the first book of *abhidharma* classifies all mental phenomena according to their karmic consequences, good, bad, or neutral. Other books deal with the various physical elements of nature.

The development of *abhidharma* is associated with Sariputra, one of the brightest of the Buddha's disciples. He lived in a city called Nalanda, where a large university—perhaps the world's first—was flourishing by the first century. The *abhidharma* books formed the basis of the physical and psychological sciences taught at Nalanda and other Buddhist universities of India. The goal, however, was not so much the advancement of the physical sciences as it was the spiritual advancement of the students. Throughout the *abhidharma* works runs the basic Buddhist teaching that no physical or mental reality is eternal, and that all are subject to constant change.

## The Third Gem: The Sangha

The third part of the Triple Gem has two components: the monastic community of ordained men (*bhikshus*) and women (*bhikshunis*), and the broader community, the universal sangha of all people who follow the Buddha's path.

### Bhikshus and Bhikshunis

Shakyamuni began accepting disciples from the time of his first sermon in the deer park at

Varanasi. Within a short time, an ordination ritual took shape in which the new disciples recited the Triple Refuge and took vows of chastity, poverty, obedience, and so on (similar vows would play an important role in Christian monasticism), and put on the distinctive robes of a monk. (In early Indian Buddhism monks' robes were usually dyed with saffron—made from the dried stigmas of certain crocuses—which produces a bright orange-yellow. Most Theravada monks still wear saffron robes, but in East Asia other colours were eventually adopted, such as red and brown. There is no special meaning to the colour, although all members of a particular branch of Buddhism wear the same one.)

### Ordained and Lay Women

Unlike many other religious traditions, Buddhism never defined women as the 'property' of men. Nevertheless, the early texts in particular indicate a profound ambiguity about the status of women in Buddhism. Shakyamuni himself is said to have cautioned the *bhikshus* against allowing themselves to be distracted by women:

> 'How are we to conduct ourselves, Lord,
>     with regard to womankind?'
> 'Don't see them, Ananda.'
> 'But if we should see them, what are we to
>     do?'
> 'Abstain from speech, Ananda.'
> 'But if they should speak to us, Lord, what
>     are we to do?'
> 'Keep wide awake, Ananda'
>     (Rhys Davids 1881: 91)

Shakyamuni is also said to have resisted the formation of an order for women, the *bhikshuni* sangha, and to have predicted that such an order would be detrimental to the survival of his teachings. On the other hand, he did agree to its establishment, and encouraged close relatives, including his stepmother, to join it, maintaining that women were no less capable than men of becoming Arhats

(saints), and that the way to nirvana was the same regardless of gender:

> And be it woman, be it man for whom
> Such chariot doth wait, by that same car
> Into Nirvana's presence shall they come.
>     (Horner 1930: 104)

Other early Buddhist texts are similarly ambiguous about women. On the positive side, they describe approvingly the support provided to the early sangha by some wealthy women. And one book of the Pali canon, the Therigatha, contains poems by early *bhikshunis*.

On the negative side, there was a distinct difference in status between *bhikshus and bhikshunis*, who were not allowed to teach their male counterparts.

Over time the *bhikshuni* sangha was allowed to die out in many Buddhist countries. The specific reasons may have varied, but in general the female order was vulnerable simply because it was relatively small and less well connected than the male order to political power. In Sri Lanka, for instance, when both sanghas were devastated by famine, the king imported a number of monks from Siam to revive the male order, but there is no evidence of any effort to revive the female sangha. Recently, some effort has been made to revive the practice of *bhikshuni* ordination in Theravada countries.

Today Theravada laywomen practise devotions at home as well as at temples. Some women join orders, wear white robes, live a pious life, serve others, and in some cases take vows of poverty and service even though they are not officially ordained. Some of these women are not interested in ordination because they feel they have more freedom to serve others if they are not bound by the *vinaya* rules.

### Ordination

Eventually, as Buddhism became more institutionalized, a preliminary level of ordination was introduced during which novices were required to master the basics of dharma before becoming *bhikshus* or *bhikshunis*. Each novice (*shramanera*) was assigned both a rigorous, demanding teacher and a supportive spiritual guide.

The full ordination ritual can be performed only in certain designated areas, which some ordination traditions still mark off with 'boundary stones', as in ancient India. The ordination ceremony takes several hours to complete. Friends and relatives of the candidates for ordination attend and pay their respects to the new sangha members, who give presents to their teachers and counsellors in gratitude for their assistance. Because seniority plays a large role in monastic life, careful attention is paid to the exact time and date of the ordination.

### The Lay Sangha

Lay Buddhists are considered members of the sangha in its wider sense, which includes all those following the path laid down by the Buddha. The

A Theravada *bhikshu* with a palm-leaf umbrella (Roy C. Amore).

sangha of all disciples includes eight categories of 'noble persons', according to which of four levels they have achieved. The four levels are 'those who have entered the stream (to nirvana)', those who have advanced enough to return (be reborn) just once more, those who are so advanced that they will never return, and those who have advanced to the state of realizing the Arhat (worthy) path. At each of the four levels, Buddhists distinguish the person who has just reached the new level from one who has matured at that level, making a total of eight classifications of noble persons.

All Buddhist traditions maintain that laypeople are capable of advancing towards nirvana. However, some expect lay members of the sangha to seek ordination at some stage, so that they can devote themselves full-time to the spiritual quest.

## Controversies, Councils, and Sects

The defection of some *bhikshus* under the leadership of Devadatta shows that sectarian problems could arise even during the Buddha's lifetime. Other divisions followed.

In the fourth century BCE, for instance, trouble arose when a *bhikshu* visiting the city of Vaishali found that his colleagues there were accepting donations of gold and silver from the lay people. He criticized them publicly, and they demanded that he apologize in front of their lay supporters. As a consequence, a meeting of all the *bhikshus* in the area had to be convened.

Because there was no central individual, court, or committee that held authority in Buddhism, the monks had to settle disputes collectively on the basis of their interpretations of the Buddha's discourses—a challenging task in an era when the scriptures had not yet been written down.

The meeting, called the Vaishali Council, decided that monastic discipline did indeed forbid the acceptance of gold and silver. Most of the Vaishali *bhikshus* agreed to abide by the ruling, but a schism soon developed when one dissident monk raised five points of controversy concerning the status of Arhats, the 'worthy ones' or saints.

Was an Arhat subject to the same limitations as an ordinary *bhikshu*? Was an Arhat susceptible to sexual misconduct? Was it possible for an Arhat to be ignorant of some doctrine or to have doubts about doctrine? Could one become an Arhat merely by instruction rather than by spiritual practice?

Behind those questions lay an issue that was to fuel even more serious divisions in later Buddhism. That issue was the level of spiritual attainment possible for Buddhists in this life. The majority of the monks took a relatively liberal position, holding out the prospect of enlightenment for ordinary people, but many of the *sthavira* ('elders' or senior monks) disagreed, arguing that attaining the Arhat level was beyond the reach of all but a few. In this way a division arose between the majority group, who formed the Mahasanghika or 'Great Sangha' sect, and the Sthavira group, who formed the Sthaviravada or Theravada sect. This debate gave the *bhikshus* a foretaste of the split that would lead to the development of the Mahayana and Theravada schools as distinctly different forms of Buddhism.

By the time of King Ashoka, in the third century BCE, there were eighteen sects, each with its own oral version of the Buddhist teachings, although from the few later-written texts that have survived, we can imagine that the versions did not differ very much. They all shared a similar ordination tradition and all followed more or less the same *vinaya* rules.

It is unlikely that the laity paid very much attention to the divisions, which were minor compared to the differences between the various denominations in Protestant Christianity. The monks of the various sects sometimes lived together in one monastery, especially at the major training centres, which evolved into Buddhist universities. The same was true of the *bhikshunis*, who always resided in their own monasteries, separate from the men.

### King Ashoka's Conversion

The spread of Buddhism within India was quite remarkable. Unlike many reformers, Shakyamuni had succeeded in gaining converts across a broad social spectrum, ranging from the lowest classes of labourers through the rich merchant class to the powerful rulers of newly formed kingdoms. But the conversion of the kings in Shakyamuni's lifetime did not necessarily mean that their successors were Buddhists as well. There was a longstanding Indian tradition that the king had a duty to defend and support all the legitimate religious traditions of his kingdom. It seems that Buddhism became one, among several others, of these legitimate dharma systems.

Approximately 150 years after the passing of Shakyamuni, Greek-speaking rulers came to power in northwestern India as a result of Alexander's conquest in 326 BCE. An Indian king of the Mauryan dynasty later drove the Greek rulers out of central India, and his son expanded the newly formed kingdom. When the latter's son, Ashoka (r. c. 273–232 BCE), inherited the throne, he embarked on a series of wars to expand his territory to the south and west. Eventually, he ruled an empire that included most of modern India.

Buddhist accounts claim that it was Ashoka's reflection on the horrible carnage of his bloody war with the kingdom of Kalinga on the eastern coast that led him to convert to Buddhism and begin promoting the ethic of non-violence. It is possible that his family had been supporters of other non-brahminical traditions such as Jainism, however, and so his conversion to Buddhism likely did not represent a major shift.

Under the patronage of Ashoka, Buddhism enjoyed its golden age in India. Buddhist accounts say that Ashoka turned from military conquest to dharma conquest. To spread the dharma of non-violence, he ordered that large stones or pillars be erected at the principal crossroads throughout his empire, with messages carved on them for the moral instruction of his subjects. Some of these stones and pillars have been recovered by archaeologists, and the messages are still readable.

In the message carved on the rock erected in the coastal Kalinga area of eastern India, he expresses remorse for the death and suffering he caused to so many people:

> When the king, Beloved of the Gods and of Gracious Mien, had been consecrated eight years Kalinga was conquered, 150,000 people were deported, 100,000 were killed, and many times that number died. But after the conquest of Kalinga, the Beloved of the Gods began to follow Righteousness (dharma), to love Righteousness, and to give instruction in Righteousness. Now the Beloved of the Gods regrets the conquest of Kalinga, for when an independent country is conquered people are killed, they die, or are deported, and that the Beloved of the Gods finds painful and grievous. . . . The Beloved of the Gods will forgive as far as he can, and he even conciliates the forest tribes of his dominions; but he warns them that there is power even in the remorse of the Beloved of the Gods, and he tells them to reform, lest they be killed (*Thirteenth Rock Edict*; de Bary 1958: 146).

He then lays out his ideals for governing his new subjects, saying that he desires security, self-control, impartiality, and cheerfulness for all living creatures in his empire. Ashoka spells out his 'conquest by dharma' and claims that it is spreading not only within the Indian continent but westward among the various Alexandrian kingdoms, whose kings he names. Ashoka states that real satisfaction in ruling over people comes only from inducing them to follow dharma:

> Thus he achieves a universal conquest, and conquest always gives a feeling of pleasure; yet it is but a slight pleasure, for the Beloved of the Gods only looks on that which concerns the next life as of great importance. I have had this inscription of Righteousness engraved that all my sons and grandsons may not seek to gain new victories, . . . that they may consider the only [valid] victory the victory of Righteousness, which is of value both in this world and the next (*Thirteenth Rock Edict*; de Bary 1958: 147).

Although he reminds his Kalinga subjects and the tribal people of the surrounding forest areas that he will not hesitate to deal firmly with rebels and criminals, he promises that his punishments will be just and moderate. Ashoka's promotion of dharma became a model for later Buddhist rulers. Like 'Dharma-Ashoka', as Buddhists later called him, they were willing to sentence criminals (and rebels) to punishment or even death, but they remained committed to non-violent practices in other matters. Ashoka himself went so far as to encourage his subjects to become vegetarian and give up occupations such as hunting.

## Buddhism and the State

### The King as Wheel Turner

Indian tradition had long used the term *chakravartin* or 'wheel turner' to refer to kings as world rulers. On one level, the image suggests a ruler whose chariot wheels encounter no opposition. On another level, however, it evokes the wisdom of the ruler who in meditation perceives a wheel turning in the heavens, and understands it to represent the orderly process of the universe. Thus the true world ruler has both the spiritual wisdom to perceive that cosmic order and the political power to impose a similar order in the world.

When the early Buddhists began to refer to Shakyamuni as a *chakravartin*, they were in one sense according him the honour due to one of his princely birth—an honour that Shakyamuni himself may or may not have sought. In another sense, however, they were redefining the concept of political power, shifting the emphasis away from unchallenged military strength and towards the notion of wisdom in the guidance of society.

From the time of Shakyamuni, Buddhism understood rulers to have special duties with regard to the dharma. Kings were expected both to provide for the physical welfare of their subjects (for example, by providing food in times of need) and to promote dharma by setting a good example and sponsoring lectures, translations, and the distribution of literature. The king who promoted dharma would be in a real sense a successor to Buddha, the definitive wheel-turner.

As Buddhism spread throughout Asia, so did its social and moral ideals regarding kingship. An East Asian Zen Buddhist story tells of a Chinese king named Wu who has dedicated himself to doing all the good works expected of a Buddhist king, probably with the goal of winning a long and pleasant rebirth in heaven. When Wu learns that Bodhidharma, a monk newly arrived from India, has taken up residence in his kingdom, he summons the monk to court and proudly shows him everything he has accomplished. Wu has established rice kitchens for feeding the poor, a new wing of the palace with rooms filled with scribes busy translating and copying the sacred Buddhist texts to be read aloud and explained to the people at Buddhist festivals, and an altar for daily worship.

After the tour, the emperor asks Bodhidharma, 'How much merit do you think I have made from all this?' 'None whatsoever!' is the famous response. Bodhidharma proceeds to explain that true merit comes only from activities that increase one's wisdom and purify the mind. It seems that the emperor has been doing all the right things for the wrong reason. With regard to Buddhism and the state, what this story tells us is that although the rulers were encouraged to support the sangha

---

## King Milinda Questions Nagasena

*The military campaigns of Alexander the Great in the late fourth century* BCE *left a number of Greek-derived regimes in eastern Iran and northwestern India. These may have been the 'Yavanas' (presumably 'Ionians') to whom the Buddhist King Ashoka reported sending missions. The following extract recounts a meeting, real or imagined, between a foreign king and a Buddhist sage.*

Now Milinda the king went up to where the venerable Nagasena was, and addressed him with the greetings and compliments of friendship and courtesy, and took his seat respectfully apart.

And Milinda began by asking, 'How is your Reverence known, and what, Sir, is your name?'

'I am known as Nagasena, O king. But although parents, O king, give such a name as Nagasena . . . [it] is only a generally understood term, a designation in common use. For there is no permanent individuality (no soul) involved in the matter.'

'If, most reverend Nagasena, there is no permanent individuality (no soul) involved in the matter, who is it, pray, who gives to you members of the Order your robes and food and lodging and necessaries for the sick? Who is it who enjoys such things when given? Who is it who lives a life of righteousness? . . . You tell me that your brethren in the Order are in the habit of addressing you as Nagasena. Now what is that Nagasena? Do you mean to say that the hair is Nagasena?'

'I don't say that, great king.'

'Or is it the nails, the teeth, the skin, the flesh, the nerves, the bones . . . or any of these that is Nagasena?'

*Continued*

And to each of these he answered no.

'Is it the outward form then (*rupa*) that is Nagasena, or the sensations, or the ideas, or the confections, or the consciousness, that is Nagasena?'

And to each of these he answered no.

'Then is it all these *skandhas* [physical and mental 'heaps' or processes] combined that are Nagasena?'

'No! great king.'

'But is there anything outside the five *skandhas* that is Nagasena?'

And he still answered no.

'Then thus, ask as I may, I can discover no Nagasena. Nagasena is a mere empty sound. . . .'

[*Now Nagasena asks the king how he travelled to their meeting. When the king says he came in a chariot, the sage asks him to explain what a chariot is.*] 'Is it the pole that is the chariot?'

'I did not say that.'

'Is it the wheels, or the framework . . . ?'

'Certainly not.'

'Then is it all these parts that are the chariot?'

'No, Sir.'

'Then . . . I can discover no chariot. Chariot is a mere empty sound.'

'It is on account of its having all these things—the pole, and the axle . . .—that it comes under the generally understood term, the designation in common use, of "chariot".'

'Very good! Your Majesty has rightly grasped the meaning of "chariot". And just even so it is on account of all those things you questioned me about . . . that I come under the generally understood term . . . "Nagasena". For it was said, Sire, by our Sister Vajira in the presence of the Blessed One: "Just as it is by the condition precedent of the coexistence of its various parts that the word 'chariot' is used, just so is it true that when the *skandhas* are there we talk of a 'being'."'

'Most wonderful, Nagasena, and most strange. Well done, well done, Nagasena' (abridged from Rhys Davids 1890: 40–55).

and actively promote dharma in their realms, the ultimate goal was the ruler's own spiritual advancement. This helps to explain why Buddhist kings sometimes abdicated at a fairly early age in order to take ordination as *bhikshus*.

### Non-violence as a Public Ethic

One characteristic of Buddhist political rule, at least ideally, was promotion of non-violence. Unnecessarily harsh punishments were forbidden, and kings were expected to release prisoners during Buddhist festivals. Justice was to be administered fairly, regardless of the social status of the accused, and quickly. A particularly pious king of ancient Sri Lanka is remembered for instructing his staff to wake him even in the middle of the night if a citizen came seeking justice. A rope attached to a bell was installed outside the palace walls so that anyone could pull it to awaken the king and present their case to him. Even today, some Buddhist festivals include the release of caged birds or other animals into the wild.

At the same time, the Buddhist king was expected to maintain an army and a police force, to defend the public against criminals and foreign enemies. There is no such thing in Buddhist scripture as a 'just war' of aggression, but many Buddhists have believed that a defensive war is not

## Map 5.1    The Spread of Buddhism

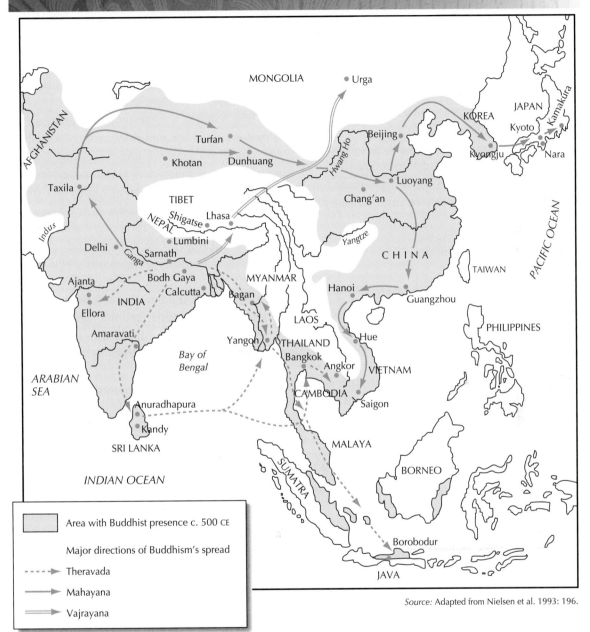

Area with Buddhist presence c. 500 CE

Major directions of Buddhism's spread

---▸ Theravada

——▸ Mahayana

═══▸ Vajrayana

*Source:* Adapted from Nielsen et al. 1993: 196.

against dharma, and that the state may use force as necessary to maintain law and order.

With very few exceptions, Buddhism spread by missionary conversion rather than by force. However, there were territorial wars among various Buddhist kingdoms of Southeast Asia, and in Sri Lanka the conflict between the Buddhist Sinhalese and Hindu Tamils has a long history.

# 🦁 DIFFERENTIATION

By Ashoka's time Buddhism had split into eighteen distinct sects. Over the following centuries all but one of these disappeared. The survivor, Theravada, represents one of the three major divisions of Buddhism that exist today. The second major school, which emerged around the first century CE, called itself Mahayana, 'Great Vehicle', in contrast to what it called the Hinayana, 'Lesser Vehicle', of Theravada and its contemporaries. The third division, Vajrayana, emerged some five hundred years later and considered itself the third turning of the wheel of dharma.

## Theravada

We know very little about the early history of the 'Way of the Elders' (Sthaviravada in Sanskrit and Theravada in Pali), but it appears to have been widespread in India by the time of Ashoka in the third century BCE. However, the Pali dialect associated with it was said to come from the ancient north Indian kingdom of Magadha, one of the four where Shakyamuni himself taught.

We do know that the Theravada tradition was conservative, as its name suggests. Rejecting all scriptures composed after the formation of the *Tripitaka*, it considers itself the preserver of Buddhism in its original form.

### Theravada in Sri Lanka

A monk named Mahinda (Mahendra in Sanskrit), who was Ashoka's son, is said to have taken Theravada Buddhism to Sri Lanka in the third century BCE. The story of his conversion of the Sri Lankan people is told in the island's *Great Chronicle* (*Mahavamsa*). Mahinda and his assistant monks are said to have travelled through the air, using psychic powers, and arrived on a large hill near the island's capital, Anuradhapura. There the king of Sri Lanka and his hunting party discover the monks and are soon converted to the Buddha's dharma.

(Mahinda's Hill [Mihintale] remains an active centre for monks and lay pilgrims in Sri Lanka today.) The next day, Mahinda enters the capital and teaches dharma to the members of the king's court, who are converted. On the following day the biggest hall available—the royal elephant stable—is put into service as a hall of dharma instruction, whereupon everyone is converted.

These legends are presumably based on historical events of the mid-third century BCE, since one of Ashoka's inscriptions claims that he sent missionaries in groups of five to seek converts far and wide, even in the Hellenistic kingdoms to the west. The king of Sri Lanka could well have been receptive to the idea of forming an alliance with the powerful emperor on the mainland, and what better way than to adopt the empire's religion and court rituals? To effect the adoption of the religion, the king ordered the building of a proper temple, dharma hall, and **stupa**, and the temple grounds were made complete with the arrival of a Bodhi tree sapling brought from India by Mahinda's sister, herself a *bhikshuni*.

After receiving the proper equipment from India, the Sri Lankan king submitted himself to a new enthronement ritual carried out according to Ashoka's instructions. In this way the island of Sri Lanka became a cultural extension of Ashoka's empire while maintaining its sovereignty. This uniting of Buddhist leadership and Indian forms of kingship set the pattern for subsequent Buddhist rulers in mainland Southeast Asia, who became the lay leaders and the chief financial supporters of Buddhism in their respective domains.

Theravada Buddhism is still the main religion of Sri Lanka, although the sangha fell on such hard times in the eleventh century that there were not enough ordained *bhikshus* to continue. Buddhist rules require a minimum of five senior *bhikshus* to officiate at an ordination. Thus *bhikshus* from Burma had to be imported to Sri Lanka to conduct a proper ordination. A similar appeal to *bhikshus* from Siam in the eighteenth century led to the revitalization of Theravada, with the establishment of a new ordination lineage. The majority of Sri Lankan monks today belong to the Siyam Nikaya ('lineage'), which has control of many of the main temples.

Sri Lanka was populated by various peoples from India, and many aspects of the island's culture reveal close ties to the predominantly Hindu mainland. Among the Hindu transplants to Sri Lanka is a version of the Indian caste system. Shakyamuni taught that people should be judged by their character rather than the social status of the hereditary occupational or clan group they were born into. In keeping with this principle, his sangha was open to all social groups. In Sri Lanka, however, the Siyam Nikaya—the most prestigious ordination lineage—today accepts only members from the Goyigama caste, the equivalent of India's vaishyas.

There are other *nikaya*s in Sri Lanka that accept members regardless of caste. The most important of these is the Ramanna Nikaya, which was founded in the nineteenth century as a lineage dedicated to various reforms, including the elimination of caste restrictions.

## Theravada in Southeast Asia

The spread of Buddhism into Southeast Asia took place in stages over many centuries. The names and boundaries of the region's kingdoms have changed frequently since that process began. 'Southeast Asia', which is a modern term, originally referred to an area under Allied military command during the Second World War. In earlier European usage the region was called 'the Indies' because of the assumption by explorers and traders from the sixteenth century onward that the cultures they encountered were all in some sense Indian. Today Buddhist culture remains dominant in much of mainland Southeast Asia, including Cambodia, Thailand, and Myanmar. It was also influential (as was Hinduism) in the Indonesian islands and the Malay peninsula, although Islamic religion and culture eventually became dominant there.

The traditional Buddhist claim is that the introduction of Buddhism in Southeast Asia dates back to the third century BCE, when King Ashoka reportedly sent missionaries to the kingdom of the Mon people, who ruled a large region spanning present-day Cambodia and Thailand; yet there is little historical evidence of Buddhism in Southeast Asia until the sixth century or so, long after Ashoka's era. The kingdoms of Southeast Asia during the early centuries of the Common Era are described as 'Indianized'. The religious affiliations of the Indianized kingdoms were sometimes Buddhist, sometimes Hindu. For example, the rulers of the impressive temple complex in Cambodia known to us as Angkor Wat were Hindu from the ninth to the twelfth century, but Buddhist thereafter. An account written by a seventh-century Chinese Buddhist pilgrim, together with some archaeological evidence, suggests that several of the early Buddhist sects were established in Southeast Asia. This diversity follows the pattern in India, where various Buddhist sects coexisted for centuries before Theravada sects eventually prevailed. Some accounts of early Buddhism in Southeast Asia stress the working of miracles, a feature of Buddhist missionary expansion found later in Tibet and elsewhere. The use of chanting to invoke blessings and protective powers was also a feature of Southeast Asian Buddhism, partly because some of the missionaries there came from the Vajrayana school, which will be discussed later.

From the eleventh century through the fifteenth, Buddhism consolidated its position in the region, and by the end of this period Theravada Buddhism was the majority religion of the Thai, Khmer (Cambodian), Burmese, and Lao (Laotian) people. It remains so today.

### Myanmar (Burma)

The region most easily reached by Buddhist missionaries from India was Burma. By the eleventh century, the kingdom of Pagan (Bagan), in what is today Myanmar, had developed ties with the Theravada rulers of Sri Lanka. A temple enshrining a sacred relic of the Buddha, a tooth alleged to be from the Buddha, became the guardian and legitimizer of the kingdom.

With the dominance of Theravada, the Pali language version of the *Tripitaka* became the official one in Burma, but in keeping with Buddhist practice elsewhere, the text was written in the local script, in this instance Burmese. The Thai and Khmer sanghas likewise copied the Pali texts using their own scripts. At first glance, these alphabets bear little resemblance to one another, but they are all derived from Indian scripts and are distantly related to the alphabets of Semitic origin used in the Mediterranean world.

## Cambodia

The area of Southeast Asia that corresponds to modern Cambodia was also influenced by various forms of Indian Buddhism as well as Hinduism before the fifteenth century. Since then, the Theravada school has been well established in Cambodia. During the period of the twentieth-century 'killing fields', all sides of the political spectrum, including the communists, looked to Buddhism for legitimacy. 'Paying respect' to the *bhikshus* is a time-honoured way for political leaders to show their continuity with Cambodia's past.

## Thailand

The Thai people are thought to have migrated into Southeast Asia from southern China, where tribal groups speaking similar dialects still live. The history of the Thai spread into Thailand, formerly Siam, traces the gradual southward movement of the Thai people and their capital cities. During the fifteenth century, Thai monks returning from Sri Lanka, where they were ordained in the Theravada tradition, gained favour with King Tiloraja, who ruled central Thailand from Chiangmai, a city well north of the modern capital, Bangkok.

Two of the most important kings of nineteenth-century Siam were Mongkut and his son Chulalongkorn. Both were active in reforming the sangha. King Mongkut (r. 1824–51) is revered by Thais under the name Rama IV and is known in the West as the king of *The King and I*—which has never been shown in Thailand because it portrays Mongkut in a disrespectful way.

Having been a monk for over twenty years, Mongkut set out to restore discipline and direction to the sangha after he became king. This endeavour led to the founding of a new ordination lineage called the Thammayut Nikaya. The name is a Thai version of a Pali word meaning 'those who adhere to the dharma'. This reform movement set the tone for modern Theravada not only in Thailand, but also elsewhere in Southeast Asia. For example, the king of Cambodia arranged for the establishment of the Thammayut Nikaya in his country in the nineteenth century.

Following in his father's footsteps, King Chulalongkorn, Rama V (r. 1868–1910), undertook to unite the various *nikayas* under a central administrative authority and standardize the training given to novices in meditation, dharma instruction, and the Pali language. The training standards and central administration are still important features in the Thai sangha.

Thai kings in the modern period, even today, have always spent time in a monastery. This monastic training is considered an important preparation for someone who, as king, will be lay head of the sangha and the guiding figure in Thai cultural life.

Buddhist discipline and orthodoxy are maintained through control of the right to ordain. Historically the kings of Burma, Cambodia, Siam, and Laos sought to regularize and consolidate religion in their kingdoms by establishing the Theravada ordination lineage as normative. Theravada may have appealed to the rulers because of its insistence on maintaining discipline and traditions and because, in adopting it, the rulers could bring their kingdoms into political alignment with other powerful kingdoms in Sri Lanka and mainland Southeast Asia.

## Laos

Laos is a small country with close linguistic, ethnic, and cultural connections to Thailand. There is inscriptional evidence of Sri Lankan *bhikshus* bringing Theravada orthodoxy to Laos over five hundred years ago. However, because of its proximity and common language, Thai Buddhism was more influential in Laos. In modern times, Laotian *bhikshus* have travelled to Bangkok to attend one of the two large universities there that train *bhikshus*.

## Summary

The history of Buddhism in mainland Southeast Asia may be summarized along the following lines. Before 1000, various early Buddhist sects as well as Mahayana and Vajrayana schools competed for support, but by the fifteenth century the rulers of the major kingdoms of the area had all embraced Theravada and imported senior *bhikshus* from Sri Lanka to re-ordain the indigenous monks in the Theravada lineage. Other forms of Buddhism gradually died out in most of Southeast Asia, and Theravada training centres and temples of national importance flourished under royal patronage.

Island Southeast Asia, by contrast, has become predominantly Muslim over the past five centuries, but both Buddhist monuments and Buddhist minorities survive. For example, although Buddhism is no longer practised in Indonesia, tourists still flock to the ruins of the majestic temple of Borobudur, which covers a hilltop with a geometrical arrangement of stupas representing the mountains that anchor the world, according to traditional Buddhist cosmology. And Malaysia has a sizable Buddhist minority, mainly among the Chinese population.

# Mahayana, The Second Vehicle

The Mahayana ('Greater Vehicle') movement appears to have emerged around the first century CE. Although its origins are unclear, we know that its members were dismissing older forms of Buddhism as Hinayana ('Lesser Vehicle') by the third or fourth century, and that around the same time it was becoming the dominant form of Buddhism across the region traversed by the Silk Road, from Central Asia to northern China. It remains the main form of Buddhism in China, Korea, and Japan.

Mahayana differed from Theravada in everything from the doctrines and scriptures it emphasized to its rituals and meditation practices. Whereas Theravada saw the discipline of the *bhikshu* as a precondition for enlightenment and liberation, Mahayana offered laypeople the opportunity to strive for those goals as well. Whereas Theravada focused on the historical Shakyamuni, Mahayana developed a framework in which he represented only one manifestation of buddhahood. Furthermore, whereas Theravada emphasized that the only way to enlightenment and liberation was through personal effort—that there was no supernatural force on which human beings could call—Mahayana populated the heavens with bodhisattvas dedicated to helping all those who prayed to them for assistance.

How did all these differences arise? A possible explanation is that Mahayana Buddhism developed from one or more of the eighteen early Indian sects. There is some evidence for a close connection between early Mahayana and two or three of the early Indian sects, especially the Mahasanghika (Great Sangha). However, it seems more likely that Mahayana Buddhism arose in southern India as part of a movement towards more liberal interpretation that spread across several of the early Indian sects.

Despite their differences, Mahayana and the earlier forms of Buddhism share a common core of values and moral teachings, practices (such as meditation, chanting, scripture study, and veneration of relics), and forms of monastic life and buildings. In short, Theravada and Mahayana are different vehicles (*yanas*) for travelling the same path to enlightenment.

## Mahayana Doctrine

### The Lay Sangha

The practice of venerating Shakyamuni at the stupas enshrining his relics had begun soon after his death. In time, many lay people began making pilgrimages to stupas with major relics, and new ones were built in all Mahayana countries. (The veneration of sacred relics was an important part of several religions in this period, including Hinduism and Christianity.) Lay Buddhists came to believe that they could earn valuable karmic merit by making a pilgrimage.

This development marked a major shift away from early Buddhism, in which the religious role of laypeople had been restricted to providing material support for the sangha and the prospects for lay progress along the spiritual path were limited. Anyone who wished to seek enlightenment more seriously was expected to 'depart the world' and become a *bhikshu or bhikshuni*. Mahayana Buddhism, by contrast, offered laypeople the possibility of pursuing spiritual development and even attaining enlightenment while living in the world.

### Doctrine of the Three Bodies (*Trikaya*)

To account for the various ways in which one could experience or refer to buddhahood, Mahayana developed a doctrine of 'three bodies' (*trikaya*). The earthly manifestation body of a buddha is called the Appearance Body or Transformation Body (*nirmanakaya*). The heavenly body of a buddha that presides over a buddha-realm and is an object of devotion for Mahayana Buddhists is called the Body of Bliss (*sambhogakaya*). These are supported by the buddha as the absolute essence of the universe, called the Dharma Body (*dharmakaya*).

The Three Bodies doctrine calls attention not only to the oneness of all the buddhas that have appeared on earth, but also to the unity of the buddha-nature or buddha-potential in all its forms. That is, the *trikaya* doctrine envisions one cosmic reality (Dharma Body) that manifests itself in the form both of heavenly beings (Body of Bliss) and of humans such as Shakyamuni (Appearance Body). By connecting the earthly Buddha to the Dharma Body or Absolute, the doctrine of the three bodies also moved Mahayana Buddhism in the direction of theistic religion—in sharp contrast to the Theravada school, which continued to revere the Buddha not as a deity but as an exceptional human being.

### Teaching by Expedient Means

The Sanskrit word *upaya* forms part of an expression frequently translated as 'skill in means' or 'skilful means'. The word was used occasionally in Theravada's Pali texts with a more general sense, but the roots of the more technical sense that the word later acquired were already present. Shakyamuni's teachings were practical, even pragmatic, and he seems to have tailored his presentation of them to suit his audience's capacity to grasp them. He urged his followers to use skill in guiding people to spiritual attainment, like the skilful boatman ferrying people to the other side of the river. The analogy of the raft or boat implies that when one has reached the other side, there is no further need of the raft for the onward journey.

### The *Lotus Sutra* and the Parable of the Burning House

A Mahayana text that places a strong emphasis on *upaya* is the *Lotus Sutra*, which treats many Buddhist teachings as provisional, that is, as steps towards a more complete understanding. As an illustration of this perspective, the *Lotus Sutra* tells a story about a father whose children are inside a burning house. He persuades them to come out by promising them chariots that he does not actually have; this false promise may be a lie, but it serves an important purpose. Similarly, those just starting on the path are taught not the ultimate truth, but temporary formulations that will allow them to advance to a point where they will be able to see the purpose of the earlier stages. From this perspective, even Shakyamuni's teaching is provisional, simply an expedient means of persuading human beings to start along the path. By treating earlier teachings as expedient means, Mahayana thinkers were able to shift the emphasis from Shakyamuni to celestial buddha figures and a notion of cosmic wisdom.

## Bodhisattvas

Early Buddhism taught that every individual makes his or her own karma. There was no supernatural source of grace. The Mahayana school, however, proposed that grace was available in the form of merit transferred to humans from bodhisattvas. Mahayana cosmology envisions a multitude of spiritually advanced beings, all of them prepared to share their great merit with anyone who prays for help.

Bodhisattvas were not unknown in early Indian Buddhism: in a previous life Shakyamuni himself had become a bodhisattva when he vowed to attain buddhahood one day, and he remained a bodhisattva until the night of his enlightenment. For most Theravada Buddhists, however, the highest goal was to reach the status of an Arhat. The Mahayana school sharply criticized this goal as self-centred, focused solely on achieving personal liberation. They maintained that those who take bodhisattva vows are dedicating themselves first and foremost to the salvation of all living beings. All Mahayana Buddhists were therefore encouraged to take the bodhisattva vow, pledging not only to attain buddhahood themselves but also to work towards the liberation of all beings.

The corollary of this innovation in Buddhist thought was Mahayana's introduction of the idea that humans could appeal to merit-filled beings in the heavens for assistance. Early Indian Buddhism had considered Shakyamuni, after his *parinirvana*, to be beyond the realm of direct involvement with human lives, and therefore had no tradition of appealing to him for assistance. In some forms of Mahayana Buddhism, by contrast, worshippers not only venerate the bodhisattvas but petition them for blessings, much as Roman Catholics venerate the saints and ask them for help.

Some important bodhisattvas have special functions. For example, Bodhisattva Manjusri is the guardian of Buddhist wisdom, and novices entering Buddhist training often call on him to guide and inspire them.

The bodhisattva known especially for compassion, Avalokiteshvara ('the Lord who looks down'), is popular in all Mahayana countries. Originally Avalokiteshvara was masculine, but in China he came to be venerated in female form under the name Guanyin. This change of gender is an example of the bodhisattva's power to take any shape necessary in order to benefit believers (the *Lotus Sutra* lists thirty-three examples of such 'shape shifting'). Known as the 'Bodhisattva of Compassion', Guanyin is the most venerated bodhisattva in Buddhist history, and has been called the 'Virgin Mary of East Asia' by Westerners, since graceful statues of her are found everywhere. Many Mahayana women feel especially close to her because she is believed to bring children to those who lack them and to care for infants who die, as well as aborted fetuses.

Bodhisattva Maitreya (the 'Friendly One') is expected to be the next buddha, the one who will turn the dharma wheel once again after the wheel set in motion by Shakyamuni has stopped turning. Some Mahayana Buddhists pray to Maitreya requesting that they be reborn when he comes, for it is easier to become enlightened when there is a living buddha to follow.

The heavens in which the buddhas and bodhisattvas reside are known as 'fields' or 'realms'. The belief in such 'Buddha realms' is another characteristic of the Mahayana school. Those who venerate a certain buddha may be reborn into his heaven. As we shall see, this is a central belief of the **Pure Land** movement, which has been especially popular in East Asia.

## Merit Transfer

Another important characteristic of Mahayana Buddhism is its extension of the concept of merit transfer. Early Buddhism taught that merit—that is, karma—is made solely by the individual, not by any external agent such as a saint or a god. The only exception to this rule was the transfer of merit for the benefit of one's dead relatives and the welfare of all beings, as in the Theravada giving (**dana**) ritual described later in this chapter. In Mahayana, by contrast, the buddhas and the bodhisattvas are believed to be capable of transferring merit from themselves to human beings. Thus devotees can appeal to their chosen bodhisattvas for assistance in the same way that Christians pray to their chosen saints to intercede for them.

## Meditation and Visualization

The Mahayana belief in various buddhas and bodhisattvas, each with his or her own heaven, gave rise to a practice known as 'vision meditation', in which the meditator would focus intensely on his or her chosen bodhisattva or buddha in the hope of being granted a vision of that figure. In the process, practitioners sought to achieve a heightened state of consciousness and develop a special rapport with the object of their devotion. Such visualization would eventually become a central element in Vajrayana Buddhism.

## Mahayana Schools in India

The above overview suggests some substantial differences between Mahayana and Theravada Buddhism, especially regarding scriptures, the nature of the Buddha, and the efficacy of prayer. But the various schools that developed within the Mahayana tradition, first in India and eventually across East Asia, also vary significantly among themselves. The **Chan** (**Zen**) school, for example, downplays the veneration of Buddha and has much in common with Theravada, whereas the Pure Land school stresses the need for reliance on Amida Buddha's help. We will begin with an overview of the more important Mahayana schools that emerged in India, then look at Mahayana as it developed in China, Korea, and Japan.

### Madhyamika

Early Buddhism taught that there were six perfections (*paramitas*), the sixth and most important of which was the perfection of a particular kind

of wisdom known as *prajna*. This wisdom—not to be confused with worldly wisdom or scientific knowledge—is accessible only to those with a highly developed consciousness or awareness.

Mahayana thinkers put great emphasis on the development of *prajna* and wrote a number of texts on the subject, beginning as early as the first century BCE with the *Perfection of Wisdom in Eight Thousand Verses*. The two that were to become the most important were the *Heart Sutra* and the *Diamond Cutter Sutra*. In all these texts, the key to the highest spiritual wisdom is awareness of the emptiness (**shunyata**) of all things.

Sometime during the later part of the second century, a brahmin from southern India converted to Buddhism and took the ordination name Nagarjuna. He wrote Buddhist devotional hymns and ethical guides, but his fame is based on philosophical works such as the *Mulamadhyamaka-karika* ('Fundamentals of the Middle Way').

Nagarjuna's philosophical position is called the 'Middle Way' (Madhyamika) because it refuses either to affirm or to deny any statement about reality on the ground that all such statements necessarily fall short of expressing ultimate truth. All realities (dharmas) are equally 'empty' of absolute truth or 'self-essence'. According to Nagarjuna's doctrine of Emptiness, everything in the phenomenal world is ultimately unreal. By a process of paradoxical logic he claims that Emptiness as ultimate reality is itself unreal, although it may be experienced directly in meditation.

Nagarjuna summed up this paradox in a famous eightfold negation:

> Nothing comes into being,
> Nor does anything disappear.
> Nothing is eternal,
> Nor has anything an end.
> Nothing is identical,
> Or differentiated,
> Nothing moves hither,
> Nor moves anything thither.
> (Chen 1964: 84)

For Madhyamika and the later Mahayana schools that developed under its influence, including Zen, enlightenment demands recognition of the *shunyata* (emptiness, nothingness) of all dharmas.

Of course Nagarjuna recognized that his own thinking was no less empty than any other. Thus he made it his philosophical 'position' to refrain from taking any dogmatic position. A modern Japanese Buddhist professor reports that as a graduate student, he told his teacher he was uncertain of where he stood in relation to the various Buddhist philosophical schools. The teacher responded by implicitly likening him to Nagarjuna: 'Your position is to have no position.'

Through his paradoxical logic, Nagarjuna asserts that *nirvana* is dialectically identical to *samsara*, or the phenomenal world. In other words, each is present in the other. This is the most characteristic Madhyamika teaching and also the most puzzling. Early Indian Buddhism had taken the two to be opposites, *samsara* being the temporal, worldly process of 'coming to be and passing away', and *nirvana* being the eternal, unchanging goal of the spiritual quest; yet Madhyamika holds that '*samsara* is *nirvana*, and *nirvana* is *samsara*'. From the point of view of conventional wisdom, the two may be distinguished, but ultimately the distinction is not tenable. In fact, claims Madhyamika, perfection of the higher wisdom brings the realization that no such distinction is tenable.

In the sixth century, a split developed around the teachings of two teachers, each of whom considered himself to be the true follower of Nagarjuna. Bhavaviveka (or Bhavya, c. 490–570) was willing to talk about levels of reality and degrees of insight, as long as it was understood that such distinctions applied only in the realm of conventional truth. That is, he accepted the mind's ability to make distinctions about reality within the realm of conventional truth, but recognized that no such distinctions could be made in the realm of absolute truth. The school he founded was known by the name Svatantrika because it accepted the validity of independent (*svatantra*) inference.

Bhavya's rival Buddhapalita (c. 470–550) rejected independent inference and argued that all statements of knowledge were ultimately self-contradictory.

## Yogacara or 'Consciousness Only'

In the late fourth century, three Indian *bhikshus* named Maitreyanatha, Asanga, and Vasubandhu founded a new Mahayana school that rivalled Madhyamika. Though usually called Yogacara ('Practice of Yoga') because it stresses meditation and uses a text by that name, it is also known as 'Consciousness Only' (Vijnanavada), because it argues that we cannot truly know either the external world or ourselves. It holds that what most people assume to be realities are in fact nothing more than ideas and images taken from a 'storehouse consciousness' (*alaya-vijnana*). As a consequence, we can never know if external objects exist. All we can ever know are the images in our consciousness—images that come from a repository shaped by past karmic actions and attachments.

For Yogacara, both the universe and the perceiver exist only in the process of perceiving. Even our 'selves' and our karma are merely reifications of momentary awareness. Sensory impressions are 'seeds' that lead to acts or thoughts:

> A seed produces a manifestation,
> A manifestation perfumes a seed.
> The three elements (seed, manifestation, and
>     perfume) turn on and on,
> The cause and effect occur at the same time.
>     (Chen 1964: 323)

According to this theory, the only way to avoid false substantialization is to so exhaust the consciousness, through yoga and spiritual cultivation, that it becomes identical to the ultimate reality called 'thusness' (*tathata*), which corresponds to the 'emptiness' of Madhyamika. Critics from rival schools argued that the concept of the storehouse consciousness seemed to contradict the traditional Buddhist doctrine of no-self (*anatman*) and come

*[handwritten marginal note: Mantra of Yogacara]*

close to affirming the Hindu notion of Atman that the Buddha had rejected. The Yogacara writers, however, were careful to point out that although, like the Atman in Hinduism, the storehouse consciousness transmigrates from birth to birth, unlike the Atman it has no eternal, unchanging substance. Buddhist ideas of the link between one birth and the next as a 'karma complex' or 'migrating consciousness' were developed by Yogacara into the notion of a storehouse consciousness.

The Yogacara school's emphasis on 'consciousness only' and the psychological origin of all perceptions may have arisen out of the experience of emptying the mind during Yogacara meditation—a practice quite different from the visualization practised in some other meditation traditions.

**Pure Land Buddhism**

Another Mahayana school developed around the veneration of a celestial buddha of 'infinite life' and 'infinite light' known in Sanskrit as Amitayus or Amitabha, in Chinese as Omitofo, and in Japanese as Amida (the Japanese spelling is the one most commonly used in English).

This school most likely began to take shape around the first century, some five hundred years after Shakyamuni's *parinirvana*.

According to an account attributed to Shakyamuni himself, Amitabha was a buddha of a previous age who in an earlier life, as a young prince named Dharmakara, had taken a series of forty-eight bodhisattva vows detailing his intention to strive for enlightenment and help others in specific ways. In a sense, some resemble a doctor's oath not to deny treatment to those who have no money to pay for it. In one of the most important vows (the eighteenth) Amitabha promises to establish a heavenly region—the 'Pure Land' or 'Western Paradise'—into which all beings who so desire can be reborn. No extraordinary effort will be required to earn rebirth in that land: admission will be free to all who have faith in Amitabha's compassionate power and make their desire for rebirth in his heaven known by thinking of him:

*18th vow*

If, after my obtaining Buddhahood, all beings in the ten quarters should not desire in sincerity and trustfulness to be born in my country, and if they should not be born by only thinking of me for ten times, except those who have committed the five grave offences and those who are abusive of the true Dharma, may I not attain the Highest Enlightenment (Bloom 1965: 2–3).

In short, Dharmakara vows that he will strive to become a completely enlightened buddha on the condition that he can remain active in the work of helping all living beings towards liberation.

Suffering, old age, and death will be unknown in the Pure Land—the *sukhavati*, as opposed to the *duhkha-vati*, the land of suffering, that is the world. There will be food, drink, and music for all; the streets and buildings will be made of jewels; and the buddha's followers will be so uplifted by his merit that their progress towards *nirvana will be easy*. This notion of the 'Pure Land' marked a remarkable transformation in the Buddhist idea of heaven. In early Buddhism, meritorious individuals could hope to be reborn in some kind of paradise. While there, however, they would be unable to 'make' new merit or develop their higher wisdom. In other words, there was no path leading from heaven to nirvana: once the inhabitants' store of merit was exhausted, they would have to return to earth and be reborn in human form in order to resume the task of accumulating merit and working towards the final goal of nirvana. The Pure Land, by contrast, offers the ideal conditions for progress towards enlightenment, and therefore rebirth on earth will no longer be necessary.

A second text, the *Shorter Sutra on the Pure Land*, spelled out what was required to benefit from Amitabha's great store of merit. Those who have recollected and repeated his name before death will, upon dying, be reborn in his Pure Land. This rebirth is not earned by the individual's meritorious works, as was the case with the path laid down by Shakyamuni. Rather, rebirth in the Pure Land is a gift made available through the infinite merits of the buddha Amitabha. Theologically, the concept of salvation through faith in divine grace is a Christian parallel.

A third text of early Pure Land Buddhism, the *Meditation on Amitayus Sutra*, offered detailed instruction in vision meditation. For those unable to undertake the rigorous training required to achieve a vision, however, it also offered an easier path. This was the formula that was to become central to Pure Land Buddhism: 'Homage to Amitabha Buddha'. Even the meritless or wicked could gain rebirth in the Pure Land through sincere repetition of the sacred formula.

The Pure Land school introduced into Buddhism a path to salvation based solely on faith. There is no equivalent to this path in the Theravada tradition. Although Theravada rituals always include recitation of the 'Three Refuges', this formula is a simple statement of homage to the Triple Gem: devotees do not expect to receive a response. The *Shorter Sutra on the Pure Land* teaches that the only condition for rebirth in the Pure Land is faith in the infinite compassion of Amitabha, shown through prayerful and meditative repetition of his name. This reliance on an external power, called 'other power', stands in sharp contrast to the self-reliance emphasized in early Buddhism. Such 'other-reliance' was described as 'cat grace', as opposed to the 'monkey grace' of self-reliance—the idea being that a baby cat is picked up and carried by its mother, whereas a baby monkey has to reach for its mother and hold on.

Over the centuries that followed, Pure Land Buddhism spread from India to China and from there to Japan. In the process, the basic concept was elaborated and refined to the point that the Indian thinkers who first developed it came to be seen more as forerunners than as founders. Pure Land became the most popular of all Buddhist schools in East Asia, and it remains the most popular school today.

## Mahayana in China

The major Mahayana schools spread along the trade routes from India to Central Asia and on to China in the early centuries of the Common Era. Once there, they tended to take on forms of thought, social norms, and architecture more reflective of Chinese culture.

### Sanlun: Chinese Madhyamika

The Sanlun ('Three Treatises') school is the Chinese extension of Nagarjuna's Madhyamika ('Middle Doctrine'). The monk Kumarajiva, famous as a translator of Buddhist texts into Chinese, introduced this teaching into China with his translation of two treatises by Nagarjuna and a third by Nagarjuna's disciple Aryadeva (or Deva, c. 300). These three works became the foundation of the Sanlun school.

Essentially a restatement of Nagarjuna's ideas, the chief teaching of the Sanlun school was that everything is empty (*shunya*), because nothing has any independent reality or self-nature. An entity can be identified only through its relation to something else. In this unreal phenomenal world we function as in a dream, making distinctions between subject and object, *samsara* and *nirvana*, but with the higher wisdom comes understanding of the higher truth called *shunyata* or Emptiness.

Kumarajiva's disciple Seng Zhao (374–414) became an outstanding exponent of this system in China, producing three texts on Madhyamika known as Zhaolun, the Treatises of Zhao. For him, the Middle Doctrine represented an effort to reconcile extremes and grasp the paradoxical reality that things both exist and do not exist—a reality that can be apprehended only through sagely wisdom, not through knowledge.

### Faxiang: Chinese Yogacara

The Chinese version of the Yogacara or 'Consciousness Only' school also has two names, Weishi ('Consciousness Only') and Faxiang ('Dharma Character'). First introduced into China in the sixth century, the school grew up around a text by

Asanga entitled *Compendium of Mahayana*. It was his perplexity over the meaning of this work that spurred a monk named Xuanzang to set out for India in search of more scriptures; on his return, the Big Wild Goose Pagoda was built in Xi'an (the Chinese terminus of the silk route) to house the manuscripts he brought back. This temple, along with its smaller companion the Little Wild Goose Pagoda, remains an important centre of Buddhism in this historic city. (The story of Xuanzang's perilous journey to India is celebrated in Chinese Buddhist art and inspired the famous novel *Journey to the West*, best known in English under the title *Monkey: A Folk-Tale of China*.)

Although Faxiang did not survive as a vital sect, it had some influence on the development of other schools of thought, including Neo-Confucianism.

### Jodo: Chinese Pure Land

In China, Pure Land is known as Jingtu and Amitabha Buddha as Omitofo. He is assisted by two bodhisattvas (*pusa* in Chinese), one of whom is Guanyin, the bodhisattva of compassion.

The recitation of praise to Omitofo is called *nianfo* in Chinese. During the recitation the devotee usually fingers a string of beads. Thus Pure Land Buddhism parallels some forms of Christianity in several ways, with a God-figure (Amida), a mediator (Guanyin), a doctrine of faith and grace, and a devotional practice not unlike the recitation of the rosary. (Some scholars think the practice of using a string of beads to keep count while reciting a sequence of prayers originated in India.)

In China, Pure Land Buddhism has had a special appeal for the masses of people who seek

Guanyin, the bodhisattva of compassion, in heaven, seated on her lotus throne and holding the jar of water she uses to bestow blessings. Other figures in this scene (displayed behind glass at a temple in Xi'an, central China) include Amida Buddha (above Guanyin) and various attendants (Roy C. Amore).

not only ultimate salvation but also a power that will assist them in everyday life. Guanyin is particularly important in this respect, especially for women. She soon came to symbolize the 'giver of children'—an adaptation that underlines the more worldly focus of Chinese Buddhism, compared with its Indian counterpart. Guanyin is associated with the medieval legend of the Chinese princess Miaoshan, killed by her parents to prevent her from becoming a nun. Sometimes seen holding a child, she recalls the Christian figure of the Madonna with child. It has been suggested that this pose reflects the influence of Christian art brought to China by missionaries in the late seventeenth and early eighteenth centuries.

## Chan

Chan Buddhism is better known in the West by its Japanese name: Zen. Its founder was Bodhidharma—the same sixth-century Indian monk who told King Wu that all his good works had earned him no merit at all. In sharp contrast to the Pure Land sect's emphasis on 'other power', Chan emphasized 'self-power' and the attainment of personal enlightenment through rigorous practice of meditation. Although there is no surviving evidence that a similar school existed in India, Chan tradition traces Bodhidharma's lineage to the Buddha's disciple Kashyapa, whose intuitive insight is celebrated in the story of the 'flower sermon' on Vulture Peak.

### THE FLOWER SERMON

This story begins with the disciples asking Shakyamuni Buddha for a dharma talk. He agrees, and the disciples prepare a place for the talk at an appropriate spot part way up Vulture Peak mountain. The list of those wanting to attend included the monks (from the earth level) as well as nagas, the mystical cobras of the underworld, and angels (*devatas*) from the heavenly realm. As the Buddha took his seat on the teaching throne, all grew silent, eagerly waiting to hear his words. Instead of speaking, however, Shakyamuni simply held up a white lotus flower.

All were dumbfounded except for Kashyapa, who in that moment experienced an intuitive flash of enlightenment. The Buddha acknowledged his understanding with a smile, and Kashyapa came to be known as Kashyapa the Great (Mahakashyapa) and the first patriarch in a lineage that stressed the achievement of the state of mind called *dhyana* in Sanskrit and *jhana* in Pali—the state reached by the young Shakyamuni while meditating under the rose-apple tree.

The Chinese pronounced the word *dhyana* or *jhana* as 'chan', and Bodhidharma is seen as the first patriarch of the Chan school in China. Bodhidharma came to China to teach what he called a 'mind to mind, direct transmission' of enlightenment, with 'no dependence on words'. Just as the Buddha relied on a single enigmatic gesture to deliver his 'flower sermon', so Bodhidharma and later Chan masters used surprising, shocking, paradoxical, or even violent actions to bring about the state of mind best known in the West by the Japanese term *satori*. One master twisted a disciple's nose so hard that the pain and indignity led to a breakthrough. Another shoved his disciple into a thorn bush, with the same result. Another would simply hold up a single finger. Other masters had their own signature methods. Many masters made impossible demands upon their students, including the master who held up one hand and demanded to be told what sound it made: this was the origin of the familiar question 'What is the sound of one hand clapping?' One master would instruct his disciples to imagine themselves hanging by their teeth from a branch suspended over some danger then being asked a question that demands a response—a question such as 'Do all persons have Buddha-nature?' If the disciple correctly answers 'Yes,' he will fall and die. But if he refuses to answer, he will seem to communicate an untruth. The master demands to know, 'What would you do?' Since there is no logical way out of this dilemma, the correct answer must be found in some place other than the rational mind.

By the early sixth century, Bodhidharma had brought this school of thought to China and had settled into a cave in the mountains above the village of Shaolin. He was known especially for meditating while facing the wall of his cave monastery. Later legend has it that after nine years of 'wall gazing meditation', his legs atrophied. This is popularly recalled in the legless, egg-shaped Japanese dolls called Darumas (*daruma* is the Japanese word for dharma). Some Japanese buy Daruma dolls on New Year's Day, then take them home and make a wish for a good year while filling in the missing pupil of one of the doll's eyes. The following New Year, they will fill in the other pupil while thanking Daruma for the good year that has passed.

Bodhidharma's teaching is summed up in these four lines attributed to him:

> A special transmission outside of doctrines. Not setting up the written word as an authority. Pointing directly at the human heart. Seeing one's nature and becoming a buddha (Robinson 1959: 332).

This formula puts into words Kashyapa's 'flower sermon' experience of the transmission of enlightened consciousness by direct contact between master and disciple, without the need for textual or doctrinal study.

Because of its distaste for book learning, Chan became known as a special transmission of enlightenment 'outside the scriptures', one that is not dependent on 'words or letters'. The special state of consciousness known as Chan is transmitted only 'from mind to mind'—from master to disciple without the intervention of rational argumentation. It advocates the 'absence of thoughts' to free the mind from external influences.

### CHAN AND THE MARTIAL ARTS

The Shaolin monastery in the valley below Bodhidharma's cave became a centre of Chan training not only in meditation but in what are now called the martial arts. The story is that Bodhidharma began teaching the students self-defence exercises

as an antidote to their long hours of sitting meditation. All the East Asian martial arts traditions trace their roots to the Shaolin monastery. Today the small mountain town of Shaolin remains a centre of martial arts training, with dozens of elementary and high schools (mostly for boys) that combine academic training in the mornings with martial arts training in the afternoons. Most of these schools are Buddhist in orientation, but two are Muslim. Students come from all over China and even beyond to attend these schools. It is said that the town of Shaolin has the highest ratio of students to population of any town or city in the world.

### THE LINEAGE OF PATRIARCHS

One day a Chinese man is said to have arrived at Bodhidharma's cave, hoping to be invited in to study under the master. But no such invitation was forthcoming. The hours passed and it began to snow, but the man waited throughout the night, shivering in the ever deepening snow. In the morning Bodhidharma finally asked him what he wanted. He explained that he wanted a teacher who would open his mind to enlightenment. Bodhidharma refused, telling him it was hopeless for someone like him, with little wisdom and feeble resolve, to expect any serious breakthrough. The man was discouraged but did not give up. After several more hours, he came up with a plan. He cut off his left arm and presented it to Bodhidharma as proof of his resolve. Bodhidharma accepted him as a disciple.

The story continues with the new disciple, now named Huike, asking Bodhidharma for help in pacifying his anxious mind. The master replied by saying, 'Bring me your mind so that I can pacify it.' Huike explained that he had long sought his mind, but he could not find it. 'So there', says Bodhidharma, 'I have pacified your mind!' The one-armed Huike went on to become the first Han Chinese patriarch, after Bodhidharma's death. In Chan paintings he is often depicted in the act of handing his severed arm to Bodhidharma. There is a small temple dedicated to Huike at the monastery in Shaolin, with a statue of him standing in the snow just outside.

The lineage of patriarchs continued and the Chan school gradually spread to other areas. Most Chan monasteries in China, Korea, and Japan were located part-way up a mountain, where the cool, dry atmosphere optimized the chances of a spiritual breakthrough. For this reason Chan Buddhism has been called the 'mountain school.'

### HUINENG AND THE POETRY CONTEST

During the era of the fifth Chan patriarch, in the late seventh century, a young boy from southern China named Huineng arrived at the Chan monastery at Shaolin, seeking admission as a novice. He was not accepted, perhaps because he spoke a southern dialect difficult for the northerners to understand. But Huineng stayed to work in the kitchen, pounding rice and helping to cook for the monks.

Huineng had made the long journey because he had learned that the monastery taught a radical new form of Buddhism that offered the possibility of a direct breakthrough to a higher level of consciousness, without undue dependence on knowledge of scriptures or the performance of rituals. He understood the essence of Buddhism to involve an intuitive, mystical experience, the 'direct pointing of the mind' that Bodhidarma had taught.

When it came time for the aging fifth patriarch to choose his successor, candidates were asked to compose a poem (*gatha* in Sanskrit) expressing their state of enlightenment. The most senior disciple wrote this verse on the wall:

This body is the Bodhi-tree;
The soul is like the mirror bright;
Take heed to keep it always clean,
And let no dust collect upon it.
(Suzuki 1991)

This poem nicely captures the Chan point of view. Rather than practising ritual veneration of the Buddha who was enlightened under a Bodhi tree long ago in a distant land, one is to think of one's own body, here and now, as the Bodhi tree, the place of enlightenment. Mirrors in old China were made of shiny metal, and they needed to be polished daily to keep dust from marring the reflections. But Mahayana Buddhism also had a long tradition of comparing the polishing of a mirror to the purifying of the mind. A bright, shiny mirror perfectly reflects reality, and a pure mind should do the same. Thus the senior disciple's poem encourages regular meditation to keep the mind clear and pure. That night, however, Huineng wrote a counter-poem on the wall nearby:

The Bodhi (True Wisdom) is not like the tree;
The mirror bright is nowhere shining:
As there is nothing from the first,
Where does the dust itself collect?
(Suzuki 1991)

This poem deepens the understanding of Chan enlightenment. It goes beyond merely bringing the enlightenment experience, symbolized by the Bodhi tree, to the 'here and now'. In denying the imagery of the Bodhi tree and the mirror, it implies that the pure mind corresponds to the state of emptiness central to the Mahayana tradition.

The fifth patriarch called Huineng into his room, acknowledged his deep understanding, and awarded him the robe and staff of the office of patriarch—but with the advice that he should go back to the South. This he did, and even though he was still a layman, he began teaching the deep state of intuitive wisdom that became known in the West as *satori*, one of its names in Japanese. Eventually he was ordained and recognized as the true sixth patriarch. It was Huineng who spread Chan to the masses and into southern China, from which it was eventually taken to Korea, where it is known as Son and to Japan, where it is known as Zen.

## Chan Buddhism

*The following extracts are from the* Platform Sutra, *an important scripture attributed to the sixth Chan patriarch, Huineng, and compiled by one of his disciples in the early 700s.*

*Meditation and Wisdom*

Good friends, how then are meditation and wisdom alike? They are like the lamp and the light it gives forth. If there is a lamp there is light; if there is no lamp there is no light. The lamp is the substance of light; the light is the function of the lamp. Thus, although they have two names, in substance they are not two. Meditation and wisdom are like this (*The Platform Sutra of the Sixth Patriarch*, sec. 15; Yampolsky 1976: 137).

*Sudden and Gradual Enlightenment*

Good friends, in the Dharma there is no sudden or gradual [enlightenment], but among people some are keen and others dull. The deluded commend the gradual method; the enlightened practice the sudden teaching. To understand the original mind of yourself is to see into your own original nature. Once enlightened, there is from the outset no distinction between these two methods; those who are not enlightened will for long kalpas be caught in the cycle of transmigration (*The Platform Sutra of the Sixth Patriarch*, sec. 16; Yampolsky 1976: 137).

### Mahayana in Korea

Physical proximity created close links between China and Korea. The Han dynasty conquered the northern part of the peninsula in the late second century BCE and Buddhism was introduced roughly two centuries later, spreading from the northern kingdom of Koguryo first to Paekche in the southwest and then to Silla in the southeast. It became most influential after Silla conquered the other two kingdoms and united the country (668–935).

The new religion expanded on an unprecedented scale during the Silla period. Among the major schools of Buddhism introduced from China were the Theravada tradition of the *vinaya* (monastic discipline), the Flower Garland (Huayan; in Korean, Hwaom) and the Faxiang (Yogacara) school, which eventually developed into a syncretic tradition. The most influential school, however, was Chan (Son in Korean), introduced

in the early seventh century. Nine Son monasteries, known as the Nine Mountains, were eventually established.

Among the Korean monks who made important contributions to Buddhist commentary in the early period was Wonhyo (617–86). In a famous text (a commentary on the *Flower Garland Sutra*) he sought to harmonize the various doctrinal trends of the period. According to Wonhyo, the different teachings all complement one another, and together they make up one whole truth, just as the Buddha-nature is present in all human beings and in the whole world:

The world itself is, essentially speaking, in everlasting Enlightenment. In other words, the essential base upon which the whole complex of relationships among the different living beings is standing, is the ultimate eternal reality which is . . . the source of life and light, . . . which make it possible for our life . . . to be truly human, to be enlightened (Rhi 1977: 202).

In the late twelfth century the Son and scholastic schools were united by a charismatic monk named Chinul (1158–1210) to create the Chogye sect, which became the orthodox form of Buddhism in Korea and remains the largest denomination today. It was also Chinul who introduced the paradoxical exercise called *gongan* in Chinese but better known in the West in its Japanese form, '**koan**' (to be discussed below).

Nevertheless, Buddhist influence withered for several centuries after the Yi dynasty (1392–1910) adopted Confucianism as Korea's state ideology. Confucian scholars petitioned the court to restrict the number of Buddhist temples, supervise the selection of monks, and reorganize the ecclesiastical system while reducing the number of sects to facilitate state control. In the fifteenth century, temple properties were confiscated, the serfs retained by monasteries were drafted into the army, and Buddhist monks were banned, especially in Seoul, the capital.

Today, the institutional form that survived, the Chogye sect, gathers in all the common forms of Buddhist religious practice in the country. In South Korea today, the monks worship the buddha Amitabha of the Pure Land, practise Son meditation, or recite *sutra*s in the same monastery, each according to his own inclinations. The situation somewhat resembles that in Chinese Buddhism, where sectarian divisions have also largely disappeared

## Mahayana in Japan

Buddhism was first introduced to Japan from Korea in the mid-sixth century. It had taken almost nine hundred years to reach the extremities of East Asia, and it had been transformed along the way. Today Japanese Buddhism is mainly Mahayana, but with influences from other forms as well.

An important landmark for Buddhism in Japan was the warm reception it received from the regent, Prince Shotoku, who in 604 issued the 'Seventeen-Article Constitution', a set of moral guidelines for the ruling class that extolled the value of harmony and urged reverence for the Three Gems. Welcoming Buddhism (as well as Confucianism) for its civilizing benefits, the prince became the centre of a Buddhist cult that still endures. The state offered protection for Buddhism, even building temples, and Japanese monks travelled to China to pursue further study.

It was during the Nara period (710–94), under the influence of Buddhism, that Japanese culture experienced its first golden age. Eventually, however, the monks' close ties with the state led many to become increasingly secularized and in some cases corrupt. The state limited the number of monks and forbade them from proselytizing among the general populace. As a result, the practice of Buddhism was for a time mainly restricted to the aristocracy.

## Tendai

The most influential Buddhist sect during the Heian period (794–1185) was Tendai, founded by the monk Saicho (766–822). After studying in China, Saicho returned home determined to reform Japanese Buddhism. Breaking with the increasingly secularized older sects established in the Nara period, he made Mount Hiei, northeast of the new capital of Kyoto, his base of operations. The temple complex on Mount Hiei eventually became a kind of fortress with its own monk-soldiers.

As in Chinese Tiantai, followers of Japanese Tendai believed in the universal attainment of buddhahood or salvation, as taught in the *Lotus Sutra*, and the harmonization of Buddhist teachings. Unlike Chinese Tiantai, however, the Japanese version incorporated esoteric beliefs and rituals drawn from certain forms of tantric Buddhism found in Tibet and Mongolia. Tendai uses both public or 'exoteric' elements (*kenkyo*) and secret or 'esoteric' elements (*mikkyo*) in its teachings and practices.

Mount Hiei also became a centre of Buddhist studies and eventually the cradle of the new sects that were to emerge later. Like the Shingon sect, Tendai taught that anyone can attain buddhahood, and focused on life in this world rather than the next. Both sought the favour of the court and the support of the nobility, and both practised magical rites intended to secure material prosperity and earthly happiness. Shingon and Tendai became the prototypes of all later Buddhist sects originating in Japan.

### Zen

Today in Japan there are two main Zen sects, Rinzai and Soto. The first is named after Linji (Rinzai in Japanese), a famous ninth-century Chinese Chan monk who is said to have entered training as a shy young boy. After training diligently for more than a year, he was permitted to meet with the master, Huangbo. When the master asked why he had come, Linji humbly requested instruction in enlightenment, whereupon the master hit him hard with his stick.

When Linji told his teacher what had happened, he was advised to try again, which led to a second beating. After three such beatings Linji decided to leave training, thinking he was not worthy. The master allowed him to leave, but requested that he first visit an old hermit monk who lived farther up the mountain. The hermit, after hearing Linji describe what had happened, exclaimed, 'Poor old Huangbo, he must have nearly exhausted himself hitting you.' This lack of sympathy so shocked and angered Linji that he experienced a breakthrough and burst out laughing. 'Why the sudden change?' demanded the hermit. 'There's not so much to old Huangbo's Zen after all' was the reply. Upon returning to Huangbo, Linji threatened to hit the master with his own stick. 'Just get back to your training,' said the master.

When Huangbo died, Linji succeeded him as master and gave his name to a new ordination lineage or sect. The Linji (Rinzai) sect stresses exactly the kind of 'sudden enlightenment', or *satori*, that he experienced in response to Huangbo's apparently irrational behaviour. Subsequent masters in his sect continued to find that they could stimulate a breakthrough to Chan consciousness by delivering unexpected blows and shouts, or otherwise confounding their pupils.

At the centre of this approach is the koan (from Chinese *gongan*): a paradoxical anecdote that is specifically designed to defy rational understanding and force the student out of normal 'heady' (reason- or word-centred) mode into a more intuitive, body-centred state of mind. The typical koan retells an incident in which, by doing something unexpected, a master sparked an enlightenment experience in his student. The point of the retelling is to evoke the same experience in successive generations of disciples. We will return to the subject of koan training in the Practice section below.

The second Zen sect in Japan is the Soto school (from Chinese Caodong), which seeks 'gradual enlightenment' through long hours of **zazen** (sitting meditation). Both sects use koans and *zazen*, so the differences lie mainly in emphasis and tradition. Soto training relies more on *zazen* and Rinzai more on koans.

The numbers of people in Japan who practise Zen are not large, but the tradition has had a profound influence on Japanese culture. Many of these cultural influences spread through the tea ceremony. The design of tea bowls, the flower arrangements, and above all the atmosphere of quiet refinement associated with the tea ritual all came to be reflected in classical Japanese culture.

### Jodo: Japanese Pure Land

In Japan, Pure Land Buddhism is called Jodo (from Chinese Jingtu), its Buddha is called Amida (from Omitofo), and the female bodhisattva is called Kannon (from Guanyin). Most Buddhists in Japan today belong to the Jodo school.

Pure Land Buddhism was introduced to Japan by a monk named Honen (1133–1212). A man

## Pure Land Buddhism: Honen's Testament

The method of final salvation that I have propounded is neither a sort of meditation, such as has been practised by many scholars in China or Japan, nor is it a repetition of the Buddha's name by those who have studied and understood the deep meaning of it. It is nothing but the mere repetition of the 'Namu Amida Butsu', without a doubt of his mercy, whereby one may be born into the Land of Perfect Bliss. The mere repetition with firm faith includes all the practical details, such as the three-fold preparation of mind and the four primordial truths. If I as an individual had any doctrine more profound than this, I should . . . be left out of the Vow of the Amida Buddha (Tsunoda 1958: 208).

of saintly reputation, Honen wanted to provide a simpler way to salvation for those unable to undertake the demanding program prescribed in the *Meditation on Amitayus Sutra*. The devotional practice that he taught relied entirely on faith in Amida's power of salvation, and consisted in chanting the 'Homage to Amida Buddha' mantra. Repeated chanting of this phrase, called the *nenbutsu* in Japanese, leads to a spiritual state of consciousness. During services, the chanting often starts slowly and then quickens to a feverish pace. (For a detailed discussion of Pure Land in Japan, see Chapter 7.)

Honen's disciple Shinran (1173–1262) further developed Pure Land Buddhism in Japan, underlining the need for the 'other-power' of Amida's grace in a 'degenerate' age when Buddhist dharma was thought to be in a phase of decline. Condemning the magical and syncretic tendencies that he saw in other schools, Shinran taught the *nenbutsu* as an act of faith and thanksgiving. In a moving passage about the salvation of the wicked, Shinran says:

People generally think . . . that if even a wicked man can be reborn in the Pure Land, how much more so a good man! This latter view may at first sight seem reasonable, but it is not in accord with the purpose of the Original Vow, with faith in the Power

of Another. The reason for this is that he who, relying on his own power, undertakes to perform meritorious deeds, has no intention of relying on the Power of Another and is not the object of the Original Vow of Amida. Should he, however, abandon his reliance on his own power and put his trust in the Power of Another, he can be born in the True Land of Recompense. . . . Amida made his Vow with the intention of bringing wicked men to Buddhahood. Therefore the wicked man who depends on the Power of Another is the prime object of salvation (Tannisho; Tsunoda 1958: 217).

Both Honen and Shinran met with opposition from rival schools and were exiled by the authorities, but they found wide support among the people. Shinran founded a new sect called Jodo Shinshu ('True Pure Land') or Shin Buddhism. He also did something revolutionary: like Martin Luther, the German priest whose reforms led to the Protestant Reformation in sixteenth-century Europe, he chose to marry, maintaining that husband and wife are to each other as the bodhisattva Kannon is to the believer. In so doing he laicized Buddhism. Although this break with the tradition of monastic celibacy was widely opposed, today most Buddhist priests in Japan are married, and temples are usually passed down through their families; the oldest son is typically called the 'temple son' and expected to train for the priesthood so that he can continue the family tradition.

Shin Buddhism grew significantly under the fifteenth-century patriarch Rennyo (1415–49), who wrote pastoral letters to the faithful and rebuilt the Honganji temple in Kyoto. Today it remains the largest Buddhist sect in Japan.

### Nichiren

Nichiren Buddhism was founded by a controversial monk with the religious name Nichiren ('Sun and Lotus'; 1222–82). He had studied on Mount Hiei but left because he believed that Tendai had abandoned the teachings of its central scripture, the *Lotus Sutra*. His own message was very simple. Whereas the Pure Land school placed its trust in Amida, Nichiren placed his in the power of the *Lotus Sutra* itself.

Like the Pure Land Buddhists who invoked the power of Amida simply by calling on his name, Nichiren sought to invoke the power of the *Lotus Sutra* by repeating the words '*namu myoho renge kyo*' ('Homage to the *Lotus Sutra*') as a chant or mantra. Nichiren inscribed this formula, called the Daimoku, on a calligraphic scroll, the Gohonzon, kept at the temple of the Nichiren Shoshu sect at Taisekiji, near Mount Fuji. Each disciple has a small Gohonzon for personal devotional use.

Starting out as a reformer, Nichiren established a new, characteristically Japanese form of Buddhism that became associated with Japanese nationalism at a time when the country feared a Mongol invasion. In the fifteenth century, with the collapse of political order during the 'warring states' period, Nichiren Buddhists rose up in arms.

Nichiren was aggressive in attacking other Buddhist sects, especially Pure Land and Zen. For this he was sentenced to death; but an apparent miracle intervened, so instead he was exiled to an island, where he wrote extensively. For him Japan was a sacred land, the land of the Lotus Sutra.

### Ji

Ji Buddhism is associated with the monk Ippen (1239–89), a practitioner of the *nenbutsu* and a preacher of simple sermons. 'Ji' refers to 'occasions', like those that gave rise to groups or assemblies that he gathered together for ritual purposes. These groups had no fixed abode and no consolidated organization. Ji Buddhism also advocated the integration of Shinto divinities with Buddhist worship.

## Vajrayana, The Third Vehicle

'Vajrayana'—from *vajra*, meaning both 'diamond' and 'thunderbolt'—is just one of several names for the third vehicle of Buddhism. The image of the diamond suggests something so hard that it cannot be broken or split, while the thunderbolt suggests a very particular kind of power. Long before the emergence of Buddhism, the thunderbolt was the sceptre of the Hindu storm god Indra, the symbol of his power. It came to be represented by a wand shaped somewhat like an hourglass, or a three-dimensional version of the familiar symbol of infinity. Such wands are used regularly by Vajrayana Buddhists in ritual. Despite the thunderbolt connection, however, the symbolism of the wand is not physical or astronomical. Rather, the curved prongs represent various buddhas, and the power that the wand symbolizes is the power of the enlightened awareness—itself unbreakable, but capable of shattering spiritual obstacles such as ignorance, greed, or hatred. It remains a central symbol in the principal Vajrayana school today, Tibetan Buddhism.

Followers of Vajrayana refer to it as the 'third turning of the wheel of dharma', the culmination of the two earlier vehicles, Theravada and Mahayana. This is exemplified in a system of Vajrayana training with three stages named after the three vehicles. In the 'Hinayana' phase of practice, beginners concentrate on basic moral discipline. In the 'Mahayana' stage, they receive instruction

A large *vajra* in the courtyard of the Swayambhunath temple in Kathmandu makes a comfortable perch for people-watching (Roy C. Amore).

in basic Mahayana doctrines. And in the third and highest stage, the Vajrayana, they learn Vajrayana doctrines and practices—the ones that Vajrayana itself considers the most advanced.

The view of Vajrayana as the third turning of the wheel also makes sense in historical terms, for it emerged at a later period than Theravada and Mahayana. Arising in India during or after the third century, Vajrayana was subsequently taken to virtually all parts of the Buddhist world: to Southeast Asia, Central Asia, and in the course of time to Japan. In many of these regions, however, Vajrayana either died out or remained a minor influence. It disappeared from Southeast Asian (Theravada) countries centuries ago, and in East Asia it had to settle for a minor role in relation to the more popular Mahayana schools.

Vajrayana became the majority religion, however, in the region of Nepal and Bhutan, and across the Himalayas in Tibet and Mongolia. Hence some refer to Theravada as 'southern', Mahayana as 'eastern', and Vajrayana as 'northern' Buddhism—northern, that is, from the point of view of the Ganges region where Buddhism first developed.

Vajrayana incorporates numerous elements that originated in India, in both Hindu and Buddhist practice, but often gives its own emphasis to them. An example is its use of mantras, sacred syllables or phrases thought to evoke great spiritual blessings when properly spoken or chanted. In many respects, the Vajrayana (also known as Mantrayana) tradition's emphasis on sound recalls the ancient brahminic tradition in which the priests' chanting of the ritual formulas in itself had a particular acoustic efficacy.

The use of mantras in Vajrayana Buddhism, however, took a very different form. A Vajrayana mantra was a closely guarded, secret teaching, passed only from master to initiated pupil. For this reason the Vajrayana tradition is sometimes referred to as 'esoteric' Buddhism.

Finally, Vajrayana is often called 'tantric' Buddhism. Like Hindu tantrism, Buddhist tantrism envisions cosmic reality as the interplay of male and female forces and teaches a set of practical techniques for tapping into the spiritual energy produced by that interplay. The image of a male figure in sexual embrace with his female consort is common in Vajrayana art. Known in Tibetan as the *yab-yum* (father-mother), this union of male and female symbolizes the coming together of the complementary elements, such as compassion and wisdom, essential to enlightenment.

Thus a central component of tantric Buddhism is the concept of sexual union. Some tantric texts suggest that since the world is bound by lust, it is to be released by lust. While the 'right-hand' school understood this symbolically, the 'left-hand' school understood it in a more literal fashion, practising ritual unions in which a man and woman visualized themselves as divine beings. Such practices, properly undertaken, would confront lust, defeat it, and transcend it. The texts that lay out such techniques are called tantras. The Tibetan canon includes a vast library of tantras under the heading Kanjur and various commentaries under the heading Tanjur.

The Vajrayana tantras classify the many buddhas and bodhisattvas in various families, which are often depicted in a sacred geometric design called a **mandala**. For example, the 'head' of the family will occupy the place of honour in the centre of the design, surrounded by the other members of the family, each of which occupies a specific position.

Practitioners meditate on a particular buddha or bodhisattva in order to achieve a vision that will help them along the path to enlightenment. The Vajrayana guru initiates the disciple into the symbolic meanings of the various members of the family and their relationships, as well as the rituals required to develop inner wisdom.

Having built up a visualization, practitioners begin to identify with their chosen figures and tap into their energies. Visualizing themselves as identical with them, practitioners become aware of the centres of power (chakras) in their own bodies and may perceive themselves to be at the centre of a sacred space defined by a mandala. At the culmination of this process of gradual enlightenment, initiates aspire to dissolve slowly into emptiness (*shunyata*), liberated from ego attachment.

A classic mandala pattern reflects tantric Buddhism's emphasis on the *Mahavairocana* ('Great Sun') *Sutra*. For example, a mandala might centre on Mahavairocana, surrounded by the buddhas of the four directions: Aksobhya in the east, Amida in the west, Amoghasiddhi in the north, and Ratnasambhava in the south, all of whom together represent the various emanations of buddhahood itself. It is also characteristic of tantric Buddhism to give female counterparts not only to the buddhas but to the bodhisattvas who accompany them; as a result, mandalas often include numerous figures.

These deities have dual aspects, pacific and angry, depending on their functions (e.g., to assist in beneficial activities or to repel evil forces). The union of wisdom and compassion, considered the key to enlightenment, is represented by the father–mother image evoked by the embrace of deities and their consorts.

### Vajrayana in East Asia

Introduced to China in the eighth century under the name Zhenyan ('true word' or 'mantra'), tantric Buddhism enjoyed only a brief period of popularity as a novelty there. In 806, however, a Japanese monk who had been studying in China introduced Zhenyan to his homeland. Shingon Buddhism, as it came to be known, flourished in Japan and is still practised there today.

Shingon tantrism is of the 'right-hand' type. For the Shingon school, enlightenment consists in the realization that one's own Buddha-nature is identical with the Great Sun Buddha, Mahavairocana, and can be achieved in this life, in this world, through the esoteric teachings of Shingon.

Zhenyan was transmitted to Korea in the same period. Known there as Milgyo, it maintained a distinctive identity until the fourteenth century, when it was amalgamated with Mahayana schools.

## Vajrayana in Tibet

Shakyamuni had been born in the foothills of the Himalayas, and he had converted his home region (now part of Nepal) a few years after his enlightenment. But the high Himalayan plateau was so difficult to reach that Buddhism made little headway there for the first 1,200 years of its history. It was not until the late eighth century that a few Buddhist texts and missionaries found their way to Tibet at the invitation of Tibetan kings.

Vajrayana is said to have been established in Tibet by a *bhikshu* named Padmasambhava. Revered as Guru **Rinpoche** ('precious teacher'), he combined instruction in dharma with magical practices involving the world of the spirits. The figure of Padmasambhava is particularly identified with a school of Tibetan Buddhism known as the Nyingma, the 'ancient' school that dates back to his time.

The indigenous religion of the region when Buddhism arrived is known as Bon (a name meaning 'truth' or 'reality'). Little is known of Bon belief and practice in that era, but most scholars agree that its ritual objectives included the safe conduct of the soul to an existence in a land beyond death. To get the soul to that realm, the Bon priests would sacrifice an animal such as a yak, a horse, or a sheep during the funeral ritual. Kings were buried in large funeral mounds that resemble Chinese tomb mounds.

The Bon religion appears to have combined and interacted with Buddhism in Tibet, but elements of it have survived to the present day. One element that distinguishes Bon from Buddhism is the claim that it originated not in India but in a mythical region west of Tibet named Ta-zig (from the same root as 'Tajikistan') or Shambhala. Today some Tibetans still identify themselves with Bon rather than, or alongside, Buddhism.

Tibetan Buddhism is divided among three main ordination lineages or orders. The best-known, the Gelugpa, was founded by the reformer Tsongkhapa (1357–1419). On ceremonial occasions, members of this order wear large yellow hats, whereas members of the Kargyu and Karma-pa orders wear red and black hats, respectively. The ceremonial hats and robes of past masters are preserved in some Buddhist monasteries.

### The Controversy over Tibet

To understand the office of Dalai Lama and the controversial Chinese claim that Tibet is a part of China, we need to understand the historic relationship between Tibet and the Mongols. As the rulers of China from 1222 to 1368, the Mongols did not invade Tibet. They did, however, appoint the head of the Shakya monastery to serve as their viceroy for the region. Some two centuries later, a Gelugpa missionary named Sonam Gyatso (1543–88) went to Mongolia and converted its ruler, Altan Khan, who created the title Dalai Lama ('Ocean of Wisdom') and bestowed it posthumously on Gyatso's two predecessors, designating Gyatso the third in the succession. With the sponsorship of the Mongol princes, the Gelugpas soon became the dominant sect in both Mongolia and Tibet.

The first Dalai Lama to become the temporal as well as the spiritual leader of Tibet was the fifth, Ngawang Lobsang Gyatso (1617–82). With Mongol aid he subdued the challenge of the rival Karma-pa lineage and constructed the famous Potala palace in Lhasa. He recognized his teacher, Lobsang Chogye Gyaltsen (1569–1662), as an incarnation of the bodhisattva Amida and gave him the title Panchen Lama. The position of the Panchen Lamas still exists, but has become controversial because the Dalai Lama and the Chinese government disagree on the identity of the legitimate Panchen Lama.

The fifth Dalai Lama also established diplomatic relations with the Manchu (Qing) dynasty, which came to power in China in 1644. As a result, Tibet became embroiled in the eighteenth-century rivalry between the Manchus in Beijing and the Oirots of Mongolia, and became a Manchu protectorate. These old Tibetan ties with Mongolia and China are the basis of modern China's claim to Tibet. The former Tibet is now divided into three Chinese provinces known collectively as the Tibetan Autonomous Region, or TAR.

# 🦎 PRACTICE

Shakyamuni himself disapproved of the rituals conducted by the brahmins of his day, especially those involving animal sacrifice. He also recognized the potential for ritual and doctrine to become objects of attachment and warned his followers against becoming dependent on them. To make his point, he told a parable about a man who builds a raft to cross a flooded river during the rainy season and then, because it has been so useful, decides to carry it with him over dry land. Doctrine and rituals, he said, are like rafts: they can be useful, but should not become a burden on the journey towards mental purification and nirvana.

Despite the Buddha's teachings, however, all forms of Buddhism soon developed their own rituals. Although there were no specific Buddhist rituals for life-cycle events such as the naming of an infant, coming of age, marriage, or death, 'blessing' rituals centring on the chanting of sacred texts developed throughout the Buddhist world to mark these occasions. Participating in these rituals came to be seen as a way of earning merit, as did the building of stupas, the painting of Buddhist scenes, the creation of images, and the copying of scriptures.

We have already mentioned the custom of releasing captive birds during important Buddhist festivals. Eventually, it became common for young people to catch birds specifically in order to sell them to pious Buddhists hoping to earn merit by releasing them.

Four places associated with Shakyamuni himself became important pilgrimage sites—Lumbini (birth), Bodh Gaya (enlightenment), Sarnath (first sermon), and Kushinagar (*parinirvana*)—and as Buddhism spread, a number of places in other countries also became pilgrimage destinations.

## Theravada Practice

The most common Theravada ritual is the Buddha-puja. Typically, when visiting a temple, Buddhists pay respect to the guardian spirit at the entrance and place flowers on altars near the stupa and Bodhi tree before proceeding into the temple to place flowers on the altar(s) there. They may also put coins into an offering box. Then they say prayers expressing their dedication to living according to the dharma. In front of the main altar, they perform the Buddha-puja, chanting praise to the Buddha and vowing to observe the 'five precepts'. Unlike the 'commandments' of the Judeo-Christian tradition, these precepts are moral rules that Buddhists voluntarily undertake to follow. The Buddhist vows to refrain from

- taking life
- taking that which is not given
- sensual misconduct (sexual immorality)
- wrong speech (lying, slander and the like) and
- intoxicants leading to the loss of mindfulness.

On holy days lay Buddhists may undertake to observe additional precepts.

Theravadins also perform a number of more elaborate 'merit-making' rituals specifically designed to produce good karma. Of these, three of the most important are almsgiving, the *dana* ritual, and the Buddha Day (Vaishakha) festival.

## Almsgiving

Traditionally, members of the sangha would leave the monastery early each morning carrying bowls to collect their daily food. As they moved slowly through the streets without speaking, their eyes downcast to maintain a tranquil, composed state of mind, laypeople would come out of their houses, put cooked food into the alms bowls, and then bow low or prostrate themselves as a sign of respect.

The practice of going for alms is increasingly rare today. It is still common in Thailand, however, and efforts have been made to revive it in Sri Lanka. In other countries, such as Malaysia, the ritual is performed in the vicinity of the temple on important Buddhist occasions. People bring rice and food packets from home and put their offerings in the alms bowls as the *bhikshus* proceed along the road near the temple.

## The Dana Ritual

The practice of giving food and other necessities to the sangha has developed into a ritual called *dana*, from the Sanskrit word for 'giving'. A *dana* might be held at a temple or a pilgrimage site, but is often held by a family in their home to celebrate some important occasion. The following description of a *dana* ceremony in a Sri Lankan home offers a glimpse of several other Buddhist rituals as well.

As the monks arrive at the door, their feet are washed by the men of the family. (If the guests were *bikshunis*, this hospitality ritual would be performed by the women of the family.) On entering the home, the *bhikshus* first bow before the Buddha altar. Then they seat themselves on the floor around the room and conduct a Buddha-puja, after which they chant from a collection of scriptures called *paritta*.

Preparations for the next ritual are made before the chanting begins and involve running a string from the Buddha image on the home altar to a pot containing water, then to the monks, and finally to all the laypeople. The monks and laypeople hold the string in their right hands during the chanting and dharma talk. The water and the string become sacred objects through the power of the chanting. The chanting is followed by a merit-transfer ritual, in which the merit made by all present through their participation is transferred 'to all living beings': 'May the merit made by me now or at some other time be shared among all beings here infinite, immeasurable; those dear to me and virtuous as mothers or as fathers are, . . . to others neutral, hostile too. . . .'

In some respects merit transfer resembles the old Roman Catholic traditions of performing penance or purchasing 'indulgences' for the benefit of deceased relatives; the Buddhist merit transfer is intended to help one's ancestors, and others, in the afterlife. Although the practice might seem to violate the early Buddhist principle that all of us must make our own karma, according to the scriptures Shakyamuni himself advocated it.

After the merit-transfer ritual, the *bhikshus* cut the string into short pieces, which they tie around the right wrist of each male. A layperson ties a string around the wrists of the women, because monks and nuns are not supposed to come into contact with members of the opposite sex. The string is left on the wrist until it falls off.

## Vesak, the Buddha Day Festival

Many Buddhist festivals developed out of earlier seasonal festivals, and there are variations from country to country. However, Buddhists in most countries celebrate the day of the full moon in the 'rains' month, known in Theravada countries as Vesak (Sanskrit Vaishakha). In English-speaking countries this festival is often called 'Buddha Day'. According to Buddhist tradition, three major events in the life of Shakyamuni occurred on that day: his birth, his enlightenment, and his *parinirvana*.

One of the rock inscriptions recounting King Ashoka's accomplishments from 259 BCE, states that he organized a procession to be held annually on Vaishakha day. In contemporary Sri Lanka, the custom is for Buddhists to travel from place to place to see special paintings depicting scenes from the life of the Buddha. Talks are given on Shakyamuni's life, and special Buddha-pujas are performed.

### Life-cyle and Death Rituals

Early Indian Buddhists continued to follow the life-cycle rituals of what we now call Hinduism, and as Buddhism spread, converts in other regions similarly continued to celebrate their traditional life-cycle rituals. Thus there are no specifically Buddhist wedding or childhood rituals. It is in part for this reason that Buddhism has co-existed with the traditional belief systems of each country where it has established itself: Sri Lankan Buddhists continue to observe Indian rituals; Thai Buddhists still worship the traditional spirits; and Japanese Buddhists still visit Shinto shrines.

There is a Theravada funeral ritual, however, based on the ancient Indian cremation ceremony. The funeral includes a procession, ritual prayers, a water-pouring ritual, final prayers, and a communal meal. But the pattern varies from country to country. Cremation is not mandatory, for example, and so burial is practised where the cost of wood is prohibitive.

A traditional Buddhist funeral in Sri Lanka illustrates the principal features of the ceremony. On the day of burial, the corpse is taken in a procession to the cemetery along a route prepared in advance by filling in potholes, cutting the grass and weeds beside the road, and placing flowers along the way. These preparations reflect traditions that have parallels in many parts of the ancient world (Christians may recall the preparations made for Jesus' procession into Jerusalem on Palm Sunday).

At the cemetery the body is placed in a temporary wooden structure above a funeral pyre. A brief service is then held that includes chants, prayers, and a ritual in which family members and friends take turns pouring holy water from one container into another while a long prayer is chanted. After the service the pyre is lit, ideally by the eldest son of the deceased. In the event that a crematorium is used instead of a funeral pyre, some aspects of the traditional ceremony, such as the water-pouring ritual, are postponed until the *dana* held on the seventh day after the death, but one or more *bhikshus* will still come to recite prayers over the body.

The loss of a loved one is always a difficult experience, but Buddhists prepare for it through years of prayer and meditation on the inevitability of death. One of Buddhism's strengths is the way it helps its followers to develop a realistic view of the end of life through rituals that remind the living of how all things pass away.

Buddhist death rituals do not end with the burial. On the sixth night after the death, a dharma-preaching service is held at the home, followed by a *dana* on the morning of the seventh day. Other memorial *dana* rituals are held at the home of the deceased after three months, on the eve of which *bhikshus* may be invited to chant all night long, and after one year. Family members and friends who live too far away to attend the funeral itself are able to participate in these memorials. After the passage of time has lessened the pain (*duhkha*) of losing a loved one, the memorial services provide an occasion for the family and friends to remember the happy times with the deceased and to enjoy a family reunion.

### Vipassana Meditation

Theravada Buddhists practise a simple form of meditation called **vipassana** ('insight' or 'mindfulness'). While sitting in a meditational posture, practitioners concentrate on their breathing, focusing either on the sensation of air passing through the nostrils or on the rising and falling of the abdomen. Although the breaths are usually counted (in cycles of ten), the point is not to keep track of the number but to focus the mind. Unlike some forms of yoga, *vipassana* does not require practitioners to slow the rate of breathing. Practitioners may also cultivate mindfulness of other parts of the body, personal emotions, or relationships with others. The goal is to live in a totally mindful way.

## Mahayana Practice

### The Bodhisattva Practice

Many of the most important features of Mahayana centre on the role of the bodhisattva. There was in early Buddhism a sense that bodhisattvas could assist others along the right path not only through instruction but through their own past merit. Mahayana greatly developed this notion, to the point that one of the chief characteristics of Mahayana is the idea that bodhisattvas share their merit with all beings. Having advanced very close to total enlightenment, they are reborn in one of the heavens, and from there they stand ready to share their great merit with all who turn to them for help. Mahayana cosmology envisions many spiritually advanced bodhisattvas, each presiding over a heavenly region, from which he or she may bestow merit on those humans who pray for help.

### Bodhisattva Vows

Another Mahayana characteristic follows directly: the practice of taking bodhisattva vows. As we have seen, early Indian Buddhism taught that in a previous era, Shakyamuni had vowed to become a buddha one day. In early Buddhism, however, Shakyamuni's 'bodhisattva vow' was understood as a special case. Few Buddhists dared to think that they themselves were destined to become the buddha of some future era: they were content to hope that they could in some future life enter the sangha and achieve the status of Arhat ('worthy one' or saint).

It was the self-centred nature of this ambition, focused on personal liberation alone, that Mahayana philosophers criticized. They argued that those who take bodhisattva vows are dedicating themselves to the salvation of all living beings. All Mahayana Buddhists—male or female, lay or monastic—were encouraged to take the bodhisattva vows declaring their intention to become buddhas some day, but also to remain active in helping to liberate all beings.

### Veneration of Bodhisattvas

In practical terms, taking the bodhisattva vow meant vowing to be reborn in a heaven from which one could transfer merit to others. Although the possibility of helping others in this world by accepting rebirth as a human was not ruled out, the advanced bodhisattvas were thought to live in a heavenly realm. This provides the background for another Mahayana characteristic, the veneration of bodhisattvas.

Early Indian Buddhism paid respect to Shakyamuni but believed that after his *parinirvana* he had moved beyond the realm of direct involvement with human lives. Therefore Theravada Buddhists do not think of themselves as praying to the Buddha. Theravada has no tradition of praying for assistance in the way that theistic religions such as Christianity, Islam, devotional Hinduism, or Shinto do. Mahayana Buddhism, by contrast, holds that numerous bodhisattvas are available to respond to the petitions of worshippers. Mahayana Buddhists can ask the bodhisattvas for blessings or assistance in much the same way that Roman Catholics pray to the saints for intervention.

Only a few individual bodhisattvas are venerated by name, and these important bodhisattvas have their special functions. Bodhisattva Maitreya, the 'Friendly One', is destined to be the next buddha. He will come after the dharma wheel set in motion by Shakyamuni has stopped turning and the world needs a new fully enlightened buddha to teach dharma. As mentioned earlier, some Mahayana Buddhists pray to Maitreya, requesting that they be reborn when that time comes, because it will be so much easier to reach enlightenment when there is a living buddha to follow.

With the emergence of Mahayana Buddhism, the distinction between the buddha who enters nirvana and the bodhisattva who has earned entry but chooses to forgo it almost disappears. The bodhisattvas have had enormous appeal as saviour figures in Mahayana Buddhism. In their compassionate self-sacrifice, they have been compared to the Christian Jesus.

## Meditation

Meditation is an important practice in all forms of Buddhism, including Mahayana. Monastic training involves careful attention to the posture of the body and the method of concentration. The goals include the quieting of the mind and the heightening of mental alertness. The ultimate goal is to break through into a state of pure mind known as the buddha-mind or emptiness (*shunyata*). In some Mahayana schools, terms such as 'buddha-nature' and 'buddha-mind' became virtual synonyms for 'enlightenment'.

The practice of meditation is particularly intense among Soto Zen monks. One famous Soto monk kept his seat cushion in the sleeve pocket of his robe so that he could practise sitting meditation (*zazen*) whenever a moment of free time presented itself. When done in groups, the leader signals the beginning of the session by striking a bell. Typically, after roughly half an hour of sitting meditation during which they have focused attention on their breathing, the bell is rung again, signalling that it is time to rise and practise walking meditation—focused on the slow lifting of the feet high off the ground—for a similar length of time. Then another bell signals a return to a period of sitting meditation.

## Koan Training and Sudden Enlightenment

The use of koans is a Zen practice that is especially closely associated with the Rinzai sect. A standard collection of koans called the Mumonkan is used in training. The first koan presented to disciples is known as 'Joshu's *Mu*'. It tells of a time when the ancient master Joshu and a disciple were walking through the monastery grounds and saw one of the stray dogs that had made the monastery their home. The disciple asks Joshu, 'Does a dog have buddha-nature?' Joshu replies '*mu*' ('no'; *wu* in the Chinese original). There are many layers to this reply. On the surface, we might say that the standard Buddhist answer to the question would obviously be 'yes', since all living beings have buddha-nature. Yet Joshu answers with a word that seems to deny that fundamental doctrine. The key to this paradox lies in the fact that *mu*, 'no', is the very word used in Buddhism to express emptiness, the 'nothingness' state of mind that characterizes the buddha mind. Thus Joshu's negation is in reality an affirmation.

What is the poor student to make of this? The correct response to the koan lies not so much in a rational explanation as in the experience of intuitively breaking through the confines of the rational mind. It is the master's task to reject all false responses to the koan until a proper response is achieved. In koan training, disciples must report to the master regularly to respond to the assigned koan. Masters have been know to shout at or hit students who respond with inadequate 'answers'. The disciples' efforts to master this first koan might go on for days, months, or years, until one day the mental breakthrough into a new level of consciousness occurs.

Roshi Robert Aitkin of the Zen Center in Hawaii tells a story from his time as one of a group of students assigned 'Joshu's *Mu*' in Japan. One of the other students, frustrated at working on the koan in silence, began to shout: 'mu! muU! muUU! muuuuuuuUU!'. As the others worked on the koan in silence, he continued to shout, day after day. In the end, the master acknowledged his breakthrough, demonstrating that there is no single correct approach. Whatever the route taken, once a student has broken through to the first level of spiritual enlightenment, a second koan is assigned.

## Relic and Stupa Veneration

In Mahayana countries, the three anniversaries of the Buddha—his birth, his enlightenment, and his *parinirvana*—are remembered on separate days, determined by the lunar calendar. Festivals honouring other buddhas and bodhisattvas are also observed, especially Guanyin's birthday. Different sects also celebrate the anniversaries of their patriarchs (for example, Nichiren in Japan).

Under the influence of the ancestor cults of China and Japan, the dead are honoured by an 'all souls' day'. In China this day is celebrated by burning paper boats to free the *preta* ('hungry ghosts') who have perished in violence. In Japan, at the feast called Obon, two altars are built, one for offerings to the dead ancestors and the other for the 'ghosts'. Traditionally, Chinese Buddhists avoided non-essential outside activity during the 'ghosts' month', to lessen the risk of encountering a ghost.

Buddhism has also adopted local customs surrounding occasions such as New Year. In China pilgrimages are made to four sacred mountains, each dedicated to a different bodhisattva. In Japan the temple gong is struck 108 times on New Year's Eve, symbolizing forgiveness of the 108 kinds of bad deeds. Many Japanese gather at temples before midnight to hear the striking of the gong, but many more watch television coverage of the ceremony broadcast from a major monastery.

### Mantra Repetition

Practice in the Pure Land tradition focuses on opening oneself to the grace of the bodhisattva Amida (Amitabha). In this tradition rebirth is not earned by meritorious works and wisdom, as was the case with the path laid down by Shakyamuni, but granted through Amida's grace. The *Meditation on Amitayus Sutra*, which explains sixteen ways of meditating to achieve a vision of Amida, is an example of a Mahayana vision text. The promise of the meditation sutra is that whoever achieves a vision of Amida will be reborn in the Pure Land.

The Japanese Nichiren school adopted the practice of chanting a mantra, but instead of honouring Amida it honours the *Lotus Sutra*. In such practice, repeated chanting of the mantra carries the chanter into a blissful state of consciousness.

During a chanting ceremony, the pace of the chant often speeds up, and the sound may reach a dramatic crescendo.

## Vajrayana Practice

The use of mandalas in Vajrayana meditation has already been outlined. In addition, this tradition makes ritual use of mantras, as well as various gestures. Mantras need not be spoken to be effective; they can be written on banners or slips of paper and hung on trees or lines, or rotated in cylindrical containers called prayer wheels.

The best-known mantra is the phrase *Om mani padme hum*. Vajrayana Buddhists interpret this phrase in various ways. The words are Sanskrit: *om* and *hum* are sacred syllables, not words per se; *mani* means 'jewel'; and *padme* is 'lotus'. So in English we might say 'O the jewel in the lotus', or simply 'Om jewel lotus hum'. But Vajrayana Buddhists offer several interpretations. Some see the jewel and lotus as symbolic of the male and female principles, and understand their union to represent the harmony of the male and female cosmic forces. Others understand it to refer to the bodhisattva Avalokiteshvara in feminine form as the 'jewelled-lotus lady'. Some believe its six syllables refer to six realms of rebirth or six spiritual perfections. Whatever the interpretation, the mantra evokes a cosmic harmony.

A unique feature of Tibetan Buddhism is the text called the Bardo Thodol ('Liberation by Hearing on the After-Death Plane'), better known as The Tibetan Book of the Dead. A set of written instructions concerning the afterlife, the Bardo Thodol is meant to be read aloud to the dying in order to help them achieve liberation during the three stages of the *bardo* state between death and subsequent rebirth.

During the first stage the dying person loses consciousness, experiences a transitional time of darkness, and then emerges into a world filled with strange objects unknown on the earthly plane. A brilliant light then appears. If the person

Buddhist nuns during morning chanting service in Lhasa, Tibet (J. Essex).

recognizes the light as the Dharma Body of Buddha, he or she will attain liberation and experience nirvana rather than rebirth. More often, however, bad karma prevents people from recognizing the true nature of the light, and instead they turn away in fear. Thus most people then pass on to a second *bardo* stage in which some consciousness of objects is regained. One may be aware of one's own funeral, for example. Peaceful deities appear for seven days, then wrathful deities appear for seven more days. These are all the Buddha in the Body of Bliss form, and those who meditate on them as such will experience liberation. Those who do not recognize them will gradually assume a new bodily form within a few weeks of death. Liberation is possible right up to the moment of rebirth, but karma keeps most people in the grip of *samsara*, the wheel of death and rebirth. In the

third stage the individual's karma is judged and the appropriate rebirth is determined.

### Choosing a New Dalai Lama

Considered to be a manifestation of the bodhisattva Avalokiteshvara, each Dalai Lama is said to be the reincarnation of the previous one. When a Dalai Lama dies, a complicated search is undertaken to find a young boy who shows signs of being his reincarnation. The candidate must display intellectual qualities and personality characteristics similar to those of the deceased, and various objects are presented to the boy to see if he chooses ones that were his favourites. Finally, the State Oracle enters a trance state in order to contact the spirits to confirm the selection. The fourteenth and current Dalai Lama, Tenzin Gyatso, was chosen in this way from a family of Tibetan descent living in

## The Fourteenth Dalai Lama

**Born:** 6 July 1935, in a peasant farming village northeast of Lhasa. His name was Lhamo Thondup.

**Signs:** After the death of the thirteenth Dalai Lama, in 1933, the head of his corpse turned to the northeast, and a senior monk had a vision that included a monastery and a house with a distinctive guttering. When the party searching for his reincarnation finally found the house, in 1938, the three-year-old boy who lived there called one member of the party by name, and picked out the toys and other objects loved by the thirteenth Dalai Lama. He was then taken from his family to the monastery to begin training.

**Instruction:** After eighteen months the boy was reunited with his family, who moved with him to Lhasa. In 1940 he was ordained as a novice and installed as the spiritual leader of Tibet. A long course of Buddhist studies followed.

**High Office:** An earthquake and threats of invasion from China prompted his installation as the political leader of Tibet in 1950, at age fifteen.

**Exile:** By 1959 the Chinese had taken over Tibet. To avoid arrest or worse, the Dalai Lama crossed the Himalayas to Dharmsala in northern India, where he continues to lead a government in exile.

**Writings:** The Dalai Lama has travelled extensively and written numerous books on Tibetan Buddhism, meditation, and philosophy as well as an autobiography, *Freedom in Exile*.

**Politics:** The Dalai Lama continues to use non-violent means to advocate for the well-being of the Tibetan people. Negotiations with the Chinese government have so far not been fruitful.

China. A senior monk's vision played a key role in locating the boy.

# CULTURAL EXPRESSIONS

Because Buddhism has been the principal religion of many Asian countries, cultural expressions of its influence are widespread.

## Stupas and Pagodas

After the Buddha's *parinirvana*, several kings requested the honour of enshrining his cremated remains in their kingdoms. This created a dilemma that was brilliantly solved by the disciple in charge of funeral arrangements. He divided the remains into seven portions. The urn that had held the cremated remains and the cloth that had covered it were also given the status of primary relics, and so nine memorials were originally built over the nine relics. But as Buddhism spread to other parts of India, additional memorials were needed to create sites for Buddhist rituals. These memorials were built over other sacred objects, such as the cremated remains of Buddha's major disciples, or even portions of the Buddhist scriptures.

The architecture of the memorials has a rich history. The Buddha had been asked before his death about the proper way to bury him, and his response was that a Tathagata's remains should be enshrined in a memorial stupa like that of a great ruler. There is evidence from as far away as Ireland that the preferred way for burying Indo-Aryan rulers was to place their remains in an above-ground crypt, which was then covered with earth to form a large burial mound. Tables or platforms for offerings were then constructed in each of the four cardinal directions near the mound.

The funeral itself lasted seven days—the twenty-eight-day lunar month was divided into four such weeks—during which the mourners walked ceremonially around the mound and placed food, water, and flower offerings on the altars. Circumambulation is always clockwise, the devotee keeping the shrine to his or her right, a much more auspicious side than the left in Indian tradition. For the same reason, monks' robes keep the right shoulder bare while covering the left.

The cremated remains were placed in small caskets, about the size of shoe boxes, richly decorated with jewels, each of which was interred in a crypt made of stone slabs. The crypt was then covered over with a large mound of earth and a layer or two of bricks, which were plastered and finally whitewashed. Then the builders erected a pole, which was fixed in a square frame on top of the mound and positioned over the crypt.

The pole represents Mount Meru, a cosmic mountain that in Indian mythology reaches from earth up towards the pole star, and around whose axis the world is thought to turn. The part of the pole that extends above its support base symbolizes the upper reaches of the heavens. The pole runs through disks of wood that symbolize the layers of heaven. (The European parallel would be the notion of 'heavenly spheres'.) There are usually nine such layers, in keeping with Indian cosmology, which envisions nine layers of heaven and nine orbiting planetary bodies. The frame, the pole, and its planes later came to be built of stone because wooden parts were difficult to maintain.

There are several ways of referring to these white memorial mounds. The Sanskrit term *stupa* and its Pali equivalent, *thupa*, are cognate with the English word 'tomb'. Another name is *caitya*, which means 'shrine', or in this case 'burial shrine'. The name used throughout East Asian Buddhism

is '**pagoda**', which derives from another Sanskrit word for a monument, *dagoba*. It connotes 'womb' in the sense that burial is the forerunner of a rebirth. Whether the memorial structure is called stupa, *thupa*, *caitya*, or pagoda, nearly every Buddhist temple precinct in the world has one.

Legends arose claiming in each case that the relic of a particular stupa could be traced back to the Buddha himself. For example, important temples in Sri Lanka and Burma claimed to have an eye tooth of the Buddha enshrined in their stupas. Major Buddhist temples developed long chronicles detailing the legendary history of the relics enshrined in their stupas.

In addition to the large main stupa, a temple complex may often have smaller ones built as memorial crypts of important Buddhists of that particular temple. These small votive stupas add to the beauty and spiritual atmosphere of the temple grounds. In popular piety, Buddhists sometimes strew flower petals at such locations and vow that they, too, will someday overcome death and achieve nirvana.

Building small stupas as an act of devotion was especially popular as a merit-making practice in Myanmar, where thousands of devotional stupas have been built through the centuries. Some are built to last, such as the ones located near the ancient Burmese city of Pagan, but most are temporary structures, such as the ones devout Buddhists make from sand at the shore. The merit comes from purifying the mind while one builds the stupa in a devotional state of mind, and so it is not necessary that it endure for long.

The shape of the stupa or pagoda underwent changes through the centuries, especially when Buddhism spread to East Asia. There, pagodas eventually developed into elegant five- or seven-storied stone or wooden towers that devotees could either climb up or circumambulate. The stories of the East Asian pagoda derive from the various levels of the heavens symbolized by the wooden disks of the original Indian stupas. Such

Bodhanath, a Tibetan-style stupa with prayer flags in Kathmandu, Nepal. The eyes towards the top of the stupa are characteristic of Nepali temples (R. Amore).

pagoda architecture exaggerated the 'heavenly section' of the original stupa, making it the main part of the pagoda.

## Temples

Buddhist monasteries grew out of the simple refuges in which early monks lived during the rainy season—usually a collection of thatched huts located on the outskirts of a city. Wealthy devotees would earn merit by paying for the construction of permanent buildings, and over time a temple complex would take shape consisting of living quarters, a small shrine, and a meeting hall. Eventually, to accommodate large numbers of lay worshippers, the small shrine developed into a large temple housing images of the Buddha. Today, besides the stupa and temple, the grounds usually contain a Bodhi tree, dharma hall, monastery, library, and refectory, and are usually surrounded by an ornamental wall with elaborate entrances.

There are some similarities among temples in different parts of the ancient world. The typical ancient temple—whether in Israel, India, or elsewhere in southern and western Asia—is a rectangular building that is entered from one of the shorter sides. (In East Asian temples, access is from one of the longer sides.) Entering through a tall portico, the worshipper comes into an outer chamber that in some cases is open to the air and can hold large numbers of people. At the far end of the building is an image of the revered figure—or, in the Hebrew temple, some sort of throne but no image—flanked by attendant deities, angels, or supernatural animals. Often, but not always, there is an altar in front of the image where worshippers or priests representing them place flowers and other offerings. Songs of praise were usually sung, and lights and incense were lit. Ritual attendants brought food and water to the image of the deity, and fanned the image during hot weather. In every way the image was housed and treated like royalty.

Although early Buddhism did not consider the Buddha to be a god, Buddhists adopted the local temple practices. They place flowers on altars or platforms at the base of the stupa and near the Bodhi tree, and then proceed into the temple to place flowers on the altar(s) there. They say prayers expressing their dedication to living according to the dharma.

Early cave temples carved in stone were clearly modelled after the shapes of wooden structures. Simple huts that earlier sangha members had dwelt in during the rainy season, when they settled down for a period of intense study and meditation, may have been a prototype. By the Gupta period in India (c. 320–540), temples took on the rectangular shape and other architectural features of Hindu temples of the time.

In some regions of India, such as Ajanta and Ellora, cliffside cave complexes were developed that included all the essentials of a temple complex, including separate caves for shrines, living areas, and even large dharma halls. The practice of carving such cave complexes into cliffsides spread with Buddhism. Similar complexes can be found in China, such as the Longmen caves, and elsewhere. Such caves took on a political role during the presidency of George W. Bush. The Taliban's destruction of some colossal Bodhisattva images carved in a cliffside in Afghanistan played a role in gaining popular support for the US decision to invade Afghanistan and drive out the Taliban.

In China, the rectangular wooden buddha hall reflected the influence of the tile-roofed imperial hall of state, with the buddha statue enshrined in the posture of an emperor. This style was the one that made its way to Japan, the best-known example being the Todaiji, the Great East Monastery in Nara, which houses a bronze image of Vairocana, the cosmic buddha, more than 16 metres (52 feet) high.

## Images of the Buddha

It was almost five hundred years after the *parinirvana* of the Buddha before the first image of him was created. Until then, it was evidently assumed, particularly in Theravada Buddhism, that no physical form could or should depict him. In the intervening years, the Buddha and his teaching were symbolized by the stupa and other noniconic forms such as his footprint, the Wheel of the Law, the Bodhi tree, or an empty seat. These representations played an important role in the decoration of the stupa as well as its surrounding fence and gates.

Scholars suggest that the representations in stone and terra cotta that came later may have been developed from wooden models of this period. This copying of wooden patterns in stone can be seen in the masonry of the important stupa complex at Sanchi in central India. The detail of its carvings, with scenes from Shakyamuni's life, hints at another transition as well, for some of the teaching scenes might be interpreted as showing the bodhisattva in human form before his enlightenment, whereas the enlightened Buddha is still not depicted.

The first Buddha icons in stone emerged during the first century CE, at a time when the devotional aspects of Mahayana Buddhism were becoming increasingly popular. Images in statues and reliefs are depicted standing, seated in the lotus position of yogic meditation, seated with dangling legs, or reclining at the moment of the *parinirvana*.

Hand gestures or **mudras**, similar to those found in Hindu portrayals of deities, became an important feature of Buddhist art. In one, the Buddha touches the earth with the fingers of his right hand, 'calling the earth to witness' as he is said to have done in his encounter with Mara on the eve of his enlightenment. Another popular image depicts the Buddha in a posture of teaching. One *mudra* shows the Buddha with his right hand raised, palm outward and fingers upward, in a gesture indicating the 'granting of protection'. This is usually combined with a *mudra* in which the left hand is extended downward with the palm outward and fingers pointed down, a gesture that is interpreted as 'fulfilling a wish'. In some cases the Buddha reclining on his side is thought to represent Shakyamuni asleep; many Hindu temples also contain a statue of the sleeping deity. More commonly, though, a reclining Buddha represents the *parinirvana*.

Buddhist iconography also includes the thirty-two major signs of Shakyamuni's status, the most obvious of which are the *usnisa* (the protuberance on the top of his head that was supposed to be the locus of his supernatural wisdom) and elongated ear lobes. Some art historians think that these features were associated with royalty (elaborate hair styles, earlobes stretched by heavy earrings), but Buddhists see them as signs of Shakyamuni's supernatural nature. Other signs include wheel images on the soles of his feet and fingers all the same length.

Buddhist iconography in China typically shows the Buddha encircled by his company like an emperor surrounded by his court. The Buddha is seated in a serene posture, flanked by his disciples Kashyapa and Ananda. Nearby stand the bodhisattvas and stern-looking Arhats (*lohans* in Chinese). The Four World Protectors or Heavenly Kings often stand guard at the entrance or along the sides of the entrance hall. Each of the four is associated with one of the cardinal directions, and each one holds a characteristic object.

## Story Illustrations

Buddhist art, especially painting and relief carving, often illustrates scenes from the life of the Buddha or from the *Jataka* ('birth story') collections that recount the previous lives of Shakyamuni. The walls of temples are often lined with such art so that visitors can see the story of the Buddha's life unfold as they circumambulate the structure.

In ancient India, stupas located away from temple grounds were surrounded by an ornamental fence carved with scenes from the *Jatakas* and the Buddha's life. The great stupa in the complex at Sanchi, in central India, offers the most important example of such art. The fences that survive today are all made of stone, but the prototypes would have been carved in wood. The narrative illustration panels in temples continue the ancient pattern.

As Buddhism spread, other cultures developed their own distinctive iconography. In China, images of Shakyamuni gradually took on a more Chinese appearance, and the figure of Guanyin developed into the graceful, standing feminine form now found throughout East Asia. There is a distinctive Korean representation of Maitreya as a pensive prince with one leg crossed over the other knee. This kind of image also spread to Japan at the time of 'Prince' Shotoku. An example is the famous wooden statue of Maitreya—the greatest of all national treasures—in Koryuji temple, Kyoto, which was founded in 622 for the repose of Shotoku.

## Zen Art and the Tea Ceremony

The highly ritualized tea ceremony was introduced by Zen monks and spread from monasteries to become one of the most familiar symbols of Japanese culture, expressed in everything from special tea bowls to distinctive tea houses. The Zen influence is also reflected in the minimalism of Japanese painting, in which empty space plays a central role, and the raked-sand gardens (the space accented only by the occasional boulder) typically found in the courtyards of Zen temples such as Ryoanji in Kyoto. Another cultural expression of Zen values is the Japanese art of flower arranging, which originated in the practice of creating floral offerings for altars and special ceremonies.

# INTERACTION AND ADAPTATION

## China

Chinese converts interpreted a number of Buddhist ideas in ways that served to harmonize them with indigenous teachings, especially those associated with Daoism (see Chapter 6). An example is what happened to the doctrine of no-soul (*anatman*) or emptiness. East Asian Mahayana Buddhists equated emptiness with nothingness (in Chinese, *wu*; in Japanese, *mu*), which in turn was paradoxically interpreted in terms of fullness or the absolute.

The Buddhist concept of the afterlife was also adapted to conform to Chinese tradition. Chinese Buddhists extended the vague notion of the underworld and a home with their ancestors into a system of many-layered heavens and hells, with a variety of saviour figures. Among them are Guanyin and the bodhisattva Dizang ('earth-store'; Jizo in Japanese), who relieves the suffering of those reborn in hell. Similarly, the scripture *Yulanpenjing* tells the story of a monk named Mulian, who after his enlightenment sought to rescue his mother from hell. This Buddhist expression of filial piety was the basis for the 'all souls' day' celebrated on the fifteenth day of the seventh month in China, Korea, and Japan, where it is known as Obon. Buddhism in turn had some influence on Chinese Daoism and folk religion, which incorporated the

Buddhist idea of rebirth on a higher or lower level of life into the traditional system of retribution for good and evil.

The Buddhist tradition of monasticism was particularly alien to a social system based on kinship and veneration of ancestors. Not only were monks required to shave their hair, given by ancestors, but the practice of celibacy put the family lineage in jeopardy. Furthermore, endowments and donations enabled monasteries to acquire large areas of land and use serf labour to work the fields. Whereas Indian society respected the monks who begged for their living, Chinese society looked down on those who did no work. In time, therefore, Chinese monks incorporated labour into their discipline, growing their own food. As a Chinese Zen master proclaimed, 'A day without work is a day without eating.'

Imperial officials saw Buddhism as a direct threat to the state's authority, as this seventh-century memorial to the first Tang emperor shows:

> Thus people were made disloyal and unfilial, shaving their heads and discarding their sovereign and parents, becoming men without occupation and without means of subsistence, by which means they avoided the payment of rents and taxes. . . . I maintain that poverty and wealth, high station and low, are the products of a man's own efforts, but these ignorant Buddhist monks deceive people, saying with one voice that these things come from the Buddha. Thus they defraud the sovereign of his authority and usurp his power of reforming the people (Hughes and Hughes 1950: 77).

Two centuries later, in 845, the Chinese state launched a campaign of persecution against Buddhism that led to the destruction of more than forty thousand temples and the laicization of 260,500 monks and nuns.

## Folk Buddhism and the Milo Cult

The image of Maitreya underwent a transformation not unlike that of the Indian Avalokiteshvara into the Chinese Guanyin. Before the seventh century, Maitreya was a heroic figure, but he reappeared in the fifteenth century as Milo, a laughing monk with a pot-belly, carrying a hemp bag and accompanied by small children. According to the legend, Milo used to travel from village to village, putting interesting objects into his sack along the way. Then, on arriving at the next village, he would give them out as presents for the children, like Santa Claus. With his happy-go-lucky nature (in Sanskrit, *maitri* means friendly), his large belly, and his affinity for children, the 'Happy Buddha' reflects the importance that Chinese culture attached both to children and to worldly prosperity. His image is still popular today on altars and as an artistic decoration, especially in restaurants. On a very different political arena, Maitreya has more than once been the focus of political rebellions in China, including the one that led to the founding of the Ming dynasty (1368).

*[handwritten margin note: China emphases → children family / → maternal (gifts)]*

## Korea

As in other countries, new cults emerged in Korea that owed their inspiration to Buddhist teachings. The best-known is Won Buddhism, which was founded in the early twentieth century. This new religion seeks to modernize the old religion by translating the *sutras* into modern Korean, emphasizing social service, especially in the cities, and permitting monks to marry. Its meditation object is an image of a black circle on a white background, representing the cosmic body of the Buddha, the *dharmakaya*. In South Korea today Buddhist practice may include elements from a wide range of traditions: in a single monastery, some monks will worship Buddha Amida of the Pure Land while others practise Son (Zen) meditation or recite *sutras*.

## Japan

### Dual Shinto

The introduction of Buddhism did not oblige the Japanese to choose between competing systems of beliefs and rituals. Instead, a syncretistic system developed called Dual Shinto that combined elements of both traditions.

Shinto shrines were built within Buddhist temples, and Buddhist *sutras* were chanted at Shinto shrines. Eventually *jingu-ji*, the 'shrine–temple' system arose, in which a Buddhist temple would be located within a larger Shinto shrine. The famous red gateways called *torii* were erected at the entrances to Buddhist temples as well as Shinto shrines. Shinto gods were worshipped alongside buddhas and bodhisattvas as their Japanese 'incarnations'. A rationale for this fusion was the concept of *honji suijaku* ('original site and local manifestations'), in which the Buddhist deities were regarded as the original 'sites' and the Shinto deities as their local forms (for details on the dynamic interaction among the various religious traditions of Japan, see Chapter 7).

### Tokugawa 'Temple Buddhism'

By the late sixteenth century, its great monasteries and armed warrior-monks had made Japanese Buddhism a sufficiently important political and military force to represent a challenge to the shoguns. Although the Tokugawa shogunate (1603–1867) preferred Confucianism as a source of ideological guidance, it eventually required that each household be registered with a Buddhist temple, partly to discourage the spread of Christianity.

Following the restoration of imperial rule in 1867–8, Buddhism again fell into disfavour, partly because of its institutional identification with the shogunate and partly because of its foreign origins. The Meiji government greatly favoured Shinto, and it ordered that Buddhist images be removed from Shinto shrines.

# ❦ BUDDHISM IN THE MODERN WORLD

## Modern Forms of Monasticism and Ordained Women

Modern Buddhism has many forms of monasticism. Even something as basic as the colour of the robes varies from country to country and sometimes from one ordination lineage to another; colours range from the traditional saffron used in most Theravada countries to dark red, grey, or black in East Asia. Even the basic practice of celibacy is not universal. Although Buddhism has historically been a monastic religion with celibate monks, in Japan monastic celibacy was abolished many centuries ago.

As a monastic tradition, Buddhism has emphasized otherworldly values while also encouraging almsgiving and the protection of life. In our own time, the Buddhist religion all over the world has been active in promoting global peace.

Currently the biggest obstacle to re-establishing a *bhikshuni* sangha is that Buddhist rules require ordinations to be performed by at least five senior sangha members of the same sex as those being ordained. This rule has worked well as a way of discouraging the formation of schismatic ordination lineages, but whenever the main female ordination line has been lost, the only way to restore it has been to import senior *bhikshunis* from another country. These are hard to find today.

Despite this drawback, Theravada Buddhist laywomen are very active in their religion, both at home and in the temples. There are organizations of women Buddhists in Thailand, for example, who live a pious life and devote themselves to the service of others. They are not ordained *bhikshunis*, but some have taken vows of poverty and service similar to those taken by Roman Catholic nuns. Some of these women are not interested in becoming *bhikshunis* because they feel they have more freedom to serve others if they are not bound by the *vinaya* rules. This option is especially appealing to women whose children are grown or who are otherwise free of family responsibilities.

The status of women in some of the Mahayana texts is somewhat higher than it is in the earlier texts. The Mahayana movement was more sympathetic than earlier forms of Buddhism towards lay people and the rituals they practised, such as stupa worship. It raised the status of all lay Buddhists, but the higher status of the laity is especially noticeable in the case of women, for the texts mention a number of outstanding laywomen.

## Jewel Brocade

*In a Mahayana text called* The Sutra of Sagara, the Naga King, *a princess named Jewel Brocade cleverly uses the Mahayana doctrine of the emptiness of all things to refute a male disciple who represents the stereotypical patriarchal position. No distinction between male and female spiritual abilities is valid, she argues, because all distinctions are ultimately invalid:*

You have said: 'One cannot attain Buddhahood within a woman's body.' Then, one cannot attain it within a man's body either. What is the reason? Because only the virtuous have eyes of Emptiness. The one who perceives through Emptiness is neither male nor female. The ears, nose, mouth, body, and mind are also Empty (Paul 1979: 236).

Mahayana considered women capable of making spiritual progress towards enlightenment in a way that Theravada did not. One reason may be that Mahayana was less dominated by monasticism, which tends to be a stronghold of patriarchal attitudes. Another reason for the improved status of women in Mahayana was that both men and women were encouraged to take the bodhisattva vow.

For reasons such as these, women were encouraged to strive towards enlightenment despite the earlier Buddhist prejudice that serious spiritual progress was not possible during a lifetime spent in a female body. Later Mahayana texts not only showed a greater acceptance of female spiritual potential, but they also took the position that ideally the bodhisattva would advance to a point beyond gender. Over time, Theravada Buddhism also moved towards acceptance of women's capacity for high religious achievement. In Thailand, for example, one particular woman is highly revered for her mastery of meditation, and young *bhikshus* go to her meditation centre for instruction.

## Buddhism in Modern India

### The Decline of Buddhism

Buddhism's intellectual and institutional influence within India lasted for several centuries after the third-century reign of Ashoka. It was only in the seventh century CE that it began to decline.

In the past, Buddhism had enjoyed royal patronage but that support gradually disappeared as its royal patrons were replaced by Muslim rulers in northwestern India. Meanwhile, Muslim armies overran and destroyed many Buddhist universities. The scholar-monks and their students were under pressure to convert to Islam or face death. Some scholars fled to Tibet or elsewhere. With its centres of learning gone and the population converting to Islam, Buddhism dwindled.

A related factor may have been the loss of lay support for the monasteries. As many of the Buddhist teachings were absorbed into Hinduism and Indian tantric practices reshaped Buddhism, laypeople may have lost their motivation to support Buddhism rather than Hinduism. We know that some of the most famous Buddhist scholar-monks emigrated to Tibet from the eleventh century onward. Their departure to Buddhist universities abroad suggests that the great Buddhist universities of India were in decline.

To escape persecution, the remaining *bhikshus* fled either to the Himalayas or to the far eastern regions of India. As a result of this migration and the loss of lay adherents, Buddhism largely disappeared from India until the mid-twentieth century. It did survive, however, in Tibet, Nepal, Bhutan, Sikkim, Assam, and in a few regions of eastern India.

### Buddhism's Return to India

### B.R. Ambedkar and the Mass Conversion of Dalits

Only in the twentieth century did Buddhism begin to develop new adherents in India. One catalyst was Dr Bhimrao R. Ambedkar (1891–1956), the lead author of the Indian constitution. Although he was born into the 'untouchable' dalit class, his keen intelligence caught the attention of a brahmin teacher named Ambedkar, who formally adopted the boy so that he could have an upper-class name. This change of name allowed him to complete on a level playing field when he went for higher education. With the help of that teacher and the local Muslim ruler, the young Ambedkar earned an undergraduate degree in India and eventually a doctorate in economics from the London School of Economics. On his return to India he became an active advocate for dalit rights at a time when his older contemporary M.K. Gandhi was pursuing the same goal. The two disagreed, however, on the best way to that goal.

Ambedkar blamed Hinduism for the discrimination that dalits faced. Hindu leaders such as

Gandhi held out the hope that Hinduism could be reformed along lines that would eliminate or at least greatly reduce that discrimination, but Ambedkar foresaw that entrenched social and economic interests would make substantial reform impossible. Therefore he turned his back on Hinduism and set out to find a religion that would not discriminate against dalits. He found in Buddhism a form of spirituality that was compatible with Indian cultural values, but that from its origins had spoken out in favour of the equality of all humans, regardless of birth status.

The history of Buddhism supports Ambedkar's view. The Buddha accepted both lay and ordained members into his movement without any regard for their caste status, and he taught his disciples to ask not about caste but about character. The names of early Buddhist leaders suggest that all social classes were attracted to the movement. Social rank within the sangha was based solely on seniority as measured by the time since ordination.

The Buddha also criticized the brahmin priests, and early Buddhist stories make fun of pompous brahmins who exploit the lower classes. One such story tells of a brahmin who gained great prestige with the king because he knew a magical charm that would cause fruit to ripen out of season. He had in fact learned the charm from a low-caste person, who revealed the charm to him only on the condition that he would answer truthfully if anyone inquired about the origin of the charm. But when the king asked where he learned it, the brahmin was too proud to admit that he had learned something from a dalit. This lie broke the magic of the charm, and the brahmin fell into disgrace. Another story tells of the Buddha asking a low-caste Chandala woman for water. This story parallels the New Testament story of Jesus taking water from a Samaritan woman at a well.

In 1956, at a large rally in the historic city of Nagpur, in the heart of Hindu India, Ambedkar and his wife publicly took the Three Refuges and the Five Precepts from a Buddhist monk, and thousands of dalits followed their example. Since then, many more dalits have converted to Buddhism, though others have turned to Islam or Christianity instead, while others remain Hindu.

Shakyamuni's critique of social inequity has also contributed to a growing appreciation among Indian scholars of his place in Indian history. During the period of Buddhist–Hindu competition before Buddhism's decline, Hindus had claimed that Buddha was actually an *avatara* (incarnation) of Vishnu. Unlike Vishnu's other *avataras*—figures such as Rama and Krishna—the Buddha was said to have played a negative role, drawing undesirable people away from the 'true' religion. That some modern Hindu scholars accept the Buddha as an important and admirable figure in the religious history of India marks a significant change.

### Restoration of Monuments and the Mahabodhi Society

Under the leadership of Buddhists from Sri Lanka, the Mahabodhi Society of India was formed in 1891 with the purpose of restoring the country's Buddhist pilgrimage sites and revitalizing Indian Buddhism. With the permission of the Indian government, the Society in 1953 took charge of Bodh Gaya, the once grand pilgrimage spot that commemorates Shakyamuni's enlightenment. It has restored several of the ancient stupas at Bodh Gaya with financial contributions from Buddhists around the world and has made the site an active pilgrimage and learning centre. The ancient pilgrimage site that commemorates Shakyamuni's birth at Lumbini has been identified in southern Nepal (on the border with India, northeast of Lucknow and southwest of Kathmandu) and has likewise been returned to active use. Sarnath (near Varanasi), the site of the first sermon, and Kushinagar (near modern Gorakhpur), the site of the *parinirvana*, have also been restored.

## Theravada in Modern Sri Lanka

After the fifteenth century, Sri Lanka was colonized by the Portuguese, Dutch, and British in turn, each of which promoted some form of Christianity. Buddhism declined in prestige but hung on, and in the late 1800s efforts to revitalize the tradition received an important boost from the founders of the Theosophical Society, Helena P. Blavatsky (1831–91) and Henry S. Olcott (1832–1907). Sinhalese Buddhists have been active ever since in publishing English-language materials on Buddhism, and they remain loyal to Theravada Buddhism despite the presence of largely Hindu India to the north and five hundred years of Christian missionary efforts under the European colonial rulers. The Sinhalese take pride in Sri Lanka's status as a stronghold of Theravada, which they regard as the purest form of Buddhism.

Despite the political problems on the island, Sri Lankan Buddhism continues its rich intellectual and ritual life. The symbolic centre of that life is the Temple of the Tooth in Kandy, in the hills 100 kilometres (60 miles) northeast of Colombo. There an eye tooth that is said to be a relic of Shakyamuni himself is enshrined under a series of miniature gold stupas. The Perahera festival celebrating the relic at the time of the full moon in August illustrates the cross-fertilization of Hindu and Buddhist customs in Sri Lanka. One of the miniature gold stupas that house the tooth is placed in a howdah on the back of an elephant and paraded through the streets of Kandy for several nights. Each night the parade becomes larger and grander, and on the final day the sacred relic is given a ritual bath in a nearby river. This bathing ritual is an ancient tradition, and one Hindu temple even takes part in the festival. The torchlight processions, in which more than a hundred richly costumed elephants parade in groups of three, interspersed with groups of musicians and dancers, are among the world's most famous religious festivals.

Since independence in 1948, there has been a revival of Buddhist influence on Sri Lankan politics and Buddhism has had considerable influence on the policies of Sri Lanka's ruling parties, which draw support from the Sinhalese majority. This has led to feelings of oppression among members of the Hindu minority, most of whom are Tamils—descendants of people from Tamilnadu in South India who migrated to the island at various times over the past two millennia. (The Sinhalese are generally thought to have come from North India.) Conflict between the government and Tamil separatists seeking an independent homeland in the northern part of the island led to more than two decades of bloodshed, although Hinduism and Buddhism alike teach non-violence. The civil war finally came to an end in 2009, but relations between the two religious communities remain severely strained.

## Theravada in Modern Southeast Asia

Theravada also remains the most important vehicle across most of mainland Southeast Asia, though East Asian Mahayana traditions are dominant in Vietnam, Malaysia, and Singapore.

The end of Burmese kingship in the late nineteenth century, the years of British rule, and long periods of military rule since independence have weakened the Burmese sangha's traditional political influence. Lately, Myanmar's economy has remained out of the mainstream of modernization and industrialization, and over the past few decades its sangha members have been cut off from significant contact with other Buddhist countries. Its people are poor and its temples have fallen into disrepair, but its *bhikshus* are still important in the traditional village-centred society.

Similarly in modern Cambodia, the overthrow of Prince Norodom Sihanouk (r. 1941–55) meant the end of Buddhist kingship with its ideal of a government that provides the basic human needs for all citizens. Since then, the Cambodian sangha's political influence has been limited. During the period of the communist Khmer Rouge under Pol Pot (r. 1975–9), many *bhikshus* were among the innocents slaughtered in the 'killing fields'. Yet by the late 1980s, the monthly newsletter of the coalition of movements opposed to the new pro-Vietnamese government, which included the remnants of the Khmer Rouge, proudly pictured Khmer Rouge soldiers and *bhikshus* working together on village projects. Today most laypeople of all political stripes remain Buddhists, and all factions appeal to Buddhist values to help legitimate their claims to power. At the village level, Buddhism continues to play its traditional role.

In Thailand Buddhism retains some political influence. The tradition of monastic training for the king continues, and members of the royal family take part in Buddhist ceremonial occasions. The most important are the rituals in which the king, at the beginning of each season, changes the clothing on the Buddha image in the famous Temple of the Emerald Buddha and gives the Buddha image a ceremonial bath. These rituals symbolize the close ties between Thai Buddhism, the Thai monarchy, and Thai nationalism.

In Laos—under communist rule since the 1960s—Buddhism has lost the governmental support that it had traditionally enjoyed throughout Southeast Asia. The traditional relationship of *bhikshus* and laity continues in the villages, however.

Finally, although Theravada has never gained a foothold in Vietnam, Theravada missionaries have recently had some success in Singapore and Malaysia, especially among English-speaking Chinese. Apparently some of the Chinese Mahayana Buddhists in Singapore have been attracted to Theravada as a purer form of Buddhism than the Chinese Mahayana schools that have incorporated numerous elements of Chinese folk religion into their practice. The Young Buddhist Association of Malaysia has been very active in encouraging dharma study among young Buddhists.

Several Buddhist reform movements are having an impact on Theravada Buddhism today. For example, retreat centres have been established in Thailand in an effort to reintroduce the practice of meditation among laypeople. The Thai reformer *bhikshu* Buddhadasa (1906–93) severely criticized what he saw as the complacency of Thai Buddhists, lay and ordained, and urged them to be more diligent in meditation and the study of dharma. Other Theravada Buddhists have concentrated on social reform. The Thai intellectual Sulak Sivaraksa (b. 1932) has argued effectively for a Buddhist vision of society in which the means of development are harnessed for the good of everyone rather than the profit of a few capitalists. He has founded several Buddhist organizations dedicated to that goal, including the Asian Cultural Forum on Development and the International Network of Engaged Buddhists.

## Mahayana in Vietnam

It is difficult to say exactly when Buddhism was introduced to Vietnam. Theravada images and monastery foundations dating from before the ninth century have been found there, but Chinese Mahayana traditions—notably Thien (from Chinese Chan) and Tinh-do (from Chinese Jingtu, 'Pure Land')—have been dominant ever since then. Thien is largely a monastic tradition, whereas Tinh-do is mainly a lay movement that spread especially during those periods when there was a dearth of educated Thien monks. However, Vietnamese Buddhism is syncretistic; the two sects have influenced each other, and all Thien monasteries also teach Pure Land practices.

In the early part of the twentieth century, Vietnamese Buddhism attempted to reform itself in the face of modern challenges, including two major challenges coming from the West—secularism and Christianity—but this effort was interrupted by the Second World War, followed by the division of the country in 1954 into a communist North and an anti-communist South, where the Roman Catholic president Ngo Dinh Diem (r. 1954–63) imposed a number of restrictions on Buddhists. It was in protest against these restrictions that, in May 1963, an elderly monk named Thich Quang Duc assumed the cross-legged lotus position on a busy street in Saigon, had gasoline poured over him, then calmly struck a match and became a human torch. A number of monks and nuns followed his example over the next months, attracting worldwide attention and contributing to the fall of the Diem government.

At the same time, these self-immolations forced Buddhists to ask what the dharma is concerning suicide. The answer is ambiguous. It is clear that Shakyamuni forbade suicide: '[Monks], let no one destroy himself, and whosoever would destroy himself, let him be dealt with according to law' (Warren 1896: 437). In the Mahayana tradition, however, the *Lotus Sutra* appears to accept suicide when it is committed for a good cause. This is the case with the Medicine bodhisattva, a popular figure in China, who vows to offer his own body to heal human beings. According to the *Lotus Sutra*:

> . . . he wrapped his body in a garment adorned with divine jewels, anointed himself with fragrant oils, with the force of supernatural penetration took a vow, and then burnt his body. The glow gave light all around to the world-spheres equal in number to the sands of eighty millions of Ganges rivers. Within them the Buddhas all at once praised him (Hurvitz 1976: 294–5).

Historically, Buddhist monks in China occasionally committed suicide as a demonstration of their piety or to protest persecutions. Sometimes they cut off parts of themselves, such as arms or fingers, and made offerings of them. It was this practice, together with the veneration of relics, that the Chinese Confucian scholar Han Yu (786–824) cited in his criticism of Buddhism in a text called the *Memorial on the Bone of Buddha*. Self-sacrifice is an important theme in the thought of Thich Nhat Hanh (b. 1926), a well-known Vietnamese monk who entered a monastery at the age of sixteen and became not only a Thien (Zen) master but a poet and a peace activist. In response to the atrocities of the Vietnam war, he developed what he called an 'engaged Buddhism' to bring the resources of Buddhist wisdom and meditation to bear on contemporary conflicts.

For Thich Nhat Hanh, the self-immolations of 1963 were acts not of self-destruction but rather of self-sacrifice, designed to call attention to the suffering of the people in Vietnam, and ought to be understood in the context of the Buddhist belief in the continuity of life beyond one human life span. Changing the world, for Thich Nhat Hanh, requires that we first change our awareness of ourselves and the world, especially through meditation and the 'art of mindful living'. Commenting on the *Heart Sutra*, he says:

> If you are a poet, you will see clearly that there is a cloud floating in this sheet of paper. Without a cloud, there will be no rain; without rain, the trees cannot grow; and without trees, we cannot make paper. If we look even more deeply, we can see the sunshine, the logger who cut the tree, the wheat that became his bread, and the logger's father and mother. Without all of these things, this sheet of paper cannot exist. . . . Everything co-exists with this sheet of paper. So we can say that the cloud and the paper 'inter-are'. We cannot just be by ourselves alone; we have to inter-be with every other thing (Nhat Hanh 1988: 3).

## Buddhism in Modern China and Korea

In the 1920s, while Chinese intellectuals were calling for intellectual pluralism and a greater openness to Western ideas, a Chan monk named Taixu ('Great Emptiness') called for reform within Buddhism. Prominent lay devotees dedicated to furthering the knowledge of Buddhism extended their activities to social work and popular education. Such activity has become part of the Buddhist mission in those areas and countries where monks and believers still have the freedom to pursue these goals.

The history of Buddhism in China raises many questions for students of the history of religions. On the one hand, Buddhism adapted itself to Chinese culture to the extent of becoming a Chinese religion while maintaining its distinct identity in the company of Confucianism and religious Daoism. On the other hand, it was never completely accepted by China's political and intellectual elites, suffered severe persecutions, and was threatened with near-extinction during the Cultural Revolution of the late 1960s. Has Buddhism's openness to acculturation served it well? What would have happened if it had been less adaptable?

Buddhism probably would not have survived in China if it had not adapted. Acculturation also accounts for its transformation from Indian to Chinese forms and its ability to contribute to Chinese civilization.

### Korea

Because North Korea has been governed by a religion-suppressing communist regime since 1945, this section will focus exclusively on the South. Under Japanese occupation (1910–45), Korean Buddhism was freed from its subjugation to Confucianism. Monks—who had been banned from Seoul during the pro-Confucian Choson dynasty (1392–1910)—were once again permitted to enter the city. However, the religion was controlled and manipulated by the occupying power. Japanese influence led to the breakdown of monastic discipline, as monks began to eat meat and marry. The renewal of Korean Buddhism had to await the country's liberation from Japan, and the process was further delayed by the devastating civil war of 1950–3. The more conservative Chogye Buddhists struggled against the married monks of the Taego order, who were based in the cities, and sought to restore the meditative, disciplinary, and scholastic orientations of traditional Korean Buddhism. It

finally won official support for its efforts in 1954, when it regained control of virtually all the major monasteries. Today Korean Son is said to have the strictest discipline of the Korean Buddhist sects. After the end of Japanese rule in 1945, partly in response to the growing influence of Christianity in Korea, Buddhists made an effort to influence students and intellectuals, especially through the spread of Son meditation.

Tension exists between Buddhists and Korea's large Christian population. Attacks on several Buddhist temples—allegedly carried out by fundamentalist Christians who see Buddhism not as a religion to be respected but as an evil to be destroyed—have led many Buddhists to feel persecuted.

## Buddhism and Modernity in Japan

In some ways, modern Japan resembles a museum of the history of religions, with exhibits that cover everything from the traditions of ancient Japan, through Indian and Chinese Buddhism, to Christianity and the secular ideologies of the West. Although Buddhism has left an indelible imprint on Japanese culture, it never became the state religion, or even the religion of the people as such. Today it is often described as the religion of the dead, whereas Shinto is called the religion of the living because of its association with the joys of life. So closely is Buddhism associated with the memorialization of the dead that the family shrine dedicated to the ancestors is called the *butsudan*— literally, the Buddhist altar. (For more on the complex interactions of Buddhism and other Japanese traditions, see Chapter 7.)

### 'Abortion Temples'

A few Buddhist temples are referred to as 'abortion temples' because they provide space on their grounds for shrines in memory of aborted fetuses. Grieving parents offer toys or treats appropriate to the ages their aborted offspring would have reached if they had lived. It may be that, in addition to honouring the unborn, parents hope to placate their spirits lest they become vengeful and seek to harm their living siblings.

### The West and the Kyoto School

An interesting development in modern Japan is the Kyoto school of Buddhist philosophy. Its founder was Nishida Kitaro (1875–1945), who came of age in the early days of the Meiji Restoration, when Japan was looking to the West for ideas to help it modernize. In this context, Nishida sought to fuse Japanese Zen Buddhist ideas with continental European philosophy. In keeping with Zen's emphasis on direct experience, he wrote of what he called 'pure experience'—'experience just as it is without the addition of the slightest thought or reflection'. For example:

> the moment of seeing a colour or hearing a sound that takes place . . . before one has added the judgment that this seeing or hearing is related to something external. . . . When one has experienced one's conscious state directly, there is not as yet any subject or object; knowing and its object are completely at one. This is the purest form of experience (Nishida, *Zen no kenkyu*; Takeuchi 1987: 456).

This approach is consistent with Zen founder Bodhidharma's call for a 'direct pointing of the mind'.

Among Nishida's successors was Nishitani Keiji (1900–90). Nishitani's interest in bridging the gap between Zen thought and Christian theology played a role in the emergence of an international Buddhist–Christian dialogue movement in the 1970s.

## Buddhism in the West

Alfred North Whitehead (1861–1947), the Anglo-American philosopher, once said that Christianity was 'a religion seeking a metaphysic', whereas Buddhism was 'a metaphysic generating a religion'.

For a long time, Western scholars were not certain whether Buddhism fitted their definition of 'religion' at all, since—despite its rituals, scriptures, and monastic traditions—it did not centre on a personal deity.

Knowledge of Buddhism in Europe and North America was almost non-existent before the middle of the nineteenth century, but in 1879 a book entitled *The Light of Asia*—a moving poetic account of the life of Buddha, by Edwin Arnold—attracted wide public attention. Even so, it was not until the beginning of the twentieth century that a few Western seekers began to publish first-hand accounts of Buddhist meditational practice. By the 1930s, Buddhist societies had been established in Great Britain, France, and Germany.

### The Spread of Zen

Buddhist influences in North America have tended to come more from the Mahayana tradition than the Theravada. This has been the case ever since the World's Parliament of Religions conference in Chicago in 1893. Among the delegates was a Zen monk named Shaku Soyen (1856–1919), who later returned to America to spread Buddhism. His young translator, Daisetsu T. Suzuki (1870–1966), became the most influential Buddhist writer in North America.

Suzuki made two extended visits to the United States, and wrote many popular books sprinkled with stories of Zen masters and the koans with which they challenged their disciples. Especially as popularized by Alan Watts, these writings caught the attention of Westerners looking for alternatives to the personal theism or institutional structures of Christianity. Some Westerners have considered Zen a form of mysticism. Others have argued against this view on the grounds that there is no experience of union with a personal god in Zen.

On the other hand, if 'mysticism' is understood as referring to the spiritual experience as a transformation of human consciousness, then Zen practitioners may well share some experience in common with Christian mystics like Johannes 'Meister' Eckhart (c. 1260–1327). Many Westerners have been interested in Zen meditational practice as well. Catholic missionaries and theologians, coming from a long contemplative tradition, have sought to learn from Zen insights and techniques. At the same time, the Zen experience has attracted the attention of experts in depth psychology, as Daoist meditation has also done.

Zen was the first form of Buddhism to make significant numbers of converts in North America, but it was by no means the only one. Nichiren Shoshu, for example, was imported by immigrants from Japan. Immigrants also brought with them various Pure Land sects. The most popular form of Buddhism in Japan, Pure Land is also the most popular form in the North American diaspora today.

### Vajrayana (Tibetan) Buddhism

Since the 1960s, two lineages of Vajrayana or Tibetan Buddhism have also gained converts in North America. The Kargyu lineage is represented both by the Naropa Institute in Boulder, Colorado, and by a community of Tibetans and converts based in Halifax, Nova Scotia, while the Dalai Lama's Gelugpa lineage has centres in New York and elsewhere.

### Ethnic Congregations

Existing alongside and independent of the converts to Buddhism are East Asian Buddhists. Beginning in the late 1880s, Chinese and Japanese immigrants settled along the west coast of North America, especially in places like Hawaii, California, and British Columbia, and gradually found the financial resources to build temples similar to those in their homelands. The ethnic congregations were quite diverse. First-generation immigrants from different lands spoke different Asian languages, and their overseas-born descendants tended to speak English. In ritual and teaching, these congregations represented many branches of Buddhism.

The most popular form of Buddhism in East Asia is Pure Land, and that popularity is reflected among the ethnic Buddhist congregations of North America. There are networks of particular ethnic groups like the Buddhist Association of America and the Buddhist Association of Canada, which serve mainly immigrants of Chinese origin, and the Buddhist Churches of America (and of Canada), which serve True Pure Land followers, who are mainly ethnic Japanese. Similar, if smaller, groups with roots in Vietnam and Laos also have their own networks. Over time, some ethnic Buddhists have adopted Christian styles of worship, with pews, hymnals, and a leader who takes on the roles expected of North American clergy. Buddhist Sunday schools were founded, Buddhist cemeteries have been consecrated, and Buddhist wedding rituals have been brought under the supervision of a *bhikshu*, now called a 'priest'.

In North America, ethnic Buddhists use their temples as community centres as well as places of worship. Visitors are welcome, but the emphasis on community affairs tends to limit congregation membership to people from the same ethnic community. Buddhist meditation centres, on the other hand, have attracted many Western converts. Umbrella organizations such as the Buddhist Council of Canada are helping to bring Western 'meditation Buddhists' into closer contact with the ethnic Buddhist congregations.

The influence of Buddhist meditation and doctrine has been greater than the relatively small number of Western Buddhists might suggest. Without necessarily becoming Buddhists, many people in the West have adopted modified versions of Buddhist meditational practices in order to calm their minds or to concentrate before athletic or artistic performances. In addition, Buddhist (and Hindu and Jaina) values such as non-violence and concepts such as rebirth and karma have spread well beyond the traditional religious context.

# Prospects for the Future

## A Renewed Sense of Mission

According to the Buddhist understanding of long-term historical cycles, Shakyamuni began a new era by setting the wheel of dharma in motion again after a period of decline. Eventually the dharma will again go into decline, until the next buddha restarts the wheel. This somewhat pessimistic view of the future stands in sharp contrast to the views of many other religions, including Christianity. Yet the notion that organized Buddhism will eventually decline does not in any way diminish Buddhists' zeal or sense of mission.

In a sense, the many volunteer associations promoting Buddhist solutions to modern problems are performing the same functions as the Buddhist kings of the past who provided financial support as well as leadership in education, economic development, and social values. Thus meditation retreat centres offer help with modern problems such as stress and overdependence on material possessions. Such centres offer instruction in basic meditational posture and breathing techniques in order to help achieve calmness, mental focus, and insight into dharma truths. Most of them emphasize the importance of breaking through the normal bonds of ego, self-centredness, and the assumption of permanence. *Bhikshu* Buddhadasa identified the fundamental problem as the attitude of 'me and mine'. This attitude may be characteristic of the human condition, but Buddhists believe that it is made worse by the materialistic and individualistic emphasis of contemporary values.

Another problem currently being addressed by some Buddhist organizations is the need for alternatives to modern schemes of economic development. Not surprisingly, they propose a middle path between the environmental and social disasters of overdevelopment on the one hand and the poverty of underdevelopment on the other. They advocate local-level, low-tech, people-oriented projects that will help everyone, and criticize all projects that serve to make the rich richer and the poor poorer.

## Cooperation among Buddhists

There is a growing spirit of co-operation among the branches of Buddhism within most countries, and networks of Buddhists from various countries are being formed. One example is the International Network of Engaged Buddhists, based in Bangkok. Many Buddhists now identify themselves first as Buddhists and only secondarily as Zen Buddhists or Theravada Buddhists. This tendency is strengthened by the growing tendency of many Buddhist periodicals and Internet sites to include articles by writers from various Buddhist traditions.

The sense of common purpose among Buddhists has been strengthened by the international exposure of the Dalai Lama, who has travelled to most Buddhist countries and in every case has been very well received. Strictly speaking, the Dalai Lama is the spiritual head of just one order of Tibetan Buddhists, but by virtue of the stature of his office and his outstanding personal qualities, Tenzin Gyatso is recognized by Buddhists everywhere as their spokesperson in some sense. His forced exile is seen as a loss for Tibet, but in the long run it may provide the impetus that Buddhism needs to regain its traditional role as one of the world's most vigorous and successful religions.

# Buddhism Today

We have traced Buddhism through 2,500 years of history from the time of Shakyamuni. The tradition has enlisted the dedication and challenged the intellect and imagination of millions of people. It has enjoyed imperial patronage and rich artistic expression. It has spread far beyond the South Asian land of its origin.

There have been setbacks. In India it was eclipsed by Hinduism and Islam. In Sri Lanka and Southeast Asia it was weakened and challenged by the Christian missions and Western values introduced during the period of colonial domination. And the loss of kingship in most of the Buddhist countries of southern Asia has undermined the political support system that existed for many centuries. Like other religions, Buddhism has also been challenged and called into question by modern, secular ways of life. Buddhists themselves do not consider the scientific world view to represent a serious challenge, since the Buddha himself taught that everything is subject to causation. But the concepts of karma and rebirth do not fit comfortably into the standard scientific world view.

It is also true that *bhikshus* are no longer the main educators, social workers, dispute settlers, and advisers in Buddhist countries, especially in the major cities; their roles have been reduced to those of ritual leaders and directors of religious education. Yet Buddhists are not converting in any significant numbers to other religions, and most make some effort to live according to Buddhist values.

What gives Buddhism its energy? What makes it work for so many people in so many countries? The answer may lie in the continuing power of the Triple Gem to shape people's spiritual lives. Buddhists feel confident in 'taking refuge' in the Buddha, not as a god but as a great human being; in the dharma as a set of living teachings that go to the heart of reality; and in the sangha as a community of people committed to following the Buddha's path as closely as possible. They also feel confident that, in the distant future, when the wheel of dharma set in motion by Shakyamuni ceases to turn, the future buddha Maitreya will appear on earth and turn the wheel yet again for the benefit of the next era.

## Sites

**Lumbini Park** in southern Nepal preserves the sacred area where the Buddha was born, with old stupas, the pond where Mahamaya bathed, a Bodhi tree, and a park surrounded by monasteries for visiting monks. This is the first of the four major pilgrimage sites of India/Nepal.

**Kathmandu** There are two great Buddhist temples in the Kathmandu area. Swayambhunath, nicknamed the 'monkey temple', sits high on a hill, its Nepali-style 'eyes' overlooking the countryside. Bodhanath is a Tibetan-style stupa surrounded by shops and cafés.

**Bodh Gaya** in northeastern India preserves the area where the Buddha was enlightened. There is the huge Bodhi tree, a temple, and a park surrounded by temples and monasteries representing different schools of Buddhism. Many Tibetans come here in the winter for a festival that is usually attended by the Dalai Lama. This is the second of the four great pilgrimage sites of India/Nepal.

**Sarnath**, the third of the four great pilgrimage sites of India/Nepal, is the deer park near Varanasi in northern India where the Buddha preached his first sermon. Sights include a new temple, several old stupas and temples, and a museum.

**Kushinagar** It was in a grove of trees near this town in northeastern India that the Buddha is said to have entered *parinirvana*. It is the fourth great pilgrimage site of India/Nepal.

**Maharashtra** state in west central India has two famous cave complexes. The Ajanta Caves, carved into a long, curving cliffside, filled with sculpture and paintings. Some caves were temples, carved and painted to look like wooden temples. Others were monasteries. Similar caves are found at Ellora.

**Kandy** The Temple of the Tooth in Kandy is the most important Buddhist site in Sri Lanka. The midsummer Perahera festival is a spectacular parade of elephants, musicians, and dancers. Both Buddhist and Hindu temples participate in the parade.

**Bangkok** On the grounds of the Grand Palace is the temple housing a famous jade sculpture known as the Emerald Buddha. Murals depicting scenes from the life of the Buddha are painted on walls surrounding one part of the palace grounds. The nearby Wat Pho is filled with interesting temples, including one with a 46-metre-long reclining Buddha image, and houses a Thai massage training centre. Across the river is the picturesque Wat Arun, the Temple of the Dawn, which features a tall pagoda that sparkles at dawn and sunset.

**Angkor Thom** in Cambodia is one of the world's great Buddhist temples. Nearby is the Hindu temple called Angkor Wat.

**Lhasa** is the site of the Potala Palace, the traditional home of the Dalai Lamas before the Chinese occupation of Tibet led the fourteenth Dalai Lama to relocate his headquarters in Dharmsala, India. Other important Buddhist sites in Lhasa include the Jokhang temple, the surrounding Barkhor pilgrimage circuit, huge monasteries, and an active nunnery.

**Shaolin**, in central China, is the home of both Zen Buddhism and the martial arts. The monastery has many buildings and statues of the early Zen patriarchs, and the town has dozens of martial-arts high schools. A two-hour hike up a mountain path leads to Bodhidharma's cave.

**Nara**, Japan's first capital, has beautiful wooden temples set in a deer park. Todaiji is a tall wooden temple housing a huge bronze Buddha statue.

**Kyoto**, Japan's second capital, has many famous temples as well, including the 'rock gardens' at Zen temples such as Ryoanji.

# Glossary

**anatman**  'No-soul', the doctrine that the human person is impermanent, a changing combination of components.

**Arhat/lohan**  A worthy one or saint, someone who has realized the ideal of spiritual perfection.

**bhikshu, bhikshuni**  An ordained Buddhist monk and nun, respectively.

**bodhisattva**  In Theravada, a being who is on the way to enlightenment or buddhahood but has not yet achieved it; in Mahayana, a celestial being who forgoes nirvana in order to save others.

**Chan/Son/Zen**  A tradition centred on the practice of meditation and the teaching that ultimate reality is not expressible in words or logic, but must be grasped through direct intuition; see also **koan** and **zazen**.

**dana**  A 'giving' ritual, in which Theravada families present gifts of food, at their homes or a temple, to *bhikshus* who conduct rituals including chanting and merit-transfer.

**dharma**  In Buddhist usage, teaching or truth concerning the ultimate nature of things.

**duhkha**  The suffering, psychological as well as physical, that characterizes human life.

**Hinayana**  'Lesser Vehicle'; the pejorative name given by the Mahayana ('Greater Vehicle') school to earlier Indian Buddhist sects, of which Theravada became the most important.

**karma**  The energy of the individual's past thoughts and actions, good or bad; it determines rebirth within the 'wheel' of samsara or cycle of rebirth that ends only when *parinirvana* is achieved. Good karma is also called 'merit'.

**koan/gongan**  A paradoxical thought exercise used in the Chan–Zen tradition to provoke a breakthrough in understanding by forcing students past the limitations of verbal formulations and logic.

**lama**  'Wise teacher'; a title given to advanced teachers as well as the heads of various Tibetan ordination lineages.

**Mahayana**  'Greater Vehicle'; the form of Buddhism that emerged around the first century in India and spread first to China and then to Korea and Japan.

**mandala**  A chart-like representation of cosmic Buddha figures that often serves as a focus of meditation and devotion in the Mahayana and Vajrayana traditions.

**mudra**  A pose or gesture in artistic representations of Buddha figures; by convention, each *mudra* has a specific symbolic meaning.

**nirvana**  The state of bliss associated with final enlightenment; nirvana 'with remainder' is the highest level possible in this life, and nirvana 'without remainder' is the ultimate state. See also *parinirvana*.

**pagoda**  A multi-storey tower, characteristic of Southeast and East Asian Buddhism, that developed out of the South Asian mound or stupa.

**parinirvana**  The ultimate perfection of bliss, achievable only on departing this life, as distinct from the nirvana with the 'remainder' achievable while one is still in the present existence.

**prajna**  The spiritual wisdom or insight necessary for enlightenment.

**Pure Land**  The comfortable realm in the western region of the heavens reserved for those who trust in the merit and grace of its lord, the celestial buddha Amitabha (Amida).

**rinpoche**  A title of respect for Tibetan teachers or leading monks.

**samadhi**  A higher state of consciousness, achieved through meditation.

**sangha**  The 'congregation' or community of Buddhist monks and nuns. Some forms of Buddhism also refer to the congregation of lay persons as a sangha.

**Shakyamuni**  'Sage of the Shakya clan', a title used to refer to the historical figure of Siddhartha Gautama, the Buddha.

**shunyata**  The Emptiness that is held to be ultimately characteristic of all things, stressed especially by Madhyamika doctrine.

**stupa**  Originally a hemispherical mound built to contain cremation ashes or a sacred relic; in East Asia the stupa developed into the tower-like pagoda.

**sutra**  A discourse attributed either to Shakyamuni himself or to an important disciple.

**Theravada**  'Teaching of the Elders', the dominant form of Buddhism in Sri Lanka and Southeast Asia.

**Tripitaka**  'Three baskets'; the collection of early sacred writings whose three sections consist of discourses attributed to the Buddha, rules of monastic discipline, and treatises on doctrine.

**Vaishakha/Vesak**  A Theravada festival held at the full moon around early May, marking Shakyamuni's birth, enlightenment, and *parinirvana*.

**Vajrayana**  The tantric branch of Buddhism that became established in Tibet and the Himalayan region, and later spread to Mongolia and eventually India.

**vinaya**  The rules of practice and conduct for monks; a section of the Pali canon.

**vipassana**  'Insight' or 'mindfulness' meditation practised by Theravada Buddhists.

**zazen**  Sitting meditation in the Chan–Zen tradition.

**Zen**  See **Chan**.

# Further Reading

Amore, Roy C. 1978. *Two Masters, One Message*. Nashville: Abindgon. Compares and contrasts the figures of Buddha and Jesus.

Batchelor, Martine. 2006. *Women in Korean Zen: Lives and Practices*. Syracuse: Syracuse University Press. A good account based on ten years of Zen practice in Korea.

Dalai Lama. 1990. *Freedom in Exile: The Autobiography of the Dalai Lama*. New York: HarperCollins.

Dalai Lama, His Holiness The. 2002. *How to Practice: The Way to a Meaningful Life*. Trans. and ed. by Jeffrey Hopkins. New York: Pocket Books.

Fisher, Robert E. 1993. *Buddhist Art and Architecture*. London: Thames & Hudson. An overview of South and East Asian developments.

Gross, Rita M. 1993. *Buddhism after Patriarchy: A Feminist History, Analysis, and Reconstruction of Buddhism*. Albany: State University of New York Press. Material for provocative debate.

Lopez, Donald S., Jr. 2002. *The Story of Buddhism: A Concise Guide to Its History and Teachings*. New York: HarperCollins.

Queen, Christopher S., and Sallie B. King, eds. 1996. *Engaged Buddhism: Liberation Movements in Asia*. Albany: State University of New York Press. Twentieth-century activism from India and Thailand to Tibet and Japan.

Seager, Richard Hughes. 2000. *Buddhism in America*. New York: Columbia University Press.

Shaw, Ronald D.M., trans. 1961. *The Blue Cliff Records: The Hekigan Roku [Pi yen lu] Containing One Hundred Stories of Zen Masters of Ancient China*. London: M. Joseph. Koans especially prized by the Japanese.

Sivaraksa, Sulak. 2005. *Conflict, Culture, Change: Engaged Buddhism in a Globalizing World*. Somerville, MA: Wisdom Publications. A recent book by an important Thai Buddhist social critic.

# Recommended Websites

http://lhamo.tripod.com/
A site focusing on women in Buddhism.

www.americanbuddhist.net
Offers a broad overview of Buddhism, including Buddhist activism.

www.buddhamind.info
A site of interest to Buddhist families.

www.buddhanet.net
A comprehensive site, including a ezine with cartoons, pictures, and much more.

www.dharmanet.org
Another comprehensive site, including video links.

www.buddhanet.net/e-learning/buddhistworld/china-txt.htm
A useful overview of the history and varieties of Buddhism in China, but does not address current issues.

www.dhamma.org
A good source on Theravada-style *vipassana* meditation.

www.freetibet.org
Site of the Free Tibet Campaign, a movement started by Tibetans in exile and their supporters.

# References

Bloom, Alfred. 1965. *Shinran's Gospel of Pure Grace*. Tucson: University of Arizona Press.

Chen, Kenneth. 1964. *Buddhism in China: A Historical Survey*. Princeton: Princeton University Press.

de Bary, William Theodore, ed. 1958. *Sources of Indian Tradition*. New York: Columbia University Press.

Dhammika, Sravasti, ed. 1989. *Buddha Vacana*. Singapore: Buddha Dhamma Mandala Society.

Horner, I.B. 1930. *Women under Primitive Buddhism: Laywomen and Almswomen*. New York: Dutton.

———, trans. 1967. The *Collection of the Middle Length Sayings (Majjhimanikaya)*. vol. 3. London: Luzac.

Hughes, Ernest R., and K. Hughes. 1950. *Religion in China*. London: Hutchinson.

Hurvitz, Leon. 1976. *Scripture of the Lotus Blossom of the Fine Dharma*. New York: Columbia University Press.

Nanamoli [formerly Osborne Moore], trans. 1972. *The Life of the Buddha as It Appears in the Pali Canon, the Oldest Authentic Record*. Kandy: Buddhist Publication Society Inc.

Nhat Hanh, Thich. 1988. *The Heart of Understanding: Commentaries on the PrajNaparamita Heart Sutra*. Berkeley: Parallax Press.

Nielsen, N.C., et al., eds. 1993. *Religions of the World*. 3rd ed. New York: St Martin's Press.

Paul, Diana Y., ed. 1979. *Women in Buddhism: Images of the Feminine in Mahayana Tradition*. Berkeley: Asian Humanities Press.

Rhi, Ki-Yong. 1977. 'Wonhyo and His Thought'. In Chai-Shin Yu, ed., *Korean and Asian Religious Tradition*, 197–207. Toronto: Korean and Related Studies Press.

Rhys Davids, Caroline A. 1964. *Psalms of the Early Buddhists*. vol. 1 (Psalms of Sisters). London: Luzac, for the Pali Text Society.

Rhys Davids, Thomas W., trans. 1881. *Buddhist Sutras*. In F. Max Müller, ed., *Sacred Books of the East*, 11. Oxford: Clarendon Press.

———, trans. 1890. *The Questions of King Milinda*, Part I. In F. Max Müller, ed., *Sacred Books of the East*, 35. Oxford: Clarendon Press.

Robinson, Richard H. 1959. 'Buddhism: In China and Japan'. In R.C. Zaehner, ed., *The Concise Encyclopedia of Living Faiths*, 321–47. London: Joseph.

Suzuki, D.T. 1991. *An Introduction to Zen Buddhism*. New York: Grove Press.

Takeuchi, Yoshinori. 1987. 'Nishida Kitaro'. In Mircea Eliade, ed., *The Encyclopedia of Religion* 10: 456–7. New York: Macmillan.

Tsunoda, Ryusaku. 1958. *Sources of Japanese Tradition*. New York: Columbia University Press.

Yampolsky, Philip, trans. 1976. *The Platform Sutra of the Sixth Patriarch*. New York: Columbia University Press.

# Chapter 6

## Chinese & Korean Traditions

❧ Terry Tak-ling Woo ❧

Next time you go to a restaurant in Chinatown, take a look around and see if there is a shrine at the door, or perhaps the back of the sitting area. Chances are good that you will see a red shrine with three incense sticks in a censer, a small plate of fruit at the front, a candle on each side, and at least one figure standing in the centre. If the figure is holding a halberd, it will represent Guan Gong, who symbolizes the Confucian virtues of loyalty (*zhong*) and sense of what is right (*yi*). A traditional cap and a flowing beard signify the Daoist lineage ancestor Lu Dongbin, while a female figure will usually represent Guanyin, the legendary Buddhist bodhisattva of compassion, who sees and hears the suffering of all sentient beings. If there is no figure, the back panel of the shrine will often carry a verse of thanksgiving addressed to the local earth god.

## OVERVIEW

When the Chinese talk about *sanjiao*, they are talking about the three (*san*) philosophies or religions (*jiao*) of Confucianism, Daoism, and Buddhism. Collectively, these are sometimes described as the elite tradition, and they stand in contrast to a much more diffuse fourth religion, often described as the little, folk, or popular tradition, that honours a myriad of spirits.

Popular Chinese religious beliefs and practices are syncretic, combining shamanistic folkways with elements from the three elite traditions (which often contradict one another). In addition, underlying all other affiliations is a near-universal tradition of ancestor veneration, which some scholars see as the fundamental 'Chinese religion'. Although devotees themselves clearly differentiate between the four religions, there are deep-rooted similarities in cultural assumptions and practices that will be discussed in some detail under Daoism.

The four religions have coexisted for millennia, for the most part peacefully. Many ordinary people consult and seek the services of religious specialists from across the spectrum, including Confucian teachers, Daoist priests, Buddhist monks, spirit mediums, astrologers, and *fengshui* practitioners, among many others. Still, it is important to remember that religious professionals—whether Confucian teachers, Buddhist monks and nuns, or Daoist priests—are often exclusive in their commitment.

Scholars have noted that Chinese religions are marked by their commitment to right action more than right belief. This is at least partly true, for even though each of the three traditions has taught a particular set of ultimately dissimilar 'right' beliefs and goals, they have all agreed on the special importance of right action. Right action is expressed in the maintenance of harmonious relations regardless of different belief systems.

This emphasis on harmonious relations reflects a common understanding that there is a variety of human temperaments and capacities. Thus the Confucian **Xunzi** talked about the myriad ways in which different people might understand various religious rites. And the *Classic of the Way and Power* or *Virtue* (the *Daodejing*, also known as the *Laozi*) attributed to Laozi, the putative founder of Daoism, speaks of the universal, all-encompassing Way (**Dao**) as necessarily inexpressible, ineffable, since any way that can be articulated is de facto partial, incomplete, relative, and not ultimate.

For their part, Mahayana Buddhists in China took guidance from the *Lotus Sutra* (*Fahuajing*) and its parable of the burning house (see Chapter 5, page 206), understanding contradictory teachings, including Daoist and Confucian ones, in the context of 'skilful means' or a hierarchy of suitability,

◀ Songshan, in Henan province, is one of five sacred mountains, revered by Daoists and Buddhists alike (© Ryan Pyle/Corbis).

# Timeline

| | |
|---|---|
| 2356–2255 BCE | Reign of China's mythical sage king Yao; some accounts place Tangun, the mythical founder of the proto-state Old Choson (Korea) in the same period |
| c. 2200–1750 | Xia dynasty (China) |
| c. 1750–1040 | Shang (Yin) dynasty (China) |
| c. 1040–256 | Zhou dynasty (China) |
| 722–479 | Spring and Autumn period |
| 551 | Birth of Confucius (d. 479); some accounts place Laozi around the same time, some place him earlier, and others say that he never existed |
| 479–221 | Warring States period |
| c. 400–100 | Huang-Lao school |
| c. 343 | Birth of Mencius (d. 289); Zhuangzi (369?–286?) was a slightly older contemporary |
| c. 310 | Birth of Xunzi (d. 219) who witnesses the carnage of the late Zhou and Qin periods |
| c. 300 | Old Choson (Korea) |
| 221–206 | Qin dynasty (China) |
| 124 | First state college for Confucian teachings established followed by state examinations |
| c. 50 BCE–668 CE | Three Kingdoms of Koguryo, Paekche, and Silla (Korea) |
| c. 48 CE | Birth of Ban Zhao (d. 112), who advocates education for women |
| 142 | Zhang Daoling founds the Daoist Celestial Masters or Orthodox Unity sect |
| 220–589 | Period of North–South disunion or Six Dynasties (China) |
| 317 | Northern China falls to invaders from North and Central Asia |
| 589–618 | Sui dynasty (China) |
| 618–907 | Tang dynasty (China) |
| 600s | Tang rulers send Daoist priests, texts, and images to Koguryo |
| 647 | Tang Taizhong, the second emperor of the dynasty, orders the construction of Confucian temples and installs in each one tablets commemorating 22 orthodox Confucians |
| 668–936 | Kingdom of United Silla (Korea) |
| 682 | United Silla establishes the National Confucian College |
| 824 | Death of Han Yu, who criticized Daoism and Buddhism and laid the groundwork for the renewal of Confucianism |
| 890–936 | Later Three Kingdoms (Korea) |
| 960–1279 | Song dynasty (China) |

*Continued*

| | |
|---|---|
| **1400s** | Both China's Empress Xu and Choson's Queen Sohye write texts entitled *Instructions for the Inner Quarters*; the former becomes one of the Four Books for Women |
| **1500s** | Choson Neo-Confucianism thrives in Village Compacts and Four-Seven Debates |
| **1529** | Death of Wang Yangming, who challenged Zhu Xi's orthodoxy with his School of Mind |
| **1644–1911** | Qing (Manchu) dynasty (China) |
| **1841** | Lin Zexu, a Confucian minister of the Qing regime, sends a letter of conscience to Queen Victoria protesting Britain's practice of selling opium in China; the Opium War and the beginning of China's Westernization follow |
| **1850–1910** | Foreign skirmishes and threats (China) |
| **1900s** | East Asia reconfigured in response to Western challenges; new religions are established and traditional ones renewed |
| **1910–1945** | Japanese colonial period (Korea) |
| **1911** | Republic (China) |
| **1945** | Split into Democratic People's Republic and Republic (Korea) |
| **1949** | People's Republic (China) |
| **1950s** | New Confucian movement in the Chinese world finds a home in New Asia College, now part of the Chinese University of Hong Kong; Korean New Confucian Kim Ch'ungnyol travels to Taiwan to study with Fang Dongmei |
| **1980s** | Revival of Daoism in China after persecution under the Heavenly Kingdom of Peace during the 1850s and the Cultural Revolution (1966–76) |

tailored to communicate with different characters and stages of development. All three traditions thus accommodated a variety of beliefs and practices through their acceptance of both natural and socio-culturally conditioned individual differences.

# 🌿 CONFUCIANISM

## Origins

Some of the seminal ideas of the philosophy that the West calls Confucianism did not originate with **Kongzi** (the name latinized as Confucius; 551[1]–479 BCE). They can be found in a collection of writings we now know as the Five Classics: the *Classic* or *Book of Changes* (*Yijing*), the *Classic of Documents* or *Book of History* (*Shujing*), the *Classic of Odes* or *Book of Poetry* (*Shijing*), the *Records* or *Book of Rites* (*Liji*), and the *Spring and Autumn Annals* (*Chunqiu*). (A sixth work, the *Classic of Music* [*Yueji*] is now lost.) Some parts of these works may predate Confucius himself, and others appear to have been added later. Nevertheless, Confucius is revered as the first of China's three foremost classical philosophers, the other two being Mencius (c. 343–289 BCE) and Xunzi (c. 310–219 BCE).

Originating during the Zhou dynasty (c. 1040–256 BCE), the Classics were first standardized during the Han dynasty (202 BCE–220 CE) and they have formed a substantial part of the state examination curriculum since the establishment of the first state college in 124 BCE. The world they describe is the same one that shaped Daoist thought, as well as later folk beliefs and practices.

Historically, the Five Classics provided both the ideology that informed Chinese government policy and the framework within which it was implemented at every level for about 2,000 years. They have also served as blueprints for good conduct within families, and as guidelines for individual moral and spiritual transformation.

The classics record a society in transition. The preceding Shang era (c. 1750–1040 BCE) beliefs in personal anthropomorphic deities, and ghosts and spirits who affect the human world, was gradually replaced by a Zhou ethos that became increasingly humanized, and which conceived of the world as operating on natural, impersonal principles. The content of the Five Classics therefore ranges from descriptions of deities, ghosts and spirits, and the rites (**li**) performed for them, to philosophical explanations of the natural principles underlying these rites.

The *Book of Rites* explains the principles behind rites, their symbolic value, and their efficacy in bringing about the ultimate goal of Confucianism: the creation of a harmonious society through careful self-cultivation not for the sake of the self, but for the sake of the society. The Five Classics were repeatedly reinterpreted over time with this goal in mind.

## Confucian Concerns

The concerns addressed in the Five Classics can be categorized in four broad areas: political, familial, individual, and cosmic. The first duty of a noble or exemplary Confucian (**junzi**) is to understand how to encourage, contribute to, and maintain peace, prosperity, and socio-political harmony.

Portrait of a Korean Confucian, attributed to Yi Che-gwan (1783–1837) (© The Trustees of the British Museum/Art Resource, New York).

The Classics make it clear that political harmony cannot be achieved by men alone, for there can be no harmony in the state without harmony in the family—and the family is the responsibility of the Confucian woman. The Classics sought to explain the principle behind this binary of the outer-political and inner-familial realms, and describe its symbolic expression in sacrifices and rituals. Rituals in general and ancestor rituals in particular were understood to have as their essential purpose or function to define, frame, and encourage right relationships. This was especially true of relations between men and women, for the relationship between husband and wife was understood by Mencius to be the most important of all human relationships.

Right relationship between husband and wife, as with all relationships, requires discipline on the part of both partners. In this fundamental way, political and familial harmony both depend on self-cultivation. For Confucians, self-cultivation means moderating human emotions, quieting the

# Traditions at a Glance

### Numbers
Confucians: Estimates range from 6 to 8 million.
Daoists: Estimates range from 2.5 to 3.5 million.
Chinese Universalist or Popular Religion: Estimates range from 385 to 405 million.
Korean Shamanism and Popular Religion: Estimates range from 1 to 7 million.

### Distribution
Confucians and Daoists live in East Asia, Australia, New Zealand, Southeast Asia, North and West Europe, North America, and a few other places. Korean and Chinese popular religions are found primarily in East Asia, with small pockets in diasporic communities in North America and Europe.

### Founders and Teachers
Mythological founders and heroes include Yao, Shun, and Yu in China, and Tangun in Korea. Famous first teachers—some mythical, some historic—include the Yellow Emperor, Confucius, and Laozi in China, and Ch'oe Ch'ung in Korea.

### Deities
For Confucians the place of a deity is filled either by Heaven or by Heaven and Earth together. For some Daoists, the Way functions as a deity; others look to what is in effect a bureaucracy of deities. Popular religions, both Korean and Chinese, include deities from various traditions.

### Authoritative Texts
For Confucians, the Classics from the Zhou and Han are the foundational texts. For Daoists, Laozi is fundamental, with variations from sect to sect. The popular and shamanistic religions tend not to be textually oriented.

### Noteworthy Teachings
None of the East Asian teachings are radically exclusive. Daoism and Confucianism share cultural and social space with each other and popular religions even if they differ doctrinally. The two elite religions hold a common utopian view of a peaceful and harmonious society in which people are devoted to self-cultivation and discipline, try to be good, live frugally, and serve the community.

heart-mind (*xin*) so as to restore its natural unity, emptiness, and tranquillity. It is in the recovery of this original heavenly emotional state that the self is transformed and brought into harmony with Heaven and Earth. This is a cosmic harmony, a harmony for all: humans, ghosts and spirits, deities, Heaven and Earth alike.

This commitment to harmony is above all a commitment to individual cultivation according to the Way. The cultivation of moral and spiritual nobility, of sagehood, requires both internal and external ritual practices: for example, both the stilling of the 'heart-mind' and the performance of sacrifices. The collective, apparently secular

Confucian will towards social harmony in this life thus arises from, is embedded in, and continues a cultural tradition rooted in the veneration of ancestors, belief in ghosts and spirits, the worship of deities, and sacrifices to Heaven and Earth. Those older other-worldly elements were not pushed aside, but coexisted alongside the goals of the newer Confucian tradition, which were decidedly this-worldly.

## Confucian Exemplars and Sages

The prototypes of the Confucian sage are three mythical sage kings named Yao, Shun, and Yu, whose stories are told in the first chapters of the *Classic of Documents*. Because the virtues they embody are civil (*wen*), familial, and filial (**xiao**) rather than military (*wu*), their stories are interpreted as implicitly criticizing rule by force. Because of this preference for government by men of exemplary virtue, the Confucian scholars came to be known as the 'soft ones' (**ru**).

Yao's reign was considered to be a success because he brought harmony to his domain and, most important, made sure that the common people he served were well fed and prosperous. In the simple agrarian community of his day, Yao led by example and his virtue radiated throughout the land.

When it came time for him to retire, the *Classic of Documents* recounts how Yao, recognizing that his own son was deceitful and quarrelsome, asked his ministers to recommend a more appropriate successor. His ministers unanimously recommended Shun, a man of humble status. When Yao asked them why Shun would make a good king, they pointed to the way he had managed to transcend his circumstances, living in harmony with his family and fulfilling his filial duties even though his father was blind (literally and figuratively) and stupid, his stepmother deceitful, and his half-brother arrogant. In other words, Shun had not allowed his situation to overcome him, but triumphed over adversity. Accordingly, Yao married his two daughters to Shun, observed his conduct for three years, and then offered him the throne.

Shun's duties as king were both religious and secular. The religious duties included performing rituals to various spirits, including not only the foremost deity, the Lord-on-High (Shangdi) but six 'venerables' who were likely symbols of exemplary historical figures and various political (though not blood) ancestors. Shun's secular duties included setting common standards for units of measure, determining political boundaries for the land, and overseeing public works such as the deepening of rivers in anticipation of the inevitable floods.

The last sage king, Yu, is associated with the largely legendary Xia dynasty—the predecessors of the Shang. Yu's father was said to have thrown the natural cycle into chaos by damming up the floodwaters, but Yu dug deep canals to channel the water away. According to a chapter in the *Documents* entitled 'The Grand Model', this story was told to King Wu, the first king of Zhou, as a lesson in governance. Understood as a blueprint for an equitable, prosperous, and harmonious society, the Grand Model was said to have been revealed to Yu as his reward for taking the 'right action' to prevent disaster: in this case, working with nature (by channelling the water) rather than against it.

## Divination and the Pantheon of Spirits

At least two related elements from the stories of the sage kings survived into later times and were reinforced by the Shang dynasty: an intense interest in 'right' governance and a belief in divine intervention through revelation to the king. We know, for instance, that the Shang kings practised divination: in fact, the king was practically the only one in that era who was believed to have the power to interpret the results of divination and forecast the future. In an effort to gain better understanding and control over both state and personal affairs, the king took on the role of a shaman who seeks to communicate with the spirits that were believed to hold the real power over the land he ruled. Religious ritual was thus an indispensable part of state governance in ancient China.

The Shang pantheon of spirits included human souls as well as natural elements and supernatural beings. At its apex, far above the natural realm, sat the sky god known as the Lord-on-High (*di*). Some scholars have speculated that he might have been the ancestor-god of the Shang clan; he was more powerful than the other deities, and the only one who could command natural elements such as the rain, thunder, and wind. Below the Lord-on-High were the nature spirits believed to animate natural phenomena such as rivers and mountains; then the celestial spirits like the sun and moon; then 'Former Lords' (*xiangong*) who were associated with the Shang but were not royal clan members; and, finally, direct ancestors, both male and female. The mystique of the cult of ancestors and divination gave the Shang kings an aura of sacredness.

Divination entailed reading the cracks created by pressing a hot brand or poker onto bone (typically cattle scapula) or the ventral part of a tortoise shell. Subjects of inquiry ranged from the king's plans or health to the prospects for a successful harvest or military campaign to the interpretation of dreams. The king might also ask approval for his actions from the spirits, suggesting that one function of divination was to legitimate the kings' activities and, by extension, their rule. The belief in spirits, the interest in divination, and the need to communicate with the supernatural world survive today in folk practices and beliefs.

In the end, the Shang dynasty fell to the Zhou. This dynastic change is explained in the *Documents* as the result of the Shang's losing the Mandate of Heaven (*tianming*) and the Zhou's earning it through virtuous deeds. When King Wu fell ill, for example, his brother the Duke of Zhou offered to die in his place in a divination to Heaven; this act of self-sacrifice so pleased Heaven that both the Duke and the King were allowed to survive.

### Virtue and the Mandate of Heaven

After King Wu died, his brother the Duke served as regent for his young nephew but returned the throne to the boy once he was old enough to rule. Such loyalty was revered in the early Confucian tradition, and the Duke of Zhou's popularity rivalled that of Confucius. The Duke, an exemplary Confucian sage, thus personified restraint, humility, and willingness to listen to advice. He declared that the Shang had lost the Mandate, that Heaven had rejected them because their later kings failed to provide for their people.

In this way moral character became the primary determinant of the right to rule. The idea that rulers were obliged to rule well as a duty to

## On the Mandate of Heaven

*The Mandate of Heaven appears in the* Classic of Documents *in the form of a public announcement legitimating the Zhou overthrow of the Yin (an alternative name for the Shang):*

Heaven has rejected and ended the Mandate of this great state of Yin. Thus, although Yin has many former wise kings in Heaven, when their successor kings and successor people undertook their Mandate, in the end wise and good men lived in misery. Knowing that they must care for and sustain their wives and children, they then called out in anguish to Heaven and fled to places where they could not be caught. Ah! Heaven too grieved for the people of all the lands, wanting, with affection, in giving its Mandate to employ those who are deeply committed. The king should have reverent care for his virtue (D. Nivison in de Bary and Bloom 1999: 36).

Heaven reflected the Zhou belief in a moral force or supreme deity that ruled the world and took an interest in human affairs. How to encourage a king to rule ethically became a central concern for Confucians. In the *Classic of Odes*, King Wen addresses the last Shang king:

> King Wen said, Woe!
> Woe upon you, Yin and Shang!
> You have been the harsh oppressor,
> you have been grasping and crushing.
> You have been in the places of power,
> you have held the functions.
> Heaven sent recklessness down in you,
> and you rise by acts of force
>     (Owen 1996: 20).

Thus the mandate to rule was taken away from the cruel and negligent Shang and passed to the good and wise King Wen of Zhou. In this political transition, the term 'god' (*di*) became increasingly associated with the earthly political ruler, while Heaven came to be portrayed as an impartial universal being or power, an intelligent cosmic moral order that is concerned with human welfare and so gives the people a caring and virtuous king.

### Ancestor Veneration

Archaeological discoveries of bronze ritual vessels as well as textual sources attest to the Shang focus on ancestral spirits and the need to placate them with sacrifices. These beliefs and practices continued into the Zhou. Traces of this ancient royal practice survive today in the popular family practice of ancestor veneration. The Zhou traced their lineage to a mythical semi-divinity named Lord Millet (Hou Ji), a culture hero who eventually became a tutelary deity of agriculture. His birth is recounted in 'She Bore the Folk', a poem in the *Classic of Odes* that describes how he was conceived when his mother, the Lady Yuan of Jiang, trod on god's footprint.

Thus the first human ancestor of the Zhou is a woman, Lady Yuan, but the male lineage begins only with her semi-divine son, Lord Millet. The more immediate historical ancestry of the Zhou line is recorded in another poem, 'The Great Brightness', which describes the royal marriages that produced Kings Wu and Wen.

More important, while the first 'historical' account in the *Documents* focuses on the mythical male sage King Yao, the first poem in the *Odes*, entitled 'Fishhawks' or 'Ospreys', is about a maiden who is so 'pure and fair' as to be a fit mate for a prince. This poem suggests that only a gentle and virtuous woman can establish the ethical atmosphere and harmonious relations required of a royal household.

Because the *Odes* volume is believed to have been edited by Confucius, the prominent

---

## How Lord Millet Was Conceived

*From 'She Bore the Folk' in the* Classic of Odes:

She who first bore the folk—
Jiang it was, First Parent.
How was it she bore the folk?—
she knew the rite and sacrifice.
To rid herself of sonlessness
she trod the god's toeprint
and she was glad.
She was made great, on her luck settled,
the seed stirred, it was quick.
She gave birth, she gave suck,
and this was Lord Millet
    (Owen 1996: 12).

## A Maiden So Pure and Fair

*From 'Fishhawks' in the* Classic of Odes:

The fishhawks sing *gwan gwan*
on sandbars of the stream.
Gentle maiden, pure and fair,
Fit pair for a prince.

Watercress grows here and there,
right and left we gather it.
Gentle maiden, pure and fair,
wanted waking and asleep.

Watercress grows here and there,
right and left we pull it.
Gentle maiden, pure and fair,
with harps we bring her company.

Watercress grows here and there,
right and left we pick it out.
Gentle maiden, pure and fair,
with bells and drums do her delight
    (Owen 1996: 30–1).

placement of the 'Fishhawks' poem has suggested to later Confucians that the 'pure and fair', 'gentle maiden' is the Queen Consort of King Wen, the first historical ancestress of the Zhou dynasty. Confucius himself is said to have praised the poem as evoking 'delight without wantonness, sadness without hurtful pain' (*Analects* 3:20). If the maiden did represent the Queen Consort, she was a fine example of womanly virtues.

### Humanization: The Transition from Shang to Zhou

With the establishment of the Zhou dynasty, the concept of Heaven gained ascendancy over the more personal 'Lord on High' of the Shang. And though the interest in divination continued, the methods and materials used for the purpose changed over time, reflecting a change in understanding of the universe. Eventually, shell and bone were replaced by the plant stalks used for divination in the *Classic of Changes* (*I Ching*)—a change that reflected a conceptual shift away from an enchanted universe towards a more rational and impersonal one.

This shift did not mean the disappearance of the ancient belief that the world was controlled by ghosts, nature spirits, and celestial beings. This belief has continued to be an integral part of Chinese religion into the present, especially in folk traditions. Nevertheless, many Zhou thinkers diverged from the Shang in this respect. A number of schools developed and thrived: Legalists stressed the power of law in the advancement of human security and well-being; Naturalists concentrated on natural elements and processes; Mohists focused on ungraded and universal love for all; Confucians promoted the importance of human relationships, beginning with familial affection. Philosophers started to see the world as regulated by impersonal processes, which they sought to understand so that they might model human behaviour and society on them.

This quest to understand natural processes was driven in part by the desire to find a natural—hence 'right'—basis on which to structure human society, with the hope of attaining universal harmony. The sixty-four hexagrams that are the basis of the *Classic of Changes*, a divination text originating in the early Zhou dynasty (c. 1000 BCE), are said to capture the metaphysical structure, transformations, and 'Way' of the universe, thereby providing both a general blueprint and a specific guide to the correct human behaviour.

## A Pattern of Complementarity

The *Classic of Changes* is made up of two parts. The first is quite old and contains the 'answers' to the divinatory questions encoded in sixty-four symbolic hexagrams that are said to represent the pattern of cosmic transformations. The second part, with a commentary attributed to Confucius, consists of general philosophical writings interpreting those answers. The building blocks of the hexagrams are eight trigrams made up of broken (--) yin and solid (–) yang lines in different combinations. Each hexagram is composed of two of these trigrams. 'Yin' means shade and 'yang' means light; the words were first used to refer to the shady and sunny sides of a mountain. The philosophical commentaries seek to explain how human affairs are reflected in and related to cosmic events through the cycles of yin and yang.

The first hexagram in the *Changes*—the creative, Heaven (*Qian*)—consists of two yang trigrams and is a symbol of the male; it is considered the most creative and assertive hexagram. The second hexagram—the receptive, Earth (*Kun*)—consists of two yin trigrams and is a symbol of the female; it is considered the most receptive and yielding of the trigrams. This binary of yin and yang is fundamental to the understanding of both the natural and supernatural worlds.

The complementary nature of the yin-yang binary permeated Zhou thinking. *Master Tso's Commentary on the Spring and Autumn Annals (Zuo zhuan* or *Zuoshi chunqiu)*, for example, refers to a belief in two souls: a corporeal soul, which is yin in character, and is the first to develop, beginning when a baby is born; and an 'anima' soul that develops as the yang energy grows. When a person dies, the yin soul stays on earth, whereas the yang soul ascends to heaven. The yin-yang binary can also be seen in ideas about gender relations. Rituals were understood to affirm and reinforce these ideas, which centred on differentiation between women and men. This gender duality, complementarity, and/or symmetry was reflected in the fact that state rites required the participation of both male and female shamans and 'invocators'. In accordance with the yin-yang principle, the functions of the two sexes were necessarily different.

The male shaman supervised animal sacrifices to the spirits of mountains and rivers and summoned spirits from all quarters. He dispelled baneful influences from houses during winter, and in spring he warded off inauspiciousness while trying to call forth auspiciousness; he also dispelled epidemics. When the king was in mourning, the male shaman would come forward with the invocator and perform rituals to help the king in his grief. The female shaman, on the other hand, performed rituals of atonement and made offerings of herbs to the spirits. She danced the rain sacrifice in the event of droughts; in the event of great calamity, she would chant and cry in supplication; and when the queen was in mourning, a female shaman would come forward with the invocator.

The grand invocator, who was male, managed the liturgies for ghosts, spirits, and terrestrial divinities. The spirits were believed to be intelligent, morally upright, and consistent; and the invocator would pray for blessings and good fortune, longevity and uprightness. The female invocator, who worked with the grand invocator, supervised the inner realm in which sacrificial offerings were made on behalf of the queen, and the latter's petitions and offerings of thanksgiving in hope of blessings. She was responsible for seasonal invocations, atonement, exorcism, and deprecations (prayers for the removal and/or aversion of bad fortune); she also dispelled pestilence. This courtly ritual complementarity of male and female ritualists was reflected and reinforced in the persons of the king and queen.

## Rites: Performance and Principles

The section on 'Principles of Sacrifice' in the *Records of Rites* explains that a ruler must seek a wife as a helpmate in both his state and familial duties. This complementarity is reflected throughout the couple's lives in the structural division of labour, in the location and prescribed realms of belonging, as well as gender differentiation in ritual performance. The king and queen were together responsible for making offerings at the ancestral temple representing the imperial family, and the altars of the land and grain representing the people and state; in this way they attended to their duties in the outer and inner realms of male and female responsibilities, respectively.

According to the *Rites*, it was the role of the Son of Heaven (*tianzi*) and his lords to provide grain for the sacrificial rites by ploughing in the regions to the south and east of the capital city and the role of the queen and the wives of the lords to provide silk for ritual vestments by raising silkworms in the region to the north. These activities were not meant to be understood literally; rather, they were symbolic expressions of sincerity, good faith, and the royal couple's particular responsibility to encourage both Heaven and Earth to treat the state and its people with benevolence.

Before the start of any state ritual, the royal couple had to observe a ten-day vigil; the king fasted and performed purification rituals outside the palace, while the queen carried out her ritual obligations inside the palace. This reinforced symbolically the principle of complementary difference between men and women, the separateness of the outer and inner quarters, and illustrated the ideal of the husband and wife working side by side in their separate realms. This yin-yang balance extended even to the foods offered to the spirits; they too had to be chosen so as to balance the forces of yin and yang.

The rituals described in the *Rites* evolved over time, as did the understanding of their place and importance in the lives of an individual, state, and society. Belief in the magico-religious value of the rituals was gradually replaced by a sense of their value in terms of discipline, education, and moral development. The deeply religious nature of Shang culture was humanized by the philosophers of the later Zhou; and particularly by Confucius. In *Master Tso's Commentary*, for example, Kong Zhiji rebukes Duke Yu when the latter remarks

that the spirits will protect him because his sacrificial offerings are 'bountiful and pure':

> It is not simply that ghosts and spirits are attracted to human beings: it is virtue that attracts them. Hence . . . the *Book of History* says, 'August heaven has no partial affections; it supports only the virtuous.' It also says, 'It is not the millet that is fragrant; it is bright virtue that is fragrant' (adapted from J. Legge in Sommer 1995: 25).

This shift from belief in the supernatural efficacy of rituals to a reliance on virtue and moral behaviour finds further support in the story of a certain marquis of Qi who is reprimanded for requesting an exorcism in response to a comet: 'If your virtue is not unclean, then why this exorcism? . . . Do not transgress against virtue, and people from all quarters will come to you' (ibid., 26).

# CRYSTALLIZATION

## Confucius

Confucius spoke of himself as a transmitter of tradition rather than an innovator. On the connection between ritual performance and goodness in people, he famously said:

> Respect without ritual becomes tiresome, circumspection without ritual becomes timidity, bold fortitude without ritual becomes unruly, and directness without ritual becomes twisted' (Sommer 1995: 46).

Confucius believed that the ancient rites embodied wisdom from the earliest Zhou tradition, and he believed they should not be abandoned. Rather, he encouraged his students to seek the meaning, spirit, and principles behind them.

Two quasi-historical elements from the earliest tradition are central to the Confucian understanding of history: the sage kings Yao, Shun, and

Yu, and the religious and socio-cultural perfection they achieved by governing in accordance with the Way. The chapter on 'The Evolution of Rites' (*Liyun*) in the *Rites* records Confucius' belief in an original utopia that was lost, then followed by the period of Lesser Prosperity.

> When the Great Way was practised, the world was shared by all alike. The worthy and the able were promoted to office and men practised good faith and lived in affection. Therefore they did not regard as parents only their own parents, or as sons only their own sons. The aged found a fitting close to their lives, the robust their proper employment; the young were provided with an upbringing, and the widow and widower, the orphaned and the sick, with proper care. Men had their tasks and women their hearths. They hated to see goods lying about in waste, yet they did not hoard them for themselves; they disliked the thought that their energies were not fully used, yet they used them not for private ends. Therefore all evil plotting was prevented and thieves and rebels did not arise, so that the people could leave their outer gates unbolted. This was the age of Grand Commonalty [**Datong**] (B. Watson in de Bary and Bloom 1999: 342–3).

Then greed and selfishness banished the Grand Commonality and inaugurated the period of Lesser Prosperity, where the exemplary rule of the sage kings became indispensable. The *Analects* (*Lunyu*) is the single most important source of Confucius' teachings on strategies required to bring security to this potentially chaotic period.

It is not surprising that the quest for a stable, secure, and peaceful society was so important to Confucius, for he lived during the chaotic Spring and Autumn period. Born Kong Qiu, he was known to his contemporaries as Kongzi or Master Kong, and some of his later followers referred to him as Kong Fuzi, 'our Master Kong'. The Chinese term designating those scholars, *ru*, evokes a commitment to learning, cultural accomplishment, and refinement, especially through the practice of six arts: ritual observance, music, archery, charioteering, calligraphy, and mathematics.

Although the English word 'analects' means 'the select part, the essence or marrow', the book's Chinese title, *Lunyu* ('conversations') is a more literal description of its contents: recollected conversations between Confucius and his disciples, as well as his interviews with some feudal rulers of his time. Confucius himself had nothing to do with the collection, which was probably compiled over a period of time at least a century after his death.

At the core of Confucius' utopian ideal was the *junzi* (translated variously as 'gentleman' or 'noble', the 'exemplary' or 'superior person'). The standard meaning of *junzi* was 'son of a lord', indicating inherited social nobility, but in the *Analects* the word takes on a new meaning: this gentleman is a person of noble character, committed to the development of *de*—another word that underwent a shift in meaning with Confucius. Originally referring to a kind of magical charismatic power, in the *Analects* it signifies a moral power derived from virtuous, ethical behaviour.

The fact that Confucius used these words in non-traditional ways, however, did not mean that the concepts behind those uses were new; as we have seen, he described himself as a transmitter rather than an innovator. The socio-political ideals he sought to promote were already present in the classic texts (*Odes*, *Documents*, *Spring and Autumn Annals*, and *Changes*). Confucius used the single word **ren**—variously translated as 'humaneness', 'benevolence', 'compassion', or 'goodness'—to capture the virtues of respect, liberality, trustworthiness, earnestness, and kindness. In his view, the most effective way to cultivate *ren* was through careful observance of *li*—the 'rites'—by which he meant not only religious rituals but also the rules of social etiquette and everyday courtesy.

Above all, Confucius emphasized the practice of filial piety or devotion. The 'Principles of Sacrifice' chapter of the *Rites* explains filial devotion as 'caring for' one's parents according to the Way (*Dao*): that is, to the greatest extent possible without neglecting one's responsibilities in other relationships (8.2.1). But it could include everything from looking after oneself and not harming one's body to protecting family members even when they had committed a crime. Confucius also understood that ritual performance was integral to the maintenance of harmony:

> Let there be no discord. . . . When one's parents are alive, one serves them in accordance with the rites; when they are dead, one buries them in accordance with the rites and sacrifices to them in accordance with the rites (2:5).

Some scholars have suggested that this focus on filial piety is one reason for the relative absence of strong affiliations to particular denominations or sects in the Chinese tradition. The popularity of institutional Daoism and Buddhism notwithstanding, the primary religious institution remained the family, and this likely contributed to the diffuse nature of Chinese religion.

Why was ritual decorum such an important part of filial piety? Confucius quotes the *Documents*: 'Be filial. Just being filial and friendly toward one's brothers has its effect on government' (2:21). In other words, true filial devotion had an extraordinary power—a power so great that even someone unable to obtain a government position (as Confucius was for much of his life) could exert a positive influence on society simply by performing his filial duty.

More specifically, Confucius suggests that those who are filial towards their parents and fraternal towards their brothers will be disinclined to offend against their superiors, and thus unlikely to create disorder. In addition to promoting harmony, this quality of loyalty would discourage involvement in movements seeking alternatives to a political system founded on the Mandate of Heaven. Thus Confucius explains that the 'noble person concerns himself with the root; when the root is established, the way is born. Being filial and fraternal—is this not the root of humaneness?' (1:2).

Above all, familial love makes the gentleman a humane person. The quality of humaneness is reflected in two characteristics: loyalty and empathetic understanding or reciprocity (*shu*) (4:15). Refining this idea, Confucius encapsulates his teachings in the 'silver rule': 'What you would not want for yourself, do not do to others' (15:23). Thus the noble person is the one who puts the self aside

A rock carving (c. 1127–1279) from the cave complex at Dazu, in Sichuan, depicts a loving son. Although the Dazu complex was predominantly Buddhist in orientation, the ideal of filial piety transcended religious boundaries (© Pierre Colombel/CORBIS).

and 'relinquishes arrogance, boasting, resentment, and covetousness' (14:2).

Who can be a noble person? Everyone. But there is a catch. Confucius teaches that all human beings are by nature similar to each other, and are set apart only through their actions (17:2). Thus even as he democraticizes the idea of nobility, he creates a hierarchy of character achieved through moral cultivation. This hierarchy is all about the mastery of self:

> Through mastering oneself and returning to ritual one becomes humane. If for a single day one can master oneself and return to ritual, the whole world will return to humaneness. . . . Look at nothing contrary to ritual; listen to nothing contrary to ritual; say nothing contrary to ritual; do nothing contrary to ritual (12:1).

Confucius believes that if the ruler wants goodness, then the people will be good because 'The virtue (*de*) of the noble (or exemplary) person is like the wind, and the virtue of small people is like grass. When the wind blows over the grass, the grass must bend' (12:19). The achievement of the Grand Commonalty thus requires that good, humane people rule over those who are small-minded, or morally inferior.

The Confucian mandate is to limit the negative consequences of the behaviour of ignoble people. When a recluse describes Confucius as 'a scholar who withdraws from particular men,' and suggests that instead Confucius should withdraw from society, Confucius sighs and responds: 'If the Way prevailed in the world, [I, Confucius] would not be trying to change it' (18:6). Personal, individual goodness and humaneness alone, therefore, are not enough: ethical nobility must be reflected in action.

What the right and appropriate action is, however, depends on the actor. One of Confucius' most famous prescriptions involves what he called the 'rectification of names' (*zhengming*): 'Let the ruler be a ruler; the minister, a minister; the father, a father; the son, a son' (12:11). In other words, each person must fulfil his or her own duties; otherwise there will be chaos.

It follows that in their relationships with one another, each party must be true to his or her own proper role. The 'Grand Model' that was said to have been given to the sage-emperor Yu after he tamed the floods mentioned five such relationships, beginning with the one between emperor and minister. The second relationship is the one between father and son; the third, between elder and younger brother; the fourth, between husband and wife; and the fifth, between friends. In each case, both parties must strive to be humane, but this quality expresses itself in different ways: as reciprocity in the senior partner, and loyalty in the junior one.

In the same way, different actors have different spheres of influence in which it is appropriate to act. Thus the queen stays in the inner realm of the palace and does not plough the fields in the south of the city, whereas the king stays outside the palace and does not practice sericulture (silk-making) to the north of the city.

## Mencius

The second most prominent classical thinker after Confucius is **Meng Ke**, addressed respectfully as Master Meng or Mengzi and latinized as Mencius. He lived more than a century after Confucius, in the fourth century BCE. By that time large conscript armies had replaced the elite chariot forces on which the rulers of the various feudal states had relied in the past, resulting in a horrific increase in the human cost of war.

In an effort to stop the carnage, Mencius travelled from state to state meeting with rulers and trying to persuade them to act in the interest of their people. He deplored the consequences of war:

In wars to gain land, the dead fill the plains;
in wars to gain cities, the dead fill the cities.
This is known as showing the land the way
to devour human flesh. Death is too light
a punishment for such men. Hence those
skilled in war should suffer the most severe
punishments . . . (4.A.14 Lau 1970: 124).

At the same time he tried to persuade rulers of the
practical value of humaneness (*ren*), expanding on
Confucius' understanding and placing rightness
(*yi*) beside *ren*.

The book *Mencius* is a collection of conversations between Mencius and his disciples, his op-
ponents in debate, and the rulers of the various
feudal states. Prominent among the issues discussed are human nature and government.

Wishing to 'follow in the footsteps of the three
sages [Yu, the Duke of Zhou, and Confucius] in
rectifying the hearts of men, laying heresies to
rest, opposing extreme action, and banishing excessive views' (ibid., 115), Mencius traced many
of the problems of his day to the human 'heart-
mind'. He identified four types of heart-mind,
each of which he associated with a particular kind
of behaviour. Thus the heart-mind of compassion
yields benevolence; the heart-mind of shame leads
to observance of rites; the heart-mind of respect
moves people to duty or right behaviour; and the
heart-mind of right and wrong brings wisdom
(*zhi*) (6.A.6 ibid., 163).

Mencius taught that no one is devoid of 'a heart
sensitive to the suffering of others'; the ancient
kings possessed this heart-mind and expressed
it in compassionate governance. In later times,
however, a great man—teacher, scholar-official, or
imperial minister—was needed to encourage the
ruler to cultivate a mature heart-mind; then, when
the prince is benevolent, dutiful, and correct, everyone else would seek to emulate him.

In this case, however, in contrast to the sce-
nario described by Confucius, the effect of the
prince's character on the people is not automatic
or magical. Mencius believed that human nature
was essentially good, but that the common people needed supervision and discipline: otherwise,
once their bellies were full and their bodies warmly clothed, they would degenerate to the level of
animals driven only by material needs and desires,
with no higher consciousness. The most effective
way of nurturing the heart-mind of the people,
Mencius taught, was neither to deprive them nor
to give them more than they needed to survive,
but to teach them to reduce their desires.

Noble rulers thus had the responsibility to educate and provide discipline for common people so
that they would not be led astray and their heart-
minds would be nurtured and grow. The noble
person would be involved by teaching them in five
ways: through transformative influence, by helping people reach their full potential in virtue, by
helping them to develop their talents, by answer-
ing their questions, and by setting an example for
those located too far away for direct contact.

Does everyone have the heart-mind to benefit from such guidance? Mencius believed so; he
thought the unsullied, heaven-given heart-mind
was a part of human nature:

Suppose a man were, all of a sudden, to see
a young child on the verge of falling into a
well. He would certainly be moved to compassion, not because he wanted to get in the
good graces of the parents, nor because he
wished to win the praise of his fellow villag-
ers or friends, nor yet because he disliked
the cry of the child (2. A. 6; ibid., 164–5).

And what of a person who does not respond to
the child? Such a person, Mencius said, is like a
mountain that has been clear-cut and then is subjected to constant grazing by cattle and sheep, so
that it never has a chance to recover its verdant
original nature: such a person has been stripped
of his natural goodness by external circumstances
that have reduced him to a state of savagery.

His belief in the ability of the mature heart-mind
to arrive at sound conclusions allowed Mencius to

take some unconventional positions. For example, he rejected the notion that filial piety demanded blind obedience. Once, when someone suggested that Shun, the son-in-law of King Yao, had defied the rule of filial piety by failing to inform his parents of his marriage to Yao's two daughters, Mencius defended Shun on the grounds that his parents' heart-minds were not well developed and therefore they would have refused him their permission to marry. Shun's own heart-mind, by contrast, was sufficiently well developed that he was justified in acting independently, according to his conscience. Similarly, Mencius argued against blind obedience to the rule that unrelated men and women should not touch one another, pointing out that it would be inhuman for a man not to rescue his sister-in-law if she were drowning. On another occasion he remarked that if everything in the *Documents* had to be accepted without critical thought, it would be better if the text had never been written. Most famously, he drew on the concept of the Mandate of Heaven to argue that rebellion is justified when the ruler is dissolute and the people are suffering. In short, according to Mencius, it is not enough simply to follow the classical teachings: we must use our heart-minds to determine the correct course of action.

Mencius is sometimes called a mystic because of the way he described the 'flood-like vital force, energy or ethers' called *qi* (or *ch'i*), which appears simultaneously to give substance to virtue and to be nourished by it:

> This is a *ch'i* which is, in the highest degree vast and unyielding. Nourish it with integrity and place no obstacle in its path and it will fill the space between Heaven and Earth. It is a *ch'i* which unites rightness and the Way. Deprive it of these and it will collapse. It is born of accumulated rightness and cannot be appropriated by anyone through a sporadic show of rightness. Whenever one acts in a way that falls below the standard set in one's heart, it will collapse (2.A.2; ibid., 77–8).

Virtue cannot be forced: it can be given substance only by following one's heart-mind and acting with integrity and rightness. It is in nourishing this vital force through constant practice of integrity and right action, Mencius suggests, that human beings can achieve cosmic oneness and harmony.

## Xunzi

Xun Kuang or Xun Qing (c. 310–219 BCE) better known as Master Xun or Xunzi, was a generation younger than Mencius. Living at the end of the horribly violent Warring States period, he likely witnessed the bloody conquest of the last feudal states by the first emperor, Qin (Qinshihuang). The book *Xunzi* was compiled and edited more than a century after his time, during the Han dynasty.

The form of this work marks a major departure from the recorded conversations of the *Analects* and *Mencius*: it consists mainly of essays in which Xunzi reflects on topics such as the original Heaven-given nature of human beings, learning, self-cultivation, government, and military affairs, as well as the origins of and the need for rites and music.

The wars that led to the Qin victory were brutal and the political intrigue of the time was vicious. It is not surprising, then, that Xunzi disagreed with Mencius on the basic goodness of human beings. Xunzi believed that human nature was evil, and that 'goodness is the result of conscious activity' (Watson 1963: 157). Nonetheless, he agreed readily with the core Confucian belief in the possibility of sagehood, and in the value of culture and learning. In his view, education and ritual were essential to the maintenance of the hierarchy required for a society to function in an orderly fashion. But he was not blind to the misuse and corruption of the Confucian system. Like Confucius and Mencius, who criticized the 'village worthy' who performed all the right actions but was insincere, Xunzi spoke out against 'rotten Confucians' and people who 'stole a reputation for virtue'.

The first chapter in the *Xunzi*, entitled 'Encouraging Learning', underlines the necessity of effort in the achievement of moral progress:

> Learning should never cease. Blue comes from the indigo plant but is bluer than the plant itself. Ice is made of water but is colder than water ever is. A piece of wood as straight as a plumb line may be bent into a circle as true as any drawn with a compass and, even after the wood has dried, it will not straighten out again (Watson 1963: 15).

It is not enough to study the Classics: some of the issues addressed in the *Odes* and *Documents* are too ancient to be relevant; the *Spring and Autumn Annals* are not easy to understand; and ritual and music performance are incomplete as guides because they provide models without explanation. Rather, Xunzi taught that to learn sagehood, 'nothing is more profitable than to associate with those who are learned' (ibid., 16).

Why do human beings need to be 'straightened'? Because, Xunzi believed, they are bent with inborn desires—for everything from profit to beautiful sights and sounds—that spark feelings of envy and hate. Xunzi believed that if these innate tendencies were not curbed and people succumbed to their extreme emotions and desires, competition for scarce objects of desire would inevitably lead to chaos. This is what he meant when he said that human beings are 'evil' by nature and must seek transformation through the guidance of sages and ritual principles: only then will they be able to cultivate courtesy and humility. Xunzi's belief that the rituals were introduced by the ancient sages specifically to prevent chaos and disorder, together with his focus on human effort, marks a conceptual departure from the supernatural notion of divine revelation in the story about Yu and the Grand Model.

In his chapter 'A Discussion of Heaven', Xunzi continues Confucius' efforts to humanize the Zhou tradition, turning sharply away from the supernatural in favour of the rational and natural. He sees Heaven, Earth, and humanity as forming a trinity in which each component has its own clearly defined role: 'To bring to completion without acting, to obtain without seeking—this is the work of Heaven' (Watson 1963: 80); as a human being, even the sage does not seek to understand Heaven, let alone to take over its 'godlike' role. Rather, humans should focus on the human world and the activities necessary for humans to live well and prosper. The noble person cherishes the power he has and does not try to usurp the power of Heaven.

> When the work of Heaven has been established and its accomplishments brought to completion, when the form of man is whole and his spirit is born, then love and hate, delight and anger, sorrow and joy find lodging in him. These are called his heavenly emotions. Ears, eyes, nose, mouth, and body . . . are called the heavenly faculties. The heart (*xin*) dwells in the centre and governs the five faculties, and hence it is called the heavenly lord (Watson 1963: 80–1).

Even though Xunzi understood the human or natural world to operate without supernatural intervention, he supported the performance of traditional rituals addressed to Heaven because he believed that they had been perfected by the ancient kings. Only a sage can fully understand the rites, he said; but the noble person finds comfort in performing them as a part of human culture, while the common person accepts them as customs that reflect the reality of the spirit world. Xunzi takes ritual and music out of the realm of magic by interpreting their functions in practical terms. Thus the purpose of teaching the rites (*li jiao*, another name for Confucianism) is to cultivate virtues—such as courtesy and humility—that discourage aggression and promote harmony. Similarly, even if the performance of rituals does not 'satisfy fully the desire of the mouth and the stomach, the ears and the eyes', it can still produce satisfaction by 'teach[ing] people to moderate their likes and dislikes and return to the proper human Way [*rendao*]' (de Bary and Bloom 1999: 344).

It is through the performance of rites that people come to perceive the differences between the eminent and the humble, elder and younger, rich and poor, important and unimportant; recognize their place in the hierarchy; and learn to accept their 'rightful' share in the society. This is illustrated by the reciprocal relationship between 'superiors' and 'subordinates' in the *Rites*:

> Sacrifice is a great benefaction. When superiors receive some benefit, they then bestow it on those below them. It is just that superiors receive the beneficence first and

subordinates receive it later; it is not that superiors accumulate excess while subordinates suffer from cold and hunger (Sommer 1995: 37).

The social privilege that gives those who are politically prominent first access to benefits is balanced by the absolute duty it creates to share those benefits with all.

Music also plays an important role in self-cultivation. Xunzi explains how music can calm and ennoble the spirit:

> Music enters deeply into men and transforms them rapidly. Therefore, former kings were careful to give it the proper form. When music is moderate and tranquil, the

## Three Schools Contemporary to the Confucians and Proto-Daoists

The Legalists rejected Confucian virtues like humaneness and rightness. Instead, they advocated war to strengthen the ruler and keep the people disciplined and submissive, and laws and punishments to keep them within bounds. They were especially interested in developing ways in which state power could be organized so that it might be concentrated in one single ruler.

The Naturalists, also known as the yin-yang *jia* (school), believed that those who adhered to the celestial and seasonal laws would flourish while those who ignored and deviated from the natural cycles would perish. Yin-yang theory was later combined with a similar theory based on five 'phases', 'agents', or 'elements' (**wuxing**)—metal, wood, earth, water, and fire—that were thought to correlate spatially to the four directions plus the centre and temporally to the four seasons and twelve months.

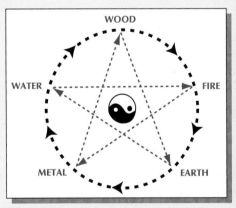

The Mohists were founded by Mo Di, whose name suggests that he may have been a prisoner or a slave. He criticized Confucians on three counts: the extravagance of their state and ancestral rituals; their skepticism regarding the existence of spiritual beings and a personal, anthropomorphic Heaven; and their tendency towards fatalism. Mo is best known for his frugality and his belief in *jianai*, an undifferentiated, ungraded love that he believed Heaven offered to all equally. This love should then be expressed by princes and kings by taking care of people's material needs.

(Illustration adapted from <http://www.users.globalnet.co.uk/~oci/fiveelementdiagram.htm>.)

people become harmonious and shun excess. When music is stern and majestic, the people become well behaved and shun disorder. . . . In such a case, the common people will dwell in safety, take delight in their communities, and look up to their superiors with complete satisfaction (Watson 1963: 114).

Xunzi, like Mencius, believed that the key to moral and spiritual development was the heart-mind. Humans are born in tranquillity but do not remain there. To return to that original state, it is necessary to cultivate a heart-mind that is empty, united, and still, unsullied by excessive emotions and desires, and broad in understanding. Rites and music are spiritual disciplines that cultivate this heart-mind and guard against chaos. Xunzi's perspective was only one of several competing for the attention of contemporary rulers. Three other schools of thought that were current in the same period are outlined in the box on page 273.

# ❧ DIFFERENTIATION

## Han Confucianism

The transition from the Qin dynasty to the Han (202 BCE–220 CE) dynasty brought political and intellectual changes that would shape imperial ideology as well as religious beliefs and practices for the next two thousand years. Trustworthiness (**xin**), a fifth virtue, was added to Mencius' four heart-minds of humaneness, right action, ritual appropriateness, and wisdom. The notions that Heaven, Earth, and human beings form a trinity and that the celestial and terrestrial powers will respond to human entreaty (*ganying*), were central to Han ideology. Han Confucian thinkers, reflecting the influence of Xunzi and a chapter in the *Rites* entitled 'The Doctrine of the Mean' (*Zhongyong*; also translated as 'Centrality and Equilibrium' or 'Centrality and Harmony'), believed that human

beings, if they were perfectly sincere in their efforts to cultivate themselves and bring about peace and harmony, could participate in the creative work and transformative powers of Heaven and Earth.

Echoing Mencius and Xunzi, Han Confucians identified economic welfare as the basis of morality. The government, and in particular the emperor, was obliged to provide for the populace both the physical sustenance and the moral education necessary for a secure, stable, and happy life. Following Xunzi, Han Confucians also promoted moral education through ritual, music, and literature.

The Han dynasty was a particularly important time in the history of Confucianism. Political or state Confucianism was established when the teaching became state orthodoxy under Emperor Wu in the first century BCE. In the process, in order to offer a holistic account of the universe and humankind's place in it, philosophers tried to synthesize the Confucian tradition with other philosophies. The result was an official Confucianism that was syncretic in nature, blending ideas from traditional texts and thinkers with belief in omens (promoted at court by masters of technical methods who were believed to be adept at manipulating the cosmos) and the notions of yin-yang and the five phases associated with the Naturalist school.

It was also during this period that some of the most influential texts were written, compiled, and edited. The idea of a Confucian canon in the form of the Five Classics was first proposed during the Han; influential non-canonical texts like the *Biographies of Exemplary* (or *Virtuous*) *Women* (*Lienu zhuan*), *Admonitions* (or *Lessons*) *for Women* (*Nu jie*), and the *Classic of Filiality* (*Xiaojing*) were written or compiled and edited in this period. *Exemplary Women* and *Admonitions* in particular defined and standardized what was expected of women, and formed the foundation of a woman's Confucian tradition that would run parallel to the men's.

Han Confucians understood Confucius to have transmitted the Zhou tradition through the canonical texts, and believed that he had a hand in the selection, compilation, and editing of all of the

Five Classics, but later scholars have shown that a good portion of their content originated after Confucius' time.

## The Compilation of the Five Classics

The Warring States that weakened the Zhou dynasty were unified by the first Qin emperor, who—in an apparent effort to minimize opposition—ordered the destruction of a great many books in his empire. Therefore the classical texts had to be reconstructed. The first classic, *Changes*, was gradually compiled and arranged in its current form over the course of the Zhou dynasty and assumed particular importance under the Han, during the first and second centuries BCE. As we have noted, it is thought to embody the metaphysical structure and the Way of the universe, and is divided into two parts: a short passage that interprets the result of the divination and, following that, ten appendices or 'wings' that elaborate on the significance of the interpretations. Traditionally, the ten wings were attributed to Confucius.

Confucius is also said to have edited or written a short introduction to each section of the second classic, the *Documents*. Recent scholarship has shown that some of the content dates from as late as the fourth century CE. Nevertheless, most Chinese through history have considered this volume to be an accurate account of China's ancient rulers, from the sage kings Yao, Shun, and Yu to the early Zhou kings. These records offer models and examples of good and bad qualities in the numerous governments and institutions.

The third classic, the *Odes*, contains about three hundred poems, mostly from the early Zhou, that Confucius is believed to have chosen and edited. They include folk songs from various states, as well as songs used in sacrificial ceremonies by the aristocracy or at banquets and other functions; both types of songs were frequently interpreted politically as the people's praise for virtuous rule or criticism against bad government.

The fourth classic, *Rites*, consists of three separate texts: *Rites of Etiquette and Ceremonials* (*Yili*) for minor officials, *Rites* (or *Institutions*) *of Zhou* (*Zhou li* or *Zhou guan*), and the *Records* or *Book of Rites* (*Liji*) that delve into the principles of rites. The contents likely date from the middle to late Zhou to early Han and took their current form over time. Confucius is credited with the compilation and editing of some of these ritual texts, whose contents range from the minutest details on how to live daily life to the broadest philosophical discussions on the meaning of state rituals and ceremonies.

The fifth and last classic, *Spring and Autumn Annals* is a terse chronicle of events in Confucius' native state of Lu from 722 to 481 BCE. Confucius is said to have compiled it from archival materials in order to express his judgments of past events. It was therefore used as a guide to moral laws and principles in the management of human affairs. Because the historical text is so brief, it is usually read with the help of three commentaries: the *Zuo*, *Gongyang*, and *Guliang* commentaries.

The adoption of Confucianism as state orthodoxy was by no means a foregone conclusion, as competing religious-philosophical groups and ideas continued to develop not only through the troubled times of the Qin but through the Han. It was the Confucians, so focused and dependent on texts, who were hardest hit by the burning of scholarly books by the first Qin emperor and the destruction in the capital (near Chang'an around the area that is now Xi'an), before the establishment of the new Han dynasty. And it was the Confucian literati who, more than any other group, took up the enormous task of retrieving and assembling lost texts during the period of political stability and economic prosperity in the third and second centuries BCE. They compiled, edited, and annotated dictionaries and great works of history belonging to other schools as well as their own.

The early 'books' were written on strips of bamboo bound together by cords or thongs, but the thongs decayed and as a result the original order of their contents was lost. When they were recovered, it was difficult to determine which version was authoritative, and different arrangements of the recovered material gave rise to different interpretations. Then there were texts written in different scripts. One legend has it that copies were found in the wall of Confucius' home in the state of Lu; these became known as the Old Text edition because, unlike the New Text copies, they were written in the archaic characters of the Zhou period rather than the standardized characters of the Qin and Han.

There was a private Old Text group based in the region of the old state of Lu, and one of its most famous scholars was a direct descendant of Confucius, Kong Anguo (156?–74? BCE); but it was **Dong Zhongshu** (195?–105? BCE), an older contemporary of Kong, who was the most influential Confucian at court.

### Dong Zhongshu

Dong, the leading official proponent of the New Text school, was most influential in persuading Emperor Wu (r. 141–87 BCE) to adopt Confucianism as state orthodoxy. Like many during the Han, Dong tried to legitimize his 'natural model' of how the world works based on the idea of correlation between the macrocosm of Heaven and Earth and the microcosm of the human body.

Focusing on questions of cosmology and the character of the natural order, Dong was most interested in self-cultivation, the development of sagehood, and good and right government. He wanted to explain how humanity—especially the emperor who was honoured as the Son of Heaven (*tianzi*)—could complete the work of Heaven and Earth and form a triad with them. Straying from Xunzi's naturalism, he believed—with the masters of technical methods—that omens were warnings sent by Heaven when the emperor deviated from the right way.

Dong set out to integrate Confucian ideas with the supernatural thinking of court diviners; the correlative thinking of the Huang-Lao movement (see the section on Daoism); and the yin-yang thinking of the Naturalist school. In following the Confucian interest in human nature and emotion through Mencius and Xunzi, Dong took ideas from both, then sought to integrate them with the Naturalist concept of vital force in the components of yin and yang.

He divided human nature into two aspects, associating feelings or emotions with yin, and humanity or love with yang. Yin, Dong said, must always be controlled and restricted; otherwise the Heavenly quality of humaneness would not manifest itself. He also used yin and yang to explain the 'Three Bonds', or primary relationships (*sangang*): emperor–minister, father–son, and husband–wife. In Dong's rendering, the senior was yang, as expressed in the emperor, father, and husband; the junior was yin, as expressed in the minister, son, and wife. It is natural and right, according to this thinking, that the yang partner should take precedence over the yin, and that the latter should be restrained and controlled.

Dong also described two cycles of the five phases. There was one of generation in which the elements give birth to each phase: as wood produces fire, fire earth, earth metal, metal water, and water wood; and another one of conquest, in which metal overcomes wood, wood overcomes earth, earth water, water fire, and fire metal. For Dong, these five phases correlated not only to human relationships but also to changes in the political realm (where the Xia was overtaken by the Yin [or Shang] dynasty, which was in turn overtaken by the Zhou) and the five viscera (heart, liver, spleen, lungs, and kidneys) of the human body. Dong associated the supremacy of human beings over all creation with the fact that the human head is large and round like Heaven.

As part of his advocacy of Confucianism as state orthodoxy, Dong encouraged the establishment of a state college that would foster Confucian scholarship. Such a college was set up in 124 BCE. By the end of that century it had an enrollment of three thousand students, and by the Latter Han (25–220 CE) the number had risen to thirty thousand. In this way the civil service came to be filled with men trained in the official Confucian curriculum, which included the Five Classics and the 'six arts'. As these men learned in Confucianism, gradually replaced the feudal aristocracy of the Zhou in government, Confucius' vision of the noble person as one defined by character and merit rather than birth moved closer to reality.

Some scholars have suggested that Emperor Wu chose Confucianism as the state orthodoxy because the Confucian idea of the Mandate of Heaven served to legitimate his authority. In fact, however, the Confucian literature expected the emperor's authority to be circumscribed by ministers who would counsel restraint and discourage extravagance. According to the tradition, it was both the right and the duty of ministers to restrain

## Map 6.1  Indigenous Chinese Religions

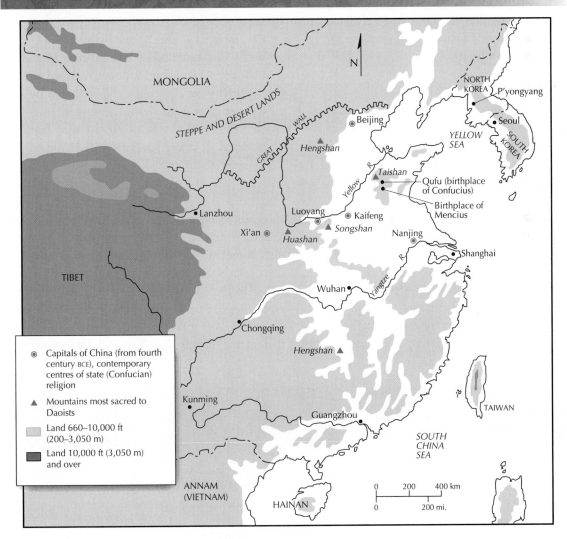

*Source*: Adapted from al Faruqi and Sopher 1974: 111.

the ruler's power by insisting on ministerial consultation. It is here that the function of Dong's yin-yang complementarity becomes clear. If the emperor and his ministers were not in harmony, as Heaven and Earth are, there would be chaos in the state. According to Han Confucianism, therefore, harmony requires that the emperor heed the counsel of his ministers, and that the husband heed the counsel of his wife.

At the close of the Han, two Old Text scholars named Yang Xiong and Wang Chong deconstructed Dong's system of correlation, separating the classical Confucian teachings from the yin-yang–five phases notions that Dong had associated with them and clearing away some of the more extravagant aspects of his theory.

### The Classic of Filiality

This focus on ministerial influence was especially clear in the influential *Classic of Filiality* (*Xiaojing*). According to tradition, this text comes from the school traced to Confucius' disciple Zengzi. By the Latter Han, *Filiality* and Confucius' *Analects* had been added to the Five Classics to make the Seven Classics. Presented in the form of what is likely an apocryphal conversation between Zengzi and Confucius, the *Classic of Filiality* broadens the definition of filial devotion outlined in the *Rites*, extends the notion of continuity between the human and spirit worlds through the veneration of ancestors, and connects filial piety to the idea of the triad formed by Heaven, Earth, and human

beings. Following the *Rites*, the classic clearly establishes filiality as the foundation of all virtues and the basis of public morality:

> The Master [Confucius] said, 'Loving one's parents, one dare not hate others. Revering one's parents, one dare not be contemptuous of others. When his love and reverence are perfected in service to parents, [the ruler's] moral influence is shed on all the people and his good example shines in all directions. . . .
>
> The Master said, 'Filiality is the ordering principle of Heaven, the rightness of the Earth, and the norm of human conduct. This ordering of Heaven and Earth is what people should follow; illumined by the brightness of Heaven and benefited by the resources of the Earth, all-under-Heaven (that is, the whole world) are thus harmonized. . . . (W.T. de Bary in de Bary and Bloom 1999: 326–27)

The text then goes on to highlight the central role that ministerial critique plays in the tradition. When Zengzi asks if a child must obey all his parents' commands in carrying out the imperative to love, respect, and comfort them so that one's reputation might be maintained, Confucius answers emphatically that like the minister who counsels his prince, so a son must remonstrate with his father so that the parent will not fall into evil ways.

### From the *Classic of Filiality*

What kind of talk is this! What kind of talk is this! Of old the Son of Heaven had seven counsellors, so that even if he himself lost the Way, he still would not lose his sway over all-under-Heaven. . . . If a father had even one son to remonstrate with him, he still would not fall into evil ways. In the face of whatever is not right, the son cannot but remonstrate with his father, and the minister cannot but remonstrate with his prince. If it is not right, remonstrate! . . . (de Bary and Bloom 1999: 328–9).

The idea of mutual guidance and remonstration, of correcting what is wrong, is thus an integral part of all relationships. This is no less true for women in their role as counsellors of the inner realm, and the men around them.

## Women

According to the *History of the Former Han Dynasty* (*Han shu*), Liu Xiang wrote the *Biographies of Exemplary Women* because he believed that women had a critical, if indirect and informal, role to play in government. To Liu's mind, the emperor would necessarily reflect the influence of his closest private counsellors, beginning with the empress. From the *Odes* and *Documents* Liu chose and included in his text models of exemplary women, some of whom had contributed to the peace and prosperity of their countries and the good reputation of their families, and some of whom had brought about the downfall of dynasties (Raphals 1998: 19). *Exemplary Women* identifies seven categories of women:

1. Maternal Rectitude,
2. Sage Intelligence,
3. Benevolent Wisdom,
4. Chaste and Obedient,
5. Chaste and Righteous,
6. Skill in Argument, and
7. Vicious and Depraved.

Under 'Maternal Rectitude' he tells the famous story of Mengmu—the widowed mother of Mencius. She is said to have moved three times, finally settling next to a school so that Mencius would grow up in the right environment for his studies. The focus on education is strong. On one occasion, Mencius answered nonchalantly 'as usual' to her question about his day at school. In response, Mengmu took a knife to the loom and destroyed the cloth she had been weaving. This dramatic action was aimed at showing by analogy that a man who does not take learning seriously is like a woman who neglects her responsibility to provide for her family. Mencius' mother is said to have been a motivating force in his life.

Another story in *Exemplary Women*, under the heading 'Skill in Argument', tells of a girl of twelve who, against her mother's wishes, was determined to admonish the king (her uncle by marriage) against his dissolute ways. She intercepted his chariot, gained an audience with him, and charged him with responsibility for 'three calamities and five evils: dissipation, extravagance, the exhaustion of the country, starvation of the common people, and wicked ministers' (ibid., 45–6). The king responded by marrying her and turning over a new leaf. Both stories illustrate the influence that a woman could exercise through intelligence and wisdom despite her yin nature and junior status in relation to her husband.

## Ban Zhao

Like a man's moral development, a woman's cultivation began at home, in the family, with herself. Self-cultivation was especially important for women because the Han Chinese believed that the cultivation of proper behaviour in a child should begin even before birth, while the child was still in the womb.

As children mature, according to a chapter from the *Rites* entitled 'Inner Maxims' (*Neize*), boys and girls should be separated: they should no longer sit on the same mat or eat together after reaching the age of seven. At the age of ten, boys were sent out to study with teachers, whereas girls were discouraged from leaving the house. While boys learnt the six arts, girls were taught the domestic skills they would need as providers of material comfort, emotional stability, and moral guidance for their families.

In addition to learning how to weave, sew, and prepare food, girls were taught etiquette—the conventions of social behaviour required for harmonious relations—and the rituals, including how to perform the sacrifices to ancestors necessary to express filial piety and keep peace with the spirits. At the age of fifteen a girl's hair was pinned up—a ceremonial rite of passage signalling that she was ready for marriage.

**Ban Zhao** (c. 48–112 CE) said she wrote *Admonitions* out of concern for her daughters, who had not had the benefit of systematic training in their roles either as wives or as daughters- and sisters-in-law in their husbands' families. Ban did not want her daughters' lack of good manners to bring shame to their ancestors, family, and clan.

Born into a leading scholarly family, Ban was said to have taken over the compilation of the *History of the Former Han* after the deaths of her father and brother. According to one later dynastic history, she worked in the imperial libraries and supervised the writing of treatises on astronomy and the chronological tables of nobles. Recognizing Ban's erudition, the emperor appointed her as tutor to the women at court, and she later served as an advisor to Empress Deng, who became regent in 106 CE and remained in power for fifteen years.

Socially prominent, well educated, and politically influential, Ban Zhao illustrates well the place of an aristocratic woman in Han society. *Admonitions* is divided into seven chapters:

1. Humility,
2. Husband and Wife,
3. Respect and Caution,
4. Womanly Qualifications,
5. Whole-hearted Devotion,
6. Implicit Obedience, and
7. Harmony with Younger Brothers- and Sisters-in-law.

Deferring to tradition, she describes three ritual customs performed at the birth of a girl and then explains the principles behind them. First, the baby girl is placed below the bed to signify that she is lowly and weak and must humble herself before others; second, she is given potsherd to play with to show that she must work hard; and third, she is announced to the ancestors to mark the importance of her role in the veneration of ancestors at home.

Ban belongs very much in the Confucian lineage, for she draws on the classical tradition, Mencius, and Dong Zhongshu. She believed that relationships are founded on the cosmic principles of yin and yang, and Heaven and Earth. Because yang is distinctive in its rigidity, a man is honoured for his strength; and as yin is characteristically yielding, a woman is considered beautiful for her gentleness. Ban writes under 'Husband and Wife':

> The Way of husband and wife is intimately connected with *Yin* and *Yang*, and relates the individual to gods and ancestors. Truly it is the great principle of Heaven and Earth, and the great basis of human relationships. Therefore the 'Rites' honor union of man and woman; and in the 'Book of Poetry' the 'First Ode' [that is, 'Fishhawks'] manifests the principle of marriage. For these reasons the relationship cannot but be an important one (Sommer 1995: 109).

She goes on to explain why husband and wife should not follow each other around even in the privacy of their own room. If they do, Ban writes, this closeness will lead to lust: the couple will take liberties with each other and '(o)ut of this licentiousness will be born a heart of disrespect to the husband. Such a result comes from not knowing that one should stay in one's proper place' (ibid.). Echoing Dong, Ban believes that a husband must control his wife, and a wife must serve her husband. This dynamic of control and service is considered crucial in the socialization of children, for the dynamic will be repeated in the parent–child and emperor–minister relationships. As Liu Xiang suggested, a woman's self-cultivation, the development of her moral character, and her influence on her husband are at the root of a good government:

> If a husband does not control his wife, then the rules of conduct manifesting his authority are abandoned and broken. If a wife does

not serve her husband, then the proper re-lationship [between men and women] and the natural order of things are neglected and destroyed (ibid.).

It is natural that a wife should serve her husband as a minister serves his lord. Ban Zhao recommends that girls be educated in their roles as women in order to prevent the chaos that would come with an improper relationship, and to ensure harmony and intimacy between husband and wife. She quotes the *Classic of Changes*:

> Should two hearts harmonize,
> The united strength can cut gold,
> Words from hearts which agree,
> Give forth fragrance like the orchid.

Over time, the name Ban Zhao became synonymous with womanly erudition. Some four hundred years after the Han, she was included in a list of exemplary women venerated in state sacrifices. And more than a millennium after her lifetime, *Admonitions* was included in a collection of readings called the Four Books for Women.

# 🌿 INTERACTION AND ADAPTATION

## Period of Disunion (220–589)

In 220 the Han fell and China entered a period of instability that was to last for almost four centuries. This was the Six Dynasties period, during which China experienced repeated invasions from Central and West Asia. Confucianism lost the state support it had enjoyed under the Han and receded to the periphery; those seeking unity and harmony increasingly looked to Daoism and Buddhism instead.

Among the latter were a group known as the Seven Sages of the Bamboo Grove who turned to Daoist texts like the *Daodejing* and *Zhuangzi*.

Another prominent and precocious thinker of this period was Wang Bi (226–249 CE), who wrote extensive commentaries not only on the *Laozi*, but also on the *Analects* and the *Changes* (revered by Confucians and Daoist alike). He was interested in the meaning and relevance of issues found in Daoist texts such as being and nothingness, naturalness, the correlation between symbols and language to reality, and the nature of a sage. Above all, Wang emphasized principle (**li**).

This *li* (a different word, written differently in Chinese from the *li* meaning rites) was traditionally used in the context of patterns in natural materials like wood and stone, but Wang used it to refer to the order and processes in the universe. Echoing the Han-era concern with the correspondences between human virtue and the ultimate nature of things, this notion of principle, *li*, would be picked up by the Song Confucians and become a central idea in Neo-Confucianism. When asked why only **Laozi** talked about nothingness and Confucius seemed unwilling to speak about it, Wang answered:

> The Sage (Confucius) embodied nothing (*wu*), so he also knew that it could not be explained in words. Thus he did not talk about it. Master Lao, by contrast, operated on the level of being (*you*). This is why he constantly discussed nothingness; he had to, for what he said about it always fell short (R.J. Lynn in de Bary and Bloom 1999: 385).

Reflecting the syncretic ethos of the time, Wang saw Confucius in Daoist terms, as a sage who implicitly reflected Daoist principles.

### Criticism of Buddhism

As Daoism and Confucianism drew closer together, both of them criticized Buddhism for its emphasis on ascetic detachment from emotions and desires and its rejection of the family and worldly service in favour of the solitary/communal context of the monastic life as the venue for self-cultivation. The

*Disposition of Error* (*Lihuo lun*) is a Buddhist defence against such criticisms, probably written during Southern Dynasties (420–589), and an early example of the ongoing disagreement and dialogue among the various religions in China. Chinese criticism of the imported tradition reflected a Confucian perspective and focused on four elements in particular: Buddhism's lack of authority and credibility, its unfilial practices, its social values, and its assumptions about the world, both material and spiritual (W.T. de Bary and L. Hurvitz in de Bary 1972: 125–38).

On the first point, the Chinese asked why, if Buddhist teachings were important, they were not mentioned in the Five Classics; Buddhism was perceived to lack authority because it did not originate in Chinese antiquity. There were also questions about the unfilial nature of Buddhist practices. To shave one's head, for instance, was construed as an act of gross disrespect for the parents and ancestors, since it amounted to harming the body given by one's ancestors. Leaving the family home and taking up the life of an itinerant monk meant uprooting what Confucians perceived to be the very foundation of a society: filial piety and the duty of ancestor veneration. And celibacy struck at the heart of Confucianism, for to leave no descendants was the most unfilial act of all. From the Chinese point of view, Buddhist ideas and practices threatened the very foundations of social harmony.

As to social values, industrious Confucians in particular disapproved of Buddhist monks' begging for food, which they interpreted as parasitism, and Buddhism's emphasis on ascetic withdrawal from productive work, which they saw as a shirking of responsibility both to the family and to the community. In their view, the Buddhist renunciation of worldly pleasures went far beyond the Confucian ideal of moderation and denied the value that Confucianism attributed to life in the world.

Finally, there was what seemed to be the extreme, even irrational nature of some Buddhist teachings. According to the *Disposition of Error*, Confucians were baffled by the Buddhist ascetic's practice of reflecting on the impurity of the body:

> The ascetic engages in contemplation of himself and observes that all the noxious seepage of his internal body is impure. Hair, skin, skull and flesh; tears from the blinking of the eyes and spittle; veins, arteries, sinew and marrow; liver, lungs, intestines and stomach; feces, urine, mucus and blood: such a mass of filth when combined produces a man. . . . awakened to the detestability of the body, concentrating his mind, he gains *dhyana* (ibid., 129).

Then there were the Buddhist concepts of cause and effect (karma) and rebirth (*lunhui*). While the former might find a parallel in the Confucian idea of the Mandate of Heaven, rebirth was clearly different. The idea that an ancestor might be reborn as a rat, or his own grandchild, would have been preposterous to many Chinese. Even more troublesome was the idea that monastics who had transcended the dusty, polluted world did not pay obeisance to the emperor. The negating of the role of the emperor at the apex of human society, as the Son of Heaven and the primary link between Heaven and Earth, cut to the heart of the Confucian world view.

These conflicts notwithstanding, Buddhist ideas did attract Chinese followers, and as those ideas began to permeate Chinese society, different spheres were allocated to each religion. Confucianism continued to play an important role in family life despite its loss of official status and support. It survived over the next four hundred years not only through individual study of the Five Classics, the *Analects*, and the *Classic of Filiality*, but also in instructional handbooks offering practical advice on everyday matters, among them the *House Instructions of Mr Yan* (*Yanshi jiaxun*).

## Instructional Handbooks for the Family

Yan Zhitui (531–591) came from a prominent family of scholar-officials and, like others of his class, was known both for his literary achievements and for his service to the state. Although the overall tone of his *House Instructions* is Confucian, the text includes a chapter on Buddhism—a clear indication of the syncretic tendencies of Chinese beliefs and practices. Like Ban Zhao, he wrote the instructions for his own children, in this case his sons.

Yan's book shows his loyalty and commitment to the Confucian cultural tradition despite the poverty and hardship he experienced, living in a politically turbulent time and serving foreign rulers. He captures the value attributed to self-cultivation when he explains that, because his parents died when he was a young boy, he was raised by his brothers, who cared for him lovingly but were not strict enough to prevent him from developing bad habits:

> After my thirtieth year gross faults were few, but still I have to be careful always, for in every instance my words are at odds with my mind, and my emotions struggle with my nature. Each evening I am conscious of the faults committed that morning, and today I regret the errors of yesterday. How pitiful that the lack of instruction has brought me to this condition! I would recall the experiences of my youth long ago, for they are engraved on my flesh and bone; these are not merely the admonitions of ancient books, but what has passed before my eyes and reached my ears (A. Dien in de Bary and Bloom 1999: 542–3).

Yan describes himself in his youth as 'uncontrolled in feelings, careless in speech, and slovenly in dress' (ibid., 542). To a Confucian, the character and psychological patterns developed through family relationships are at the heart of culture and civilization: 'if a father is not loving, the son will not be filial; if an elder brother is not friendly, the younger will not be respectful; if a husband is not just, the wife will not be obedient' (ibid., 545). The habits developed in youth last a lifetime; therefore it is essential to cultivate harmonious relationships from earliest childhood.

# China Reunited (589–907)

In 589 China was reunited for the first time since the fall of the Han nearly four hundred years earlier, and in 618 the Tang came to power. Both Daoism and Buddhism were to reach new heights of popularity over the centuries that followed. The new imperial family, which claimed to be descended from Laozi, adopted Daoism as the official state religion. At the same time, Buddhism remained prominent at the elite as well as the popular level as monks from a variety of sinicized Buddhist schools became attendants at court and Buddhist elements were incorporated into state ceremonies.

Confucianism also experienced an important revival in this period. The second Tang emperor, Taizhong, established an academy in the 600s for scholar-officials where the curriculum relied on the classic Confucian texts, the students venerated Confucius as well as the Duke of Zhou, and—for the first time in Chinese history—it became possible for a commoner to work his way into officialdom. Taizhong also ordered all prefectures and districts to build Confucian temples for sacrifices to be performed by the literati. In 647 he installed in each temple twenty-two tablets commemorating orthodox Confucians of the Han era. A century later, in 739, the title of King of Manifest Culture (*Wenxuan wang*) was bestowed on Confucius, who now effectively displaced the Duke of Zhou as the 'uncrowned king' (*suwang*) of Chinese civilization.

One of the responsibilities of the Confucian officials was to oversee rituals. Four new types of worship that drew on earlier dynastic ritual systems were established at the royal clan temples during the Tang dynasty: honouring Earth (through the gods of the land and harvest), Heaven

Ritual vessels and tablets on display at China's second-largest Confucius temple, in Jianshui, Yunnan (Alamy).

(*jitian*), Confucius, and imperial ancestors. Within a century the Confucian temples began to display carved images of honoured figures, similar to the images in Buddhist temples representing buddhas, enlightened beings, and Arhats. Among the figures so honoured were Confucius himself, Yan Hui (his favourite disciple, who died young), his seventy-two disciples, and ten historical figures admired by Confucians and known as the 'Wise Ones'. These images remained in the temples for seven or eight hundred years, but were eventually replaced by portraits in an effort to differentiate Confucian temples from Buddhist ones.

In time, the Confucian curriculum for bureaucrats was expanded to include a total of twelve works, among them the *Analects* and *Classic of Filiality*. The revival of interest in Confucian thought was reflected in three writers of particular interest to us here: Madame Zheng, the wife of a government official, who likely composed the *Classic of Filiality for Women* (*Nu xiaojing*) during the late seventh century; **Han Yu** (768–824), a prominent scholar-official displeased with the elements of superstition in folk Buddhism and intent on the recovery of Confucianism; and Han's contemporary Song Ruozhao, the daughter of an official, who wrote the *Analects for Women* (*Nu lunyu*) in the early ninth century.

## Madame Zheng *and the* Classic of Filiality for Women

Modelled in both form and content on the *Classic of Filiality*, the *Filiality for Women* sets out the correct behaviour for various classes of women from the empress and the wives of high officials to commoners. The central figure in the text is Ban Zhao, who is imagined as a teacher in conversation with a group of women. Her advice reflects the perennial

Confucian themes of cosmic harmony, ritual propriety, and humaneness:

> Now filiality embraces Heaven and Earth and enriches all human relationships. It moves ghosts and spirits and affects birds and animals. 'Show respect according to the dictates of propriety'; 'think three times and then act'. Be affable and gentle, modest and deferential, humane and understanding, filial and affectionate. Then you will have perfectly embodied correct moral behaviour and be without blame. . . . (T. Kelleher in de Bary and Bloom 1999: 825).

In a conscious effort to create a female Confucian tradition retroactively starting from Ban Zhao, Madame Zheng emphasizes the importance for women of purity or chastity, filial piety, intelligence and wisdom, so that they may guide their husbands by example. The exemplary wife encourages her husband in good behaviour and guides him with 'a sense of modesty and deference, [so that] he will refrain from being contentious' (ibid., 826). She uses music and rites in the broad sense—including everything from the regular practice of formal courtesy in the household to the performance of religious rituals—to moderate his emotions, so that he will be pleasant and easy to get along with. When the women in attendance ask if they are to obey their husbands' every command, Ban Zhao responds indignantly—'What kind of talk is that!' Then, echoing the original *Filiality*, she cites numerous historical examples of wives who remonstrate with their husbands and explains:

> If a husband has a remonstrating wife, then he won't fall into evil ways. Therefore, if a husband transgresses against the Way, you must correct him. How could it be that to obey your husband in everything would make you a virtuous person? (ibid., 827)

## Han Yu and the Critique of Buddhism and Daoism

Han Yu is especially important in the history of Confucianism because he lived in a period when Daoism and Buddhism were flourishing; the former as the state religion and the latter as the religion of choice among both the elite and the masses. Although Confucian principles had been reintroduced into government, they had little popular currency. In an effort to bring Confucian teaching back to the centre of Chinese life after nearly six hundred years on the periphery, Han Yu wrote *Essentials of the Moral Way* (*Yuandao lun*). In it he answers the question 'What is the teaching of the former kings?' as follows:

> To love largely is called a sense of humaneness; to act according to what should be done is called rightness. To proceed from these principles is called the moral Way; to be sufficient unto oneself without relying on externals is called inner power. . . . Its methods are the rites, music, chastisement, and government. Its classes of people are scholars, peasants, craftsmen, and merchants. . . . (C. Hartman in de Bary and Bloom 1999: 569)

Han Yu also outlines the basics of the Confucian tradition: listing classical texts; modifying the five relationships (leaving out friends and adding teacher and pupil, and guest and host); and tracing the lineage from the sage king Yao to the Duke of Zhou, and Confucius to Mencius (Xunzi and Yang Xiong, the Han Confucian, were Confucians, he notes, but in his opinion they did not understand the essence of the teaching).

In addition Han Yu criticized Daoists and Buddhists because, in their respective quests for quietude and withdrawal from the world, they neglected the productive work required to provide the necessities of life. He chastises Emperor Xianzong for sending some monks to greet the relic of the finger bone of the Buddha, reminding him of Confucius' advice to respect spiritual beings but keep them at a distance. He also reminds the emperor to set an example for the common people, who are ignorant and dull, and will be swayed by his actions.

### Song Ruozhao and the Analects for Women

*Analects for Women* (*Nu lunyu*) is usually attributed to Song Ruozhao, though some say that her sister Ruohua actually wrote the text. Like Ban Zhao, Song came from a scholarly family. She was appointed to the court as scholar, and after an audience with the emperor was assigned to teach the imperial princesses. There are eight sections to the treatise:

1. Establishing Oneself as a Person,
2. Learning How to Work,
3. Ritual Decorum: Learning Proper Etiquette,
4. Rising Early to Begin Household Work,
5. Serving One's Parents-in-Law,
6. Serving a Husband,
7. Instructing Sons and Daughters, and
8. Managing the Household.

The work begins with an echo of 'Fishhawks', the first poem in the *Odes*: 'To be a woman, you must first learn how to establish yourself as a person. The way to do this is simply by working hard to establish one's purity and chastity. By purity, one keeps one's self undefiled; by chastity, one preserves one's honour' (T. Kelleher in de Bary and Bloom 1999: 828). Song then goes on to emphasize self-mastery, discipline, ritual propriety, and harmony in serving one's elders, husband, in-laws, and friends. Most pointedly, she writes that the 'authority/responsibility to instruct (sons and daughters) rests solely with the mother' (ibid., 830). Thus, like Ban Zhao, Song suggests that female education is essential for the health of the empire.

## Early Song Confucianism

Towards the end of the Tang, under the influence of Daoist priests, the Emperor Wuzong moved to put an end to the spread of Buddhism in China. In 845 he issued an edict that summarized the charges laid against the foreign religion by defenders of China's indigenous social values:

> We have heard that up through the Three Dynasties [Xia, Shang, and Zhou] the Buddha was never spoken of. It was only from the Han and Wei on that the religion of idols gradually came to prominence. So in this latter age it has transmitted its strange ways, instilling its infection with every opportunity, spreading like a luxuriant vine, until it has poisoned the customs of our nation. . . .
>
> Now if even one man fails to work the fields, someone must go hungry; if one woman does not tend her silkworms, someone will be cold. At present there are an inestimable number of monks and nuns in the empire, each of them waiting for the farmers to feed him and the silkworms to clothe him, while the public temples and private chapels have reached boundless number, all with soaring towers and elegant ornamentation sufficient to outshine the imperial palace itself . . . (B. Watson in de Bary and Bloom 1999: 585–6).

The disdain, envy, and fear of institutional Buddhism are palpable. Under the edict more than 4,600 public temples throughout the empire were demolished; 26,500 monks and nuns were laicized and subjected to a new Twice-a-Year Tax; 40,000 private temples were destroyed, releasing a considerable amount of fertile land for public use; 150,000 temple servants, male and female, were freed and likewise made subject to Twice-a-Year Tax. Wuzong's policy was reversed by his successor, but the damage had been done: Buddhism in China had been profoundly wounded. The prime beneficiary, however, was not Daoism, which was stripped of its status as the state religion after the fall of the Tang. Over the next two hundred years, Confucianism built on the contributions of people like Taizhong, Madame Zheng, Han Yu, and Song Ruozhao to become the dominant ideology. The ongoing development of Confucianism culminated in the emergence of what is known in China as *Lixue* (the School of Principle, Learning, or Study) and in the West as Neo-Confucianism. Thinkers of this school (also known as the Cheng-Zhu school) sought to find the principle underlying the world. An early proponent was Cheng Yi (1033–1108):

> There is principle in everything, and one must investigate principle to the utmost. There are many ways to do this. One way is to read books and elucidate moral principles. Another way is to discuss people and events of the past and present, and to distinguish which are right and which wrong. Still another way is to handle affairs and settle them in the proper way. All these are ways to investigate the principle of things exhaustively (Jochim 1986: 51).

The systematic development of Song Neo-Confucianism would reach its apex in the twelfth century with **Zhu Xi** (1130–1200), but much of his work drew on thinkers from the preceding century, among them Zhou Dunyi (1017–73), Zhang Zai (1020–77), and the brothers Cheng Yi and Hao, who studied with Zhou. Although the Neo-Confucians traced the roots of their philosophy to the ancient writings, their subjects in many cases reflected Buddhist and Daoist concepts. Thus Zhou Dunyi advocated what he called 'quiet-sitting'—a practice clearly modelled on Buddhist meditation—and used a Daoist diagram describing the creation of the material world as the basis of an important work, an essay entitled 'An Explanation of the Diagram of the Great Ultimate' (see box). With that essay, Confucianism took a definitive step away from its original humanism and towards a more metaphysical, recognizably religious orientation.

For Zhou, the Great Ultimate and the Ultimate Non-being are identical. Through movement, yang is generated from the Ultimate Non-being/Great Ultimate. When its limit is reached, it becomes quiet and yin is generated. When yin reaches its limit, then activity, or yang, begins again. Thus the alternation between stillness and movement produces yin and yang, which in turn give rise to the five vital forces of fire, water, earth, metal,

## From Zhou Dunyi, 'An Explanation of the Diagram of the Great Ultimate'

The Ultimate of Non-being and also the Great Ultimate! The Great Ultimate through movement generates yang. When its activity reaches its limit, it becomes tranquil. Through tranquillity the Great Ultimate generates yin. When tranquillity reaches its limit, activity begins again. So movement and tranquillity alternate and become the root of each other, giving rise to the distinction of yin and yang, and the two modes are established (W.T. Chan in Sommer 1995: 185).

and wood, each with its specific nature. When Ultimate Non-being interacts with the essences of yin-yang and the five phases, a mysterious union occurs, from which Heaven and Earth come into being.

The interaction of these two material forces in turn creates all things, resulting in endless transformation. Embodied in human beings, the five agents are expressed in the five moral principles of humaneness, right action, ritual propriety, wisdom, and faithfulness. And those principles reach their highest expression in the sage who, having perfected the qualities of balance and harmony in himself, is able to use them to benefit the world.

Three central elements of Confucianism are at play here: the belief in endless change, the focus on the qualities of the sage, and the emphasis on emotional balance. The importance of the latter in Confucian thought can be seen in the chapter from the *Classic of Rites* entitled 'Centrality and Equilibrium' (*Zhongyong*). Whereas Buddhism sought to transcend human emotions, Confucianism sought to realize them fully by bringing them to consummate proportion: when 'centrality and harmony are perfected, everything in heaven and earth finds its place and all things flourish.' 'Centrality' refers to a state in which the emotions of pleasure, anger, sorrow, and joy have not yet been aroused; and 'harmony' is the state when these emotions have arisen and have reached an appropriately measured degree (see Sommer 1995: 37). It is this state of emotional balance that allows the sage to move through the world in tranquillity.

Just as Zhou adapted the Daoist idea of creation, so Zhang Zai adapted the Buddhist concept of the unity of all things. In *The Western Inscription* (*Ximing*), for instance, Zhang writes: 'Heaven is my father and Earth is my mother, and even such a small creature as I find an intimate place in their midst'; and 'All people are my brothers and sisters, and all things are my companions' (W.T. Chan in Sommer 1995: 188). Following the classical and Tang Confucians, Zhang extends the metaphor of the family to the level of the state, emphasizing the society's duty to care for its young, old, infirm, and disadvantaged members.

## Zhu Xi and the School of Principle

The School of Principle (*Lixue*) explicitly linked *li*, the principles or patterns of nature, to human relationships and theories about education and government. Zhu Xi (1130–1200) synthesized the ideas of the early Song thinkers and brought to fruition a Confucianism with a metaphysical bent.

Zhu focused on the nature, place, and function of self in the Great Ultimate, yin and yang, and the rudimentary elements of heaven and earth in Zhou's diagram. His thinking on this subject was not new. Like the Han Confucians, he understood human beings to be part of the fabric of the universe. Despite his interest in Zhou's Buddhist-style 'quiet sitting', Zhu is quintessentially Confucian in his focus on self-cultivation. He also recalls Xunzi in his focus on the importance of heart-mind in self-cultivation; the immanence of Heaven in human nature; and the threat that human desires pose to balance, security, and harmony in society. Despite these affinities to Xunzi, however, he gave priority to Mencius' teachings about the four heart-minds.

In addition Zhu emphasized 'Centrality and Equilibrium' as well as another chapter from the *Rites* entitled 'The Great Learning' (*Daxue*), in which self-discipline or self-cultivation is seen as the first link in a chain that extends from the individual through the family to the state and recalls the ideal of the Grand Commonalty. A famous passage from 'The Great Learning' explains how proper self-cultivation through the investigation of things (*gewu*) benefits all under Heaven (*tianxia*)— that is, the whole world:

> Once things are investigated, knowledge can be extended. When knowledge is

extended, thoughts can be made sincere; when thoughts are sincere, the mind can be rectified. When the mind is rectified, one can develop the self; once the self is developed, the family can be managed. When the family is managed, the state can be governed well; when the state is governed well, peace can prevail throughout the land. (Sommer 1995: 39)

For Zhu Xi, the 'investigation of things' included both thinking about the world around us and reading the classical texts, nine of which he identified as especially important: the Five Classics and what became known as the 'Four Books': the *Analects*, *Mencius*, 'The Great Learning', and 'Centrality and Equilibrium'. (The Twelve Classics of the Tang era became the Thirteen during the Song with the addition of *Mencius*; thereafter, the Thirteen Classics retained their special status until the fall of the Qing in the early twentieth century.)

## Confucianism into the Contemporary Era

Neo-Confucianism continued to thrive from the Song through to the Ming dynasty (1368–1644). And after the Ming fell to the invading Manchus or Qing, the latter would in turn rely on the indigenous teaching to govern and to legitimate their rule over the Han Chinese.

The education of women received renewed attention during the Ming. Empress Xu, the wife of Yongle (r. 1402–24) the third Ming emperor, wrote *Instructions for the Inner Quarters* (Neixun) under the inspirational example and influence of her mother-in-law, the wife of the founding emperor of the Ming dynasty. Empress Ma often remonstrated with her cruel, hot-tempered husband Taizu, believing it was her duty to serve as inner counsellor and Mother of the people. Empress Xu's *Instructions* reflects the same sense of a woman's broader responsibilities. When a set of 'Four Books for Women' (Nu sishu) was compiled during the Ming, Empress Xu's work was one of them, along with Ban Zhao's *Admonitions*, Song Ruozhao's *Analects*, and Madame Zheng's *Filiality*, though the latter would eventually be replaced by 'A Handy Record of Rules for Women' (Nufan jielu), written by a woman identified only as the mother of a certain Wang Xiang.

Meanwhile, Neo-Confucianism continued to develop. Approximately three centuries after Zhu Xi's death, **Wang Yangming** (1472–1529) challenged his view of the process of self-cultivation. Wang introduced the idea that knowledge of the good (liangzhi) was innate and that the attitude of sincerity would naturally develop out of it. He argued that the heart-mind's awareness of the good trumps both thinking about the world and book knowledge. In other words, if our intuition tells us what is good, our moral sense is innate and does not need to be learned. Therefore in-born understanding that generates earnestness, good faith, and impartiality takes precedence over the investigation of things and should be encouraged.

When asked to explain the meaning of *mingde*, translated as 'clear character' or 'bright virtue' in the first sentence of the Great Learning—'The Way of the great learning lies in clarifying bright virtue (*mingde*), loving the people, and abiding in the highest good'—Wang answered that since 'human beings form one body with Heaven and Earth', the mind 'is naturally intelligent, clear, and not beclouded'; therefore the mind 'is called the "clear character (*mingde*)"' (Sommer 1995: 229). Wang's school is usually referred to as the School of Mind (Xinxue, also known as the Lu-Wang school).

The ability of Confucianism to adapt to changing times, manifested in its assimilation of Daoist and Buddhist concepts foreign to its classical teachings, reasserted itself time and again. This flexibility would resurface as Chinese society became increasingly urban and commercialized through the Song to Qing dynasties, and the traditional Confucian reliance on the mystical influence of a personally virtuous ruler guided by the counsel of his ministers proved inadequate. Political focus started to shift from the personal to the institutional.

### Huang Zongxi and Change in the Qing Dynasty

The Qing Confucian Huang Zongxi (1610–95) was one scholar who questioned the traditional reliance on the virtue of the emperor, as the son of Heaven, to ensure good governance. He stressed instead the need for reform and the introduction of constitutional law to constrain the absolute authority of the ruler. Huang was unsuccessful in his call for changes. In his concern for the people, the Qing minister echoed all Confucians but most particularly Mencius, who wrote that 'The people are of supreme importance; the altars to the gods of earth and grain come next; last comes the ruler' (Lau 1970: 196). For Huang, the welfare of the common person took precedence over religious ritual; religion existed to serve people, not the other way round:

> Whether there is peace or disorder in the world does not depend on the rise or fall of dynasties but upon the happiness or distress of the people. . . . If those who act as ministers ignore the 'plight of the people', then even if they should succeed in assisting their prince's rise to power or follow him to final ruin, they would still be in violation of the true Way of the Minister' (W.T. de Bary in de Bary and Lufrano 2000: 9).

For ministers simply to counsel the ruler was not enough: they should be prepared to act against the emperor when he acted against the interest of the people. In other words, ministers should act as agents of Heaven, upholding or rescinding the Mandate of Heaven as required.

After more than a hundred years of prosperity and relative peace during the high Qing in the 1700s, the need for change was reinforced when the British began selling opium to the Chinese in a bid to balance their trade deficit with China. In 1841, a minister named Lin Zexu (1785–1850) wrote to Queen Victoria protesting this practice:

> The wealth of China is used to profit the barbarians [the British]. That is to say, the great profit made by barbarians is all taken from the rightful share of China. By what right do they then in return use the poisonous drug [opium] to injure the Chinese people? Even though the barbarians may not necessarily intend to do us harm, yet in coveting profit to an extreme, they have no regard for injuring others. Let us ask, where is your conscience? (S.Y. Teng and J. Fairbank in deBary and Lufrano 2000: 203).

Acting as a true Confucian minister, morally aware and conscientious, Lin appealed to the queen's moral sensibility, arguing that since opium was not allowed in Britain, then it was all the more reprehensible that the British would try to sell it to the Chinese. Like the Han Confucians who were ridiculed for being antiquarian and impractical, the minister fought a losing battle.

The repercussions of this high-minded approach were dire. The British declared war and the Chinese were hopelessly outgunned. The Opium War (1839–42) is a watershed in East Asian history. The victory of the British augured the inevitable and irreversible fall of the dynastic system and a profound reassessment of traditional ways of thinking. Confucianism soon came to be described as 'the teaching of rites that cannibalizes people.'

The final military nail in the coffin was Japan's victory in the Sino-Japanese War of 1894–5. That Japan—a former vassal state—had successfully modernized along Western lines and defeated China meant that radical reforms were necessary. While some thinkers urged the abandonment of all things traditional, however, others argued that some aspects of China's cultural heritage should be preserved. Kang Youwei (1858–1927) was one such reformer.

## Reaction to the West in the Nineteenth Century

Kang admired the West for its orderliness, prosperity, and attainments in science and technology, and he attributed this human progress in part to Christianity. Likewise, he believed that the adoption of Shinto as Japan's state religion had contributed to that country's success in modernizing (see Chapter 7). Therefore he recommended that Confucianism be shaped in such a way that it might be adopted as China's national religion. He argued for the 'Way of the Grand Commonality . . . utmost peace-and-equality, utmost justice, utmost humanness, and the most perfect government'. In his best-known work, *The Grand Commonality*, Kang reached back to the *Rites* and the New Text school of Dong Zhongshu and projected the traditional idea of a golden past into the future. In another book, *Confucius as a Reformer*, he described Confucius as follows:

> Confucius was the founder of a doctrine. He was a godlike sage king. He complements Heaven and [E]arth and nurtures the myriad things. All men, things, and principles are embraced in the Great Way of Confucius. He is, therefore, the most accomplished and perfect sage in the history of mankind. . . . Wherein lies the reason for this? It lies in the fact that scholars knew the Six Classics (including *Music*) were written by Confucius. This was the opinion of all before the Han dynasty. Only when a scholar recognizes that the Six Classics were written by Confucius can he understand why Confucius was the great sage, the founder of the doctrine, and the model for all ages; and why he alone was called the supreme master (C. Tan in deBary and Lufrano 2000: 266–7).

Here was a Confucius who could walk alongside Jesus. Kang responded to the encounter with Christianity by seeking to find common ground with it, just as the earlier Confucians Zhu Xi and Han Yu had sought to accommodate Buddhist ideas of monasticism, rebirth, and so on. Kang was optimistic; he believed that Western knowledge could be integrated into the Confucian Way:

> Being that I was born on the earth, then mankind in the ten thousand countries of the earth are from the same womb but of different bodily types. Being that I have knowledge of them, then I have love [*qin*; a word normally reserved for family members] of them. All that is finest and best of the former wisdom of India, Greece, Persia, Rome, and of present-day England, France, Germany, and America, I have lapped up and drunk, rested on, pillowed on; and my soul in dreams has fathomed it (ibid., 271).

Kang was not the first Confucian to envision a universal family; as early as the eleventh century, Zhang Zai wrote that 'All people are my brothers and sisters, and all things are my companions'. To advance the ideal of the 'Grand Commonality', Kang called for the abolition of 'nine boundaries': of nation, class, race, gender, family, property, unjust laws, species, and suffering. (In the spirit of this idealism, he demanded the abolition of the cruel practice of footbinding.)

Kang's campaign for radical political and social reform following the military defeat and psychological devastation of the Opium War was continued by his student Tan Sitong (1865–98); Tan welcomed the teachings of Christianity as well as Confucianism, Daoism, and Buddhism. He criticized the theory of the Three Bonds and saw the husband–wife relationship in particular as contrary to the ideal of the Grand Commonality: 'When a husband considers himself the master, he will not treat his wife as an equal human being.' Tan argued the point historically, suggesting that in ancient China a wife could ask for a divorce, and that widows in those earlier times could choose to remarry—a freedom that effectively ended with the Song Confucians' zealous propagation of virtuous widowhood. Tan was especially critical of the Song-era idea that for a woman 'to die in starvation is a minor matter, but for her to lose her chastity by remarrying would be a serious matter' (D. Reynolds in de Bary and Lufrano, 2000: 284).

## Post-dynastic China: The 'New Confucians'

Sun Yatsen, the founding father of modern republican China, identified three principles as fundamental to democracy: nationalism, citizen rights, and the welfare of human beings. He found precedents for democracy in China's Confucian philosophers, specifically Mencius and Neo-Confucian Cheng Yi, and argued that the three principles represented 'a completion of the development of . . . three thousand years of Chinese ideas about how to govern and maintain a peaceful world' (Bell and Hahm 2003: 9).

Sun Yatsen's insights notwithstanding, state Confucianism was disestablished and Confucius himself was roundly criticized following the fall of the Qing and the formation of the Chinese Republic in 1911. During the 1950s, Fang Dongmei, a professor of Chinese philosophy, encouraged the development of New Confucianism in Taiwan after the communist takeover in mainland China; and a 'Manifesto for a Reappraisal of Sinology and the Reconstruction of Chinese Culture' was published in English under Carsun Chang (Zhang Junmai), a professor who was teaching in North America. The Manifesto outlined the ideas of a group of 'New Confucians' (xinru) based at New Asia College (now a part of the Chinese University of Hong Kong).

Even though they identified themselves as New Confucians, the authors of the Manifesto were careful to include Daoism and Buddhism as important components of Chinese culture. Under the heading 'What We Expect from World Thought', they wrote that 'The expansion of Western civilization has brought the peoples of the world into close contact and unfortunately has also produced much friction.' To overcome this friction and achieve world peace, the New Confucians argued that we must go beyond philosophy and science and

> attain an attitude of respect and sympathy toward other cultures and thereby acquire genuine compassion and commiseration toward mankind in adversity. . . .
>
> The human existence as formed by 'establishing Man as the Ultimate' is that of a moral being that, at the same time, attains a higher spiritual enlightenment; for this reason, it can truly embrace God, thereby attaining 'harmony in virtue with Heaven'. Hence, this human existence is simultaneously moral and religious existence (J. Berthrong in de Bary and Lufrano 2000: 559).

The New Confucians' use of the Christian term 'God' is an example of the way they responded to the West by adopting Western concerns and categories—not unlike those Confucians who, centuries earlier, integrated Daoist and Buddhist ideas, institutions, and categories into their thought.

## Confucianism in the Diaspora

The New Confucians entered into conversation with the West with an understanding of Chinese culture as a Confucian-Daoist-Buddhist civilization. In this syncretic spirit they pointed to five qualities that Chinese spirituality could contribute that might serve as complements to specific Western values (in parentheses): Daoist-style retreat (Western progress); wisdom (intellect); mildness and compassion (assertive love, often mixed with a will to power); perpetuating ancestral spiritual will (speed and efficiency); and the ideal of the world as one family (nationalism).

The New Confucians have sympathizers and descendants in North America. The most easily identifiable group, known as the Boston Confucians, is based at Harvard and Boston University in Massachusetts; one prominent member, Tu Wei-ming, has written on contemporary issues such as human rights and gender. Despite their strong representation within elite academic institutions, however, it is difficult to say how influential Confucianism will be in the West.

The fortunes of Confucianism in the Chinese world have varied widely. It has remained strong in Taiwan, though more as a philosophy than a religion, and its values are well integrated into local Buddhist practices and beliefs. In Singapore, it had the support of President Lee Kuan Yew and for a time was listed on census forms as a religious category, but this practice was discontinued when it became clear that few people identified themselves as followers of a Confucian religion. In Hong Kong, Confucianism has long been recognized as a religion for census purposes, but here too very few people self-identify as Confucian, so this practice is expected to end soon.

The Communist government was for decades antagonistic towards Confucianism; since the 1980s, however, it has reintroduced the symbolic celebration of Confucius' birthday and it now encourages both academic study and popular discussion of Confucianism. Apparently the Chinese government hopes that the Confucian ethos of care and virtue will act as a corrective to perceived problems of ruthless capitalism, excessive consumption, and corruption. In the early twenty-first century, the mainland government has established Confucius Institutes around the world, many of which are affiliated with universities.

It is difficult to say whether this new tolerance on the part of the Communist state, in conjunction with the policies and actions of Chinese governments in Singapore and Taiwan, and other

Children at a private kindergarten in Wuhan, in the central province of Hubei, learn the Confucian classics (© ZHOU CHAO/epa/Corbis).

communities especially the ones in diaspora, will encourage a revival of the teaching. It is unclear what Confucianism can represent, apart from a personal philosophy, in an era when elements crucial to traditional practice (including the imperial state and its rituals) have long been disestablished; ties to place and family have in many cases been broken through migration; and values antithetical to its core teachings are in the ascendant. Even so, it appears that a new chapter on Confucianism is being written.

# 🐉 Daoism

## Introduction

The current research on Daoism is very exciting. New findings offer new ways of understanding the roots of the tradition and the relationship between what were historically understood to be its two branches: philosophical (*jia*) and religious (*jiao*). This research shows that the traditional dichotomized picture of an elite philosophy and a popular, vulgarized, and debased religious version is simplistic and misleading. Ongoing scholarship demands a re-evaluation of traditional accounts of the beginnings of Daoism and its relationship to later developments.

Traditionally, Daoist philosophy has traced its origins to the third and fourth centuries BCE, whereas Daoist religion has usually been traced to the second century CE (the Latter Han dynasty) and two groups: the Celestial Masters (also known as the Orthodox Unity) and the Yellow Turbans. Recent research has revealed that philosophers at the Jixia Academy in the state of Qi were discussing ideas related to both philosophical and religious Daoism as early as the fourth century BCE, during the Warring States period.

The state of Qi occupied land that had been part of Confucius' home state of Lu (roughly what is now Shandong province in northeast China).

The term 'Daoist' was not used during this period, but there are references to the school of Huang-Lao. Named for the mythical 'Yellow Emperor' Huangdi and the legendary (historically dubious) philosopher Laozi, the Huang-Lao teachings correspond roughly to what we now consider philosophical Daoism. In the early fourth century, King Xuan of Qi (r. 320–301) following the example of King Wei (357–320) offered the thinking men of his time sinecures at the Jixia Academy, encouraging them to discuss the problems of the day and find solutions to them. Among those scholars—who came from different states, north and south—were the Naturalist Zou Yan, Mencius, Xunzi, and a 'Daoist' student of the Huang-Lao teachings named Huan Yuan.

### Philosophical Daoism

The early history of philosophical Daoism has conventionally been associated with two main sources: the *Classic of the Way and Power* (*Daodejing*), a multi-layered, multi-authored verse text that is traditionally attributed to Laozi (the 'old master'); and the **Zhuangzi**, named for the thinker whose ideas it purportedly represents. Both texts consist of disparate parts by different authors, but the *Zhuangzi* is distinctive in its frequent use of humorous anecdotes.

This conventional view is changing, however. At least three new textual sources have proved helpful in reconstructing the early development of philosophical Daoism. Two of them are found in the *Guanzi*, a collection of writings that has traditionally been attributed to a very early (seventh century BCE) historical figure named Guan Zhong, but that more likely originated during the fourth century and arrived at its current form during the first century BCE. The *Guanzi* was categorized as Daoist during the Han era but was later reclassified as Legalist. For this reason it was neglected by students of Daoism, but recent research has found that two of its sections, both dealing with mental discipline, are directly relevant to them. The first, entitled *Techniques of the Mind I* (*Xinshu, Shang*), is written in verse but includes prose commentaries and addresses both the broader concerns of government and methods of self-cultivation. The second, *Inward Training* (*Nei-yeh*), focuses exclusively on spiritual cultivation; it is written in verse and clearly bridges the streams of philosophical and religious Daoism.

The third new textual source for the study of classical Daoist development is a bundle of silk manuscripts discovered in Hunan province in 1973 and containing the teachings of the Huang-Lao group. Including both verse and prose, the *Huang-Lao Silk Manuscripts* (*Huang-Lao boshu*) were, like the *Daodejing* and the later chapters of *Zhuangzi*, written and compiled over time. Our knowledge of classical Daoism in both its philosophical and religious aspects will undoubtedly improve as scholars continue to study these and other new texts.

## Religious Daoism

Religious Daoism is widely associated with colourful rituals; belief in deities, ghosts, and spirits; and the pursuit of immortality. Thus it may appear to be diametrically opposed to philosophical Daoism, with its focus on ideas such as the nature of virtue, the cultivation of the heart-mind, and the use of such teachings in politics. Yet in fact religious and philosophical Daoism do share a number of fundamental ideals, beliefs, and practices, including self-discipline, transcendence of one's ordinary self, not-doing (**wuwei**), and the idea that religion and politics are embedded in one another. These fundamentals can be found not only in the *Daodejing* and *Zhuangzi*, but in *Inward Training*, *Techniques of the Mind I*, and *Huang-Lao*.

What distinguishes religious from philosophical Daoism is the fact that it incorporates two markedly non-philosophical traditions: a southern tradition of shamanism and a northern tradition known as the way of magic and immortality (*fangxian dao*). Quite unlike the (northern) divinatory shamanism of the Shang and Zhou eras, this southern shamanism is distinctly non-philosophical and resolutely religious; its character can be seen in a collection called *Songs of the South* or *Songs of Qu* (*Quchi*), which features lavish descriptions of gods and goddesses, 'serpentine cloud banners', 'soaring phoenixes', and 'rainbows of multicoloured streamers'.

The second tradition was the domain of various 'masters of technical method', including magicians, doctors, diviners, geomancers, astrologists, and exorcists, who specialized in the search for an elixir of everlasting life. The combination of these two very different traditions in what came to be called religious Daoism only adds to the difficulty of understanding the early history of Daoism.

## Connection between Philosophical and Religious Daoism

The nature and origins of the two Daoist streams are complex, as is the relationship between them. Recent scholarship on *Inward Training*, however, has suggested a possible bridge over the divide separating the two streams of Daoism.

*Inward Training*—a short poetic work of twenty-six sections focusing on meditation—contains elements that are present in both the philosophical and religious streams. Scholars have suggested that it may be the first writing on meditation in China. They believe that the ideas about self-cultivation expressed in it are likely related to the philosophical stream represented by the *Daodejing* and *Zhuangzi*, and by extension the *Techniques of the Mind I* and writings in the *Huang-Lao*. They also believe that practices within the religious stream were probably influenced by the references in *Inward Training* to the cultivation of three elements: vital essence (*jing*), vital energy, and numinous essence or spirit (*shen*). When the six texts—*Inward Training, Daodejing, Zhuangzi, Songs of the South, Techniques of the Mind*, and the *Huang-Lao* manuscripts—are read alongside each other, they suggest a movement that drew from multitudinous sources and was consciously syncretic in its development.

# Origins

## *Early Developments*

The combination of those texts with the southern shamanistic tradition and the northern tradition of the masters of immortality produced not just two but several distinctive streams in early Daoism. Three recurring elements have been identified in the classical Daoist texts: the concept of the Dao as the One and the primary force in the universe; the importance of inner discipline to empty out the ordinary heart-mind of distractions, allowing space for the deep tranquillity natural to human beings and necessary to experience unity with the One; and finally, the use of the first two elements for benevolent government.

In light of these elements, three ways of categorizing the concerns in the classical texts have been suggested: Individualist, Primitivist, and Syncretist. The Individualist stream is mystical and concerned primarily with inner cultivation and the experience of union with the cosmos; it is basic to all six of the classical texts listed above. The second stream takes the basic Individualist perspective and adds an appeal for a simple agrarian way of living. This Primitivist stream can be seen in the *Laozi* as well as chapters 8 to 10 and the first part of 11 in the *Zhuangzi* and may be later than the first. The third and last stream combines teachings of Laozi and Zhuangzi with other schools and is found in the later chapters of the *Zhuangzi*, *Techniques of the Mind I*, and *Huang-Lao*. This Syncretist approach likely came after the first two and can be dated to the early Han dynasty.

The exact chronology of the various writings is not known, but the *Daodejing* and *Inward Training* are generally considered to be the earliest. Anecdotes in the *Zhuangzi* describing encounters between Confucius and Laozi would make the two men contemporaries; but scholars now question

the historical authenticity of the latter. The first seven chapters of the *Zhuangzi*, if they were in fact composed by Zhuang Zhou (known as Zhuangzi; 369?–286? BCE) are also of some antiquity.

Finally, the *Songs of the South* are traditionally attributed to Qu Yuan (340?–278 BCE), a famously righteous Qu minister, but most of them were probably written about a century after his death. Thus the poems are likely of a slightly later period than the other texts. Brief descriptions of the six sources follow.

## *Inward Training* **in Daoist and Confucian Contexts**

This short text is embedded in the *Guanzi*, a collection of miscellaneous writings that was until recently neglected in the study of classical Chinese religions. It is important for our introductory study because it bridges philosophical and religious Daoism, and provides clear examples of the cultural beliefs and practices from the Zhou era that Confucians and Daoists shared.

*Inward Training* deals with the cultivation of the heart-mind. This focus on self-cultivation, as we noted at the start of this chapter, is common to all three of China's elite religious traditions. The theme of inner cultivation in particular is evident in the Daoist emphasis on the notion of 'holding fast to the One', and can be found in the *Daodejing*, *Zhuangzi*, *Techniques of the Mind I*, and *Huang-Lao* sources. Other themes from *Inward Training*, however—notably the concepts of the vital essence, vital energy or breath, and the numinous (or the spirit)—are uncommon in the philosophical texts. Instead, they became core features of religious Daoism, in which the integration of these three elements through certain meditational and dietary practices was believed to confer longevity and even immortality or transcendence.

A description of meditation from Section 19 highlights the particular Daoist notions of the body and spirit: vital breath, the numinous, and blood:

By concentrating your vital breath as if
   numinous,
The myriad things will all be contained within
   you.
Can you concentrate? Can you unite with
   them?

. . .

It is not due to the power of the ghostly and
   numinous,
But to the utmost refinement of your essential
   vital breath.

. . .

When the four limbs are aligned
And the blood and vital breath are tranquil,
Unify your awareness, concentrate your mind,
Then your eyes and ears will not be
   overstimulated.
And even the far-off will seem close at hand
   (Roth 1999: 82).

While the elements of body and spirit are Daoist, the focus on awareness, concentration, and
control of sensory stimuli is present in both Daoism
and Confucianism. The Daoist, like the Confucian,
is seen here as moving away from the shamanistic possession of the 'ghostly and numinous' and
moving towards a kind of mystical union with the
Way or Dao, in which 'The myriad things will all be
contained within you'. This passage offers evidence
of a common cultural background and points to
a shared concern with meditative concentration,
cultivation of a tranquil, unified state of mind, and
the minimizing of external stimulation. It echoes
specifically Xunzi's advice to calm one's mind. This
same focus on self-cultivation is reinforced in Section 15, where the image of a floodlike vital essence
coursing through the body recalls the floodlike vital energy evoked by Mencius:

For those who preserve and naturally generate
   vital essence
On the outside a calmness will flourish.
Stored inside, we take it to be the well spring.

Floodlike, it harmonizes and equalizes
And we take it to be the fount of the vital
   energy (ibid., 74).

In addition, the *Inward Training* recalls early
Confucianism in its attribution of a kind of magical, mystical efficacy to the virtue of an exemplary
person. The emperor in particular was believed to
be capable of 'righting' conditions in the empire
without expending any vital energy, simply by virtue of his own attainment of harmony. Section 9
uses the same terms as the Confucians to describe
the noble or exemplary person (*junzi*) who culti-
vates this power-virtue (*de*):

Only exemplary persons who hold fast to the
   One are able to do this.
Hold fast to the One; do not lose it,
And you will be able to master the myriad
   things.
Exemplary persons act upon things,
And are not acted upon by them,
Because they grasp the guiding principle of
   the One (ibid., 62).

Like the ideal Confucian ruler, the exemplary
Daoist possesses a virtue-power that influences the
lesser person in the same way that the wind causes
the grass to bend. This idea of mystical efficacy is
extended and reinforced in section 18:

Rewards are not sufficient to encourage the
   good;
Punishments are not sufficient to discourage
   the bad.
Yet once this flow of vital energy is achieved,
All under the heavens will submit.
And once the mind is made stable,
All under the heavens will listen (ibid., 80).

*Inward Training* thus reveals a multitude of similarities between Daoists and Confucians. This is
further reinforced in Section 22 in a passage that

is remarkably reminiscent of the Centrality and Equilibrium in the *Rites*. This description of the significance of rites and music in Daoist practice would not be out of place in Confucian text:

> . . . to bring your anger to a halt, there is
>     nothing better than poetry;
> To cast off worry there is nothing better than
>     music;
> To limit music there is nothing better than the
>     rites;
> To hold onto the rites there is nothing better
>     than reverence;
> To hold onto reverence there is nothing better
>     than tranquillity.
> When you are inwardly tranquil and
>     outwardly reverent
> You are able to return to your innate nature
> And this nature will become greatly stable
>     (ibid., 88).

*Inward Training* suggests none of the antipathy towards Confucians that, as we will see, can be found in Laozi and Zhuangzi. Instead, it hints at a shared desire for tranquillity and the recovery of one's original or Heavenly nature. Later forms of Daoism, however, included many beliefs and practices that would have been profoundly offensive to some later Confucians, among them the incorporation of sexual practices into religious ritual, the ingestion of cinnabar (a poisonous substance) to attain immortality, and the practice of mental discipline with the goal of escaping or transcending this mundane world.

### Laozi and the *Daodejing*

If the apparent incongruity of such practices raises questions about how they all fit into the category of Daoism, it may be helpful to remember the famous first line of the *Daodejing*: 'The way that can be spoken is not the constant Way.' The dynamism and fluidity implied by this holy ineffability are abundantly evident in Daoism.

The putatively Confucian *Yijing*, for example, is preserved in the *Daozang*, a large and unwieldy collection of works by writers considered to be Daoist. So too are two typically 'non-Daoist' thinkers: Han Feizi (d. 233 BCE), a thinker from the Legalist school whose text includes two chapters of commentary on the *Daodejing*; and Mozi, who taught universal love (*jianai*; see the section below on Popular Religion and Other Movements). If the Confucians were syncretic, the Daoists were even more so.

Unlike the authors (or editors) of *Inward Training*, Laozi takes a dim view of Confucian rites: 'The rites are the wearing thin of loyalty and good faith/ And the beginning of disorder' (Lau 1963: 99). Yet, like the Confucians, he considers the rooting of the Way in the person, family, village, and state to be indispensable, for it ensures that 'the offering of sacrifice by descendants will never come to an end' (ibid., 115). The sage of the *Daodejing* shares the ideal of discipline: the only difference is that he seeks to achieve it not through humanly created rites but through the cosmic all-embracing Way.

There seems to have been a genre of literature consisting of wise advice collected from elders during the late fourth century and early third century BCE. The *Daodejing* may be one such anthology. It deals with the sage in his/her relationship to the Way and virtue-power as these elements relate to government. Since the 1970s, five redactions of the *Laozi* have been recovered from two archaeological sites. The version we work with today is a later edition that likely took shape during the first century CE and was given its final form during the third century. It is a short text divided into two sections, and seems to take its title from the first substantive word in each section: *dao* from Book I and *de* from Book II (*jing* means simply 'classic'). The two characters *dao* and *de* offer some insight into the nature of the text.

The term *dao* acquires new dimensions in the *Daodejing*. No longer simply a way or path, as in the Confucian way or the Daoist way, it takes on cosmic proportions, becoming the creative aspect of Heaven, even the Creator. It also takes on a personality: this Way is variously described as 'empty', 'deep', and 'darkly visible', and exhibiting a 'weakness' that overcomes strength.

> The way begets one;
> One begets two;
> Two begets three;
> Three begets the myriad creatures.
> The myriad creatures carry on their backs the
>     yin and embrace in their arms the yang and
>     are the blending of the generative forces of
>     the two
>         (Lau 1963: 103).

> Turning back is how the way moves;
> Weakness is the means the way employs
>     (ibid., 101).

The term *de* in the *Daodejing* refers to virtue-power, but this is no ordinary virtue. It embodies the mystic inner power attained through integrity and alignment with the unseen world of the numinous, the power that allows a sage ruler to infuse his realm with the harmony he has achieved by 'doing nothing'. (It's important not to take this phrase literally: here 'doing nothing' refers to a state of mind or being in which it is possible to be permeated by the Way, so that one acts in concert with the Way, without self, intention, or ulterior motives.)

The Daoist sage models himself on the Dao, encouraging it to dwell in him by making himself empty like the hub of a wheel, the hollow of a cup, or the space in a room. Soft as the water that flows over and around rocks, yet in time wears them down, and occupies ravines and valleys, benefiting all things, this sage is spare in his desires. Overturning convention, he knows the honoured male but keeps to the traditionally subservient and humble female. He knows the symbolic goodness of white but keeps to the 'hoodwinking', unenlightened black (ibid., 127). He embraces the One and remains an uncarved block. He refuses to be sculpted with conventional virtues—though Laozi makes it clear that he also teaches conventional values:

> What others teach I also teach.
> 'The violent will not come to a natural end.'
> I shall take this as my precept
>     (Lau 1963: 103).

Yet even as the *Daodejing* counsels against violence—just as the Confucian sages did in their time—it criticizes as 'false adornments' the Confucian concepts of the wise sage and righteous benevolence. It also finds fault with the value commonly attributed to profit and ingenuity, boldly declaring that they, along with learning, should be exterminated. Simplicity, the Daoist sage suggests, should replace these false values:

> These three [the Confucian sage, benevolence,
>     and ingenuity], being false adornments, are
>     not enough
> And the people must have something to which
>     they can attach themselves:
> Exhibit the unadorned and embrace the
>     uncarved block,
> Have little thought of self and as few desires as
>     possible
>         (Lau 1963: 75).

Unlike the Confucian who works primarily with the good and virtuous, the Daoist sage 'abandons no one' (ibid., 84). He is said to have three treasures: compassion (*ci*, the same character used in Buddhism), frugality, and 'not daring to take the lead in the empire' (ibid., 129). He is 'drowsy', 'muddled', 'foolish', and 'uncouth' (ibid., 77). He is inconspicuous, does not consider his own way to be the right way, neither does he brag, or boast, or contend with others (ibid., 79). He is self-effacing and 'avoids excess, extravagance, and arrogance' (ibid., 87). Such a sage is capable of surviving even the tumult of the Warring States.

Shaking off the conventional preference for what is high and pure, the sage holds on to what is low and impure. He shuns the positive and keeps to the negative. Beyond that there is yet another perspective:

> The whole world recognizes the beautiful as the beautiful, yet this is only the ugly; the whole world recognizes the good as good, yet this is only the bad.
> Thus Something and Nothing produce each other;
> The difficult and the easy complement each other;
> The long and the short off-set each other;
> The high and the low incline towards each other;
> Note and sound harmonize with each other;
> Before and after follow each other.
> Therefore the sage keeps to the deed that consists in taking no action and practises the teaching that uses no words
> (Lau 1963: 58).

Here, embracing the One is associated with 'taking no action' and using 'no words'—suggesting a transcendence beyond that of the negative over the positive. The sage in concert with the One lives in a world of no action and no word, that embodies both white and black, male and female and so overcomes a dichotomous complementarity.

### Zhuangzi

The current working copy of the *Zhuangzi* comes from an edition by Guo Xiang (d. c. 312 CE). Chapters 1 to 7, known as the inner chapters, and 17 to 22 are deemed to be from the school of Zhuangzi. The sages of the two philosophical texts, Lao and Zhuangzi, are similar but not the same. The sages or holy people of the *Zhuangzi* shun politics and take on a hermitic quality. More strikingly, the personalities who offer sagely wisdom range from ordinary folk like cooks and cripples, to Confucius, to Lao Tan (understood to be Laozi), to mythological rulers like the Yellow Emperor and goddesses like the Queen Mother of the West (Xiwangmu). The fanciful and historical exist side by side like black and white, female and male.

The sage in Laozi who aims to transcend dichotomy is found also in Zhuangzi. The latter elaborates, using 'this' and 'that' as counterpoints:

> Everything has its 'that', everything has its 'this'. From the point of view of 'that' you cannot see it, but through understanding you can know it. . . . [The sage] illuminates all in the light of Heaven. He too recognizes a 'this', but a 'this' which is also 'that', a 'that' which is also 'this'. His 'that' has both a right and a wrong in it; his 'this' too has both a right and a wrong in it (Watson 1968: 39).

The sage allows his mind to wander in simplicity, blending with the vastness that is the Way. He follows things as they are and makes no room for personal views. In contrast to Laozi, with his 'doing nothing', Zhuangzi describes a state of self-soness or spontaneity (*ziran*). Though the principle is not inconsistent with the Confucians' ideal of following the pattern in nature, in expression it is remarkably different. The story of Cook Ding illustrates well the Daoist point: when the prince goes to him for advice, Cook Ding counsels him to govern in the way he carves an ox: by the hollows of the joints. Instead of hacking through on the basis of preconceived notions and rules, without examining the ox itself, the ruler should size up the empire just as he would an ox, to find out where the hollows are.

The state in which it is possible to make a clear assessment of the empire or ox is one of Oneness through emptiness (*xu*). This is different from the Buddhist concept of emptiness. Rather, as in *Inward Training*, this emptiness is achieved by using the body to discipline the heart-mind. Here Zhuangzi adds an unexpected non-sectarian twist, setting Confucius up with his favourite disciple, Yan Hui. When the latter asks about the meaning of fasting, Confucius replies:

> Make your will one! Don't listen with your ears, listen with your mind. No, don't listen with your mind, but listen with your spirit. Listening stops with the ears, the mind stops with recognition, but spirit is empty and waits on all things. The Way gathers in emptiness alone. Emptiness is the fasting of the mind (ibid., 57–8).

In his attention to the spirit, the sage in *Zhuangzi* takes an approach more reminiscent of *Inward Training* than of the practically focused Confucius and Laozi. This other-worldly orientation is confirmed in the image of the Holy Man who lives on Gushe Mountain, far away from human society. His skin is said to be 'like ice and snow', and he is 'gentle and shy like a young girl':

> He doesn't eat the five grains, but sucks the wind, drinks the dew, climbs up on the clouds and mist, rides a flying dragon, and wanders beyond the four seas. By concentrating his spirit, he can protect creatures from sickness and plague and make the harvest plentiful (ibid., 33).

This is the sage as spiritual and cosmic healer. The themes of health, long life, and immortality are introduced in the *Zhuangzi* through reference to the mythical Yellow Emperor, who does not appear in either *Inward Training* or the *Daodejing*. This sage-emperor is the putative author of the medical text *Inner Canon of the Yellow Emperor* (*Huangdi neijing*); yet it is said that when he attained the Way, he 'forgot his wisdom': content to be remoulded (ibid., 89) he 'ascended to the cloudy heavens' (ibid., 82).

This account of the Yellow Emperor's ascension is offered alongside the more prosaic observation that 'Life and death are fated—constant as the succession of dark and dawn, a matter of Heaven.' Juxtaposing the ordinary and the extraordinary, the mortal and the immortal, the material and the spiritual, he also points out humanity's inherent limitations. Like the summer cicada who can know nothing of spring and autumn, he writes,

> a man who has wisdom enough to fill one office effectively, good conduct enough to impress one community, virtue enough to please one ruler, or talent enough to be called into service in one state, has the same kind of self-pride as these little creatures (ibid., 31).

Zhuangzi himself, when invited to take a government position, is said to have responded by telling the story of the dead tortoise (a symbol of long life) that was wrapped in cloth and kept in the ancestral temple of the king. Zhuangzi asks the officials who have offered him the position whether the tortoise would prefer to be thus honoured or to be alive and dragging its tail through the mud. The officials answer that it would prefer to be alive. Zhuangzi then ends the interview by stating that he would like to continue fishing by the river and dragging his tail in the mud. Throughout the *Zhuangzi*, political engagement and adherence to conventional norms are associated with death and disfigurement, either physical or spiritual.

Thus—unlike his Confucian contemporaries Mencius and Xunzi, who sought to offer 'sagely' advice to the princes of the Warring States period—Zhuangzi stepped back and asked whether the various conflicting solutions offered by the thinkers of the day might actually be adding to the chaos. Instead of proposing solutions, he offered stories conveying profound insights in lighthearted yet direct and forceful terms.

## From the *Zhuangzi*

*One chapter attributed to Zhuangzi is entitled 'Fit for Emperors and Kings'. It concludes with a little story about the impact that even well-intended sameness and conformity can have on one's physical and spiritual well-being.*

The emperor of the South Sea was called Shu [Brief], the emperor of the North sea was called Hu [Sudden], and the emperor of the central region was called Hun-tun [Chaos]. Shu and Hu from time to time came together for a meeting in the territory of Hun-tun, and Hun-tun treated them very generously. Shu and Hu discussed how they could repay his kindness. 'All men,' they said, 'have seven openings so they can see, hear, eat, and breathe. But Hun-tun alone doesn't have any. Let's try boring him some!'

Every day they bored another hole, and on the seventh day Hun-tun died (Watson 1968: 97).

### Women and the Feminine in the Classical Texts

The subject of women is not addressed in either *Inward Training* or the *Daodejing*, although the latter does talk abstractly about the 'mother' and the 'spirit of the valley', which it describes as both the 'root of heaven and earth' and the 'mysterious female' that never dies (Lau 1963: 62). Nor does Zhuangzi concern himself much with women. Wives are mentioned in passing as companions in life, and are then grieved in death. The yin-yang dichotomy seems to have been generally accepted and was clearly reflected in the division of labour and social roles. Women are seen as weavers, working in the domestic realm; and men as farmers, working outside the home.

'This' and 'that'—representing subject and object, self and other—were also applied to the realm of the conventional and unconventional in the relations between women and men. The Daoist Liezi is described as taking over the domestic realm of the feminine after he attains mature spiritual understanding.

He went home and for three years did not go out. He replaced his wife at the stove, fed the pigs as though he were feeding people, and showed no preferences in the things he did. He got rid of the carving and polishing and returned to plainness, letting his body stand alone like a clod. In the midst of entanglement he remained sealed, and in this oneness he ended his life. (Watson 1968: 97)

This association of sacred oneness with animals and the feminine is not surprising. Nor is Zhuangzi's implied criticism of Confucian-style 'carving and polishing', given the Daoist preference for not-doing and the natural. The theme of men seeking union with the feminine, and women with the masculine, becomes prominent in the poems of the south. Images of female power and divinity in themselves—without reference to men—appear only in the chapter entitled 'The Great and Venerable Teacher', which mentions a Queen Mother of the West who heads the pantheon of goddesses and a teacher called the Woman Crookback. These are mythical characters, however: unlike the Confucian classics, the *Zhuangzi* does not celebrate any historical woman.

### The *Songs of the South*, *Huang-Lao Silk Manuscripts*, and *Techniques of the Mind I*

The *Songs of the South*, *Techniques of the Mind I,* and *Huang-Lao Silk Manuscripts* were likely compiled through the late Zhou, Qin, and early Han periods (between the fourth century BCE and the second century CE). The last two are syncretic and similar to the *Daodejing* and *Zhuangzi* in various ways, but the *Songs* are distinctive in their literary quality and descriptions of love between deities and humans.

The *Songs* are dedicated to anthropomorphic spirits of heaven, earth, and water. These gods and goddesses from the south were drawn in sumptuous details, and intimately involved with their human lovers. In 'The Lady of the Xiang', a man seeks union with the goddess of the river Xiang:

> A child of the lord descends upon the
>     northern shore;
> Her eyes' subtle glances yearn for me.
> . . .
> Mounting her chariot together we will roam.
> . . .
> The seasons of time allow but a fleeting
>     encounter
> Would that I might wander freely
>     (Sommer 1995: 89).

The man goes on to describe how he will build a bower for the goddess on the water and lists all the varieties of flowers he will choose, some for appearance and others for fragrance.

In another poem, 'The River Earl', the human figure is a woman in love with a male river spirit:

> With you I roam the nine rivers,
> Balanced on the rising winds and poised
>     above the waves;
> Riding a water-canopied with lotus,
> Drawn by a brace of dragons, sea-serpents at
>     their sides.
> . . .

> With you I roam the banks of the river,
> The rushing, thawing waters churning as they
>     descend.
> . . .
> Waves in torrents come to welcome me;
> Fishes, shoal upon shoal, are my bridesmaids
>     (ibid., 90).

In both poems, the human partners wander freely with their divine lovers, unconstrained by sociocultural conventions. The title of the first chapter in the *Zhuangzi*, 'Free and Easy Wandering', suggests a similar ethos of emancipation from the material realm, perhaps in anticipation of Daoist transcendence or immortality.

The *Huang-Lao Silk Manuscripts* were sealed in a tomb in 168 BCE. The ideas they record are drawn from a wide range of schools, but their underlying theme is said to be Laozi's idea of the tranquil sage king who governs through non-action.

Like Dong Zhongshu and the New Text Confucians, the Huang-Lao scholars believed in the triad of Heaven, Earth, and humanity. The Daoists went further, imagining that the macrocosm of the universe was reflected in the microcosm of human society or even the individual human body and using the yin-yang and five phases system to discern correspondences between Heaven, Earth, and human beings. They were active at court during the first sixty years of the Han dynasty (second century BCE), but seem to have disappeared after Emperor Wu made Confucianism the state religion. Until these manuscripts were excavated in 1973, none of their contents were known.

Like the Huang-Lao teachings, *Techniques of the Mind I* reflects the Daoist concerns outlined in *Inward Training*, the *Daodejing*, and the *Zhuangzi*. Echoing the *Daodejing*, it seeks to explain how self-cultivation—specifically, the practice of restraining desire and emptying the mind—can help an enlightened ruler attain the tranquillity necessary to respond harmoniously to any situation in its 'self-so-ness'. The text has two parts, one written in verse and tentatively dated to the mid-third century BCE and the other a line-by-line prose commentary dated to 180 BCE.

## Differentiation

### Han Dynasty Daoism and Confucianism

Huang-Lao thinkers were influential at the early Han court. In 139 BCE—two years into Emperor Wu's reign—Liu An, King of Huainan, submitted to the emperor (his nephew) a copy of the *Huainanzi*—a collection of twenty-one essays on topics ranging from cosmology and astrology to inner cultivation, government, and political thought. Like the older texts, its message is the need for a sage ruler to still his passions and rid himself of prejudice so that he can respond appropriately to all situations. The collection was intended to offer a Daoist sage king a comprehensive guide to just and effective governance.

The essays are generally believed to have been composed by Daoist adepts and scholars under Liu An's direction, though some historians believe they were actually Huang-Lao texts presented to Emperor Wu in an effort to thwart the rise of Confucianism. In any event, the content of the *Huainanzi* is very similar to the account of Daoism written by Sima Tan, who held office of Grand Historian from 140 to 110 BCE; in fact, some think this was the text he had in mind when he wrote 'On the Six Lineages of Thought'.

Sima identifies syncretism as a primary feature of Daoism. A follower of the Huang-Lao school and a contemporary of Dong Zhongshu, he describes the Daoists of his time as flexible in their actions and policies, changing with the seasons, adapting to changes in the world, and exemplifying the foundational belief that the Way is always in transformation and cannot be fixed. He adds that Daoists derived many of their techniques of self-cultivation from the five other schools. They followed the cosmic cycles of the yin-yang and five phases of the Naturalists, chose the best ideas from the Confucians and Mohists, and integrated into their system the basic ideas of the Terminologists (*Mingjia*) and Legalists.

The Daoists' goal, according to Sima, was to permit the 'numinous essence within people to be concentrated and unified' so that they might 'move in unison with the Formless and provide adequately for all living things' (de Bary and Bloom 1999: 279). According to Sima, the language of 'numinous essence' and the 'Formless' is unique to the Daoists, as is the focus on meditation. And although the goal of providing for others recalls the Confucians, the Daoists included among those 'others' not just human beings but all living things.

As for the ascendant New Text Confucians, Sima commented that they 'are erudite yet lack the essentials. They labour much yet achieve little. This is why their doctrines are difficult to follow completely' (ibid.). In short, Sima Tan, the Huang-Lao believer, distanced himself from purposeful 'right' action and made clear his preference for the Daoists:

> The essentials of the Great Way are simply a matter of discarding strength and avarice and casting aside perception and intellect. One relinquishes these and relies on the techniques [of self-cultivation]. When the numen (*shen*, 'spirit') is used excessively it becomes depleted; when the physical form labours excessively it becomes worn out. It is unheard of for one whose physical form and numen are agitated and disturbed to hope to attain the longevity of Heaven and Earth (de Bary and Bloom 1999: 279–80).

The concern for health and longevity in this account is paradigmatically Daoist. And while Confucians would agree on the importance of renouncing avarice, they would argue in favour of strength (especially for men), perception, and intellect. Thus, even though Daoists and Confucians alike talk about the universal Way and the welfare of others, their approaches to self-cultivation are quite different. The Confucian focus on the primacy of ritual performance and the Daoist focus on the fasting of the mind reflect the contrasting ways in which the two religions understood nature and its patterns, and what each considered important.

Nevertheless, underlying both traditions is a broad emphasis on self-cultivation for the sake of harmony in the universe. Both Confucians and Daoists seek to control the heart-mind, especially the passions, in order to attain the tranquillity necessary to achieve union with the Way. Both believe that oneness with the Way and, consequently, with Heaven and Earth, allows us to transcend our ordinary selves in order that we may serve others. The ideal of universal harmony and the notion that it is the role of human beings to mediate between Heaven and Earth are shared by Confucians and Daoists alike.

### Daoism beyond Texts

### Belief in 'Transcendents' (Immortals)

Even after the Huang-Lao school had been overshadowed by the Confucians, the interest in immortality and mysticism evident in the earliest

A sculpture of the 'Eight Immortals' of Daoism on display in Singapore as part of New Year's celebrations. Representing men and women of different ages and stations in life, the Immortals play a role not unlike that of Christian saints, serving as patrons of various groups and trades (© Kevin R. Morris/CORBIS).

Individualist works continued. By the end of the first century BCE the Yellow Emperor was venerated as the founder of the Xia dynasty. For Daoists he became the Primordial Ancestor, skilled in the arts of longevity and immortality, and the father of alchemy. He was also credited with inventing the Chinese calendar, sacrificial and funeral rites, the compass, and musical scales, among other things.

Daoist lore also has it that the Queen Mother of the West, the head of the pantheon of female immortals and the guardian of access to transcendence, visited Emperor Wu in 110 BCE because he was absorbed in the quest for eternal life. Another story relates how the next-highest-ranking female transcendent, the Lady of Supreme Basis, appeared to the Emperor and, denouncing him as 'licentious, extravagant, and violent', informed him that he would never achieve immortality, no matter how many Daoists he invited to court (Cleary 1989: ch. XI–XII). Goddesses were clearly central to the practice of religious Daoism, even if they were scarce in the classical texts.

Two documents attest to the Han court's continuing interest in immortality: *Records of the Grand Historian* (*Shiji*) by Sima Tan and his son Sima Qian; and the *Lives of the Immortals*, attributed to Liu Xiang (the author of the *Biographies of Exemplary Women*). Sima Qian described men from Yan and Qi during the Spring and Autumn and Warring States period as practising the way of the transcendents 'who shed their mortal forms and melted away' (Kirkland 2004: 185).

The *Immortals* was probably written in the second and third centuries CE, after the time of Sima Qian, and modelled on Liu Xiang's *Biographies of Exemplary Women*.

It includes an account of the Yellow Emperor being escorted to Heaven by a celestial dragon. Also included in the collection is the immortal Prince (*Wangzi*) Qiao, a historical figure closer in time to the Han, who is described as alighting on the peak of a mountain on a white crane (another symbol of longevity), waving to his relatives before ascending to heaven like the Yellow Emperor. This same prince is mentioned in the poem 'Far Off Journey', likely written during the time of Emperor Wu:

> I can follow Wang Ch'iao (Qiao) and sport
>     with him.
> I dine on the six vital forces and drink mists
>     and vapours,
> Rinse my mouth with the principal yang
>     forces and imbibe the morning haze.
> I safeguard the halcyon clarity of the spiritual
>     and numinous,
> And refined vital forces enter and coarser
>     dregs are expelled
>         (Sommer 1995: 92).

These few lines illustrate the syncretism characteristic of Chinese religious culture, reflecting influences from the indigenous shamanistic milieu, meditative principles, and yin-yang theory, as well as belief in transcendence. These poetic and religious elements would find expression in later schools like the Highest Clarity (*Shangqing*).

## Meditation and Worship: Practices and Beliefs

The goal of meditation, according to the classical texts, was to return vital essence, vital energy, and the numinous spirit to their natural states, before awareness and worldly activities dissipated them. The Daoist seeks to return to the Dao through a process of reversal—as a sculpture might seek to recover its original unity and return to the block of marble from which it has been carved. The practitioner seeks to go from form to essence, from essence to vitality, from vitality to spirit, and from spirit to emptiness or the Void.

This ultimate Void is formless but can be visualized as the highest deity: the Great One, Supreme Unity or Supreme Oneness (Taiyi). The classical texts suggest various ways of achieving this oneness, including the maintenance of original unity by 'holding fast to the One (*shouyi*)'; 'sitting and forgetting'; visualizing the cosmos within one's body; and following the circulation of vital energy in the body. In the Han era it was thought that a long period of inward concentration would lead to the formation of an embryo containing or representing the True Self, which could develop into an immortal. Harking back to *Inward Training*, this True Self was said to be born when the spirit has been purified, united with and indistinguishable from vital energy and essence. This Self was referred to by various names: Holy Embryo, Spirit Embryo, Golden Embryo, Golden Elixir, the True Person Cinnabar of the North, the Golden Pill, the Pearl.

## The Celestial Masters and Yellow Turbans

Over time, the Confucian underpinnings of the Han regime were challenged by a combination of political corruption, natural disasters, and military turbulence. The resulting economic and social turmoil provoked uprisings across the empire, some of which reflected a significant Daoist influence. At the same time, a text (now lost) called the *Classic of the Great Peace* (*Taipingjing*) was circulating that prophesied the coming of a celestial master who would bring peace to a time of surging chaos.

Two millenarian and messianic movements were likely influenced by *Great Peace*: the Celestial Masters and the Yellow Turbans (or Way of Taiping). Founded in 142 CE, the Celestial Masters sect (later renamed Orthodox Unity) traced its origins to the deified Laozi or Lord Lao (*Laojun*), who was said to have appeared to **Zhang Daoling** and given him a covenant establishing a new relationship between the gods and the people. A central feature of this covenant was the abolition of the traditional blood sacrifice. No longer would the gods be influenced by the offerings made to them. Rather, over time they came to operate as a kind of celestial bureaucracy to whom the faithful could present their appeals just as they did to state bureaucrats in ordinary life. Priests too were expected to offer their services without monetary reward; for subsistence they relied on the devotees, who were required to donate five bushels of rice each year (for this reason the group is sometimes referred to as Five Bushels of Rice Daoism).

Initiates of the Celestial Masters gained access to esoteric sacred texts. Practices included chanting and meditation, and the *Daodejing* was used in liturgy. Purity chambers were provided for the cultivation of the Spirit Embryo. Talismans (*fu*) drawn on paper and offered to the gods and goddesses served as contracts between deities and the faithful, guaranteeing protection.

Although some have described the Celestial Masters as a 'health cult' and others have emphasized its members' concern with sin, the two are closely connected, since disease of any kind—personal, social, or civil—was understood to be the consequence of sin. Deities from the three Offices of Heaven, Earth, and Water were believed to record human wrongdoing. Those who had committed offences expiated their sins by writing them down; each sin was written on three pieces of paper, each of which was then submitted to one of the three Offices: one paper would be burnt, one buried, and one submerged in water. The communal confession of sins was also used, along with talismans, to heal the sick.

In the late second century, Zhang Daoling's grandson Zhang Lu, the third Celestial Master, took control of the Sichuan region and established a theocracy. Community and social welfare were promoted through projects like road and bridge repairs, and food and shelter were provided for the hungry and destitute. The membership was divided into twenty-four parishes, each headed by a 'Great Libationer' (male), with female and male officers at lower levels. By 215, however, a powerful warlord named Cao Cao was threatening to take the region by force. To avoid an invasion, Zhang surrendered. The Cao family (who later established

the Wei dynasty) made Daoism the state religion and intermarried with the Zhangs. Nevertheless, around the year 300 the Celestial Masters, leaders and members alike, were dispersed across northern China, and in this way the sect spread to all corners of the land. Since the fourth century the Celestial Masters sect (eventually renamed Orthodox Unity) has been guided by a set of commandments that, in addition to the usual injunctions against killing, adultery, and stealing, includes prohibitions against retaining numerous servants and concubines, the buying and selling of slaves, and a variety of environmentally harmful practices such as burning fields and mountain forests, cutting down trees for no good reason, and urinating on plants or in water that people may drink. Having survived over 1,800 years, the Orthodox Unity remain active in southern China and Taiwan today.

The Yellow Turbans movement (Taiping Dao), based in Shandong in northeastern China, was established by the Zhang brothers Jue, Liang, and Bao, with the express purpose of challenging the Han regime in the name of the Yellow Emperor. They wore yellow turbans because, according to calculations based on the Naturalist yin-yang five phases system, a new dynasty associated with the colour yellow and the element earth would overthrow the Han (associated with blue, green, and wood). Like the Celestial Masters, the Yellow Turbans focused on confession, repentance of sins, meditation, and chanting, but they also believed in inherited guilt. Their conversion efforts attracted a massive following, but it was short-lived. When the Yellow Turbans rose in rebellion in the year 184 (believed to mark the beginning of the new sixty-year cycle in the Chinese calendar), they were crushed and the movement disappeared.

## Crystallization

### *Six Dynasties Period (220–589)*

In 220, as we have seen, northern China fell to the first in a series of invasions from Central and West Asia. Amid the chaos and instability of this era, state Confucianism was in disarray, and Buddhism was able to establish a foothold in China.

Daoism, for its part, took a variety of directions. Old interests and concerns were not abandoned; the quest for transcendence remained a focal point—a quest pursued in some cases through self-cultivation and in others through the ingestion of substances such as cinnabar, known today as mercuric sulphide (some tales of the Yellow Emperor suggest that cinnabar contributed to his ascent into heaven as an immortal). But under the influence of Buddhism Daoists also began reinterpreting doctrine, rebuilding community rituals, and establishing new institutions, including the first Daoist temple, constructed in the fifth century. Daoist leaders affiliated themselves with various foreign dynasties, including the Niu-Song and Toba Wei in the 400s, and the Liang in the 500s, and Daoism remained active politically. Like Confucianism, however, it also began to turn inward, focusing more on individual cultivation.

At the same time, Zhuangzi's notions of spontaneity, spiritual freedom, and non-attachment to convention were gaining popularity. They encouraged eccentric behaviour, especially in literary men such as the Seven Sages of the Bamboo Grove—one of whom was said to roam around naked in his hermitage. Having fled the turmoil of northern China for the south, the Seven Sages engaged in Pure or Light Conversation (*qingtan*) on metaphysical and non-political topics and reflected Confucian and Buddhist as well as Daoist influences.

The *Liezi*—the third most important Daoist text, after the *Daodejing* and *Zhuangzi*—was compiled in the 300s, bringing together stories about Liezi, a Daoist philosopher mentioned in the *Zhuangzi*. Meanwhile, Daoism continued to be active in the north. Celestial Masters Daoism became the state religion of the foreign Toba Wei in the 400s and was established across the countryside.

Interest in meditation also continued. The sixth-century *Secret Instructions of the Holy Lord on the Scripture of Great Peace* harked back to the

teachings of the *Inward Training*. Like the Han-era *Classic of Great Peace*, it taught that to 'pursue long life you must love energy, venerate spirit, and value essence'. By 'holding fast to the One', practitioners of meditation could 'go beyond the world and ascend to heaven!' (Kohn in Sommer 1995: 147). Describing seven lights that practitioners should see in meditation, the text warned that those who saw only darkness should take medicine, for this was 'the light of human disease, disorder, and nervousness' (ibid., 148). Similar ideas were characteristic of two new schools that emerged during this time.

## Two New Schools: Highest Clarity and Numinous Treasure

Between 364 and 370 a medium and shaman named Yang Xi—a literate servant of a large aristocratic clan—received scriptures from the immortal Lady Wei of the Heaven of Highest Clarity. The goal for Yang and his Highest Clarity school was to become a true being or perfected person (*zhenren*) through three practices: visualizing the gods of the Big Dipper and associating them with different organs in the body; absorbing vital energy and light from the sun and moon; and using 'outer alchemy'—the ingestion of elixirs based on substances such as cinnabar—to facilitate flights of ecstasy to the star deities who controlled human destiny. Like the Holy Man of Gushe Mountain, Highest Clarity devotees would also fast or abstain from grains and eat only very small amounts of food. It was believed that the adept's body, made light and radiant as a result of this diet, would be able to ascend, glittering, to the heavens.

This interest in heavenly ascent was reflected in a poem that was said to have been revealed to Yang Xi. Echoing the *Songs of the South*, the 'Song of An, the True Consort of Ninefold Fluorescence' takes the form of a love song addressed by a 'transcendent' (immortal) to her human lover, and includes a reference to Mount Sumeru, the centre of Buddhist cosmic geography—another indication of Buddhism's influence on Daoism.

This was not the only such evidence. A few decades after Yang Xi, Ge Chaofu claimed to have received a series of revelations involving the Buddhist concepts of karma, rebirth, and *kalpa* (cycles of time). Whereas the focus in the Highest Clarity sect was on the individual, Numinous Treasure (*Lingbao*) sect looked outward to the community and all of humanity, suggesting a synthesis of Daoist and Buddhist concerns. One of this sect's texts, the *Scripture for the Salvation of Humanity* (*Durenjing*), describes a great cosmic deity who is so concerned for the salvation of human beings that he sends an emissary to reveal the teaching from the Dao itself. This teaching focused especially on rituals of two kinds: purification (*zhai*) and communal renewal (*jiao*).

The goals of the Numinous Treasure purification rituals were typical of the earlier Han dynasty: preventing disease, warding off natural calamities, and ensuring the salvation of ancestors. They were performed around a temporary altar and started with a cleansing of the body through bathing and fasting. The heart-mind was then purified through the confession of sins and a communal feast celebrating the reinstatement of harmony between the gods and human beings. In community renewal rituals, deities were invited down into the altar, incense was offered, and the faithful who sponsored the rituals were granted audiences with the gods, during which they would request boons for the community.

It was during this period that the first effort was made to collect a Daoist 'canon'. Lu Xiujing (406–477) tried to create a set of common texts by organizing the existing writings into the 'Three Caverns' of Perfection, Mystery, and Spirit (paralleling the Three Baskets of Theravada Buddhism). The Cavern of Perfection and the Cavern of Mystery contained the writings of the Highest Clarity and Numinous Treasure sects, respectively, while the Cavern of Spirit contained talismans whose functions and efficacy were explained in the *Writs of the Three Sovereigns* (*Sanhuang wen*), a text concerned with the summoning of spirits and the ritual use of talismans. Writings of the Celestial Masters were included in supplements, and three more supplements were eventually added, one each for the *Daodejing*, the *Scripture of Great Peace*, and writings from the Great Purity (*Taiqing*) alchemical tradition. Soon after Lu's efforts, and a hundred years after Yang Xi, Tao Hongjing (456–536) collected and edited Yang's revelations in the *Pronouncements of the Perfected* (*Zhen Gao*).

## Interaction and Adaptation

### The Tang Dynasty

The Tang dynasty was a high point for Daoism. The imperial family, which shared the surname Li with Laozi, claimed to be his descendants, and Daoism once again became the state religion. Highest Clarity patriarchs either held government posts or were invited to the capital, Chang'an (now known as Xi'an) to attend the emperors. One of the most famous patriarchs of the period, Sima Chengzhen (647–735), emphasized the personal practice of inner alchemy, meditation, and longevity techniques in two essays, 'On the Essential Meaning of the Absorption of Energy' (*Fuqi jingyi lun*) and 'On Sitting in Oblivion' (*Zuowang lun*).

Emperor Xuanzhong (713–756), the renowned Brilliant Emperor, wrote a commentary on the *Daodejing*, invited Sima to court, and sponsored Daoism to an unprecedented extent. Princesses were ordained Daoist priestesses and performed state rituals for the blessing and protection of the empire. The *Daodejing* was briefly included in state examinations, and a network of Colleges of Daoism was established. By 739 there were 1,137 abbeys for male Daoist monastics and 550 for women. There were also popular women teachers like Huang Ling-wei (c. 640–721), who had a coterie of women disciples. The worship of deities continued, and the Queen Mother of the West, the goddess first mentioned in the *Zhuangzi*, remained popular with both women and men. Classical Daoism reached its height of power and popularity during the Tang, but it was not until the Song dynasty that it would experience any substantial new development.

## From the Song Era to the Present

### Complete Truth School

The school of Complete Truth (Quanzhen; also translated as Perfect Realization, Perfect Truth, or Complete Clarity), like Orthodox Unity, is still active today. It is associated with the White Cloud Abbey in Beijing and is distinctive in its monasticism. It was founded by Wang Zhe (1113–70), who was known by his Daoist name Double Yang (Chongyang), and was a contemporary of many of the Song Neo-Confucians. Wang expressed his understanding of the cultivation of immortality or transcendence as follows:

> Leaving the world does not mean that the body departs. . . . When you realize the Tao, your body will be in the sphere of the ordinary, but your mind [hsin] will be in the realm of the sages. Nowadays, people want to avoid death forever and at the same time leave the ordinary world. They are very foolish, indeed, and have not even glimpsed the true principle of the Tao (Kirkland 2004: 188).

Wang Chongyang discouraged the magical, supernatural understanding of the practice of transcendence. He encouraged his disciples to read from across all three traditions including the *Daodejing*, the *Classic of Filiality*, and the Mahayana Buddhist *Heart Sutra* (*Xinjing*). In his 'Fifteen Precepts for Establishing the Teaching', Wang started with the ideal of harmony in spirit and vital energy, which comes when the body is well rested. This, he wrote, can be achieved by entering a Daoist monastery and avoiding damage to vital energy through overexertion. He also discussed health (recommending the use of herbs for healing); living a simple life and not seeking a lavish external one; developing and maintaining good Daoist friends; nurturing one's Nature and living out one's

Destiny; pacifying one's mind; and leaving behind the mundane world. The 'basic motif of the art of self-cultivation', he wrote, is the 'search for the hidden meaning of Nature and mind' (Sommer 1995: 202).

### Women

Where Confucianism has Ban Zhao, the Daoists have Sun Buer or 'Not-two' (1119–83). Sun was the wife of Wang Chongyang's disciple Ma Danyang or 'Singular-yang'. In time, her spiritual attainments exceeded those of her husband, and she became one of Wang's most famous students—the only woman among his 'Seven Perfected' disciples. Her story is an interesting one, for it underlines the particular difficulties that women of faith were expected to encounter in their search for enlightenment.

One day Sun heard Wang say that an immortal was expected to emerge in the city of Loyang, far from where she lived in Shandong. When she told Wang that she wished to go and cultivate transcendence there, however, he withheld permission. He explained that she would be the target of men's desire and that she would be molested and raped. It would be a waste of her life to take up practice, for she would want to kill herself from the shame of such harassment and violation. Wang refused to let her go.

Undeterred, Sun went directly from the meditation hall to the kitchen and asked the servants to leave her. Once alone, she heated some oil in a wok and, when it was hot enough, poured cold water into it. Closing her eyes, she let the hot liquid splatter onto her face, burning and scarring her skin. Recognizing her sincerity, Wang taught her the methods of inner alchemy. He then counselled her to hide her knowledge so that people would not know that she was a seeker of the Way.

When her husband returned, she schemed to be left alone, stopped grooming herself, and pretended to be insane. When Ma told Wang that Sun had lost her mind, Wang answered that she could not otherwise become an immortal. Eventually, she managed to slip quietly out of the house and travel to Loyang, where she continued to behave as if she were mad and therefore was left alone by most of the townspeople. As Wang had anticipated, she was accosted by two men who harassed all women they encountered; but Sun escaped them and was saved by enormous hailstones. After this supernatural intervention, the men felt chastised and spread the story about her special nature, after which she was left alone for twelve years in Loyang.

### Revival of Orthodox Unity

Other new ritual traditions continued to do well through the late Song and into the early Yuan period, but this changed when Kublai Khan, the Mongolian ruler, extended his government to the south. There he consolidated his control over religious life by giving authority only to the Orthodox Unity on Dragon and Tiger Mountain (Lunghu shan), which had persevered through the dominance of Highest Clarity and Numinous Treasure. After the Mongols were overthrown, the Orthodox Unity's exclusive authority continued under the Ming, and its leader was entrusted with the compilation of the Daoist Canon (*Daozang*), which was printed under the auspices of the Emperor Yongle in 1445.

Even as Neo-Confucianism became entrenched during the Qing dynasty (1644–1911), Daoism continued to inspire popular morality books (*shanshu*), gymnastics, meditation, breath exercises such as *qigong*, and the movement of vital energy through the body, as in the practice known in the West as Tai Chi (*taiji*) or the Great Ultimate. It suffered enormous setbacks, however, in the period that followed the Opium Wars of the mid-nineteenth century, when reform movements inspired by the West began to attack traditional beliefs and practices. Modernizing movements such as the Christian-inspired Taiping Rebellion, communism, and scientism were particularly critical of Daoism, which they perceived as a body of superstition, hostile to progress. The deadliest blow came during the Cultural Revolution (1966–76), when temples and shrines of all kinds—syncretic folk, Daoist, Confucian, and Buddhist—were either destroyed or severely damaged. Daoism is now rebuilding not only in China but also around the world, most notably in Europe and North America.

# MOHISM AND CHINESE POPULAR RELIGION

## Mohism

Mohism coexisted with Confucianism and Daoism and was active and influential during ancient times, but disappeared after the Han. Mo Di or Master Mo (Mozi, 470–391 BCE) taught an ungraded, undifferentiated love, a love of all without distinction. He believed that Heaven willed people to love one another, and that those who failed to do so would be punished. In his view, the ultimate objective of government was the provision of shelter, food, and security for all, and members of a society should work to save each other from harm and deprivation.

## Popular Religion

Popular religion in China might be characterized as a loose collection of beliefs and practices that pertain to and privilege the power of deities, ghosts, and spirits. It is non-institutional and draws various elements from more established religions like Confucianism, Daoism, Buddhism, and, more recently, Christianity. One important element is the belief that human spirits or souls can, after death, continue to intervene uncontrolled in the human world or be harnessed for the benefit of the living. An everyday expression of this belief can be seen in the restaurant shrines described at the beginning of this chapter, but it can also give rise to politically charged sectarian and millenar-ian movements such as the White Lotus Society and the Heavenly Kingdom of Great Peace—the movement behind the Taiping Rebellion.

### The White Lotus Society

The White Lotus Society was a Buddhist group with a largely lay following based on the belief in the messianic Future Buddha, Milo (Maitreya in Sanskrit), and Manichaean ideas about the coming of a King of Light. Its clergy married, it offered social services usually covered by the fam-ily, and it favoured unorthodox vernacular scrip-tures featuring common folk motifs. Although the White Lotus Society played a substantial role in the overthrow of the Mongolian Yuan dynasty (1269–1368) and the establishment of the native Ming, the first Ming emperor feared its power and sought to suppress it. By the late Ming, the group itself seems to have disappeared and the name 'White Lotus' had become a kind of general pe-jorative term, used by officials to refer to any sus-pect religious groups, including Christians newly arrived on Chinese soil.

### The Taiping Rebellion

Five hundred years after the White Lotus Soci-ety helped to overthrow the Yuan, the movement for the Heavenly Kingdom of Great Peace (*Taip-ing tianguo*) (1850–64) played a similar role, pro-moting rebellion against the Qing regime. It came into being after the Opium War, when the conces-sions demanded of China in the Treaty of Nanjing (1842) signalled the utter defeat of the Chinese government. Like the White Lotus Society, this movement contributed significantly to the weak-ening and eventual fall of the incumbent dynas-ty. Its founder, Hong Xiuquan, claimed to be the younger brother of Jesus, sent to establish an egali-tarian kingdom of great peace that reflected influ-ences from the Daoist past as well as the Christian present. In its enthusiasm for establishing the True Teaching, it set out to eradicate all others. The

rebellion that erupted in 1850 continued until 1864, killing an estimated twenty to thirty million people and destroying thousands of Daoist and Buddhist temples in southern China.

### The Relationship between Popular and Elite Religion

Popular religious traditions often express, in ad-dition to local personalities and customs, the universal ideals of elite traditions. Yet there are telling differences between them. The elite tra-ditions have their own texts and are relatively distinct from one another. Folk religious move-ments, by contrast, tend to syncretize a variety of sometimes incongruous ideas pertinent to their cause, and rely on oral, non-written teachings even when semi-classical texts are available to them. Elite traditions are based on a canon; each has a reliably fixed system of beliefs and prac-tices, and therefore they maintain a good mea-sure of orthodoxy. Folk beliefs and practices, on the other hand, tend to be fluid in nature and often lack any clear standard of orthodoxy. While the goals of sagehood, immortality, and enlight-enment transcend ordinary life and demand self-restraint, the goals of folk religion tend to be more prosaic, focusing on health, happiness, long life, prosperity, and status. Their rituals tend to be more emotional and dramatic: for instance, the exorcisms conducted in cases of 'spirit pos-session', or the funeral rituals in which actors stage attacks on hell.

Nevertheless, folk and elite religions are inti-mately connected on many levels. Ancestor ven-eration, for instance, is common to all Chinese religions. Ancient folk beliefs in ghosts and spir-its, and shamanistic ritual practices formed the early foundations of today's elite religions, while many contemporary popular religious movements (such as Falungong) draw inspiration from those beliefs and practices even though the elite tradi-tions no longer hold them to be literally 'true'. Many of the exemplary figures associated with elite traditions—sages, teachers, monks, nuns— were born into popular folk traditions, and in many cases they eventually became folk deities. The ritual specialists engaged to perform ceremonies such as funerals are not bound to one religion as in the elite beliefs and practices, and they often perform rites for people who are not religiously affiliated. Finally, elite religious texts have provided material for use in many areas of popular culture, from folk ritual to education (e.g., morality books) to entertainment (e.g., theatre).

# 🦋 CONCLUSION

The ancient popular beliefs and practices at the roots of China's elite religions came from many different places and cultures. Yet all these diverse traditions share a single aspiration to harmony— individual and communal, mundane and cosmological. Furthermore, all see the achievement of that goal as depending on the disciplined transcendence of self. Though individual groups have varied in their specific goals and methods, they have all tended to share the belief that the way to harmony lies in harnessing the basic human desires—for material well-being, health, familial joy, personal security, social stability, spiritual maturity and release—and directing them towards the care of family, friends, community, and state.

# 🦋 KOREAN RELIGIONS

This section will concentrate on the historical development of religions on the Korean peninsula, though it will also take a brief look at the rapidly changing non-traditional religious culture of contemporary South Korea. (North Korea will not be discussed, since the communist government's antipathy towards religion makes it impossible to know anything about contemporary beliefs and practices.)

In the early 2000s, census data showed that nearly half of South Korea's population professed to have no religion. Those who did claim an institutional affiliation were almost equally divided between Christianity (mainly Protestant, especially Pentecostal) and Buddhism. Other unspecified affiliations accounted for less than 1 per cent of the population, while Confucianism came last at a negligible 0.3 per cent and the indigenous shamanic folk tradition was statistically invisible. The apparent lack of institutional affiliation and personal dedication to two foundational sets of beliefs and practices, Shamanism and Confucianism, is striking. Yet by all accounts both these traditions continue to be pervasive in contemporary Korean life.

The statistics' failure to capture the religious culture of Korea is revealing, however, because it calls into question the way 'religion' (*chonggyo*) is understood as a category in public life. More research is needed to clarify how respondents interpret 'religion' and what they mean when they describe themselves as having no religious affiliation.

This section will discuss the historical importance of Shamanism and Confucianism and assume their continued significance. Although Daoism will also be discussed, it appears never to have had a strong presence in the region.

## Introduction

Theoretically, traditional Korean religiosity can be classified as non-theistic at the elite level and polytheistic at the popular. In practice, though, Korean religiosity, like its Chinese counterpart, tends to be syncretic. Thus neither of these categories can be assumed to exclude the other, and it is even possible to identify a quasi-monotheistic belief in a purposeful and creative Way (or Heaven, or Heaven-and-Earth) co-existing with both the polytheistic belief in ancestral spirits and nature deities and the non-theistic belief in an impersonal natural Way.

Traditional Korean beliefs and practices have tended to accommodate devotees' needs, whether for salvation, self-perfection (physical and spiritual), peace of mind, material well-being, or human fellowship. Thus, for example, Korean Buddhists have been able to seek salvation or release in the afterlife without rejecting this-worldly Confucian notions of filial piety and loyalty. The same is true of contemporary Korean Christians. Pentecostal Christianity has been especially popular in Korea, perhaps because many of its practices are remarkably similar to traditional shamanistic practices.

# Foundation Myths, Daoism, and Shamanism

## Korea and China: A Shared History

Ancient Korean culture shows traces of influences both from continental East Asia and from the Scytho-Siberian peoples of Central Asia. Migration from China to the Korean peninsula was underway as early as the Zhou dynasty, and political relations between the two populations have from the beginning reflected both kinship and antipathy, relatedness and differentiation. The earliest written records of Korea are Chinese. Sima Qian's *Records of the Grand Historian* describes Wiman, one of the later kings of the proto-state of Old Choson, as a refugee from northern China who ruled over Chinese refugees and indigenous inhabitants at Wanggom (present-day Pyongyang) in the sixth and fifth centuries BCE.

The Wu family shrine in the Chinese coastal province of Shandong, built in 147 CE, further illustrates the connection between these ancient peoples, for the content of the Old Choson foundation myth of Tangun is carved into slabs of stone there. A third Chinese source, the sixth-century *History of the Wei Dynasty*, tells how the mythical Tangun established Old Choson during the time of China's mythical sage king Yao.

## Foundation Myths

### Tangun and Old Choson (?c. 2333 –?50 BCE)

An early Korean source, now lost, told a different story, however. This source, known as the *Old Record*, started with Tangun's divine ancestors, his grandfather Hwanin and father Hwanung. Hwanin knew that Hwanung wanted to descend from heaven and live in the world of human beings, so he chose one of the highest mountains, Mount T'aebaek, and settled his son there, in a cave.

But Hwanung was not alone in the cave. A bear and a tiger were also living there, and they asked him to transform them into human beings. To that end, Hwanung gave them a bundle of sacred mugworts and twenty cloves of garlic, with instructions to eat these foods and avoid the sunlight for a hundred days. After twenty-one days the bear became a woman, but the tiger failed to avoid the light and therefore was not transformed. The woman remained alone, unable to find a husband, so she prayed under the altar tree for a child; Hwanung responded by transforming himself, lying with her, and giving her a son, Tangun Wanggom.

This foundation myth became a marker of national identity in the thirteenth century, during the time of the Mongol invasions, when it appeared in two Korean histories in slightly different versions. According to the version in *Memorabilia of the Three Kingdoms* (*Samguk yusa*), by the monk Iryon (1206–89), the god Hwanung descends into the human world and marries a she-bear who gives birth to Tangun (a bear cult is still current among the Ainu people of Japan as well as some Siberian tribes in Russia). Yi Sunghyu (1224–1300) in his *Songs or Rhymed Record of Emperors and Kings* (*Chewang ungi*) gives a variant account in which the great king Hwanung gives medicine to his granddaughter to change her into a human being; she then marries a god of the sandalwood tree and bears Tangun (a tree cult was prevalent in the southern portion of the Korean peninsula). By contrast, Kim Pu-sik's official *History of the Three Kingdoms* (*Samguk sagi*), compiled in 1145 and

Confucian in inspiration, does not include any story about Tangun.

### King Tongmyong (Koguryo-Paekche) and King Hyokkose (Silla)

The proto-state of Old Choson was followed by the Three Kingdoms (c. 50 BCE–668 CE) of Koguryo, Paekche, and Silla. The foundation myth for Koguryo (found in a collection that dates from the thirteenth century) tells how its founder Chumong, who later took the title of King Tongmyong, was born from an egg after the sun—Haemosu, the Son of Heaven—shone on the breast of his mother, the eldest daughter of the River Earl. In both style and content, this poem recalls the *Songs of the South* and the first poem in the *Odes* ('Fish-hawks'). After ruling for nineteen years, Tongmyong forsakes his throne and rises to heaven. The founder of Paekche, King Onjo, is said to have been the son of Chumong and therefore to have shared this divine heritage.

Silla's foundation myth, like Old Choson's, was recorded in Iryon's *Memorabilia*. Like King Tongmyong, King Hyokkose ('Bright'), the founder, is born from an egg, a red one in this case. His birth is announced by an eerie lightning-like emanation

---

## The Lay of King Tongmyong

*From the Collected Works of Minister Yi of Korea*

In early summer, when the Great Bear stood in the Snake,
Haemosu came to Korea,
A true Son of Heaven.
He came down through the air
In a five-dragon chariot,
With a retinue of hundreds,
Robes streaming, riding on swans,
The atmosphere echoed with chiming music.
Banners floated on the tinted clouds.

. . .

North of the capital was the Green River,
Where the River Earl's three beautiful daughters
Rose from the drake-neck's green waves
To play in the Bear's Heart Pool.
Their jade ornaments tinkled.
Their flowerlike beauty was modest—
They might have been fairies of the Han River banks,
Or goddesses of the Lo River islets.
The king, out hunting, espied them,
Was fascinated and lost his heart.
Not from lust for girls,
But from eager desire for an heir.

   (Lee et al. 1993: 24)

from a well. When the people crack open the egg, they find inside it a beautiful boy with a radiant appearance. When they bathe him he emits light; the 'birds and beasts danced for joy, heaven and earth shook, and the sun and the moon became bright' (Lee et al. 1993: 33). Soon after, a dragon appears near a well and brings an infant girl from under her left rib. The child's features are exceptionally lovely except for a beak-like lip, which falls off after she is bathed in the river. When the two reach the age of thirteen, they marry and become king and queen.

### Daoism

Korea's foundation myths contain a variety of shamanistic elements that also occur in Daoism, including nature deities (the River Earl), marriage between gods and human beings (Hwanung and the bear-woman), and ascension into heaven (King Tongmyong). In Silla, the people believed in the Holy Mother, a mountain goddess and guardian of the country. She was said to live on a mountain to the west of the capital, recalling the Queen Mother of the West in the *Zhuangzi*.

These apparently Daoist elements have led some scholars to suggest that the cult of the Holy Mother is a composite of an indigenous mountain deity and a Daoist immortality cult. In *Memorabilia* there is an account of the holy mother coming to the aid of a Buddhist nun seeking to repair a Buddha Hall. This holy mother, who appears in a dream, is said to be the daughter of a Chinese emperor who learnt the way of immortality. After settling in Korea, she gives birth to a holy man who becomes the first ruler of Silla; the story suggests that 'perhaps' this was Hyokkose.

This mythological syncretism is reinforced in Silla's history. In the 700s Kim Chisong, a vice-minister of state, kept one image each of Amitabha, the Buddha of the West, and Maitreya, the Buddha of the Future. He read Mahayana literature but also enjoyed Laozi and the first chapter of the *Zhuangzi*, 'Free and Easy Wandering'. Echoes of Daoist scripture continued into the 1400s, during the staunchly Neo-Confucian Choson (or Yi) dynasty, when one minister, disappointed in his ruler, left the court to spend the rest of his life wandering as a monk, writing poetry, and telling stories,

---

## Holy Mother of Mount Fairy Peach

*The following text comes from the* Samguk yusa. *The phrases 'art of the immortals' and 'art of longevity' refer to Daoism: by emphasizing that the Holy Mother embraced both Daoism and Buddhism, the passage underlines the syncretic nature of Korean religion.*

During the reign of King Chinp'yong [579–632], a nun . . . wished to repair a hall for the Buddha . . . but could not carry out her desire. A beautiful immortal fairy, her hair adorned with ornaments, appeared in the nun's dreams and consoled her: 'I'm the holy goddess mother of Mount Fairy Peach [Mount West], and I am pleased that you would repair the Buddha Hall. . . .' The holy mother, originally the daughter of a Chinese emperor, was named Saso. Early in her life she learned the art of the immortals and came to live in Korea, where she stayed for a long time. . . . When Saso first came to Chinhan, she gave birth to a holy man who became the first ruler of Silla—perhaps he was Hyokkose, who married Aryong. . . . Saso donated gold to make a Buddha image, lighted incense for the living beings, and initiated a religion. How could she be merely one who learned the art of longevity and became a prisoner in the boundless mist? (Lee et al. 1993: 94)

and other literary men retired from official life to engage (like the Seven Sages of the Bamboo Grove) in conversation on matters metaphysical.

In addition, murals in Koguryo tombs suggest that the Daoist cult of immortality merged with local Korean beliefs in prognostication. And the Tang court sent a memorial asking about Daoism in Korea, along with an adept and seven other envoys, plus a copy of the *Daodejing*. In the same period, a Buddhist monastery in the region of what is now the border between North Korea and China was converted into a Daoist temple, and in 643, at the request of the Koguryo king, eight Daoist priests were dispatched there from China. By 650, the Daoist influence at the Koguryo court was so strong that the monk Podok, who opposed the state's adoption of Daoism, fled and sought refuge in Paekche.

A female shaman performs a prayer for peace at a festival in Seoul marking the first full moon of the lunar year (© JEON HEON-KYUN/epa/Corbis).

Along with Daoism, practices such as geomancy (influenced by the Naturalist yin-yang five phases) and prognostication continued to attract popular interest throughout the United Silla period (668–936). During the Koryo period, King Yejong (r. 1105–1122) was such a devout Daoist that in 1110 China's Emperor Song Huizong sent him two Daoist priests. Yejong sponsored the construction of Pogwon Temple (1110–17), which when completed was able to accommodate more than ten priests. Some courtiers suspected that the king wanted Daoism to replace Buddhism as the state religion.

## Shamanism

### The Native Tradition

As Daoism found its place at court, folk Daoism's focus on deities, ghosts, and spirits found deep resonance in Korean shamanism (*mugyo*). There were native songs (*hyangga*) and dances dedicated to communication with deities and spirits. Each village had its own tutelary deity: a local mountain god or goddess in inland regions and a dragon king by the sea. A pair of spirit-generals, female and male, were responsible for all activities below and above the earth, respectively.

Traditional household deities included the gods of the hearth, the roof beam (in the main room of the house, where guests were received and family corpses laid out), and the outhouse. Shamans (*mudang*) were summoned in cases of demonic disturbance and they regularly performed rituals (**kut**) at annual community celebrations and ceremonies of thanksgiving. Meanwhile, distinctive fragments of Daoist practice endured, embedded in practices such as the use of alchemy in medicine, gymnastics, and breath exercises like *taiji* and *qigong*, all of which became part of Korean culture.

### Modern New Religions

There are more than two hundred new religions in South Korea today. They too are syncretic, reflecting a mix of traditional and new influences, including Christian beliefs. Folk shamanism in particular has emerged as a rallying point in response to the West and globalization. Some modern progressives urged the revival of folk traditions rather than 'foreign' Confucianism as a way of reclaiming Korean culture, though others, who saw shamanism as mere superstition, called for it to be rooted out. Na Ch'ol's (1813–1916) Religion of the Great Ancestors (Taejonggyo), which some call the oldest religion in Korea, combined ancient indigenous myths with Christian beliefs, depicting God as Korean and presenting the heavenly triad of Hwanin, Hwanung, and Tangun as an alternative to the Christian Trinity. At the same time Daoism lives on in movements like Dahn World, which focuses on inner alchemy and humanity's progress towards an 'enlightenment revolution'.

## Confucianism

Korea has the largest network of Confucian shrines in the world today. The process of Confucianization stretched over a millennium, beginning during the Three Kingdoms period. After the Ming dynasty fell to the Manchurians in 1644, Korea prided itself on being the world's only true Confucian nation.

### Three Kingdoms, United Silla, and Koryo

Koguryo established a government school for Confucianism in 371 but was not generally Confucian in its ethos of government. Paekche and Silla, however, both had Confucian bureaucracies. In 682 Silla set up the National Confucian College (later University); and in 717 portraits of Confucius, ten Confucian philosophers, and seventy-two Confucian worthies were brought from China and installed there. Korean students travelled to Chang'an, the Chinese capital, to study and sit for the civil examinations, which qualified them to become scholar-officials in both countries.

It was during the Koryo period, when Buddhism was at its height in Korea, that Confucianism became firmly rooted. King T'aejo (r. 918–943), who defeated Silla and founded Koryo, was an ardent Buddhist, but he also encouraged Confucian learning. Thus he rejected Silla's tradition of governance by a hereditary aristocracy and adopted instead the examination-based bureaucratic system of the Tang. In addition, T'aejo is said to have left for his successors a list of 'Ten Injunctions' that reflected his syncretic approach, bringing together Buddhist, Confucian, and indigenous perspectives. The first injunction, for example, clearly honours the Buddhist tradition:

> The success of the great enterprise of founding our dynasty is entirely owing to the protective powers of the many Buddhas. We therefore must build temples for both Son [Meditation] and Kyo (Textual) Schools and appoint abbots, that they may perform the proper ceremonies and themselves cultivate the way (Lee 1985: 132).

The third injunction pays tribute to the Confucian tradition:

> 3. In matters of royal succession, succession by the eldest legitimate royal issue should be the rule. But Yao of ancient China let Shun succeed him because his own son was unworthy. This was indeed putting the interests of the state ahead of one's personal feelings. Therefore, if the eldest son is not worthy of the crown, let the second eldest succeed to the throne. If the second eldest, too, is unworthy, choose the brother the people consider the best qualified for the throne.

The fourth injunction, however, emphasizes the primacy of indigenous Korean experience:

> 4. In the past we have always had a deep attachment for the ways of China and all of our institutions have been modelled upon those of T'ang. But our country occupies a different geographical location and our people's character is different from that of the

Chinese. Hence, there is no reason to strain ourselves unreasonably to copy the Chinese way . . . (H. Kang in Lee 1993: 263).

The fifth injunction then pays respect to the land, implicitly evoking the indigenous shamanistic tradition:

> I carried out the great undertaking of reunifying the country by availing myself of the latent virtue of the mountains and streams of the Samhan [three kingdoms in the south of Korea] (Lee 1985: 108).

T'aejo was both pragmatic and humanistic in his principles. When the last Silla king surrendered, T'aejo made him the governor of the old Silla capital and granted him substantial acreage. He also appointed as local magistrates many of the heads of powerful Silla and Paekche clans, giving them considerable autonomy.

Confucianism received a further boost in the eleventh century when **Ch'oe Ch'ung** (984–1068), a high-ranking official known as the Korean Confucius, established a private Confucian academy. Two hundred years later, An Hyang (1243–1306) and his contemporary Paek I Chong introduced Zhu Xi's Neo-Confucian teachings into Korea during the reign of King Ch'ungnyol (1274–1308), who erected a national shrine to Confucius in what is now Seoul.

While Neo-Confucianism flourished, the Buddhist community began to attract criticism for its involvement in profit-making ventures that ranged from investments in horse breeding and trading in surplus grain to brewing and money-lending. Chong Tojon (d. 1398), a Neo-Confucian minister, criticized Daoism as well as Buddhism for worshipping purity and annihilation:

> . . . there is nothing a human being desires more than life and nothing he hates more than death. Buddha strove to escape death and birth, which means that he feared death.

Lao Tzu strove for longevity, which means he craved life. If this is not worldly gain, what is it? ('Philosophical Rebuttal of Buddhism and Taoism', in Lee et al. 1993: 456).

Accusing both Buddhism and Daoism of seeking 'worldly gain', Chong argued that Zhu Xi's Neo-Confucian philosophy was the only solution to social problems. This vehement attack marked the end of a long tradition of tolerance in Korean Confucianism.

## Choson

### Antipathy to Buddhism

The founder of the Choson dynasty, also named T'aejo (r. 1392–8), introduced a registration system that banned the building of new temples and stopped the growth of the monastic population. His son, T'aejong, continued the effort to control Buddhism. Many temples were disestablished, and their estates and workers, including slaves, were confiscated; the examination of monks for state service was strictly regulated; certain rituals were prohibited; and activities and temples were confined to specific areas.

Around the same time, Buddhist funerals and memorial rituals were discontinued and families began installing shrines for ancestral tablets in their homes. Eventually, the first son became responsible for the performance of the rites of ancestor veneration (*chesa*), and the only one with the right of inheritance. This system of primogeniture put an end to the Koryo system, under which female and male offspring alike were entitled to inherit property, and couples could hold property jointly.

### Korean Neo-Confucianism

Cho Kwang-jo (1482–1519) continued the process of Confucianization by rooting out superstitions that were incompatible with Confucian beliefs and practices. He encouraged government by moral suasion and instituted a system of local self-government based on the idea of a village code (hyangyak), outlined in a work of the Chinese Neo-Confucian philosopher Zhu Xi entitled *Lu Family Compact with Additions and Deletions*. At the heart of this endeavour was a notion of reciprocity or mutuality expressed in four objectives: mutual encouragement of morality, mutual supervision of conduct, mutual decorum in social relations, and mutual aid in times of hardship or disaster.

Zhu Xi's influence extended well beyond the world of practical politics into the metaphysical realm. In particular, his ideas regarding human nature inspired a famous exchange of letters between the Korean philosophers Yi Hwang (or T'oegye; 1501–70) and Yi I (or Yulgok; 1536–84). At the centre of this exchange, known as the 'Four–Seven Debate', was the relationship between the four heart-minds—which, according to Mencius, reflect the fundamental goodness of human nature—and seven emotions (happiness, anger, sorrow, fear, love, hate, and desire)—which, according to 'Centrality and Equilibrium', cause some human actions to be less than good.

Both taking Zhu Xi as their starting-point, Yi Hwang and Yi I arrived at different conclusions. Yi Hwang argued that principle or pattern in nature (***i***) rises and material force (***ki***) follows, implying that human nature is mixed from the beginning. Yi I, on the other hand, argued that if principle pervades everything, is uniform and undifferentiated, then it must be material force that initiates action, implying that human nature is originally wholly good.

Behind the philosophers' quest for a deeper understanding of human nature was the commitment to psychological-moral transformation of the self—the Neo-Confucian equivalent of the self-cultivation emphasized in classic Confucianism. The focus on self-improvement was not limited to men.

In early Choson Korea, as in Ming China, women's education became a focal point. Three prominent publications written by or for women in this period were Queen Sohye's (1437–1504) *Instructions for the Inner Quarters* (*Naehun*); a letter written by Song Siyol (1607–89) on the occasion of his eldest daughter's marriage, emphasizing the importance of a mother's influence on her children; and a letter by Lady Hyegyong (1735–1815) to her nephew in which she sought to impress on him the importance of Confucian virtues: being honest and conscientious, respectful of elders, affectionate and filial at home, a loving guide to younger cousins, and generous and compassionate to paternal aunts.

A similar focus on moral education was evident in other parts of Korean society as well. Yu Hyongwon (1622–73), for instance, used Confucian

---

## Zhu Xi on Human Nature

Following Zhou Dunyi, Zhu Xi believed human beings—like everything else in the universe—to be the product of the interaction between heavenly 'principle' and the material forces of yin-yang and the five elements. Thus human beings possessed both principle and material force. Like Mencius, Zhu Xi believed human nature to be the expression of heaven-given principle and therefore intrinsically good. Human action, however, was not necessarily good. Zhu Xi attributed this apparent contradiction to the effects of material force on the three aspects of human personality: heavenly nature (i.e., principle), human feelings, and mind. As Zhu put it: 'Nature is the state before activity begins and feelings are the state when activity has started, and the mind includes both of these states' (W.T. Chan in Sommer 1995: 192). The mind is the master and 'unites and apprehends nature and the feelings, but it is not united with them' (ibid.); the mind brings nature and feelings together, but remains a separate entity.

ethics to argue against slavery. Under a government run by a true king, Yu wrote, slavery would be unthinkable:

> At the present time our country regards slaves as chattels, but they are human beings the same as we are. Under what principle can you treat a human being like chattel [?] . . . in our country at the present time the custom is that when you ask a man how wealthy he is, he always answers by telling you how many slaves and how much land he owns. Therefore, you can also see how mistaken and sick our laws and customs are (Ch'oe et al. 2000: 161).

Meanwhile, as Neo-Confucianism became increasingly entrenched at the state level and Daoism was gradually assimilated into Choson culture, Buddhist monastics argued for reconciliation of the various religions—in effect, syncretism. As the monk Hyujong (1520–1604) put it in his *Mirror of Three Religions* (*Samga kwigam*): 'An ancient man said: "Confucianists plant the root, Taoists grow the root, and Buddhists harvest the root"' (Lee et al. 1993: 662). The dominance of Confucianism continued, however.

## *Post-Choson to the Present*

### Confucianism Challenged

Korean responses to the West varied. Yun Ch'iho (1865–1945) favoured wholesale Westernization and an end to the relationship with China (by that time the 'Sick Man of East Asia'), in which Korea was implicitly expected to play the subordinate role. If Koreans were oppressed, poor, dirty and filthy, Korean women degraded, Korean families weak, and Korean officials treacherous and cruel, Yun argued, Confucianism was to blame.

Yun's antipathy towards Confucianism was perhaps not unreasonable. During its occupation of Korea from 1910 to 1945, Japan used Confucianism as an imperial tool, renovating the old Royal Confucian Academy and establishing institutions such as the Society for the Promotion of the Confucian Way.

### Transnational Confucianism

Other Korean scholars agreed that Korea's adherence to teachings of Zhu Xi, which came to be considered 'conservative', had held it back. However, they believed that a transnational Confucianism based on the traditional values of filial piety, chastity, and frugality could illuminate the whole world. Among those men was Pak Unsik (1859–1925). Pak himself preferred the Confucianism of Wang Yangming, who had been neglected and overshadowed by Zhu Xi in Korea.

Wang Yangming had elaborated on the passage from the 'Great Learning' that begins: 'The Way of the great learning lies in clarifying bright virtue, loving the people, and abiding in the highest good' using the Neo-Confucian categories of 'principle' and 'nature':

> The highest good is the ultimate principle of manifesting character and loving people. The nature endowed in us by Heaven is pure and perfect. The fact that it is intelligent, clear, and not beclouded is evidence of the emanation and revelation of the highest good. It is the original substance of the clear character which is called innate knowledge of the good (W.T. Chan in Sommer 1995: 230).

Pak Unsik saw hope in the 'manifesting' of the naturally 'clear character'. The exemplary person, Yangming wrote, makes no distinctions between his person and the myriad things in exercising his 'innate knowledge of the good'. He commiserates with other people in their suffering, with birds and animals about to be slaughtered, with broken plants and even shattered tiles and stones. Pak was not alone in his choice of Confucianism as a response to modernity.

Kim Ch'ungnyol, a professor of East Asian philosophy who had studied with the New Confucian Fang Dongmei in the 1950s and 1960s, was an activist in the Korean democracy movement in Korea during the 1970s and 1980s. He believed that Confucianism could serve as an antidote to the excesses of capitalist industrialization. But the movement for the revival of Confucianism in Korea is not monolithic.

So Chonggi was critical of authoritarian rule but, like Pak, believed that Confucianism could be good for Korea. Differentiating between 'royal', 'official', and 'scholar' Confucianisms, he criticized all three for being singular and narrow in their focus on 'ethical politics', 'ritual politics', and 'eremitic politics', respectively. In their place he proposed a Confucianism of the people (*minjung*) based on their moral purity and creative capacities.

The recent establishment of an Institute of Confucian Cultural Studies as part of a nationwide network—headquartered at Songgyun'gwan University's Academy of East Asian Studies—suggests a revival of scholarly interest in Confucianism. However, recent census data show that popular support for Confucianism as a religion is slim.

# CONCLUSION

Korea has undergone tremendous transformations over the last fifteen hundred years, developing from a federation of states suffused with shamanic beliefs to a Buddhist-dominated unified Koryo to a Neo-Confucian Choson. Contemporary religious culture in South Korea remains pluralistic and syncretic. The traditional religions—shamanism, Buddhism, and Confucianism—have not yet disappeared. But Christianity has flourished, and there are now more than two hundred active new religious movements. How the various religions will interact with one another remains to be seen.

Students wearing traditional costumes perform during one of the regular celebrations of Confucius held at Songgyun'gwan University in Seoul (© Seoul Shinmun/epa/Corbis).

# Sites

## CHINA

**Beijing** The Imperial Palace complex, also known as the Forbidden City, includes the Tiantan (Altar or Temple of Heaven), where the Ming and Qing emperors performed the grandest sacrifices. The city is also home to the Taimiao, the ancestral temple of both dynasties; a Confucian temple dedicated to scholar-officials; various Daoist and Buddhist temples; and the tombs of the later Ming emperors.

**Qufu** The complex of monuments in the birth place of Confucius, in Shandong, includes a temple, a cemetery, and a family mansion. The cemetery contains Confucius' tomb and the remains of more than 100,000 of his descendants.

**Nanjing** The first capital city of the Ming, whose emperor, Hongwu, is buried here in the Xiaoling Tomb. Scholar-officials were trained in this thriving ancient metropolis, at the Confucian Academy. The Jinghai Temple is dedicated to the goddess of the sea, in honour of China's great Muslim seafaring admiral, Zhenghe.

**Wudangshan** Mount Wudang in Hubei is known for its many Daoist monasteries. It is also home to an organized complex of palaces and temples, built mostly during the Ming, and contains Daoist buildings from as early as the seventh century. The buildings include some of the finest examples in Chinese art and architecture.

**Xi'an** The capital for numerous dynasties, the city and its environs are home to the famous terracotta warrior guardians; numerous Daoist and Buddhist temples; and Huashan, one of the five sacred mountains of Daoism.

## KOREA

**Seoul** The Changdeogung Palace (Palace of Prospering Virtue) complex was established by T'aejong, the first king of the Choson dynasty. It includes Jongmyo, the oldest and most authentic of preserved Confucian royal shrines, which are dedicated to the ancestors of Choson. It houses tablets bearing teachings of the royal family.

# Glossary

**Ban Zhao** (c. 48–112 CE) An influential female Confucian scholar who wrote *Admonitions* (or *Lessons*) *for Women*.

**Dao/dao** Either the 'Way' in the sense of the Ultimate or the 'way' in the sense of the path taken by followers of a particular tradition.

**Datong** The Grand Commonality; an age of complete harmony, in which all people are as they should be: faithful, trustworthy, loving, conscientious, and cared for.

**Dong Zhongshu** (195?–105? BCE) The most prominent Confucian of the New Text school, who helped establish Confucianism as the state religion.

**Han Yu** (768–824) Played a pivotal role in the revival of Confucianism in a period when both Daoism and Buddhism were popular.

**i** The Korean transliteration for *li* ('principle'). See the second explanation for **li**.

**junzi** A person of exemplary behaviour, especially in Confucianism; traditionally translated in English as 'gentleman', implying the virtues of the upper class; a superior person, or one of virtue and exceptional character.

**ki** The Korean transliteration for *qi*; see **qigong**.

**Kongzi** The first teacher of Confucianism, known in the West as Confucius (551–479 BCE).

**kut** The ritual in which Korean shamans or *mudang* communicate with spirits.

**Laozi** The 'Old Master'; the putative patriarch of Daoism and author of the *Daodejing* who may or may not have been a real historical figure.

**li** The single English transliteration used for two different Chinese characters. The first sense, 'rites', involves ritual practice and decorum. The second,

'principle', refers to the meaning of patterns in natural materials like wood or stone and was used by the Neo-Confucians to designate the universal force or element that pervades the cosmos.

**Meng Ke** (c. 343–289 BCE) The second most prominent Confucian thinker, also known as Master Meng, Mengzi, and Mencius; he believed that human nature is originally good.

**qigong** A 'breath' discipline or set of exercises used to enhance health and spiritual well-being; also the vital or material energy or force that animates everything in the universe.

**ren** The central Confucian virtue, usually translated as humaneness, benevolence, goodness, or compassion.

**ru** The 'soft ones'; a term denoting Confucian scholars.

**sangang** The three primary relationships, between emperor and minister, father and son, and husband and wife.

**taiji** The 'Great Ultimate', which 'coexists' with the Ultimate of Non-being; also the term for the slow-motion exercise widely known in English as Tai Chi.

**Wang Yangming** (1472–1529) The Ming Confucian who challenged Zhu Xi's approach to self-cultivation and established the Neo-Confucian School of Mind.

**wuwei** 'Not-doing' as a way of being in the world: a state not of 'doing nothing' but of acting without intention or self-interest; an ideal for both Daoists and Confucians, though most prominently associated with the former.

**xiao** Filial piety; a child's love for its parents expressed in respect and duty; the cornerstone of Confucianism, considered a virtue by all Chinese religions.

**xin** The single English transliteration used for two different Chinese characters. The first, translated throughout

this chapter as 'heart-mind', is associated with both the thinking and feeling capacities; the second means trustworthiness, a quality valued by Confucians and Daoists alike.

**Xunzi** (c. 310–219 BCE) The third most important classical Confucian thinker, Xunzi maintained that human nature is evil.

**yi** A moral sense of what is right, what is required and appropriate for a situation; most often used in conjunction with *ren*.

**yin-yang wuxing** 'Yin' and 'yang' originally referred to the shady and sunny side of the mountain, but in time came to be associated with female and male qualities and, more broadly, complementary forces in the universe. *Wu* means 'five', and *xing* can be translated as 'element', 'agent', 'force', or 'phase'. Together, the various components of the term specify the dynamic quality of the universe and is an integral part of the Naturalist school popular during the Han dynasty.

**Zhang Daoling** Founder of the oldest surviving Daoist school; according to tradition, he established the Way of the Celestial Masters after Laozi appeared to him in a vision in 142 CE.

**zhong** The loyalty expected of all but especially of the junior partners in the five relationships: minister, son, younger brother, wife, and younger or less experienced friend.

**Zhuangzi** (369?–286?) The second most important early Daoist thinker, after Laozi; also the title of the book attributed to him.

**Zhu Xi** (1130–1200) The systematizer who was the most important member of the Neo-Confucian School of Principle.

**ziran** Self-so-ness or spontaneity, acting without societal constraints and in concert with the Way; most often associated with the Daoist philosopher Zhuangzi.

# Further Reading

Bell, Daniel A., and Chaibong Hahm, eds. 2003. *Confucianism for the Modern World*. Cambridge: Cambridge University Press. Draws from Chinese, Korean, and Japanese texts and histories to argue that Confucianism is relevant to our world.

Buswell, Robert E., ed. 2007. *Religions of Korea in Practice*. Princeton: Princeton University Press. Contains primary-source selections regarding ordinary devotional beliefs and practices together with critical analyses; also includes a helpful introductory essay by Don Baker.

Elman, Benjamin A., ed. 2002. *Rethinking Confucianism: Past and Present in China, Japan, Korea, and Vietnam*. Los Angeles: UCLA Asian Pacific Monograph Series. Delves into issues of gender and national variations, and asks who represents Confucianism.

Kirkland, Russell. 2004. *Taoism: The Enduring Tradition*. London: Routledge. An introductory text by an author who believes Daoism has been misrepresented and seeks to offer a new perspective.

Kohn, Livia, ed. 1993. *The Taoist Experience: An Anthology*. Albany: SUNY Press. Primary sources (with brief notes) for a range of philosophical, liturgical, and alchemical texts, mostly from medieval Daoism.

Lopez, Donald S., ed. 1996. *Religions of China in Practice*. Princeton: Princeton University Press. Includes essays on the religious practices of ethnic minorities such as the Manchus and Yi; Stephen Teiser's introductory essay provides a helpful overview.

Miller, James. 2003. *Daoism: A Short Introduction*. Oxford: Oneworld. Covers the historical development, political involvement, and physical practices of Daoism as well as its understanding of nature.

Wu, Ch'eng-en. 1970 [1943]. *Monkey*. Arthur Waley, trans. New York: Grove Press. A fictional look at popular religious beliefs and practices in medieval China.

Yao, Xinzhong. 2000. *An Introduction to Confucianism*. Cambridge: Cambridge University Press. Focuses on China; Korea and Japan are dealt with very briefly.

Yu, Anthony. 2005. *State and Religion in China*. Chicago and La Salle, IL: Open Court. Argues successfully that religions in China have always been closely involved with worldly politics.

# Recommended Websites

www.orientalarchitecture.com
Asian Historical Architecture offers photographs of numerous religious sites in China, Korea, and other countries in Asia, with brief historical notes and descriptions of how the buildings are used.

www.clickkorea.org/
A general interest site sponsored by the Korea Foundation with essays on Korean religions; to access, select the main category 'Thought & Religion', then choose from six subcategories.

www.stanford.edu/~pregadio/index.html
'The Golden Elixir: Taoism and Chinese Alchemy' is hosted by Fabrizio Pregadio of Stanford University, who gives a concise introduction to Daoism and includes an impressive list of sources on alchemical beliefs and practices in Daoism.

eng.taoism.org.hk
The Taoist Culture and Information Centre offers an insider view of Daoism's history and place in the world today. The site is sponsored by the Daoist Temple Fung Ying Seen Koon in Hong Kong and maintained with the help of scholars from North America, Europe, and China.

afpc.asso.fr/wengu/wg/wengu.php?l=bienvenue
'*Wengu zhixin*' ('Review the Old, Learn the New') is hosted by Association Française des Professeurs de Chinois and contains several original Chinese texts with English and French translations. The scholarship is traditional, but the site offers convenient access to texts.

# References

al Faruqi, I., and D.E. Sopher, eds. 1974. *Historical Atlas of the Religions of the World*. New York: Macmillan.

Bell, Daniel A., and Chaibong Hahm, eds. 2003. *Confucianism for the Modern World*. Cambridge: Cambridge University Press.

Ch'oe, Yongcho, Peter Lee, and W. Theodore de Bary, eds. 2000. *Sources of Korean Tradition*. Vol. II. New York: Columbia University Press.

Cleary, Thomas. 1989. *Immortal Sisters: Secret Teachings of Taoist Women*. Berkeley: North Atlantic Books.

de Bary, William Theodore, ed. 1972. *The Buddhist Tradition in India, China and Japan*. New York: Vintage Books.

————, and Irene Bloom, comp. 1999. *Sources of Chinese Tradition*, 2nd edn. Vol. 1. New York: Columbia University Press.

————, and Richard Lufrano, comp. 1999. *Sources of Chinese Tradition*, 2nd edn. Vol. 2. New York: Columbia University Press.

Fung, Yu-lan. 1934/1953. *A History of Chinese Philosophy*. Vol. 2. Derk Bodde, trans. Princeton: Princeton University Press.

Jochim, Christian. 1986. *Chinese Religions. A Cultural Perspective*. Englewood Cliffs, NJ: Prentice-Hall.

Kirkland, Russell. 2004. *Taoism. The Enduring Tradition*. New York and London: Routledge.

Lau, D.C., trans. 1970. *Mencius*. Middlesex and New York: Penguin.

————, trans. 1963. *Lao Tzu: Tao Te Ching*. Middlesex and New York: Penguin.

Lee, Ki-Baik. 1985. *A New History of Korea*. Edward Wagner, trans. Cambridge, MA: Harvard University Press.

Lee, Peter H., et al., eds. 1993. *Sourcebook of Korean Civilization*. Vol. I. New York: Columbia University Press.

Owen, Stephen, ed. and trans. 1996. *An Anthology of Chinese Literature*. New York, London: W. W. Norton & Company.

Raphals, Lisa. 1998. *Sharing the Light: Representations of Women and Virtue in Early China*. Albany: SUNY Press.

Roth, Harold D. 1999. *Original Tao: Inward Training and the Foundations of Taoist Mysticism*. New York: Columbia University Press.

Sommer, Deborah, ed. 1995. *Chinese Religion: An Anthology of Sources*. New York, Oxford: Oxford University Press.

Watson, Burton, trans. 1968. *The Complete Works of Chuang Tzu*. New York: Columbia University Press.

————. 1963. *Xunzi: Basic Writings*. New York: Columbia University Press.

# Note

1. This is the standard birth date for Kongzi, though some scholars prefer 552, based on scientific dating of an eclipse mentioned in the records of the time.

# Chapter 7

# Japanese Traditions

❧ John K. Nelson ❧

# OVERVIEW

## The Rousing Drum

In a small city deep in the mountains of central Japan, tens of thousands of laughing, chatting, yelling, and quietly expectant people fill the evening streets for the festival of the 'rousing drum'. At 9:30 p.m. an enormous drum—a metre and half in height—will emerge from the city's main Shinto shrine, having been blessed by priests in solemn rituals. It will then be hoisted and affixed to a platform that will be carried through the streets by as many as one hundred and seventy men. Adding to the weight of the platform will be two male strikers, one on each side of the drum, and eight 'guardians' representing local officials. But the weight is only part of the challenge faced by the bearers, for as the drum makes its way through the streets it will be 'attacked' by neighbourhood teams with their own (smaller) drums mounted on platforms, who will attempt to fight through the mass of guardians at ground level and occupy a position of honour immediately behind the main drum.

Fuelled by generous amounts of sake, the ensuing clashes seem anything but conducive to community solidarity. The festival is like a steam vent designed to release the pressure created by class and economic differences. In fact, injuries are common; parked vehicles are frequently damaged, and houses belonging to greedy landlords or stingy merchants may be vandalized. Old-timers still remember with pride the year when festival-goers trashed the local police station. Yet the rousing

The *okoshidaiko* or 'rousing drum' festival takes place in Furukawa township, Hida city, Gifu prefecture. Smaller drums from neighbourhood associations try to assume a coveted position behind the main drum, which represents the city government and main Shinto shrine (Hida city, Gifu prefecture).

◀ Shinto shrine attendants at a multi-faith ceremony in Nagasaki commemorating the victims of the 1945 bomb (Franck Robichon/epa/Corbis).

# Timeline

| | |
|---|---|
| **c. 8000 BCE** | Hunter-gatherers produce sophisticated cord-pattern pottery, arrowheads, and human figures with possible religious significance |
| **c. 450–250 CE** | Immigration from north Asia introduces new technology, cultural forms, language, religious rituals, etc. |
| **c. 250–600** | Kofun period; rulers interred in massive burial mounds (*kofun*), with grave goods and clay models (*haniwa*) of attendants that indicate complex local hierarchies in this life and the next |
| **538** | Introduction of Buddhism; Yamato clan establishes its dominance over other clans |
| **594** | 'Prince' Shotoku (*Shotoku taishi*) promotes Confucian principles alongside Buddhism; later acknowledged as patron saint of Buddhism in Japan |
| **600s** | Early temple-building; ruler referred to as 'heavenly sovereign' (*tenno*) |
| **710–794** | Nara period; capital city, Heijokyo, located on site of present-day Nara |
| **712, 720** | Compilation of two key texts (*Kojiki, Nihon Shoki*) used to legitimate imperial rule and aristocratic privileges; more than a thousand years later, these texts would be used in the campaign to revitalize 'Shinto' |
| **752** | Dedication of Todaiji temple and completion of its Great Buddha image |
| **785** | Saicho, founder of Tendai sect, establishes a temple on Mount Hiei |
| **794–1184** | Heian period; capital city, Heiankyo, moved to what is now in Kyoto |
| **834** | Kukai, founder of Shingon sect, establishes a monastery on Mount Koya |
| **1039** | Tendai monks attack monasteries of rival Buddhist sects |
| **1052** | Beginning of the 'Final Decline of the Buddhist Dharma' (age of *mappo*) marked by fires, famines, earthquakes, wars, pestilence, etc. |
| **1175** | Honen begins propagating 'Pure Land' Buddhism |
| **1185–1333** | Kamakura period, characterized by dominance of the samurai class; capital moved to Kamakura |
| **1200** | Eisai establishes Rinzai Zen school with support of the samurai |
| **1233** | Dogen establishes Soto Zen school |
| **1253** | Nichiren forms a sect centred on recitation of the *Lotus Sutra* |
| **1254** | Honen's disciple Shinran introduces True Pure Land Buddhism |
| **1274, 1281** | Attempted invasions by Mongol armies are thwarted when violent storms, called 'divine winds' (*kamikaze*), sink many of their ships |
| **1430–1500** | Major fires, famine, epidemics, social disorder; Onin War (1467) devastates Kyoto and marks start of regional power struggles |
| **1474–1550** | True Pure Land peasant protest movement spreads throughout the country |

*Continued*

| | |
|---|---|
| 1542 | Systematization of Shinto shrines, priestly certification via Yoshida clan |
| 1549 | Christianity enters Japan with the Jesuit Francis Xavier |
| 1573–1602 | Gradual centralization of political power; Oda Nobunaga, Toyotomi Hideyoshi, and Tokugawa Ieyasu establish military regimes that subdue regional lords |
| 1603–1867 | Edo Period; Tokugawa clan dominates all political, military, and bureaucratic activity; country closed to outside trade in 1633 |
| 1638 | Shimabara rebellion; Christianity banned |
| 1644–1860 | Rise of neo-Confucian teachings as challenge to Buddhist dominance |
| 1705 | First major pilgrimage of commoners to Ise |
| 1812 | Beginning of movement to revitalize Shinto |
| 1853–1867 | Commodore Matthew Perry arrives in Japan and demands open ports; Christian missionaries return; regional wars between feudal and imperial forces end with defeat of Tokugawa shogunate |
| 1868 | New Meiji government orders separation of *kami* and buddhas, resulting in destruction of many temples and religious art throughout the country |
| 1879 | Establishment of Yasukuni Shrine, where the spirits of military dead are venerated |
| 1890–1944 | State campaign to establish ideology centred on notions of imperial divinity, Japan as a sacred country, and military conquest |
| 1936–1945 | War in the Pacific, ending in the systematic destruction of most major and many minor Japanese cities |
| 1945–1953 | Allied occupation of Japan; emperor renounces divinity; disestablishment of Shinto as state religion |
| 1995 | Aum Shinrikyo attack on Tokyo subways; government passes new laws regulating religion organizations and activity |

drum festival is an annual event, promoted by both municipal and tourist associations as representing 'the spirit of Furukawa'.

## Mr Sato's Funeral

After nearly a week of preparation, the funeral for Mr Sato Hideo (in Japan, the surname precedes the given name) is unfolding with the precision of a military operation. In a building constructed specifically for funerals, on the grounds of a large temple, the casket sits at the front of a hall decorated by hundreds of white chrysanthemums. A portrait of Mr Sato, smiling and grandfatherly, has been placed in the centre of the display, surrounded by candles and food offerings that recall a Buddhist altar.

Professional funeral directors, men and women wearing black suits, black armbands, and white gloves, direct the proceedings in soft yet commanding voices. Hired by the family and subcontracted by the temple, they have orchestrated every part of the ceremony: the syrupy background music, the guest books, the arrangements for voluntary

# Traditions at a Glance

### Numbers
(All numbers are based on self-assessment by various religious groups. Because most Japanese religions are complementary rather than exclusive, the numbers of adherents reported by various sects may reflect periodic participation rather than ongoing membership.)

Shinto: Estimates range from 3.5 million self-described adherents to more than 100 million if annual New Year's visits to shrines are counted as indicating 'Shinto' affiliation.

Buddhism: Estimates range from 85.1 million, based on a 1999 government assessment of membership in the major denominations, to more than 100 million.

New Religions: Estimates range from 10 to 30 million worldwide.

Christianity: Generally estimated at a little under 1 million nationwide.

### Distribution
Buddhism, Shinto, and 'new' religions are practised in every part of Japan, as well as in overseas communities. Japan itself counts approximately 75,000 Buddhist temples and more than 80,000 Shinto shrines, although many of the latter do not have resident priests.

### Founders
Shinto is an ethnic religion, with no founder, that developed through the clans, ancestors, and political affiliations of the Japanese people. Important founders of new Buddhist schools include Saicho (Tendai), Kukai (Shingon), Eisai (Rinzai Zen), Dogen (Soto Zen), Honen (Pure Land), Shinran (True Pure Land), Nichiren (Nichiren).

### Deities
Shinto has a vast number of deities, many of which are specific to local communities. The Sun Goddess, Amaterasu, has been promoted as the supreme deity since the late 1800s because of her affiliation with the imperial household. However, one of the most widely distributed deities is Hachiman, associated with military valour.

The primary deities in Buddhism include the Medicine Buddha, the Cosmic Buddha, and Amida, the Buddha of the Pure Land, along with various bodhisattvas associated with compassion, deliverance from hell, or healing.

### Authoritative Texts
Since the nineteenth century the primary texts for Shinto have been the *Kojiki: Record of Ancient Matters* and the *Nihon Shoki*. Individual Buddhist denominations and 'new' religions all have their own primary texts.

### Noteworthy Teachings
Shinto emphasizes harmony with nature, sincerity, and ritual purity. Each Buddhist denomination (Tendai, Shingon, Rinzai Zen, Soto Zen, Pure Land, True Pure Land, and Nichiren) and 'new' religion (Tenrikyo, Omotokyo, Rissho Koseikai, etc.) likewise emphasizes key points to differentiate their mission from competing sects. These range from secret teachings about the nature of reality, to faith in the Buddha of the Pure Land, to an absolute reliance on the *Lotus Sutra*, to the importance of memorial rites for ancestral spirits, and so on.

donations, the refreshments for guests, transportation to the crematorium for relatives.

As the mourners file in, three at a time, each one takes a pinch of sand-like incense and sprinkles it on glowing charcoal before bowing to the portrait. Although ceiling exhaust fans are set on high, smoke soon fills the room—but no one leaves for fresh air. In three hours, after the funeral has concluded and the body has been cremated at a high-tech facility nearby, family members and close relatives will use special chopsticks to select astonishingly white bone fragments for the urn.

All the identities Mr Sato assumed in the course of his eighty-three years—son, brother, soldier, father, businessman, civil servant, poetry aficionado, grandfather, gardener, world traveller—are now consigned to the past as he takes on his final role, that of 'ancestor'. This will remain Mr Sato's identity for the next thirty-three years—the time it will take before his spirit fully leaves this world and enters into the undifferentiated collectivity of the family's 'distant' ancestors. Until then, his spirit must be venerated regularly through rituals, offerings, and grave visitations, lest it take offence and seek retribution.

## Performing Belief

A young woman in her early twenties, dressed completely in black except for red shoes and screaming red hair, walks towards a large public park with a Fender guitar slung over her shoulder. It's early Sunday afternoon and her band, the Killers, is about to put on a concert of very loud, atonal music known as 'Visual Kei'—similar to punk, but less structured and rhythmic. She hopes that a talent agent she's invited to several previous performances will finally show up and offer them a contract. How could he resist, after he's seen the drummer (a cute girl with a green mohawk, yellow bikini top, and numerous body piercings) launch an exploding canister above the crowd, releasing a giant paper spider web, while the 'music' becomes a car-crash of metal, sirens, and sparks flying from a spinning metal wheel?

As is her custom before one of these park performances, she veers off the main path and enters the compound of a small temple. Using a ladle from a stone basin filled with clean water, she purifies her hands and mouth. Then, in the main hall, she joins her hands together and bows to the bodhisattva of compassion, Kannon, who bestows her mercy on all who ask. Before leaving, she makes sure to stop in front of a small shrine to Benten, deity of music and performance, where she bows, claps her hands twice, throws a coin into the coffer, and asks that today's concert be the best ever, that the talent agent actually show up, and that he give them the break they need. Were a foreign researcher to stop her and ask if she is 'religious', she would likely say 'no way!' before telling him, in no uncertain terms, to get lost.

## Persistent Themes

The preceding vignettes present a challenge to Western cultural assumptions about the nature of 'religious' belief and practice in general. Over the five centuries since Martin Luther launched the Protestant Reformation, most Westerners have come to think of religion as a matter of personal belief, based on individual experience and needs. A recent poll conducted in the US discovered that 42 per cent of the population has changed religions from the one in which they were raised. We often ask in casual conversation, 'So what religion are you?' and we usually respond with equal respect to almost any answer (short of answers that involve Satanism, animal sacrifice, or bodily mutilation). After all, belief is a personal matter, and a mature democracy is supposed to honour every citizen's right to freedom of religion.

Contrast this perspective with that of a typical Japanese, who, after ringing a bell at a Buddhist temple late on the evening of 31 December, finds it quite natural to visit a Shinto shrine in the first minutes of the new year. Over the previous year the same person probably celebrated Christmas, Halloween, and even Valentine's Day, in addition to more traditional Buddhist festivals such as Obon, when the spirits of the departed are honoured. She looks forward to a Christian wedding ceremony followed by a Shinto-style sharing of cups of sake. And at the end of her life, if she is traditional, she expects to be buried in the family plot at a local Buddhist temple, though she could also choose to be buried in a communal grave for women only. She regularly consults the online horoscopes and occasionally has her palm read. Yet she would almost certainly agree with the musician in the park that she is not religious.

In fact, the Japanese language had no equivalent to the word 'religion' until the 1880s, when, as part of a government modernization campaign, the characters meaning 'teachings' (*kyo*) and 'sect' (*shu*) were combined to form *shukyo*. Lack of specific 'religion', however, does not necessarily mean a lack of religious belief, feelings, or orientation (Pye 2004). Japan has no fewer than eight major and sixteen minor schools of Buddhism; countless 'new religions', most of them founded in the wake of that modernization campaign; and more than 8 million different **kami**—the individual spirits associated with specific natural phenomena, powers, and places. So it's not surprising that people might feel confused when asked whether they adhere to the teachings of one particular sect. Most Japanese people have no trouble tolerating doctrinal diversity at the popular level. Nor do most of their religious traditions impose regulations about what is and is not allowed.

It's important to emphasize from the start that, in Japan, religious belief generally takes a back seat to religious activity. Taking action—if only to purchase an amulet from a Shinto shrine or a Buddhist temple—may significantly reduce anxiety about an upcoming examination, a relationship problem, or a health condition. The choice of shrine or temple to visit in order to obtain the most beneficial blessing for a particular situation is often determined by local custom or the recommendations of neighbours, relatives, or co-workers, based on their own experience.

The traditional approach to Japanese religions would emphasize the most important doctrines, institutions, incidents, and leaders associated with each of the three major traditions: Buddhism, Confucianism, and Shinto. This chapter will certainly touch on all of these. However, recent scholarship has questioned the validity of this approach. Scholars now generally agree that for much of Japanese history, these grand traditions—one of which did not exist as such until the late nineteenth century—were neither discrete nor autonomous. In fact, these traditions, with their specific doctrines and ritual practices, have been subordinate to the themes outlined below for more than a thousand years.

## Seeking Benefits

Central to most religious traditions in Japan is the pragmatic desire to secure various benefits, either in this world or in the next. It matters little to the average person whether a particular shrine is devoted to the Buddha or to a particular local *kami*. What matters is the efficacy of prayers offered there in helping the petitioner deal with a particular situation, whether healing an illness, winning a battle, starting a new business, taking an examination, finding a marriage partner, or conceiving a child. A person may visit both temples and shrines, engage priests to perform rituals, and make regular offerings until the desired outcome is obtained—or until it seems clear that those efforts have failed. Then he or she may well have little to do with any organized religion until the next problem arises. 'Turning to the gods in a time of trouble' is a well-known expression that summarizes the pragmatic attitude of the average person in Japan towards religious institutions and beliefs.

To those who identify themselves as Christians, Jews, or Muslims, this kind of behaviour may smack more of self-interest than of religion. Where are the moral codes, the commandments, the sacred texts that guide all aspects of life? Where is the congregation of fellow believers with whom the faithful can share their sorrows and joys? How is it possible to draw from multiple religious traditions without violating at least some basic principles?

One way to understand the diversity of religion in Japan is to imagine religious life as a market-place in which consumers decide which shops to patronize on the basis of cost, product availability, and benefits received. Variables of time, place, and occasion also enter into consumers' calculations: thus a religious 'product' appropriate for the end of summer—for example, the ritual called for to pro-tect the ripening rice crop from insects, typhoons, or fire—is not the same ritual required to protect one's business from financial trouble or one's soul from the flames of hell. Just as consumers go to different stores, depending on the kinds of goods they need to buy, so Japan's religious consumers know which traditions offer the appropriate assis-tance for the situation at hand.

A person may shop around for the right reli-gious 'product' or service, but once a decision is made, a reciprocal relationship is created that entails certain obligations and expectations. In exchange for tangible assistance from a spiritual agent—whether *kami*, bodhisattva, or buddha—one must show one's gratitude not only by per-forming various formal rituals but by treating that agent with special respect. Japanese literature is full of exemplary stories in which an ungrateful or arrogant person who has offended one or more of the deities ends up chastened and contrite.

## Religious and Spiritual Agents

Let's look more closely at the spiritual agents that require such attention and care. One of the most fundamental themes of Japanese culture and civi-lization has been the idea that there is a kind of life-energy that circulates throughout the phe-nomenal world, and that humans can align them-selves with it through worship of the *kami*. Highly mobile, fluid, and capable of entering any object useful for exercising their power, *kami* can be found in flowing water, rain, mountains, clouds,

fire, earth, and wind, as well as certain animals that serve as their agents, messengers, and avatars. Their peaceful side (**nigimitama**) is beneficial and helps humans prosper, while their destructive side (**aramitama**) can only be endured and appeased through rituals.

## Mythology

We see a clear example of these dynamics in the myths explaining the origins of what would be-come 'Japan'. The basic contours of Japan's creation myth first took shape in the **Kojiki**, a collection of regional stories compiled in 712 CE with the purpose of legitimating the dominance of the Ya-mato clan by associating it with the divine origins of Japan. However, these stories were not widely known until the nineteenth or even the twentieth century, when they were circulated as part of the nation-building campaign to create a cultural heri-tage that citizens of the new nation could share.

The positive and peaceful side of the primor-dial *kami* couple, Izanagi and his 'wife' Izanami, can be seen in their creation of the islands and the primary elements of the phenomenal world. After a false start produces a 'leech baby', which must be cast aside, the two successfully create all the di-mensions of the natural world: seas, straits, winds, trees, mountains, plains. Then suddenly, with nei-ther warning nor rationale, Izanami gives birth to the deity of fire and in the process suffers burns that lead to her death. As her grieving partner con-signs her to the land of the dead, he laments: 'Alas, I have given my beloved spouse in exchange for a mere child!' (Philipi 1985: 57).

The destructive side of the *kami* is then revealed in several examples. First, the enraged Izanagi kills the fire deity and journeys to the gates of Yomi (the netherworld) to beseech his wife to return so that they can continue creating the world. Although she has eaten from the hearth of Yomi, she agrees to ne-gotiate with the gods of the underworld on the con-dition that Izanagi does not look at her. Of course he cannot resist taking a peek and is shocked to see

## Map 7.1    Japan: Major Cities and Religious Sites

*Source*: Adapted from Young 1995: 211.

her corpse full of 'squirming and roaring maggots' (ibid., 62). As he attempts to flee the underworld, she cries out, 'He has shamed me!' and, furious at this betrayal of trust, sends her 'hags' to stop him. After several narrow escapes, Izanagi leaves the land of the dead and uses a huge boulder to block the opening. As a final example of a *kami*'s vengeful side, Izanami vows that she will cause 1,000 of Izanagi's subjects to die each day, but he counters that he will cause 1,500 to be born.

Izanagi then bathes in a river to purify himself after this ghastly encounter with death and its defilements. As he does so, the female *kami* of the sun, **Amaterasu**, is born from his left eye; she will become the primary deity associated with the imperial family. She is followed by the male moon *kami*, which springs from Izanagi's right eye; then the last imperial *kami*, associated with the land, issues from his nose. Izanagi rejoices: 'I have borne child after child, and finally . . . have obtained three noble children' (ibid., p. 71).

What we learn from this myth is that the *kami* are constantly at work in the natural world, and that they are responsible for both its blessings and its destructive powers. *Kami* may also enter into human beings, enabling them to perform heroic tasks, such as unifying warring clans or chiselling a tunnel through solid rock so that a riverside community can gain access to a road. Whenever the well-being of individuals, families, and communities is threatened, you can be sure that the *kami* will be petitioned for help.

# ORIGINS

Japan itself has no written records from the first four centuries of the Common Era. However, Chinese histories from the fourth century describe 'the land of Wa' (Japan) as ruled by a female queen who used 'black magic and witchcraft' to control the *kami* and thus maintain power. The belief that early kings and 'emperors' (second to fifth century CE) embodied the *kami* served to legitimize their rule as a function of divine will.

When these rulers died, earthen mounds of all sizes and shapes (more than ten thousand in all, called **kofun**) were built to house their tombs, into which were deposited various items that they would need in the netherworld. Unlike their counterparts in Egypt and China, however, the Japanese did not sacrifice human beings to accompany their masters to the next life. Instead, they relied on clay models called **haniwa** to provide the servants, musicians, shamans, and soldiers that the ruler would require for life in the next world. These early rulers became guardian spirits of the clans, communities, and regions they once ruled, assuming positions alongside the local *kami*. We can still visit some of their ancient burial sites: at Mount Miwa near Nara (in central Japan) and Yoshigaoka (in northwestern Kyushu), at Asuka and Sakai (both located in central Japan, these rivalled the Great Pyramid of Cheops in the number of slave labourers their construction required), and near Miyazaki (in eastern Kyushu).

## From the *Nihon Shoki*

*Japan's second oldest book after the* Kojiki *(712), the* Nihon Shoki *('Chronicles of Japan', 720) provides a more accurate account of the reigns of early emperors.*

This Dharma is superior to all others. It is difficult to grasp and difficult to attain. Neither the Duke of Zhou nor Confucius was able to comprehend it. It can give rise to immeasurable, limitless merit and fruits of action, leading to the attainment of supreme enlightenment. The treasure of this marvelous Dharma is such that it is as if one owned a wish-fulfilling gem that granted every desire. Every prayer is granted and nothing is wanting. Moreover, from distant India to the three kingdoms of Korea, all receive these teachings and there is none who does not revere and honor them (*Nihon Shoki* account in Bowring, 2006: 15).

These traditions changed dramatically after 538 CE, when the ruler of what is today western Korea wrote to the Japanese king praising Buddhism as a religion 'superior to all others'. Buddhism offered a whole new set of deities and rituals that could be petitioned to protect the ruler and maintain the status quo. The clans especially devoted to *kami* worship did not simply roll over and submit to this foreign religion; there was prolonged contention and conflict over how to accommodate new foreign influences within the existing local orders.

For its first 150 years in Japan, Buddhism was sustained mainly by clans with ties to Korean immigrants from earlier centuries. But in time its new rituals, its promises of 'liberation' and 'salvation', and its unique teachings attracted increasing state patronage. Meanwhile, a steady stream of immigrants fleeing ongoing wars in southern China and the Korean peninsula brought to Japan valuable cultural knowledge—in everything from architecture and philosophy to astrology and divination to courtly protocol—that contributed significantly to the development of the fledgling state.

Japan's first Buddhist temple was constructed in 596 CE with the assistance of Korean builders, and the first Buddhist rituals were conducted there by specialists (both men and women) from the Korean kingdom of Paekche. Incredibly, temples established in these early years are still in existence at places like Shitennoji (in Osaka), Horyuji (in Nara, which incidentally houses the world's oldest wooden building, from the early seventh century), and Todaiji (also in Nara).

## Todaiji

It's worth pausing for a moment to look more closely at the founding of the Todaiji temple, because it brings together many of the themes we've

The Great Buddha (Vairocana) that overlooks the interior of Todaiji temple in Nara is nearly 15 metres (50 feet) in height (John K. Nelson).

been discussing. Ostensibly a 'Buddhist' institution, designed to house a monumental bronze statue of the Cosmic Buddha (Vairocana), the temple was conceived by the emperor Shomu in the early 740s in response to a series of earthquakes and poor crops. Before starting construction, he sent a high-ranking priest to the distant island of Kyushu to ask a powerful *kami* named Hachiman whether the project should proceed. Not only did the *kami* approve, he demanded to be transported to the construction site so as to oversee the local deities and keep them from interfering. His shrine still stands on a hillside overlooking the reconstructed temple (which, at two-thirds the size of the original structure, remains the world's largest wooden building, and has been designated a World Heritage Site by the United Nations).

What we see at Todaiji is the use of Buddhism both as a source of additional protection in the form of rituals and prayers, and as a worldview that, without discrediting older ideas about the *kami*, adapted them to fit into a Buddhist cosmos. Japan's kings took advantage of both religious systems to help control the many variables threatening the stability of their regimes: from poor harvests and inclement weather to epidemic disease, court intrigues, and continuing immigration—as well as threats of invasion—from the continent.

Despite the many centuries that have passed since the completion of the Todaiji temple in 752, aspects of this story are still relevant today. Temples and shrines—major and minor, Buddhist and Shinto alike—still conduct rituals for the health of the emperor and the stability of the nation. Rituals continue to be seen as generating a variety of benefits that address this-worldly concerns. And though Westerners tend to see the two dominant religious traditions in Japan as discrete entities, most Japanese do not distinguish between them. As a result there is considerable interaction between Buddhist and Shinto concepts and activities.

# Other Spiritual Agents

The role of the **bodhisattva** in Mahayana Buddhist traditions was discussed at some length in Chapter 5. In Mahayana thought, a bodhisattva is an enlightened being who chooses to delay entry into nirvana in order to help all the living beings who have not yet been released from worldly suffering.

The bodhisattva with the greatest reputation for intervening in human affairs is undoubtedly Kannon the Compassionate, who arrived in Japan from China under the name Guanyin but originated in India as a bodhisattva called Avalokiteshvara. Although, as divine beings, bodhisattvas have no sex, they have generally been imagined as male. In a culture with a strong tendency to associate qualities such as generosity, caring, and sympathy with women rather than men, however, depictions of Kannon's features in sculpture and painting over time became increasingly feminine. Today Kannon is usually depicted as female.

In Japan, Kannon is committed to alleviating the suffering she perceives (*kan*) and hears (*on*). Countless 'miracle' tales testify to her powers of intercession, especially in desperate situations, when people are facing calamity and death. She was very popular with the warrior class since she confers the 'gift of fearlessness' in the midst of terror and trouble. The economic golden years of the 1980s saw a revival of interest in Kannon: her cult was promoted at pilgrimage sites and in temples, and giant statues of her were erected in various places, some reaching 108 metres in height (108 is the number of the human frailties that Kannon is said to help overcome) (Reader 1991: 191, 157, 36).[1] While all the traditional attributes of Kannon are still present, her benign, all-embracing, and motherly qualities have received special attention, attracting a new generation of devotees; her persona has also been used to promote tourism.

Another bodhisattva who has provided comfort to millions of Japanese is known as Jizo (Ksitigarbha in Sanskrit), or, more respectfully and affectionately, Ojizo-sama. Known for his ability to descend into hell and free tormented souls, he also protects children and travellers. With his shaved head, staff, and wish-fulfilling jewel (which lights the darkness), Jizo is an easily recognizable figure, and statues of him can often be seen standing at crossroads or near main thoroughfares. In addition, since the 1970s he has taken on the job of conducting the souls of children and aborted fetuses to salvation. Anyone visiting a temple in Japan today is likely to see neat rows of Jizo statues, many with bibs, little berets on their shaved heads (he is a monk, after all), and offerings of coins or pebbles at their feet. A woman who has aborted a pregnancy or suffered a miscarriage may arrange for a temple to care for the soul of the fetus; for a fee of perhaps thirty dollars a month, the temple will perform periodic rituals and offerings to appease the unhappy and potentially dangerous spirits of the unborn.

## Unsettled Spirits

How can the spirit of an unborn child be dangerous? This tradition has complex roots, combining native Japanese, Korean, and Chinese folk beliefs and practices with Daoist dynamics and Buddhist demonology. In ancient times, the spirits of people who had lost their lives to powers beyond their control were thought to become angry and very possibly vengeful. In order to calm these spirits, periodic rituals of acknowledgment and pacification were necessary. This belief appears to have been in place since prehistoric times, and it permeates Japanese attitudes towards death even today. One of Japan's most respected scholars of death and dying, Gorai Shigeru, believes that all Japanese funeral and memorial rites reference this tradition, in which the spirits of the dead must be placated before they can become benevolent ancestral influences (Shigeru 1994: 105).

Before Buddhism was imported in the early sixth century, spirit appeasement had been the exclusive domain of shamans, who engaged in *kami* veneration. Yet even after Buddhism's adoption for the protection of the state, first by the Soga aristocracy and later by the Fujiwara, the need to calm and control potentially vengeful spirits (especially those of assassinated rivals or powerful enemies killed in battle) remained high on the list of state-sponsored ritual activities. To neglect or ignore these spirits was to invite retribution in any number of forms: storms, earthquakes, droughts, infertility, sickness. Accordingly, controlling unsettled spirits has been one of the most enduring responsibilities for all Japan's religious traditions.

In addition to the influence of local cults and Buddhism, Japanese culture absorbed from the mainland certain concepts and practices that we now associate with religious Daoism. The need to control and exorcise spirits is only one part of this cultural and religious heritage. Attention to the movement of the stars is manifest on the ceilings of imperial tombs and helps to link the Japanese court to its counterparts in Korea and China, where the same constellations can be found. Stories about magical peaches ('Momotaro') and time-travel ('Urashima Taro') also contain themes that can be traced to Daoist ideas about immortality and alchemy. Even elements of the material culture that symbolize the imperial household—the mirror, sword, and jewel, as well as the colour purple—have roots in continental Daoist practices, which themselves were influenced by the older traditions of shamanism (Senda 1988: 133–8).

## CRYSTALLIZATIONS

The fluid, richly syncretic nature of Japanese religious traditions makes it impossible to isolate a single moment of 'crystallization'. At best we can identify a series of crystallizing moments occurring over a period of nearly 1,500 years.

Perhaps the first of those moments came during the formative Nara period (710–794). In 701, the government had set up a ministry to manage the shrines of the *kami*. At the same time, a council of senior Buddhist priests formed the Sangha Office to oversee the behaviour, training, and duties of Buddhist monks. The growing Buddhist organization was represented through various bureaus (library, textiles, art and architecture) within the Ministry of Central Management.

This administrative control and oversight helped to set the stage for the Nara and Heian periods. The same basic administrative structure would remain in place for nearly 350 years, reasserting itself whenever a strong centralized government took charge. Knowing all too well from Chinese history about the potential of religious organizations and ideas to undermine the state, the early Japanese rulers carefully monitored all religious appointments and construction projects, none of which was permitted to proceed without bureaucratic supervision.

## Tendai and Shingon

For roughly three centuries, from its introduction in 538 until the late ninth century, Buddhism was the preserve of the Nara elite, who commissioned Buddhist temples dedicated to their ancestors, consigned their second or third sons to Buddhist monasteries, and sponsored Buddhist art as a way to cultivate religious merit, even as they continued to worship the indigenous *kami* responsible for such crucial matters as weather and agricultural production.

In 804, however, two monks named Saicho (767–822) and Kukai (774–835) travelled to China with diplomatic missions in order to study new interpretations of Buddhist practice. They returned separately to 'the land of the rising sun' with some important new perspectives, one of which—for the first time—emphasized the written word: specifically, the power of a Buddhist teaching known as the *Lotus Sutra*, which had originated in north India, been translated into Chinese (in 209 and again in 406 CE), and was thought to be a vehicle

for enlightenment and salvation simultaneously. The *Lotus Sutra* preached that there is only one vehicle to salvation—the body in which we live here and now—and that we all have the potential to become buddhas ourselves. The priests who had mastered the teachings advocated in the *Lotus Sutra* saw themselves as instrumental to the welfare of the state.

When Saicho and Kukai returned from China, they brought with them volumes of teachings and commentaries, paintings, mandalas, ritual implements, and certifications from Chinese masters of their facility with these new and powerful traditions. It might sound like little more than a wholesale borrowing of the religious 'software' from another culture, but the traditions founded by these two monks—Tendai by Saicho and Shingon by Kukai—helped to domesticate Buddhist teachings and rituals in very pragmatic ways.

For one thing, both Tendai and Shingon taught a kind of short-cut approach that put the possibility of enlightenment and salvation within the reach of the common person: anyone (not just monks and nuns) could actually *become* a buddha in this lifetime. Through a combination of incantation, ritual gestures, meditation, visualization, and austerities, individuals could connect with and obtain benefits from deities in other spheres of existence. Whereas previous schools of Buddhism viewed the human body as highly problematic because of its fragility, desires, and impermanence, the new doctrines, which we now identify as 'tantric' or 'esoteric', attributed a spiritual value to the physical body: much as geothermal steam and seismic activity can be transformed into electricity, bodily desires could be harnessed through ritual and directed towards the quest for salvation and enlightenment.

The fact that both sects chose to establish their headquarters on sacred mountains—Tendai on Mount Hiei, northeast of what is today Kyoto, and Shingon on Mount Koya, some 70 kilometres from Kyoto—suggests that they continued to respect the local *kami*. Indeed, we can see the consolidation of the relationship between Buddhism and *kami* worship as a third crystallization, which has continued throughout Japanese social and religious history.

The Japanese phrase **honji suijaku** (which comes from the *Lotus Sutra* and means 'manifestation from the original state') helps to explain the implications of this relationship. *Honji*, meaning the 'original ground', refers to the fundamental reality and power of various buddhas and bodhisattvas, while *suijaku* refers to the 'trace' or particular form in which the deity chooses to manifest him or herself in Japan. Thus the *kami* of a particular mountain or powerful clan came to be seen as the 'provisional manifestation' (*gongen*) of a particular buddha or bodhisattva. Today Buddhist and Shinto deities are clearly differentiated, but for many centuries the *honji suijaku* principle made them interdependent, although the Buddhist deities were usually superior.

The powerful Fujiwara clan established both a shrine honouring its principal *kami* (the Kasuga Grand Shrine in Nara, c. 768) and a major Buddhist temple (Kofukuji), where rituals were performed to memorialize ancestors, heal illness, exorcise spirits and so forth. Each of the Kasuga *kami* had a specific domain and function, either in sustaining the legitimacy of the Fujiwara regime or in controlling forces and events (insurrections, diseases, earthquakes, etc.) that might threaten the clan's power.

As Buddhism expanded from the ninth century onward, it increasingly overshadowed the traditional ritual practices centred on *kami*. The *honji suijaku* principle was applied to local shrines as a way to both incorporate their deities and give them a way to achieve salvation along more obviously *Buddhist* lines. The four main *kami* of Kasuga—two associated with agriculture and two with war—were linked to Buddhist counterparts: Shakyamuni Buddha, Kannon the Compassionate, the Medicine Buddha, and the Buddha of the future.

A number of rituals honouring *kami* and buddhas could be performed by priests of either tradition. We are fortunate to have the early eleventh-century diary of a high-ranking noblewoman who served as the chief spiritual medium (*saiin*) at the

A young *bugaku* dancer performs on the grounds of Osaka's Shitennoji temple. Established in 593 CE, the temple has been in continuous operation ever since (John K. Nelson).

## Taboo Words for Male and Female Priests at Key Shinto Shrines

In an effort to resist total assimilation into the influential new tradition, the priests and priestesses of major shrines developed a kind of code for referring to Buddhism without adopting its vocabulary. Thus Shakyamuni Buddha became the 'Central One', a temple a 'tiled roof', and sutras 'dyed paper'. Buddhist monks, with their shaved heads, were called 'long hairs', death became 'getting well', and illness was 'slumber' (Felicia Bock, cited in Bowring 2005: 191).[2] Using these terms, the participants in a *kami* ritual could acknowledge the importance of Buddhist concepts while keeping a certain distance from them.

Kamo Shrine in Kyoto, a shrine ranked second in importance only to the Grand Shrine of Amaterasu at Ise (pronounced *ee-say*). A devout Buddhist concerned with reaching salvation in the Pure Land (about which we will hear more in a moment), she nonetheless served in a ritual capacity for the Kamo deities for nearly four decades.

# ❧ DIFFERENTIATION

## New Sects in the Kamakura and Muromachi Periods

Around the world, people deeply affected by changing political, economic, and cultural conditions have often been open to innovations in religious belief or practice that promise to help them cope with challenging new circumstances. In Japan, not just one but three new types of Buddhist practice emerged during the Kamakura period (1185–1333): Pure Land, Nichiren, and Zen. Significantly, these are the three principal forms of Buddhism still practised in Japan today. At the same time, innovations in *kami* worship laid the foundations for what would eventually come to be known as 'Shinto'.

The relative stability of the Heian period ended in a war that overthrew the courtly families in power since the early days of Japanese civilization and resulted in the destruction of numerous temples, including the magnificent Todaiji. Once the imperial capital of Kyoto was under the control of

the new regime, which drew its power from the warrior elite that we call **samurai**, they promptly shifted the centre of political power north to Kamakura, a region near what is today Tokyo. For the aristocrats, priests, doctors, and merchants still living in the Kyoto region, this was an unmitigated disaster. Yet they knew that conflict, corruption, and vice would be the order of the day because a popular Buddhist teaching had predicted that the year 1052 would mark the beginning of the degenerate age known as **mappo**, during which the Buddhist dharma would decline. Social chaos and bloody political disorder were accompanied by a series of natural disasters, including earthquakes typhoons, pestilence, and famine. Living at a time before the science behind such disasters was understood, people sincerely believed they were trapped in a kind of hell on earth.

## Pure Land Salvation

It is no wonder, then, that a new interpretation of Buddhism promising salvation in a Pure Land gained widespread acceptance among elites and commoners alike. Prior to this development, Buddhism had been almost exclusively the faith of the former. While there had been individual monks who worked with the common people—men like Gyoki (668–749), renowned as a bodhisattva for his charity and public works, and Kuya (903–972), who used song and dance to convey the dharma to the lower classes—it was not until Genshin (942–1017) organized Pure Land beliefs into a coherent system that Buddhism began to attract wide public attention. To make the doctrine of salvation more compelling, his *Essentials of Salvation* (*Ojo yoshu*, completed in 985), described in graphic, often terrifying detail the six realms of existence (hell, hungry ghosts, demonic beings, animals, human beings, and heavenly beings) through which every living creature must pass, in multiple incarnations, before reaching the perfection of the Pure Land.

For the first time in Japan, groups of Buddhist monks began to concern themselves with the salvation of the ordinary person, but it took another two hundred years before a new institutional form emerged that gave practical expression to their concern. It was a Tendai monk, frustrated by his sect's preoccupation with politics and managing the profits from its vast landholdings, who developed Pure Land Buddhism as we know it today. Honen (1133–1212) believed it was impossible for people in an age of *mappo* to attain salvation by traditional means (following the precepts, chanting

sutras, meditating, worshipping the Buddhist deities), so he emphasized repeated recitation of the **nenbutsu**. Honen argued that the saving grace of Amida did not discriminate according to social rank, past karma, or present activity: sincere faith and repeated recitation of '*Namu Amida Butsu*' alone were enough. In this way Honen opened the door to what was then the radical notion of universal salvation.

This concept might sound pleasingly democratic to modern ears, but it was seen at the time as subversive of the entire monastic enterprise. Taken to its logical conclusion, the principle of universal salvation meant there was no difference between a lay person and a learned monk. Thus Honen was banished from the Kyoto region in 1207, along with one of his prominent disciples, Shinran (1173–1262). Earlier that year, Shinran had scandalized both temple and courtly communities by marrying—a 'degenerate' practice that was fairly common among monks (as was keeping

The Amida Hall of the Isshinji temple in Osaka is dedicated to the Buddha of the Pure Land (John K. Nelson).

a concubine) but was *never* made public. Shinran reasoned that if the power of Amida Buddha was great enough to save even those of the lowest social status, then marriage would make no difference in achieving salvation.

Honen's exile lasted only four years, but Shinran was banished for seven. According to popular biographies, he used this time to preach and organize among farmers and fishermen, refining his 'True Pure Land' doctrine to the point of maintaining that a *single* sincere repetition of the *nenbutsu* would secure salvation. Shinran believed human beings to be incapable of mustering the disciplined 'self-power' (*jiriki*) necessary for attaining salvation: therefore we must rely on 'other-power' (*tariki*) for deliverance from suffering.

In the tumultuous disorder of the Kamakura period (and beyond), Pure Land teachings gained wide popular support, but detractors were still powerful. In 1227, monks from the Tendai temples on Mount Hiei desecrated Honen's grave and burned copies of his major works. Pure Land practice was spread around the country via small groups called *ko*, where emphasis was on *nenbutsu* practice. Around 1450, the eighth hereditary leader of the Pure Land movement, Rennyo (1415–99), began to systematize the teachings and organize the scattered Pure Land communities into a well-disciplined religious group. Taking advantage of a time of widespread civil unrest, he drew on the existing networks of Pure Land followers to create a kind of militant security force dedicated to protecting the sect's Honganji temple (in what is today the city of Osaka).

The result was a new development in Japanese Buddhism: bands of armed peasants and low-ranking samurai loyal to the True Pure Land tradition rose up against those they considered to be oppressors. These were not the first Buddhists to take aggressive action: as early as 1039, 'monk warriors' from the Tendai monastery on Mount Hiei had attacked rival sects and temples, and even challenged the legitimacy of the imperial court itself. Four centuries later, however, the True Pure Land

insurrection was led not by monks but by masterless samurai and common people. With nothing to lose and salvation guaranteed through their faith in Amida Buddha, fearless True Pure Land militias were able to hold their own against experienced armies and sometimes even overwhelm them. By 1500 they controlled several provinces as well as what is today the city of Osaka, where their fortress temple was never breached, although they were finally defeated and brought at least partially under control by the warlord Oda Nobunaga (1534–82) in the 1580s.

## Rinzai Zen and Kamakura Culture

Zen Buddhism established itself in Japan in much the same way as Pure Land, but with an important difference: Zen was imported directly from China, and its development benefited from the leadership of Chinese masters who immigrated to Japan in the thirteenth century. Although the seeds of Zen can be found in Tendai doctrines as early as the ninth century (when a practice referred to as 'constantly sitting' was introduced), it was not until the latter part of the twelfth century that the tradition took root in Japan, imported by an enterprising Japanese monk who had encountered it during a visit to China in 1168.

The word 'Zen' is the Japanese version of the Chinese *chan*, which is itself a translation of the Sanskrit term for meditation, *dhyana*. Whereas the Pure Land traditions emphasized recitation of the name of Amida Buddha as the path to salvation, the Chan/Zen tradition emphasized the practice of seated meditation as the path to enlightenment and, eventually, salvation. The cultural exchanges that had led to the introduction of the Tendai and Shingon sects to Japan four hundred years earlier—along with many other cultural innovations in areas from architecture and music to medicine and astrology—had been ended by government decree in the ninth century in response to the Tang dynasty's persecution of Buddhism. The next time Japanese monks and bureaucrats ventured to China was in 1168, after Japan had experienced its own political upheaval.

One of the religious members of the 1168 delegation was a Tendai monk named Eisai (1141–1215). He expected to find the traditions from which Tendai and Shingon had originated in the ninth century, but discovered that Chan was now the dominant Buddhist tradition. The persecution that began in 845 had targeted the esoteric traditions because of their lavish wealth, landholdings, political meddling, and 'parasitic' monks and nuns who did nothing for society. Chan temples, by contrast, were located mostly in rural areas, where their monks worked with their hands and displayed none of the elaborate trappings that had become attached to other traditions.

Although Eisai stayed in China for only six months, he studied Chan doctrines for the next twenty years while continuing to fulfill his duties as a Tendai priest. A second trip to China in 1187 gave him the opportunity to study with an eminent Chan master in the Linji (Rinzai in Japanese) tradition, who certified Eisai's enlightenment before he returned to Japan in 1191. In addition to his knowledge of Chan, Eisai imported other Buddhist and Confucian teachings—as well as a plant from which a hot drink could be made to keep sleepy monks awake during meditation. His work 'Drink Tea and Prolong Life' is credited with promoting tea in Japan; and the tea ceremony (developed a century later) was deeply influenced by Zen aesthetics and symbolism.

In an effort to legitimate his new school of Buddhism and attract the patronage of the military rulers in Kamakura, Eisai wrote a treatise entitled 'The Propagation of Zen for the Protection of the Country'. Emphasizing outer discipline and inner wisdom, this work caused his temporary exile from all Tendai temples in the Kyoto region. After a short time in Kamakura, where he secured patrons for his teachings and established a small temple, he returned to Kyoto and in 1202 built the city's first Zen temple, Kenninji, in what is today

The Kenninji temple in Kyoto marked its 800-year anniversary by commissioning this powerful painting by Koizumi Junkasu for its ceiling (John K. Nelson).

the Gion entertainment district. Its many rebuildings have maintained a number of cultural treasures as well as beautiful examples of classic Zen landscape gardens and architecture.

It's worth asking why a samurai warrior would be attracted to a somewhat austere Chinese tradition focused on the achievement of 'sudden enlightenment' through the practice of seated meditation (*zazen*) and the mental exercise of the koan. One reason was that the kind of mind cultivated through those practices was conducive to a particularly rich type of artistic expression. Zen-inspired poetry, stories, paintings, and sculpture were valued for their subtle and elegant evocation of concepts such as emptiness, the cycle of rebirth (*samsara*), impermanence, and enlightenment (*satori* in Japanese), and those who associated themselves with such art easily acquired a highly valued aura of refinement. At the same time, in a society that accorded the highest status to the warrior,

Zen-style discipline was valued as a way of training the mind and body to endure hardship, pain, and even the reality of death.

Just as two schools of Pure Land Buddhism developed in close proximity to each other, so it was with Zen. Although Eisai never renounced his Tendai roots, he is regarded as the founder of the Rinzai lineage.

## Soto Zen, the Gradual Path

The other major Zen school, also based on a Chinese tradition, promotes 'gradual enlightenment' through the practice of 'just sitting' without any conceptual or metaphoric stimulation. The story of Soto Zen and its founder Dogen (1200–53) is problematic in that the only accounts we have are those of the tradition itself.

According to the standard accounts, then, Dogen studied on Mount Hiei in the Tendai tradition, but was troubled by a persistent question: if humans are born with an innate Buddha-nature, as Tendai doctrines maintained, why should it be necessary for them to make any effort to achieve enlightenment? After studying at Kenninji with Eisai's successor, the young monk somehow gained a place with an official mission to China in 1223, in the course of which he encountered the Caodong tradition. Whether Dogen actually made the trip or this part of the tale was invented by later Soto leaders to legitimize their tradition is unclear; in any event, the Caodong emphasis on integrating body and mind via *any* activity became central to the kind of liberation promoted by Dogen. Supposedly, a conversation with a monastery cook helped him understand the importance of 'enlightened activity' and led to his own spiritual awakening.

On his return to Kyoto in 1227, it became apparent to Dogen that his Soto Zen could not hope to compete with the increasingly influential Rinzai school. Leaving the capital voluntarily, he discovered local aristocrats and wealthy landowners outside the cities who were more receptive to his new way to liberation than the samurai had been. The Eiheiji monastery he founded (near present-day Fukui city) is still the headquarters of the Soto sect, and continues Dogen's emphasis on 'just sitting' *zazen* coupled with rigorous study and physical labour.

The Rinzai tradition was assisted in its institutional development by its ongoing relationship with the ruling samurai class in Kamakura. Adopted from China, Rinzai's temple-building and political alliances prospered because of the 'Five Mountain' monastery system, which made five top temples into administrative outposts of the government. The Five Mountain temples, through their many subtemples and affiliations, helped to

### Dogen and the Cook

As a young monk travelling in China, the founder of the Soto Zen school, Dogen, encountered an old priest who was serving in the office of *tenzo* (head cook). Dogen felt the *tenzo* was working too hard for a person of his age, so he asked him, 'Reverend sir, why don't you do *zazen* or read the ancient texts? What is the use of working so hard as a cook, drying these mushrooms in the blazing sun?' The *tenzo* laughed for a long time and then he said, 'My foreign friend, it seems you don't really understand Zen practice or the words of the ancients.'

Hearing the elder monk's words, Dogen felt ashamed and surprised. He asked, 'What is practice? What are words?' The *tenzo* said, 'One, two, three, four, five.' Dogen asked again, 'What is practice?' and the *tenzo* replied, 'Everywhere, nothing is hidden' (adapted from Dogen 1996).

monitor local conditions and implement new laws for the military rulers. The same system was soon applied to several major Zen temples in Kyoto as well, including Nanzenji, Tenryuji, and Japan's first Zen temple, Kenninji.

In the countryside the popularity of Soto Zen grew rapidly after priests in the early fifteenth century introduced a new practice that would help to transform the religious landscape of Japan. Dogen's teachings were important within a monastic setting, but local warlords, wealthy farmers, and other patrons were—like most upper-class Japanese—more concerned with salvation than with enlightenment. In part because Zen offered direct, intuitive transmission of enlightenment, its priests were said to embody the very mind of Shakyamuni Buddha. Who better, then, to lead the spirit of a deceased loved one towards the ultimate liberation? In this era, only the clergy were entitled to funeral services; therefore the corpse was symbolically ordained as a monk or nun (Bodiford 1992). This brilliant innovation not only gave common people access to funeral and memorial services but helped to gain a wide following for Soto Zen.

## Nichiren

The last new Buddhist sect of the Kamakura period was founded by a charismatic priest who drew on the Tendai tradition of reciting mantras but saw the teachings of the *Lotus Sutra* as the only possible path to salvation, not only for the individual but for the nation. Believing that it provided an all-encompassing guide to both secular and spiritual affairs, Nichiren (1222–82) instructed his followers to study its teachings and chant the mantra 'namu myoho renge kyo' ('Hail the marvellous teaching of the *Lotus Sutra*!'). To Nichiren, other types of Buddhism were merely provisional, introductory teachings, no longer relevant in the age of *mappo*.

After being expelled from his monastery in Kyoto, he travelled to Kamakura where he preached on street corners the radical message that 'the nenbutsu is hell, Zen is a devil, and Shingon is the nation's ruin'. He was exiled twice for subversive teaching and avoided execution only because of a divine intervention that, according to his own account, shattered the executioner's sword as it was about to fall on his neck. Nichiren's 1260 work, 'On Establishing the True Dharma to Bring Peace to the Nation' (*Ankoku-ron*), established him as a pioneer in politicizing religion. If the nation suffered invasions, plagues, and social disorder, he argued, it was the fault of the ruler who had not adopted the *Lotus Sutra* as his guide to sound governance.

When the Mongol dynasty actually invaded Japan in 1274, Nichiren's warnings were seen as a kind of prophecy, and he was pardoned. Weary of continual confrontation, he accepted an offer of land at Mount Minobu (not far from Mount Fuji). The temple he established there became both a memorial to Nichiren's teachings and a training facility for the next generation of disciples. Men like Niko, Nissho, and Nichiko proselytized widely, and though they were persecuted by the authorities and ostracized by other Buddhist sects, they succeeded in establishing a network of temples throughout central Japan. However, each had different ideas about what should be emphasized, leading to centuries of factionalism. It's important to note that some of Japan's most prominent 'new religions'—Soka Gakkai (which has branches all over the world and counts a number of Hollywood celebrities among its adherents), Rissho Koseikai, Nichiren Shoshu—trace their roots to one or another of these sectarian denominations.

## Confucianism and the Beginnings of Shinto

We've focused thus far on the development and differentiation of Buddhist sects in the Kamakura and Muromachi periods. But there were two other developments—the introduction of Confucianism and the beginnings of Shinto—that also deserve attention for their influence on the development of the modern Japanese state.

You will remember that a number of Chinese Chan masters came to Japan in the thirteenth century to head Rinzai Zen temples, and that Japanese Tendai monks in the same period once again travelled to China to obtain new teachings and texts. Among the fruits of this cultural exchange were the teachings of Confucius. Although Confucian ideas (dating from the fifth century BCE) had been present at the very beginning of Japanese civilization in the sixth century CE, they did not develop into a distinct body of knowledge or ritual practices. During the political and social disruptions of the Kamakura and Muromachi periods, however, Japan's ruling classes began to take a new interest in religions and philosophies that promoted order in society.

Confucian values, as interpreted by the scholar Zhu Xi (1130–1200), laid out the 'Way' that every member of society—ruler, minister, parent, friend, child—should follow, as determined by his or her position in that society. Awareness of the responsibilities in each relationship would promote reciprocity between superiors and subordinates, which in turn would foster a stable and harmonious society. Zen monks found these teachings to resonate with their own monastic and religious traditions, and so they were taught within the Five Mountain system and recommended to rulers by their Buddhist advisers for nearly four hundred years. We will see in the next historical period how these Confucian seeds grew into a vast tree that branched out to cover all of Japanese society.

## The Emergence of 'Shinto'

And what of the older religion based on the ritual veneration of natural and human spirits called *kami*? Recent scholarship has demonstrated that it was only in the medieval period that 'Shinto' began to take form as a distinct and self-conscious organization. After the fall of the imperial forces in 1185, the Ise Grand Shrines, dedicated to the sun goddess Amaterasu, lost their main source of financial support, and by the early fifteenth century were in obvious decline. Fearful of further decay, their priests devised new strategies to attract support from wider sources.

Since the early eleventh century, the imperial household had made regular pilgrimages to the Kumano shrines some 80 kilometres to the west, rather than Ise. Therefore the priests opened up Ise to visits from samurai and lower-ranking officials and developed new rituals for them. Purification was of primary importance, but now, in recognition of the institutional power of Tendai and Shingon and the doctrine of *honji suijaku*, Ise ritual practices were coupled with Buddhist notions of enlightenment so that, instead of competing, the two traditions complemented one another. At one time there were more than three hundred Buddhist temples on the Ise shrine grounds.

With its emphasis on rituals rather than texts, the 'way of the *kami*' had always lacked the kind of conceptual structure that was so highly developed within Buddhism. By creating their own theological rationale, Ise priests reversed the *honji suijaku* principle that the *kami* were lesser manifestations of the original buddhas and bodhisattvas. They argued that *kami* were indigenous to the land of Japan, and that although they could have Buddhist counterparts, they were not subordinate to Buddhist deities. With new doctrines in place, pilgrimage at an all-time high, and increasing interest in the power of Ise's main deities to provide benefits even for common people, a foundation was in place for the *kami* tradition to assume a new importance in the life of the nation. An organized system began to emerge in 1542, when the central government granted the powerful Yoshida clan the authority to appoint and demote shrine priests outside of Ise. Today, in part because of Ise's appeal as a source of Japanese cultural identity and its association with imperial mythology, the Ise Grand Shrines receive over five million visitors annually.

The ascent of the sacred mountain of Fushimi Inari Shrine in Kyoto is lined with *torii* gateways, each one donated by an individual or organization. Inari is the *kami* of rice, business, and prosperity (John K. Nelson).

# 🌿 PRACTICE

The opening pages of this chapter described several contemporary religious practices involving access to benefits, control of spirits, and petitions to deities concerning problems. Many of these customs can be traced back to the end of the Muromachi period (1333–1573), with further elaboration in the Tokugawa (1600–1867) and modern (1868–1945) eras. As a way of reviewing and expanding on those themes, let's revisit two of the most important for individuals and institutions alike: access to benefits and veneration of spirits.

The variety of benefits (*riyaku*) that worshippers may seek is almost endless: from good health and financial prosperity to individual salvation in the afterlife, fertility and beneficial weather to enlightened governance. Equally diverse are the religious practices believed to help bring about these conditions. Here are just a few examples.

- Individuals, families, businesses, entire communities, or even political leaders can contract religious specialists to conduct rituals at a temple or shrine. In most cases, petitioners address their request to a particular spiritual agent (buddha, bodhisattva, or *kami*) believed capable of exerting a beneficial influence on the situation in question.

- By purchasing amulets or talismans, individuals can establish an informal relationship with the deity of a particular temple or shrine. Like a kind of battery, however, the spiritual energy invested in these objects becomes depleted over the course of a year, so that purchasers must return regularly for replacements.

- Undertaking a pilgrimage to a sacred place is another way of accessing benefits in this world and beyond. We saw how imperial pilgrimages to the Kumano and Ise shrines became popularized in the medieval and modern periods. Even today, the 88 sacred temples of the island of Shikoku are regularly visited by more than 100,000 pilgrims a year. Some walk the entire route of 1,400 kilometres at once, but most take buses or private transportation and complete the route in segments, as time permits. Smaller, less demanding pilgrimage routes exist all over Japan, each of which is believed to provide pilgrims with some kind of spiritual benefit.
- Monetary donations and the performance of good deeds for a temple/shrine or its priests are thought to generate merit beneficial to one's spiritual condition.
- Grand festivals (*matsuri*) involving the entire community generate benefits not only for those who participate but even for those who do not. Although many Buddhist temples also have adopted this practice, it is especially common for Shinto shrines to periodically remove their central object of worship and place it in a portable shrine that can be paraded through the community. In large communities, the *matsuri* can be a major annual event commanding a staggering degree of financial, personal, and administrative commitment. The 'rousing drum' festival mentioned at the beginning of this chapter involves an entire city of 74,000, while the Tenjin Matsuri held in central Osaka attracts crowds of nearly two million.

A second widespread religious practice is the veneration and memorialization of spirits. Unlike Western religious traditions, in which the spirits of the deceased have no lingering engagement with this world, the religious traditions of East Asia and

Barrels of sake are often presented as offerings to the resident deities at both temples and shrines. After the ritual presentations have finished, the contents are distributed to parishioners and priests (Liba Taylor/Corbis).

Japan in particular maintain that the spirits of the dead continue to play an active part in the lives of the living. Whoever the deceased may have been in life—a religious leader, a soldier killed in war, the sweetest grandmother in the world—his or her spirit may become angry or vengeful in death; therefore periodic rituals are required long after the funeral to ensure that this does not happen. If the spirits are satisfied, they can become benign and beneficial allies to those who show them the proper respect.

One of Japan's great holidays is the Obon festival, held in mid-August in most parts of the country, when the spirits of the dead are said to return to this world to enjoy some entertainment—perhaps a community dance on the grounds of a temple or in a public park—and receive ritual offerings of food and drink made on behalf of their loved ones. In addition, individuals and families regularly memorialize departed family members at household altars (*butsudan*). In the past, the size and shape of home altars followed sect guidelines, but today more and more people are choosing to express their spirituality through altars designed to complement the interiors of their homes.

# CULTURAL EXPRESSIONS

The household altar is just one example of the material impact that religious traditions and practices have had on Japanese culture. From paintings and sculpture, architecture and landscape design, to ritual attire and habits of personal hygiene derived from purification rituals, the list of cultural influences is almost endless. Let's consider just a few of the things that a visitor to Japan would likely encounter in the course of a week.

Even before leaving the international airport, a visitor might see an example of *ikebana*, the Japanese art of flower arranging. Having developed in Buddhist temples, where the spare, deceptively simple arrangements were used in memorial services, the practice of *ikebana* eventually filtered through all social classes. Today there are many different styles of *ikebana*, but most still share a few basic features, including organic materials (not necessarily flowers—stems and leaves are at least as important), sensitivity to the season, balanced composition, and poetic or religious symbolism (a classic three-part arrangement, for instance, is likely to symbolize heaven, earth, and humanity).

A similar combination of natural materials, restrained composition, and religious symbolism is found in the Japanese garden. The art of garden design also developed first at temples, where a few artfully placed rocks in a bed of gravel might symbolize islands in the sea of eternity. Gardens were later constructed in imperial palaces and, as the centuries passed, on the estates of wealthy aristocrats, samurai, and merchants. Today even the most humble residence will often have a carefully tended garden that evokes ancient cultural values. The temple has also been a major influence on architecture. The sweeping roof lines, overhanging eaves, and verandas of the classic temple have constituted the dominant paradigm for builders for over a thousand years. Inside the house, one room would typically be modelled on the abbot's quarters in a temple, with a hanging scroll painting in an alcove, an *ikebana* arrangement, and open space conveying a calming sense of space in harmony with form. Even ultramodern high-rise condominiums still try to incorporate the alcove into their designs.

The influence of Japan's religious traditions can also be seen in both literature and popular culture. The minimalism of image and language in the *haiku*, for example, is said to derive from Zen's emphasis on penetrating to the essence of reality. In its seventeen syllables, the *haiku* typically gives us both sharply defined detail and a connection to a wider universe, as in this example, composed by one of Japan's most noted poets, the former Zen priest Basho, in the late 1600s:

The sea darkens;
the plaintive calls of the wild ducks
are faintly white.

Another art form that uses minimalism to evoke deep emotions and reflection on the nature of reality is Noh theatre, in which Buddhist themes are prevalent. The slow, mesmerizing cadences of the masked actors—who speak in a manner reminiscent of the ritual chanting heard at a temple or shrine—usually convey a lesson of some kind, whether about karma, the consequences of desire, or the spiritual power of priests.

Our final examples from popular culture are the post-war phenomena of *anime* and *manga*. Both genres abound in references to religious practices, individuals with spiritual powers gained through ascetic training (*shugyo*), and divinities who use their powers for both good and evil ends. The early comics of Osamu Tezuka (1928–89) and the feature films of animator Miyazaki Hayao (b. 1941; *Totoro, Princess Mononoke, Spirited Away*) are full of allusions to Japan's religious and spiritual history.

# ❧ INTERACTION AND ADAPTATION

## Christianity, New Religions, and Native Learning

It's now time to bring our discussion of Japanese religious traditions more fully into the modern period. We often talk about 'globalization' as a phenomenon of the late twentieth century, but in fact the worldwide exchange of people, ideas, and goods began several centuries earlier. In the fifteenth century, while Japan was in the midst of a series of wars over local territory, European powers such as Spain, Portugal, Holland, and England were navigating the globe, claiming new territory for their kings and the Christian church. The first Europeans to reach Japan were some shipwrecked Portuguese sailors who arrived there in 1543, but they were soon followed by Jesuit missionaries led by Francis Xavier (1549). The Jesuit strategy for missionary work combined religious proselytizing along with the lucrative incentive of trade via Portuguese ships travelling between Macao (near what is today Hong Kong), India, Mozambique, and Europe.

## Christianity's Rise and Fall

Had Japan not been in a state of ongoing internal conflict, it is doubtful that the Jesuits would have been permitted to enter Japan at all. Yet because of a unique convergence of social and political factors, they were able to broker agreements with a number of local warlords. It was also a stroke of luck that the first Europeans arrived during the rise to power of Japan's first military unifier, Oda Nobunaga. Highly distrustful of the Tendai warrior-monks as well as the True Pure Land militias, Nobunaga saw Christianity as a wedge into the strength of Buddhism in Japan. He also tolerated the missionaries because he profited handsomely from the trading opportunities that came with them.

By 1571 Nobunaga's military and economic power had grown to the point that he was able to attack Mount Hiei, destroying every building on the mountain (along with priceless manuscripts, pictures, and sculptures) and killing more than three thousand priests and attendants. The example was not lost on the Pure Land sect, which had also become politicized and taken up arms: only one more major battle was required to bring them under control. It also served as a warning to the early Christian missionaries.

Although Nobunaga died in 1582 (assassinated by one of his own vassals), his chief aide quickly established himself as a visionary leader and patron of religion. Toyotomi Hideyoshi (1537–98) not only continued the unification effort that Nobunaga had begun, but he embarked on a building and consolidation campaign among Buddhist and Shinto sects that led to the construction of many of the temples and shrines we see today. So great were his economic resources that he even tried twice to take the Korean peninsula in preparation for an invasion of China (neither attempt succeeded).

Hideyoshi's tolerance extended beyond Buddhism to Christianity, which by 1590 may have acquired as many as 100,000 converts, though not all the conversions were voluntary: some were forced by local warlords seeking to facilitate trade first with the Portuguese and later with the Spanish and Dutch. However, after a Spanish ship ran aground in Shikoku in 1596 and its captain threatened military reprisals to be delivered by an armada stationed in the Philippines, new legal restrictions were imposed on Christian missionaries. A number of European missionaries and Japanese converts were expelled and some were put to death.

The third of Japan's great unifiers, Tokugawa Ieyasu (1548–1616), at first tolerated Christianity (because of the lucrative trade), but in time he came to see its priests as meddlesome and disruptive of the social order. His successors cracked down hard, beginning in the 1620s, requiring all adults to register at the local Buddhist temple; those who resisted or refused to step on an image of Jesus or Mary were arrested and threatened with torture if they did not recant their Christian faith.

In 1637 an estimated 25,000 oppressed peasants and rogue samurai warriors took over an abandoned castle in Shimabara, Kyushu, and tried to mount an armed insurrection. Using Christian symbols on their flags, this rag-tag army held off the government's forces for nearly seven months. Dutch ships were called in to bombard the rebel fortifications, but with little effect. It was only when the rebels ran out of food and gunpowder that an army of more than 125,000 was able to storm the fortifications and kill all those within, effectively ending the last resistance to the Tokugawa regime.

With the defeat of the Shimabara rebels, Japan closed the door not only on Christianity but on Europe. From 1641 to 1853, the only port open to the outside world was Dejima, a small artificial island near Nagasaki, and it was rigidly controlled. Christianity did not entirely disappear, however. Rather, it went into hiding in remote valleys and on far-flung islands. Believers adopted Buddhist practices but continued reciting mass and worshipping images of the Virgin Mary disguised as the bodhisattva Kannon.

## Unification and Stability

As part of its effort to impose stability after half a century of political turmoil, the Tokugawa shogunate set out to impose laws that would restructure Japanese society into four distinct classes: samurai, farmers, artisans, and merchants. This structure (like the temple registration law) was inspired by the Confucian doctrines introduced to Japan by Chinese Zen priests some four hundred years earlier. In addition, a number of newer Confucian texts discovered in Korea during Hideyoshi's attempted invasions were now re-interpreted in ways that would promote, above all other values, the overall stratification and regulation of society. Each social class was given specific guidelines regarding occupation, travel, and civic duties, with infractions punishable by the confiscation of property, imprisonment, or execution. Likewise, the central government imposed regulations on both Buddhist and Shinto institutions, requiring them to adopt a hierarchical organizational model that held sect leaders and branch priests alike accountable for adhering to the rules. The Tokugawa **shoguns** had Zen priests as some of their closest advisers in the early years. Buddhist priests continued to provide counsel, but as the regime tightened its control over the nation, it also sought advice from neo-Confucian scholars.

The overall mood of society was changing as well. During the medieval period, Buddhism had flourished because its doctrines of salvation in the next life offered hope to people whose prospects in this life were bleak. Now, with growing economic prosperity in the cities and order imposed by a police state (although there were still periodic rebellions in the countryside because of heavy taxes and famines), neo-Confucianism became more relevant to Japan. Scholars and intellectuals developed ideologies that were critical of Buddhism and emphasized what they considered to be truly 'Japanese'.

We have already seen how Buddhism benefited from state patronage but also suffered because of its involvement in political affairs. Temple-building increased dramatically with the imposition of the temple-registration requirement; the numbers of Soto Zen temples alone increased from several thousand to 17,500 in this period. At the same time, however, the increasing emphasis on political rather than spiritual matters was reflected in a breakdown of morality among many priests (Williams 2005). As one seventeenth-century Confucian scholar noted, 'the freedom with which they eat meat and engage in romantic affairs surpasses that of even secular men' (Jansen 2000: 217). Although Buddhism remained central to ritual life, it was losing its vitality. It is not surprising, therefore, that alternative religious perspectives and practices began to emerge towards the end of the Tokugawa period.

## New Religious Expressions

The first of the 'new religions' originated in an 1838 revelation to the wife of a wealthy farmer. Nakayama Miki said that 'God the Parent' (oyasama) had chosen her to transmit divine truths about how to live happily and honorably. She was imprisoned a number of times for her beliefs but, as the Tokugawa regime ended, she succeeded in establishing the religion known as Tenrikyo. The religion called Kurozumikyo traced its origins to a revelation 'received' by a Shinto priest (he claimed to have experienced 'divine union' with Amaterasu). And Konko-kyo (1859) was based on a privileged communication between a farmer and a kami who supposedly turned out to be the saviour of mankind.

Scholars in particular were eager for new philosophies that would explain the meaning of life and the individual's purpose in society. The first wave of neo-Confucian thought promoted a vision of harmony between the basic principles of the universe (purity, honesty, sincerity, moderation)

and the role of the individual, whose true inner nature was said to demand acceptance of his or her place in the social order. Disseminated through essays, teaching academies, and government policies, these seventeenth-century ideas encouraged the development of inner constraints based on the individual's intellect, reason, morals, and sense of propriety. Government officials produced almanacs and calendars promoting neo-Confucian principles regarding social regulation, and counselled village head men accordingly. Hayashi Razan and Yamazaki Ansai were key figures in this movement, as was Yamaga Soko (1622–85), the scholar who codified samurai ethics to create the 'way of the warrior' known as **bushido**.

The next movement, 'Native Learning' or **Kokugaku** (literally, 'study of one's country') argued the superiority of all things Japanese over their foreign counterparts, including the superiority of native spiritual traditions over Buddhism and Confucianism. Some scholars argued that for convincing evidence of Japan's superiority, one needed only to consider the story of Noah and the flood, which Japan had survived untouched. Likewise, the reason Japan had not produced medical breakthroughs was that it was essentially pure and less polluted than other countries (ibid., 209). Scholars like Motoori Norinaga (1730–1801) tried to use ancient texts like the Kojiki (which contains the rather bizarre foundation myth of Izanagi and Izanami) to discover fundamental truths about the will of the kami regarding the roles of a ruler and his subjects. The logical implication was that the solution to the country's growing political problems and the threats it faced from abroad lay in direct imperial rule—although to voice this opinion publicly would surely have led to charges of treason.

In 1825, during the last decades of the 250-year-old shogunate, the scholar and samurai Aizawa Seishisai (1781–1863) advocated the unification of religion and the state, as in the colonial powers from Europe that were slowly encircling and threatening Japan's sovereignty. He urged the adoption of Shinto as the national faith and the sun deity Amaterasu as the primary *kami* as a way to enhance national polity (*kokutai*). Although these ideas created controversy at the time, they later became central to the leaders of samurai clans in the far west and south.

In 1868, following a brief civil war, those clans overthrew the Tokugawa regime. Well aware of how far behind Japan had fallen during its period of isolation, and fearing colonization by European and American powers, the new government embarked on an unprecedented program of industrialization, militarization, and nation-building. Legitimized by a new emphasis on the emperor's status as a direct descendent of the *kami* (exactly as Aizawa had recommended four decades earlier), this agenda would dramatically alter Japan and the Asian region in both positive and negative ways.

# 🦋 RECENT DEVELOPMENTS

How does a government create a nation of citizens where only feudal loyalties had existed before? This was the daunting challenge that faced the social architects of the Meiji government (1868–1911). Whereas the previous regime had been named after the dominant clan, the new government named itself after the emperor Meiji in acknowledgement of the 'divine' authority that legitimated the policies of the state. In its effort to promote a kind of national cult based on the emperor and his associations with various *kami* and Shinto precedents, the state subjected Buddhism to a brief but dramatic period of persecution, in part because it had served the Tokugawa so well. Institutions that had been fully syncretic—combining Buddhist and *kami* worship—were now split apart. Their ritual specialists were either forced into lay life or re-educated as government-certified Shinto priests. Even more extreme was the destruction promoted by over-zealous officials and carried out by mobs. Temple grounds all over Japan are still scattered

with the remains of Buddhist statues decapitated during this period.

The government embarked on ambitious programs of education, industrialization, and militarization modelled on Western precedents. Shinto was designated the official religion of the state, although adherence to it was described by the state as a matter of 'civic duty' rather than religious conviction. Not everyone supported these policies, of course. However, a series of wars with China (1894–95), Russia (1904–5), and Korea (1910)—which cost the lives of approximately eighty thousand young men while gaining Japan overseas resources that it would use to expand its manufacturing base—inspired a general patriotic fervour that drowned out opposition voices.

It was during this period that the government sponsored the establishment of a shrine dedicated to the veneration of the spirits of soldiers who had died in the service of the nation. Although Shinto shrines had traditionally avoided association with the impurity of death, at the Yasukuni Shrine in Tokyo Shinto-style rituals were combined with Buddhist ancestor worship and shamanic traditions of spirit appeasement and control. After all, as young men cut down in the prime of life, Japan's military dead were at high risk of becoming unsettled and vengeful. The emperor and his household, high-ranking government officials, and leading businessmen, intellectuals, and even Buddhist priests all visited the shrine regularly to pay their respects during the war years.

Shrines throughout the country were coerced into participating in a 'spirit-cycle' that saw ancient local festivals appropriated for the purposes of civic and national unity. There was no greater glory (according to the government and educational curriculum) than to die for the nation and be enshrined at Yasukuni. An imperial edict on education instructed the youth of Japan that, 'should emergency arise', they were expected to 'offer [themselves] courageously to the State; and thus guard and maintain the prosperity of Our Imperial Throne coeval with heaven and earth' (Hardacre

1989: 122). The well-known 'divine wind' (*kamikaze*) missions undertaken in desperation at the end of the Second World War to attack American naval vessels in the Pacific were extreme expressions of this ideology.

More recently, Japan's prime minister from 2001 to 2006, Koizumi Junichiro, insisted on visiting the Yasukuni Shrine once a year. Each visit set off violent anti-Japanese demonstrations in China and Korea—both of which had been occupied by the Japanese military during the war—and China broke off all high-level diplomatic ties for nearly five years. They objected not so much to the practice of honouring the military dead as to inclusion of fourteen men identified by allied courts after the war as 'class-A' war criminals. These men were the ones who were said to have orchestrated and carried out Japan's punitive and bloody military campaigns against its neighbours.[3]

## Postwar Restructuring

After Japan's devastating defeat in 1945, a period of occupation by the Allied forces laid the groundwork for its transformation into a stable democracy. The emperor was obliged to renounce his divinity and Shinto was stripped of its status as the *de facto* state religion. In the spiritual void that followed a war in which so much had been lost, constitutional guarantees of religious freedom encouraged a proliferation of new religious movements. Among them were Soka Gakkai and Rissho Koseikai (both based on the *Lotus Sutra*), Shinnyo-en (derived from Shingon), and others such as Mahikari (True Light) and Perfect Liberty Kyodan (Obaku Zen), each of which claims more a million followers today.

Much of the success of these movements can be attributed to the sense of community they provide to people uprooted by urbanization and industrialization, and the strength they offer individuals to deal with life's problems. Some smaller movements, however, have seen it as their role to serve as agents of radical personal and social transformation. The

most extreme example was the Aum Shinrikyo cult ('the Supreme Truth of Aum'), established in 1987, which was responsible for a number of crimes and murders, including a sensational sarin gas attack on the Tokyo subway system in 1995 that killed twelve people and injured five thousand. According to the group's leader, Asahara Shoko, Japanese society was so thoroughly corrupt that it demanded to be 'cleansed' by an apocalypse. As a result of these attacks, the Japanese government began instituting more rigorous measures to monitor all religious organizations.

## Concluding Remarks

Today the religious traditions of Japan appear to be entering a new and somewhat experimental phase. Ancient shrines and temples still attract many visitors, but most are more interested in history and art than religious experience. A number of younger Buddhist priests are encouraging their temples to engage more directly with the problems of society, offering community services, providing sanctuary for victims of domestic violence, and working to protect the environment against unnecessary development. In urban areas, local festivals mounted by Shinto shrines continue to attract broad-based participation, especially among women who for generations were barred simply because of their gender. In many rural areas, however, it is becoming difficult to find enough people even to carry the portable shrine. Meanwhile, new religions continue to develop on the strength of savvy public relations, charismatic leaders, and the social support offered by a community of like-minded believers.

Even so, there is an increasing tendency to move away from traditional religious affiliations, especially from the financial demands they impose. It is predicted that, as Japan's baby-boomers age and pass away, their funeral rituals will become less identifiably Buddhist and more like the eclectic services typical of North America and Europe. Many rural Buddhist temples no longer have resident priests and have been forced to sell lands and buildings. Although young people are distrustful of organized religion in general, partly because of a series of financial scandals and partly because of the Aum terror attack, many still seem interested in more individual spiritual pursuits. Books related to the occult, fortune-telling, and the spirit world always sell well. This suggests that the most ancient of all Japan's religious traditions—'turning to the gods in times of trouble'—will likely remain a guiding paradigm.

## Sites

**Neighbourhood temples and shrines.** One of the easiest ways to become acquainted with Japanese religious traditions is to visit local (Buddhist) temples and (Shinto) shrines. They are usually open to the public and at festival time may offer opportunities for direct participation.

**Nara** Japan's capital from 710 to 784, Nara is the site of many famous buildings. The **Todaiji Temple**, said to be the world's largest wooden building, houses a colossal Buddha image. Both **Kofukuji** and **Horyuji Temples** feature ancient five-storied pagodas, and the latter is home to the world's oldest wooden building. **Kasuga (Shinto) Shrine** hosts a famous lantern festival in late summer. There is even a festival dedicated to the deer that roam freely through Nara Park.

**Kyoto** Japan's capital from 794 to 1869 abounds in temples and shrines. **Toji** is a Buddhist temple with Japan's tallest pagoda. **Ryoanji** is a Zen temple with a world-renowned rock and sand garden. The picturesque (but tourist-thronged) **Kinkakuji**, or **Golden Pavilion**, was built as a shogun's palace and is now part of a Zen temple. Japan's first Zen temple (**Kenninji**), its second most important Shinto shrine (**Kamigamo**), and the famous **Kiyomizu Temple**, built on the side of a mountain overlooking the city, are also worth seeing, along with the **Imperial Palace** and **Nijo Castle.**

**Ise Shrines** Associated with the imperial *kami* Amaterasu, these ancient shrines in south-central Japan receive over five million visitors a year.

**Izumo Shrine** Located in Shimane prefecture on the Japan Sea coast, Izumo Shrine is one of Japan's oldest, mentioned in several myths and ancient accounts of the founding of the nation.

**Kamakura** Kyoto had been the centre of political and religious power in Japan for only two hundred years when a samurai-led army from the north seized power and moved the capital to Kamakura. Between 1185 and 1333, the once-small fishing village became home to grand temples, shrines, and palaces. One of the most famous large Buddha statues in the world can be found in Kamakura, some 50 kilometres southwest of Tokyo.

**Nikko** Nikko's religious architecture and dramatic mountain setting have become major tourist attractions. **Rinnoji** is a Buddhist temple founded in the eighth century by the famous monk Shonin, who also established the nearby **Futarasan Shrine**, dedicated to the *kami* of the surrounding mountains. The **Toshogu**, the tomb of first Tokugawa shogun, is open to visitors. Look for the beautiful ceremonial bridge and the famous carving of the three monkeys who 'see no evil, hear no evil, and speak no evil'.

# Glossary

**Amaterasu** Female deity of the sun, born from the eye of the primordial deity Izanagi following his purification; enshrined at Ise as the patron deity of the imperial family.

**aramitama** The rough or violent side of the *kami*, responsible for natural disasters, illness, political disorder, etc.

**bodhisattva** A Buddhist 'saint' who has achieved spiritual liberation but chooses to remain in this world to help alleviate the suffering of individuals.

**bushido** Literally, the 'way of the warrior'; an ethical code that combined a Confucian-style emphasis on loyalty with the discipline of Zen.

**haniwa** A clay effigy representing a servant, soldier, etc., interred with a ruler in the burial mound period to serve him in the afterlife.

**honji suijaku** Literally, 'manifestation from the original state'; the concept that *kami* are manifestations of buddhas or bodhisattvas.

**jiriki** Literally, 'self-power'; the principle that individuals can attain liberation through their own abilities and devotional activities.

**kami** The spirits that animate all living things, natural phenomena, and natural forces. Shrines were built to accommodate their presence during rituals.

**kofun** Burial mounds, dating from the second to the sixth centuries CE.

**Kojiki** A collection of stories commissioned to legitimate the imperial regime by linking it with Japan's mythical origins. It was published in 712 CE but was soon replaced by the *Nihongi* and remained largely forgotten until the eighteenth century.

**Kokugaku** Literally, 'learning about one's country'; the intellectual movement of the eighteenth and nineteenth centuries that privileged Japanese culture and ideas over those from abroad.

**mappo** The period of 'decline of the (Buddhist) dharma', thought to have begun in 1052; a time of social disorder, during which individuals could not achieve liberation without the aid of buddhas and bodhisattvas.

**nenbutsu** The key prayer of the Pure Land traditions: *Namu Amida Butsu* ('praise to the Amida Buddha').

**nigimitama** The benevolent side of the *kami*, associated with peace, prosperity, good health, and ample harvests.

**Nihongi** An ancient text (c. 720 CE), also called *Nihon Shoki*, commissioned to present a more positive and systematic account of the Yamato clan's rise to power than the one set out in the earlier *Kojiki*.

**samurai** A popular term for the *bushi* ('warrior'), who served regional warlords in various capacities; samurai made up the top 5 per cent of society during the Edo period (1603–1867).

**shogun** The supreme military commander of Japan, appointed by the emperor and effectively ruling in his name.

**tariki** The 'outside power', offered by buddhas and bodhisattvas, without which individuals living in the age of the Buddhist dharma's decline (*mappo*) would be unable to achieve liberation.

# Further Reading

Bowring, Richard. 2006. *The Religious Traditions of Japan, 500–1600*. Cambridge: Cambridge University Press. A comprehensive and highly readable account of Japanese religious history covering more than 1,000 years.

Covell, Stephen. 2005. *Japanese Temple Buddhism: Worldliness in a Religion of Renunciation*. Honolulu: University of Hawaii Press. A rare examination of contemporary temple Buddhism, with an emphasis on the Tendai sect.

Jaffe, Richard. 2002. *Neither Monk nor Layman: Clerical Marriage in Modern Japanese Buddhism*. Princeton: Princeton University Press. An engaging analysis of the tension between the historical image of Buddhist priests as monks and the modern expectations that priests will have families and run their temples like businesses.

Nelson, John. 1996. *A Year in the Life of a Shinto Shrine*. Honolulu: University of Hawaii Press. A study of what goes on behind the scenes at a major Shinto shrine in the city of Nagasaki.

————. 2005. *Spirits of the State: Japan's Yasukuni Shrine.* 28 min. Documentary film, distributed by Films for the Humanities (www.films.com). A documentary, made for university audiences, about the controversy surrounding the Yasukuni Shrine, where the spirits of the military dead are enshrined and venerated by the state.

Reader, Ian. 2005. *Making Pilgrimages: Meaning and Practice in Shikoku.* Honolulu: University of Hawaii Press. A detailed study of the Shikoku pilgrimage, including the religious significance of the 88 sacred temples that make up the route.

Schnell, Scott. 1999. *The Rousing Drum: Ritual Practice in a Japanese Community.* Honolulu: University of Hawaii Press. An insider's look at a major festival in a small mountain city and what it means to the cultural identity of the local people.

Swanson, Paul, and Clark Chilson, eds. 2006. *The Nanzan Guide to Japanese Religions.* Honolulu: University of Hawaii Press. The most recent compilation of scholarly articles on many topics related to Japanese religions.

Thal, Sarah. 2006. *Rearranging the Landscape of the Gods: The Politics of a Pilgrimage Site in Japan, 1573–1912.* Chicago: University of Chicago Press. A comprehensive history of the wrenching changes forced on a formerly Buddhist temple, now converted to a major Shinto shrine.

Watsky, Andrew. 2004. *Chikubushima: Deploying the Sacred Arts in Momoyama Japan.* Honolulu: University of Hawaii Press. One of the best studies of the artistic, architectural, and aesthetic contributions of the sixteenth-century Toyotomi regime to the religious landscape of Japan.

Williams, Duncan. 2005. *The Other Side of Zen: A Social History of Soto Zen in Tokugawa Japan.* Princeton: Princeton University Press. Surprising and often shocking in its account of corruption and exploitation among priests from the sixteenth to the nineteenth centuries, this study reveals the 'dark' side of institutional Zen, which dominated Japanese society for more than 250 years.

# Recommended Websites

www.nanzan-u.ac.jp/SHUBUNKEN/publications/jjrs/jjrsMain.htm
A semi-annual journal dedicated to the academic study of Japanese religions.

www2.kokugakuin.ac.jp/ijcc
The English-language website for the Institute of Japanese Culture and Classics at Kokugakuin University, specializing in Shinto studies. Many online publications.

global.sotozen-net.or.jp/eng/index.html
The English-language website of the Soto Zen school introduces key teachings and practices. (Each Buddhist denomination has a similar site; many temples also have their own sites.)

www.jodo.org
An English-language website offering a variety of resources on Pure Land Buddhism.

www.onmarkproductions.com/html/buddhism.shtml
A photolibrary devoted to artwork, especially sculpture, depicting Buddhist and Shinto deities in Japan.

# References

Bodiford, William M. 1992. 'Zen in the Art of Funerals: Ritual Salvation in Japanese Buddhism'. *History of Religions* 32.

Bowring, Richard. 2005. *The Religious Traditions of Japan: 500–1600*. Cambridge: Cambridge University Press.

Dogen, Eihei. 1996. '*Tenzo kyokun*: Instructions for the *Tenzo*'. Yasuda Hoshu and Anzan Hoshin, trans. White Wind Zen Community. Retrieved online at http://www.wwzc.org/translations/tenzokyokun.htm.

Hardacre, Helen. 1989. *Shinto and the State: 1868–1945*. Princeton: Princeton University Press.

Jansen, Marius. 2000. *The Making of Modern Japan*. Boston: Harvard University Press.

Kamens, Edward. 1990. *The Buddhist Poetry of the Great Kamo Priestess: Daisaiin Senshi and Hosshin wakash*. Michigan monograph series in Japanese studies no. 5. Ann Arbor.

Philipi, Donald L. 1985. *The Kojiki*. Tokyo: Tokyo University Press.

Pye, Michael. 2004. 'The Structure of Religious Systems in Contemporary Japan: Shinto Variations on Buddhist Pilgrimage'. Occasional Paper No. 30, Centre for Japanese Studies. University of Marburg.

Reader, Ian. 1991. *Religion in Contemporary Japan*. Honolulu: University of Hawaii Press.

Senda, Minoru. 1988. 'Taoist Roots in Japanese Culture'. *Japan Quarterly* 35, 2.

Shigeru, Gorai. 1994. *Nihonjin no shiseikan* ('Japanese views of death'). Tokyo: Kadokawa Shoten.

Williams, Duncan. 2005. *The Other Side of Zen: A Social History of Soto Zen in Tokugawa Japan*. Princeton: Princeton University Press.

Young, W.A. 1995. *The World's Religions*. Englewood Cliffs: Prentice-Hall.

# Notes

1. One of these colossal statues of Kannon appears at the end of the 2006 film *Kamikaze Girls* as background for the battle between an all-girl motorcycle gang and one of the protagonists.

2. For more on the *saiin* tradition, see Edward Kamens, *The Buddhist Poetry of the Great Kamo Priestess: Daisaiin Senshi and Hosshin wakashu*, Michigan monograph series in Japanese studies no. 5 (Ann Arbor, 1990).

3. For a treatment of this topic suitable for classroom use, see my documentary film *Spirits of the State: Japan's Yasukuni Shrine* (2005, Films for the Humanities).

# Chapter 8

# *Current Issues*

Amir Hussain ❧ Roy C. Amore

Most of the chapters in this volume have concentrated on individual religious traditions. In this concluding chapter we will widen our focus and look at the way different traditions are handling some important current issues.

## ❧ RELIGION AND POLITICS

Once upon a time, many in the West regarded religion as a kind of cultural fossil. Aesthetically rich, anthropologically intriguing? Yes. But relevant to today's hard-nosed world of economics and politics? Hardly at all. Those of us who studied religion were often asked how we could waste our lives on something that had so little to do with the modern world. In the secular intellectual climate of the 1960s, some philosophers and even theologians announced that God was dead. That announcement proved to be premature.

Religion has been a major factor in many of the events that have shaken the world over the last thirty years. One such event occurred in 1979, when the Shah of Iran was deposed in an 'Islamic Revolution'. That a nation of forty million people would be ready to sacrifice lives and livelihoods to defend religious values was a concept utterly alien to development economists and politico-military strategists in the West. Meanwhile, not only in Iran but elsewhere, Muslims were turning their backs to modernity and secularism in general and to the modern West in particular. In increasing numbers, Muslim men from Algeria to Zanzibar started to grow beards and wear turbans, and more Muslim women than ever before adopted the hijab (head scarf).

A second event of 1979 that was to have profound repercussions was the Soviet Union's invasion of Afghanistan. From across the Muslim world, volunteers were taken to Afghanistan and trained by the United States to fight for the country's liberation. They were called *mujahidin*, and at

the time—before the end of the cold war—they were widely seen as what US President Ronald Reagan called 'freedom fighters'.

Among the supporters of Afghanistan's 'holy war' was Osama bin Laden (b. 1957), a wealthy Saudi who helped fund and train *mujahidin*. The Soviet troops were withdrawn in 1988, but bin Laden emerged as the leader of Al-Qaeda ('the base'), an extremist organization. In 1996 bin Laden issued a *fatwa* (religious legal opinion) calling for the overthrow of the Saudi government and the removal of US forces in Arabia; in 1998 he declared war against Americans generally; and in 2001 he was accused of masterminding the 9/11 attacks. In response to those attacks, the United States went to war first in Afghanistan and then in Iraq. To understand the modern world, we now realize, we need to take into account the meanings that traditional religions have for their adherents.

Another eventful year was 1989, when the communist order of eastern Europe and the Soviet Union began to crumble. Hopes for democracy, peace, and progress were high. But when the restraints of the socialist order were loosened, old identities resurfaced, and with them passions that most outsiders had assumed to be long dead. Feuds and ethno-religious divisions in the Balkans, the Caucasus, and Central Asia erupted into bitter conflict. Samuel Huntington, in his book *The Clash of Civilizations*, argued that the old world order based on the conflict between communism and capitalism had been replaced by a new one based on the differences among civilizations—and civilizations are defined mainly along religious lines.

Islam is not the only religious tradition that has experienced a revival in recent years. In India, advocates of Hindu nationalism have formed

◀ **Buddhist monks in northeast Thailand constructed the Wat Pa Maha Chedi Kaew temple complex entirely of recycled bottles** (Bronek Kaminski/Barcroft Media Ltd).

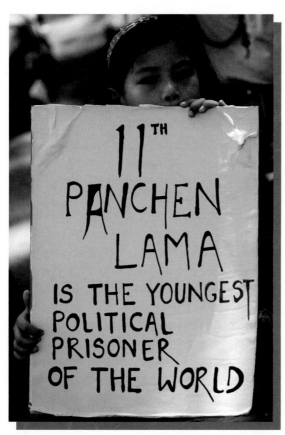

At a protest in New Delhi in 2009, Tibetans in exile called for the release from Chinese detention of Gedhun Choekyi Nyima (b. 1989), recognized by the Dalai Lama as the Panchen Lama—Tibet's second-highest spiritual leader (REUTERS/Arko Datta).

governments at both the state and the national level. In Sri Lanka, the struggle of Hindu Tamil separatists to establish an independent homeland sparked a resurgence of Buddhist fervour among the Sinhalese majority, which—for the first time in history—elected several monks to parliament. And in China religious minorities such as the Muslim Uighurs and the Buddhist Tibetans have renewed their struggles against the repressive tendencies of the national government.

# 🌿 FUNDAMENTALISM

In most cases the leading figures in the resurgence of religious fervour have come from the ultraconservative or 'fundamentalist' end of the religious spectrum. A brief review of the rise of fundamentalism may help to explain why.

The term 'fundamentalism' originated in the United States, where a series of booklets entitled *The Fundamentals* was published in 1910. Affirming the 'inerrancy' (infallibility) of the Bible and traditional Christian doctrines, the booklets were distributed free to Protestant clergy, missionaries, and students through the anonymous sponsorship of 'two Christian laymen' (William Lyman Stewart and his brother Milton, both of whom were major figures in the Union Oil Company of California). By 1920 advocates of inerrancy were being described as 'fundamentalists'.

Fundamentalism is a modern phenomenon, a reaction against the values associated with secularism and modernity. Above all, perhaps, what fundamentalists reject is the modern tendency to locate ultimate authority in human institutions such as courts and legislatures rather than divine scriptures and religious leaders. If they interpret their scripture as condemning homosexuality, for example, they resist all efforts to legalize same-sex marriage as a human right. Fundamentalists do not necessarily denounce science, but on specific issues where science differs from their interpretation of scripture, they side with scripture as the ultimate authority. For Christian fundamentalists, the main conflict with science has centred on the perceived conflict between the biblical stories of creation and the consensus of modern science. They understand the Bible to affirm that the world was created by God in six days, only a few thousand years ago, and that everything that exists originated at that time. By contrast, science maintains that the universe has existed for many billions of years, that our planet formed some time later, and that all life on earth was the product of evolution through countless generations.

The test case for fundamentalism came in 1925, when a high-school teacher named John T. Scopes was brought to trial for violating a newly enacted Tennessee law that banned the teaching of evolution on the grounds that it contradicted the Bible. The court found for the prosecution, conducted by the famed orator William Jennings Bryan (1860–1925) against the defence of Clarence Darrow (1857–1938), and fined Scopes $100. So extensive was the news coverage of the case, however, that fundamentalism itself was effectively put on trial in the court of public opinion, where Darwin, Scopes, and Darrow emerged the clear victors. In particular, it was the idea that humans were not the special creations of God but a species of primate descended from the same common ancestor as gorillas and chimpanzees that underlay the Scopes case and earned it the nickname the 'monkey trial'. Scopes's conviction was overturned in 1927 on the technical grounds that the fine was too high, although it would be another forty years before the Tennessee law banning the teaching of evolution was repealed.

The word 'fundamentalism' can have various meanings, but almost all of them are pejorative: even conservative Protestants tend to describe their own views as evangelical and use 'fundamentalist' only to refer to more extreme views. In addition to denoting an orthodoxy based on the inerrancy of scripture, 'fundamentalism' generally suggests orthopraxy—conformity to a straitlaced code of social and personal conduct—and a militant defence of their tradition as they understand it. Fundamentalists have been known to attack as diabolical those they believe to be subverting that tradition by expressing doubt or taking more liberal positions on some issues.

Fundamentalists perceive a struggle between good and evil forces in the world, and they have a greater-than-average readiness to believe that evil is tangibly manifested in social groups and forces with which they take issue, such as advocates of homosexual rights or free choice in abortion. They also tend to believe that the apocalypse—a final battle between the forces of good and evil in this world—is imminent.

Since the 1970s the term 'fundamentalist' has been widely used to describe ultraconservative movements in religious traditions other than Christianity—especially those that have taken their beliefs into the political realm. Some scholars object to the use of a term with specifically Christian roots to refer to different traditions. Nevertheless, from the popular perspective there are enough similarities among the various ultraconservative movements around the world to justify the term's extension to other cultures.

# BIOETHICS

Another important challenge facing religious communities in the twenty-first century is the unprecedented power over human life and death made available by developments in biological research and medical technology. This power is especially troubling for the Western religions, which have traditionally considered humans to be sacred, set apart from all other beings. In Islam, for example, the human being is created expressly to serve as God's representative on earth:

> Behold, your Lord said to the angels: 'I will create a vicegerent on earth.' They said: 'Will You place therein one who will make mischief there and shed blood while we celebrate Your praises and glorify Your holy name?' God said: 'I know what you do not' (Q. 2:30).

Central to the notion of the human being as sacred is the notion of the soul. The Christian understanding of the soul was economically expressed by the Anglican writer C.S. Lewis: 'You don't have a soul, you are a soul. You have a body.' Hinduism likewise teaches that the soul (*atman*) is the eternal and therefore the more important part of the human being; in fact, one of the Hindu terms for soul is *dehin*, meaning 'that which possesses a body'. In Islam, the soul is believed to enter the body at a certain stage of its development in the womb:

'And truly We created the human being out of wet clay, then we made it a drop in a firm resting place, then We made the seed a clot, then We made the clot a lump of flesh, then We made (in) the lump of flesh bones, then We clothed the bones with flesh, then We caused it to grow into another creation, so blessed be God, the best of the creators' (Q. 23:12–14).

Modern Muslims take great pride in the history of science and medicine associated with Islam. Following an injunction of the Prophet Muhammad 'to seek knowledge even unto China' (that is, to the end of the then-known world),[1] Muslims never really experienced the kind of tension between religion and science that Western Christianity did. To discover scientific truths about the world was to learn more about God who created the world. Thus universities were established in the Islamic world as early as the ninth century; one of the earliest accounts of the duties of the doctor was written by a ninth-century physician named Ishaq ibn Ali Rahawi; and in the tenth century another Muslim physician named al-Razi (known in the West as Rhazes) wrote numerous treatises on medicine, pharmacy, and medical ethics.

The Islamic system of moral deliberation is even older. Jonathan Brockopp, in his edited volume *Islamic Ethics of Life: Abortion, War and Euthanasia* (2003), identifies the sources of Islamic ethics as the Qur'an and the traditions of the Prophet Muhammad (*hadiths*), together with the commentaries on those texts written over the centuries. Traditionally, the scholars and jurists who interpret these texts in order to rule on the ethical questions brought before them have tended to prefer cases and examples over abstract principles.

Perhaps this traditional preference for the specific over the general helps to account for Muslims' reluctance to approach medical issues from the perspective of 'bioethics' (as is usually done in the West). Rather, the tradition has been to let God and the family decide. Although advances in medicine are welcomed and the doctor's expertise is honoured, the wishes of the individual or the family have taken priority over the opinions either of doctors or of Islamic religious scholars. And because it is impossible to know God's will, Muslims have preferred what Brockopp calls a 'stance of humility' when it comes to deciding questions of life and death.

In the West, arguments for the patient's right to die are often based on the concept of human dignity. Among Muslims, however, human life is valued not for its own sake but because it is a trust given by God; similarly, human dignity is not inherent in the individual but a product of his or her relationship with God. While active euthanasia (mercy killing) would be forbidden, therefore, a brain-dead patient kept alive only by medical technology could be removed from artificial life support if that were the family's wish.

Nevertheless, 'Let God and the family decide' is not always adequate to the conditions under which most North Americans, including Muslims, now live and die. Amyn Sajoo, in his book *Muslim Ethics: Emerging Vistas* (2004), writes not only as an academic but as an insider to the Muslim tradition, and he shows it responding to medicalized death in a more activist mode. Sajoo reprints extracts from the *Islamic Code of Medical Ethics* adopted by the Islamic Organization for Medical Sciences in 1981. The organization upheld the traditional position on euthanasia: 'A doctor shall not take away life even when motivated by mercy.' With respect to the artificial prolongation of life, however, it advised the doctor

to realize his limit and not transgress it. If it is scientifically certain that life cannot be restored, then it is futile to diligently keep on the vegetative state of the patient by heroic means of animation or preserve him by deep-freezing or other artificial methods.

Thus in cases where the family wishes to continue life support even when there is no hope of recovery, it may not necessarily have the final word: the doctor may become the primary decision-maker.

Another organization that is working to bring traditional religious standards and ideals into modern medical situations is the Islamic Medical Association of North America (IMANA). IMANA has developed a number of principles and policy statements (available on its website) to guide Muslim medical practice and help to answer questions about current controversial issues. This organization may not represent a universal Muslim consensus about such issues, but it is a vivid example of accommodation and creative adaptation to new circumstances.

The situation with Eastern religious traditions is somewhat different. One reason is that modern medical technologies have only recently arrived in Asia, and still are not readily available to many people. Abortion, however, has long been an issue for Buddhists and Hindus. All Eastern traditions condemn the practice, but abortion is relatively common in most Asian countries, especially Japan, India, and South Korea.

The Buddhist scriptures have little to say about abortion itself, but the Buddhist ethic of non-violence has been understood to apply to abortion no less than to any other form of harm. In the Theravada countries of Southeast Asia abortion is typically illegal, but covert abortions are common. Japanese Buddhists have developed a special memorial service, called *mizuko kuyo*, for aborted fetuses, and some temples set aside special areas where family members may go to honour their memory.

As well as all the usual motivations for abortion, Hindus in India face two additional pressures. One is the persistence of an unusually onerous dowry system under which the family of a bride is expected to provide the groom's family with generous compensation. Because the family can rarely afford to pay the entire debt before the wedding, the payments are often spread over several years, like a mortgage. The dowry system is not sanctioned in traditional Hindu law, but neither governmental legislation nor the condemnation of Hindu leaders has been able to put an end to it. Thus the birth of a daughter means that the family faces the prospect of a terrible burden when she comes of marital age. Not only will it have to pay for both the wedding and the dowry, but after marriage the girl will go to live with—and work for—the groom's family. Conversely, a baby boy brings the prospect not only of receiving a significant financial reward when he marries, but of gaining an additional labourer or income earner in the form of his wife.

Under these circumstances it is hardly surprising that many families use modern medical technology to find out the sex of a prospective child before birth, and that some give in to the temptation to abort female fetuses. The other factor contributing to the rise of abortion in India is the government's ongoing effort to address over-population problems. Unlike China, India has not resorted to forced birth control, but it has put in place incentives to limit reproduction. For example, a village that manages to keep its birth rate low is eligible to receive special grants for community development projects, such as roads, wells, or community centres. Thus community leaders sometimes put heavy pressure on women who already have children to undergo sterilization in order to prevent additional pregnancies. This approach may have the unintended effect of encouraging abortion.

# THE ENVIRONMENT

After creating the first humans, according to the Bible (Gen. 1.28), God gave them 'dominion . . . over all the earth': the fish of the sea, the birds of the air, and every living thing. This verse was traditionally interpreted as a grant of power and a licence for unlimited exploitation of the earth's resources, but today it is generally understood differently, as a command to take responsibility for the environment.

An influential early advocate of this 'greener' interpretation was Lynn White, who in 1967 published an article entitled 'The Historical Roots of Our Ecologic Crisis', in which he argued that the traditional reading of Genesis had played a significant part in the degradation of the earth. This article prompted a shift in attitude among many Jews and Christians, towards an understanding of 'dominion over the earth' that emphasized stewardship of God's creation rather than exploitation of it. This awareness can be seen in churches such as the Canadian Memorial Church in Vancouver, which has embraced an environmental mission 'To cultivate a spiritual understanding of Creation, and to adopt and promote awareness of a spiritually-principled approach to planetary sustainability.'

According to the Qur'an, God offered the responsibility for this universe as 'a Trust to the heavens and the earth and the mountains; but they refused to undertake it, being afraid thereof' (Q. 33:72). Thus the 'Trust' passed to the one part of creation that was willing to take it: the human being. The verse concludes with the following words: 'The human being was indeed unjust and foolish.' In suggesting that we would behave foolishly and without justice to the earth, this passage underlines the necessity of wisdom and justice in the exercise of the profound responsibility that humans have been given.

Faced with the evidence of humans' failure to serve as responsible stewards, Muslims today, like Jews and Christians, are reflecting on their fundamental religious teachings and discovering in them the bases for a new environmental ethic. So, for example, the web page of the Muslim group Green Deen (*deen* is the Arabic word for religion), based in southern California, states that its mission is 'to raise awareness and change the current environmental conditions by promoting a healthier, greener and more environmentally conscious lifestyle'.

In sharp contrast to their Western counterparts, most Eastern religious traditions have never made any radical distinction between humans and other animals. Hinduism understands all animals to have a soul (*atman*), and reincarnation may take place in either a human or an animal body. Jainism goes even further, teaching that plants as well are animated by a kind of soul. Jainism and Buddhism alike emphasize the ethic of non-violence, and denounce any human activity that causes unnecessary harm to living things.

A number of Buddhists, including the Dalai Lama and Sulak Sivaraksa, have applied the Buddhist ethic of moderation to environmental issues. Sulak argues that human greed is responsible for the redirection of vast quantities of natural resources to support the demand for cash crops, causing suffering on the part of local people as well as harm to the environment. One of the first to bring these ecological concerns to wide public attention

Appa Sherpa, a Nepali high-altitude guide, holds a vase filled with Buddhist offerings that he planned to carry to the summit of Mount Everest in an effort to restore the sanctity of the Himalayas and raise awareness about climate change (REUTERS/Gopal Chitrakar).

was the economist E.F. Schumacher, in his book *Small Is Beautiful* (1973). Schumacher called for a 'Buddhist economics' designed to meet the needs of all the planet, as opposed to a traditional business economics designed to maximize profits. But of course this approach is not confined to Buddhism: M.K. Gandhi's preference for small-scale, locally based technology, together with his call for all to work for the benefit of all, has inspired many organizations around the world dedicated to environmental responsibility and human-centred development.

# 🌿 GENDER AND SEXUALITY

In 2000, two advertising campaigns in Los Angeles featured images of veiled women. One campaign was for the opening of the renovated Aladdin Hotel and Casino in Las Vegas, a day's drive across the desert. Billboards featured the head and shoulders of an attractive Middle Eastern woman with an enticing smile, wearing a delicate veil that covered her hair and lower face. The image was a classic example of the 'erotic Orient' myth—the harem girl whose sensuality so shocked (and sometimes titillated) the Victorians.

The other campaign was for the *Los Angeles Times*. Entitled 'Connecting Us to the Times', it included television commercials as well as print ads and billboards. In each case, an image of bikini-clad women on a beach was juxtaposed with an image of women covered from head to toe in full black robes. In many ways, this campaign was more troubling than the first example. It's no surprise that a Las Vegas casino would use sex to sell itself, but why would a respected newspaper choose that approach? In this case, the veiled women suggested a suppressed sexuality that underlined the overt sexuality of the women in bikinis. The ads were criticized not only by Muslim groups, but also by two hundred *Times* employees

who objected to the use of women's bodies—covered or uncovered—to sell their product. As a result, the *Times* cancelled the campaign.

These examples are recent and specifically North American, but the distorted images they present point to a tendency to distort the image of Muslim women that is rooted in prejudice and misunderstanding.

When discussing the roles and lives of Muslim women today, it is essential to keep in mind that individual circumstances vary just as widely for them as for any other group. To be a woman in North America is a very different experience for a university professor than it is for an unemployed mother of four who never finished high school. Or look at the roles of women in political life. Both in Canada and the United States, women are theoretically equal to men, yet neither country has elected a female leader. (Kim Campbell's short stint as prime minister in 1993 was the result of the midterm resignation of Brian Mulroney, not a national election.) By contrast, Indonesia, Pakistan, Bangladesh, and Turkey—all with predominantly Muslim populations—have elected women as leaders. It would be no less simplistic to assume that North America is necessarily progressive in its treatment of women than it would be to assume that the Muslim world is necessarily oppressive.

Another issue centred on gender made headlines in 2005, after Dr Amina Wadud led a mixed-gender Muslim prayer service in New York City. The event caused a great deal of controversy, not only because it broke the Islamic convention that women may lead prayer only among other women or within their own family, but because men and women sat beside one another rather than in separate rows, and because some of the women left their hair uncovered, contrary to the rule that women should veil themselves for prayer. Since then a number of similar events have been held in Toronto as well as New York City. This is a classic example of the issues centred on gender roles and expectations that are likely to become increasingly important for North American Muslims.

Karva Chauth is a North Indian Hindu festival celebrating married women's devotion to their husbands. Participants observe a 24-hour fast, during which they pray for their husbands' well-being (REUTERS/Ajay Verma).

Many religious traditions are also beginning to rethink their positions on sexuality. Islam is among the majority of Western religious traditions that recognize only heterosexual relationships as valid, and Muslims often speak out against homosexuality. However, there are Muslims who identify themselves as gay–lesbian–bisexual–transgendered–intersex–questioning (GLBTIQ), and they are forming support groups. One such group, with branches in several Canadian cities including Toronto and Vancouver, is Min al-Alaq, which takes its name from a Qur'anic phrase (96:2) that translates literally as 'from the clot'. The implication is that members consider all believers, whatever their sexual orientation, to come 'from the same clot of blood'.

According to its founder, Min al-Alaq does not openly advertise its meetings, or even its existence, for fear of attracting the attention of homophobes within the Muslim community. Instead, information is passed along to 'fellow travellers', and counselling and support are offered on an individual basis. A conversation with another member of Min al-Alaq underlined the tremendous religious isolation that comes with being a gay Muslim in North America. While his partner was a Christian member of an 'affirming congregation' open to all, regardless of sexual orientation, this man had no 'affirming mosque' that he could attend. Although he could pray with other Muslims in the mosque, he could feel 'welcomed' religiously only in his partner's church.

Al-Fatiha ('the opening') is a group for GLBTIQ Muslims based in Los Angeles. A non-Muslim who hosted a meeting at his home in Los Angeles in 2001 later said he was interested to hear the group discussing 'gay Sunni Muslims versus gay Shi'i Muslims'. A few years earlier, he said, 'they were all just "gay Muslims", but now they can be more divisive . . . along the same lines as gay Christians who are now gay Baptists, gay Methodists, [or] gay Adventists.'

An increasingly important source of support for gay Muslims is the Internet. With access to the Net (and the anonymity that it provides), people around the world can have access to groups such as the South Asian Gay and Lesbian Association of New York (its site includes a description of the first GLBTIQ Muslim conference, held in Boston in 1998) and Queer Jihad. Based in West Hollywood—an area where gay people have a strong voice in local government and community affairs—Queer Jihad defines itself as 'the queer Muslim struggle for acceptance: first, the struggle to accept ourselves as being exactly the way Allah has created us to be; and secondly, the struggle for acceptance and tolerance among Muslims in general'.

Homosexuality has played a major role in Christian church politics as well. The international family of churches led by the Archbishop of Canterbury, the head of the Church of England, has been particularly hard hit by controversy over homosexuality. Until recently these churches constituted one big family known as the Anglican Communion, but in recent years a major split has taken place, largely over the question of whether or not the Church should bless same-sex marriages and ordain persons openly living in same-sex relationships. James Packer, a well-known conservative Anglican theologian, officially resigned his membership in a Vancouver-area diocese in 2008 because its head favoured allowing the ritual blessing of same-sex unions. Earlier that year several conservative congregations broke away from the Anglican Church of Canada to form the Anglican Network of Canada. They recognize a South African bishop as their spiritual head and pride themselves on adhering to biblical tradition, which in their view considers homosexuality a sin. (In fact, although some local divisions of the Anglican Church of Canada have endorsed same-sex

blessings, so far the Church as a whole has not done so.)

Most Eastern traditions are just beginning to discuss such issues. In fact, it is only recently that India has officially recognized the existence of homosexuality within its borders. Buddhist ordination rules prohibit the admission to the sangha of a category of persons that has been understood to include homosexuals and transsexuals. But most sanghas insist that monks and nuns remain celibate in any case, so questions about sexual orientation rarely arise. (The one exception is Japan, where married Buddhist priests are common.) In general, Buddhist societies in Asia are socially conservative and frown on homosexual relationships, although the Buddhist culture of Thailand has a long tradition of accepting males who cross-dress as females.

A major factor in India's movement towards greater openness has been the Bollywood film industry. Just a few years ago, the leading lady in an Indian film could not be kissed on camera, but now physical expressions of affection—even suggestions of gay or lesbian sexuality—are increasingly common. Still, many traditionally minded Hindus and Muslims are shocked by the new openness.

# RELIGIOUS DIVERSITY

'Aren't all religions pretty much the same?' Most students of religion will be asked this question, or some version of it, more than once in their careers. As scholars we might want to unpack the proposition: what aspect of religion are we talking about—teachings? practices? implications for society? Still, it would probably be safe to assume that the questioner considers all religions to be of equal value and deserving of equal respect. And in the multicultural society of twenty-first-century North America, most of us would probably agree. This was not the case a hundred years ago, when North American society was overwhelmingly Christian and most of the Christian churches were actively engaged in missionary work. Missionary activity presumes a difference among religions—a difference so consequential that believers cannot keep silent about it, but must spread the word.

For its first three centuries, Christianity was an affinity-based movement whose members were not born into it but actively chose to join. In the early fourth century, however, with the imperial favour of the emperor Constantine (r. 306–37), the missionary religion became a state religion as well. Christianity converted several entire populations by first converting their rulers. In its earlier centuries, Islam likewise succeeded in persuading a significant number of nations to convert, perhaps partly because it offered improved juridical status, including especially tax exemption, to those who became Muslims. Christianity's spread after the 1490s was closely associated with European military and cultural expansion. Priests accompanied soldiers in Mexico and Peru, and the sponsoring Spanish and Portuguese regimes took it as their responsibility to save the souls of the indigenous peoples whose bodies they enslaved. The cultural-religious imperialism of Catholic countries in the sixteenth century was matched in the nineteenth by that of Protestant England, notably in Africa.

Muslim rule in northern India began with the establishment of the Delhi sultanate in the thirteenth century. This was the first region where Islam did not succeed in converting the entire population. Only in the Indus Valley, Bengal, and the mid-southern interior did Muslims become the majority; the rest of the subcontinent remained predominantly Hindu.

In the later centuries of its expansion, Islam grew not through military conquest, but through trade and the missionary activity of the Sufis in

## Missionary Religions

The fact that a mere three traditions—Buddhism, Christianity, and Islam—claim the allegiance of over half the world's population reflects the success of their missionary activities. All three are 'universal' rather than 'ethnic' religions: that is, they direct their messages to all human beings, regardless of heredity or descent. And all three were strongly motivated from the start to spread their messages far and wide.

By the time Buddhism emerged in what is now northern India, Indian society was already stratified into four broad social classes. Whether those distinctions had ethnic connotations in the time of the Buddha may be debated. What is clear is that Buddhism set caste and class status aside as irrelevant to the achievement of spiritual purity and liberation.

Christianity began as a sect of Judaism, a religion focused almost exclusively on the relationship of one particular nation to God. But the early Christians decided that it was not necessary to be a Jew in order to become a Christian. Early Christian teaching understood the new covenant to apply to all humans who accepted Jesus as their Lord, regardless of ethnicity.

Islam believes the Prophet Muhammad to have been the last in a long line of prophets sent by God to different peoples. And although the Qur'an explicitly addresses the people of Arabia, it was understood from the start to incorporate the messages delivered to other groups by earlier prophets and to represent God's final revelation to humanity at large. It is not ethnic identity but submission to the One God that renders humans acceptable in the sight of God. Thus the community established by the Prophet could expand far beyond Arabia.

particular. The devotional life of the Sufis resonated with the Hindu and Buddhist meditational piety already present in Southeast Asia and provided Islam with an entrée to that region, in which it became dominant. Similarly in Africa south of the Sahara, traders and Sufis were the principal vehicles of Islam.

In general, Buddhist, Muslim, and Christian missionaries have been more successful in recruiting converts from the traditional religions of small-scale tribal societies than from the other major religions. The reasons may have something to do with the material culture and technologies—including writing systems—of the major civilizations, which have conferred powerful advantages on those who possess them. Scriptural literatures have given the major traditions a special authority among cultures that were primarily oral, allowing them to use the content of their scriptures to shape social values. The early missionary spread of Theravada Buddhism is credited to King Ashoka. We do not know enough about the indigenous traditions in many of the regions where Theravada spread to determine why its teachings were accepted. In the case of China, however, it seems that the Daoist interest in magic and healing techniques may have helped Mahayana Buddhism gain an initial foothold.

In the twentieth century, some Christian denominations began to curtail their missionary activity, partly because the returns on the resources invested were too small. Generations of European missionary effort in the eastern Mediterranean had made almost no inroads into Islam. And in the years around 1960, when many African countries were struggling for independence from European rule, Christian missionaries in West Africa particularly suffered from identification with colonial interests as well as the former slave trade. Thus Christian missionaries in Africa were largely replaced by an emerging generation of indigenous church leaders. Another factor in the Christian churches' retreat from missionary work, however, was an increasing respect for other communities and traditions.

## Dialogue in a Pluralistic Age

Today we often use the term 'pluralism' to denote a combination of two things: the fact of diversity, and the evaluation of that diversity as desirable. This use of the word, which has become standard since the mid-twentieth century, reflects a convergence of developments and trends.

But let us be clear about what we mean by it. First, pluralism is not the same thing as diversity. People from many different religions and ethnic backgrounds may be present in one place, but unless they are constructively engaged with one another, there is no pluralism.

Second, pluralism means more than simple tolerance of the other. It's quite possible to tolerate a neighbour about whom we know nothing. Pluralism, by contrast, demands an active effort to learn.

Third, pluralism is not the same thing as relativism, which can lead us to ignore profound differences. Pluralism is committed to engaging those differences, to gain a deeper understanding both of others' commitments and of our own. It is also important to recognize that pluralism and dialogue are happening around the world, not just in North America.

The current situation has been shaped by increasingly intimate intercultural contact. Within the lifetimes of people still alive today, transportation and communication have been transformed almost beyond recognition. As late as 1950, travel between North America and East Asia was rare, but now tens of thousands of people fly across the Pacific every day. And new technologies allow us to be in touch with almost any part of the world in an instant. Migration has also increased significantly. Since the end of the Second World War, the demographic profile of European and North American cities has been transformed by the arrival of populations from other parts of the world who have brought their Muslim, Hindu, Buddhist, and other traditions with them. Though apprehensive at first, Western societies have made some progress towards understanding those traditions.

Change in the evaluation of diversity is reflected in many aspects of contemporary life, large and small. In some cases old institutions have been retained, but with new rationales. For instance, Sunday—the Christian day of religious observance—remains the day of reduced business activity in many jurisdictions. The arguments for legislation preserving Sunday store closing, however, now involve fairness, family time, and opportunities for recreation.

We should distinguish pluralism from secularism. Secularism means the exclusion (in principle) of all religious groups, institutions, and identities from public support and public decision-making. Pluralism, on the other hand, means equal support, acceptance, and participation in decision-making for multiple religious groups. Whereas recreational arguments for Sunday closing are secularist, arguments for school holidays on the Jewish New Year or the Muslim festival ending the Ramadan fast are pluralist. Up to a point, secularism and pluralism go hand in hand in the West because both seek to limit the role that Christianity can play in setting the society's standards. Where they differ is in what they propose as alternatives. Pluralism places a parallel and a positive value on the faith and practice of different communities. It often does so on the assumption that any religion is beneficial to society so long as it does no harm to other religions. It can also presume that the effort to understand a neighbour's religion—whatever it may be—is beneficial to society. Essentially, pluralism downplays the differences between religions and focuses instead on the values they share. In its scale of priorities, the value of harmony in the society as a whole is more important than the commitments of any particular religion.

## Interfaith Dialogue

The word 'dialogue' comes from a Greek root meaning to argue, reason, or contend. Some Christian writers have pointed to the apostle Paul as an early proponent of interfaith dialogue because he is described as 'arguing and pleading about the kingdom of God' with the Jews (Acts 19:8–9). Paul was a missionary, however, and missionaries—by definition—believe they are possessed of a truth that it is their mission to spread. Missionary argumentation therefore bears little resemblance to dialogue in the modern sense, which demands openness to other points of view.

Dialogue is also a literary form, almost always designed to advance the author's point of view. The Greek philosopher Plato was a master of the dialogue form, using questioners and objectors as foils (or comedic 'straight men') to demonstrate the invincible logic of his own ideas and those of his mentor Socrates.

The Hindu *Upanishads* also take the form of dialogues, and they too were composed to advance specific arguments. The early Christian writer Justin Martyr in his dialogues with the Jew Trypho; the Buddhist sage Nagasena who answers the questions of King Milinda (Menander); and the Khazar king in the *Kuzari* of Yehuda Ha-Levi—in each case the questioner is like a puppet whose only function is to bring out the views that the author is already committed to.

True openness to alternative points of view is rare in any of the premodern traditions, but we do find instances of it. One highly significant example is the Mughal Indian emperor Akbar (r. 1556–1605). As a Muslim ruler of a mainly Hindu population, Akbar could have taken a tolerant stance towards Hindu spirituality on purely practical grounds, but he was a genuine seeker of religious insight. Therefore he summoned to his court representatives of all the religious communities within his domain and pursued conversations with them late into the night. From those conversations Akbar drew the components of an eclectic new religion that he called Din-i Ilahi ('divine faith'). Although Akbar's synthesis did not endure for long after his death, it reflected a remarkable phenomenon in his society: a widespread perception that despite their communal boundaries, Hindus and Muslims shared a devotional spirituality.

Conservative Muslims disapproved of Akbar's openness to heretical views. This is nothing new. Traditional religions may encourage disputation when the outcome is not in question. But Akbar's explorations were open-ended. A dialogue in which both sides are equal is something that orthodoxy cannot control. To those committed to a fixed position, such dialogue implies a threat.

The World's Parliament of Religions, convened in Chicago in 1893, was an adventure in dialogue that brought together representatives of many—though not all—of the world's faiths to present their religious goals and understandings. The conference reflected the existing religious scene and at the same time affected its future development by creating opportunities for Vedanta to present itself as the definitive form of Hinduism, Zen to claim to represent Buddhism, and the Baha'i faith to appear as an overarching synthesis of religion.

Understanding of interfaith dialogue has grown considerably since 1948, when the World Council of Churches was formed. Experienced dialogue participants emphasize that such exercises require both parties to set aside their claims to exclusivity: each must work to understand the other on his or her own terms. Both participants must also be open to the possibility of revising their views in the light of what they learn in the encounter—though this is easier said than done. Even the best-intentioned participants may be tempted to read their own views into others'. The influential Roman Catholic theologian Karl Rahner (1904–84), for instance, referred to people of other faiths as 'anonymous Christians'—Christians who simply did not recognize the fact. By the same token, could not Rahner himself have been an anonymous Buddhist?

The goal of dialogue in the modern sense is 'understanding'. But 'understanding' can be a slippery term in the context of religion. Academic students of religion understand particular traditions by explaining them: by describing as accurately as possible what they require of their adherents and how they have developed to become what they are. For those people, understanding may be informed by sympathy, but it is not the same as participation or identification. Similarly, the participants in dialogue understand each other by identifying one another's commitments, but that is not to say that they identify with those commitments. Particularly in the area of Jewish–Christian–Muslim dialogue, there have been calls for complete solidarity on complex and hotly debated issues, characterized by one critic as 'ecumenical blackmail'. Does true understanding of Judaism require uncritical endorsement of

Archbishop Desmond Tutu of South Africa meeting with the Dalai Lama in Vancouver in 2004 (REUTERS/Lyle Stafford).

Israel's policies towards the Palestinians? If one truly 'understands' Islam, must one agree with Iran's theocratic government and its suppression of democracy? Does understanding Hinduism mean accepting polytheism or animal sacrifice? No. Real understanding is not a matter of agreement or acquiescence, but a quest for a patient and appreciative relationship that can persist despite disagreement.

## The Question of Value

For more than three decades, the 1978 Jonestown tragedy—in which 914 members of a religious community called the Peoples Temple died in a mass suicide—has stood as a challenge to the idea that all religions are equally valuable and deserving of respect. The community's founder, the Reverend Jim Jones (1931–78), who took his own life alongside his followers, had aspirations to overhaul the world order that were compatible with a reformist and utopian strand in Protestant (and Marxist) thought; one of his objectives in founding the movement had been to improve the living standards of the poor. But he also sought from his followers an uncritical dedication to his personal leadership that many found disturbing. Having moved the community from the US to rural Guyana in 1972, Jones ordered the mass suicide when he became convinced that evil forces were closing in and the only honourable escape was death.

History repeats itself. The Jonestown story recalls the Jewish Zealots at the fortress of Masada who are said to have committed mass suicide when they were surrounded by Roman troops in 73 CE. Suicide and the psychology of martyrdom have been linked at various times by Christian groups, and in other traditions as well. A similar interpretation has been applied to the conduct of the followers of David Koresh (Vernon Wayne Howell, 1959–93), eighty-five of whom perished with him when their heavily armed religious commune outside Waco, Texas, was stormed by US law enforcement forces for firearms violations in 1993.

To approve of Masada's defenders while condemning the 'Branch Davidians' at Waco would amount to deciding what constitutes a provocation worth resisting to the death.

Jim Jones and David Koresh were both leaders of movements that sought to recruit and retain converts. That is not unusual in missionary religions: Buddhism, Christianity, and Islam have all done the same, as have numerous 'new religious movements' since the late 1960s. If modern pluralistic society proclaims the freedom to preach or follow religion without state intervention, fairness demands that the same freedom be extended to all.

Nevertheless, my freedom to practise or promote a religion is limited by the freedom of others to know what I am offering and to refuse it if they so choose. In a pluralistic society, religious groups forfeit their right to acceptance if they engage in coercion (psychological or physical) or illegal activities (such as narcotics abuse, firearms abuse, or tax fraud). Critics of movements such as the Unification Church (the 'Moonies'), or the International Society for Krishna Consciousness (the Hare Krishna movement), or the Church of Scientology are particularly alarmed when recruits are instructed to sever all ties with their families—even though there have been parallels to such demands in the early Christian movement and in some religious orders, and the families of such recruits have often resorted to equally coercive methods to retrieve and 'deprogram' them.

By the early twenty-first century, some of the new religions had achieved a degree of institutional maturity and public acceptance. Most of these organizations were compatible with mainstream religions in that they helped their members cope with their lives and encouraged good citizenship. Like mainstream religions, in one way or another they addressed the human condition.

The last point is important. Religions are not all the same, but many may be humanly acceptable if they in fact benefit human beings; an appropriate test is suggested by Jesus' words in the

Sermon on the Mount: 'you shall know them by their fruits' (Matthew 7:16). On some occasions, when they have lived up to their ideals, all the major traditions have passed that test; on other occasions, when they have fallen short of their ideals, the same traditions have failed. Typically, though, the various traditions see their distinguishing features as eminently valuable in themselves. If all religions were of equal worth, if there were no fundamentally important differences, why would anyone choose one of them over another? Pluralism may be socially desirable, but it poses a serious theological challenge. Does it really require us to modify our own doctrinal claims?

We personally are convinced that it does. Affirmations of religious 'truth' that used to be understood as statements of fact are now increasingly regarded as perspectival—true 'for me'—rather than universal claims. Today, thinkers from various backgrounds are presenting their traditions as symbolic accounts of the world and metaphorical narratives of the past. What is more, they argue that this is the way the various traditions should have been seen all along, and that literal interpretation has always been a mistake.

Pluralism demands that religious traditions adapt to a world that is becoming ever more interconnected. Here we think of the work of Wilfred Cantwell Smith (1916–2000), perhaps the greatest Canadian scholar of religion in the twentieth century. Professor Smith founded the Institute of Islamic Studies at McGill University in Montreal. He then moved to Harvard University, where he directed the Center for the Study of World Religions. One of his most important books was *Towards a World Theology: Faith and the Comparative History of Religion* (1981). In it he argued that our various religious traditions were best understood in comparative context, 'as strands in a . . . complex whole':

> What they have in common is that the history of each has been what it has been in significant part because the history of the others has been what *it* has been. This truth is newly discovered; yet truth it is, truth it has throughout been. Things proceeded in this interrelated way for many centuries without humanity's being aware of it; certainly not fully aware of it. A new, and itself interconnected, development is that currently humankind *is* becoming aware of it, in various communities.

Although current events make us painfully aware of the differences that separate the world's religions, it is more crucial today than ever to appreciate the complex connections they share. That is exactly what we are trying to do in this book: to deepen understanding of our interconnected religious worlds.

# References

Brockopp, Jonathan. 2003. *Islamic Ethics of Life: Abortion, War and Euthanasia*. Columbia: University of South Carolina Press.

Sajoo, Amyn. 2004. *Muslim Ethics: Emerging Vistas*. London: I.B. Tauris in association with The Institute for Ismaili Studies.

Schumacher, E.F. 1973. *Small Is Beautiful: Economics as if People Mattered*. New York: Harper and Row.

Smith, Wilfred Cantwell. 1981. *Towards a World Theology: Faith and the Comparative History of Religion*. London: Macmillan, and Philadelphia: Westminster.

# Note

1. Some Islamic scholars have questioned the authenticity of this *hadith*.

# Credits

W.H. McLeod. Extracts from *Textual Sources for the Study of Sikhism* (Manchester: Manchester University Press, 1984). Reprinted by permission of W.H. McLeod, University of Otago.

Nanamoli. Extracts from *The Life of the Buddha* (Kandy: Buddhist Publication Society Inc.). Reproduced with the permission of the Buddhist Publication Society Inc., 54 Sangharaja Mawatha, Kandy, Sri Lanka.

Stephen Owen, ed. and trans. Extracts from *An Anthology of Chinese Literature* (New York, London: W.W. Norton & Company, 1996).

S. Radhakrishnan, ed. Extracts from *The Principal Upanisads* (Harper & Brothers Publishers/George Allen & Unwin, 1953).

Caroline A. Rhys Davids. Excerpt from *Psalms of the Early Buddhists* (Pali Text Society, 1964). Reprinted by permission of the publisher.

Deborah Sommer, ed. Extracts from *Chinese Religion: An Anthology of Sources* (New York, Oxford: Oxford University Press, 1995).

Barbara Stoler Miller. Extracts from *The Bhagavad-Gita: Krishna's Counsel in Time of War*. Translation copyright © 1986 by Barbara Stoler Miller. Used by permission of Bantam Books, a division of Random House, Inc.

Ryusaku Tsunoda, ed. Extracts from *Sources of Japanese Tradition*. Copyright © 1958 by Columbia University Press. Reprinted by permission of the publisher.

Burton Watson. Extracts from *Xunzi: Basic Writings*, translated by B. Watson. Copyright © 1963 by Columbia University Press. Reprinted with permission of the publisher. Extracts from *The Complete Works of Chuang Tzu*, translated by B. Watson. Copyright © 1968 by Columbia University Press. Reprinted with permission of the publisher.

Every effort has been made to determine and contact copyright owners. In case of omissions, the publisher will be pleased to make suitable acknowledgement in future editions.

# Index